西部地区农产品物流可持续发展政策研究

Study on Sustainable Development Policy of Agricultural Products Logistics in Western Region

王 静 著

方志出版社
Publishing House of Local Records

图书在版编目(CIP)数据

西部地区农产品物流可持续发展政策研究 / 王静著.
—北京:方志出版社,2015.12

ISBN 978-7-5144-1722-7

Ⅰ.①西… Ⅱ.①王… Ⅲ.①农产品—物流—可持续性发展—研究—西北地区②农产品—物流—可持续性发展—研究—西南地区 Ⅳ.①F724.72

中国版本图书馆 CIP 数据核字(2015)第 232297 号

西部地区农产品物流可持续发展政策研究

著　　者: 王　静
责任编辑: 罗　滔

出 版 人: 冀祥德
出 版 者: 方志出版社
地址　北京市朝阳区潘家园东里9号(国家方志馆4层)
邮编　100021
网址　http://www.fzph.org
发　　行: 方志出版社发行中心
电话　(010)67110500
经　　销: 各地新华书店
排　　版: 北京宝蕾元科技发展有限责任公司
印　　刷: 北京京都六环印刷厂

开　　本: 700×1000　1/16
印　　张: 30.75
字　　数: 520 千字
版　　次: 2015 年 12 月第 1 版　2015 年 12 月第 1 次印刷

ISBN 978-7-5144-1722-7　定价:98.00 元

第四批《中国社会科学博士后文库》编委会及编辑部成员名单

序　言

2015 年是我国实施博士后制度 30 周年，也是我国哲学社会科学领域实施博士后制度的第 23 个年头。

30 年来，在党中央国务院的正确领导下，我国博士后事业在探索中不断开拓前进，取得了非常显著的工作成绩。博士后制度的实施，培养出了一大批精力充沛、思维活跃、问题意识敏锐、学术功底扎实的高层次人才。目前，博士后群体已成为国家创新型人才中的一支骨干力量，为经济社会发展和科学技术进步作出了独特贡献。在哲学社会科学领域实施博士后制度，已成为培养各学科领域高端后备人才的重要途径，对于加强哲学社会科学人才队伍建设、繁荣发展哲学社会科学事业发挥了重要作用。20 多年来，一批又一批博士后成为我国哲学社会科学研究和教学单位的骨干人才和领军人物。

中国社会科学院作为党中央直接领导的国家哲学社会科学研究机构，在社会科学博士后工作方面承担着特殊责任，理应走在全国前列。为充分展示我国哲学社会科学领域博士后工作成果，推动中国博士后事业进一步繁荣发展，中国社会科学院和全国博士后管理委员会在 2012 年推出了《中国社会科学博士后文库》（以下简称《文库》），迄今已出版四批共 151 部博士后优秀著作。为支持《文库》的出版，中国社会科学院已累计投入资金 820 余万元，人力资源和社会保障部与中国博士后科学基金会累计投入 160 万元。实践证明，《文库》已成为集中、系统、全面反映我国哲学社会科学博士后优秀成果的高端学术平台，为调动哲学社会科学博士后的积极性和创造力、扩大哲学社会科学博士后的学术影响力和社会影响力发挥了重要作用。中国社会科学院和全国博士后管理委员会将共同努力，继续编辑出版好《文库》，进一步提高《文库》的学术水准和社会效益，使之成为学术出版界的知名品牌。

哲学社会科学是人类知识体系中不可或缺的重要组成部分，是人们认识世界、改造世界的重要工具，是推动历史发展和社会进步的重要力量。建设中国特色社会主义的伟大事业，离不开以马克思主义为指导的哲学社会科学的繁荣发展。而哲学社会科学的繁荣发展关键在人，在人才，在一批又一批具有深厚知识基础和较强创新能力的高层次人才。广大哲学社会科学博士后要充分认识到自身所肩负的责任和使命，通过自己扎扎实实的创造性工作，努力成为国家创新型人才中名副其实的一支骨干力量。为此，必须做到：

第一，始终坚持正确的政治方向和学术导向。马克思主义是科学的世界观和方法论，是当代中国的主流意识形态，是我们立党立国的根本指导思想，也是我国哲学社会科学的灵魂所在。哲学社会科学博士后要自觉担负起巩固和发展马克思主义指导地位的神圣使命，把马克思主义的立场、观点、方法贯穿到具体的研究工作中，用发展着的马克思主义指导哲学社会科学。要认真学习马克思主义基本原理、中国特色社会主义理论体系和习近平总书记系列重要讲话精神，在思想上、政治上、行动上与党中央保持高度一致。在涉及党的基本理论、基本路线和重大原则、重要方针政策问题上，要立场坚定、观点鲜明、态度坚决，积极传播正面声音，正确引领社会思潮。

第二，始终坚持站在党和人民立场上做学问。为什么人的问题，是马克思主义唯物史观的核心问题，是哲学社会科学研究的根本性、方向性、原则性问题。解决哲学社会科学为什么人的问题，说到底就是要解决哲学社会科学工作者为什么人从事学术研究的问题。哲学社会科学博士后要牢固树立人民至上的价值观、人民是真正英雄的历史观，始终把人民的根本利益放在首位，把拿出让党和人民满意的科研成果放在首位，坚持为人民做学问，做实学问、做好学问、做真学问，为人民拿笔杆子，为人民鼓与呼，为人民谋利益，切实发挥好党和人民事业的思想库作用。这是我国哲学社会科学工作者，包括广大哲学社会科学博士后的神圣职责，也是实现哲学社会科学价值的必然途径。

第三，始终坚持以党和国家关注的重大理论和现实问题为科研主攻方向。哲学社会科学只有在对时代问题、重大理论和现实问题的深入分析和探索中才能不断向前发展。哲学社会科学博士后要根据时代和实践发展要求，运用马克思主义这个望远镜和显微镜，增强辩证思维、创新思维能力，善于发现问题、分析问题，积极推动解决问题。要深入研究党和国家面临的一系列亟待回答和解决的重大理论和现实问题，经济社会发展中的全局性、前瞻性、战略性问题，干部群众普遍关注的热点、焦点、难点问题，以高质量的科学研究成果，更好地为党和国家的决策服务，为全面建成小康社会服务，为实现“两个一百年”奋斗目标和中华民族伟大复兴中国梦服务。

第四，始终坚持弘扬理论联系实际的优良学风。实践是理论研究的不竭源泉，是检验真理和价值的唯一标准。离开了实践，理论研究就成为无源之水、无本之木。哲学社会科学研究只有同经济社会发展的要求、丰富多彩的生活和人民群众的实践紧密结合起来，才能具有强大的生命力，才能实现自身的社会价值。哲学社会科学博士后要大力弘扬理论联系实际的优良学风，立足当代、立足国情，深入基层、深入群众，坚持从人民群众的生产和生活中，从人民群众建设中国特色社会主义的伟大实践中，汲取智慧和营养，把是否符合、是否有利于人民群众根本利益作为衡量和检验哲学社会科学研究工作的第一标准。要经常用人民群众这面镜子照照自己，匡正自己的人生追求和价值选择，校验自己的责任态度，衡量自己的职业精神。

第五，始终坚持推动理论体系和话语体系创新。党的十八届五中全会明确提出不断推进理论创新、制度创新、科技创新、文化创新等各方面创新的艰巨任务。必须充分认识到，推进理论创新、文化创新，哲学社会科学责无旁贷；推进制度创新、科技创新等各方面的创新，同样需要哲学社会科学提供有效的智力支撑。哲学社会科学博士后要努力推动学科体系、学术观点、科研方法创新，为构建中国特色、中国风格、中国气派的哲学社会科学创新体系作出贡献。要积极投身到党和国家创新洪流中去，深入开展探索性创新研究，不断向未知领域进军，勇攀学术高峰。要大力推进学术话语体系创新，力求厚积薄发、深入浅出、语言朴实、文风清新，力戒言之无物、故作高深、食洋不化、食古不化，不断增强我国学术话语体系的说服力、感染力、影响力。

“长风破浪会有时，直挂云帆济沧海。”当前，世界正处于前所未有的激烈变动之中，我国即将进入全面建成小康社会的决胜阶段。这既为哲学社会科学的繁荣发展提供了广阔空间，也为哲学社会科学界提供了大有作为的重要舞台。衷心希望广大哲学社会科学博士后能够自觉把自己的研究工作与党和人民的事业紧密联系在一起，把个人的前途命运与党和国家的前途命运紧密联系在一起，与时代共奋进、与国家共荣辱、与人民共呼吸，努力成为忠诚服务于党和人民事业、值得党和人民信赖的学问家。

是为序。

张江

中国社会科学院副院长

中国社会科学院博士后管理委员会主任

2015 年 12 月 1 日

摘 要

本研究成果在深入考察西部地区农产品物流客观现实和相关研究基础上，系统回顾和借鉴现代物流与经济发展理论、可持续与可持续发展理论、制度变迁与创新理论；从交易视角和功能范式上界定研究的基本范畴和分析基点；科学地定义和解释西部地区农产品物流可持续发展的概念内涵、基本特征，揭示其均衡过程、内在规律；借鉴国际经验，形成研究启示；运用历史分析和计量检验方法，从制度和数量方面，实证西部地区农产品物流关系结构失调及特征，剖析其根本原因、深层原因和直接原因，进而创建了可持续发展模式，设计区位化双层物流联盟的组织模式及其区域协控中心的运行平台，并围绕可持续发展机制的生成，以观念创新和政府职能转变为前提，制定和实施可持续发展战略的基本思路。从宏观制度环境、农村经济和农产品物流这三个方面提出了政策建议，形成以营造宏观制度环境为保证，建立综合决策机制加快体制创新；以化解西部地区农村经济约束为基础，建立立体保障机制改善发展质态；以强化西部地区农产品物流功能为突破，建立整体运行机制实现管理创新的可持续发展机制的建设路径。

一 研究的基本结论

1. 西部地区农产品物流可持续发展的内涵与机理：是西部地区农产品物流理想状态的实现过程，受产业环境、信用关系和微观基础的约束

西部地区农产品物流可持续发展，是西部地区农产品物流与农村经济可持续发展主体，在制度可持续框架下，综合运用各种可能的可持续发展

手段，使西部地区农产品物流与农村经济关系达成理想状态，具有在开放系统中制度、技术作用下西部地区农产品物流通畅，其总量、结构和速度配合适当构成良性循环的理想状态特征。其实现过程是一个不断受西部经济发展的要求和外部干扰因素影响、不断进行关系状况判断，具有内部结构复杂、多层次相交叉、在变革—创新中不断循环往复的“前期—后期渐进式”系统运动过程。从“均衡过程”看，是宏观制度环境下西部地区农产品物流与农村经济相互促进达成的最优供求均衡。从“内在规律”看，西部地区农产品物流可持续发展，必须以良好的产业环境、信用关系和微观基础为条件。

2. 农产品物流可持续发展的国际经验借鉴与启示：经济发展中农产品物流可持续发展模式具有多样性，但成长路径具有一致性

发达国家（地区）农产品物流可持续发展逐渐形成产销一体化趋势、物流运行虚拟化趋势、绿色物流发展趋势。发达国家（地区）经济发展过程中都十分重视农产品物流的可持续发展，善于把握农产品物流与农村经济的关系。发达国家（地区）都十分重视通过法律去规范农产品物流的可持续发展，可持续手段的选择经历了从单一的市场或政府协调到政府、市场等多种综合运用的过程。发达国家（地区）都十分重视社会性物流和双向性物流在农产品物流可持续发展中的作用，并由狭义的运销支农逐步发展为以交易为特征的农产品物流与农村经济互惠发展。农产品物流可持续发展模式是可持续发展系统遵循可持续发展原理，在可持续发展主体推动下能动地适应其“生态环境”而不断演进的结果。

3. 中国农产品物流制度变迁的演化过程分析：中国农产品物流与农村经济制度变迁模式不同，在时间、结构及其相互影响上失调

农产品物流制度变迁在不同体制下总是表现为机构的不断反复调整，农产品物流制度变迁在三个不同层次上表现为二元结构系统的演进，农产品物流制度变迁以政府主导的自上而下的强制性制度变迁为主，农产品物流制度变迁是强制性制度变迁力量强于诱致性制度变迁的过程。农产品物流制度变迁过程中的关系结构表现出：不仅农产品物流与农村经济制度变迁模式互不适应（主体、路径和动机不同），而且农产品物流与农村经济制度变迁存在结构失衡（需求结构、供给结构和区域结构失衡）。直接导致了农产品物流制度变迁在时间上滞后于农村经济制度变迁，使得农产品

物流制约了农村经济制度变迁的进程。

4. 转型时期西部地区农产品物流数量关系实证：转型时期西部地区农产品正规物流受内外因素影响未能与农村经济相互促进可持续发展

转型时期的西部地区农产品正规物流未能促进农村经济发展：首先，西部地区农产品物流来源未能促进农村经济发展。物流网络里程的增加并不必然代表农村经济发展；农产品货物周转量不仅没有促进农村经济的发展，反而阻碍了农民收入和农村经济总产值的增长。其次，西部地区农产品物流运行未能促进农村经济发展。农产品物流产值与农民收入以外的其他农村经济发展指标没有明显关系；农产品物流产值占农村经济总产值的比重提高，即农产品物流深化对农民收入增长产生的是负面的影响。转型时期的西部地区农村经济发展未能促进农产品正规物流发展：首先，西部地区农村经济发展未能直接促进农产品物流发展。农产品货物周转量水平的提高并不必然代表农产品物流发展；农村经济总产值增长不能促进农产品物流产值增长。其次，西部地区农村经济发展未能间接促进农产品物流发展。农村消费与农产品货物周转量、农产品物流产值不存在重要联系；农村投资与物流网络里程、农产品物流产值不存在重要联系。转型时期的西部地区农产品物流与农村经济关系受外因制约：受整体经济发展和整体物流发展的制约，西部地区农产品物流在整体物流中处于从属地位和被整体物流隔离的状态，“二元物流结构”制约了农产品正规物流向农村经济发展所需要的方向发展；关系失调主要是由于国民经济发展通过“二元物流结构”中的农产品正规物流，实施了对农村经济的极化效应。

5. 西部地区农产品物流关系结构失调原因分析：西部地区农产品物流关系结构失调源于制度环境、农村经济和农产品物流的共同约束

西部地区农产品物流关系结构失调的根本原因是宏观制度环境约束，具体表现为初始条件不足和发展战略使然；二元经济约束和分层治理冲突；思想认识不足和传统观念限制。深层原因是农村经济发展制约，具体表现为西部地区农村经济在波动中增长，但发展水平极不平衡；西部地区农民收入稳步增长，但城乡人均收入极不平衡；西部地区农村产业结构发生变化，但农村经济比较利益低下；西部地区农业生产条件进一步改善，但农村市场主体发育不良。直接原因是农产品物流功能不足，具体表现为西部地区农产品物流深化改革滞后：多元化农产品物流结构不合理、农产

品社会性物流发展不到位、农产品双向性物流发展难度大、农产品经济性物流发展不协调。西部地区农产品物流市场体系建设不完善：西部地区农产品物流市场上物流交易规模小、西部地区农产品物流市场体系发育不健全。西部地区农产品物流监管与调控体系功能不强：西部地区农产品物流监管体系构造不完备、西部地区农产品物流调控体系功能不强。

6. 西部地区农产品物流可持续发展的模式创建：西部地区农产品物流可持续发展模式，特征表现为一致性的实现机理和多样性的实现形态

西部地区农产品物流可持续发展模式，是西部地区农产品物流可持续发展实现机理的外在表现，其形态取决于可持续发展的具体目标、可持续发展的外部环境约束、可持续发展手段的最优组合、可持续发展主体的自身能力等因素，应依据可持续发展的实现机理，在可持续发展模式总体框架下探索不同条件下的具体实现形态。西部地区农产品物流可持续发展模式的基本类型分为：基础推动战略的梯度推进与节点带动模式、创新推动战略与组织推动战略的综合模式。通过西部地区农产品物流可持续发展模式的提升策略、结构创新，实现西部地区农产品物流区位化双层物流联盟的模式优化、机制优化。西部地区农产品物流区位化双层物流整个联盟体系的联盟过程是一个不断发展，不断螺旋上升的过程。西部地区农产品物流可持续发展的构建或探索过程具有一致性，有规律可循。

7. 西部地区农产品物流可持续发展的模式运行：西部地区农产品物流可持续发展的模式运行体系，特征表现为集成化的运行管理和一体化的运行保障

西部地区农产品物流可持续发展的具体实现形态取决于模式创建要有基础运行平台作保证，应依据“模式”的提升策略与结构创新，设计西部地区农产品物流区位化双层物流联盟的运行平台——西部地区农产品供应链的区域协控中心。为此，探索西部地区农产品物流可持续发展模式的运行设计，具体包括西部地区农产品供应链的区域协控中心的运行体系、形成机制、实现机制、约束机制；在此基础上分析西部地区农产品物流可持续发展模式的运行管理，具体包括基于区域协控中心的区位化双层物流联盟的运作风险、空间优化；最后进行西部地区农产品物流可持续发展模式的综合评价，具体包括西部地区农产品物流可持续发展评价指标体系的构建、综合评价方法。基于“模式”的运行设计、运行管理、综合评价

的分析，通过整合各成员的资源、技术与信息，科学设计西部地区农产品区域协控中心的运行平台，以保障西部地区农产品物流区位化双层物流联盟模式的优化实施，整个运行体系表现出集成化的运行管理和一体化的运行保障，实现西部地区农产品物流可持续发展。

二 研究的重要观点

1. 西部地区农产品物流可持续发展是经济社会可持续发展的内在要求和重要内容

西部地区农产品物流可持续发展是西部大开发后续发展的重要基础之一，是有效提高资源配置效率、解决人口膨胀、促进经济社会可持续发展的重要途径。第一，西部地区农产品物流发展是促进结构调整推动整个农业系统均衡协调发展的重要基础。第二，西部地区农产品物流发展是提高居民生活质量、增加农民收入的重要内容。第三，西部地区农产品物流发展已成为开发利用西部地区内陆港（无水港）、解决农村资源短缺的重要途径。第四，西部地区农产品物流发展是农业实现区域化、专业化生产和产业化发展，提高农产品的市场竞争能力的重要保证。第五，西部地区农产品物流发展是农村剩余劳动力转移的战略重点。

2. 西部地区农产品物流可持续发展必须建立基于交易视角和功能范式的农产品物流发展观

在交易视角下西部地区农产品物流是一种交易；西部地区农产品物流交易具有规模经济效应；信用交易是农产品物流的本质特征；西部地区农产品物流的外在特征是交易的表现形式和组织方式。基于交易视角，西部地区农产品物流的概念内涵在功能意义上从以下几个方面理解：第一，西部地区农产品物流是具有促进西部农村经济发展功能的物流。第二，西部地区农产品物流是西部农村经济与整体物流的交叉系统。第三，西部地区农产品物流是内部功能结构复杂多样的系统。

3. 西部地区农产品物流可持续发展符合可持续发展的一般原理，但具有自身的独特性

西部地区农产品物流与农村经济是中国“二元结构”“转型”“WTO”和“西部大开发”背景下，既与整体物流、经济密不可分，又具有独特

微观基础和内在结构的复杂系统，两者互动发展，既可相互促进又可相互制约，既可独立又可共同地对整体物流和经济构成影响。经济转型过程中，西部地区农产品物流关系结构失调的原因复杂多样。失调源于制度环境、农村经济和农产品物流的共同约束，从根本上讲是制度抑制长期积累的结果。

4. 西部地区农产品物流可持续发展模式的总体框架，特点在于发挥西部特殊优势

西部地区农产品物流可持续发展模式是以制度可持续为中心，以市场导向、企业运作、环境支撑、农民参与为基础，多种可持续手段配合使用的总体框架。发挥西部特殊优势，以策略联盟构筑其区位化双层物流联盟的组织模式、区域协控中心的运行平台，实行统一、协调、控制的物流运作，推动农产品电子商务平台、运销标准与规范平台对接，实现西部地区农产品物流可持续发展。

5. 实现西部地区农产品物流可持续发展，关键在于机制与模式构建

可持续发展的基础是市场经济条件下，政府、西部地区农产品物流主体和农村经济主体功能的发挥，核心在于制度可持续，重点是政府行为与市场行为的可持续。发挥政府职能，实现“集约型”“差别物流”是走出“失调陷阱”、走向“可持续发展”的切入点。但治本在于现代市场制度在西部农村的确立和完善，以及“二元”经济、物流结构的“一元化”。

三　研究的主要创新

1. 研究视角的创新：建立了基于交易视角和功能范式的逻辑起点与分析框架

本课题在“功能范式”的基础上，引入新制度经济学方法，从界定研究的基本范畴和研究基点入手，建立了基于交易视角和功能范式的分析框架，实现了研究范式的转换，超越了停留在哲学层面上的既有西部地区农产品物流与农村经济关系的一般研究，开辟了研究的新视野。

2. 研究理论的创新：揭示了西部地区农产品物流可持续发展的内涵与机理

本课题在吸收既有研究成果定义基本概念的基础上，运用新古典经济学方法和系统科学理论，规范性界定了西部地区农产品物流可持续发展的概念内涵和基本特征，进而揭示出其均衡过程、内在规律的实现机理，深化了对可持续发展的认识，并为相关研究提供了借鉴。

3. 研究实证的创新：证实了西部地区农产品物流关系结构失调原因及其特征

本课题运用新制度经济学的历史分析方法，在全面深入考察中国农产品物流制度变迁历程，分析其基本特征、影响因素和相互关系的基础上，从制度层面，发现了农产品物流关系结构失调及其特征。运用回归分析、协整（cointegration）检验、格兰杰（Granger）因果关系检验等计量经济学工具，从数量层面，实证了转型时期西部地区农产品物流关系结构失调及其特征。

4. 研究对策的创新：设计了西部地区农产品物流可持续发展的组织模式与运行平台

本课题在理论和实证基础上，构建了西部地区农产品物流可持续发展模式总体框架。设计了西部地区农产品物流区位化双层物流联盟的组织模式，打造产业链层面的物流联盟、绿色通道层面的物流联盟，使物流功能得到完善和充分发挥。设计西部地区农产品供应链的区域协控中心的运行平台，降低物流成本提高竞争力、实现农产品快速调配和优化、强调农产品生命周期管理和质量安全追溯体系。

5. 研究结果的创新：明确了西部地区农产品物流可持续发展的路径

本课题基于研究视角、理论、实证及对策，明确了西部地区农产品物流可持续发展机制建设的基本思路是以观念创新和政府职能转变为前提，制定和实施可持续发展战略。形成以营造宏观制度环境为保证，建立综合决策机制加快体制创新；以化解西部地区农村经济约束为基础，建立立体保障机制改善发展质态；以强化西部地区农产品物流功能为突破，建立整体运行机制实现管理创新的可持续发展机制的建设路径。并基于这一路径构建了可持续发展模式，围绕可持续发展机制的生成，提出了系统化的可操作性政策建议。

本课题在研究中，无论是揭示西部地区农产品物流可持续发展的基本范畴、概念内涵、基本特征和实现机理，证实其结构失调原因，构建总体模式，设计区位化双层物流联盟的组织模式及其区域协控中心的运行平台，还是形成建设机制和实现路径的深化，其里面所要阐释的内容和所要揭示的道理，都有个性化的表现和独特的主张。

四　研究的政策建议

1. 西部地区农产品物流可持续发展机制建设的基本思路

(1) 由“效率优先、兼顾公平”向“公平高效、规范透明”转变。切实赋予并保护好西部地区农民公正平等、规范透明的市场主体地位；切实赋予并保护好西部地区农产品物流与农村经济公正平等、规范透明的产业地位；切实赋予并保护好西部地区不同产权主体公正平等、规范透明的市场地位。

(2) 由“城乡分割、相对独立”向“城乡统筹、空间集聚”转变。以可持续发展为原则制定和实施经济发展战略；以城乡统筹为手段化解农产品物流二元结构；以空间集聚为方法实现农产品物流关联效益。

(3) 由“粗放型、不协调发展”向“集约型、可持续发展”转变。建立西部地区农产品物流区位化双层物流联盟的组织模式；建立西部地区农产品供应链的区域协控中心的运行平台；建立健全以生态评价为中心的矛盾梳理体系。

2. 以营造宏观制度环境为保证，建立综合决策机制加快体制创新

(1) 以“制度建设”为核心，构建和完善可持续发展体制。平衡“生态文明”与“经济增长”的价值取向；构建“市场为基础”与“政府为主导”的实现平台。

(2) 以“能力建设”为重点，强化政府的可持续发展职能。科学界定可持续发展中的政府职能；优化可持续发展中的政府治理结构。

3. 以化解西部地区农村经济约束为基础，建立立体保障机制改善发展质态

(1) 建立西部地区农村经济发展的基础，加大西部地区农村资金筹集和管理。改变农村资金投入方式，建立“土地银行”；广拓农村资金筹集渠道，建立“专项基金”。

(2) 改善西部地区农村经济发展的质态，加速西部地区农村生产要

素流动。引导农村剩余劳动力转移，促进农民就业；立足农业和农村全产业链，提升比较优势；聚拢农业和农村核心科技，打造行业地标。

（3）激发西部地区农村经济发展的活力，壮大西部地区农村市场经济主体。增加农村经济主体的人力资本，强化市场能力；优化农村经济组织的运行模式，增进市场运作。

4. 以强化西部地区农产品物流功能为突破，建立整体运行机制实现管理创新

（1）形成现代物流观念，把握西部地区农产品物流改革意义。一是按物流发展规律改革西部地区农产品物流建立制度物流观念。二是按农村经济需求改革西部地区农产品物流建立功能物流观念。三是按产业发展规律改革西部地区农产品物流建立产业物流观念。主要包括：建立农产品综合生产防范体系，推进西部地区农产品产销链的产前变革；建立农产品物流运行虚拟化治理模式，推进西部地区农产品产销链的产后变革；农产品物流体系重构，产销一体化破解“菜贱农伤”之困；建立西部地区农产品物流突发事件应急机制，消除产销失控现象。

（2）优化西部地区农产品物流结构，重构西部地区农产品物流组织体系。一是建立西部地区农产品物流组织体系的制度基础必须优化西部地区农产品物流产权结构。包括：确立西部地区农产品物流发展的制度基础；优化西部地区农产品物流发展的产权结构。二是扩展西部地区农产品物流组织体系的服务范围必须优化西部地区农产品物流业务结构。包括：扩展西部地区农产品物流服务的业务领域；拓宽西部地区农产品物流机构的经营与业务范围；成立西部地区慈善性质的农产品物流机构形成特色的可持续扶贫的道路。三是提高西部地区农产品物流组织体系的核心能力必须优化西部地区农产品物流产业结构。包括：提高西部地区农产品物流制度核心竞争力；提高西部地区农产品物流企业的核心竞争力。

（3）改进西部地区农产品物流监管，提高西部地区农产品物流运行效率。一是建立西部地区农产品物流监管方式：刚性管理与柔性管理。当前西部地区农产品物流的监管方式创新的基本方向，就是要在新的历史时期建构出一种政府主导的、规范有序的自上向下、自下向上的平行轨道的“双轨”格局。二是优化西部地区农产品物流监管模式：大通道管控与双窗口开放。大通道是指联结中国东部与西部、联结亚欧大陆的通道，双窗

口是指联合中国东部、西部两个窗口，开放式走西口。西部地区农产品物流要依托大通道与双窗口优势，大力发展窗口经济、通道经济，形成一个由极点增长模式和带状发展模式结合的“双窗口—大通道—区域间联动—沿腹地轴线纵深型”的西部地区农产品物流开放带。促进区域间的协调发展，更好地适应西部地区农产品物流的可持续发展。三是完善西部地区农产品物流监管机制：提升人力资本与强化行为规范。建立西部地区农产品物流监管与西部地区农产品物流市场的可持续发展，是目前西部后续开发背景下实现西部地区农产品物流可持续发展的有效途径。

关键词： 西部地区　农产品物流　可持续发展　政策研究

Abstract

The research results in the in – depth investigation in the western region agricultural product logistics based on objective reality and related research, a systematic review and how to use the theory of modern logistics and economic development, sustainable and the sustainable development theory, theory of institutional change and innovation. From the perspective of transaction and the definition of research on functional paradigm of basic category and analysis basis points, scientific definition and explanation in the western region agricultural products logistics concept connotation, basic characteristics of sustainable development, the article reveals its equilibrium process, inherent law. It draws lessons from international experience, forms the research revelation. Using historical analysis and measurement methods, from the aspects of system and the quantity, the empirical relationship between the western region agricultural products logistics structural imbalance and characteristics, it analyzes its basic reason, deep and direct reasons, then create the sustainable development model, design localization of double logistics alliance organization modes and their area of control center platform, and centers on the generation of the mechanism for sustainable development on the premise of ideas innovation and change of government function, develops and implement the basic ideas of sustainable development strategy. From the macroscopic system environment, the rural economy, it puts forward policy suggestions on the three aspects of agricultural products logistics to build system of macro environment in order to ensure the formation, set up the system of comprehensive decision – making mechanism to speed up the innovation To resolve the western region rural economic constraints, on the basis of the establishment of a three – dimensional security mechanism to improve the development quality and the state. The article's purpose is to strengthen the western region of agricultural products logistics function as the breakthrough, to establish the overall operating mechanism to achieve the sustainable development of the management innovation mechanism for the construction of the path.

Ⅰ. The Basic Research Conclusion

1. The connotation and mechanism of the sustainable development of agricultural products logistics in the western region of China: the realization of the ideal state in the western region agricultural logistics process, the industrial environment, and the relationship between the credit constraints and micro foundation

In the western region sustainable development of the logistics of agricultural products, agricultural product logistics is the main body in the western region and rural economy sustainable development. Under the system of sustainable framework, with the integrated use of a variety of possible means of sustainable development, the western region of agricultural products logistics and rural economic relations reached an ideal state, under the effect of the open system, technology in the western region of agricultural products logistics unobstructed, the total amount, structure and speed with appropriate constitute of the ideal characteristics of a virtuous cycle. Its implementation process is a constant demands of the development of western economy and external interference factors, ongoing relationship condition judgment, and it has complex internal structure, multi – level phase cross, and in the change, innovation constantly " stage, progressive stage" system loop in motion process. From the" equilibrium process", it is the macroscopic system environment in the western region of agricultural products logistics and promotes rural economy to achieve the optimal balance of supply and demand. From the " inherent law " in the western region sustainable development of the logistics of agricultural products, there must be a good industry environment, the credit relations and the micro basis for the condition.

2. The international experience for reference and enlightenment for the sustainable development of agricultural products logistics: economic developing mode of sustainable development of agricultural products logistics has diversity, but consistent growth path

Developed countries (regions) production and marketing integration trend of sustainable development of the logistics of agricultural products gradually formed virtualization trend, the development trend of green logistics and logistics operation. (area) in the process of economic development in the developed countries attach great importance to the sustainable development of the logistics of agricultural products, it is good to deal with the relationship between agricultural products logistics and the rural economy. Developed countries (regions) have attached great importance to passing a law to regulate the sustainable development of the logistics of agricultural products, sustainable means choose experienced one from a single market or government coordination to the government, market and other integrated use of the process. Developed countries (regions) have attached great importance to social logistics and biphasic role in the sustainable development of the logistics of agricultural products, and the special distribution of agriculture gradually developed as the trade of agricultural products logistics is characterized by the development of rural economy reciprocity. Sustainable development of agricultural products logistics mode follows the principle of sustainable development, the sustainable development system under the sustainable development of the main body to promote activity to adapt to the" ecological environment" and the result of evolution.

3. The evolution of Chinese agricultural products logistics system

vicissitude process analysis: China's agricultural products logistics and the rural economic system change mode, time, structure and influence each other and disorder

Agricultural products logistics system change under the different system always show the agency's repeated adjustment, agricultural products logistics system vicissitude in three different levels for the evolution of the dual structure system, agricultural products logistics system vicissitude the government – leading top – down mandatory institutional change is given priority to, the agricultural products logistics is a mandatory institutional change power stronger than the induced institutional change process of institutional change. Relational structure in the process of agricultural products logistics system vicissitude showed: not only agricultural products logistics and the rural economic system change mode does not adapt to the subject, paths and different motives, but also the imbalance in the structure of agricultural products logistics and economic institutional change in rural areas (demand structure, supply structure and regional structure imbalance) . It directly led to the agricultural products logistics system change on the time lag behind the rural economic system change, making the process of agricultural products logistics restrict the rural economic system change.

4. The quantitative relationship between the western region agricultural products logistics empirical: during the period of transition in the western region during the period of transition affected by internal and external factors failed to promote with rural economy and produce normal logistics and rural economy sustainable development

Transition period of the western region of agricultural products logistics formal failed to promote rural economic development: first, the source of agricultural products logistics has failed to promote rural economic development in western China. Logistics network mileage increase is not necessarily representative of the rural economic development; Quantity of agricultural products failed to promote the development of rural economy, but hinder the growth of farmers' income and rural economic output. Second, agricultural products logistics operation failed to promote rural economic development in western China. Agricultural products logistics production and farmers'income of the rural economic development indicate there is no obvious relationship; Logistics of agricultural products output value increase in the proportion of total output value of the rural economy, and the agricultural products logistics deepening is a negative impact on the farmers' income growth. Transition of rural economic development in western China has failed to promote the development of agricultural products logistics formal: first of all, the rural economy development in western China failed to directly promote the development of agricultural products logistics. The improvement of agricultural product quantity does not necessarily represent the agricultural product logistics development; rural economic output growth does not promote agricultural products logistics output growth. Second, the rural economy development in western China failed to indirectly promote the development of agricultural products logistics. Between rural consumption and quantity of agricultural products, agricultural products logistics production there is no important link; Among rural investment and logistics network range, the output value of agricultural products logistics contact there is no important link. Transition period of the western region of agricultural products logistics and rural economic relations is conditioned by external causes: the restriction of the overall economic development and the overall logistics development, the western region agricultural products logistics that occupies a subordinate position in the whole logistics and the overall logistics state of isolation," binary logistic structure" restricted the agricultural products normal logistics to develop in the direction of rural economic development needs; Dysfunctional relationship is mainly due to the national economic development by" dual logistics structure" in formal logistics of agricultural products, the implementation of the polarization effect of the rural economy.

5. Cause analysis of structural imbalance the western region of agricultural products logistics: common constraints from structure disorder of

the western region agricultural products logistics, the institutional environment, the rural economy and agricultural products logistics

The root cause of the western region of agricultural products logistics relationship between structural imbalances is macroscopic system environmentconstraints, embodied due to lack of initial conditions and development strategy; Dual economic constraints, and hierarchical governance conflict; Ideological understanding shortage and limitation in traditional concepts. Deep reason is that rural economic development constraints, embodied in the western region rural economic growth in the volatile, but the uneven level of development; in the western region there has been a steady rise in farmers' income, but urban and rural per capita income is highly uneven; there are rural industrial structure changes in the western region, but the rural economy of comparative advantage is low; to further improve agricultural production conditions in the western region, but rural market main body dysplasia. Direct cause is the insufficient agricultural products logistics functions, embodied in western region of agricultural products logistics deepening reform lag: the diversification of the structure of agricultural products logistics, agricultural products to the social development does not reach the designated position, agricultural products logistics two - way logistics development is difficult, the agricultural economy of logistics development. The western region of agricultural products logistics market system is not perfect, the western region agricultural products logistics market size is small, and the western region agricultural products logistics development of the market system is not sound. The western region of agricultural products logistics function of supervision and regulation system is not strong, the western region agricultural products logistics incomplete regulatory system construction, and the western region agricultural logistics control system function is not strong.

6. Creation of mode In the western region for the sustainable development of agricultural products logistics: the western region sustainable development of agricultural products logistics mode, characteristic

performance for the realization of the implementation mechanism of consistency and diversity

In the western region sustainable development of agricultural products logistics mode, the mechanism of sustainable development of the western region of agricultural products logistics is to achieve the external performance, its shape depends on the specific goals of sustainable development, the sustainable development of the external environment constraints, the optimal combination of the sustainable development means sustainable development, the main body of factors such as their own capabilities, should be based on the realization of the sustainable development mechanism, the sustainable development mode under the framework of the overall exploration under the condition of different concrete realization form. Western region basic types of the sustainable development of agricultural products logistics mode can be divided into: the basis to promote strategic gradient propulsion and node drive mode, the innovation push strategy and organization to promote strategic integrated mode. Through promotion of the sustainable development of agricultural products logistics mode in western strategy, structure innovation, there will be the realization of the localization in the western region agricultural products logistics double logistics alliance model optimization, the mechanism of optimization. The western region of agricultural products logistics localization double logistics alliance of the entire alliance system is a continuous development, the process of spiral. Building or exploration for the sustainable development of the western region of agricultural products logistics process is consistent, and there are rules to follow.

7. In the western region of agricultural products logistics mode of sustainable development: the sustainable development of western region of agricultural products logistics mode system, features of the operation of the integrated management and integrated operational support

Concrete realization of the sustainable development of the logistics of agricultural products in western form depends on the mode to create basic operating platform should be, should be based on" model" strategy and structure innovation, the design of the western region of agricultural products logistics localization of double logistics alliance platform in the western region of agricultural products supply chain area control centre. Therefore, to explore the operation of the sustainable development of the western region agricultural products logistics mode design, concrete including regional coordinated control center of the agricultural products supply chain in western regions of the operation of the system, mechanism, implementation mechanism, constraint mechanism; On the basis of the analysis of the western region sustainable development of agricultural products logistics mode of operation and management, including localization double logistics alliance based on region coordinated control center of the operation risk, optimize space; Finally, to the western region's agricultural products logistics comprehensive evaluation of sustainable development model, including the establishment of evaluation index system of sustainable development, western region of agricultural products logistics, the comprehensive evaluation method. Based on the operation of the" mode" design, operation and management, it makes an analysis of the comprehensive evaluation, through the integration of resources, technology and information of each member of scientific design of control center in the western region agricultural area operation platform in order to ensure the western region of agricultural products logistics localization double logistics alliance mode optimization, the running system shows the integrated operation management and the integration of the security, and realizes sustainable development of agricultural products logistics in the western region of China.

Ⅱ. The Research Important Point

1. The sustainable development of agricultural products logistics in the western region of China is the internal requirement of sustainable economic and social development and the important content

In the western region sustainable development of the logistics of agricultural products is one of the important basis for subsequent development of west development, is effective to improve efficiency of resource allocation, to solve the population expansion, promote economic and social sustainable development important way. First, the agricultural products logistics development in western China is to important foundation to promote the structural adjustment, and the whole agricultural system equilibrium coordinated development. Second, agricultural products logistics development in western China is the important content to improve the residents'quality of life, and increase farmers'income. Third, agricultural products logistics development in the western region has become the development and utilization of inland port (anhydrous port), to solve the shortage of rural resources important way. Fourth, the agricultural products logistics development in western China is the important guarantee for an agricultural regionalization, the specialized production and industrialization development, and improvement of the agricultural product market competition ability. Fifth, the western region ' s agricultural products logistics development is the strategic key of rural surplus labor transfer.

2. In the western region sustainable development must be established based on agricultural products logistics transaction perspective and the function model of agricultural products logistics development

Under the transaction perspective the western region's agricultural products logistics is a kind of trade; the western region's agricultural products logistics trade has economies of scale; Credit transaction is the essential characteristics of agricultural products logistics; the external characteristic of the western region of agricultural products logistics is transaction form and way of organization. Based on transaction perspective, the concept of the western region of agricultural products logistics connotation understanding on the functional meaning from the following several aspects: first, the western region's agricultural products logistics is the function of the logistics of promoting the western rural economic development. Second, the western region's agricultural products logistics is a cross of western rural economy and the overall logistics system. Third, the western region of agricultural products logistics is an internal function structure of complex systems.

3. The western region's sustainable development of the logistics of agricultural products is in accordance with the general principles of sustainable development, but has its uniqueness

Agricultural product logistics in the western region and rural economy is China's" dual structure"," transition"," WTO" and" western development" under the background, and the overall logistics and economic are inseparable, but also has a unique micro foundation and inner structure of complex system, the interactive development, can promote each other and restrain each other, can be independent but also collectively with the overall logistics and economic implications. In the process of economic transformation, reasons of the western region's agricultural logistics behind the imbalanced relationship structure are complicated. Disorder is the result of the institutional environment, the rural economy and agricultural products logistics common constraints is fundamentally system restrain of the result of long – term accumulation.

4. The overall framework of sustainable development of the western region's agricultural products logistics mode, characteristic lies in the western special advantage

The western region of agricultural products logistics system of sustainable development model is sustainable as the center, market – oriented, enterprise operation, environment support, farmers'participation as the foundation, the use of multiple means of sustainable overall framework. Play the special advantage in the west and strategic alliance to build its localization of double logistics alliance organization mode, the operation of the regional coordinated control center platform, unified, coordinate and control the logistics operation, promote agricultural e – commerce platform, marketing standards and specification docking platform, realize sustainable development of agricultural products logistics in the western region of China.

5. The key to realize a sustainable development of the logistics of agricultural products in the western region lies in the mechanism and pattern

Sustainable development is the foundation of the market economy condition, the government, the western region of agricultural products logistics main body and the rural economy main body function of the play, the core lies in the system of sustainable, the focus is on the government's sustainable behavior and market behavior. Playing he functions of the government, to achieve" intensive", "logistics" difference is out of the trap" disorder", to" sustainable development" comes in. But its root lies in the establishment of the modern market system in the western rural and perfect, and the" dual" economy, the logistics of the structure of the "unified".

Ⅲ. The Main Innovation

1. The innovation of the research angle of view: based on transaction perspective and functional paradigm of logical starting point and analysis framework

This topic in the" functional paradigm", on the basis of introducing the method of new institutional economics, from the basic categories and research basis of defining the research, based on transaction perspective analysis framework and function model, implements the transformation of research paradigm, beyond the stay on the philosophical level both in the western region of agricultural products logistics and general research of rural economic relations, has opened up a new field of vision of research.

2. The research of the theory of innovation: reveals the connotation and mechanism of the sustainable development of agricultural products logistics in the western region of China

This topic in the absorption, on the basis of both the results of the study are to define the basic concept, by using the theory of new classical economics method and system for scientific and normative definition of the concept of sustainable development of agricultural products logistics in the western region of connotation and basic characteristics, and then reveals its equilibrium process, the realization of the inherent law of mechanism, deepens the understanding of sustainable development, and provides the reference for related research.

3. The empirical research innovation: to confirm the relationship between the western region of agricultural products logistics structural imbalance causes and characteristics

This topic using historical analysis method of new institutional economics, in the comprehensive look at China's agricultural products logistics system vicissitude process, analyzes its basic characteristics, influence factors and on the basis of mutual relations, from the system level, found that the relationship between the agricultural products logistics structure disorder and its characteristics, using the regression analysis, integration, integration test, Granger, Granger causality test and other econometric tools, from the aspects of quantity, the empirical relationship between agricultural product logistics in the western region during the period of transition structure disorder and its characteristics.

4. The countermeasures of innovation: the design of sustainable development of the western region of agricultural products logistics organization mode and operation platform

This topic on the basis of theoretical and empirical, builds the sustainable development of the western region of agricultural products logistics mode framework, designs the localization in the western region agricultural products logistics organization mode of double logistics alliance, makes level in the industry of logistics alliance on the level of logistics alliance, the green channel, makes the logistics to improve and give full play to the function. Design of the agricultural products supply chain in western area of control center platform reduces logistics cost to improve competitiveness and realizes the rapid deployment and optimization of agricultural products, emphasizes on agricultural product lifecycle management and the quality and safety traceability system.

5. The results of innovation: clear the path for the sustainable development of western region of agricultural products logistics

This topic is based on the research Angle, theory, empirical and countermeasures, has been clear about the agricultural product logistics in the western region sustainable development mechanism of the construction of the basic train of thought based on the premise of ideas innovation and change of government function and formulates and implements the strategy of sustainable development. To build system of macro environment as the guarantee, set up comprehensive decision - making mechanism to speed up the system innovation, to resolve the western region rural economic constraints, on the basis of the establishment of a three - dimensional security mechanism to improve the development quality, and the state; To strengthen the western region of agricultural products logistics function as the breakthrough, to establish the overall operating mechanism to achieve the sustainable development of the management innovation mechanism for the construction of the path. And based on the path to build a sustainable development model, around the generation of the mechanism for susta-inable development, the maneuverability of the systematic policy sugg-estions are put forward.

This topic in the study, whether it is revealed in the western region for the sustainable development of agricultural product logistics basic category, concept, connotation, basic features and implementation mechanism, confirms the cause structural imbalance, and builds the overall pattern, designs localization of double logistics alliance organization modes and their area of control center platform, or forms mechanism and realization path of deepening, the inside has to illustrate contents and reveals the truth, has personalized and unique position.

Ⅳ. Study of Policy Recommendations

1. In the western region agricultural product logistics basic train of

thought of the construction of the mechanism for sustainable development

(1) From the" priority to efficiency and due consideration to fairness" to "fair" efficient, standardized transparent transformation. To give and to protect western region farmers fair and equal, specifications transparent market main body status; To give and protect the agricultural product logistics in the western region and rural economic justice equal status, standard transparent industry; To give and fair and equal protection in the western region of different ownership, standard transparent market position.

(2) By the" urban and rural segmentation, relatively independent" to" urban and rural areas as a whole, the spatial agglomeration". Based on principles of sustainable development to develop and implement the strategy of economic development; Agricultural product logistics in urban and rural areas as a whole as the means to resolve binary structure; Method with spatial agglomeration so as to realize the agricultural products logistics associated benefits.

(3) From the" extensive, uncoordinated development" to" intensive and sustainable development". Established localization double logistics alliance organization mode of the western region's agricultural products logistics; Establishing regional coordinated control center of the agricultural products supply chain in western operation platform; Establishing and perfecting the carding system centered on ecological assessment of contradiction.

2. To create a system of macro environment as the guarantee, establish comprehensive decision – making mechanism to speed up the institutional innovation

(1) "System construction" as the core, build and perfect the system of sustainable development. Balance of " ecological civilization " and " economic growth" value orientation; Build a" market – based" and" the government as the leading" the implementation of the platform.

(2) Focusing on the " capacity building ", strengthen the sustainable development of the government function, scientific definition

of sustainable development of the functions of the government, and optimization of the sustainable development of government governance structure.

3. On the basis of dissolving the western region's rural economic constraints, the establishment of a three – dimensional security mechanism to improve the development quality, and the state

(1) To establish the basis of economic development in western rural areas, increase funding and management in western rural regions, changing the mode of rural capital investment, establishing the" land bank"; obtaining the rural fund – raising channels, and establishing a "special fund".

(2) To improve the quality of the rural economic development in western states, accelerate the production factors flow in western rural regions. Guide the rural surplus labor transfer, promote rural employment; Based on agriculture and rural industry chain, enhance the comparative advantage; Gather core science and technology, agriculture and rural landmark building industry.

(3) Stimulate the vitality of economic development in western rural areas, strengthen the market economy main body in western rural regions. To increase rural economic subject of human capital, strengthen market capacity; To optimize the mode of the rural economic organizations, improve market operation.

4. To strengthen the western region's agricultural products logistics functions as the breakthrough, to establish the overall operating mechanism to achieve management innovation

(1) The formation of modern logistics concept, the western region of agricultural products logistics reform. One is according to the logistics system of agricultural product logistics law reform in the western region to establish logistics concept. Second, according to the reform of rural economic demand in the western region of agricultural products logistics function logistics concept is established. Third is in the western region agricultural products logistics industry development course reform to

establish industry logistics concept. It mainly includes: to establish agricultural comprehensive production prevention system, to promote the western region agricultural production and marketing chain of prenatal change. Virtualization to establish agricultural products logistics operation management mode, to promote the western region agricultural production and marketing chain of postpartum change, agricultural products logistics system reconstruction, production and marketing integration crack "vegetables base farmers hurt" trapped; Establish emergency mechanism of the western region's agricultural products logistics, and eliminate the phenomenon of production out of control.

(2) The optimization of the structure of the western region agricultural products logistics, and reconstruction in the western region agricultural products logistics organization. One is to establish a system of the agricultural products logistics organization system in western foundation it must optimize the structure of the western region agricultural products logistics property. It includes: establishing the system of the agricultural products logistics development in western China; To optimize the structure of agricultural products logistics development in western China. Second, it is extended in the western region of agricultural products logistics organization system service scope, it must optimize the structure of the western region agricultural products logistics business, including: expand the business areas of western region of agricultural products logistics service; Broaden the management of the western region of agricultural products logistics organization and scope of business; West charitable nature of the agricultural products logistics agency forming features of sustainable in the way of poverty alleviation. Three is to improve the core competence of the agricultural products logistics organization system in western must optimize the structure of agricultural products logistics industry in the west, including: to improve the core competitive capacity of the western region of agricultural products logistics system; Increase in the western region of agricultural products logistics enterprises core competitiveness.

(3) Improvement in the western region of agricultural products logistics supervision, improvement of the efficiency of the western region's agricultural products logistics. One is to build the western region agricultural products logistics mode of regulation: rigid management and flexible management. The current regulation mode of the logistics of agricultural products in western regions of the basic direction of innovation, is to be in the new historical period to construct a government – led, standardized and orderly, from bottom to top downwards on the" dual – track" pattern of parallel tracks. Second, optimization of the western region agricultural products logistics mode: channel control and double window open. Passage refers to connecting east China and west, connecting the Eurasian channel, double window is refers to the joint of eastern China, two Windows in the west and open characteristics. The western region of agricultural products logistics and double window depends on channel advantages, vigorously develop the window economy, channel, form a growth model by pole and ribbon development model of combination of" double window – big channel – regional linkage – channel hinterland along the axis depth" in the western region of agricultural products logistics open zone. Promote the regional coordinated development, better adapt to the sustainable development of the western region of agricultural products logistics. Third is to perfect the western region of agricultural products logistics supervision mechanism, human capital and improving code of conduct. Established in the western region agricultural products logistics and the sustainable development of the western region of agricultural products logistics market, is currently the subsequent western development under the background of effective ways to realize the sustainable development of the western region agricultural products logistics.

Key Words: In the western region; The logistics of agricultural products; Sustainable development; Policy research

目　录

Contents

第一章　总　论

第一节　研究的问题与背景

一　问题的展示

本课题是关于西部地区农产品物流可持续发展政策的研究，研究的基本定位是：以农村经济为中心，以农产品物流为重点，以可持续发展为主线，通过理论与实证分析，探索市场经济条件下，西部地区农产品物流可持续发展的机制与模式。选择和研究本课题主要基于下列几点原因。

（一）西部农村经济发展与西部地区国民经济发展不相适应

农村经济发展是经济发展理论和发展中国家普遍面临的一个不可逾越的根本性问题。理论逻辑和历史事实清楚地表明，中国国情下①的农村经济发展，对中国经济和社会发展始终具有特殊②的重要意义③。但中国农村经济在推动中国经济以独特的“中国模式”创造“中国奇迹”的同时，

---

① 中国是一个农业文明悠久，农业传统深厚，既有漫长的封建历史和近30年的计划经济经历，又有一百多年追求现代化的艰苦摸索和30年渐进式市场化改革的成功实践，经济社会呈现典型“二元”特征，正在经历全面“转型”，但仍将长期处于社会主义初级阶段的发展中的小农大国。

② 在中国13亿人口中近8亿人在农村，农业是国民经济的基础，农村经济发展对整个经济、社会发展始终构成重要影响，而且，特有的人口与资源禀赋、经济结构和制度、文化和意识形态，以及独特的发展历程，使得中国农村经济问题既不同于亚洲、非洲和拉美的发展中小国，也不同于印度、巴西等非社会主义的发展中大国，更不同于欧美等发达的市场经济国家，与发展经济学的理论假设和经典结论也相差很大，既没有现成的模式可以移植，也没有现成的理论可以套用。

③ 中国自古号称“以农立国”，历史上的革命和现实中的改革都开始于农村，成败也取决于农村。

20世纪90年代，尤其是90年代后半期以来，农村经济发展出现了与国民经济发展不相适应的景象，突出表现为：农业经济发展速度放慢；农民收入增长幅度减缓；城乡收入和消费差距扩大；农业劳动生产率相对下降；农业对农民收入增长贡献降低；工业化与城市化发展不相协调。在这种宏观背景下，西部农村经济发展与西部地区国民经济发展也受到严重影响，不仅使西部农村发展遇到了前所未有的困难和矛盾，而且，没有从西部地区实际出发，没有充分运用市场机制调动社会力量，使“三农”问题成为影响西部地区社会成员利益、制约西部地区国民经济发展全局的关键问题，最终成为社会关注的热点、理论研究的难点和政治决策的重点①。

（二）发展滞后的西部地区农产品物流制约西部农村经济发展

当前西部农村经济发展与西部地区国民经济发展不相适应，很大程度上是西部地区农产品物流关系结构失调所致。物流是国民经济发展的核心。“现代物流是衡量一个国家或地区现代化程度的重要标志，是国民经济发展的动脉和基础产业。而农产品物流在国民经济发展中具有举足轻重的作用，尤其是在西部地区经济发展中更是具有重要的战略地位，它关系到本地区经济运行效率、农业产业化发展和农民的根本利益。”[1]物流与经济关系的理论成果和历史事实，尤其是过去30多年的经济发展史实表明：物流与经济可持续发展在经济发展中始终具有重要意义，保持物流与

① 1982—1986年中共中央国务院连续5年出台关于农村问题的1号文件后，2004—2005年又再度连续出台针对农村问题的1号文件，充分表明党中央、国务院对“三农”问题的重视。2000年1月，国务院西部地区开发领导小组召开西部地区开发会议，研究加快西部地区发展的基本思路和战略任务，部署实施西部大开发的重点工作。实施西部大开发战略，加快西部的经济发展，让西部人民尽快富裕起来，是促进我国各地区经济协调平衡发展，缩小东西部之间经济发展的差距，实现我国社会主义现代化三步战略，建成中等发达国家的战略决策。西部是传统的农业区和贫困地区，农业开发是西部大开发的一个重要组成部分，它直接关系到农民生活水平的提高，关系到西部地区经济与社会的协调发展，关系到我国社会主义现代化建设的进程和全面建设小康社会战略的实现，只有搞好西部农业开发，不断地巩固农业基础地位，才能从根本上实现西部地区的经济繁荣和社会稳定，最终完成西部大开发的历史重任。因此，西部大开发的成败，最为关键的不是大中城市的发展，而是西部农村有没有根本性的变化，西部农民能不能真正富裕起来。实施我国西部地区大开发战略，是党中央在世纪之交作出的具有全局意义的重大决策，对于优化地区生产力布局，缩小地区发展差距，加强民族团结，推进改革与发展，保持国家长治久安，具有重大的政治、经济和社会意义。

经济可持续发展的物流改革，已经普遍成为世界各国推行经济市场化的重要步骤。但值得注意的是，中国农村经济改革以及由此推动的中国经济改革，是在没有触动“物流”的背景下展开的，并因此产生了西部、中部与东部经济市场化的差异。20世纪90年代以来，伴随着国内改革开放的逐渐深化，尤其是西部大开发经过10年的发展，西部地区特色农业、特色制造、特色旅游等产业迅速崛起，支撑起中国经济版图发展的新模式。西部地区由于具有发展特色农业的明显的区域比较优势和成本优势，国家确定了重点发展西部七大特色农业基地并已形成七条产业带，农产品生产能力显著提高。西部地区的谷物、棉花、油料、肉类、禽蛋、水果等主要农产品在全国居领先地位，这些农产品大部分都要通过物流进入最终消费领域。但从西部地区目前的农产品物流运行状况看，农产品物流发展还是较为缓慢，运行质量较低。首先是由于西部地区城乡二元结构的现实状况，农产品物流长期以来粗放型发展及投入不足，不仅影响城乡联动发展，而且影响物流业的整体发展水平和效益，始终处于“冰山”状态。其次是现有农产品流通体系是计划经济体制下由国家统购统销的流通体系经过诱导性制度变迁政策的引导逐步演变形成。随着市场的快速演变，影响了消费结构和消费趋势变化以及农产品加工产业链延伸，这一流通体系和格局已经显示出与现代农产品流通“大生产、大流通”不相适应。农产品物流总值是反映农产品物流整体发展规模和水平的重要指标，西部地区农产品物流总值占社会物流总值的比例不超过3%，反映出农产品物流发展规模偏小，总体效率较低，不适应经济发展的要求[2]。尤其是加入WTO以后，物流开放程度不断加大，面对日益显露的西部地区农产品物流问题，以市场化、信息化、全球化、绿色化为特征的农产品物流改革，使西部地区农产品物流在改革中逐渐显露出农产品物流落后既有深刻的历史原因，又有现行的管理体制方面的原因，更有技术落后的因素。表现出农产品物流行业在过低进入障碍和过高退出障碍的双重作用下的“低收益和高风险”性；社会性农产品物流金融发展不到位；业务非农化；缺乏持续发展能力。当前，发展滞后的西部地区农产品物流已成为制约西部农村经济运行的重要因素，并阻碍着西部经济的长期可持续发展。农产品物流关系结构失调的矛盾日益暴露并不断激化。直接表现为：农产品物流缺少农村经济支撑→农产品物流脱离农村经济发展→农村经济发展缺乏物流支持→农产品物流的关系结构陷入不可持续的恶性循环。

（三）西部地区农产品物流与西部农村经济发展原理尚不清楚

解决西部地区农产品物流发展不持续问题，关键在于从西部地区农产品物流发展原理及其可持续发展机理出发，找出导致问题的原因，借鉴国际经验，构建可持续发展的机制与模式，提出具有理论和实证支持的政策措施。但遗憾的是，西部地区农产品物流发展原理至今尚不清楚。

现有文献的研究揭示，国外对农产品物流的研究较早，农产品物流研究的历史从物流的概念产生时就已经开始，它起源于美国、发展在日本、成熟在欧洲。1901 年，J. F. Growell 在《农产品流通产业委员会报告》中首次涉及农产品配送问题，详细论述了农产品配送成本的各类影响因素，从此拉开了人们对农产品物流认识的序幕。1916 年，L. D. H. Weld 在《农场产品的市场营销》中论述了市场营销时间效用、场所效用、所有权效用的概念和营销渠道的概念，从而肯定了农产品通过物流在创造产品的市场价值中的时间价值及空间性价值中的重要作用。1962 年，美国管理学大师德鲁克在《财富》杂志上发表《经济的黑暗大陆》的文章中指出，物流是降低成本的最后领域，物流是“经济界的黑大陆”“一块未被开垦的处女地”。物流价值的观点引起了众多专家学者的重视。20 世纪 80 年代后，农产品物流随着物流理论研究的不断深化而发展，但农产品的自然特性（储存期短、易腐烂变质等）决定了农产品物流同一般的物流相比有一些特殊性。一是在供应链管理方面。供应链思想早期注重从内部运营效率的层次分析，如 Miehell and Jones 提倡在农业中进行纵向整合；供应链发展期则注重以农产品链的市场定位及生产的自然属性为基础进行均衡分析，如 Koeing and Van Wiik 提出战略联盟，Den Ouded 进一步认为需要在供应链合作机制中加入信息代理，Singh 加强了对信息流作用研究。二是在成本控制与管理方面。农产品自然属性导致农产品物流存在更多的不确定性，Crowell 首次讨论了农产品配送的成本和影响因素；Ellram 认为良好的组织合作关系能降低交易总成本、Van Der Vorst 提出整合信息沟通体系对降低物流成本有促进作用；Brad Gilmour 则认为物流效率是中国内陆农产品是否具有竞争力的决定因素。三是在物流金融应用方面。1942 年 Friedman、1948 年 Raymand and Albert 等人，对存货质押融资和应收账款融资业务进行了广泛的研究。2004 年，Buzacott 确定了物流金融业务中的利率和贷款额度等重要指标，对研究农业尤其是农产品物流发展的金融支持问题有借鉴意义。

国内对农产品物流进行研究是在2000年以后出现的，主要是借鉴国外成果进行国内的实证检验，基本上停留在新古典经济学的分析框架内。一是供应链管理与成本控制方面。李洪波等运用博弈论和信息经济学的思想方法，确立了供应链内各企业长期有效合作的内在机制；武拉平提出农产品运输成本是影响农产品市场整合的重要因素；王新利则明确提出采用作业成本法核算农产品物流成本；胡小平、尹志超通过实证研究认为流通费用是决定农产品竞争力的一个关键因素；丁俊发认为农产品物流不仅能使农民生产的任何产品都实现其价值与使用价值，也可以使农产品在物流过程中增值，还能降低农产品生产与流通的成本，提高农业生产的整体效益。二是在借鉴各国制度经验方面。从国内宏观层次研究看，多采用描述性分析，朱信凯考察了日本农产品批发市场；黄祖辉等分析发达国家农产品流通体系变迁；贾会棉等介绍了欧美和东亚农产品物流模式；王滨分析了荷兰农业物流。这些研究集中在国外农产品物流管理制度和发展经验的借鉴上，进而对我国提出相应的政策建议。三是在区域范围研究方面。从国内微观层次研究看，多采用叙述性统计分析，刘文敏以上海为例指出联盟物流模式和现代农产品配送模式是今后的取向；郭淑媛从物流系统最优化的角度构筑河北省农产品物流的运作模式；刘飞翔以福建永辉集团为例选择其生鲜农产品的自营物流模式；向平以四川为例强调现代农产品配送中心的重要作用；秦代红、刘学以成都市为例，分析了农产品物流当前的问题，并提出了加快发展农产品物流业、提高农业竞争力的对策；梁琳娜认为西部农产品物流问题是影响西部经济发展的重要问题，提出强化西部农产品物流系统化管理，降低流通成本，提高农产品价值，发展农产品物流业，成为推动西部经济发展的重要途径；李虹就湘西自治州农产品物流的现状，探讨了目前农产品物流存在的问题，并提出了相应的对策；张春颖、王秀云、李娜采用SWOT法较为全面地对我国西部欠发达地区农产品物流发展的现状进行了分析，并对农产品物流中心的现状进行了剖析，提出了促进我国西部发达地区农产品物流发展及物流中心建设的措施；张春颖、王秀云通过分析我国西部特色农产品冷链物流的发展现状，提出发展的对策，为加快我国西部特色农产品冷链物流的发展提供参考。四是物流技术方面。从国内长期以来实行食物安全的发展战略看，主要集中在保障供给的数量安全方面，影响了农产品物流技术与物流链管理，农产品供应链的信息技术、电子商务技术还处于技术引进和初级研发阶段。孙元欣、吕永成、杜小芳、李艳霞等分别研究了库存和财务等具体环节，但缺乏全流程的集成研究。尽管周欢、张晟义、王新利等开始关注农产品质量安全问题，大多集中在生产和消费领域而忽视了对流通的考察，更没有关注西部地区农产品物流对农产品质量安全的促进作用及其对农产品质量安全追溯体系建立的重要性。五是物流金融应用方面。李碧珍提出解决中小企业融资困难的重要途径是“融通仓”；邹小梵、唐元琦提出的“物流金融”被正式确定为新的研究平台；唐少麟、乔婷婷采用风险控制研究了开展中小企业物流金融的可行性，物流金融理论在实践中的另一个重要应用是物流银行业务的开展。

通过对相关文献进行回顾我们发现，已有研究理论主要侧重于两类：一类基于交易成本经济学和不完全契约理论研究农产品物流；一类基于博弈论和信息不对称理论研究链上冲突，实现协调。研究方法主要有：随机模型、几何规划技术、成本分析方法，更为重要的是作业成本分析法。毫无疑问，既有的理论成果，对于研究和探索西部农产品物流可持续发展理论具有非常重要的学术价值和现实意义。但在这些研究中，国外研究只侧重于农产品物流发展对农村经济增长的促进作用及其因果关系，大多研究以比较完备的市场制度和完善的物流市场为前提，忽视了研究农产品物流可持续发展的重要性。而国内更多的研究属于针对某一具体问题的一般性对策研究，未能涉及西部地区正处于战略“转型”之中的经济体制，一方面，要面对国内经济市场化的冲击；另一方面，又要迎接加入 WTO 后物流经济开放带来的挑战，西部地区农产品物流可持续发展问题，与世界上任何国家都不相同，甚至与中国的中部、东部地区也不尽相同。文献中对于西部农产品物流问题的关注，特别是对西部农产品物流服务供给不足问题的分析，大多着眼于西部农产品物流机构视角，所遵循的是以结构—功能—绩效分析为特征的机构范式，研究视角主要集中在西部地区农产品物流促进农村经济方面，而农产品物流功能及其生成机制的研究没有被重视，鲜有从农村经济角度探索西部地区农产品物流发展的研究。学术界为研究西部地区农产品物流可持续发展机制与模式问题留出了相当大的空间。可见，对于西部大开发 10 年来西部地区农产品物流发展的研究，无论是在微观、宏观层次，还是各个管理方面，理论和实践研究都比较贫乏，对其研究一直处于不系统状态。因此，本研究将试图在全面梳理并综合各种观点的基础上对于这些问题进行深入研究。

（四）可持续发展问题研究应向机制与模式层面深化

目前，可持续发展已被越来越多的人所接受，并逐渐成为国际公认的经济伦理规范。“可持续发展”核心是“协调发展”，代表了当今“发展”和“发展研究”的方向。中国经济社会发展中，随着国际上可持续发展理念的提出，我国政府将可持续发展战略作为实现经济社会长远发展的基本国策，并在2007年2月发行的《中国可持续发展总纲（国家卷）》中进一步提出了我国可持续发展的战略目标，并进行了一系列理论和实践探索。我国实施可持续发展战略涉及经济社会的各个方面，它同样引导着我国现代物流的发展方向。但在总体上，对“可持续发展”的研究和认识，仍然停留在“发展观”的哲学层面和宏观分析的理论层面，还未深入涉及政策操作层面的机制与模式问题，更未涉及农产品物流领域，西部地区农产品物流可持续发展的机制与模式远未被人们所认识。现实的需要和研究的短缺，构成了选择和研究本课题的全部理由与意义。需要特别说明的是，西部大开发战略实施10年以来，西部特色农业获得了巨大的发展和变化，从物资经济学的角度系统地研究西部地区农产品物流可持续发展，对支持西部大开发后续政策研究具有重要的理论价值和现实意义。首先，研究西部地区农产品物流可持续发展的基本特征，发现其内在规律，总结国际经验形成启示，是丰富和发展中国特色社会主义经济理论体系的需要。其次，研究10年以来西部地区农产品物流的客观现实有助于形成可持续发展模式总体框架及其区位化的组织模式和运行平台，并据此提出农产品物流可持续发展路径及政策以解决现实问题，促进我国西部经济未来发展，实现整个国家经济和社会和谐发展。这不仅为本研究提供了思想和理论指导，而且也进一步验证了选择和研究本课题在方向上的正确性、时间上的及时性和价值上的重要性。

二　研究的背景

（一）时间背景

本研究跨越新中国成立以来，主要是1978年以来，1992年中国社会主义市场经济体制确立后，西部地区农产品物流发展的各个阶段。考虑到研究结论对支持西部大开发后续政策研究的针对性、时效性和对未来的指导意义，将重点考察2000年西部大开发战略全面实施以来[①]，尤其是2006年12月8日国务院常务会议审议并原则通过《西部大开发“十一五”规划》后[②]，西部地区农产品物流的关系结构。为了更好贯彻2010年7月5日中共中央、国务院明确提出深入推进西部大开发的战略部署和思路[③]，更好地刻画和揭示西部地区农产品物流发展的内在特征，本研究在相关的制度考察中，还将研究的时间背景适当延伸到中国农产品物流和农村经济发展的历史长河之中，以历史的视角来考察和解释现实问题。

（二）空间背景

本研究以我国西部地区12个省、自治区和直辖市[④]，即“跨行政区域的经济带”[⑤] 意义上的西部地区农产品物流发展为研究对象。本研究中

---

① 2000年10月，中共十五届五中全会通过的《中共中央关于制定国民经济和社会发展第十个五年计划的建议》，把实施西部大开发、促进地区协调发展作为一项战略任务，强调：“实施西部大开发战略、加快中西部地区发展，关系经济发展、民族团结、社会稳定，关系地区协调发展和最终实现共同富裕，是实现第三步战略目标的重大举措。”

② 2006年12月8日，国务院常务会议审议并原则通过《西部大开发“十一五”规划》。目标是努力实现西部地区经济又好又快发展，人民生活水平持续稳定提高，基础设施和生态环境建设取得新突破，重点区域和重点产业的发展达到新水平，教育、卫生等基本公共服务均等化取得新成效，构建社会主义和谐社会迈出扎实步伐。部大开发总的战略目标是：经过几代人的艰苦奋斗，到21世纪中叶全国基本实现现代化时，从根本上改变西部地区相对落后的面貌，建成一个经济繁荣、社会进步、生活安定、民族团结、山川秀美、人民富裕的新西部。

③ 2010年7月5日至6日，在西部大开发战略实施10周年之际，党中央、国务院召开西部大开发工作会议，胡锦涛总书记和温家宝总理发表了重要讲话。这次会议，站在我国改革开放和现代化建设全局，全面回顾了西部大开发的巨大成就，深刻阐述了西部大开发的丰富经验，明确提出了深入推进西部大开发的战略部署和思路，对于我们在新的历史起点上，推动西部大开发再上新台阶，具有十分重要的意义。

④ 综合考虑经济发展水平、地理区位和民族地区发展因素，国务院西部地区开发领导小组办公室将西部开发的范围定义为陕西、甘肃、青海、宁夏、新疆、内蒙古、四川、重庆、云南、贵州、广西、西藏等十二个省、区、市以及湖南、湖北两省的部分少数民族自治州，其国土面积538万平方千米，占全国国土面积的56%；目前有人口约3.67亿人，占全国人口的28.56%。西部地区自然资源丰富，市场潜力大，战略位置重要。但由于自然、历史、社会等原因，西部地区经济发展相对落后，人均国内生产总值仅相当于全国平均水平的2/3，不到东部地区平均水平的40%，迫切需要加快改革开放和现代化建设步伐。

⑤ 实施西部大开发，就是要依托亚欧大陆桥、长江水道、西南出海通道等交通干线，发挥中心城市作用，以线串点，以点带面，逐步形成我国西部有特色的西陇海兰新线、长江上游、南（宁）贵、成昆（明）等跨行政区域的经济带，带动其他地区发展，有步骤、有重点地推进西部大开发。

的“西部地区农产品物流”不是一成不变的空间概念，而是始终处于不断发展变化之中的，在西部农村经济不同的发展阶段，其内涵、形态和特征各有区别的动态概念。本研究认为正是这种发展变化及其区别，对西部地区农产品物流可持续发展构成了重要的影响，从而自然构成了本研究的重要内容。但本研究的空间背景并不完全局限于此，而是一方面将西部地区农产品物流与西部农村经济置于整个国民经济当中，从经济、社会发展全局的角度，从总体和宏观上加以考察和研究；另一方面结合西部地区经济社会发展和产业经济运行，从中观上进行研究和探索，同时还将从政府、农户和企业行为角度，构建西部地区农产品物流可持续发展的微观基础；再一方面，本研究还将从世界范围内，对农产品物流可持续发展的实践进行考察和总结，为研究提供国际经验借鉴。

（三）理论背景

本研究以前人相关的理论成果和实践经验为宝贵资源，从中汲取有用成分用于支撑本研究，并试图取得创新的理论和方法营养。本研究将这些理论资源集中概括为现代物流与经济发展、可持续与可持续发展、制度创新与变迁理论三大理论体系。其中既包括由马克思和恩格斯开辟的，后来马克思主义者继承和发展的马克思主义的相关理论及其研究方法；又包括西方经济学中各种流派的理论、观点与政策主张，还包括现代系统科学的理论和方法。研究中将在严格分析这些理论产生、发展背景和运用条件的基础上，紧密结合中国实际和本研究特点，努力加以吸收利用，并力争取得突破和创新。

（四）现实背景

当今西部大开发最大和最重要的背景是“改革开放和现代化建设”[①]。“改革开放和现代化建设”的核心是社会主义市场经济体制的建立和完善，以及与之相伴随的对外开放和随之而来的“全球化”冲击。在本研

① 当前和今后一段时期，是西部地区深化改革、扩大开放、加快发展的重要战略机遇期。要重点抓好基础设施和生态环境建设；积极发展有特色的优势产业，推进重点地带开发；发展科技教育，培育和用好各类人才；国家要在投资项目、税收政策和财政转移支付等方面加大对西部地区的支持，逐步建立长期稳定的西部开发资金渠道；着力改善投资环境，引导外资和国内资本参与西部开发；西部地区要进一步解放思想，增强自我发展能力，在改革开放中走出一条加快发展的新路。

究中，前者构成了研究的体制背景，后者构成了研究的开放背景。

从体制背景上看，本研究正处于西部地区战略“转型”的阶段，转型是一项庞大的系统工程，经济转型是根本，社会、生态、文化转型是保证。西部大开发战略实施十年来，党中央，国务院高瞻远瞩，总揽全局，强化基础，重点突破，先后出台实施了一系列政策指导意见，国家相关部委也相应制定促进西部大开发的各种政策措施。为了更好整合各职能部门资源以及协调中央和地方之间的关系，国务院在2000年1月成立“国务院西部地区开发领导小组办公室”，由朱镕基总理亲自出任组长，副总理温家宝任副组长，中共中央，国务院19个部门的主要负责人为领导小组成员，有力推进西部大开发规划和政策的实施。2000年10月26日，国办转发了《国务院关于实施西部大开发若干政策措施的通知》[①]，此后国务院西部开发办出台《关于西部大开发若干政策措施的实施意见》（2001年8月8日）、《国务院关于进一步完善退耕还林还草试点工作的若干意见》（2000年9月10日）、《国务院关于进一步完善退耕还林政策的若干意见》（2002年4月11日）、《退耕还林条例》（2002年12月6日通过）、《关于应对金融危机保持西部地区经济平稳较快发展的意见》（2009年9月30日）等。各有关部门和地方各级政府在贯彻西部大开发实施意见和规划的过程中也出台了相应的政策措施。西部大开发总体规划可按50年划分为奠定基础、加速发展、全面推进现代化三个阶段[②]。实施西部大开发是一项长期艰巨的历史任务，也是一项规模宏大的系统工程。尽管体制“转型”尚未完成，但社会主义市场经济体制的建设和完善已经进入快车道。所以，本研究将回首计划经济体制，总结在计划经济体制中西部地区

① 《国务院关于实施西部大开发若干政策措施的通知》，通知中明确西部大开发的重点任务：加快基础设施建设；加强生态环境保护和建设；巩固农业基础地位，调整工业结构，发展特色旅游业；发展科技教育和文化卫生事业。

② 西部大开发总体规划可按50年划分为三个阶段：一是奠定基础阶段：从2001年到2010年，重点是调整结构，搞好基础设施、生态环境、科技教育等基础建设，建立和完善市场体制，培育特色产业增长点，使西部地区投资环境初步改善，生态和环境恶化得到初步遏制，经济运行步入良性循环，增长速度达到全国平均增长水平；二是加速发展阶段：从2010年到2030年，在前段基础设施改善、结构战略性调整和制度建设成就的基础上，进入西部开发的冲刺阶段，巩固提高基础，培育特色产业，实施经济产业化、市场化、生态化和专业区域布局的全面升级，实现经济增长的跃进；三是全面推进现代化阶段：从2031年到2050年，在一部分率先发展地区增强实力，融入国内国际现代化经济体系自我发展的基础上，着力加快边远山区、落后农牧区开发，普遍提高西部人民的生产、生活水平，全面缩小差距。

农产品物流发展恶化的教训；立足转型经济，实证转型时期西部地区农产品物流数量关系状况和存在的问题；面向市场经济，寻求市场经济中西部地区农产品物流可持续发展的对策。研究中充分考虑中国经济、社会“转型”过程中，经济体制既呈现出向市场经济体制迅速“转轨”的趋势，又不可避免地要出现带有计划经济体制痕迹的“混合”体制特征和由体制“转轨”带来的物流“真空”。但本研究并不始终停留在“转型”体制背景之下，而是以市场经济体制的理论模型为参照，研究和探索西部地区农产品物流发展的内在关系，并以此为基础构建适合西部地区实际的可持续发展的机制与模式。

从开放背景上看，伴随着改革的深化，西部大开发体制机制创新和对内对外开放不断加强①。从中央政府的角度出发，在农业领域，农业部在“十五”期间采取十大措施支持西部大开发，包括组织实施天然草地保护工程，计划5年内在西部地区治理和建设草地2.2亿亩（0.15亿公顷）；加强粮食基地建设，包括成都平原，河西走廊，新疆南部地区，陕西关中地区，宁夏河套灌区，内蒙古河套灌区等区域；建设特色农产品生产基地，其中包括：优质棉花生产基地，优质果园，蔬菜良种繁育基地，鲜切花基地，中药材良种繁育基地和天然橡胶基地等。大力发展旱作节水农业，通过加强旱作农田基本建设，完善节水补充灌溉配套设施，抗旱品种选育和推广以及配套完善土壤肥料监测等措施，搞好200个旱作农业示范县建设；积极推进生态农业的发展，“十五”期间在西部地区建设100个生态农业示范县；加快发展西部地区养殖业；积极发展农产品加工业和乡镇企业；加强农业社会化服务体系建设；大力开展基层农技人员和农民的职业培训。伴随着国民经济的快速发展、世界贸易组织的正式加入、与周边国家和地区自由贸易区的加快建立以及粮棉等重要农产品流通体制的深化改革，农产品市场化程度和贸易自由化程度得以快速提高，对现代农产品物流产生了内在的需求。2001年12月11日正式加入WTO，意味着中国开始主动参与经济全球化，对外开放进入新阶段，西部农业和农村经济发展也进入崭新历史阶段。从西部农村经济角度看，一方面，加入WTO，

① 积极探索投资体制改革，推进财税体制改革，加大转移支付力度。特别是近年来，东西部地区互动发展呈现出良好势头据不完全统计，2000年至2007年，东部地区到西部地区投资经营的企业累计近20万家，投资总额15000多亿元，西洽会、西博会、中国—东盟博览会等已成为东西互动合作和吸引外商投资的重要平台。西部地区累计实际利用外商直接投资约180亿美元。

西部农业不仅面临巨大的国内市场竞争压力，而且国际市场竞争更趋激烈，农产品市场竞争呈现国内市场国际化和国际市场国内化的格局，西部农业必须按比较优势来组织生产，实现规模化、产业化、国际化和市场化，传统的农业生产经营和组织管理方式面临全面的挑战。另一方面，加入 WTO 后的进一步开放，必然要求加快城市和国有工业企业改革，从而对西部农村经济发展提出更高的要求，外来资本和技术对城市经济和非农产业的改造与嫁接，在一定程度上还会产生“马太效应”，加大西部农业和农村经济与整个西部经济发展的差距。从西部地区农产品物流角度看，加入 WTO 后，长期处于政策壁垒保护下的西部地区农产品物流将不可避免地要受到物流国际化、全球化和一体化的冲击，西部地区农产品物流也不可避免地要迎接严峻的挑战。这种挑战，一方面来自加入 WTO 后，中国物流业将全方位开放，西部地区农产品物流不可避免地要受到外资物流机构介入的冲击；另一方面来自物流开放条件下，国有物流出于自身生存与发展需要，为迎接 WTO 挑战而进行改革，所带来的西部地区农产品物流“真空”；再一方面就是来自 WTO 背景下西部农村经济发展对农产品物流的新要求。开放背景下，西部地区农产品物流发展，面临着更加严格的约束条件。本研究将在这些约束条件下，分析其内在关系，探索可持续发展的机制与模式。

第二节　研究的目标与假设

一　研究的目标

本研究的总体目标：用科学的理论和方法，系统地探索市场经济条件下西部地区农产品物流可持续发展的机制与模式，为西部地区农产品物流可持续发展战略和政策制定及实施提供理论和实证依据。为此，本研究解决以下关键问题：一是回顾和借鉴国内外已有理论和相关研究，确立本研究的逻辑起点。二是确立研究范式，界定西部地区农产品物流可持续发展的基本范畴和研究基点。三是分析西部地区农产品物流可持续发展的概念内涵、基本特征，揭示可持续发展的实现机理。四是在系统考察国外农产品物流可持续发展经验的基础上，比较分析国际经验，形成研究启示。五是判断西部地区不同阶段农产品物流发展状况及其影响，分析西部地区农产品物流发展不持续的原因。六是建立西部地区农产品物流可持续发展模式总体框架及其区位化的组织模式。七是科学设计保障区位化组织模式实施的运行平台。八是构建西部地区农产品物流可持续发展的机制与模式，并提出相关政策建议。

二　研究的假设

本研究的基本假设：一是物流与经济是有条件的互动发展、互为因果关系。西部地区农产品物流发展，既符合物流与经济关系的一般原理，又具有自身的独特性。西部地区农产品物流、农村经济是中国“二元结构”“转型”“西部大开发”和“WTO”背景下，既与整体物流、经济密不可分，又建立在自身微观基础之上的结构系统，两者互动发展，既可相互促进，又可相互制约；既可独立，又可共同地对整体物流和经济构成影响。二是西部地区农产品物流可持续发展，是西部地区农产品物流关系结构的理想状态及其实现过程。可持续发展既是制度、技术和结构变迁相互协调持续的过程，又是多样化实现手段相互协调持续的过程。其基础在于市场经济体制条件下，政府、农产品物流主体和农村经济主体功能的发挥，核心在于制度可持续。三是经济转型过程中的西部地区农产品物流关系结构发展失调。其原因复杂多样。直接原因是西部地区农产品物流脱离农村经济；深层原因是西部地区农村经济发育程度低；根本原因是宏观制度环境约束。四是在消费结构和消费趋势变化下，建立西部地区农产品物流的可持续发展模式总体框架及其区位化的组织模式。通过整合各成员的资源、技术与信息，科学设计保障区位化组织模式实施的运行平台。五是西部地区农产品物流关系结构失调，从根本上讲是制度抑制长期积累的结果。西部地区农产品物流可持续发展，关键在于机制与模式构建，核心在于制度可持续。制度可持续，既不能脱离宏观制度环境，但又必须独立运动；发挥政府职能，实现“集约型”“差别物流”是走出“失调陷阱”、走向“可持续发展”的切入点。但治本在于现代市场制度在西部农村的确立和完善，以及“二元”经济、物流结构的“一元化”。本研究将以适用于中国西部地区的研究结论为起点，建立理论和分析框架，用新的视角、思路、理论和方法来论证这一假设。

第三节 研究的思路与方法

一 研究的思路

本研究的基本思路：围绕可持续发展，广泛挖掘和科学吸收、利用已有理论资源，以适合于中国西部地区的研究结论为起点，在充分认识到西部地区农产品物流关系结构特殊性的基础上，将西部地区农产品物流、农村经济置于整个宏观经济物流背景之中。从政治经济学的角度以经济社会发展对西部大开发的总体要求为指导，借鉴西方经济学合理的方法和理论，联系客观现实深入剖析基本概念，在充分认识西部地区农产品物流发展理论内涵的基础上，深入探索西部地区农产品物流与农村经济的互动原理及其微观基础，从交易视角和功能范式上准确界定西部地区农产品物流可持续发展的理论内涵，揭示其可持续发展的实现机理，构建本研究的理论框架，并进一步借鉴农产品物流可持续发展的国际经验形成研究启示，完善和检验理论框架；在此基础上，运用制度分析和计量分析方法，基于实证数据系统地研究经济转型过程中的西部地区农产品物流发展状况，揭示关系结构失调的表现，分析失调的影响及约束原因；依据可持续发展的原理和国际经验，构建基于功能范式的，西部地区农产品物流可持续发展总模式及其区位化的组织模式和运行平台，并据此有重点、分层次地指出可持续发展的机制与模式及其发展战略，并提出针对性的政策建议。

本研究在深入客观实际进行调研和进行系统的理论回顾与借鉴基础上，努力遵循“是什么—为什么—怎么样—如何办”的知识创造和认识过程，按应用经济学研究从理论—实证—对策的一般程序展开研究，研究的技术路线是：确定分析的基本方法—揭示概念内涵与实现机理—通过实证数据客观剖析约束原因—确定可持续发展模式总体框架建立组织模式—设计运行平台—基于前述研究提出可持续发展机制与模式建设路径以及政策建议。因此，可以概括为图 1－1。

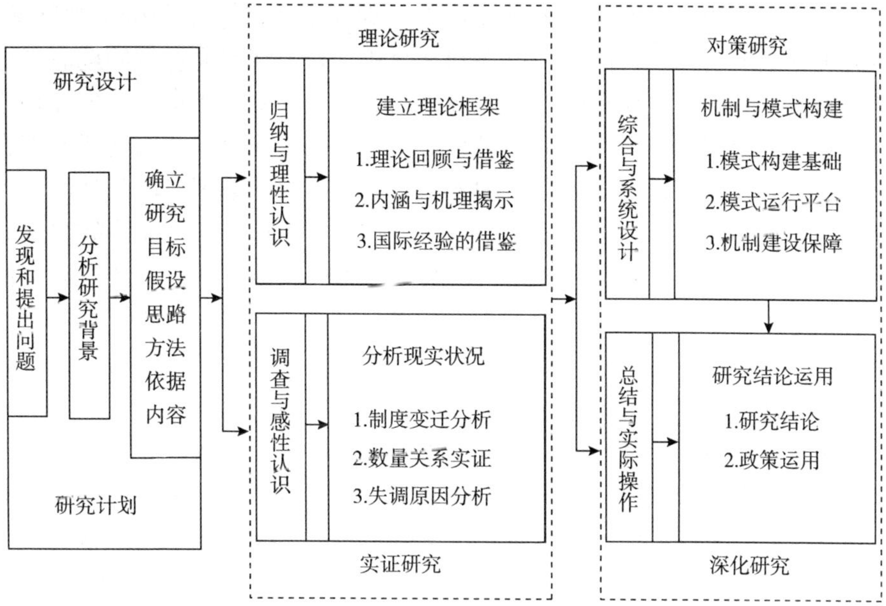

图 1-1 西部地区农产品物流可持续发展政策研究的技术路线

二 研究的方法

本研究遵循辩证唯物主义与历史唯物主义的基本原理，以马克思主义分工理论、流通理论为理论指导，借鉴了现代物流学、经济发展学、新制度经济学、现代管理学、统计学等基本理论和方法，对现代西方经济理论及其哲学思想的吸收，在可持续发展理论框架下，加强多学科理论和方法的综合运用。一是在研究路径上，将规范研究和实证研究相结合。实证分析是客观地描述现象，回答“是什么”的问题；规范分析则在于形成一种解释这些现象的理论，回答“应该是什么”的问题。本研究以西部地区农产品物流发展中的现实问题为出发点，以实现西部地区农产品物流可持续发展为目标，在规范研究的基础上展开实证研究，并以实证结论去检验规范研究结论[3]。二是在研究视角上，将历史分析与逻辑分析相统一。前者通过概念、推理、判断等形式再现研究对象发展变化的本质特点，确定其规律性；后者则按照研究对象的历史发展进程揭示其规律性。本研究力求历史与现实相结合，即立足现实，用历史方法分析和解释现实问题，但又不拘泥于历史；微观与宏观相结合，即在宏观背景中分析微观问题，在微观基础上解释宏观问题；经济和社会相结合，即研究经济问题时考虑社会因素，分析社会现象时考虑经济原因；理论和实证相结合，即在理论分析基础上展开实证，用实证结果来证明理论的正确性，从而使研究能在纷繁复杂的农村问题中把握主线和方向，揭示出西部地区农产品物流可持续发展的机制与模式。具体方法主要表现在：在理论回顾与借鉴的基础上，确定研究的逻辑起点，界定本研究的基本概念，进而运用新古典经济学的理论和分析范式，构建西部地区农产品物流可持续发展的理论框架；运用农产品物流可持续发展的国际经验去检验理论框架；运用历史分析和计量经济分析的方法和手段，实证西部地区农产品物流发展的现实表现和影响；运用新制度经济学的视角和分析工具，揭示西部地区农产品物流关系结构发展失调的原因，寻求可持续发展的机制与模式，构建可持续发展的战略，提出对策建议。规范研究注重概念界定和内涵揭示，并以此为基础展开数理推理；实证研究在规范研究的基础上展开，将定性的、定量的、时序的和横断面的分析相结合；定性分析注重制度和历史分析方法的运用；定量分析强调数据可靠、方法实用、手段先进，以博弈论、因果分析、聚类分析、网络层次分析 ANP 等为主。

第四节　研究的依据与内容

一　研究的依据

本研究的数据资料以国家法定或权威数据为主，主要来自历年的《中国统计年鉴》《中国商业年鉴》《中国物流年鉴》《中国经济年鉴》《农业统计年鉴》《中国农产品加工业年鉴》《中国农产品价格调查年鉴》《中国农村统计年鉴》《中国仓储协会统计年鉴》《经济普查公报》《农业普查公报》等，部分数据来自经典著作、权威性学术期刊和研究报告，并加以引注。这些经典著作有西方经济学、微观经济学、制度经济学、产业经济学、区域经济学、现代物流学等多方面的专业论著、译著和教材；

权威性学术期刊有《经济研究》《管理世界》《中国社会科学》《中国农村经济》《农业经济问题》等；研究报告有中国社会科学院农村发展研究所和国家统计局农村社会经济调查总队所著的《农村经济绿皮书》，国家发展和改革委员会经济运行局、南开大学现代物流研究中心编辑出版的《中国现代物流发展报告——迈向全面开放的中国物流市场》，中国物流与采购联合会按年度编辑出版的《中国物流发展报告》。研究中还使用了一些实际调查数据，包括相关研究和本研究组织的调查，对其来源和取得方法都将给予说明。研究中必要的定性资料，主要是国家法律和政策公开的文件、权威性的报告、公告、专业研究报告和科学论文等。

二 研究的内容

本研究的内容包括总论、理论研究、实证研究、对策研究和附录五部分，共分为十二章。

第一部分：总论。包括：第一章。详细介绍研究的问题与背景，研究的目标与假设，研究的思路与方法，研究的依据与内容。

第二部分：理论研究，共三章。包括：第二章，理论回顾与借鉴；第三章，西部地区农产品物流可持续发展的内涵与机理；第四章，农产品物流可持续发展的国际经验借鉴与启示。通过比较系统回顾和借鉴现代物流与经济发展理论、可持续与可持续发展理论、制度变迁与创新理论；从交易视角和功能范式上界定研究的基本范畴和分析基点；科学地定义和解释西部地区农产品物流可持续发展的概念内涵、基本特征，揭示其均衡过程、内在规律；比较分析国际经验，形成研究启示。

第三部分：实证研究，共三章。包括：第五章，中国农产品物流制度变迁的演化过程分析；第六章，转型时期西部地区农产品物流数量关系实证；第七章，西部地区农产品物流关系结构失调原因分析。以国家统计局规定为指导，推算当前西部地区农产品物流总值及它们在社会物流总值的比重。运用历史分析和计量检验方法，从制度和数量方面，实证转型时期西部地区农产品物流与农村经济的关系结构，剖析其根本原因、深层原因和直接原因。

第四部分：对策研究，共四章。包括：第八章，西部地区农产品物流可持续发展的模式创建；第九章，西部地区农产品物流可持续发展的模式运行；第十章，西部地区农产品物流可持续发展的机制建设；第十一章，研究结论与政策运用。基于供应链管理研究成果的系统分析，在消费结构和消费趋势变化下，建立西部地区农产品物流的可持续发展模式总体框架及其区位化的组织模式；基于成本控制与管理、物流技术研究成果的综合分析，通过整合各成员的资源、技术与信息，科学设计保障区位化组织模式实施的运行平台；围绕前述研究结论，分析西部地区农产品物流可持续发展机制与模式建设路径，以及与之相对应的系统化的可操作性政策建议。

第五部分：附录。包括：第十二章。作为课题的补充项目及珍贵资料。附录一：西部地区农产品现代物流发展模式相关案例；附录二：西部地区农产品市场与基地联盟相关案例；附录三：西部地区农业产业化龙头企业；附录四：西部地区农业产业化示范单位。

第二章　理论回顾与借鉴

科学研究和理论创新必须以前人的成果为基础。本研究是在深入考察西部地区农产品物流客观现实，以及相关研究的基础上提出的。研究展开的首要问题是对前人的相关研究成果进行梳理、综合和分析，为确立研究的逻辑起点、建立研究的理论框架，提供有效的理论借鉴。根据研究目标和理论假设的逻辑推演，本研究可借鉴的理论资源是现代物流与经济发展理论、可持续与可持续发展理论、制度变迁与创新理论。本章将围绕这三大理论，概括性挖掘和展示本研究的理论源泉。

第一节　现代物流与经济发展理论

农产品物流研究的历史从物流的概念产生时就已经开始，自现代物流业的理论研究与实践产生以来①，现代物流与经济发展理论是一个始终和经济理论交织在一起的重要组成部分，其重要性伴随着经济发展中物流地位的日益提高而不断增强；其内涵伴随着经济、物流发展而不断深化，其内容涉及经济学、物流学的各个领域、各个方面，是一个门类庞杂、流派众多、内容深刻、观点纷繁的理论体系。本节将主要围绕马克思经济学和西方经济学两大主线展开论述。

---

① 现代物流业的理论研究与实践最早起源于美国，发展在日本，成熟在欧洲，20 世纪 70 年代初被引入我国。20 世纪 80 年代中期以来，随着经济全球化和信息化进程的不断加快，物流业作为具有广阔前景和增值功能的新兴服务业，在全球范围内获得迅速发展，被称为“现代物流革命”和“第三利润源泉”。

一　当代马克思经济学中的现代物流与经济发展理论

马克思经济学是指由马克思和恩格斯等经典作家开创，并经马克思主义者继承、完善和不断发展形成的关于经济运行与发展规律的理论体系。马克思经济学中的流通理论与经济增长思想博大精深，对现代物流与经济发展理论有着深远的影响。以下主要以马克思的经典理论和邓小平等中国马克思主义者在社会主义市场经济条件下的主要观点为主线展开。

（一）经典马克思主义的流通与经济关系理论

马克思所处的时代，“物流（Logistics）”① 的概念还未形成，人们对“物流（Logistics）”的认识还停留在商品流通中的商流层次上，作为独立的物流与经济发展的理论还没有形成，追述其渊源可以从流通与物流系统的边界理论开始。马克思的流通与经济关系理论是通过生产的社会性即生产关系、交换关系、分配关系、消费关系来反映的。贯穿于马克思关于商品、货币、资本和剩余价值的理论之中，和马克思主义哲学一脉相传。其核心是“经济决定流通，流通反作用于经济”②。

1. “经济决定流通”源于马克思的分工交换理论

马克思基于分工的极端重要性→分工与协作创造生产力（集体力）→社会分工（商品交换作为媒介）与生产组织内部分工（资本家或管理部门的共同指挥作为媒介）的交互作用→分工制度内涵的推理过程，认为“一个民族的生产力发展水平，最明显地表现于该民族分工的发展程度。任何新的生产力，只要它不仅仅是现有生产力的扩大（例如开垦新的土地），都会引起分工的进一步发展”[4]。“分工与协作不仅提高生产力，而且创造生产力，并且这种生产力是‘集体力’”[5]。“在工场内部的分工中

---

① 翻译实践中，“物流”或“Logistics”作为一组可以对译的中英文词汇来使用。物流一词起源于第二次世界大战期间美国的军事应用（physical distribution，PD），直译为“物资分配”，日本将其定为“物流”。战后，物流在企业界得到应用和发展，现在多以“Logistics”表示。从严格的专业意义上看，“Logistics”和“PD”应注意其区别，谨慎使用。详见叶怀珍主编：《现代物流学》，北京：高等教育出版社，2003 年，第 1 页；林勇著：《物流管理基础》，湖北：华中科技大学出版社，2008 年，第 1 ~ 3 页。

② 马克思的流通与经济发展理论的现代语言表达和概括，马克思的文献中并没有直接给出这样的论述。

预先地、有计划地起作用的规则，在社会内部的分工中只是在事后作为一种内在的、无声的自然必然性起着作用，这种自然必然性可以在市场价格的晴雨表的变动中察觉出来，并克服着商品生产者的无规则的任意行动”[6]。在资本主义商品经济中以商品交换作为媒介实现社会分工的总体联系，而在生产组织内部以资本家或管理部门的共同指挥作为媒介实现生产组织内部分工的总体联系[7]。“分散的交换行为产生出银行和信用制度”[8]，“随着商业和只有着眼于流通而进行生产的资本主义生产方式的发展，信用制度的这个自然基础也在扩大、普遍化和发展”。这种“扩大、普遍化和发展”表现为“商品不是为取得货币而卖，而是为取得定期支付的票据而卖”[9]。银行信用的产生能够动员整个社会资金，为商品流动乃至整个社会再生产过程的继续和扩大服务。马克思认为分工不仅是单个企业的生产组织制度，也是整个经济活动的生产组织制度。同时，分工不是没有历史背景的生产要素组合，而是以特定的经济制度尤其是生产资料所有制为前提的，是所有制在具体生产组织上的反映[10]。根据马克思的理论逻辑，商品经济不仅决定了以信用制度、生产组织制度为特征的“流通”的产生，而且还直接决定其规模、结构和发展速度。马克思的分工理论揭示了农产品物流必须是各物流主体在分工的基础上进行协作，对引导农户从自营农业的小经济部门向分工、合作的协调式方向发展，扩大生产经营规模，促进农产品物流模式不断创新、完善，具有重大的指导意义[11]。

2. “流通反作用于经济”源于马克思的流通理论

（1）马克思主义流通理论的分析逻辑。马克思基于物物交换→简单的商品流通→发达的商品流通制度的推理过程，认为“流通本身只是交换的一定要素，或者也是从总体上看的交换”[12]。“每个商品形态变化形成的循环同其他商品的循环交错在一起，这个全部过程表现为商品流通。”[13]由此可见，马克思把交换作为研究流通理论的起点。随着社会分工与交换的进一步扩大，商品经济的发展使得简单的商品流通出现了货币流通的形式，并进而演化到发达的商品流通即资本流通。流通形成发展演进过程真实的表明了商品流通的发展程度标志着商品经济发展的历史进程。①商品流通的一般规定性与形成。交换中等价物的形成→买卖的形成→商品流通的形成。正如马克思所指出的，“商品交换是在共同体的尽头，在他们与别的共同体或其他成员接触的地方开始的”[14]，交换等价物的形成使得物物交换（W—W）变为以货币为媒介物的交换（W—G—W）。“流通实际上只是把交换价值一次表现在商品规定上，另一次表现在货币规定上的形式过程”[15]，买卖的形成使得商品所有者只有首先完成第一形态变化，才有可完成第二形态变化，演化为商品流通的形成。②商品流通的特殊规定性与形成。马克思进一步考察了资本主义流通的特殊规定性，创立了资本流通理论。发达商品流通是由简单商品流通发展而来的。买卖两次行为的断裂→交换目的的变化→交换发展成为流通的必然性。简单的商品流通中的“卖”和“买”作为两次行为隐藏着两次行为断裂的可能性，同时也意味着交易中存在着自由性。有可能通过先买后卖的方式获取价差，使得货币增加，即形成了发达的商品流通形式（G—W—G′）。由物物交换到简单的商品流通，再到发达的商品流通是交换发展的必然。发达的商品流通就是资本的流通，资本流通过程作为价值增值的实现过程，“在交换中则表现为各资本彼此按照一定的和限定的比例进行交换。”[16]③商业资本与商业作用。马克思认为商品流通实际上是流通过程中产业资本与商业资本的有机结合，也就是总流通过程，“总过程表现在生产过程和流通过程的统一；生产过程成为流通过程的媒介，反之亦然”[17]。商业这种商品流通形式提高社会效益和经济效益的作用，主要表现在三个方面。一是商业的存在对于加速商品转换为货币的过程，从而加速社会再生产过程具有重要作用。二是商业的存在可以相对地减少社会投入流通领域的资本或资金的数量，从而有利于生产规模的扩大。三是商业的存在还有利于社会分工的发展和生产专业化程度的提高，从而有助于社会分工生产率的不断提高。马克思指出：“资本主义生产方式以大规模的生产为前提，同样也以大规模的出售为前提；因此是以出售给商人，而不是出售给消费者个人为前提。”[18]

（2）流通是经济社会运行的方式。①流通是所有者的循环更迭的运动过程。简单商品流通与发达商品流通的运动形式不同：前者起点是商品，终结是商品，而后者起点是货币，终结是货币；前者是流通的结束标志着进入消费的阶段，而后者是货币在本次运动终结时又将成为新一次运动的开始。因此，这种运动形式是循环往复无止境的。由于发达商品流通的起点与终点都是同质货币，其实际意义在于量的差别。因此扩展成过程“货币—商品—货币—商品”被看作流通的特殊形式。这种循环运动着的交换过程，“作为交换行为的系列，在交换中，在不同的交换时刻，所有者会改变。”[19]正是所有者的不断更迭，消费者作为货币的所有者才能在商品流通结束时成为商品的所有者。②流通是社会各成员之间的利益关系体系。“商品流通是一系列无休止的社会性交换行为，流通是商品所有者全部相互关系的总和”[20]，在商品流通过程中买卖双方是以对立形式出现的，“这两种角色不是固定的，而是在商品流通中经常由人们交替扮演的”[21]“商品不能自己到市场上去，不能自己去交换，因此，我们必须寻找它的监护人”[22]。这种极其复杂的商品流通中交换关系的社会性质，表现出买卖双方、生产者、经营者和消费者以及不同所有者各成员之间的利益关系体系。③流通是商品经济的运行方式。货币对交换的介入使得作为一次成功的行为 W—W 变为卖 W—G 和买 G—W 两次行为，一个商品的第一形态变化，同时也是另一商品的第二形态变化。商品流通由 G—W 和 W—G 两个价值形态的转变构成，前者是通过购买生产资料和生活资料实现实物替换；后者是通过售卖商品转让使用价值并实现商品价值。流通关系是“产品所必须通过并由以取得一定社会性质的一定的社会过程”[23]。流通的社会性就是社会过程，就是社会经济的运动过程。商品流通过程是物质替换过程和价值补偿实现过程的统一。

（3）流通揭示了社会经济运行规律。①商品经济特征在于商品流通。马克思分析资本主义经济是从分析商品开始的，商品是“用来交换，能满足人们某种需要的劳动产品”[24]。商品交换是商品所有者彼此让渡使用价值和实现价值的过程。因此，商品必须转手，这种转手就形成商品交换。商品经济是“以交换为目的，具有商品生产、商品交换和货币流通的经济形式”[25]。商品流通是由商品交换和货币流通构成，因而，商品经济实质可以理解为是商品生产和商品流通的经济。首先，商品流通是以货币为媒介的商品流通，货币的形成是交换发展的必然。由商品交换发展为商品流通是商品交换发展的必然。其次，商品交换与商品生产缺一不可，二者构成社会再生产总过程。从多个再生产组成的经济循环及周转角度看，如果把整体的生产过程看作是流通，那么生产仅仅是流通的要素，揭示了流通的重要性。在马克思的商品流通理论中，流通不仅是再生产过程的必要环节，而且是引领生产发展的关键因素，同时还是优化生产要素组合的有效途径。一是商品流通是再生产过程的必要环节。生产和流通是社会再生产的两个基本方面和环节，二者之间密切联系，相互影响，共同决定着社会经济活动的规模、质量和效益。生产决定流通，流通对生产具有反作用。具体表现为：流通是生产的前提、流通是社会生产连续性进行的必要前提。二是商品流通是引领生产发展的关键因素。马克思认为：在社会再生产形成过程中，由于“不断扩大产品销路的需要，驱使资产阶级奔走于全球各地”[26,27]。三是商品流通是优化生产要素组合的有效途径[28]。②资本流通是发达的商品流通。资本流通的形成是由简单的商品流通（W—G—W）阶段发展到发达的商品流通形式（G—W—G′）阶段，这种由商品流通发展为资本流通的形式和本质都会产生变化，人们的交换目的也开始产生转变，变化的核心是由最初追逐使用价值→到最终追逐商品价值（价值增值）。资本的流通费用和流通时间表现在：一是流通费用（纯粹流通费用、生产性流通费用）的性质及其补偿完全不同。二是流通决定和制约着社会再生产的速度。三是商品本身对资本的流通时间的限制。四是经济发展的关键是节约流通费用和缩短流通时间[29]。马克思认为可以通过发展商业、特别是大商业，改进交通运输和通信业、发展专门的社会中介组织、建立信用制度等措施和办法，达到加速资本周转、缩短流通时间、节约流通费的目的[30]。③资本主义的根本弊病在于商品流通不实现。按照马克思的分析，资本主义基本矛盾表现在为生产社会化和资本主义私人占有制之间的矛盾。从生产角度看，资本主义生产不可避免地造成社会资源的浪费，盲目投资、盲目扩大、盲目竞争，社会资源并不能真正做到最优配制，但这一问题尚不能从根本上动摇资本主义经济。从流通角度看，真正对资本主义经济起动摇作用的是流通，生产出来的东西卖不出去，产品交换不能实现，导致资本主义经济危机，社会生产力遭到巨大破坏。因此，资本主义的基本矛盾使得商品流通最终不能实现。

马克思主义将资本主义经济的动态归结为由其本身所决定的、不断演进的阶级关系，进而更广泛的社会生产关系，强调对经济发展规律的理解不能脱离生产关系的运动规律。在这点上，马克思主义具有自己独特的优势：单纯的技术或者“生物学”的因素是无法对经济增长这个历史过程给出一个全面而合理的解释的；只有结合对资本主义的生产关系的调整和发展的认识，才能更深入和全面地理解资本主义经济增长率的上升和下降，也就是资本主义发展的经济现象。在马克思主义经济增长的基本模型中资本主义体系所能达到的或者潜在的最大的资本积累和社会总资本的增长速度是由资本主义经济体系的生产力发展水平、资本主义社会的生产关系以及这种生产力与生产关系之间的相互关系决定的。卡尔·马克思在其《资本论》中提出了社会总资本的再生产和流通理论，他不仅描述了扩大再生产的基本途径——增加积累和提高生产要素产出率，以及与此相对应的外延和内涵两种扩大再生产方式，而且强调指出扩大再生产的顺利进行必须保持各部门之间的动态平衡。马克思的论述不仅为社会主义国家的经济学家所接受。如苏联的菲尔德曼、波兰的卡莱茨基、匈牙利的科尔奈等，而且也被作为现代经济增长理论开端的哈罗德—多马模型以及新古典增长理论所接受。

（二）当代中国马克思主义者的现代物流与经济发展理论

马克思流通理论当代视角表现出流通概念的层次性、流通力量先导性、流通产业协调性、流通组织效率性、流通范围世界性[31]。当代中国马克思主义者的现代物流与经济发展理论精髓是："物流是国民经济发展的核心。"

1. 邓小平对马克思主义流通经济理论的发展

邓小平——当代中国马克思主义①的创立者[32]。邓小平在把马克思主义普遍原理同中国具体实际相结合的过程中，既坚持了马克思主义最基本的立场、观点和方法，同时又以新的理论和实践对马列主义、毛泽东思想进行了丰富和发展。邓小平理论同毛泽东思想一样，都是中国化的马克思主义。邓小平理论不仅是中国化的马克思主义，而且是反映了当代中国历史要求和时代特点的当代中国的马克思主义，把中国化的马克思主义推进到了一个崭新的发展阶段。邓小平继承和发展了马克思主义流通经济理论、毛泽东关于商品生产和商品交换的思想[33]。毛泽东在领导中国革命和建设的过程中，历来重视对经济问题的思考，特别是对商品经济问题进行了长期的探索，毛泽东商品经济思想观点有以下几方面[33-36]：商品关

---

① 所谓"当代中国"始于1956年；当代中国的基本问题是建设、巩固和发展社会主义，是怎样在中国实现现代化；"当代中国的马克思主义"的内涵是马列主义基本原理与当代中国实际和时代特征相结合的产物，是毛泽东思想的继承和发展，是党中央领导集体和全党全国人民智慧的结晶，是中国共产党和中国人民最可珍贵的精神财富；当代中国马克思主义集中体现在三卷《邓小平文选》之中；"创立者"含义：一是党在思想理论上的杰出代表者，二是党和人民群众集体智慧的概括总结者，三是主要科学论断的提出者。

系是社会主义普遍存在的经济关系①——两种所有制的存在是商品生产和商品交换存在的主要前提②——价值规律在社会主义商品经济中的普遍作用③——敢于使用有积极意义的资本主义范畴的思想④——企业自主权和企业制度改革思想⑤。邓小平始终强调以经济建设为中心，把大力发展生产力、促进经济增长视为社会主义初级阶段的根本任务，其流通经济思想就服务于这一根本任务[37]。邓小平的流通经济思想观点有以下几方面[38-40]：科学预见了流通国际化的发展趋势⑥——科学地阐明了我国参与国际流通经济的方式⑦——分析了当代西方国家技术转移过程与资本流通互相融合的客观规律⑧。邓小平的流通管理思想、技术流通与服务流通思想、资本流通思想、国际流通思想等在我国参与国际流通体系、吸引国

① 毛泽东强调："我们对于社会商品，只能实行等价交换，不能实行无偿占有，在社与队、队与队、社与国家之间，在经济上只能是买卖关系，必须遵守等价交换原则。"（参见毛泽东同部分省委第一书记的谈话记录，1959 年 3 月 5 日）

② 毛泽东认为，"只要还存在两种所有制，商品生产和商品交换就极其必要、极其有用。""商品生产，要看它是同什么经济制度相联系，同资本主义制度相联系就是资本主义的商品生产，同社会主义制度相联系就是社会主义商品生产。"

③ 毛泽东在谈到国家与农民的关系问题时指出："苏联的办法把农民挖得很苦……我们对农民的政策不是苏联的那种政策……工农业品的交换，我们采取缩小剪刀差，等价交换或者近乎等价交换的政策。"

④ 毛泽东指出："外国资产阶级的一切腐败制度和思想作风，我们要坚持抵制和批判，但是这并不妨碍我们学习资本主义国家的先进的科学技术和企业管理方法中合乎科学的方面。工业发达国家和企业，用人少，效率高，会做生意，这些都应当有原则地学过来，以利于改进我们的工作。"

⑤ 毛泽东认为："我们不能像苏联那样，把什么都集中到中央，把地方卡得死死的，一点机动权也没有。""把什么东西统统都集中在中央或省市，不给工厂一点权力，一点机动余地，一点利益，恐怕不妥。""各个生产单位都要有一个与统一性相联系的独立性，才会发展得更加活泼。"并提出了"两参一改三结合"企业制度改革主张。

⑥ 邓小平认为："任何一个国家要发展，孤立起来，闭关自守是不可能的，不加强国际交往，不引进发达国家的先进经验、先进科学技术和资金，是不可能的。""一切有利于发展社会生产力的方法，包括利用外资和引进先进技术，我们都采用。这是个很大的试验，是书上没有的。""我们同国际上的经济交往更加频繁，更加相互依赖，更不可分，开放政策就更不会变了。"

⑦ 邓小平认为："计划经济不等于社会主义，资本主义也有计划；市场经济不等于资本主义，社会主义也有市场。""应该建立国际经济新秩序，解决南北问题，还应该建立国际政治新秩序，使它同国际经济新秩序相适应。""现在国际垄断资本控制着全世界的经济，市场被他们占了，要奋斗出来很不容易。像我们这样穷的国家要奋斗出来更不容易，没有开放政策、改革政策，竞争不过。""从国际经验来看，一些国家在发展过程中，都曾经有过高速发展时期，或若干高速发展阶段。日本、南朝鲜、东南亚一些国家和地区，就是如此。"

⑧ 邓小平认为："西方国家在资金和技术上就是互相融合、交流的。"

际资本、实施流通管理等多方面发挥了重大作用，是我国进行流通体制改革、完善市场经济体制、开拓国内外市场的重要政策基础和理论依据，是对马克思流通理论的重要补充和发展[41]。

2. 当代中国马克思主义者的现代物流与经济发展理论

（1）物流随流通的出现而发展。我们从马克思的流通理论中可以挖掘出流通内涵的高级性，首先是作为商流的流通，其次是作为商流、物流、信息流合一的流通。但是，马克思的流通概念更侧重于商流过程的分析而没有深入分析商品的实体运动即物流。从经济实践看，现代商品流通是集有形要素与无形要素于一体的全要素流通，无形要素流通在现代流通中占的比重越来越大。在商品流通中，原来以有形要素实物流转为主的商流分解为商流、物流、信息流，商品交易分解为现货交易和期货交易。在资本流通中，原来以产业资本为基本形态的资本循环和周转，分解成有形资本的流通和虚拟资本的流通。在各种交易中，原来充当一般等价物的货币，分解为与金银保持一定比例的有形货币和代表信用关系的无形货币。资本流通是以商品流通为前提，而物流是商品流通的实物表现形式，物流是商品使用价值的实现过程。物流最初伴随生产而发展起来，而在商品流通规模化之后，物流又更多地伴随于流通。

（2）现代物流是流通形式的一场革命。流通革命可以定义为受产业革命和消费革命制约，并对产业革命和消费革命发挥能动作用的，是集业态创新、组织创新和制度创新为一体的流通系统革命。流通革命带来了流通领域内一系列深刻的变化，从而引起了流通方式的重大变革。流通革命所导致的这些变化主要表现在零售业态的多样化、批发机能的复合化、物流功能的社会化、商业组织的网络化，形成流通运行过程的延伸与拓展——供应链一体化的现代物流运行过程。流通革命之前，商流和物流是合在一起的，物流依附于商流，由生产者自己承担。在流通革命的进程中，原来依附于商流过程中的物流过程摆脱了对生产和销售的依赖，从商流中独立出来，成为承担储存保管、流通加工、运输配送、委托代理等一揽子作业的物流企业。物流业的产生使流通领域内部的社会分工进一步深化，从而大大提高了流通效率，物流被誉为经济领域的“黑暗大陆”。现代物流业是20世纪90年代应用了现代管理技术和现代信息技术而发展起来的新兴产业，它以先进的管理技术和组织方式，对资源进行优化整合，从整体上改变了企业的运行方式，是流通方式的一场革命。由于它降低了产品的总成本，因而物流业也成为除制造业利润、商业利润之外的“第三利润源”。现代物流业对增强国力和国际竞争力产生积极作用，因而现代物流业得到了迅速的发展。

（3）物流是国民经济发展的核心。当代中国马克思主义者的现代物流与经济发展理论精髓是：“物流是国民经济发展的核心。”“核心”在静态上是指——物流产业是国民经济中新兴的重要服务部门，具有辐射性强、关联度高、连带性大的特点；在动态上是指——物流是国民经济的动脉和基础，是各种生产要素集结、整合与聚变的载体；从积极的方面看是指——现代物流是经济发展的支柱，是现代经济新的增长点；消极的方面看是指——现代物流活动的诸多方面都会对环境造成负面影响，会对社会经济的可持续发展产生消极影响[42]。这一论断深刻揭示了现代物流与经济的辩证关系，确立了现代经济发展中现代物流先导的价值观。赋予了物流在市场经济条件下，物资有形或无形地从供应者向需求者进行的物资物质实体的流动，定位创造物资的空间效用、时间效用、形质效用的重任，指出了物流在一定程度上可以超然于实物流转为主的商流运动，从而形成实物流导向价值流的超前定位范式，明确了物流作为深化经济体制改革的助推器和引致经济增长的放大器功能，形成了研究和解决现代物流与经济发展的理论基础。中国共产党第十六次代表大会和十六届三中全会所提出的“科学发展观”和“统筹发展”，以及在此基础上形成的“32 字方针”和若干经济、流通政策主张，尤其是 2010 年颁布《物流业调整和振兴计划》，更进一步明确了新时期中国经济发展中处理现代物流与经济发展的思想和理论基础，是马克思主义流通与经济关系理论的又一次创新和发展。

马克思的流通与经济关系理论为本研究提供了极具普遍而深刻意义的理论和方法指导，但本研究注意到，目前社会分工不断深化、流通发展实践日益丰富，人口、资源、环境问题影响到了经济的可持续发展。马克思的研究是以资本主义为背景，基于市场行为的流通与社会再生产的关系，政府行为没有纳入分析框架，也没有具体测定其关系的强弱，更没有直接涉及农村领域。马克思的研究出现以后，“物流”已经远远超出流通的范畴，更何况当前我国农产品物流与农村经济的关系，还具有自身的独特性。尤其是西部大开发战略实施 10 年来，西部特色农业得到快速发展，农产品生产能力显著提高。农业和农村经济发展进入新阶段，西部大开发后续研究也逐渐转向农产品物流问题。虽然对农产品物流问题的重视和研究已经开始，但无论是在微观、宏观层次，还是各个管理方面，理论和实践研究一直处于不系统状态，有关支持西部地区农产品物流可持续发展的政策研究非常缺乏。当代中国马克思主义者的现代物流与经济发展理论，为本研究提供了更具体的指导。本研究的任务不是诠释政策，也不停留在对前人理论和思想的总结与梳理，而是要在此基础上，具体探索西部地区农产品物流可持续发展的机制与模式，为理论和政策的创新提供科学支持。因此，本研究将更多地注重马克思流通与经济关系理论的基本原理和研究方法的运用，并以此为指导，广泛吸收和鉴别西方现代物流与经济发展理论成果，挖掘蕴藏其中的理论资源。联系中国西部地区农产品物流与农村经济实际加以整合利用和创新，而不是教条性地照搬马克思的只言片语。

二　西方经济理论中的现代物流与经济发展理论

借鉴国内通用的表达方法，本研究所涉及的西方经济理论，一般泛指经济学体系中，除马克思经济学以外的经济理论体系。西方经济学也是研究交换的，但严格地说，在欧美国家并没有（或很少有）研究商品流通的专门理论，其原因在于欧美国家的经济理论（主流经济理论）和马克思经济理论的研究视角不一致。西方经济学研究交换，主要研究的是交换的双方，即供求，这和马克思主义经济学研究生产与消费的中间环节——交换，及其总体——流通有很大区别。对现代物流与经济发展的探索贯穿于西方经济理论的发展全过程①，其理论也正是在这一过程中不断地深化和完善。现代物流的发展经历了20世纪30年代以前的物流理念的启蒙与产生阶段（Physical Distribution，PD萌芽期），20世纪30—80年代的物资流通阶段（PD成长期）→物流阶段（Logistics推广期），20世纪80年代至今的供应链阶段（Supply Chain成熟期）。本课题以20世纪30年代和80年代为两个分水岭，将其发展分为三个阶段，

① 本研究内容并没有对经济增长和经济发展概念进行严格的区分，经济发展与经济增长是世界各国都经历过而且目前仍然在经历着的社会实践过程。从本质上看，二者都是通过资源的优化配置和合理使用使社会财富积累，以满足人们日益增长的多样性需求的过程，经济发展与经济增长是一致的。

围绕其主流展开其理论体系。

（一）20世纪30年代以前的物流与经济发展理论

20世纪30年代以前的物流与经济发展理论主要是在物流产生阶段，围绕早期经济增长思想、分工理论展开的，将物流纳入市场营销的研究范畴之中，为研究经济发展另辟蹊径。基本内容依其发展过程可以概括如下。

1. 物流理念的启蒙与产生阶段——市场分销阶段：(20世纪30年代以前)

物流研究和实践的发展至今经历了100多年的时间①。19世纪末至20世纪初，美国迎来了大量生产、大量流通、大量消费的时代，出现了直接进入流通领域的制造商，同时也出现了一些除生产和销售之外的第三方——专业运输者。最早关于物流的概念是1915年，美国营销学者阿奇·萧（Arch W. Shaw）在其著作《市场分销中的若干问题》（哈佛大学出版社1915年出版）中首次提出了physical distribution of goods的概念。有的人把它译成“实体分销”，有的也译成“物流”，这就是最早的物流概念，其实质是“分销物流”。他认为在市场分销中，存在两类活动，一类叫作创造需求，一类叫作物资实体分配。学者L. H. H. Weld进一步充分肯定了物流创造产品的市场价值、时间价值及场所价值（《农产品的市场营销》，1916）。1929年，著名营销专家弗莱德·E. 克拉克（Fred E. Clark）在其著作Principle of Marketing中将流通机能划分为“交换机能”“物流机能”“辅助机能”三部分，使物流活动的研究真正上升到理论高度，为研究经济发展另辟蹊径。这一阶段的研究体现在物流作为附属功能的定位，并没有延伸物流系统化的概念。

2. 宏观经济发展的相关理论

（1）早期经济增长思想。人们对经济增长问题的认识和讨论是在古典经济学产生以前就开始的[43,44]。重商主义者的经济增长观点是贸易财富的积累。古典经济学杰出代表和理论体系的创立者亚当·斯密最早提出经济增长概念，英国资产阶级古典政治经济学的完成者大卫·李嘉图认为经济增长原因是将剩余部分追加到生产中所形成的资本积累。德国

① 追溯到J. F. Growll在1901年，美国政府报告“工业委员会关于农产品配送的报告”中揭开了人们认识物流的序幕。

历史学家李斯特则认为经济增长的决定性因素是生产力①。从19世纪初到19世纪末和20世纪初的新古典主义学派认为经济增长的原因是资本家把一部分收入储蓄起来进行积累，以及资本家对企业的组织管理活动。

（2）分工理论。①古典经济学的分工理论。1776年，亚当·斯密就已经提出分工程度②，其基本逻辑是，分工带来的专业化导致技术进步，技术进步产生报酬递增，而进一步的分工则依赖于市场范围的扩大[45]。所以，分工和专业化是推动经济增长和财富增加的主要因素[46]。1890年，马歇尔在亚当·斯密分工理论的基础上提出了分工专业化程度③。1928年，杨格认为分工包括人的专业化水平、不同专业种类数（同产品种类数）和生产的迂回度（间接生产链条的长度）三个方面，并总结出被后人称为“杨格定理”的观点：递增报酬的实现取决于分工演进；分工水平取决于市场大小，市场大小反过来取决于分工水平；需求和供给是分工的两个侧面。杨格定理意味着，如果缺乏足够高水平的分工和足够大的相关市场，不仅新技术发明不了，即便发明了，在商业上也不能被大范围地推广[47]。1984年，杨小凯证明了分工水平达到最优的方法④。从古典经济学理论中可看出，分工导致专业化而提高生产率，分工与交易效率（运输条件）相关，分工产生的递增报酬源于分工水平提高与市场范围扩大之间的正反馈效应，或者说分工的网络效应[48]。②新古典经济学的分

① 亚当·斯密（1776）在其经典著作《国富论》中提出经济增长概念，指出经济增长本质是劳动分工、资本积累以及技术进步。大卫·李嘉图（1817）在《政治经济学及赋税原理》认为经济增长原因是资本家将其净收入中除了消费外的剩余部分追加到生产中所形成的资本积累。李斯特（1841）在其著作《政治经济学的国民体系》中总结了李斯特作为德国关税同盟经济顾问时丰富的实践经验，比较了当时欧洲大陆各国以及美国的兴衰，在批驳自由市场教条的同时，形成了完整的国家主义经济学说，对于遏止亚当·斯密学说对德国工业的威胁，协调德国政界、实业界和舆论界的意见，化解德国地主对保护主义的反对，起到了只手擎天的作用。弗里德里希·李斯特认为经济增长的决定性因素是生产力，认为古典政治经济学派只讨论“价值”，不注意生产力，是一种狭隘的理论，李斯特提出了独特的生产力理论，他认为一国的发展程度取决于它的生产力发展水平，而不是所积累的财富的多寡，财富的生产力比财富更重要。从这一概念出发提出了一个对后世具有深远影响的经济增长理论框架，这一框架包括实物、资本、科学技术、精神资本、政治法律制度以及文化心理差异等因素。

② 亚当·斯密（1776）提出分工的程度由市场大小决定，市场大小又取决于运输条件。

③ 马歇尔（1890）认为：给定相对生产和消费量，分工水平和生产力由分工的好处和分工引起的交易费用之间的冲突所决定。也就是说，分工问题研究的是选择专业方向和在选定专业中的专业化程度。

④ 杨小凯（1984）证明当分工的边际效益等于边际交易费用时，分工水平达到最优。

工理论。新古典经济学把制度、交易费用、交易效率和一般均衡等概念引入分工理论[49]，认为生产率是由分工水平决定，而分工水平又由交易效率决定[50]。分工的加深带来交易次数的增加，在市场均衡中，如果交易效率很低，则分工产生的专业化的好处完全被交易费用抵消，因此人们会选择自给自足；如果交易效率很高，则分工的好处大于交易费用，此时人们会选择分工[50]。从影响交易效率的范围来看，有制度、组织模式、交易机制、生产模式等影响因素①，但最主要的因素应该是制度[51,50]。但是，该理论没有涉及市场制度安排、企业制度结构对经济的影响，没有研究企业组织边界的问题，引起了制度经济学家的质疑。

3. 物流与经济发展理论

（1）物流对经济发展的促进论。根据早期经济增长思想，社会专业化分工是经济增长的基本动力之一②，实现社会专业分工的前提是物流发展，只有物流得到真正发展才能保证社会专业分工的运营正常化。根据古典经济学的分工理论，按照新兴古典经济学关于分工和专业化的思想③，物流发展扩大了市场的范围，促进了进一步的劳动分工，因此物流的发展可以促进经济增长和发展。

（2）经济发展对物流的影响论。在人类早期社会阶段，生产力水平极低，经济增长程度与社会专业化程度也非常低，人们生产的有限产品主要用于自己消费，而不需要考虑运输、仓储问题，因此，简单的社会分工对物流的要求很少。在资本主义初期阶段，由于生产力水平的逐渐提升，

---

① 诺思在其著作《经济史中的结构与变迁》中认为，有效率的组织需要在制度上作出安排和确立所有权，以便造成一种刺激，将个人的经济努力变成私人收益率接近社会收益率的活动。杨小凯、张永生在其著作《新兴古典经济学与超边际分析》中认为，在经济转型的过程中，由于缺乏良好的价格体系和完善的法律系统，从定价和法律执行的角度出发，交易成本将十分高昂。这就意味着，经济转型过程中的企业更倾向于利用人际关系网络作为自身经营战略的一部分，而不是通过市场去获取资源或开展战略结盟。这样，分工网络的规模和网络效应就受到很大的限制，因而影响分工的水平和生产率的提高。所以，好的制度安排保证了高交易效率，降低了交易成本，有利于促进分工和提高生产率。

② 从早期亚当·斯密提供增长的动力为劳动分工、资本和技术进步，一直到新经济增长理论从专业化和劳动分工演进为出发点对经济增长的研究，这些经济增长理论虽然在研究内容上有很大区别，但却存在一个共同点，即都认为社会分工是带来经济增长的一个主要源泉。

③ 分工是交换的产物，分工和专业化能够加速知识的积累，带来收益的递增；但协调分工又需要成本（即交易费用），分工的深化会引起交易费用的增加，交易费用取决于交易机制的效率；分工的好处和交易费用增加之间形成两难冲突，构成分工演进的基本约束；在这个两难冲突中，分工的深化取决于交易费用与分工收益的相对比较，呈现出一个自发演进的过程。

带来了经济增长，但产品总的数量有限，产品生产出来总可以分销出去，并不关心分销运输成本和效益，没有表现出物流的重要性。直到20世纪初，在一些发达的资本主义国家，生产力发展到比较高的水平，社会总产品数量达到比较饱和的程度，社会的总需求也相应有较大程度的增长，生产的产品不一定都能分销出去，市场竞争激烈，而且再靠提高生产技术已经有一定难度。于是人们开始关注分销工作，降低分销成本、提高分销经济效益。对物流的要求越来越高，对物流的要求必然带来物流的不断发展。

（二）20世纪30—80年代的现代物流与经济发展理论

从20世纪30年代开始的现代物流与经济发展理论经历了物流理论形成与实践初步推广阶段——由产品配送阶段（Physical Distribution）进入到综合物流阶段（Integrated Logistics Management），在现代经济增长理论、产业组织理论、交易费用理论等经济发展理论基础上[52-56]，现代物流与经济发展理论的中心从市场分销转向了物流结构，形成以黑暗大陆理论、物流冰山理论、第三利润源理论的物流发展理论。具体内容依其发展历程可以概括为以下几个方面。

1. 物流理论形成与实践初步推广阶段（20世纪30—80年代）

（1）产品配送阶段（Physical Distribution）：20世纪30—70年代。1935年，美国营销协会（AMA）与对PD进行正式定义①。进入20世纪50年代后，由美国为主的从事第一阶段物流研究逐渐发展到各国对物流的系统研究。1961年，斯马凯伊、鲍尔索克斯和莫斯曼对PD进行了详尽的研究②。1962年，德鲁克提出著名的“经济的黑暗大陆”学说③。1963年，美国成立了国家物流管理委员会④。日本1956年首次引入物

---

① 美国营销协会（AMA，1935）对PD定义为“包含于销售之中的物资和服务，从生产地点到消费地点流动过程中所包含的种种经济活动”。通过全美输送物流协会（American Society of Traffic Logistics，1946），对专业输送者进行资格认定，为美国物流业发展培养专门人才。

② 斯马凯伊、鲍尔索克斯、莫斯曼（1961）在其专著Physical Distribution Management：Logistics Problems of the Firm中对PD进行了详尽的研究，第一次从系统的角度论述了物流总成本分析的概念。

③ 彼德·德鲁克（1962）在“经济的黑暗大陆”一文中也强调了应当高度重视流通及流通过程中的物流管理，从而对实业界和理论界又产生了一次重大的推动作用，使他们逐渐认识到物流是“第三利润源”。

④ 美国成立了国家物流管理委员会（National Council of Physical Distribution Management，1963）是世界上第一个物流专业组织。

流概念[①]，与此同时英、德、法等欧共体国家的也开始了物流研究。这一阶段的物流研究和物流实践仍以分销过程为主，物流管理的特征是注重产品到消费者的物流环节，目的是对与实物配送有关的一系列物流活动进行系统管理，以最小的成本确保把产品有效地送达消费者，企业内部物流并不包含在物流管理之中。当人们正在专注地研究分销领域中的物流问题、发展各种专业物流理论和技术的时候，企业内部生产物流理论悄然兴起[②]。20 世纪 60 年代随着计算机应用的普及和推广，人们逐渐把计算机应用到制订生产计划上来，美国生产管理和计算机应用专家 Oliver W. Wight 和 George W. Plosh 首先提出了物料需求计划（Material Requirement Planning，MRP）的概念，而 IBM 公司则首先在计算机上实现了 MRP 处理，从此产生了 MRP 技术，并且在企业中得到了应用和发展，到了 80 年代，发展到了 MRPⅡ、MRPⅢ。20 世纪 70 年代物流概念发展进入第二个阶段。

（2）综合物流阶段（Integrated Logistics Management）：20 世纪 70—80 年代。基于企业产、供、销等全范围、全方位的物流问题，Logistics 的概念比较切合当时物流发展的实际情况。1974 年，唐纳德·鲍尔索克斯（Donald J. Bowersox）在 Logistics Management 一书中对“Logistics”做了比较全面的论述。1985 年美国物流管理协会（CLM）正式对“Logistics”作出定义[③]。基于 MRP 产生了 20 世纪 80 年代的配送资源计划（Distribution Resources Planning，DRP），并且相应又发展出 DRPⅡ、DRPⅢ。这些先进的管理技术与方法的产生和应用，大大地改进了物流系统的管理水平。

---

① 1956 年日本首次引入物流概念，称为“物的流通”；1970 年成立了两个最大的物流学术团体“日本物流管理协会”和“日本物的流通协会”，日本企业重视提高物流服务的水平，逐步开展了城市之间和城市内部的配送活动，大大提高了物流服务的水平。

② 1965 年美国 J. A. 奥列基博士（Joseph. A. Orlicky）提出独立需求和相关需求的概念，并指出订货点法的物资资源配置技术只适用于独立需求物资。而企业内部的生产过程相互之间的需求则是种相关需求。相关需求应当用相关需求的物资资源配置技术。

③ 1985 年，美国物资配送管理协会（NCPDM）更名为美国物流管理协会（CLM），将“Logistics”定义为“为满足顾客需求而规划、实施以及控制原材料、在制品库存、产成品以及相关信息，从产出地到消费地高效、低成本流动及存储的过程”。物流突破了商品流通的范围，把物流活动扩大到生产领域。物流活动不仅从产品出厂开始，而是包括从原材料采购、加工生产到产品销售、售后服务，直到废弃物回收等整个物理性的流通过程。企业界与学术界认识到，把物料管理与实物配送结合起来管理可以大大提高物流效率与效果。同时，全球性竞争的加剧也使采用新的物流管理技术、改进物流系统成为必要。

但这时的物流管理只限于企业内部，这个阶段开始用 Logistics 代替 Physical Distribution，标志着综合物流概念的确立。20 世纪 80 年代后，Logistics 的物流概念从美国走向世界，Logistics 已经成为世界公认的物流标准用语。

综合物流阶段物流活动的综合程度表现在任何不同环节的物流主体以及由这些环节共同组成的物流链，都是坚持以优化物流活动作为始终一致的努力方向。1999 年，鲍尔索克斯等①提出物流作为一种能力、一种核心能力两种定位时起到不同的作用来说明物流活动的综合程度[57]。2003 年，戴维·J. 布隆伯格等②明确了综合物流的定义[58]。这一阶段的研究主要是形成了理论体系与初期实践，特征是基于实物配送引入物料管理的新概念和新技术（如图 2－1 所示）。

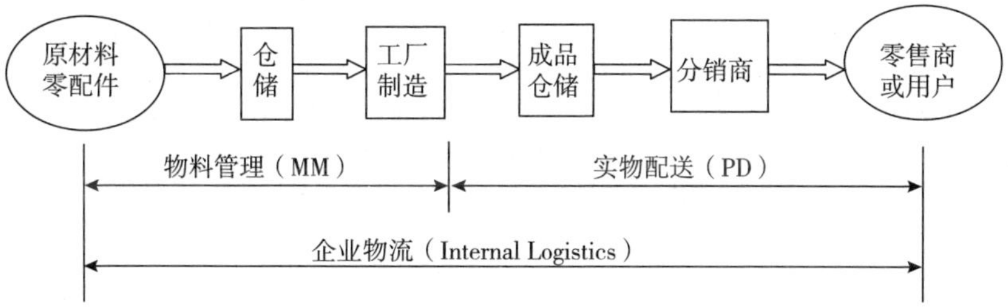

图 2－1　综合物流阶段

2. *宏观经济发展的相关理论*

（1）现代经济增长理论。现代经济增长理论的重点在于研究实现经济稳定增长的长期条件，也就是在长期中如何达到较低的失业率和通货膨胀率以及在适当经济条件下的经济增长率这一目标。为了表示各经济变量之间的相互关系，经济学家建立了各自的经济模型，并用它来概括经济增长的理论。20 世纪 30—60 年代末是现代经济增长理论研究时期，是从拉

---

① 鲍尔索克斯等（1999）认为，物流是作为一种能力在一个企业内部进行定位的，它对创造顾客价值的一般过程做出贡献；当物流作业被高度一体化并定位成一种核心能力时，它就能够对企业或行业的战略优势起到奠基石的作用。

② 戴维·J. 布隆伯格等（2003）给综合物流的定义是：为了满足客户需求而获取资本、原料、人员、技术和信息的过程；为实现顾客的需求而对商品和服务的生产网络优化的过程；以及利用这种网络及时满足顾客需求的过程。通过企业内部物流一体化所推动的综合物流与供应链管理实践在制造业领域已取得了良好的效果。

姆齐模型和哈罗德—多马模型开始的[①]。20 世纪 50 年代后期美国经济学家索洛和丹尼森研究美国的经济增长，其理论占据统治地位近 30 年[②]。早期哈罗德—多马模型与新古典模型的共同点是，认为促进经济增长的第三个因素——技术进步，是外在决定的、偶然的、无成本的资源。在 1957 年索洛的著作中，技术进步被看成是增长模型中的主要决定因素。1962 年诺贝尔经济学奖得主肯尼思·阿罗发表《学习的效果》是众多内生经济增长理论和技术进步模型的理论基础[③]。1965 年宇泽提出了研究内生经济增长的思想是以人力资本为中心，对新经济增长理论影响很大[④]。

（2）产业组织理论。西方产业组织理论最早萌芽于 1890 年马歇尔《经济学原理》一书中的“生产要素理论”，马歇尔第一次正式把组织一

① 拉姆齐对经济增长的理论贡献是 1926 年发表的“储蓄的数学理论”一文，这篇文章奠定了研究最优积累和最优增长问题的方法论基础。哈罗德最早建立数学模型来研究经济增长同各种经济要素之间的关系，从而将经济增长理论引入“现代”时期。哈罗德—多马经济增长模型建立在凯恩斯的就业理论和国民收入决定论的基础上，是经济增长的长期化和动态化的描述。哈罗德—多马经济增长理论强调资本积累在经济增长中具有压倒一切的重要性。发展学派突出了提高储蓄率的必要性，在这个过程中，它们都反映了当代发展经济学的要旨。罗斯托和赖维斯把提高储蓄率当作经济由起飞进入持续增长的关键。新古典增长模型的出现，破除了资本积累被夸大了的作用。

② 罗伯特·索洛模型提出，当外生的技术以固定比率增长时，经济将在平衡增长路径上增长，而当外生技术水平固定不变时，经济将趋于停滞，投资仅能补偿固定资产折旧和装备新工人，技术进步是经济增长的主要动力。丹尼森等人通过对美国经济增长的实证分析证实和巩固了索洛的观点。正因为该模型强调了技术进步对经济增长的决定性作用，故被称为“技术决定论”。新古典增长理论的另一个重要假设是在机会均等的条件下，各国没有技术水平的差别。因此各国有很强的使经济发展水平和增长率趋于一致的倾向。而事实正与之相反，这是新古典增长理论无法解释的地方。

③ 肯尼思·阿罗（1962）在《经济研究评论》上发表了题为《学习的效果》的文章，这篇文章现在被广泛认为是众多内生经济增长理论和技术进步模型的思想源头。阿罗认为，学习是经验的产物，学习只有在实践活动中才会发生，知识在实践中的积累是很普遍的现象。随着知识的积累，单位产品的生产成本随生产总量而递减。生产经验的增长也是生产过程中的一种投入，这种生产经验的积累可以被投资或产量的积累指数化。阿罗模型中的学习过程包含两种效应：一是由于生产了更多的资本品而积累了更多的知识，使得下一代资本品所包含的技术水平得以提高；二是由于知识的共享性，所有劳动力和固定资产的效率在生产最终产品时都有所提高，这就是所谓的“溢出效应”。

④ 宇泽最早将人力资本用于研究技术进步和经济增长问题，他在 1965 年的《世界经济评论》上发表了《经济增长总量模型中的最优技术变化》一文，在他的增长模型中引入了教育部门，假定社会配置一定的资源到非生产的教育部门，教育部门对生产的贡献是通过提高生产部门的技术水平而间接实现的。宇泽提出了研究内生经济增长的新思路，即以人力资本为中心，这一思想对新经济增长理论也产生了很大的影响。

词引进经济学研究领域，最早提出了“组织”的四要素论，他认为组织包括企业内的组织形态、企业间的组织形态以及产业间的组织形态和国家的组织形态，马歇尔对组织的外延界定较为宽泛①。20 世纪 20 年代美国企业的第二次兼并浪潮，垄断阻碍了资源的优化配置。面对严峻现实的挑战，1933 年英国剑桥大学经济学家琼·罗宾逊和 E. 张伯伦提出了垄断—竞争新理论，尤其是张伯伦在其《垄断竞争理论》著作中提出了“垄断竞争”“产品差别”等概念和理论观点，修正和发展了西方经济学的垄断—竞争理论，成为现代产业组织理论的主要来源，而且张伯伦还率先开展了经济理论实证分析方法的研究，分析模式被看作是 SCP 分析模式的雏形并推动着产业组织理论向市场结构方向发展。因此，张伯伦本人也被认为是现代产业组织理论的奠基人。产业组织理论体系的最终形成，是以 20 世纪 30 年代以后西方一些学者的实证研究结论为基础的。其形成的标志是贝恩（J. Bain）1959 年出版《产业组织理论》②，提出了完整的“结构—行为—绩效”范式。贝恩还把上述三个范畴与国家的产业组织政策联系起来，从而系统地构建了产业组织理论的基本框架，至此，以哈佛大学为主要基地的正统产业组织理论基本形成。哈佛学派 SCP 范式的产业组织理论影响了整整一代经济学家和决策者，同时也不断受到批评与挑战③。20 世纪 60 年代以来的一些经济学家针对哈佛学

---

① 马歇尔对产业理论研究的贡献不仅仅是提出了“工业组织”的概念，最重要的是他提出了著名的“马歇尔冲突”，即规模经济与竞争的矛盾问题。马歇尔虽然开创了产业组织研究之河，但受到当时所处经济发展即自由主义盛行，垄断还是个别现象的局限，并没有形成完整的产业组织理论。

② 1959 年贝恩在总结已有的产业组织理论研究成果尤其是哈佛学派的理论研究成果的基础上，出版了《产业组织》一书，该书第一次完整而又系统地论述了产业组织体系，阐明了产业组织研究的目的与方法，提出了“市场结构、市场行为、市场绩效”等基本范畴。贝恩认为市场结构决定企业的市场行为，企业的市场行为决定市场绩效，而市场结构又取决于特定情况下的市场供求环境。

③ 到 20 世纪 70 年代，产业组织理论的发展分化成两个分支，一个分支是代表主流学派，沿着 SCP 范式继续前进的“新产业组织理论”，其代表人物有考林（Cowling）、沃特森（Waterson）等人。另一个分支是以芝加哥学派为首的非主流产业组织理论，还包括新制度学派和新奥地利学派。其代表人物是芝加哥学派的斯蒂格勒、德姆塞茨（Demsetz）、布罗兹恩（Y. Brozen）等。新产业组织理论比传统的产业经济学更关注产业经济学的理论发展。如企业理论、市场理论、交易成本理论、企业间关系以及合同与组织间关系等都在这一阶段得到重视并取得了进一步的深化。如果从另一个角度来看，传统产业组织理论关注的是企业间关系、企业界行为、市场结构和绩效三者的互动关系，而新产业组织理论出现，企业界内部的“黑箱”问题才被提到议事日程，开始研究企业内部和企业之间两方面问题。

派产业组织理论在理论方法及微观基础等方面存在的缺陷，在不放弃SCP分析框架的前提下，对正统学派的产业组织理论进行了修正和补充。

（3）交易费用理论。①威廉姆森等的交易费用理论。在科斯交易费用理论①的基础上，威廉姆森提出了有限理性和机会主义行为的假设。威廉姆森认为人的认识是“意欲合理，但只能有限地做到”；人不仅是自私的，而且只要能够利己，就会不惜一切去损人，人的这种“本性”可称为“机会主义”。在有限理性和机会主义行为的假设前提下，威廉姆森进一步分析了在信息不充分和信息不对称环境下，有限理性和机会主义的治理问题。威廉姆森认为制度的创设、习惯的形成，可以有效地抑制交易中的机会主义行为，保证交易的顺利完成和利益的获得。威廉姆森进一步发展了科斯的交易费用理论。他认为资产专用性表明资产具有专门的用途，其收益依赖于它所支持的专门交易。“资产专用性对交易费用经济学的重要性无论怎样强调也不过分。”[59]威廉姆森认为资产专用性可以分为人力资产专用性、物质资产专用性、地点专用性及特殊资产专用性。治理结构是一种交易的组织模式，通常它是分布在企业和市场之间的交易组织形式，即除市场和一体化组织这两极端外，两者之间还存在着一系列连续的、数个市场和组织相混合的制度形式。它主要有四种交易协调的组织模式，即市场治理结构、三边治理结构、双边治理结构和一体化治理结构。威廉姆森在研究交易和治理结构的有效搭配时，主要考虑了影响交易费用的两个因素，即交易频率与资产专用性。交易频率维度中的偶尔交易与重复交易，结合资产专用性维度中的非专用型交易、混合专用型交易和高度专用型交易，描述了六种交易类型，当交易不确定性客观存在的时候，一体化治理能够有效地减少机会主义行为引致的交易费用，

---

① 科斯在1937年发表的《企业的性质》一文中提出了交易费用概念。科斯认为市场和企业是可以相互替代的两种资源配置方式，其选择是由市场的交易成本和企业内部化的成本的均衡点决定的。当一笔交易的企业行政协调的成本低于市场机制的成本时，这笔交易将趋向采用企业行政协调进行，反之交易将趋向采用市场来进行。由于信息不对称、机会主义等原因，就出现了交易费用。所谓交易费用，是指通过市场机制组织交易所支付的成本，包括收集交易信息、谈判、签约、管理必要的后勤和履行合约的监督费用。同时科斯认为，通过签署长期的合同，企业就可以避免为寻找伙伴、谈判等支付的费用，进而降低交易费用。

适用于资产专用性较强的产品；对于资产专用性较低的产品采用市场机制治理都是最为有效的；对于资产专用性大小处于两者之间的中间形态而言，比较适合采取混合模式治理结构。1978 年克莱因、克劳福德和阿尔钦持提出了专用性资产的合同后机会主义行为及治理办法①，当交易费用在较大程度上受资产专用性程度影响时，采用企业的形式，则所费交易成本会较低。②中间组织理论。威廉姆森在《交易费用经济学：契约关系的规则》一文中提出了混合模式治理结构，即“双边规制”和“三方规制”两种介于市场和企业之间的中间性组织形式，这是中间组织思想的萌芽。此后，各国专家学者围绕企业集群、战略联盟、网络组织、企业集团、虚拟企业、特许权安排等不同形式的研究丰富了中间组织理论。日本学者今井贤一认为中间性组织是兼具市场与组织特征的东西，从另一日本学者丸川知雄②、我国学者王询③的理论分析中可以看出[60,61]，中间组织的本质是出于对交易成本和组织成本的节省而对市场和企业的替代，一般适用于内部交易成本不太高而市场交易成本不断上升的情况。与企业和市场相比，中间组织具有以下优势：管理成本和关系构筑成本低，有利于企业获取生产所需的资源；关联企业的资源联合，有利于资源利用效率的提升；增强了企业的环境适应能力，有利于企业应对市场的不确定性。当然，这种中间组织也存在着不足：由于不能使用权力限制或者命令，组织目标的实现或组织成员间利益关系的调整，都需要花费成本；而且，中间交易关系的形成，强化了与老客户的原有的人力资产和物力资产等交易特定资产，且这些资产大都不

---

① 克莱因、克劳福德和阿尔钦持（1978）在《纵向一体化、可占用性租金与竞争性缔约过程》一文中将机会主义行为分为事前和事后两种，即合同订立前和合同执行中两种。他们认为专用性资产的合同后机会主义行为是指缔约后的违约和敲诈行为，这种行为产生的原因是资产专用性，具体的理由是存在着所谓“可占用准租金”。克莱因等人认为抑制缔约后的机会主义行为及因其引致的交易费用的办法是订立长期合同和垂直一体化。

② 日本学者丸川知雄认为：“企业与企业之间的关系可以采取介于一体化（合并）和偶然而短暂的市场交易关系这两个极端之间的各种形式，这就是‘中间性组织’形式，其中包括参股、控股、承包制、长期合作等从紧密到松散的各种形式。这些中间性组织的共同点是在企业之间互相保持独立性的条件下，建立比较长期而稳定的交易关系。”

③ 我国学者王询从传统经济学的企业与市场关系出发，把市场交易方式称为“古典的市场”，把企业交易称为“古典的企业”。王询认为，在“古典的市场”中，行动者是完全独立的，而在“古典的企业”中，行动者则无独立性；两者之间存在着具有“相对独立性”的广阔中间地带，在这中间地带里，企业之间存在着程度不等的非市场协作关系。

能转为他用，相关投资成本成为沉没成本。中间组织理论对现实经济社会中经济组织和交易的多样性和复杂性的分析，为我国农产品物流模式创新提供了渠道选择的理论借鉴[62]。

3. 现代物流与经济发展理论

（1）“黑暗大陆”理论。1962 年，管理大师德鲁克在《财富》杂志上发表《经济的黑暗大陆》的文章中指出，消费者所支付的商品价格中，约 50% 是与商品流通活动有关的费用，物流是降低成本的最后领域，物流是“经济的黑暗大陆”“一块未被开垦的处女地”。

（2）物流冰山理论。日本早稻田大学西泽修教授对物流成本进行专门研究，提出“物流冰山”理论。①物流成本的两个部分。物流冰山主要体现了物流成本，包括两个部分：一是显性成本。显性成本是能够看得见的成本，一般包括装卸费、搬运费、保险费、运输费、配送费、采购费、包装费等等。二是隐性成本。隐性成本是容易被忽视的部分，它包括人工费、管理费、折旧费、盘点费、信息费、积压费、缺货损失费、货损费等等。②两个成本的关系。物流成本的问题，可以用冰山来做形象的比喻。它说我们看见的物流成本，只是冰山的一角。海水上面的冰山是显性成本，海水下面的冰山是隐性成本。而下面的冰山体积要远远大于上面的体积。现行的会计制度海无法体现这些隐性成本。③降低隐性成本是重中之重。我们要不断挖掘冰山下面的那些隐性成本，就要保证货物及时到位。从另外一个角度来讲，大量的库存积压，会形成资金流、现金流的困难，我们可以把库存变成现金，由于这些现金可以做其他的投资，这在管理上称为机会成本。

（3）第三利润源理论。1970 年，日本早稻田大学西泽修教授提出了物流是企业的“第三利润源”理论①。①第一利润源——材料成本。第一

① 西泽修（1970）在他的著作《物流——降低成本的关键》一书中提出了“第三个利润源”理论。他指出：1950 年，日本在美国的经济援助和技术支持下，很快实现了企业机械化、自动化生产，企业经营的第一利润源是降低制造成本。然而，自动化生产手段制造出来的大量产品引起了市场泛滥，产生了对大量销售的需求，1955 年日本从美国引进了市场营销技术，这一时期企业经营的第二利润源是增加销售额。1965 年起，日本政府开始重视物流，1970 年后，日本进入了物流发展时代。这一时期，降低产品制造成本的空间已经非常有限，增加销售额也已经走到尽头，企业迫切希望寻求新的利润源。通过降低物流成本实现“第三利润源”的提法，恰好吻合了当时企业经营的需要。故西泽修的“第三利润源”说一提出，就备受关注，广为流传。

利润源，管理学上称为材料成本，通过节省材料来降低产品的成本。产品成本降低，销售价格就更有竞争力。一般材料的成本往往占产品成本的50%到70%。如果成本稍微下降一两个百分点，销售价格竞争力就提高了。因此在工业革命的阶段，人们非常注意通过降低材料成本获得利润。②第二利润源——人工成本。到了工业革命的后期，人们发现人工成本也可以大幅度下降。可以通过一些方法，在降低人工成本的同时，提高工作效率。比如，可以调整人力结构，精减人员，并进行培训提高人员的水平，从而提高工作效率，这种做法不但节约了开支，而且有效地提高了效率。③第三利润源——物流成本。物流成本是企业的第三利润源，它不是直接的利润，但可以通过降低成本来提高利润。通过成本的最小化，达到利润的最大化。

（三）20世纪80年代以来的现代物流与经济发展理论

第二次世界大战以后，技术进步与科技发展带来的物流革命，现代物流开始进入物流管理理论成熟阶段，供应链管理（Supply Chain）已经成为企业普遍的运营实践模式，从而使20世纪80年代以来的物流发展理论，沿着宏观经济发展相关理论的深化与现代物流与经济发展理论的发展两个方向展开，并深化了对物流影响经济微观机理的认识。

1. 物流供应链成熟阶段：(Supply Chain)（20世纪80年代至今）

随着工业化的进程及社会化的分工协作，产生了物流管理的系统化思想，一体化概念得到了广泛应用。1983年和1984年，Peter Kraljic与Roy D. Shapiro分别在哈佛商业评论上发表论文，首先提出了供应管理。1985年迈克·波特（Michael E. Porter）在其著作《竞争优势》（Competitive Advantage）中提出价值链（Value Chain）的概念。William C. Copacino对Supply Chain Management（SCM）进行了定义。1985年W. D. Harries和J. R. Stock发表了《市场营销与物流的重组——历史与未来的展望》，1983年日本采用大型量贩式网上订发货系统，欧共体的物流应用了物流供应链的概念，1998年美国物流管理协会（CLM）在物流概念中融入了供应链理论①。面临经济全球化企业的竞争越来越激烈，为增强自身的核心竞争优势，企业间必须进行更多的协同与合作。而仅仅认为供应链是制造企业中的一个内部过程的传统供应链概念已不适应当前竞争的需要。到目前为止，尚未形成统一的、权威的供应链定义，许多学者从不同的角度给出了许多不同的定义。美国史迪文斯②、美国供应链专家 Robert & Nichols③ 的研究可以看出供应链概念发生了转变，主要是考虑了供应链的完整性和其中所有成员操作的一致性[63-65]。英国著名物流专家哈理森④、马丁·克里斯托弗⑤、菲力普⑥的研究体现出现代供应链的概念更加注重围绕核心企业的网链关系[63,66,67]。美国供应链管理专业协会解释了供应链概念⑦。主要具有供应链的用户需求目标特征、供应链的动态性特征、供应链的复杂性特征、供应链的合作性特征、供应链的信息特征、供应链的

① W. D. Harries 和 J. R. Stock（1985）在《市场营销与物流的重组——历史与未来的展望》中运用历史经验证明了市场营销与物流活动的相关性，首次提出了营销与物流的一体化概念，该文的发表推动了物流供应链过程的一体化研究与实践的开展。1983 年，日本开始了以大型量贩式为中心的网上订、发货系统，物流企业发展到 5 万多家，从业人员约 105 万人，货运量达到 34 亿吨，开始在全国乃至国外开展物流业务，形成了多渠道、多层次、多形式、工商齐办的现代化物流一体化网络系统。欧共体的物流在这一阶段为了追求物流系统的集成化和一体化，开始应用了物流供应链的概念，发展联盟型和合作型的物流新体系，通过改变原来分散的物流管理方式提高物流效率。1998 年，美国物流管理协会（CLM）对物流概念重新进行了定义，提出“物流是供应链流程的一部分，是为了满足客户需求而对商品、服务及相关信息从原产地到消费地的高效率、高效益的正向和反向流动及储存进行的计划、实施与控制过程”。

② 史迪文斯认为：“通过增值过程和分销渠道控制从供应商的供应商到用户的用户的流就是供应链，它开始于供应的源点，结束于消费的终点。”

③ Robert & Nichols 将供应链定义为：“供应链包括了产品从原材料阶段一直到最终用户手中这一过程中，与产品的流动和转化以及伴随的有关信息的活动。信息在供应链上可以向下流动，也可以向上流动。供应链管理是通过改善供应链关系而对这些活动进行集成，从而获得持续的竞争优势。这一定义强调了从原材料获取到产品到达用户这一过程中，与物流和信息流有关的所有活动。”

④ 哈理森将供应链定义为：“供应链是执行采购原材料、将它们转换为中间产品和成品并且将成品销售到用户的功能网链。”

⑤ 克里斯托弗认为：“供应链是指涉及将产品或服务提供给最终消费者的过程和活动的上游及下游企业组织所构成的网络。”

⑥ 菲力普认为：“供应链中战略伙伴关系很重要，通过建立战略伙伴关系，可以与重要的供应商和用户更有效地开展工作。”

⑦ 美国供应链协会对供应链的概念有这样的解释：“供应链——目前国际上广泛使用的一个术语，囊括了涉及生产与交付最终产品和服务的一切努力，从供应商的供应商到客户的客户。供应链管理包括管理供应与需求，原材料、备品备件的采购、制造与装配，物件的存放及库存查询，订单的录入与管理，渠道分销及最终交付用户。”

虚拟特征。其结构模型①如图 2－2。

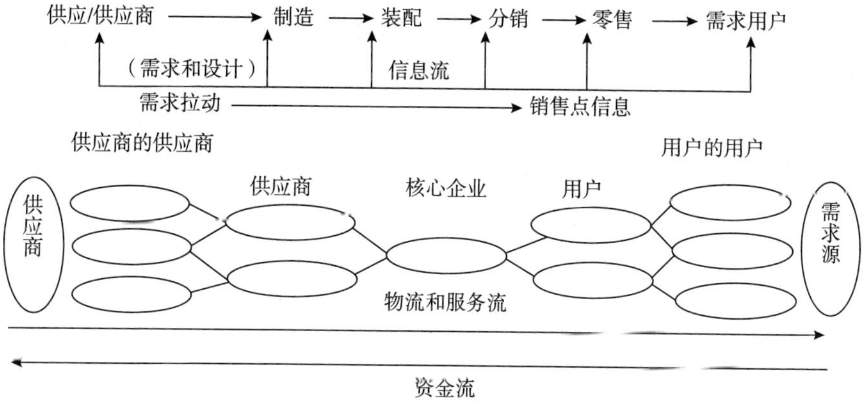

图 2－2 供应链的网链结构模型

随着供应链发展与激烈的全球竞争，供应链管理的概念开始出现②。设计物流、供应、生产、计划、需求等领域。其中包括计划、合作、控制物料和信息，细分为职能与辅助领域。达到降低总交易成本、提高用户服务水平的目的。2005 年 1 月，四十多年历史的美国物流管理协会（CLM）正式更名为美国供应链管理专业协会（Council of Supply Chain Management Professionals，CSCMP）。这也揭示了 21 世纪国际物流发展的主流趋势已经变成供应链整合管理。随着信息技术、计算机与网络通信技术的发展，供应链管理已经成为企业普遍的运营实践模式，现代物流开始进入供应链时代。

① 根据供应链的定义，供应链由所有加盟的节点企业组成，其中一般有一个核心企业，节点企业在需求信息的驱动下，通过供应链的职能分工与合作，以资金流、物流和服务流为媒介实现整个供应链的不断增值。

② “供应链管理”一词由 Keith R. Oliver 等人于 1982 年首次提出。自 20 世纪 80 年代以来，激烈的全球竞争使生产制造商逐渐认识到买卖双方之间相互协作与战略伙伴关系的重要性，供应链管理的概念开始出现在生产制造商与其供应商建立的战略伙伴关系中，进而产生了物流一体化概念。供应链管理不同于传统的企业管理，它更强调整体效率提高和整体成本的下降，以最终客户为中心，进行供应链整体的集成与协调，突破传统基于职能部门的管理模式，要求各链节企业围绕物流、信息流、资金流以及工作流进行信息共享与经营协调，实现全过程的战略管理。在管理过程中，通过采用集成的思想和方法实现柔性的与稳定的供需关系。现在的供应链管理把供应链上的各个企业作为一个不可分割的整体，使供应链上各企业分担的采购、生产、分销和销售的职能成为一个协调发展的有机体。

2. 宏观经济发展相关理论的深化

（1）新经济增长理论。20世纪80年代以来，现代物流发展理论的一个重要特点是直接对物流技术和物流市场建模，而传统物流理论只对物流技术和物流市场进行比较简单和明确的处理。20世纪80年代兴起的以保罗·罗默（Romer，1986）和罗伯特·卢卡斯（Lucas，1988）为代表的“新经济增长理论”，美国经济学家保罗·罗默1990年提出了技术进步内生增长模型，从效用函数入手，通过建立具有微观基础的、结构严谨、论证规范的模型，并在模型中引入了诸如不确定性、不对称信息和监督成本与完全竞争相悖的因素，把经济增长建立在内生技术进步上。新经济增长理论包括以保罗·罗默（1986）、巴罗（1991）等为代表人物的知识积累模型①、以卢卡斯（1988）、罗默（1990）、琼斯（1995）等为代表人物的人力资本模型②、以杨小凯与博兰德（1991）、贝克尔和墨菲（1992）为代表人物的分工演进模型③。因此，对物流技术和物流市场的形成可以做出规范性的解释，研究内生物流体系如何发展并作用于经济增长的，使政策主张更加接近现实④。

（2）新产业组织理论。新产业组织理论出现在20世纪80年代，新产业组织理论的发展主要体现在以下四个方面：一是在分析框架上改变了单向、静态的研究模式，认为SCP框架是一个循环的流程，S、C、P之间并不仅仅是一个简单的S—C—P的单向决定，而且还存在着P—C—S这样一个反向决定；二是在理论基础上，以科斯为代表的新制度经济学派运用

---

① 知识积累模型的基本结论是技术进步可以提高投资的收益，投资又会引致知识积累，知识增加加快了技术进步的进程，在这种正反馈中，经济系统出现了一个良性循环，从而长期稳定地提高经济增长率。因此，一国要实现经济的长期增长，必须不断地追加投资。

② 人力资本模型很好地解释了各国经济发展的差异，解释了美、欧、日等发达资本主义国家和地区，在近现代曾持续了一百多年的经济增长现象，对中国、印度等大国为何在此期间却一直落后，以及一些最不发达国家为何至今仍锁在低收入陷阱里甚至经济退步等现象具有一定的解释能力，对这些国家的政策制定也有较好的参考价值，其局限性在于人力资本的测算与加总问题。

③ 劳动分工理论研究了经济增长的微观机制，使用了消费生产者的概念，模型存在着竞争均衡和帕累托最优的一致性。

④ 经济可以实现内生增长的观点是新经济增长理论的核心思想，大多数人认为内生的技术进步是实现经济增长的决定因素。以上这些新经济增长模型共同观点是经济增长是经济系统的内生变量决定的，政府实施的某些经济政策对经济增长具有重要的作用。这种以知识为基础的新的经济增长理论鼓励新知识的积累以及知识在经济中的广泛运用，促进了高新技术革命的发展和知识经济时代的到来。

交易成本理论和委托—代理理论，对企业的存在及其边界进行了解释；三是研究重心转向厂商主义，即从重视市场结构转向重视企业行为的分析；四是研究方法上将博弈论、计量经济学和信息经济学的分析方法有机地贯穿于产业组织研究中[68]。

3. 现代物流与经济发展理论的发展

（1）协同学理论。在“协同学”中，协同是指在复杂系统中，各组成要素、各子系统在运行过程中合作与协调，从而产生出新的结构和功能。协同意味着经济组织如果有创新能力且善于识别发展机会，就可以更有效地利用它所拥有的资源和技能，不断扩大其规模。美国战略理论研究专家H. 伊戈尔·安索夫（H. Igor Ansoff）出版《公司战略》① 中第一次提出协同的经济学含义，安索夫认为基于协同理念的战略，能够产生一种联合作用的效应，这种效应大于由部分资源独立创造的总和，有利于公司更充分地利用现有优势开拓新的发展空间。2000 年，安德鲁·坎贝尔、凯瑟琳·萨姆斯·卢克斯在著作《战略协同》中正式定义了协同概念，“协同是企业如何通过识别自身能力与机遇的匹配关系来成功地拓展新的事业。”[69]随后，日本战略专家伊丹广之（Itami Hiroyuki）也对协同进行了界定，他认为协同是发挥资源最大效能的方法，其效应可以分为“互补效应”和“协同效应”两部分。“通俗地讲，协同就是搭便车，当从企业一个部分中积累的资源可以被同时且无成本地应用于企业的其他部分的时候，协同效益就发生了。当若干领域可以同时使用某种资源而不会影响其他领域对这种资源的使用时，协同效应就产生了。互补性资产主要是通过对可见资产的使用来实现的，而协同效应则主要是通过对隐形资产的使用来实现的。”[70]罗伯特·巴泽尔（Robert Buzzell）则从协同价值的角度进一步研究了协同。他认为，“协同创造价值主要有四种：对资源或业务行为的共享、市场营销和研究开发的扩散效益、企业的相似性以及对企业形象的共享。”[71]协同理论能够提高现代物流模式的运作效率，从而有效地促进经济发展。从系统的观点看，协同力是指在一定的环境作用下，物流由物流主体、物流客体、物流载体等要素构成的有机整体，这些要素之间相互关联，相互作用。从

① H. 伊戈尔·安索夫（H. Igor Ansoff）在 1965 年出版《公司战略》一书中，首次确立了协同的经济学含义，即企业整体的价值有可能大于各部分价值的总和。

价值的角度看，物流的价值实现是通过广泛的空间定位、库存安排和快速商品调拨等。物流全球化发展的趋势要求物流组织必须实施协调手段，对物流资源进行整合，通过物流资源的协调、开发，提高我国物流业的整体效益，进而提升我国物流业的竞争优势，实现经济协调持续发展。

（2）产业融合理论。早期的产业融合研究主要集中在计算机、印刷和广播等产业领域。随着信息技术的快速发展，产业融合涵盖的范围逐渐扩大，综合性日益增强，学术界对其内涵的研究也更为全面、深刻。比较具有代表性的含义界定有：1978 年，麻省理工学院媒体实验室的 Negrouponte 用三个圆圈来描述计算、印刷和广播三者的技术边界，认为三个圆圈的交叉处将会成为成长最快、创新最多的领域[72]。植草益认为产业融合是通过技术革新和放宽限制来降低产业间的壁垒，加强产业企业间的竞争合作关系[73]。马健认为产业融合是产业之间在技术、业务、市场上的融合[74]。上述概念分别从产业融合的动力、前提条件、实质内容及结果进行了界定。本研究认为，产业融合应该是在技术进步、政府管制放松及管理创新的前提下，发生在产业边界和交叉处的一种技术融合，这种融合能够有效地改变原有产业的产品特征及市场需求，形成新型的竞争与合作关系，并最终实现产业间在市场、产品及业务方面的全面融合。基于产业融合的物流金融协同创新是指物流业和金融业在现代信息技术基础上通过产品融合和市场融合扩大产业边界，形成资源共享、同步响应基础上的产品创新、技术创新、市场创新、流程创新和管理创新。加快物流与金融保险、产品加工业、运输仓储业、流通配送业及零售业的融合，建立以企业为主体、市场为导向的物流金融协同创新体系，形成我国物流金融协同创新的基本体制架构，是增强我国物流业核心竞争力、经济协调持续发展的必然选择。

（3）相互关系理论。一是物流作用于经济的理论。现代物流对宏观经济增长的作用①。首先，现代物流在经济增长中的基础保障作用。在社会化大生产中，生产、分配、交换、消费构成了人类经济循环的一个完整

① 刘南（2007）认为当前对现代物流与宏观经济增长关系的研究中，关注于现代物流对经济增长的作用文献相对比较多，一般通过经济增长的相关理论，对现代物流的发展与经济增长之间的关系进行理论分析，进而得出现代物流在经济增长中发挥的作用。

过程，物流具有把这几个环节有机结合起来的功能，可以认为物流是社会经济的主要纽带①。物流网络体系是实现社会专业化分工的前提，对经济发展起到保障的基础性作用。其次，现代物流对经济增长的促进作用。第一，现代物流的本质是社会分工发展同时又促进分工进一步深化，从而进一步促进经济的增长②。第二，现代物流的发展促进了现代化大工业的发展。第三，现代物流的发展加快了全球经济一体化的进程。第四，现代物流的发展可以改善投资环境，促进地区招商引资和外资的流入。第五，现代物流的发展对社会人力资本投资产生重大影响作用。第六，现代物流对经济增长还存在对其他方面的影响③。二是经济作用于物流的理论。宏观经济增长对现代物流发展的影响作用④。首先，经济的快速增长带来物流需

---

① 社会专业化在不同地区的分工，必然带来货物在空间的位移，专业化分工越高，货物的集散在规模上就越大，在空间上就越广，而物流的作用被解释为克服需求和供给之间的时间性、空间性距离的过程，因此可以说只有完善的物流系统，才能够保证社会专业化分工的实际进行，才能保证货物在空间上的有效的配置，从而带来经济增长。

② 物流发展到现代物流阶段，出现了一种新的组织方式——物流联盟，而物流联盟的出现正是交易费用与分工收益相互协调发展的结果现代物流对普遍降低交易成本所做的贡献可以在物流联盟企业之间的交易过程和交易主体行为的考察中得到证实。一方面，从交易的全过程看，现代物流的发展有助于物流联盟企业的各个合作伙伴之间在交易过程中减少相关交易费用。由于物流合作伙伴之间经常沟通与合作，可使搜寻交易对象信息方面的费用大为降低；提供个性化物流服务建立起来的相互信任和承诺，可以减少各种履约风险，即便在服务过程中产生冲突，也会因为合同时效的长期性而可通过协商加以解决，从而避免仲裁、法律诉讼等行为所产生的费用。另一方面，从交易主体行为看，物流联盟的出现将促使伙伴之间的"组织学习"，从而提高对方对不确定性环境的认知能力，减少因交易主体的"有限理性"而产生的交易费用，即物流联盟企业之间的长期合作将在很大程度上抑制交易双方之间的机会主义，这使得交易双方由于机会主义而产生的交易费用控制在相对较低的程度。

③ 除了以上分析现代物流对经济增长的促进作用外，现代物流对经济增长的作用还包括一些其他的内容。例如，现代物流的发展往往伴随技术进步的出现，而技术进步也是经济增长的一个重要动力，亚当·斯密提到最后一个经济增长的动力就是技术进步，同样处于早期经济增长思想的马克思以及熊彼特也都是通过技术进步论述经济增长的原因。现代物流的发展除了对经济增长产生促进作用外，还对经济增长的方式产生重要影响，这主要体现在现代物流的发展可以通过降低交易成本带来经济增长方式的转变。一个结构稳定、高效运作的物流网络，不仅可以减少组成要素之间的磨损和交易成本，减少用户使用网络资源和要素的成本，还可以放大各要素的功能，提高要素和整个网络的收益，实现"1+1>2"的作用。

④ 王槐林等（2001）认为现代物流被认为是经济发展到一定阶段的产物，经济发展对现代物流的影响一方面体现在经济的大幅度增长将带来对物流需求的增加，而物流需求的增加可以推动现代物流的发展；另一方面体现在经济的发展水平决定了现代物流的发展水平。经济的大幅度增长，必然导致巨大的物资产品的流动，也就必然导致物流量的增加，这是经济发展的必然规律，也是物流发展的必然规律。

求的增加。自20世纪70年代以来，经济与技术的发展更多地要求物流服务方式以及它们与社会物流系统的各环节之间更有效、更合理地衔接配合。市场经济条件下经济迅速增长，社会化专业分工的深化带来物流需求不断增加。其次，经济的发展状况决定了物流的现代化程度①。物流的发展需要基础设施的投资、完善，只有经济发展到一定的水平才能够进一步推动物流的发展②。三是现代物流与宏观经济增长的相互作用机制。第一，现代物流与经济发展的双向作用关系。对现代物流和经济增长关系研究的很多文献表明，现代物流与宏观经济增长的关系并不是简单的单向促进作用，它们之间是相互作用、相互促进的双向作用关系。例如张文杰③、靳伟④、桂寿平等⑤从不同角度证实这种存在的相互关系。第二，现代物流与经济发展的基本因果关系。系统动力学在物流研究中应用比较广泛，其中较典型的有克莱顿·希尔模拟模型，哈佛大学的物流系统模拟模型等⑥，系统动力学在研究现代物流与经济增长的相互关系可以用以下的因果关系图进行描

① 牟惟仲（2003）认为物流是经济总体架构中的一个组成部分，因此受经济对其发展的决定性作用，从政策、人财物力支撑、发展空间等诸方面显现。在经济发展的各个不同阶段，对物流的需求不同，相应的产业政策，对物流的重视程度也不同，因此物流的发展状况也不同。

② 从西方发达国家物流发展的历程可以看出经济增长对物流的刺激作用，例如，在20世纪60年代，欧洲主要国家全面由“卖方市场”转变为“买方市场”，这使得消费品市场竞争变得日益激烈，产生了对“高效率、低费用”提供服务的需求，谁能够高效率、低费用的向市场提供产品，谁就拥有竞争力。因此，产生对物流发展的巨大需求。从那时候起，物流伴随着经济的快速发展也不断向前发展。

③ 张文杰（2002）运用经济学与交易理论对经济和物流之间的相互关系做了分析，总结得出经济和物流之间的相互作用关系表现在：经济的全球化、区域经济的一体化、区域中的企业对利润和核心竞争能力的追求，以及我国经济发展的现实促进了现代物流的发展；同时现代物流的发展也改变着经济的增长方式、促进新的产业形态的形成、优化区域产业结构、促进以城市为中心的区域市场的形成和发展。

④ 靳伟（2002）也认为经济、贸易和物流三者是紧密相连、密不可分的，经济的发展会带动贸易，贸易发展后，物流伴随发展，三者之间互为因果、相辅相成；同时，三者也存在互补性，取长补短、互为裨益、互相依赖关系。

⑤ 桂寿平等（2002）分析了经济增长和物流的关系，并根据物流系统与系统动力学的特点，对物流系统建立相应的模型，并且对广州市现代物流和经济之间的关系做了实证分析，研究了广州市现代物流发展的方向。

⑥ 在物流系统优化的研究中常用的系统动力学模拟模型有：库存模型，复杂的排队等待问题模拟模型，物流费用分析模拟模型。系统动力学模拟技术在物流管理的应用有如下方面：物流大系统的优化、物流设施的平面布置、库存控制系统、仓库规划、装卸搬运系统的分析，装配流水线作业计划等。近年来，计算机模拟技术在建模方法、模拟优化方法、模拟语言发展、模拟结果分析等方面均有很大发展，并开发了一些专用于物流系统的模拟模型。

述如图2－3所示。

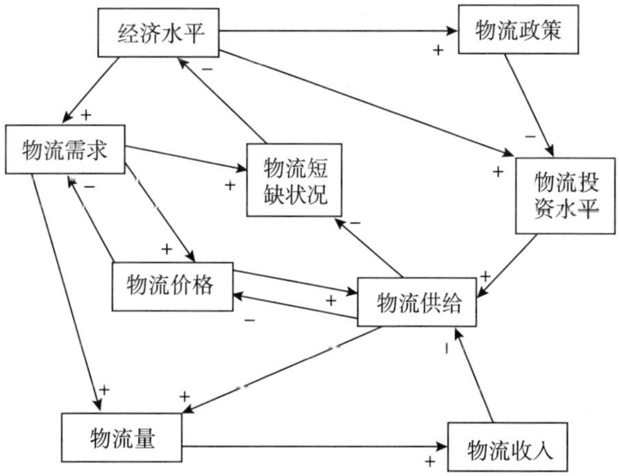

图2－3 物流与经济发展的基本因果关系①

4. 物流功能论

物流功能或职能理论，是揭示物流影响经济的微观机制理论。该理论贯穿于现代物流与经济发展理论的全过程，20世纪80年代以来，它得到了新的认识。该理论认为：信息成本和交易成本是物流市场和物流机构出现的原因；物流市场和物流机构的出现就是为了解决由信息成本和交易成本所带来的问题；不同类型的信息成本和交易成本导致了不同类型的物流契约、物流市场和物流机构。物流体系促进经济发展的最基本功能可以概括为：在不确定性存在的情况下，在时间和空间上配置资源，通过"资本积累"和"科技创新"两个途径来影响经济的增长。西方农产品物流发展理论代表人物利马（Lira）、拉森（Tage Skjoett－Larsen）、道格拉斯（Douglas N. Lambert）、玛格丽塔（Margaret A. Emmelhainz）、约翰（John T. Gardner）等认为：农产品物流涉及从生产、加工、储存、运输到销售的整个物流链，其中存在的交易费用大小和契约关系的完全程度影响着农

① 因果关系图可以看出现代物流与经济增长之间的作用关系，一方面现代物流对经济增长的基础和促进作用可以通过物流发展带来物流体系的完善，从而对经济增长产生作用；另一方面经济增长通过对物流需求的增加促进物流的发展。结合两个方面，可以通过"物流短缺"即物流供给能力和物流需求之间的差距来对现代物流发展和经济增长之间的关系进行解释。资料来源：谢如鹤等编，《物流系统规划原理与方法》，中国物资出版社，2004（3），15。

产品物流的运作和发展①。菲利普（Phillip）、勃杰和施拉德（Boehlje and Schrader）认为：由于交易费用存在，一方面导致了一个低效均衡，另一方面，随着交易费用的增加，促使人们创新不同的经济组织与交易方式②。托马斯和格弗埃（Thomas and Grinffin）认为：整个农产品物流链条是由不同的、独立利益的主体构成的一个动态系统，因而博弈天然存在，提高整个链条的运行效率的关键问题是协调与集成。瑞尼克斯等（Rcynircs）、利马（Lim）、陈（Chen）等利用博弈论和信息不对称理论从不同的视角研究如何解决链条上的冲突，实现协调③。在现代物流的发展历程中，系统思想和系统方法为实现物流活动的系统化和整体最优化提供了理论基础，尤其是在 Logistics 的物流概念确立以后，现代物流的发展从物流基本功能各自分离的状态进入了有机结合的阶段。物流体系的功能可以具体细分为获取信息和配置资源、分散和共担风险、运营监督和约束、方便产品和服务交易、创造需求与供需综合平衡五个方面。

第一，物流获取信息和配置资源的原理。高信息成本是在搜索和处理足够的投资信息情况下产生的，物流中介可以通过规模经济使搜索和处理信息成本降低，并在物流体系中鉴别最有能力的企业，使资本进行有效配置加快经济发展[75]。

第二，物流分散和共担风险的原理。在信息成本和交易成本出现的情况下，物流市场和物流制度有助于风险交易、风险规避、风险分散及风险共担。由于物流过程的不确定会产生物流的流动性风险，加之信息不对称和交易成本会阻碍资产的流动也会加强流动性风险，在这种情况下，只有

① 利马（Lira）通过显示原理分析了物流链上的契约结构，给出实话实说的可能性；韦弗和赫达逊（Weaver and Hudson）对供应链中的契约协作进行了理论和实证分析；拉森（Tage Skjoett - Larsen）基于资产专用性利用交易成本理论分析了物流关系的形成和维持；道格拉斯（Douglas N. Lambert）、玛格丽塔（Margaret A. Emmelhainz）、约翰（John T. Gardner）等则从物流链上各方的利益格局和企业制度环境出发作了开创性研究，指出成功物流关系的条件是第三方物流制度安排的保障。

② 菲利普（Phillip）提出通过建立战略伙伴关系，与重要的供应商和用户更有效地开展工作，从而提高绩效，并且艾伦（Alan McKinnon）对英国食品供应链运输效率进行了分析；勃杰和施拉德（Boehlje and Schrader）主张将食品供应链的研究重点由市场转到链条的纵向协调，严格控制产品质量并对链条进行内部整合以提高整体的运作效率。

③ 瑞尼克斯等（Rcynircs）分析了产品配送和质量控制的协调问题，利马（Lim）研究了第三方物流的合同设计：陈（Chen）等则建立了一个单一供方的分销系统的合作机制：不完全信息下的供应商的最优批量折扣模型是由克贝特（Corbett）给出的；克莱门特（Clement E. Ward）从整合出发考察了牛肉、猪肉和禽类，认为牛肉业的整合比可规模化生产的猪肉业和禽业更困难。

采用有效的物流市场和物流制度才能减少风险，提高物流体系长期的流动性安全，能够吸收大量资本投入，促进经济发展。另外，物流体系是多元主体共同利益上的联合，其本质是经济利益一体化经营，通过交易、分散等方式建立“风险共担，利益共享”基本原则。一是要根据“风险共担，利益共享”的基本原则，在“龙头”单位和各参与者主体之间建立互利互惠的利益关系。二是“龙头”和农户要共同坚持“共担”与“共享”原则。

第三，物流运营监督和约束的原理。物流除了降低事前得到信息成本以外，还能降低事后对企业、经理的监督成本。物流经营系统的正常营运，多主体互利互惠关系靠营运约束机制来实现。参与各方从一开始就界定产权，使企业真正成为产权明晰、自主经营、自负盈亏、自立发展的经济主体，使物流系统真正成为“风险共担，利益共享”的经济共同体。从“龙头”企业与农户的联结关系和要素组合方式来看，物流经营采用的运行方式有：市场约束机制；合同（契约）约束机制；股份合作约束机制；租赁约束机制；专业承包约束机制。

第四，物流方便产品和服务交易的原理。物流体系会便利交易，降低交易费用的物流可以推动专业化、技术创新和经济增长。物流的出现大大降低了交易成本，导致了更大程度的专业化，专业化需要更多的交易，物流具有交易费用的降低与技术创新的优势。物流体系降低交易成本这一特征正是适应了更大的专业化，从而提高了生产力。同样生产力的提高对物流的发展也有正的反馈作用：当建立物流市场的成本是固定时，只用拿出人均收入中一小部分资金来投资这个物流市场固定的成本，经济发展刺激了物流发展。

第五，物流创造需求与供需综合平衡的原理。即物流动员运销的原理，是将聚敛分散运销者的资金并引向投资。在物流的发展过程中，可以根据物流的服务目的、服务功能、技术手段等特征，将物流分为“传统物流”与“现代物流”。传统物流体现了一种满足需要的“需要满足功能”，以尽可能低的物流成本，给顾客以尽可能好的物流服务为目的；而“现代物流”则通过动员运销、促进运销、支援运销的“创造需求功能”和使需要、供给相互配合的“供需综合平衡功能”，目的在于提高效益，并把满足顾客要求放在首位，以此提高企业效益[76]。因此，物流的发展过程本质上就是扩大信用的交易过程，从最初的获取信息→经过信任、信用、信誉、增进信任→到最终的扩大信用交易，在这个过程中物流中介建立良好的声誉并获得政府的支持至关重要，这样才能改善资源配置和促进物流创新发展。

考察西方现代物流与经济发展理论可以发现，其对现代物流与经济发展的认识从“无”→“有”→“复杂”，认识方法从经验观察→理论抽象→实证检验→通过实证发现新理论。但本研究也注意到，西方现代物流与经济发展理论，以市场经济下投资驱动的工业化为背景，市场制度是外生的，政府行为没有纳入分析框架，现代物流与经济发展中的制度因素没有被充分揭示。西方农产品物流发展理论，基本上还停留在现代物流与经济发展理论的一般应用和经验与政策总结层面。近年来，虽然中国现代物流与经济发展理论发展较快，但分析范式不是停留在“经济决定流通、流通反作用于经济”的哲学层面上，就是被束缚在计划经济思维模式下的“国家干预”框架内，或是照搬西方现代物流与经济发展理论；在西部地区农产品物流理论研究和实践探索上，主要是从机构视角研究西部地区农产品物流对农村经济应发挥的作用，忽视了西部地区农产品物流发展的农村经济因素，农产品物流供给不足的问题变成了农产品物流机构多与少的问题；对西部地区农村经济的农产品物流功能需求以及农产品物流如何发挥其功能的研究十分薄弱。

第二节　可持续与可持续发展理论

可持续与可持续发展理论集合了多种学科的相关理论和方法，是解释和解决可持续与可持续发展问题的思想、理论和方法的总称。本研究在经济发展理论、系统科学理论的基础上对可持续与可持续发展理论进行论述和展示。

一　经济发展理论中的可持续与可持续发展理论

（一）传统的可持续与可持续发展理论

传统的可持续与可持续发展理论在本研究中是指没有明确的可持续发展理念，但其概念早在传统的经济增长模型中就已经存在了。经济学对经济增长的研究自然是最富权威性的，但并不是完备无缺的。经济学通常视经济过程为孤立的、自行循环的过程，其与环境系统的相互影响往往为过去的研究所忽视。美国经济学家乔·奇斯库·罗根提出一个有价值的见解：经济学家的这种忽视可能因借鉴经典力学的思想方法所致。在传统的经济学研究中，经济学家往往认为经济过程不产生环境性质的变化，也不为所处环境性质的变化所影响。经济过程为一种与外部隔绝、自成系统以及与历史无关的过程，一种既无外流，又无内流，在消费与生产之间自行循环的过程。因此，大多数经济思想把经济过程看作一种与自然界“不相往来”的过程。使“经济学的理论”① 发展为“经济增长理论”（又称增长经济学）在现代西方宏观经济学中占有重要一席，它主要研究发达的资本主义国家经济长期发展的条件和趋势。西方经济学界一般将英国经济学家哈罗德在1939年发表的《论动态理论》一文作为经济增长理论的标志。在此之前，凯恩斯在《就业、货币和利息通论》一书中认为，只要政府调节总需求，就可以使资本主义经济活动达到充分就业的均衡状态。根据凯恩斯的理论，只有当I = S，即当投资等于储蓄，或者说储蓄全部用于投资时，经济活动就能达到均衡状态。哈罗德认为，凯恩斯的分析是短期静态分析，具有一定的局限性，因此有必要使它长期化、动态化。

所谓长期化，就是把人口数量、资本数量和技术条件等因素看作变量。所谓动态化，就是把经济活动看成是时间上具有连续性的活动，着重研究经济稳定增长的条件和长期增长的趋势。哈罗德以凯恩斯提出的I = S这个均衡条件出发，进一步指出，投资的变动不是由产量（或收入）的绝对水平决定的，而是由产量（或收入）的变化率的“引致”作用决定的，从而提出 $G = \frac{S}{V}$（G 表示国民收入的增长率，S 指储蓄倾向，V 表示资本—产量比率）这个均衡增长模型。它表明要实现均衡的经济增长，国民收入的增长率就必须等于储蓄倾向与资本—产量比率的二者之比。

哈罗德模型用数学形式表明了劳动、资本、储蓄、投资与产量增长率之间函数关系，但只局限于两种生产要素，即劳动和资本的考察，而没有考察其他生产要素与经济增长的关系。更为重要的是，哈罗德模型所阐明的经济增长是一种单纯的经济量的增长，随之发生的社会影响和环境变化均不在考察之列。因此，尽管哈罗德模型视经济过程为持续过程，但仍然

① 关于国民经济“增长”和“发展”问题的原理、规律，以及据此作出政策推论的学说。

没有超越一般经济学视经济过程为孤立过程的传统。继哈罗德模型之后，新古典经济增长理论虽然在模型本身的构造上有所发展，但其研究思路仍没有突破。

（二）现代的可持续与可持续发展理论

现代可持续发展思想的产生有其深刻的社会历史背景和迫切的现实需要。第二次世界大战以后，一些工业化国家出现了一股从未有过的“增长热”。在这个时期，烟囱产业曾被作为“朝阳”工业而受到推崇，以工业化为主要内容的经济增长取得了明显效果。经济发展把一个受战争创伤的世界，在短短几十年里推向了一个崭新的、前所未有的工业化时代。然而，世界系统并非线性的简单系统，而是非线性的复杂系统。工业化和城市化进程大大加剧了耕地、淡水、森林和矿产的消耗，环境污染和生态破坏问题愈趋严重，在某些区域内已影响到人类的生存。历史事实表明，整个工业文明是在人视自然为奴隶而统治自然的思想基础上发展起来的，这种建立在掠夺资源、破坏环境、损害生态基础上的发展，主宰了工业社会几百年的历史进程，已经走到了尽头。一些有识之士开始对传统经济发展模式和经济发展与资源环境的关系进行反思，变革这种传统发展思想与战略的潮流势不可挡。它既带来挑战和机会，又充满矛盾和危机。在这种情况下，传统的发展观与发展模式日益遭到冲击，已经不能适应当代世界经济、社会、科技、生态、文化等各方面发展的客观要求，这就迫使人们去寻求新的发展模式，研究新的发展观，进行新的战略选择。于是，发展观的改变与发展就应运而生，并形成新发展观。作为世界发展经济的共同战略指导思想——“可持续发展”战略指导思想，正是近30年来世界环境与发展运动实践的产物。其具体产生过程包括了如下三个阶段：

1. 舆论准备阶段

世界经济的发展进入20世纪60年代末，世界范围内的生态与经济的矛盾已经明显地显现出来。当时针对可能产生的生态经济危机问题，出现了一场关于人类社会发展前途的大讨论。1962年，美国海洋生物学家R. 卡逊（R. Carson）在《寂静的春天》一书中指出：由于化肥、农药和杀虫剂的大量使用，将造成对生物的大量杀伤，以至于在许多地方再也听不到蛙鸣鸟唱的春之交响曲，春天将变得死一般寂静。这本书在当时引起巨大轰动，它标志着人类生态意识的觉醒和“生态学时代”的开端。1966

年，美国经济学家鲍尔丁把全球经济比喻为“宇宙飞船经济”。①改变“增长型”的经济，而采取“储备型”的经济；②改变传统的“消耗型”经济，而代之以“休养生息”的经济；③实行“福利量”的经济，而不能像过去只着重于“生产量”的经济；④放弃过去的“单程经济”，而建立起一种既不会使资源枯竭，又不会造成环境污染、生态破坏的能够循环使用各种物质的“循环经济”。1968 年，意大利经济学家佩切伊发起组织了一个世界性的民间团体——罗马俱乐部①。他们通过对人类生存困境的研究，系统地论证了经济高速增长带来的消极后果。以“罗马俱乐部”为代表的悲观派观点认为，当代世界经济任其发展下去，地球上的经济增长在 100 年内就要达到极限。因此主张不能继续增长。针对增长极限论，以美国学者赫曼·卡恩和经济学家朱利安·林肯和西蒙等为代表的乐观派则提出了“经济发展决定论”，它实际上是传统经济理论的延伸，认为经济增长可以弥补其伴随的一切副作用，世界发展不会因资源、人口、土地的限制而降低发展速度，技术和资本可以代替一切，当前人类社会的发展正面临着“无限繁荣的机会”，发展的“极限”不会到来。两派的长期激烈争论为世界可持续发展战略指导思想的形成做了思想和舆论上的准备。

2. 全球保护环境的行动阶段

1972 年 3 月，罗马俱乐部出版了《增长的极限》一书。书中指出：人口呈指数增长，而地球资源却十分有限；污染呈指数增长，而地球的自净能力又十分有限，从而使资源锐减，环境恶化。再这样下去，地球这艘宇宙之舟就有倾覆的危险，全球性的灾难将在 21 世纪来临。为避免人类社会“灾难性的崩溃”，他们提出了经济“零增长”模式。该书的出版在世界上产生了极大的反响，并由此引发了对全球未来趋势的广泛大论战，这些论述在反思传统发展观的过程中产生了重大的影响。此后，几个主要的事件直接推动了可持续发展观的产生。1972 年 6 月联合国召开了“人

① 1968 年，正当工业国家陶醉于战后经济快速增长和随之而来的“黄金时代”时，来自西方不同国家的约 30 位企业家、科学家、教育家和经济学家等学者聚会罗马，成立了一个非正式的国际协会——罗马俱乐部（The Club Rome），共同探讨了关系全人类发展前途的人口、资源、粮食、环境等一系带根本性的问题，并对原有经济发展模式提出了质疑。1972 年丹尼斯·米都斯（Dennis L. Meadows）代表罗马俱乐部（The Club of Rome）发表的《增长的极限》（The Limits to Growth），对传统的发展模式的怀疑，实际上也是这一理念的反映。

类环境会议”①，会后联合国规定了每年6月5日为“世界环境日”，并成立了联合国环境规划署，负责处理世界环境方面的事务[77]。从此，一个世界性的环境保护运动就蓬勃发展起来。

3. 全球环境与发展行动统一的阶段

1974年，罗马俱乐部提出了“有机增长”的《人类处于转折点》出版。1981年，美国世界观察研究所所长、农业经济学家R. 布郎（Lester R. Brown）的《建立一个可持续发展的社会》的问世标志着可持续发展观的初步形成。因此，从20世纪80年代开始，“可持续发展”这一观点得到了有关国际组织、政府首脑、科研机构以及企事业单位的广泛关注。1987年《我们共同的未来》报告经第42届联大通过后成为世界各国在环境保护和经济发展方面的纲领性文件。报告呼吁世界各国维护资源、保护环境，开辟可持续发展的道路，把可持续发展作为一个关键性的概念提出来，并对其内涵做了界定和详尽的理论阐述。报告指出：“目前保护和保持人类进步，满足人类需要，以及实现人类抱负所做的许多努力，无论是富国还是穷国都是不持久的。他们在业已掠取过度的环境资源账户上掠取得太多、太快……他们可以在我们这一代的结账单上显示盈余，但我们的孩子们则将继承赤字……我们目前极度浪费的结果正在迅速使我们的子孙后代没有选择的余地。”人们的生态环境意识有了很大提高，各国政府在保护生态环境方面也做了大量工作。但是全世界范围的生态与经济矛盾并没有消除，全球生态环境的状况还在继续恶化，并且愈来愈明显地制约着经济社会的可持续发展。为此，1992年6月联合国又召开了“环境与发展大会”，其突出的成就是把环境与发展密切结合起来，这是人们从20年来世界环境与发展运动实践中取得的一个突破性的认识。据此，大会明确提出了“可持续发展”的指导思想，为新的历史时期世界环境与发展运动指出了正确的奋斗目

① 联合国在瑞典首都斯德哥尔摩召开了“人类环境会议”，它是世界各国政府第一次聚集在一起共同讨论环境问题的会议，标志着世界保护生态环境的运动从思想准备转入实际行动。会议通过了《联合国人类环境宣言》和《人类只有一个地球》的报告。这次会议没有直接提出可持续发展的问题，但会议的《宣言》已经爆发出了某些今天我们所说的可持续发展思想的火花。会议报告中写道：“实际上联合国对这次会议的要求，显然是要确定我们应当干些什么，才能保持地球不仅成为现在适合人类生活的场所，而且将来也适合子孙后代居住。”呼吁各国政府和人民为维护和改善人类环境，造福全体人民，造福后代而共同努力。

标。这一目标随即就被各国作为发展经济的共同指导思想肯定了下来，可持续发展成为经济发展理论中的主导思想。可持续发展的内涵既包括经济发展，也包括社会的发展和保持、建设良好的生态环境，经济发展和社会进步的可持续性与维护良好的生态环境密切相连。经济发展应包括数量的增长和质量的提高两部分，数量的增长是有限度的，而依靠科学技术进步去提高发展的经济效益、社会效益、生态效益才是可持续的。可持续发展是受内部和外部因素制约的，其发展的速度并非是匀速的，由于不同的作用方式其发展可能为波浪式、跳跃式或螺旋式的，也可能出现暂时的停滞，但最终发展表现为前进的[78]。如图 2－4 所示。

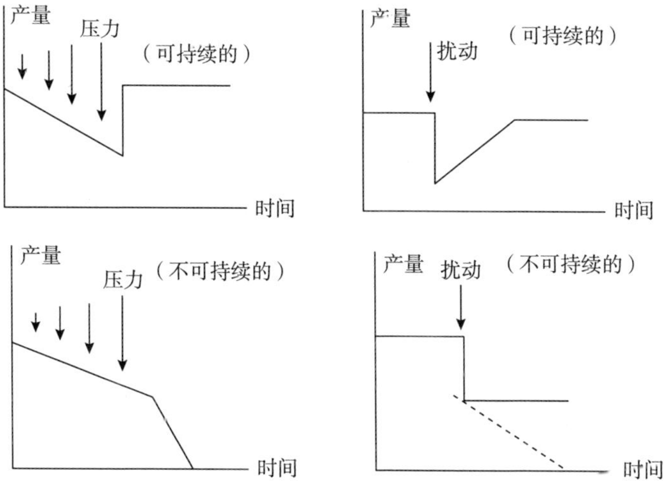

图 2－4　持续性的解释图示

当今人类推进传统发展思想与战略向现代发展思想与战略的转变，就必须选择可持续发展思想与战略。这是人类发展的历史性的重大转折，是人类创建生态文明，取代现存的工业文明的必由之路。这是因为，可持续发展思想与战略具备了现代发展思想与战略的丰富内涵：第一，可持续发展的主体是人的全面发展，实行这种战略的最终目的是要实现人类发展的全面需求，即物质需求、精神需求和生态需求；第二，可持续发展否定了把经济发展作为发展的唯一目标，把国民生产总值增长作为发展的唯一尺度，把自然环境作为资源取之不尽的“供奉者”和存在废物的“垃圾桶”

的传统发展思想与战略。强调发展既是经济可持续，又是生态可持续和社会可持续等多元可持续发展；第三，可持续发展强调当代人在追求当今发展的同时，要努力做到使自己的机会与后代人的机会相平等，决不允许当代人为实现当今发展而剥夺了后代人本应合理享有的同等发展的机会；第四，可持续发展的实质，是为了解决经济社会发展需求的无限性与自然生态供给能力的有限性之间的矛盾，缓解生态与经济的基本矛盾，实现生态与经济协调发展[79]。

马克思虽然没有具体论述可持续与可持续发展问题，但马克思的理论对可持续与可持续发展理论影响是极其深刻的①。马克思揭示了社会简单再生产实现条件[Ⅰ(V+m)=Ⅱ(c)]、社会扩大再生产条件[Ⅰ(c+V+m)=Ⅱ(c+△c)、Ⅱ(c+V+m)=Ⅰ(V+m/x+△V)+Ⅱ(V+m/x+△V)]，研究社会再生产条件和两大部类关系充分体现了可持续思想、方法与分析范式。邓小平“计划多一点还是市场多一点，不是社会主义与资本主义的本质区别，计划经济不等于社会经济，资本主义也有计划，市场经济不等于资本主义，社会主义也有市场。计划和市场都是经济手段”的精辟论断以及先富和后富的辩证思想等，是对马克思的可持续与可持续发展理论进一步丰富和发展。1992年联合国“环境与发展大会”以后，我国政府率先响应，制定了中国的可持续发展战略，发布了《中国21世纪议程——中国21世纪人口、环境与发展白皮书》。并且在1996年的第八届全国人民代表大会第四次会议上，把可持续发展战略纳入到了国民经济和社会发展计划。从此，可持续发展就作为我国发展经济的重要战略指导方针肯定了下来。中国共产党第十六次代表大会和十六届三中全会所提出的“科学发展观”和“统筹发展”则是这一理论在中国现实背景下的最好表述和体现②。这样也就为我国的西部大开发提供了正确的战略思想，它的实施也必将引导我国

---

① 王伟光（2004）提出基于唯物辩证法，马克思认为：发展是事物内部矛盾不断产生、发展和解决的对立统一过程；是一种运动状态，但又不是一般的运动状态，而是特指事物向前、向上，由低级向高级，不断推陈出新，不断进步的运动状态；任何发展都是系统的发展，系统构成要素在发展中相互联系、相互制约、相互作用，构成了系统的整体发展；发展必须是兼顾的、对称的、照顾他方的发展，否则就是畸形的，甚至是倒退和停顿的。

② 科学发展观，从本质上说，就是坚持以人为本，全面、协调、可持续的发展观，其立足点是人的全面发展，核心是协调，手段是统筹，目标是可持续，重点是城乡发展、区域发展、经济社会发展、人与自然和谐发展、国内发展和对外开放五大领域。科学发展观真正揭示了现代可持续发展的永恒主题，形成了完整而系统的发展观。

西部地区农产品物流走上可持续发展的正确方向。

二　系统科学理论中的可持续与可持续发展理论

系统科学理论①反映了整体和相互关联性的系统思想，它要求全面地而不是局部地看问题、连贯地而不是孤立地看问题、发展地而不是静止地看问题、灵活地而不是呆板地看问题。很多学科正在以系统科学理论作为分析手段，为研究复杂的自然或社会现象力求找到更适合本学科发展的有效方法论支持。

可持续与可持续发展理论在系统科学理论中侧重于可持续方法论。

1. 一般系统论

系统论研究系统的一般模式、结构与规律以及各个系统之间共同的特征。一般系统论“整体大于局部之和”的命题和系统的整体性、开放性和动态性原理，为从整体、系统内部结构、功能和系统与外部的关系角度把握可持续与可持续发展，提供了新的方法和分析框架。

2. 信息论

信息论研究信息、信息熵、通信系统、数据传输等问题，将信息传递作为一种统计现象，总结出估算通信信道容量的方法。

3. 控制论

控制论研究动物（包括人类）和机器内部的控制与通信的一般规律。可持续是一个控制的过程，根据信息和控制的关系，可以分为人为的、有组织的和集中的“前期渐进式可持续”，自发的、无组织的和分散的“后期渐进式可持续”，以及将两者相互结合以克服各自缺点的“前期—后期渐进式可持续”。

4. 协同论

协同论研究不同事物共同特征及其协同机理，探讨各系统从无序发展到有序时的相似性。系统控制的目标是使系统或系统要素间实现协同，形成一种有序的自组结构，该结构是指在远离平衡条件下，借助外

---

① 是指有中国著名科学家钱学森所概括的，在自20世纪40年代以来的一般系统论、信息论和控制论的基础上，产生和发展起来的包括耗散结构论、协同论、突变论等在内的一批新兴科学理论和方法的统称，是被公认为能有效探索系统问题的、跨学科的、具有方法论意义的“新工具”，一般将其分为一般系统论、控制论和自组织理论。

界的物质流、能量流、信息流维持的一种时间、空间功能有序的结构，即是耗散、协同结构。它随着外界条件的输入而不断进化发展，并能进行“自组织”，导致系统的熵值不断减少。系统进入自组织状态，使系统不断结构化、层次化，从无序到有序、从低有序到高有序，进而产生出新的更高的系统结构和功能。因此，自组织的形成过程，即是持续发展的过程，内因和外因的作用在这过程中缺一不可，同时起作用。协同理论的这些思想和研究方法丰富了可持续与可持续发展理论，为此本研究将充分吸收利用，从系统的角度揭示西部地区农产品物流可持续发展的机制与模式。

前人的可持续与可持续发展理论为本研究提供了很好的理论借鉴，本研究将以此为起点，结合西部地区农产品物流实际，探索西部地区农产品物流可持续发展的机制与模式。

第三节　制度变迁与创新理论

经济思想史始终贯穿与制度及制度变迁的有关问题。本研究主要从马克思经济学和新制度经济学[①]方面对制度变迁与创新理论进行论述和展示。

一　马克思经济学中的制度变迁与创新理论

经典马克思主义的制度变迁与创新理论。马克思虽然没有应用制度变迁与创新的概念，但是马克思的经济学核心思想是“生产力决定生产关系，生产关系必须适应生产力”，马克思主义经济学的基本特征在于联系生产关系研究生产力、联系上层建筑研究经济基础，在生产力与生产关系、经济基础与上层建筑的对立统一关系中把握经济的发展与制度的变

① 制度经济学在广义上包括以凡勃伦、康芒斯和米契尔为首的早期制度经济学（Institutional Economics），也称旧制度经济学；以艾尔斯、贝尔、米恩斯、加尔布雷斯和熊彼特为首的后制度经济学（Neo Institutional Economics）；以诺思、威廉姆斯、阿尔奇安和德姆塞茨等为主要代表的新制度经济学（New Institutional Economics）。

迁。因此，这是一部完整的制度变迁与创新的经济学①，经典马克思主义的制度变迁与创新理论与新制度经济学是一致的②。

当代中国马克思主义者的制度变迁与创新理论。以邓小平为代表的中国马克思主义者所推动的社会主义市场经济体制建设，在本质上就是由计划经济体制向市场经济体制的制度变迁与创新，无论是在制度变迁与创新的理论上，还是在实践上，也无论是在社会主义发展史上，还是在人类制度文明建设史上，都十分富有特色[80]。中国正在进行的创建社会主义市场经济体制的改革，实质上是在计划经济体制基础上，通过制度创新来实现向市场经济体制"转型"的制度变迁[81]。20世纪80年代以来，中国的经济发展无疑是这一制度变迁与创新的结果。以邓小平建设中国特色社会主义理论为基础，当代中国的马克思主义制度变迁与创新理论，正是这场改革的理论指导，其内容极其广泛和深刻，本研究结合需要，将其主要思想概括为：①制度创新的前提是观念创新和理论创新，而建立在知识积累、更新与尊重事实基础上的"解放思想、实事求是"，是观念创新、理论创新的基础。②计划经济和市场经济都是手段，市场体系是市场机制在资源配置中发挥基础作用的载体，建立市场经济体制，必须不断探索所有制的实现形式，允许并鼓励各种所有制经济共同发展，培育和发展市场体系。③制度变迁与创新必须以发展生产力为宗旨，必须在改革、发展、稳定相协调的前提下，在各种体制相协调的基础上，在效率与公平的协调中，综合人类现有制度资源中的优势成分，促进经济发展。④制度创新，一方面，不能脱离中国实际去照搬照抄别国模式和经验；另一方面，由于市场和计划都是资源配置的手段，其创新程序、行为规则、运行机制和组织结构等，是可以相互参照或移植的。制度创新和变迁是一个不断开放的过程。⑤市场经济离不开

① "看到了资本主义总需求会持续出现不足的矛盾，并认为解决矛盾的唯一方法就是制度变革。"（斯蒂格利茨，1997）。在马克思看来，制度属于生产关系范畴，生产力和生产关系的对立统一构成生产方式。社会生产方式的变革和发展总是从生产力的变革和发展开始的。生产力决定生产关系，生产力的发展必然引起生产关系的变革。马克思所揭示的生产力和生产关系的联系，用新制度经济学语言就是效率与制度的关系（茅以轼，1999）。

② 正如L. E. 戴维斯（I. E. Davis）和D. C. 诺斯（Douglas C. North）所说："马克思和恩格斯提供了成为列宁灵感的信仰体系，解释了世界存在的方式和未来的道路。虽然马克思没有提供成功实现社会主义社会转变或建设的蓝图，但他提供了意识形态领域的基本框架，特别是关于所有权变革的理论基础。"（L. E. Davis、Douglas C. North，2004，中译本）

政府的宏观调控，政府职能必须转变，而中国的改革在很大程度上是政府主导型改革。因此，既要改革政治体制，又要发挥政府的作用，注重利用已有组织资源和制度兼容的特点，实现对制度变迁方向与进程的有效制导和控制，保持新旧体制的有效衔接和过渡。⑥制度创新与内外环境条件密切联系，不同环境条件下创新不是均衡的。制度创新必须选择正确的起点和路径，在实践中不断摸索[82]。

“在详细描述长期变迁的各种现有理论中，马克思的分析框架是最有说服力的。”[83]道格拉斯的这一评价是恰如其分的。但本研究也意识到，马克思这一理论的主要目的，是为了从逻辑上洞悉人类社会整体制度发展变化的规律。因此，马克思制度的变迁与创新理论只是一个宏观动态的整体制度变迁与创新理论模型，对于微观比较静态的制度分析和微观制度安排的规律与特征的分析有所忽视，并且其分析框架比较粗放。因此，研究中需要进行具体化、微观化和现实化[84]。当代中国马克思主义的制度变迁与创新理论，是以中国实践为基础的理论，并充分吸收了当代先进制度的文明成果，其理论和方法毫无疑问对本研究建立制度分析框架是有益的，但它并没有直接给出本研究所需要的具体结论。本研究将在马克思主义制度变迁与创新理论的指导下，综合运用制度变迁与创新的理论成果，分析西部地区农产品物流发展失调的制度原因，探索可持续发展的制度路径。

二　新制度经济学中的制度变迁与创新理论

以制度需求为重点的制度变迁与创新理论。从制度需求角度看，新制度经济学①认为：制度是关于交易活动的规则，在此基础上提出制度创新②，

① 虽然加尔布雷思等人的理论曾经被称之为新制度经济学而风行一时，但时过境迁，现在新制度经济学成为以科斯为代表的制度经济学派的专有名词，而把科斯之前的制度经济学一律称为旧制度经济学。新制度经济学的内容包括制度的构成与起源、制度变迁与创新、产权与国家理论、制度与经济发展的关系等理论。

② 基于“科斯定理”（Coase's theorem），新制度经济学得出了“制度是重要的”结论，并在此基础上引入熊彼特（Joseph Alois Schumpeter，1883—1950）在《经济发展理论》中提出的“创新理论（Innovation Theory）”，认为“制度创新（Institutional Innovation）”是指制度的变革、改革，其结果是制度总体或基本特征的变化，即用新的更有效率的制度来代替原有的制度，以取得更大的制度净收益，也就是通过提供更有效的行为规则而对经济发展做出贡献。

形成制度变迁①与创新的需求机制②，制度变迁与创新是制度主体对获利机会自发和渐进反应的演进过程，是一个需求诱致性的过程[85-90]。

以制度供给为重点的制度变迁与创新理论。从制度供给角度看，新制度经济学认为：制度因素③有重要作用。美国经济学家道格拉斯·C. 诺思（Douglass C. North）在研究中发现了制度因素的重要作用[91]。“度变迁是指一种制度框架的创新和被打破”[92]。诺思认为制度环境是制度变迁的外生变量，制度变迁的内在动因是经济组织和政治组织等变迁主体希望获得最大的“潜在利润”，即外部利润。国家作为制度及制度变迁的主要供给者，其变迁动机也是为了追求福利和效用最大化。我国学者林毅夫从经济人的成本——收益分析角度对制度变迁进行了解释，制度变迁可以分为诱致性制度变迁和强制性制度变迁④。在林毅夫看来，为了弥补诱致性变迁所带来的制度供给不足问题，政府应该凭借其强制力、意识形态等优势，采取强制性制度变迁以减少或遏制搭便车现象，降低制度变迁的成本[93]。因此，制度供给不仅是一个需求诱致性的过程，而且是一个强制性的过程。

在物流领域，新制度经济学的制度变迁与创新理论，一方面被直接应用于物流制度，尤其是物流治理结构的研究；另一方面则发展了物流创新理论。该理论认为物流本身就是一种制度化的产物，物流发展是物流创新的结果，而物流创新的原始动力来自于物流消费的需要，包括来自真实经

---

① “对旧的价值体系带来干扰，这种价值的扰动产生两个结果：首先受到扰动后产生了投入与产出的价值差，即利润或亏损；其次是若出现利润，大家就会争相模仿最后导致利润消失。在这一过程末了，新的价值体系确立，向零利润经济复归，从而形成了变迁”（汪丁丁，1995），也就是说只有当制度创新被大多数人所接受并模仿，才能产生制度变迁。

② 打破了原有制度均衡，从而导致潜在利润的产生；而这些潜在利润难以在现有的制度安排结构中实现，从而引诱经济主体力图通过制度变迁来获取其潜在利润（Ronald H. Coase、A. A. Aichian、Douglas C. North 等，1996）；制度创新是制度创新者为了获得追加的或额外的收益（L. E. Davis、Douglas C. North，1994），而对现行制度进行的变革。

③ 制度供给主要依赖于创新主体的形成及其相互间的协调与共同努力、知识基础与创新成本、社会各既得利益集团的权力结构或力量对比等因素。

④ 林毅夫认为诱致性制度变迁是由原有制度安排下无法得到的潜在利润引起的，但诱致性制度变迁通常会碰到外部效果和搭便车问题，造成创新者报酬降低。“诱致性制度变迁指的是现行制度安排的变更或替代，或者是新制度安排的创造，它由个人或一群（个）人，在响应获利机会时自发倡导、组织和实行。与此相反，强制性制度变迁由政府命令和法律引入和实行。”“如果诱致性创新是新制度安排的唯一来源的话，那么一个社会中制度安排的供给将少于社会最优。国家干预可以补救持续的制度供给不足。”

济转移价格风险和信用风险，增强资产流动性，提高创造价值、实现价值需要，以及保证信用、存储货物、物畅其流、融通资金、提高效率、超前消费等需要，还包括测量自己的判断和预期，发挥自己智慧和能力的需要[94,95]。物流创新受到技术、竞争、管制等多种因素的影响。但从根本上讲，物流创新是以降低交易成本为特征的，与经济制度相互影响、互为因果的制度创新[96]。物流创新的内在逻辑决定了经济物流化、物流全球化、经营一体化的物流发展必然结果。物流创新是一把“双刃剑”，在通过提高物流资产的选择性、替代性，来分摊价格风险、降低物流成本，进而推动物流市场发育，提高物流、经济效率的同时，也加大了物流系统的不稳定性和物流管理成本，以及对社会资源过多的吸收消耗，并可导致物流障碍，影响经济可持续发展。因此，有效地物流创新应该是物流工具和物流监管制度相协调的创新。从新中国成立60年来我国农产品流通制度的创新看，由“政府主导型”农产品物流模式→“双轨制”农产品物流模式→“社会专业化”农产品物流模式发展演进，是合乎我国农业经济发展规律的新的制度创新。由于技术进步等因素的作用，原来有效的传统物流运作模式就会变成非最有效的。农产品物流金融模式就是在这种新的有利的经济机制条件下，产生的一种诱致性制度变迁。因此，它并非是主观臆造的，也不是政府强制实行的，而是经济发展的内在动力所引致和推动的自发性制度创新。实践证明，这种制度更适合于我国现代农产品物流和农村金融发展的需要，具有完全的科学性和合理性，是我国农产品物流业产业升级的必由之路。

新制度经济学的制度变迁与创新理论，在产权与交易费用概念基础上，将制度作为经济发展的内生变量，以制度均衡为目标，运用成本收益分析方法，从制度需求和供给两个方面，揭示出制度变迁与创新的诱致性和强制性过程的成因、原理、机制及其路径、模式、影响因素与变化规律，构建了制度分析的基本框架，提供了一整套能对现实经济，尤其是对转型经济，做出了切合实际解释的分析，并且在某种程度上和马克思主义经济学的制度分析框架和工具保持了一致性[97-101]。显然，运用其分析框架和工具来解释西部地区农产品物流发展失调的原因，构建可持续发展的机制与模式，对本研究将是积极有效和必需的。但本研究也意识到该理论尤其是其中的制度设计理论，本身还处于不断发展、完善和探索之中，在物流领域的应用和研究还很不深入，而且还容易将制度变迁与创新分析引入基于“理性主义”和“演绎主义”的“构建主义”的误区[102]。事实上，成熟的制度绝不是仅靠理论推演就能构建出来的，而是在实践中建立起来的，制度设计必须紧密结合实际。因此，本研究将在马克思主义制度变迁与创新理论的指导下，紧密结合西部地区农产品物流发展实际，对该理论加以应用。

本章最后需要强调的是：以上三大理论只是根据研究需要所做的划分。事实上，三者有着密不可分的联系，共同为西部地区农产品物流可持续发展理论框架的规划、设计和构建提供了资源，其中现代物流与经济发展理论侧重于构建这一理论框架的边界和基础，而可持续与可持续发展理论、制度变迁与创新理论则在此基础上提供方法和支柱。在此基础上，本研究将紧密结合西部地区农产品物流和农村经济实际，从西部地区农产品物流的理论内涵入手，具体构造本研究的理论框架，探索西部地区农产品物流可持续发展的机制与模式。

第三章　西部地区农产品物流可持续发展的内涵与机理

分析西部地区农产品物流可持续发展的内涵与机理，为探索西部地区农产品物流可持续发展建立概念基础。本章将要研究的问题是：究竟应该把西部地区农产品物流放在怎样的一个框架下进行分析？如何界定西部地区农产品物流可持续发展的概念内涵？西部地区农产品物流可持续发展状态有哪些基本特征？能否找到西部地区农产品物流可持续发展过程的内在规律揭示其实现机理？如何界定对这些问题的解答不仅能从理论上对其基本范畴和分析基点做一个阶段性的判断，还能为现实中特别是西部大开发后续发展背景下，更加灵活有效地制定政策提供一些参考性的理论依据。

第一节　西部地区农产品物流可持续发展的分析基点

一　交易视角的西部地区农产品物流内涵

（一）对既有分析范式的讨论

准确定义“西部地区农产品物流”，是本研究展开的首要前提。千百年来，西部地区经济一直以农业为主导。研究发现，虽然西部地区农产品物流在中国历史悠久，但“西部地区农产品物流”作为一个概念被广泛运用，是2003年1月8日中央农村工作会议之后的事①。随着农产品物流理念在西部地区深入人心，国内一些学者开始关注西部地区农村和农产品物流的问题，提出改善西部地区农产品物流现状的策略[103-107]。长期以来，在“农产品物流，即农产品的物理性流动”的主流农产品物流观②基础上，“西部地区农产品物流”概念就被自然生成“西部地区农产品物流就是西部地区的农产品物流”。这种望文生义、同义反复的定义，不仅失去了西部地区农产品物流的自身特性与独立泡畴，而且存在对“西部地区的”③ 指向不明与对“农产品物流”理解流于形式的问题。首先在“西部地区的”内涵上含糊不清，一是没有指明具体空间，农产品物流是存在西部地区还是存在于西部地区农村地理空间的？二是没有指明具体身份，是冠以西部地区“农”字招牌还是从属于西部地区农村经济主体的？三是没有指明具体业务，是在西部地区农村从事业务还是其他兼而有之的业务活动。其次在“农产品物流即农产品的物理性流动”理解上只是概括了农产品物流活动的形式，却将其本质隐藏起来，没有深刻地认识到农产品物流的实质并不是农产品的物理性流动，而是农产品物质实体及相关信息的跨时交易活动，“包括一系列物质运动过程、相关的技术信息组织和处理过程以及各个环节上的物流管理活动。”[108]显然，仅依此形式化的定义难以把握“西部地区农产品物流”的内涵，更难以进一步透视出西

① 张敏（2010）：“2003年1月8日中央农村工作会议明确提出了‘加强农业流通体系的建设’之后，关于我国农产品物流的研究达到了一个新的高潮。”张春颖、王秀云、李娜（2010）：“2003年1月8日的中央农村工作会议的一项重要内容就是加强农业流通体系建设。各级地方政府也都加强了对农产品物流基础设施、市场体系、信息体系的建设；一些专业物流企业开始涉足农业物流领域；一些传统储运企业、粮食系统、供销系统的企业也都加快了向第三方物流转变的步伐。”

② 根据《中华人民共和国国家标准物流物流术语》（2001）中的物流定义，行业百科将农产品物流界定为：农产品物流是物流业的一个分支，指的是为了满足消费者需求而进行的农产品物质实体及相关信息从生产者到消费者之间的物理性流动。就是以农业产出物为对象，通过农产品产后加工、包装、储存、运输和配送等物流环节，做到农产品保值增值，最终送到消费者手中。张倩（2004）：农产品物流是指为了满足用户需求，实现农产品价值而进行的农产品物质实体及相关信息从生产者到消费者之间的物理性经济活动。具体地说，它包括农产品生产、收购、运输、储存、装卸、搬运、包装、配送、流通加工、分销、信息活动等一系列环节，并且在这一过程中实现了农产品价值增值和组织目标。李学工（2009）：农产品物流是指为了满足用户需求，实现农产品价值而进行的农产品物质实体及相关信息从生产者到消费者之间的物理性空间位移的经济活动。

③ “西部地区”是中国三大经济行政区域之一，与东部地区、中部地区相伴、相对而生的，具有经济、社会属性和历史特征的地理空间系统。包括重庆、四川、贵州、云南、广西、陕西、甘肃、青海、宁夏、西藏、新疆、内蒙古十二个省、市、区。

部地区农产品物流可持续发展的机制与模式。

深入分析发现，导致这一问题出现的原因在于2003年以来虽然西部地区农产品物流改革从未停止，但对西部地区农产品物流范式的研究，仍然是依据传统农产品物流理论，以“农业”为对象、以流通为特征、以人为定身份、以行政手段赋予职能、以地理意义上的农产品物流机构为载体的机构范式。基于既有文献“我国食品物流业面临的问题，我国整体物流水平和物流机构还很不健全。”[109]“以发展农产品物流为核心业务的农业合作社、农民协会、农村供销合作社以及专业运输公司、仓储公司、配送中心等专业物流组织匮乏。”[110]因而研究西部地区农产品物流的问题，尤其是西部地区农产品物流服务供给不足的问题，认为其根源是农产品物流机构不足的原因。“物流企业和组织是发展农业物流业的关键。要采取多渠道、多形式、多元化的办法，打破所有制、地域、行业界限，尽快培育一批陕西省的农产品物流企业。”[111]“一方面，我们要根据湘西自治州农业产业现状，加强农产品市场建设。其次，是大力发展农村中介组织。再次。是培养农民经纪人队伍。最后，我们要积极发展农民合作经济组织。”[105]由此看来，西部地区农产品物流要发挥功能，必须遵循机构—功能—行为绩效的分析范式，在现有机构视角的框架下通过其行为绩效判断其功能实现的效应。

然而，西部大开发以来，西部地区农产品物流组织体系重构的不懈努力，非但没有解决西部地区农产品物流供给不足的问题，“农产品买卖难”“菜贱伤农”的现象时有发生，难免会回到“大而全、小而全”的传统组织形式，反而导致了物流机构“低收益和高风险”的事实，清楚地表明机构范式的“西部地区农产品物流”，不仅难以成为求解西部地区农产品物流问题的逻辑起点，而且此种同义反复的定义，分析范式的偏差，第一，导致了将西部地区农产品物流等同于西部地区农业物流，忽视了西部地区农村经济中的其他物流需求。第二，导致了将西部地区农产品物流等同于西部地区农产品物流机构，将单纯的西部地区农产品物流机构增加理解为西部地区农产品物流发展等同于，试图从构建新的西部地区农产品物流机构求解农产品物流服务供给不足的问题。第三，导致了将西部地区农产品物流机构的界定等同于西部地区农村身份的人为认定。这种界定不仅造成西部地区农产品物流政策缺少有效载体使其功能无法落实，还人为地加剧了西部地区城乡物流分割的“二元”结构。生产地与消费地的明确分隔，西部地区农产品物流职能被人为划定在“西部地区农村”但未必具有相应意愿和能力的物流机构范围内，形成有限的农产品物流资源配置，物流机构间的市场竞争有失公平，导致西部地区农产品物流存在严重的“道德风险”和“逆向选择”，农产品流通不畅，给各方面造成巨大损失。西部地区农产品物流机构非农化倾向和西部地区农产品物流资源外流严重，西部地区农产品物流功能被弱化。因此，西部地区农产品物流理论和实际工作的相关系列问题都与“西部地区农产品物流”缺乏科学界定有关，必须选择恰当的视角和范式科学界定其内涵。

（二）交易视角中的西部地区农产品物流

基于西部地区农产品物流的现实，一直是农产品物流供给不足。因此，本研究选择交易①视角来定义“西部地区农产品物流”。

1. 西部地区农产品物流是一种交易

首先，不同产权主体是其存在的必要条件。目前西部地区农产品物流企业还处于发展期，无法承担起全部的责任，于是以各种形式存在的物流服务提供者更多地充当了物流企业的角色。农产品物流市场形成了多方物流与工商企业、个体物流同台竞争的多元化格局，现有的物流主体可以划分为：传统的国有流通企业；传统运输领域的国有企业；个体私营运输类或仓储运输公司；专业化的第三方物流公司；专业经济合作组织、行业协会；经纪人。其次，所有权的分散性与生产集中性的矛盾，风险能力和经营能力分布的不对称性是其存在的充分条件。西部地区农业生产中突出的矛盾之一就是小规模经营与大规模生产、大流通矛盾。规模小是指农产品生产、经营、流通普遍零碎化，没有规模效益；大群体指参加农业生产的主体众多，离散性强，缺少联合，组织化程度低，导致生产盲目性，容易造成农产品买难和卖难的交替出现[112]。这种农产品的“小生产”和“大市场”的矛盾决定了农产品流通过程呈现出由分散—集中—分散的交易特点。由于农产品自身的生物特性和特殊重要性决定了农产品物流具有很大的风险，除自然风险外，还包括农副产品的市场风险（价格风险）、农产品生产资料的质量风险和供应延误风险等，这就需要物流技术与物流装

---

① 研究中的“交易”是新制度经济学意义的“交易”，是指人与人之间的交互行为，是制度分析的基本单位。本研究中的“交易”可以理解为西部农产品物流与农村经济主体之间的交互行为。

备达到一定的经营水平。但事实上这种风险能力和经营能力分布往往是不对称的，造成供给不适应需求、市场价格波动大、物流经营者的预期利润降低，不利于形成有序的市场竞争和培育市场主体[113]。

2. 西部地区农产品物流交易具有规模经济效应

首先，西部地区农产品物流交易是西部农村经济活动的函数，“规模经济”的存在和产权主体对“规模收益”的追求，是西部地区农产品物流存在和展开的内在动力。农产品生产不同于工业生产的特点，决定了农产品供应主体的分散性①，农业生产的这种异质性导致以家庭为单位的生产制度的普遍存在[114-116]。供给主体除了自己消费外，每个农户都要出售自己的剩余农产品，然而从农产品产出到终端消费的每个环节中，按照农户个人的生产量与市场衔接，不可能实现农产品生产、加工、流通以及销售的规模化，横在其间的是巨大的交易成本，因此他们必须使自己进入农产品物流体系。其次，交易次数与交易双方的信息对称性决定西部地区农产品物流交易成本。交易成本形成的7项原因是：有限理性、机会主义行为、不确定性及复杂性、少数的寡占交易关系、信息不对称、气氛、资产专用性[117]。有限理性使得长期契约成本增加，小数量谈判及投机主义的联合效果使得短期契约成本增加。交易次数决定农产品物流交易成本，而不是交易规模。值得强调的是，事前信息不对称导致逆向选择，事后信息不对称导致道德风险。农产品物流运营存在着大量信息不对称状况，具体表现在农产品质量安全、银企借贷、农产品物流外包、农产品物流组织创新等方面的信息不对称，信息对称性程度也同样决定农产品物流的交易成本。

3. 信用交易是农产品物流的本质特征

在制度约束下以信息为先导，建立在信任、信誉基础上的信用交易是西部地区农产品物流的本质特征。马克思认为信用是一种有条件的信任，是一种独特形式的运动，是一种经济关系，也是一种社会关系。这表明信

① 德国的大卫（Ed David）在《社会主义与农业》（1922）第二章“有机生产与机械生产的本质差异”中，将机械生产的工业与有机生产的农业进行比较，把有机生产的农业的异质性归纳为9点：1. 劳动过程是季节性的，而非持续性的。2. 劳动形式呈现出多样性，并且不断地变化。3. 在田间的劳动和劳动手段必须移动。4. 生产过程必须遵循作物的自然生长规律。5. 作业场所开阔，即使雇佣农业劳动力，也不可能对其作业进行全面的监督。如果一定要进行监督，则需要大量的时间和成本。6. 在农业经营中人与自然的全面结合。7. 受自然因素的制约，农业生产力的提高是缓慢的和有限的。8. 土地报酬呈现出递减规律。9. 农地的扩大（外延性扩大）将会导致与现有农地的竞争。

用是建立在双方互相信任基础上的，并且是以偿还为条件的[118]。就信用本身而言，可以分为广义的信用与狭义的信用，前者是在不同期限内，以契约为保障的经济交易行为。后者是在特定期限内，兑现付款或还款承诺的能力形式，即资本信用[119]。由此可见，信用可以减少流通过程的中间费用，加速资本的自由转移。目前西部地区农产品物流由于存在众多的主体，具有明显的交互性、跨期性、不确定性；因此，农产品物流信用交易表现出风险性、交叉引致性、扩散性、一定程度的可控性的典型特征。交易双方的信息能力、风险能力、谈判能力以及所受约束的有效性和外部不确定因素的冲击，直接决定了交易的缔约过程和结果。

4. 西部地区农产品物流的外在特征是交易的表现形式和组织方式

机构是专业性农产品物流供给主体，是社会分工合乎逻辑的结果，是交易与治理结构的有效匹配。治理结构，即市场治理结构、三边治理结构、双边治理结构和一体化治理结构。威廉姆森在研究交易和治理结构的有效搭配时，主要考虑了影响交易费用的两个因素，即交易频率与资产专用性[120]。描述了六种交易类型，农产品物流组织应该采取不同的治理结构与不同的交易类型相匹配，如表3－1所示[121]。

表3－1　　治理结构（契约关系）与交易的有效匹配

类型		投资特征		
交易特征		非专用型	混合型	专用型
交易频率	偶尔	市场治理结构（古典缔约活动）	三边治理结构（新古典契约）	
	重复		双边治理结构（关系契约）	一体化治理结构（关系契约）

从交易方式与治理结构的匹配来看，对于偶尔发生和重复发生的非专用型交易，市场治理是主要的治理结构。交易条件通过多次“讨价还价”达成，如农产品运输等公共物流服务；偶尔进行的混合型和高度专用型农产品物流交易，适合采用三边治理结构，如农产品综合物流代理服务。对于重复发生的混合型和资产专用型程度较高的农产品物流交易，交易重复进行的特征使专用型治理结构的成本能够收回，双边治理结构是比较适当的交易协调方式，而当物流资产专用性进一步提高且交易频繁时，纵向一体化方式更适合，如某些农业产销一体化企业的农产品自营物流组织。结果看出，只要在具备农产品物流交易条件下交易达到一定的规模，市场就

会诱导出相应的农产品物流机构；相反，若不具备农产品物流交易条件，强制性输入某种新的农产品物流机构，不会扩大交易规模，还可能使这种农产品物流机构陷入困境。

基于此，本研究认为："西部地区农产品物理性流动"只是西部地区农产品物流形式的概括，而"西部地区农产品物流"本质属性应是在信息约束、信任约束、信誉约束和制度约束的共同作用下形成"规模经济"的信用交易，包括这些活动在制度安排下所形成的经济系统（与其他经济系统具有平等交换关系的系统）、运动形式（农产品、资金、信息的流出方和流入方，连接两者的农产品物流中介机构和农产品物流市场，形成产品流、资金流、信息流、信用流，提高生产效率、满足客户需求的形式）总称。西部地区农产品物流实质是信用关系制度化的产物。依此定义，本研究认为西部地区农产品物流供给不足的问题，其实质是农产品物流交易条件不足的问题①。针对农产品物流的交易特点，进行交易条件的创造，才是解决问题的根本所在。

（三）功能意义上的西部地区农产品物流

基于交易视角，西部地区农产品物流的概念内涵在功能意义上从以下几个方面理解：第一，西部地区农产品物流是具有促进西部农村经济发展功能的物流。西部地区农产品物流机构、组织体系和物流工具只是农产品物流功能的实现形式，是西部地区农产品物流需求决定了农产品物流机构、组织体系和物流工具的形态，而不是相反。第二，西部地区农产品物流是西部农村经济与整体物流的交叉系统。西部地区农产品物流既属于西部农村经济，是西部农村经济系统中的子系统；同时，西部地区农产品物流又属于物流范畴，是整体物流系统中的一个单元。第三，西部地区农产品物流是内部功能结构复杂多样的系统。西部地区农产品物流包括一系列内涵丰富的物流产品和服务，如农产品生产、收购、运输、储存保管、包装、装卸搬运、流通加工、配送、分销、物流信息服务等，以及与之相对应的物流组织体系。

为便于进一步从理论上把握西部地区农产品物流的内部结构，本研究首

① J. D. 冯皮斯克（1983）："并不在于机构的简单增设，当着眼于交易水平的提高"，"机构作为一种特殊的交易主体，其本身数目的多少并不必然与交易的规模相对应。"

先按其职能分工，将农产品物流分为农产品行政性物流和农产品业务性物流。前者是政府的物流管理组织体系和运行机制的总称。具体包括政府的物流管理当局（中央政府主管部门），以及行业性的物流自律机构及其运行机制，如中国物流与采购联合会、中国仓储协会、中国储运协会、中国国际货运管理协会、中国集装箱协会、中国铁路运输协会、中国交通运输协会等行业协会①。后者是具体从事物流交易活动的物流组织体系及其运行机制的总称。其中又可分为社会性物流、双向性物流、经济性物流，社会性物流是政策性的非营利性物流，双向性物流是合作性的非营利性物流，经济性物流也可称为营利性物流，既包括正规的营利性物流、运输、邮政机构及其运行机制，在我国现实的农产品物流中，主要是传统运输领域全国性的国有企业如中国邮政、铁路系统、中储等将业务延伸到农产品物流市场的经营业务，以及传统的国有流通企业改革中出现的国有粮食公司和供销社逐步演变成的物流企业。严格地讲，以营利为目的农村供销合作社也归入此类。也包括非正规的营利性物流组织及其运行机制，如各种以营利为目的的民间物流。

其次，根据法律地位分为正规物流和非正规物流。正规物流主体是指受到中央政府主管部门的控制和物流法规约束的物流机构，其又可以分为经济性（营利性）、社会性和双向性（非营利性）物流机构。在我国现有农产品物流体系中，前者如传统的国有流通企业改革中出现的国有粮食公司和供销社逐步演变成的物流企业、传统运输领域全国性的国有企业如中国邮政、铁路系统、中储等改变经营模式将业务延伸到农产品物流市场；后者为国有粮食企业、国有商业公司、农村供销合作社从事农产品业务的部分。非正规物流主体在中央政府主管部门监管和物流法规约束之外的物流服务供给方，主要是指如农户、加工型企业的自营物流、个体私营运输类或仓储运输公司、专业化的第三方物流公司、各种联合会、经纪人等民间物流活动。其最重要的特征在于其主体地位没有得到正式制度承认和保障，甚至被排斥在正式制度安排之外。

① 李学工（2009）："在我国，行业协会是贯彻政府物流政策的半行政组织，在农村物流中发挥着不可替代的作用。"它们在信息资讯、鉴定认证、物流交易、法律保险、合作交流、推广宣传等服务方面充分发挥了自身优势，及时传递市场消费变化信息，把握需求动态；通过鉴定认证服务为会员提供农产品安全鉴定认证，同时也为消费者提供了农产品物流监控追溯系统的安全保证；利用电子交易平台发布实时的市场交易信息，为物流企业的生鲜农产品找到销路，减少交易的成本，实现效益的最大化等。

此外，农产品物流根据其生成机制，还可分为农产品内生物流与农产品外生物流。农产品内生物流是指西部地区农村经济发展过程中，根据农村经济发展的实际需要而自发产生的农产品物流活动及其组织机构。如一体化农产品物流、农产品物流联盟。农产品外生物流则是指从农村经济系统外强行植入的农产品物流活动及其组织体系。根据农产品不同类型还可以分为生鲜农产品的物流组织、工业加工原料农产品的物流组织、粮食物流的组织等。根据所有制，分为农产品的私有物流、公有或国有物流、外资物流，以及介于三者之间的各种形态的混合所有制物流。根据投资，主体多少还可以分为私人独资、国有独资、外商独资，以及各种混合的股份制。根据经营主体可以分为民营物流、国营或外商经营物流等不同形式。这些形式相互交叉，构成了农产品物流系统的复杂结构。

二 西部地区农产品物流发展的制度内涵

（一）西部地区农产品物流发展的制度属性

“西部地区农产品物流发展”是本研究中又一个基础性概念。“西部地区农产品物流发展”从形式上看是“物流发展”与“经济发展”[①] 在“西部地区农产品物流”上的体现。研究发现，既有的“西部地区农产品物流发展”概念被简单地定义为“西部地区农产品的物流发展”或“西部地区农产品物流的发展”，也是在宏观经济增长相关理论[②]下的“物流

① 发展经济学认为：经济发展是指伴随着经济、社会结构和政治体制等全方位变革的经济增长，不仅意味着产出的增加，而且意味着随产出增加而出现的产出与收入结构，以及政治、文化等制度因素的变化。新制度经济学认为“以往对经济发展原因的研究都集中在资本积累、技术进步及专业化与劳动 分工等方面，而这些因素与其说是经济增长的原因，倒不如说是经济增长本身。经济增长的根本原因是制度的变迁，一种能提供适当的个人刺激的有效产权制度是促进经济增长的决定性因素”（Douglas C. North，1990）。奥地利学派的米赛斯和哈耶克等自由主义者认为：经济发展就是分工和交换的扩张，即哈耶克称之为“合作秩序”的市场制度扩展或演进过程。在当代，“经济发展”又赋予了“追求生活质量、可持续性、公平分配和民主参与”的内涵，联合国开发计划署在此基础上提出了“人文发展”的概念。

② 如果说经济增长是一个单纯的“量”的概念，那么经济发展就是一个比较复杂的“质”的概念。一般认为，经济发展不仅包括经济增长的速度、增长的平稳程度和结果，并且还特别包括一国或地区的人民的平均生活质量，如教育水平、健康卫生标准等，以及整体经济结构、社会结构等的总体进步。从经济学所强调的观点来看，经济发展是经济持续增长的结果，居民生活水平的提高，经济结构、社会形态等的进步也都很大程度上依赖于经济增长。

发展"① 冠以"农产品"的简单定义。无疑，宏观经济增长相关理论意义是极为深刻的，但也注意到这一定义侧重现代物流与宏观经济增长的相互关系，反映的是物流发展的数量方面，表现出物流发展就是物流结构的变化，没有真正揭示物流发展背后的制度因素，因此，在一定程度上还只是"增长"意义上的"农产品物流发展"。

基于"西部地区农产品物流"概念内涵，"西部地区农产品物流发展"的内涵不仅要把握其"量"的方面，而且还必须从交易视角深入到制度层面把握其"质"的方面。"西部地区农产品物流发展"是西部地区农产品物流交易的扩张，表现在交易量和交易活动范围或空间领域的扩大，以及交易手段（农产品物流工具）的不断创新，更表现为农产品物流交易主体对交易的"规模收益"与风险损失的权衡。农产品物流发展的原始动力是"规模经济"，农产品物流发展的根本限制是"风险损失与交易成本"，提高"规模经济"的收益和降低"风险损失与交易成本"是促进农产品物流发展的关键。

随着西部地区农产品物流交易的扩张，信息不对称性、不确定性与风险性也相应增加，无法保证农产品物流交易的"信任度"，导致农产品物流交易成本增加。为了减少交易成本，需要改变农产品物流交易中的现有信任关系：交易双方之间的信任→对双方以外的农产品物流工具的信任→农产品物流中介机构的信任→农产品物流交易中的委托—代理关系。信任度越高，委托—代理效率越高，交易成本越低，农产品物流的"规模效益"越好，农产品物流交易发展和扩张越大，为持续这种发展和扩张，就必须监督和强化委托—代理中的信任关系[122]。于是农产品物流监管以及农产品物流制度以及实施制度的专业化农产品物流监管机构便产生了。农产品物流便从原始意义上的农产品物流活动，发展成为依靠制度增进信任，促进农产品物流交易活动不断扩张，追求规模净收益最大化系统的现代意义上的农产品物流体系。从西部地区农产品物流发展过程可以看出，西部地区农产品

① 王槐林等（2001）、牟惟仲（2003）分析了宏观经济增长对现代物流发展的影响作用。张文杰（2002）、靳伟（2002）、桂寿平等（2002）分析了现代物流与宏观经济增长的相互作用机制。刘南、赵成锋、陈远高（2007）分析了现代物流对宏观经济增长的作用。

物流发展是信用的发展①，实质就是农产品物流制度的完善过程：（前提）实体经济存在规模经济+经济主体追求规模收益+（根本）信息→信任→信用→信誉+（保证）减少交易不确定性+降低交易风险+降低交易成本=（完善）农产品物流制度[123]。

（二）功能意义的西部地区农产品物流发展

基于“西部地区农产品物流发展”的制度属性，从功能范式意义上有以下理解：西部地区农产品物流发展无法超越西部经济发展战略和与之相适应的制度安排，受到宏观制度环境的影响和冲击，必须以政府行为的有效性为前提，必须和西部农村经济发展保持适应，实现促进西部农村经济发展的目标。

1. 西部地区农产品物流发展是促进结构调整推动整个农业系统均衡协调发展的重要基础

（1）促进结构调整推动增长方式转变。我国的国土资源分布不均衡，西部地区气候干旱，地广人稀，人口只占全国总人口的28.4%，而土地面积占全国土总面积的56.5%。西部地区耕地面积占全国耕地的28.4%，林地占全国林地的38.3%，牧草地占全国牧草地的72%。就人均占有量而言，西部地区人均土地为28.8亩（1.92公顷），人均耕地、林地、牧草地分别是2.0亩（0.13公顷）、4.7亩（0.31公顷）、10.3亩（0.69公顷），为全国平均水平的0.3倍、1.7倍和1.3倍[124]。我国农村剩余劳动力1.5亿，西部地区所占比重最高为49.93%；西部地区城乡居民收入差距2008年达到3.31∶1，加上其他因素已达到了5∶1或6∶1[125]；发达国家农产品产值与农产品加工产值之比为1∶3到1∶4，而西部地区则为1∶1左右；果蔬产品的损耗率也数倍于发达国家。农产品物流作为一种先进的组织方式和管理技术，对于优化农村资源配置，提高农业经济运行质

① 由“特殊主义信用”向“普遍主义信用”的发展。“特殊主义信用”指建立在对特定交易者或交易物人格化信任基础上的信用，由于建立信任的前提——信息，一般是通过血缘、亲缘、情缘、地缘、业缘等特定关系获得的，所以，这种信用基础上的农产品物流通常只发生在某一特定的狭小范围，主要依靠伦理道德等非正式制度来保障。“普遍主义信用”指独立于交易者或交易物身份特殊关系的，建立在对非特定交易者或交易物信任基础上的信用，由于建立信任的前提——信息，一般是在外在力量有效的监督、强制与激励约束下获得的。所以，这种信用通常可以在一个较广泛的范围内发生，其范围大小受制于外在力量监督、强制和激励约束，其有效性必须依靠法律规章和政策等正式制度来保障。

量，推进农业结构调整与经济增长方式的两个根本性转变具有重要意义[126]。

（2）推动整个农业系统均衡协调发展。农产品现代物流一体化不但能提高农产品的流通水平，还能推动整个农业系统均衡协调发展。现代物流运作模式还以其专业化、规模化、信息化、标准化程度高，运输及配送的速度快、辐射面广、效率高等特点，为农产品的仓储、运输、集散、配送等提供极为有效的一体化解决方式。农产品现代物流依靠地域广阔的信息网络以及快捷准确的运输配送方式，有效地解决产地和销地之间的物理隔离和逻辑隔离问题，架起生产与消费两个环节之间的桥梁；农产品现代物流的信息化和专业化发展还能够有效降低小而分散的农户盲目生产的损失、仓储的损耗以及运输过程中的损耗，从而降低整个农业产业链的成本；农产品现代物流还能依靠其一体化的发展方式为物流的各环节及各经营主体提供及时、准确的有效信息，提高各经营主体的决策水平，提高整个产业链的经济效益；农产品现代物流还以其标准化的服务方式使各个环节相互协调、准确对接，高效联盟，提高整个农业产业链的运行效率。因此，发展农产品现代物流对于减少市场运营过程中的不确定性和盲目性，有效地提高农产品的流通速度，降低农产品流通的成本和流通损失，提高农产品的流通效益具有重要的推动作用[127]。

2. 西部地区农产品物流发展是提高居民生活质量、增加农民收入的重要内容

西部地区农产品物流提供的农产品数量大，质量高，不但对改善人们的饮食结构，提高生活质量发挥着越来越重要的作用，而且在提高农产品附加值带动农民增收方面潜力巨大。农民单纯出售初级农产品，市场吸引力有限，农民的收入也有限[128]。如果在农产品物流过程中实现加工增值服务的同时，创造一种利益协调机制，创造一种组织形式让农民获得一部分增值利润，则可以大大提高农民的收入，大幅度提高农业生产的积极性，实现降低损失、减小成本、提高经济效益。西部地区果蔬产品市场放开比较早，果蔬产品的物流在农产品物流中发展的速度也比较快，但由于储存、包装的保鲜水平差，运输的专业化程度低，使果蔬产品从采收、运输、储存、批发到消费者手中，物流环节的损失率非常高。在消费环节上，西部地区也有较高的废弃物流，存在着数量惊人的无效物流成本。以陕西省为例，目前，陕西省认证的无公害农产品、绿色食品和有机食品基

地面积已达45.33万公顷，已建设37个省级无公害农产品示范基地，11个省级无公害农产品标准化示范区。同时创建了太白、合阳、旬邑、彬县、白水和洛川6个全国无公害水果、蔬菜示范基地县和出口示范基地县。陕西省认证绿色食品总数已达177个，企业84家，年生产能力226万吨。按照陕西省3750万人口平均，陕西省可为全省每人每年提供约60公斤绿色食品。农产品物流成本约占总成本的30%—40%，其中在采摘、运输、储存等物流环节上的损失率为25%—30%；而发达国家的物流成本一般占总成本的10%左右，损失率则控制在5%以下。以现行的物流成本水平估算，全部合理开发利用高效的农产品物流系统后可增加收入25.74亿元[129]。

3. 西部地区农产品物流发展已成为开发利用西部地区内陆港（无水港）①、解决农村资源短缺的重要途径

西部地区与十多个国家接壤，陆地边境线长达12747公里，形成边境线长而无港口现象。由于西部地区特殊的地理位置和自然条件，使得农副产品具有得天独厚的优势，并且在全国农产品贸易量中占有很大的比例，西部农产品出口大部分经过港口到达国外，农产品外贸物流发展有着巨大的内在需求与外在动力。目前，建立“西安国际港务区”，将国际港口服务功能内移，将陕西及西部地区进出口贸易与国际货运航线直接对接，实现航空、铁路、公路与海运的有效连接，西安也将成为适应跨国战略经营需求的国际物流体系的重要组成部分。西部地区农产品物流依托西安国际港务区的优势，在逐渐扩大的内陆港物流商圈中，将形成周边及其腹地的物流产业和农业产业的集聚现象，形成农产品物流优化布局、优势互补的供应链间的结构模式。将成为开发利用西部地区内陆港（无水港）、解决农村资源短缺的重要途径[130]。

4. 西部地区农产品物流发展是农业实现区域化、专业化生产和产业化发展，提高农产品的市场竞争能力的重要保证

（1）调节农产品地域差异及供需矛盾。西部地区农业发展的根本出

① 内陆港，有的地方称其为“无水港”或者“国际陆港”，通常在靠近铁路、公路、机场、江河码头等交通运输枢纽附近开发建设，兼带货运代理、通关、订舱、海陆空多式联运、国内外贸易、各类增值服务等方便客户的港口运营功能。“无水港”或者内陆港等建在内陆地区，尽管不是滨海港口，但具有和沿海港口基本相似功能，为付货人提供信息、通关、内陆堆场等一体化服务的现代物流中心便应运而生。

路在于农业实现区域化、专业化生产和产业化发展。区域化、专业化生产是横向整合农业生产资源的有效手段，是发挥西部不同区域资源禀赋的比较优势，提高农业生产规模效应的有效方式，但产品的市场化和区域间消费结构的平衡问题必须有与之相适应的物流支持。农业产业化是沿着农业产业链方向进行的纵向资源整合，有利于提高整个农业产业链的效率和效益，有利于提高产业链的综合竞争力，但产业链间的联结和协调也需要强有力的物流支持[131]。农产品物流是联结农产品生产与消费的关键环节，也是农业产业链协调、供应链稳定的有力保障，是保证整个农业系统有效运行的关键因素。农产品现代物流是农业区域化、专业化生产和产业化发展的重要组成部分，是推进整个农业区域化、专业化生产和产业化发展的加速器。农产品物流不仅可以实现农产品的空间转移，还可以有效调节农产品的供需矛盾。在过去物质短缺年代，满足人们温饱需求的农业生产是主要矛盾。随着生产水平不断提高、生产规模不断扩大，如果仍重视生产而不重视解决物流的问题，商品便不能马上进入市场到达消费领域，容易造成积压和浪费，甚至引发整个经济链条出现问题。农产品除了生产者自我消费的小部分外，其余都要经过市场转变成商品，从生产者转移到消费者手中，实现其经济价值。物流与生产和消费有着高度的相关性，市场将生产和消费有机地连接在一起并通过物流来实现商品的转移，如果物流过程不畅，也会出现“买难”和“卖难”的矛盾，生产者的生产动机和利益以及消费者的生活和利益都将受到严重影响。

（2）不断提高农产品的市场竞争能力。加入 WTO 后，农业产业的生产经营已经融入国际竞争的大环境下，国内市场国际化的竞争将变得越来越明显。通过对农产品现代物流流通渠道、供应链组织、物流节点的研究，寻求西部地区最佳的农产品物流渠道，并对各个物流节点进行合理规划、设计一套有利于调动各方积极性的利益分配及激励约束机制，提高农产品供应链的稳定性，变目前的一次博弈为动态多次博弈，降低农产品物流过程中的交易成本、物流成本，从而大大降低流通时间和在途损耗，提高农产品的价格竞争力，积极应对来自国内外市场的激烈竞争。

5. 西部地区农产品物流发展是农村剩余劳动力转移的战略重点

充分利用西部地区区位优势和农产品资源优势，大力发展农产品物流，能提供相当大的就业机会，可有效地缓解人口增长、劳动力过剩带来的就业压力。农产品现代物流与传统的农产品流通的最大区别就在于不仅强调农产品的位移，而且强调在位移过程中对高新技术、信息化等的引进，以及价值、使用价值的增值。同时，随着农业自身的发展以及农业合作组织的发展，农产品物流应当是内生于农业系统的。农产品物流业的发展，能够提供大量的就业岗位，而这些装卸、搬运、运输、包装、配送加工的工作对技术水平、文化素质要求不高，有利于吸纳农村剩余劳动力，解决农村劳动力转移问题，并同时在集聚地（产地批发市场、物流园区、配送中心）带动城镇化建设。以蔬菜物流走廊带为例，依托蔬菜生产基地，在云南元谋、甘肃河西走廊和青海发展反季节蔬菜、无公害蔬菜和野菜，开发300多万亩（20多万公顷）生产基地与物流园区对接、联盟能够安排产业劳动力100多万人，而间接转移的劳动力数量更大。在当前大宗农产品过剩、农民收入增幅减缓的形势下，围绕物流产业发展起来的产前、产中、产后服务业等几十个行业如果能迅猛发展壮大，对转移农村剩余劳动力、缓解就业压力将有重大意义。

第二节　西部地区农产品物流可持续发展的概念内涵

一　可持续发展的内涵与特征

（一）可持续发展的概念界定

发展是人类经济社会追求的永恒主题，传统发展观的目标仅限于产值的增长和物质财富的增加。可持续发展（Sustainable Development）概念是在20世纪80年代被提出的，内容涉及了人口、资源、环境、经济和社会等各个领域，所以对其内涵并没有共识性的定义。从自然属性定义可持续发展，“可持续地使用，是指在其可再生能力（速度）的范围内使用一种有机生态系统或其他可再生资源”（国际自然保护同盟IUCN，1991）。“保护和加强环境系统的生产更新能力”，即可持续发展是不超越环境系统再生能力的发展（国际生态学联合会INTECOL和国际生物科学联合会IUBS，1991）。从社会属性定义可持续发展，《保护地球——可持续生存战略》“在生存不超出维持生态系统涵容能力的情况下，提高人类的生活质量”，进而提出了可持续生存的 9 条基本原则（世界自然保护同盟、联合国环境规划署和世界野生生物基金会，1991）。从科技属性定义可持续发展，“可持续发展就是建立极少产生废料和污染物的工艺或技术系统。”（美国世界资源研究所，1993）。从经济属性定义可持续发展，《经济、自然资源、不足和发展》“在保护自然资源的质量和其所提供服务的前提下，使经济发展的净利益增加到最大限度。”（巴比尔 Edward B · Barbier，1989）。“为全世界而不是为少数人的特权所提供公平机会的经济增长，不进一步消耗自然资源的绝对量和涵容能力。”（普朗克 Pronk 和哈克 Hag，1992）。《世界末日》“自然资本不变前提下的经济发展，或今天的资源使用不应减少未来的实际收入。”（皮尔斯 Pearce 和沃福德 Warford，1993）。《世界发展报告》“建立在成本效益比较审慎的经济分析基础上的发展和环境政策，加强环境保护，从而导致福利的增加和可持续水平的提高。”（世界银行，1992）。尽管对可持续发展的定义不尽相同，但就当前来看，1987 年布伦特兰夫人提交联合国的《我们共同的未来》的报告中所给出的可持续发展定义仍最为大家所接受。其定义是：可持续发展是“既满足当代人的需求，又不对后代人满足其自身需求的能力构成危害的发展”。具体来说，就是谋求经济、社会与自然环境的协调发展，维持新的平衡，制衡出现的环境恶化和环境污染，控制重大自然灾害的发生。如何实现可持续发展？《中国 21 世纪议程》认为，主要是在保持经济快速增长的同时，依靠科技进步和提高劳动者素质，不断改善发展质量，提倡适度消费和清洁生产，控制环境污染，改善生态环境，保持可持续发展的资源基础，建立“低消耗、高收益、低污染、高效益”的良性循环发展模式。我国国民经济和社会发展“九五”计划和 2010 年远景目标规划把可持续发展作为跨世纪的战略任务。同时，可持续发展业已成为人类迈向 21 世纪的行动纲领。

综合既有的“可持续发展”定义，本研究认为：“可持续发展”作为新型“发展观”①，概念可以概括为：以实现人类理想为系统演进的总目

① 发展观是从哲学角度对发展的诠释，是人们对经济社会发展总的看法和根本观点。随着人类社会的不断进步，人们对发展的认识不断深化，发展的内涵越来越充实。“可持续发展”是一种体现不同时代人类理想的、没有终极内涵、具有层次性的动态概念。“可持续发展”是“协调发展”的最高目标，“协调发展”是实现可持续发展的最基本手段，而“科学发展观”则是引领人们实现这一目标的根本态度、原则和价值指向。

标，在遵循客观规律的基础上，通过经济发展的同时能控制人口增长、提高人口素质、合理利用资源、保护和改善环境，使社会与经济能够形成持续、快速、健康发展的多元目标和互相协调，实现系统及其内部构成要素之间的关系不断朝着理想状态演进的动态过程。作为中国基本战略之一的可持续发展，既从经济增长、社会进步和环境安全的功利性目标出发，也从哲学观念更新和人类文明进步的理性化目标出发，全方位地涵盖了“人口、资源、环境、发展”四位一体的辩证关系，并将此类关系在不同时段和不同区域的差异，融合在整个发展演化的共同趋势之中。作为国家的一项基本发展战略，它除了具有十分坚实的理论基础和知识内涵外，面对实现战略目标的总体要求，应当进一步规定实施战略目标的方案和规划，从而组成一个完善的战略体系，在理论上、实证上、应用上去寻求实施战略过程的最大“满意解”。

（二）可持续发展的基本特征

1. 可持续发展战略体系的特征

从可持续发展的基础理论出发，拟定的战略体系具有三个最为明显的特征：发展度、协调度、持续度。

（1）发展度。所谓发展度，就是指保持增长、提高经济增长的质量和较好地满足就业、粮食、能源、饮用水和健康的基本生存需求，从这三方面去满足人类不断增长的需求和生活质量的不断提高。我们所拟订的战略体系，必须能表达如何衡量一个国家或区域的“发展度”（数量维），即能够判别一个国家或区域是否在真正地发展？是否在健康地发展？以及是否在保证生活质量和生存空间不断改善的前提下发展？总之，它必须澄清一个容易混淆的观念，即认为可持续发展似乎不强调经济增长、社会进步和财富积累，这显然是与可持续发展理论的本质背道而驰的。

（2）协调度。协调度由调控人口的数量增长，不断提高人口的素质和始终调控环境与发展的平衡这两方面去体现，以此达到人与自然之间的协调以及人与人之间的协调。因此，可持续发展应能衡量一个国家或区域的“协调度”（质量维），即要求在统一尺度比较下定量地诊断能否维持环境与发展之间的平衡？能否维持效率与公平之间的平衡？能否维持市场发育与政府调控之间的平衡？能否维持当代与后代之间的利益分配上的平衡？这一特征与区域的“发展度”相比有所侧重，如果说发展度更加强调“量”的概念即财富规模的扩大，协调度则更加强调内在的效率和“质”的概念，即强调合理优化资源的配置、调控经济的增长方式，采取合理的财富积聚、建立财富的公平分配制度以及财富在满足全人类需求中的行为规范。

（3）持续度。持续度由维持、扩大和保护地球的资源基础与集中关注科技进步对于发展瓶颈的突破两方面去体现。一方面通过物质基础的储备，另一方面通过知识基础的储备，为可持续发展的健康延续提供潜在的能力，以此实现可持续发展战略的持续性。毋庸置疑，可持续发展应能衡量一个国家或地区的“持续度”（时间维），即判断一个国家或地区在发展上的长期合理性。这里所指的长期，近者可能包含五代或者十代人的时间，远者直至整个人类的未来。持续度更加注重从“时间维”上去把握发展度和协调度。换言之，可持续发展战略目标中所关注的发展度和协调度，不应只是在短时间内的发展速度和发展质量，它们建立在充分长时间维上的调控之中。

可持续发展战略理论体系中所表明的三大特征，即数量维（发展度）、质量维（协调度）、时间维（持续度），从本质上表征了对于可持续发展战略目标的完满追求。由上述三维空间所构建的可持续发展战略，其最大贡献是从理论构架和操作方式上对可持续发展的“指标体系”作出了符合理性的深层次的解析。

2. 可持续发展意识的主要特征

可持续发展意识是反映人、社会、自然环境、经济的相互关系和社会思想、理论、情感、意志、知觉等观念形态的总和。在联合国的一些文件中，常称为世界文明、全球道德、共同人性等。人类的环境意识是在热爱自然、保护环境的活动中产生的；可持续发展意识是在经济的高速增长造成了环境的巨大破坏之后，人类在反思环境和经济发展的关系中逐步成熟起来的。可持续发展意识有以下主要特征：

（1）综合思维。把人类、社会、自然环境和经济作为一个有机整体，统一考虑，注重协调约束各自的行为限度，达到一个动态的发展平衡。这种思维方式表现在社会发展战略的选择上就是要综合决策。

（2）价值观。可持续发展的价值评定不仅以人类为尺度，而是以更深层次的“人类—自然”系统为尺度；不仅是以人类的利益为目标，而是以人类与自然的和谐发展为目标。在价值观念上，既承认自然界对于人类的各种价值，也承认自然界自身存在的价值，即它对地球生命支持系统具有的存在价值，对于生命和自然界可持续生存的价值。既然自然资源是有限的和有价的，就必须珍惜、保护、有偿使用。在利用自然资源的过程中，重在追求效率与公平，避免浪费与破坏。可持续发展价值观的建立，将决定公众的行为取向，是公众参与的动力源泉。

（3）经济观。经济增长是生产值（如国民生产总值）的提高，它并不等同于经济发展。不能以损害和牺牲环境的方式去追求经济增长。在经济核算中，环境成本应当内部化，应当考虑自然资源的使用成本、用户成本（机会成本）、风险成本等。经济发展中应寻求集约型的发展模式，生产过程中应采取清洁生产技术。经济发展的目的是在人类、社会、环境系统相互协调的前提下，提高人类的生活质量。

（4）道德观。可持续发展要求人们具有高度的文化水平和道德水平，明白自身的活动对于自然、人类社会的生存、发展的长远影响与后果，认识自己对社会和子孙后代的崇高责任，并能自觉地为社会的长远利益而牺牲一些眼前利益和局部利益。人们应当改变超前消费、炫耀富裕、过分追求物质利益、以牺牲环境来换取高额利润的各种不道德行为。人类应当建立环境道德观，不应为自身的利益而损害自然环境。道德调节的范围要从人与人的社会关系，扩展到人类、社会与自然界的关系。这种道德观的目标是人类、社会和环境的协调。建立可持续发展的道德观和价值观，是人类社会在逐步接受可持续发展思想之后的又一进步，只有每个人都对自己生活的地球，对人类大家庭的幸福和对于未来报有强烈的责任感，才能形成一个巨大的可持续发展的意识源泉，进而推动可持续发展战略的实施。

3. 可持续发展理论的主要特征

（1）坚持发展是主题。发展是人类共同和普遍具有的基本权利，也是人类运行的规律。任何国家，任何时期都应坚持发展，经济零增长论是没有根据的。可持续发展鼓励经济增长，而且它是国家实力和社会财富的体现。同时，可持续发展不仅重视增长数量，更追求改善质量、提高效益、节约能源、减少污染，改善传统的生产和消费模式，实施清洁生产和文明消费。

（2）坚持持续发展是根本。可持续发展的核心是“可持续”，“可持续”就是长期延续。可持续发展要以保护资源为基础，与资源与环境的承载能力相协调。因此，发展的同时必须保护环境，包括控制环境污染、改善环境质量、保护生命支持系统、保护生物多样性、保护地球生态的完整性，保证以可持续的方式使用可再生资源，使人类的发展保持在地球承载能力之内。

（3）坚持整体、协调、综合发展的具体道路。可持续发展强调是发展的整体性、协调性和综合性，寻求的是经济、社会、环境、资源、人口的全面发展。可持续发展要以改善和提高生活质量为目的，与社会进步相适应。可持续发展必须与解决当代世界上大多数人口的贫困联系在一起。对于发展中国家来说，贫困与不发达是造成资源与环境恶化的基本原因之一。只有消除贫困，才能构筑起保护环境和建设环境的能力。

（4）坚持合理使用自然资源和保护环境是实现可持续发展的基础。丰富的自然资源和良好的生态环境是人类社会赖以存在和发展的基础。可持续发展各特征之间相互联系不可分割，孤立地追求经济增长必然导致经济崩溃；孤立追求生态持续不能遏止全球环境衰退。生态持续是基础，经济持续是条件，社会持续是目的。人类共同追求的应该是自然—经济—社会复合系统的持续、稳定、健康发展。

综合以上分析，可持续发展的基本特征表现为：一是综合性：可持续发展是人与环境的综合发展。二是多层次性：可持续发展是总系统目标下的各系统及其内部组成要素间关系的多层次协调。三是依赖性：可持续发展是基于发展所依赖的资源和环境承载能力的发展。四是统一性：可持续发展在时间和空间上表现为层次性、动态性及其形式多样性的统一。五是系统性：可持续发展系统是具有复杂内部结构的自组织系统。六是反向性：可持续发展的反向是发展不可持续。

二　西部地区农产品物流可持续发展的内涵与特征

（一）西部地区农产品物流可持续发展的概念界定

由“可持续发展”的内涵、特征，不难得出：市场经济体制条件下，可持续发展必须建立有机的内部运行机制和良好的外部发展关系。国民经济发展必然要求西部地区农产品物流、农村经济与之保持可持续，否则，以工业化为特征的经济发展将落入“李嘉图陷阱”①，而处于不断调整和波动之中[132-134]。西部地区农产品物流可持续发展，是指西部地区农产品物流部门在促进西部农村经济和整个西部经济可持续发展的前提下，形成的农产品物流与农村实体经济系统，在各自内部组成要素持续协调，以及两者在总量和结构上分别相互持续协调的基础上，实现农产品物流利益的最大化与整体经济、物流系统演进保持可持续的系统演进过程。为了简化研究过程，本研究将包括西部地区农产品物流在内的整个西部农村经济与西部经济的可持续发展作为研究的目标，并将西部农村经济发展的其他因素予以抽象，着重探讨在可持续发展目标下，西部地区农产品物流可持续机理。这样，西部地区农产品物流可持续发展可以表述为：保持西部农村经济发展，适应西部经济发展要求的西部地区农产品物流与农村实体经济关系理想状态及其实现过程。农产品物流与农村实体经济之间的相互关系是相互依存、相互制约、平等互利的产业经济关系。西部地区农产品物流可持续发展的内涵是在不损害后代利益的前提下，利用市场机制适度地开发利用农产品物流资源，保证当代人对物流产品及服务的需求，实现农产品物流资源供需平衡和良性循环。其本质是农村资源在农产品物流与农村实体经济部门的可持续性优化配置。具体可表现为：西部地区农产品物流与农村实体经济总量平衡、结构适应；速度适宜、持续、平稳；机制有效、组织合理、管理有力、功能完善、行为规范。其核心是经济发展过程中，正确判断和处理好西部地区农产品物流与农村经济关系的问题。其首要的问题是根据西部地区农产品物流可持续发展机理，借鉴国际成功经验，正确判断和把握西部地区农产品物流与农村经济的关系，分析失调的原因；其次是在此基础上，依据可持续发展机理，针对现实存在的问题，构建可持续发展的机制与模式。

由功能意义的西部地区农产品物流发展理解，可以看出，西部地区农产品物流可持续发展是西部大开发后续发展的重要基础之一，是有效提高

---

① 对经济发展中工农关系的研究分为两个阶段，第一阶段是18—19世纪40—50年代，以李嘉图为代表的古典经济学家对工业化先驱国家早期经济发展中工农关系的研究；第二阶段是20世纪40年代后，以张培刚为代表的发展经济学家对当代经济发展中的工农关系所做的探索。研究的共同结论是：农业是影响工业化的重要因素。由于李嘉图最早进行这一研究，因此一般把工业化过程中的工农关系危机称为“李嘉图陷阱”。

资源配置效率、解决人口膨胀、促进经济社会可持续发展的重要途径[135]。如果将可持续发展背景下，经济发展对农产品物流发展的需求设为 Q，那么，Q 既包括经济发展对农产品物流发展需求的总量特征，又包含结构特征。农村经济系统用 X_{ai} 表示，a 表示农村经济部门，i 表示农村经济系统的内部构成要素，$i=1$，2，3……n，可以从农村经济主体、农村经济的产业结构、区域结构、制度构成等方面分类，每个方面又由若干基本要素构成。农产品物流系统用 X_{fj} 表示，f 表示农产品物流部门，j 表示农产品物流系统的内部构成要素，$j=1$，2，3……m，可以从农产品物流供给主体、农产品物流业务和物流工具、农产品物流的区域构成、制度构成、交易方式等方面分类，每个方面也同样由若干基本要素构成。用 y，z 分别表示农产品物流和农村经济发展的资源和环境。这里的资源和环境，既包括自然的，也包括社会经济的，尤其是物流资源和制度环境。R 表示资源和环境承载能力，T 为时间变量，L 为空间变量，F、G 表示函数关系，则西部地区农产品物流可持续发展内涵的一般数学表达为（3－1）：

$$MaxQ = F(X_{ai}, X_{fj}, Y, Z, T, L) \qquad (3-1)$$

其中：$i=1$，2，3，……N；$j=1$，2，3，……M；

$X_{ai} \geqslant 0; X_{ai} \geqslant 0; Y \geqslant 0; Z \geqslant 0;$

约束条件为：

$$X_{ai}^2 + X_{fi}^2 \leqslant R^2 \qquad (3-2)$$

$$R = G(Y, Z) \qquad (3-3)$$

$$F(X_{ai}, X_{fi}) - [F(X_{ai}) + F(X_{fj})] \geqslant 0 \qquad (3-4)$$

$$F_a(X_{ai}) - [F_a(X_{a1}) + F_a(X_{a2}) + F_a(X_{a3}) + \cdots\cdots + F_a(X_{aN})] \geqslant 0 \qquad (3-5)$$

$$F_f(X_{fJ}) - [F_f(X_{f1}) + F_f(X_{f2}) + F_f(X_{f3}) + \cdots\cdots + F_f(X_{fM})] \geqslant 0 \qquad (3-6)$$

（二）西部地区农产品物流可持续发展的基本特征

1. 可持续发展是内部结构复杂的系统运动过程

依据本研究对西部地区农产品物流发展概念内涵的分析，借助系统科学理论框架分析可见，西部地区农产品物流可持续发展系统，具有复杂的内部结构，是一个开放、复杂的、灰色的、非线性的自组织系统，是以目标一致、功能齐备、结构合理、效益统筹、利益兼顾等为原则。通过系统内部（物流主体系统、物流作业系统和物流信息系统三个分系统）以及系统之间（农产品物流系统、农村经济系统）的物质、能量和信息交换来实现的。这里的可持续发展系统由西部地区农产品物流、农村实体经济以及政府三大系统构成。可持续发展主体为农产品物流供给主体、农村实体经济主体（也即农产品物流需求主体）以及政府。可持续发展的手段依据现代经济学理论无非包括市场手段和人为手段，以及介于两者之间的各种过渡形式，具体而言，包括政府可持续、市场可持续、企业可持续、准市场组织可持续、关系网络可持续和社会可持续，归根到底是制度可持续。可持续发展的目标是满足经济系统可持续发展对农村经济发展的要求[136]。因此，可持续发展过程的实质是：西部地区农产品物流与农村经济可持续发展主体，为实现各自的利益，基于可持续发展的共识和对西部地区农产品物流可持续发展机理的把握，分析和判断农产品物流与农村经济关系状况（协调和失调），进而针对农产品物流与农村经济关系状况及其发展失调的原因，在制度可持续框架下，综合运用各种可能的可持续发展手段，使西部地区农产品物流与农村经济关系达成理想状态，具有在制度和技术作用下西部地区农产品物流通畅，其总量、结构和速度配合适当构成良性循环的理想状态特征。由此可见，可持续发展过程受西部经济发展的要求和外部干扰因素影响，是一个不断进行关系状况判断，在变革—创新中不断循环往复的渐进式发展的过程。

2. 可持续发展是多层次相交叉的系统运动过程

西部地区农产品物流可持续发展，从可持续内容上看，表现在：系统功能的可持续、系统结构的可持续、系统地位的可持续、系统时间的可持续、系统空间的可持续相互交织的方面；从可持续层次上看，可以概括为如图 3－1 所示的西部地区农产品物流与农村经济分别在微观、中观和宏观层次上不同组合的可持续发展。表现在微观主体到整个西部经济的不同层次上，即有西部地区农产品物流与农村经济系统的总体可持续，也有西部地区不同层次的经济或行政区域范围内的农产品物流与农村经济可持续发展，以及西部地区农产品物流内部结构与农村经济内部结构即产业层次上的可持续；还可以在微观上表现为某一农村经济活动中的农产品物流与农村经济的可持续发展，或农产品物流供给主体与农村经济活动主体之间的可持续。从内部构成要素来看，上述可持续发展又是以西部地区农产品物流系统内部构成要素的可持续为基础的。西部地区农产品物流系统内部有自己的运行领域，在物流技术、物流基础设施、物流政策等方面又是融入整个社会物流系统之中的。

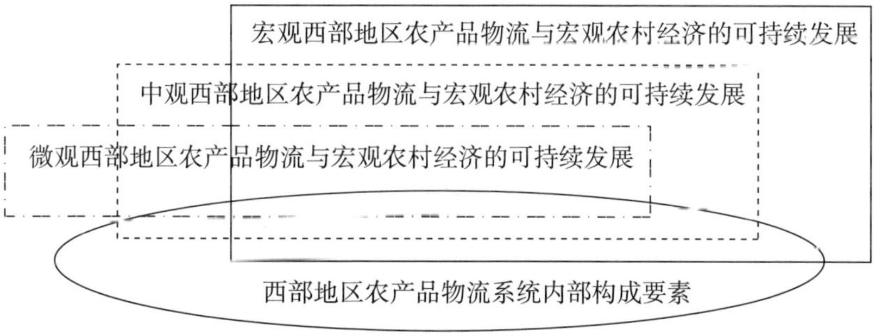

图 3－1　不同层次西部地区农产品物流可持续发展的可能形式

3. 可持续发展是变革—创新中渐进式的系统运动过程

就西部地区农产品物流而言，由于农业本身的发展、超市等新型零售业态的介入、城市居民食物消费结构与消费方式的变化、信息技术应用于物流实践的拓宽，物流体系面临变革的压力，需要改变各物流主体融入物流链能力、实现农产品物流过程增值、获取农产品新利润等的制度创新①。在市场经济体制条件下，必须建立有机的内部运行机制和良好的外部发展关系的西部地区农产品物流可持续发展机制，农产品物流部门在促进农村经济和整个国民经济可持续发展的前提下，形成的农产品物流与农村实体经济系统，在各自内部组成要素持续协调，以及两者在总量和结构上分别相互持续协调的基础上，实现农产品物流利益的最大化与整体经济、物流系统演进保持可持续的系统演进过程[137]。根据信息与控制的关系，可持续可分为“前期渐进式可持续”“后期渐进式可持续”以及克服两者不足而将两者相结合形成的“前期—后期渐进式可持续”三种形式（如图 3－2）。表现出“前期渐进式”→“后期渐进式”→“前期—后期渐进式”演进形态。

① 李学工（2009）：“在我国，行业协会是贯彻政府物流政策的半行政组织，在农村物流中发挥着不可替代的作用。”

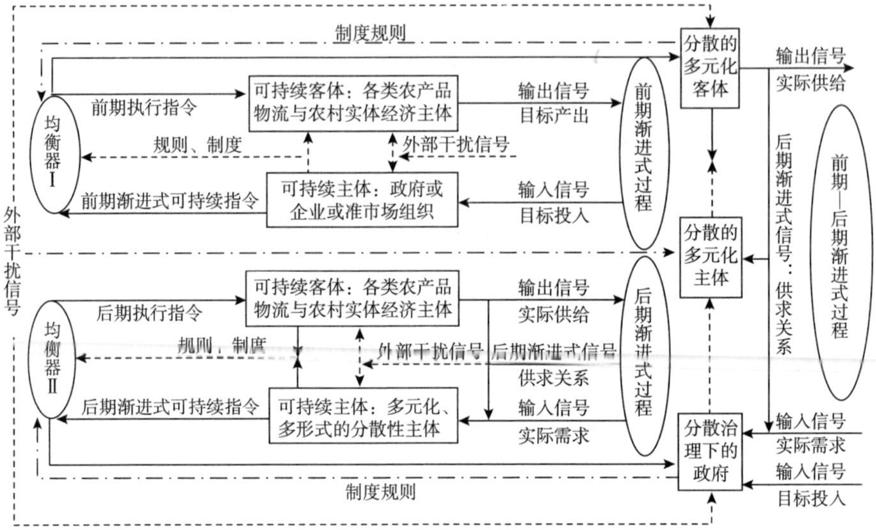

图3－2　前期渐进式→后期渐进式→前期—后期渐进式可持续发展过程

表3－2　　西部地区农产品物流可持续发展典型特征与演进形态识别

	前期渐进式可持续	后期渐进式可持续	前期—后期渐进式可持续
可持续主体	由一部分组成：政府、企业、准市场组织	由一部分组成：多元化、多形式的分散性主体	由两部分组成：分散治理下的政府；分散的多元化可持续主体
可持续客体	各类农产品物流与农村实体经济主体	各类农产品物流与农村实体经济主体	分散的多元化客体
可持续过程	集中	分散	集中—分散
输入信号	目标投入	实际需求	目标投入、实际需求
均衡器	一个（均衡器Ⅰ）：计划、命令、法规等人为手段	一个（均衡器Ⅱ）：价格、供求、竞争等市场手段或社会关系、道德情感之类的社会运行手段	两个（均衡器Ⅰ、均衡器Ⅱ）：第一个是政府的前期渐进式均衡器，第二个是多元化可持续主体的后期渐进式均衡器
可持续机制（可持续指令）	依据发展战略、规划或计划的目标，由单一可持续主体的某种组织形式为载体集中发出	多元化的可持续主体根据其追求的目标，由多元化可持续主体构成的体系为载体各自分散发出	第一个均衡器将政府的可持续指令转化为前期渐进式执行指令，采用前期渐进方式作用于分散的多元化可持续主体。分散的多元化可持续主体的输入信号，来自于市场供求关系信号和政府输入的政府可持续执行指令信号

续表 3-2

	前期渐进式可持续	后期渐进式可持续	前期—后期渐进式可持续
输出信号	集中的可持续指令信号经过决策系统的均衡器转化为执行指令，作用于集中的可持续客体，即农产品物流与农村经济主体，形成实际目标输出	分散的可持续指令信号经过体系化的均衡器转化为执行指令信号，作用于分散的可持续客体，即多元化农产品物流与农村经济主体，形成市场供给	第二个均衡器将分散的多元化可持续主体分散的后期渐进式的可持续指令，先转化为后期渐进式的执行指令，再作用于分散的可持续客体，即多元化的西部地区农产品物流与农村经济主体，形成市场供给
运行效率	取决于均衡器运行规则（制度）的有效性	取决于均衡器运行规则（制度）的有效性	取决于两个系统的可持续。政府的“前期渐进式可持续”功能发挥，即政府“前期渐进式可持续”执行指令是否得当，是至关重要的
影响因素	受到外部干扰信号——市场需求和外部环境变化的影响	受到外部干扰信号的影响，但这种影响既可以作用于输入信号，也可以作用于执行命令	外部干扰信号分别影响政府、分散的多元化可持续主体（同时也是可持续客体）
满足条件	①由输入到输出的信息传递不存在损耗；②决策系统的变换算子计算正确无误；③决策系统能及时把握并有效纠正干扰信号引起信号偏差	①输出信号掌握及时，输入信号正确；②均衡器高效运行；③主体多元，而且充分理性	必须满足前述两种可持续的条件
优点	事前性、强制性和目的明确、可持续时间反应性好、市场需求影响度高	满足以上条件就能不断适应外部环境变化，排除外部干扰，自动、高效地实现可持续发展	结合了“前期渐进式可持续”和“后期渐进式可持续”各自的优点，克服了各自的缺点
缺点	由于其运行条件的苛刻性、外部环境的复杂性和信息传递的多层次性、高损耗、易干扰性，往往效率比较低，只能在特定的领域有条件地使用	上述条件不存在容易产生波动性震荡。由于输入信息所依赖的是前期色输出信息，往往存在“蛛网问题”，可持续时间反应性不高。由于这一过程中信息传播和利用的分散性，决定了可持续不可避免地具有盲目性	

资料来源：本文研究整理。

“前期渐进式可持续”，是人为的、有组织的、集中可持续，在本研究中可对应于政府可持续、企业可持续和准市场组织可持续。“后期渐进式可持续”，是自发的、无组织的分散可持续，在本研究中对应于市场可持续、社会可持续和关系网络可持续。“前期—后期渐进式可持续”，是利用“前期渐进式可持续”和“后期渐进式可持续”功能上的互补性将两者相结合的产物。西部地区农产品物流可持续发展属于“前期—后期渐进式”形态。政府的“前期渐进式可持续”功能发挥，即政府“前期渐进式可持续”执行指令的强弱、及时与是否得当，至关重要。

第三节 西部地区农产品物流可持续发展的实现机理

一 西部地区农产品物流可持续发展的均衡过程

（一）西部地区农产品物流多重均衡与可持续发展

首先，西部地区农产品物流与农村经济的相互作用机理。研究西部地区农产品物流与农村经济两者之间的关系首先需要分析两种模式：第一种“需求追随”强调西部地区农产品物流发展是农村实体经济发展的结果。农村实体经济发展意味着市场规模的扩张和以此为基础的分工和交换的发展，以及由分工和交换发展所带来的产品差异的扩大和规模经济的出现[138-140]。因此，处于分工和交换之中的，追求规模经济的农村经济主体对农产品物流服务的需求，导致了农产品物流的发展。但这一过程同时又是交易活动的不确定性增加和交易成本上升的过程，农村经济发展必须越过这一“门槛效应”（threshold effect）① 的限制，农产品物流交易、农产品物流机构、相关的农产品物流服务和农产品物流制度安排才能被诱导出来，这一阶段的农产品物流发展是被动于经济发展的[141-148]。第二种

① 农产品物流体系运行需要消耗一个相当于被中介资金数量的一个固定比例的成本，农产品物流中介和农产品物流市场的组建存在很高的固定进入费用和交易成本，只有农村经济发展使人均收入的增长能够支撑这一成本，农产品物流体系才能有利可图，即在农产品物流发展与农村经济发展之间存在“门槛效应”（threshold effect）。

“供给领先”强调了西部地区农产品物流机构和相关物流服务的供给，这种外在的供给先于农产品物流的需求，对农产品物流发展，进而对农村经济发展起促进作用。因此，两者在农村经济发展的不同阶段扮演不同的角色，供给引导型的农产品物流发展在农村经济增长的初期处于主导地位，需求跟随型的农产品物流发展在农村经济发展的成熟期将逐渐居于主导地位，但即使是在早期的供给领先模式中，宏观制度环境对农产品物流机构的放松管制，尤其是允许真正市场主体的准入，仍是相当重要的[149-153]。进一步研究西部地区农产品物流发展与农村经济发展的关系，可以看出，农村经济发展，一是促进了专业化和劳动分工，推动了西部地区农产品物流体系的发展；西部地区农产品物流的发展，反过来又进一步促进了农村经济的发展。二是提高了农村经济主体的收入水平，诱导了西部地区农产品物流的扩张；西部地区农产品物流发展则通过资本积累、市场扩张和技术进步三个基本因素实现经济增长[154-157]。总之，西部地区农产品物流与农村经济的相互作用机理是在宏观经济、物流环境和相应的制度安排下，西部地区农产品物流和农村经济的交易主体，在一定交易环境中进行相应交易活动的结果[158-160]。

其次，西部地区农产品物流可持续发展的供求均衡。现实中的西部地区农产品物流与农村经济关系是处于开放系统中的关系，不仅两者相互作用，而且还受到宏观经济、物流环境及其制度安排的影响。根据上述定义，西部地区农产品物流与农村经济关系集中表现为西部地区农产品物流需求与西部地区农产品物流供给的数量关系。西部地区农产品物流的全部意义，从最终目的上讲，无非是为实体意义上的农村经济过程服务的，是满足农村经济发展的物流需求的过程。但是，在理论上，西部地区农产品物流既存在直接因农村实体经济发展需要，同时在提供媒介、运输、配送、采购、包装、交易等服务的农村直接物流过程，也存在支撑这一过程或为之服务的，在物流系统内部进行的如保险、融资、交易、结算等间接地为农村实体经济服务的农村间接物流过程。与之相对应，西部地区农产品物流供给和需求也必须分为直接的和间接的两个部分，其直接的部分分别相当于一般经济学上最终产品和最终需求，而间接的部分则分别相当于中间产品和中间需求[161-163]。西部地区农产品物流与农村经济供求分析，还可以从西部地区农产品物流需求与供给的实际构成角度进行。从农村经济发展的实际需要角度看，西部地区农产品物流需求不外乎是农民消费性农产品物流需求、农业生产性农产品物流需求以及农村社会发展性农产品物流需求[164]。而西部地区农产品物流供给则不外乎农产品正规物流供给和农产品非正规物流供给[165]。西部地区农产品物流需求与农村经济结构和西部地区农产品物流供给结构有关，而西部地区农产品物流供给则取决于农产品正规和非正规物流的供给能力及其结构[166]。总之，西部地区农产品物流可持续发展的供求均衡必须建立在西部地区农产品物流结构与农村经济结构相适应的基础上，宏观制度通过改变交易环境影响西部地区农产品物流发展与农村经济发展的关系。

再次，西部地区农产品物流可持续发展的多重均衡。上述分析可以看出：西部地区农产品物流的供求均衡是受供求双方多重因素的影响而相互作用，没有唯一均衡解，可以在不同水平上实现均衡。从西部地区农产品物流与农村经济相互作用机理的分析表明，西部地区农产品物流体系建立的固定成本，使西部地区农产品物流发展和农村经济发展之间存在一个“门槛”限制，更进一步地讲，西部地区农产品物流与农村经济关系同时受到双方发展水平的作用，可能存在不同水平下的多重均衡状态。一是从技术选择的角度分析，可以进一步解释这种多重均衡机制[167]。当西部地区农产品物流体系没有充分发展时，人们在进行风险分散时，可以选择风险小而生产能力相对较低的某些不太尖端的技术，这种以技术的灵活性来降低风险的方法，形成了农村经济体系中缺乏效率的结构，这种结构在某种程度上削弱了西部地区农产品物流体系的发展，从而导致一个低水平的均衡。相反，一个发达的西部地区农产品物流体系能够刺激投资者选择更加尖端、更有效率和风险更高，同时收益也更高的技术，从而又进一步促进了西部地区农产品物流发展。因此，如果西部地区农产品物流发展能够越过收入“门槛”的限制，农村经济发展就会促使农村经济由低水平向高水平均衡转变。二是从规模经济的角度分析，同样可以解释这种多重均衡[168]。由于西部地区农产品物流体系的成本决定于西部地区农产品物流交易次数和交易规模，即：如果农村实体经济系统拥有足够的资金存量和大规模的投资需求，那就必然会内生一个与之相适应的西部地区农产品物流体系，因为这个西部地区农产品物流体系所需要的固定成本，能够被足够多的农村经济主体和交易活动来分摊；而这又进一步促进了农村经济活动主体更多地利用西部地区农产品物流体系，以扩大规模经济，提高资本的产出率。相反，如果农村经济系统没有足够的规模和资金存量与投资需求，西部地区农产品物流体系的成本就无法分摊，一方面投资者难以利用西部地区农产品物流体系，另一方面西部地区农产品物流体系自身也难以发展，西部地区农产品物流与农村经济处于低水平的均衡。

依据本研究对西部地区农产品物流可持续发展的定义，并不是西部地区农产品物流与农村经济的所有均衡关系都是可持续发展，只有在西部地区农村经济发展和西部地区经济社会发展相适应条件下的均衡才是可持续发展，而且这种均衡不仅表现在总量上，还要表现在结构上，并且是具有高度稳定性的长期均衡，但其均衡关系原理和影响因素同样适用于解释可持续发展。

（二）西部地区农产品物流可持续发展的均衡机理

首先，从农村实体经济来看，如果由于制度创新、投资增加、技术进步、结构变迁等原因导致内部结构失调，则必然出现农村实体经济的产品结构性供求失调，在消费者选择机制的作用下，供不应求的产品价格上升，投资收益率相应提高，而供过于求的产品则相反。在利益机制的驱动下，投资者会增加对供不应求产品的投资，生产者则扩大供不应求产品的生产，而对供过于求的产品则进行相反的调节，直至产品供求关系达到市场均衡水平，实现农村经济系统内部的可持续。

其次，从西部地区农产品物流系统来看，如果由于资本投入、物流组织、制度和工具创新，导致西部地区农产品物流系统内部结构失调，必将引起西部地区农产品物流产品供给结构失衡，原有西部地区农产品物流资产的风险和收益状态被打破，致使投资者对风险低、收益高的物流产品增加投资，而减少对风险高、收益低的物流产品的投资，使物流产品的价格发生相应的变化，直至物流市场供求均衡，实现西部地区农产品物流系统内部的可持续。

再次，从西部地区农产品物流与农村实体经济的关系上看，如果西部地区农产品物流供给过度，即过多的资产被配置到西部地区农产品物流领域，而农村实体经济发展所需要的资本投入不足，一方面，必然会出现农村实体经济因资本短缺而萎缩，产品和服务价格因生产能力不足而上升，从而使实体经济投资效率提高，资本将从西部地区农产品物流领域流向农村实体经济领域，致使农村实体经济资产价格上升；另一方面，由于西部地区农产品物流供给过度，在经济物流化的驱动下，物流资产价格进一步上升、膨胀，引发物流投机，致使资产价格和价值严重背离。直至西部地区农产品物流与农村经济资本配置比例达到理想状态，即实现可持续发展。此外，如果西部地区农产品物流与农村经济关系是西部地区农产品物流抑制，而导致西部地区农产品物流供给不足，即西部地区农产品物流发展难以满足农村实体经济的需要，农村资源配置将无法达到最优。由于存在西部地区农产品物流抑制，西部地区农产品物流服务价格则因供给不足而提高，西部地区农产品物流产品投资收益率提高。在不存在制度刚性和西部地区农产品物流市场进入限制时，理性的投资者就会增加西部地区农产品物流产品投资，减少对农村实体经济的投资，从而导致农村资本市场上由于资金流入减少，资产价格下降，预期收益率提高；而农村实体经济由于产品供过于求，产品价格下降，在收入效应的作用下，理性消费者为实现效用在时间上的最大化，必然减少当期消费，而增加对西部地区农产品物流产品的投资，使农村资金从实体经济领域流向物流领域。直至西部地区农产品物流与农村经济资本配置比例达到理想状态，即实现可持续发展。

上述可持续发展的均衡机理，是一种理想状态的抽象，在现实中这些条件并不存在。其一，西部地区农产品物流可持续发展系统是开放的，与外界存在巨大的物质、能量和信息交换，并且往往是资本流出多，流进少，系统极其容易受到外部冲击，而处于不稳定状态。其二，由于信息不充分、不对称，或信息获取滞后，以及利益集团压力，市场主体参与市场博弈的地位不平等等因素，导致制度供给滞后，供给结构不合理的情况十分普遍。西部地区农产品物流和农村经济制度弹性不可能是充分的，制度的适应性存在时滞，制度约束客观上普遍存在。其三，由于资源的自然属性以及制度障碍的存在，西部地区农产品物流系统的资源流动并不是自由的，而是有障碍和成本的[169-171]。因此，实现西部地区农产品物流可持续发展的关键在于制度可持续。实现可持续发展必须通过制度创新，创造西部地区农产品物流可持续发展系统运行的理想条件。

二　西部地区农产品物流可持续发展的内在规律

（一）西部地区农产品物流可持续发展的影响因素

1. 西部地区农产品物流可持续发展的产业环境

西部地区农产品物流可持续发展，就是在一定宏观经济、物流环境及其相应制度背景下，农产品物流供给与农产品物流需求，即农村经济主体在一定条件下相互“交易”的结果。从西部地区农产品物流与农村经济“交易”的实际来看，西部地区农产品物流与农村经济系统的外部环境、内部结构决定着各自的资源禀赋和风险分布状态，也决定着交易双方的风险承受能力、支付能力和谈判能力，从而形成西部地区农产品物流与农村经济“交易”的基本条件。加之城乡之间、工农之间的“二元”结构，也为西部地区农产品物流与农村经济“交易”打上了历史的烙印[172]；渐进改革的推进，尤其是加入 WTO 后物流改革的深化以及西部大开发的后续推进，无疑又在西部地区农产品物流与农村经济“交易”条件中，引入了新变量，从而对西部地区农产品物流与农村经济关系及其可持续发展构成了重要影响[173]。西部地区农产品物流可持续发展实际上是西部地区农产品物流与农村经济“交易”双方互为约束的条件下，通过对西部地区农产品物流交易量与交易价格等决策变量进行选择，从而实现双方受益最大化的过程。

西部地区农产品物流可持续发展的产业环境受到结构变动、政府管制的影响。农村经济主体参与西部地区农产品物流“交易”的最高价格承受水平，由其生产经营活动的收益分布状态和机会成本决定。西部地区农产品物流供给主体对“交易”价格的最低接受水平，在物流资源可以自由流动的条件下，主要取决于物流资源投资于其他领域的机会成本。西部地区农产品物流需求主体使用西部地区农产品物流资源的平均净收益应大于或等于西部地区农产品物流供给和需求主体从事该“交易”的机会成本之和。农村产业结构、区域结构、就业结构的多样化，对西部地区农产品物流需求主体使用物流资源的平均净收益率，提出了更高的要求：如果农村经济活动的平均收益率得不到相应提高，就会加剧西部地区农产品物流资源外流；如果农村经济结构在地区和产业上不是同质的，那“交易”将首先在平均收益率高的地区和产业达成；如果西部地区农产品物流需求主体的经营能力不是同质的，达成“交易”的首先是能依靠经营能力获得较高平均收益率的经营者；如果西部地区农产品物流需求主体从事生产经营活动的资本来自自身积累部分越多，则西部地区农产品物流供给主体越愿意提供物流供给，而且，物流需求主体的“交易”地位也将随之提升。因此，物流结构是否合理对西部地区农产品物流可持续发展意义重大。西部地区农产品物流供给能满足西部地区农产品物流需求，首先需要农村经济发展提供一个足够的空间。由于资源禀赋、制度安排以及市场规模等原因的约束，农村经济不仅与城市经济存在巨大差异，而且其发展在地区、产业和不同经营者之间也不平衡，从而使西部地区农产品物流与农村经济发展呈现出明显的“马太效应”[174,175]。因此，政府要在交易规模不变的情况下实行管制，就必须以财政支持为基础的社会性物流与之匹配[176-178]。

2. 西部地区农产品物流可持续发展的信用关系

西部地区农产品物流可持续发展的信用关系受到信用风险、交易方式与交易动机的影响。“交易”意义上的西部地区农产品物流可持续发展，西部地区农产品物流与农村经济“交易”的缔约过程本身就是交易双方对“交易风险”的判断过程①，“交易风险”对西部地区农产品物流与农村经济关系构成了重要的影响。在存在信用风险的条件下，西部地区农产品物流需求主体更多地选择参加西部地区农产品物流交易，而西部地区农产品物流供给主体参与交易的约束更加苛刻，将更多地选择退出交易。而“交易”是双方的，任何一方的退出，交易规模都会因此而萎缩。因此，需求主体与供给主体的交易是否达到一定的信用水平对西部地区农产品物流可持续发展非常重要。西部地区农产品物流交易方式、动机对西部地区农产品物流可持续发展构成重要影响，长期交易、关联交易、团队交易、抵押交易更加有助于可持续发展[179,180][123][181]，生产性交易动机比生活性交易动机更有利于可持续发展。

需要特别说明的是：产权是交易的前提，交易在本质上就是产权交换。以上是在产权既定前提下，基于规范的物流交易合约的分析，其基本假设条件是存在一个以自由选择、自愿交换、自愿合作为前提，以分散决策、自发形成、自由竞争为特点的完善的市场；交易合约的达成是交易双方根据自身利益要求和市场竞争规则，通过实力竞争和讨价还价确定下来的，是双方互为约束条件、同时追求收益（或效用）最大化的结果。整个过程体现着平等、自由、理性与互利的契约原则。然而，“互利只是达成有效交易的必要条件，而非充分条件，充分条件是所有权的完整性。”[182]在经济体

① 作为一种缔约过程，由于契约的不完备性、不对称性，以及经营能力、市场风险和自然风险等原因，在合约缔结后存在不能履约的问题，即存在“交易风险”。“交易风险”包括有能力履约而拒绝或部分拒绝履约和由于能力不足而完全或部分不能履约两种类型，前者可称为“信用风险”，由于“经济人”的机会主义行为所致；后者可称为“经营风险”，因经营能力以及不可抗拒的自然或市场风险所致。

制转轨过程中的中国西部农村地区，这一充分条件并不必然地具备，相反，倒是地方政府这一产权边界模糊的“准市场主体”[183]的普遍干预行为带来的政府缺位、越位的尴尬。因此，完善产权制度，规范政府行为，这在西部地区农产品物流与农村经济关系中具有基础性的意义。

（二）西部地区农产品物流可持续发展的微观基础

1. 西部地区农产品物流需求主体的行为特征

依据对西部地区农产品物流需求的分析，西部地区农产品物流需求是指因农村经济发展而直接产生的物流需求。在理论上，政府是提供公共服务的部门，但从西部农村实际情况来看，政府直接参与了农村经济和农产品物流活动。因此，本研究也将其纳入西部地区农产品物流与农村经济交易主体的分析框架，但由于政府的特殊性，对其行为分析将单独进行。以下就按西部地区农产品物流需求主体的构成①，分别分析农户②、农业产业化组织的行为特征。

（1）西部地区农户的农产品物流需求行为分析。农户是分析西部地区农产品物流可持续发展微观机理的逻辑起点[184,185]，当存在要素市场高度发达（生产要素在城乡市场可以自由流动）、要素市场不十分发达（城乡市场处于分割状态）时，西部地区农户的农产品物流需求行为不同。目前，西部农村面临劳动力过剩、资本短缺的实际情况，因此，在不同市场条件下西部地区农户的农产品物流需求行为过程首先表现为劳动力对资本的替代，其相互作用的结果是要素投入对产出增长的贡献为零，产出增长主要依靠技术进步，在农户的农业产出不足以维持农户家庭消费和社会负担需要时，农户首先选择的通过剩余劳动力的非农就业来获得收入，以维持收支平衡；只有市场充分发达，农户才有可能通过运销来扩大生产性投资。在以上情形中，如果农村非农产业不断发展，或跨越城乡市场的成

① 西部地区农产品物流的需求主体就是农村实体经济主体，是由从事农村经济活动的农户，农业产业化组织，以及直接参与农村经济活动的政府构成。

② 严格意义上的农户和农民是有区别的，“中国的社会单元是家庭而不是个人”“家庭结构是一种尊卑等级制，而不是由契约关系决定的个人独立制”（Fair－bank J. K，1980）。因此，在本研究中，农村经济活动的主体是农户，而不是以个体存在的农民，但对农户的讨论，必须以农民为基础进行。农户是农村经济的基础性主体，研究任何农村问题都离不开农户这个基本单位，其行为都是基于特定的文化和外在约束下理性选择的结果，并不是孤立和不变的。

本不断降低，则处于城乡生产要素市场分割，农村非农产业充分发展条件下的生产要素投入水平和生产要素的边际生产率为零时的投入水平之间的实际投入，形成农村生产要素投入的实际水平，向生产要素市场高度发达，劳动和资本可以在城乡市场自由流动时的投入水平靠近；农村生产要素投入的实际价格或收益向城乡经济一体化、市场一体化即市场高度发达，劳动和资本可以在城乡市场自由流动时的生产要素价格靠近；实际产出向生产要素市场高度发达，劳动和资本可以在城乡市场自由流动时的产出水平靠近。可见，农户的经济物流行为受市场发育的影响，同时也受工业化和农村非农产业发展水平、农户家庭消费和社会负担以及思想观念的影响。分析发现，市场发育、非农产业发展、农户思想观念的转变直接决定了西部地区农户的农产品物流需求经济行为。

（2）西部地区农业产业化组织的农产品物流需求行为。农业产业化组织被认为是实现农业现代化的有效形式①，2003 年中国农业产业化组织达到 28 万个，龙头企业 11 万家，销售收入突破 5.7 万亿元，提供的农产品及加工制品占农产品市场供应量的 1/3，占主要城市“菜篮子”产品供给的 2/3 以上。近几年以来，龙头企业在促进农业发展、带动农民增收、保障农产品供给、维护市场稳定方面作用越来越突出，效果越来越明显[186]。在新古典经济学的厂商理论中[187]，农业产业化组织的行为和所有企业一样，被假定为具有人格化的目标函数——追求利润最大化。其行为被看成投入与产出之间的一种技术关系，并没有揭示决定其行为的内部结构。现代企业理论和产业组织理论认为[188-190]：农业产业化组织是一系列契约的有机组合②。农业产业化组织的治理结构（governance structure）直接决定了各自的行为与绩效；而专用性资产（asset specificity）和交易的不确定性的存在，必然会导致契约是不完备的和由此而产生的机会主义（opportunism）行为。所以，非市场或准市场的治理结构就会替代市场，

① 农业产业化组织是指农业产业化过程中出现的，以解决小生产与大市场矛盾为目的，以市场为导向，以利益为纽带，以契约为形式，以农业企业为龙头，以农业生产基地为依托，以农户为基础，将农业产前、产中和产后有机联结起来，克服农业利益被分割的各种农业生产经营一体化的新型组织形式的总称。

② 农业产业化组织是一系列（不完全）契约（合同）的有机组合（nexus of incomplete contracts），是一种以人与人之间的交易关系为基础的契约关系，其行为是一定约束条件下追求效用最大化的企业成员及企业与企业、企业与政府、企业与其他市场交易主体之间博弈的结果。

形成纵向和横向的一体化，一方面表现为农村企业规模扩张，另一方面表现为准市场的即介于市场和企业之间的产业组织形成，农业产业化组织便是这样一种治理结构。而治理结构和交易都是有成本的，成本在多大程度上可以被其收益抵消，取决于交易频率以及在这一过程中所产生的制度安排。频率越高成本越小，收益越大，有效的制度安排越容易形成，市场发育也就越好。频率小的交易只能在企业内部进行。因此，农业产业化组织的形成和规模受制于治理成本与生产成本，而这又与交易频率和促进交易的制度安排有关，其行为取决于其治理结构的有效性①。

2. 西部地区农产品物流供给主体的行为特征

西部地区农产品物流供给主体包括行政物流主体和业务物流主体。前者是指政府的物流管理组织体系和运行机制的总称。包括政府的物流管理当局以及行业性的物流自律机构及其运行机制。后者是指是具体从事物流交易活动的物流组织体系及其运行机制的总称。包括农产品正规物流主体、农产品非正规物流主体，都可以分为营利性和非营利性两种。营利性物流就是经济性物流或产业性物流。既包括正规的经济性物流机构及其运行机制，也包括非正规的营利性物流组织及其运行机制。非营利性物流是指社会性、双向性物流。以下就按西部地区农产品物流供给主体的构成，对这些物流主体分别进行讨论。政府作为行政物流主体，由于其特殊性，将单独进行讨论。

（1）西部地区农产品正规物流主体的行为分析。首先，西部地区农产品正规营利性物流主体。西部地区农产品经济性物流主体。正规营利性物流主体行为除具有前述企业理论所揭示的一般特征及其内在决定机制外，还具有以下独特性。一是以追求利润最大化为目标。二是高度集中。三是主要为较高阶层正规农产品生产企业服务。四是难以充分了解当地农产品物流需求者的信息，面临“逆向选择”与“道德风险”。当

① 这些企业中的农业企业由于农产品生产和加工具有周期长、季节性强，以新、活产品为主，储存、运输、保鲜难，市场风险大，利润率低，但经济社会发展又不可或缺等特点，在一般情况下，需要政策扶持才能得到健康发展。在农业产业化发展过程中，将农户、企业和市场以及生产基地有机联系起来，并按市场要求进行专业化、商品化、标准化和企业化生产。在产业化组织形成的初期，其主要的物流需求是产业化发展的基础设施性的投入和生产规模扩张的需求；产业化形成后，主要是市场扩张、规模化生产、技术进步、基础设施更新改造、企业多元化发展等扩张型物流需求，需要更加高级的现代物流服务与之相适应。

正规物流市场利润与期望收益率之间的关系存在“道德风险”和“逆向选择”时，不仅导致物流配给，进而降低物流市场效率，甚至会导致物流市场消失。五是正规物流主要是依靠制度信任。卢曼（Luhmann）将信任分为人际信任（Interpersonal trust）和制度信任（Institution trust）。前者是以人与人交往建立起的感情联系为基础的信任；后者是以人与人交往中所受到的制度（行为规范、法规纪律等）约束为基础的信任。根据不完全契约理论可以发现，不仅交易契约的达成需要成本，而且契约的维护、执行以及违约后的裁定也都需要成本，履约过程中必然存在机会主义行为，产生制度缺失。必须通过长期交易和反复博弈，才能增强交易双方自我履约的信任机制[191]。西部地区农产品物流需求主体更多的是依赖于人际信任，原因在于中国西部农村总体上仍属于传统社区，农户流动性不大，行为受传统道德约束。比较注重声誉，社区范围的交易具有典型的“人格化”特征，主要受非正规制度约束。但超出社区这种自我履约机制就失去效率，必须凭借正式制度约束。其次，西部地区农产品正规非营利性物流主体。第一，西部地区农产品社会性物流主体。西部地区农产品物流市场在西部地区农产品物流资源配置中，由于竞争不充分和西部地区农产品物流机构本身的特性，不能有效地配置物流资源，存在着“西部地区农产品物流市场失灵”。农产品社会性物流主体存在的前提：首先是提供“公共物流产品”①。其次是为弱势群体的物流需求提供供给②。在西部地区农产品社会性物流存在的情况下，社会性投资主体往往优先获得农产品社会性物流资源③。但农产品社会性物流并非是纯公共物品（即萨缪尔森意义上的具有非排他性和非竞争性的物品

① 主要是包括为保障农户收入稳定及增长、促进农村基础设施改善、维护农村社会稳定、保障农产品安全、推进农业战略性结构调整、促进农业科技推广和农村企业产品升级换代、推进农村工业化和乡村城市化而产生的物流需求提供物流服务。

② 从农产品物流需求主体来看，这里的弱势群体的物流需求主要是指农村贫困户、农村中小企业、农业产业化的龙头企业的物流需求。

③ 根据政府的干预目标，农产品社会性物流资源往往被社会性投资主体优先获得。经济性投资又可称为产业性投资，是以经济效益为主要决策目标的投资，一般由各投资主体在竞争的市场环境中自主进行。社会性投资则是以社会效益为主要决策目标的投资，一般处在国民经济优先发展的领域或者公共产品的生产领域，其经济的内在收益率大都明显低于竞争性生产领域，往往投资激励不足。但该类投资在维护国民经济的稳定运行、保护幼稚产业或者提供公共服务等方面表现出较高的社会效益。

和服务），而是一种准公共物品（介于纯私人物品和纯公共物品之间，既具有排他性又具有竞争性的物品和服务）。西部地区农产品社会性物流主体所承担的功能可以通过市场机制来解决。西部地区农产品社会性物流主体行为特征如下。一是不以追求利润最大化为目标，实现政府赋予的政策支农任务。二是资金来源具有一定的政府性。三是农产品社会性物流主体行为内在地存在“道德风险”、“委托—代理”成本偏高性[192]。第二，西部地区农产品双向性物流主体。西部地区农产品双向性物流主体的行为特征概括为：一是组织上实行自愿原则。二是管理上实行民主原则。三是经营上实行互助原则。四是分配上实行经营利润按公共积累、按交易量返还盈利、股息分红、弥补亏损原则。本研究认为：这种发展趋势已经超出了双向物流的范围，而异化为营利性或经济性物流。因此，双向物流作为一种特殊的物流形式，追求的是社区性或者说是社区的社会效益的特性。它具有由经济主体自发形成，自愿组合的特点，与中国计划经济时期形成的国有或集体所有物流也有本质区别。在西部地区农产品物流市场中处于弱势地位的农村经济主体有效的自觉、自主、自立、自助的物流组织形式是农产品双向性物流，因此，西部地区农产品双向性物流必须采取符合合作制原则的组织形式，形成有效的双向物流制度。

（2）西部地区农产品非正规物流主体的行为分析。农产品非正规物流，同样可以分为营利性和非营利性两种。由于非正规物流中的非营利性物流供给主体行为是由维护社会公平、救助弱势群体等理念驱使的，具有超出一般“理性”范围的特征，在西部地区农产品物流中只能起辅助和补充作用。因此，在这里只分析营利性非正规物流的行为特点。西部地区农产品非正规物流主体的行为特征概括为：一是交易手续方便简洁、组织结构简单灵活。二是交易分散性强且本地化特点显著。三是多采用互助性物流，往往都有比较密切的社会关系①。由“囚徒困境”可知，这种硬约束②

① 这种关系可能来自宗族、血缘、社区、职业、年龄或宗教等，相互了解程度远远大于物流机构和客户之间的关系。能够克服“道德风险”和“逆向选择”，减少“搭便车”的机会，降低风险，提高物流配置效率。

② 在法律约束之外，只遵循双方自愿达成的交易规则，当出现违规时，违约方会因不守信用，遭到谴责、排斥，而身名狼藉，甚至可能丧失自己的财产、劳动力、社会地位，乃至生命受到暴力伤害。尽管这些行为被法律所禁止，但法律往往只能对行为后果发挥作用，难以介入其过程。因而，对违规者而言是一种硬约束。

可以限制机会主义，促进信用关系的改善和信用体系的建立①。农产品非正规物流因拥有正规物流所不具备的特征，而具有某些效率优势和存在与发展的空间。但必须注意，农产品非正规物流行为存在明显的局限：一是难以满足农村经济发展的大规模物流需求。二是分流了农产品正规物流的物流资源，在一定程度上制约了正规物流发展，弱化了物流政策效应。三是由于缺少正规制度约束，一旦无序发展，会导致大量纠纷，容易引发危机和一系列社会问题，加大农村经济、社会的运行成本。四是农产品非正规物流导致物流交易过程中的税收流失。五是只能在特定区域发生作用，在分割的小规模市场中才具有竞争性，由于跨市场的交易成本非常高，所以资源配置的范围和能力十分有限。因此，农产品非正规物流存在的种种局限，在经济发展中应加以引导和予以规范。

3. 西部地区农产品物流发展中的政府行为

(1) 经济体制与政府行为。在传统的国家理论中，在阶级分析的视野中，在主流经济学分析框架中，在以现代西方民主为核心的国家理论中，以公共选择理论为代表的现代国家理论中分别论述了“政府”概念[193,194]。判断西部地区农产品物流与农村经济关系并做出反应的只能是中央政府，其调节也只能通过“命令—服从”的行政手段和依靠层层委托—代理关系建立起来的经济计划来进行[195]，各级地方政府和农村经济与西部地区农产品物流主体只能是贯彻和落实计划、完成计划任务。就西部地区农产品物流与农村经济关系而言，在市场经济条件下，政府行为的意义在于履行纠正西部地区农产品物流与农村经济关系中“市场失灵”的政府职能。依据市场经济理论的逻辑和西部地区农产品物流的特点，西部地区农产品物流与农村经济关系中的政府行为，应限制在为西部地区农产品物流和农村经济主体创造最合适的竞争环境的范围以内。对经济体制“转型”而言，最重要的就是政府—市场的动态关系。因此，不仅建立关于市场经济的共识，推进市场经济体制的建立和完善，自然成为政府行为的重要内容[196]。而且，伴随市场经济体制的建立和完善，市场行为将逐步替代政府那些超出纠正“市场失灵”范围

① 提高履约的可靠性，并具有既让有违约倾向的交易者望而却步，又限制了根本不具备物流能力的人进入物流市场的示范效应，从而促进了信用关系的改善和信用体系的建立。社区的约束力越强，履约率就越高，以便长期保持稳定的物流关系。

的行为。但在这一过程中，政府必须在保持新旧体制有效衔接，防止出现体制“真空”带来混乱的前提下，积极主动地退出属于市场行为的领域，保持政府行为与市场行为有效配合与协调持续，自然成为政府行为的重要内容，并显得尤其重要。因此，在西部地区农产品物流可持续发展中，适时地判断市场经济的发育程度，界定政府行为在西部地区农产品物流与农村经济中的作用领域、方式和程度，包括政府退出的领域、方式和程度，对西部地区农产品物流可持续发展具有深刻的影响和十分重要的意义。

（2）分层治理与政府行为。在分层治理结构中，中央政府由于直接面对外部竞争压力和内部政治、经济和社会发展的需求，不仅自然地承担经济发展职能，而且还是政府行为最终的无限责任承担者。由于农业和农村经济与工业化的内在联系，以及物流在现代经济中的核心地位，使得中央政府在推进工业化过程中，不得不考虑如何保持农业和农村经济发展与工业化相协调持续的问题，防止落入“李嘉图陷阱”[197]。在物流发展方面，既要利用物流促进经济发展，实现政府目标，又要保持物流稳定，避免物流障碍。而农村经济发展，离不开农产品物流发展。因此，西部地区农产品物流可持续发展也必然被列入中央政府行为的目标函数之中。此外，由于实现分层治理，中央政府必须把经济发展的目标，层层具体落实到地方政府，并下放相应的权力和资源，给予必要的激励，形成过渡时期中国地方政府推动经济增长的主体格局，造就目前中国特有的以地方行政利益为边界的市场竞争关系和经济增长方式。从这一意义上讲，包括农村经济在内的经济发展目标，要通过层层分解，下放给地方政府的水平分层治理结构去实施。但是，由于物流的“核心地位”“规模经济”的内在要求、系统的内在脆弱性，以及物流风险的扩散性，中央政府必须建立起独立于地方政府的垂直物流监管和控制系统，以保持物流稳定和对经济发展的宏观调控能力，即包括西部地区农产品物流在内的物流发展是通过垂直分层治理结构实施的。因此，在西部地区农产品物流与农村经济关系中，中央政府和地方政府职能并不对称。“政府”作用在本研究中西部地区农产品物流需求和供给的行为主体并不完全一致。前者主要是各级地方政府的农村经济行政管理部门，后者主要是独立于地方政府的中央政府各级物流监管当局。在分层治理中，保持垂直治理的农产品行政物流主体和水平治理的农村实体经济管理部门相互间的行为协调持续性，对西部地区农产品物流可持续发展尤为重要。最后需要强调的是，在市场经济条件下，西部地区农产品物流与农村经济关系中的政府行为，是通过建立在市场制度基础上的农业和农村产业政策及相关物流政策来实施的，其有效程度取决于制度和政策制定与执行者的态度和人力资本。因此，加强人力资本投入，形成学习机制，真正行使政府职能对西部地区农产品物流可持续发展同样重要。

第四章　农产品物流可持续发展的国际经验借鉴与启示

"他山之石，可以攻玉"，"攻玉"的过程就是借助他人经验帮助自身不断完善的过程。本章以美国、加拿大、法国、荷兰、日本为发达的市场经济国家的代表，以韩国、中国台湾为新兴的市场经济国家（地区）的代表，并按北美农产品物流模式、欧盟农产品物流模式、东亚农产品物流模式的地区分布，分别介绍这些国家（地区）农产品物流可持续发展的实践，总结其成功的经验，探索其机制与模式及其成长的路径，进一步检验并丰富和深化农产品物流可持续发展的理论框架，为构建中国西部地区农产品物流可持续发展机制和模式提供借鉴和启示。

第一节　北美农产品物流可持续发展的典型——农产品物流可持续发展的北美模式

一　北美发达国家农产品物流可持续发展概况

美国农业人口不足3%，之所以能拥有世界上最大、最强和最现代化的市场农业，与美国政府高度重视农业发展，强调物流与农业可持续发展密不可分[198]，政府的支持性政策使美国农产品物流得到快速发展。美国城乡经济高度市场化、一体化，农产品物流可持续发展主要表现在以下领域。

（一）政府政策支持及完备的法律法规

19 世纪初，美国农产品的运销就开始采用现代期货交易①，最早出现的农产品销售合作社至今已近 200 年，美国农场主合作社的发展经历了一个发生、发展和壮大的过程[199]。第一阶段是美国农业实现商品化的时期（1810 年—1870 年），主要任务是解决农产品的销售。一些州先后通过了立法，为农场主合作社合法化和以后的发展铺平了道路。第二阶段是农业机械化蓬勃发展的时期（1870 年—1890 年），1867 年美国农业陷入了第一次危机，出现了“格兰其”和“农场主联盟”两个保护农场主利益的社团②，但当时的大多数合作社并没有因此成功的。第三阶段是 20 世纪初内燃机为美国农业机械化带来革命性影响的时期（1890 年—1930 年），经历了 1920 年沙皮洛运动③，1922 年美国国会通过的卡帕—沃尔斯坦德法④、1929 年美国爆发了历史上最严重的经济危机后通过的农产品销售法⑤对美国农场主合作社的发展具有重要意义。第四阶段是合并和提高效率的时期（1930 年至今），随着农场主供应与销售合作社的发生与发展，其他各类农场主合作社也迅速发展了起来⑥。

---

① 美国现代期货交易始于 19 世纪初，并同芝加哥的商业发展和中西部的谷物交易密切相关。由于芝加哥位于五大湖的下端，紧靠中西部肥沃的农业区，自然这一战略位置使它迅速发展成美国谷物集散地。芝加哥期货交易所现在已经是世界农产品价格的形成中心，对全世界的农产品价格都有导向作用。

② “格兰其”（1867 年成立）和“农场主联盟”（1873 年成立），在它们的支持下纷纷成立农场主合作社。到 1890 年，全国大约有 1000 多个合作社组织，但是当时的合作社大多由于管理不善、内部分裂和资本缺乏等原因而很快失败了，只有少数是比较成功的。

③ 1920 年，美国农场局联盟召集主要来自中西部、东部合作社代表开会，加州几个农场主合作社的律师阿隆·沙皮洛建议成立一个强有力的高度集中的垄断性合作社，使它能控制整个作物的 90% 以上，以便于管制价格。

④ 卡帕—沃尔斯坦德法规定，凡是符合：①不管合作社成员在合作社中拥有多少股份每个只能有一票表决权，且合作社每年分配给社员的红利不超过 8%；②为非社员的服务量不超过为社员服务的总量的条件，农场主合作社都可以避免受谢尔曼反托拉斯法条文的限制。从而在法律上为农场主合作社开了绿灯。在以后的一段时间里，农场主合作社进行了整顿，不仅合作社的规模扩大了，而且合作社数目也有了较大的发展。

⑤ 法律规定，成立农场局，拨款 5 亿美元，向合作社提供贷款，鼓励他们建造仓库，储存剩余农产品以控制供应。但由于经济危机的加深而归于失败，不过合作社却得到较大的发展，1931 年合作社数目增加到 11950 个，社员人数达到 300 万人，营业额总共达到 24 亿美元。

⑥ 1955 年降至 1 万个以下，1970 年为 7790 个，1981 年只有 6211 个。但就社员人数而言，在 20 世纪 50 年代中期以前总的趋势是增加的，1956 年达到 773 万人。以后逐年减少，到 1981 年社员人数减少为 534 万人，并继续呈现减少的趋势。

表 4－1 1997 年美国农产品物流流量情况①

商品类别	货值（亿美元）	货运量（百万吨）	周转量（亿吨公里）	平均运输距离（英里）
粮食谷物	596	490	2001	125
饲料	668	220	468	79
活动物、活鱼	62	6	15	272
其他农产品	1023	202	808	438
肉、鱼海鲜及制品	1838	79	364	137
面粉、面包等	1099	103	485	122
食品及油脂	3464	397	1241	127
烟草	564	4	10	296
化肥	273	179	436	116
合计	9587	1680	5828	1712

资料来源：根据美国统计局（U. S. Census Bureau）《1997 运输商品流量调查》，1999. 12. 09。

多年来，美国纷纷通过政府制定相关政策、法律法规和制度规范促进农产品物流发展。美国制定《商品交易法案》②，通过政府对市场的规范限定了农产品的物流渠道，甚至依靠法律力量对农产品的物流模式进行强行规定，增强了对物流渠道的管理，减少了农产品流通过程中的盲目性和随意性，减少了农产品物流的社会总成本。为了适应现代物流的发展需要，2005 年，美国制定了《国家运输科技发展战略》③，美国不断通过政府宏观政策的引导，确立以现代物流发展带动社会经济发展的战略目标。同时，高度重视农产品质量安全。为了确保农产品安全和市场秩序，北美国家均把农产品安全管理放到了突出的位置，非常注重通过法律法规加强农业的标准化管理，在标准化生产方面逐步完善了相应的法规。如美国颁布了《联邦鸡蛋生产检验法》《饲料法》《肥料法》《鱼类检验法》等三十多部联邦法律法规以及各地方的法律法规，以确保农产品安全和市场秩序，也为国外农产品进入美国市场建立了坚实的技术壁垒。在加强农产品

① 1997 年美国国内物流流量按货物价值计算农产品排在第五位以后，其原因是农产品的价值小，尤其是附加值小于其他工业品。但是，如果按运输周转量计算，农产品中的粮食物流排在第二位、食品和油脂排在第四；按承运量计算粮食排在第五位。可见在美国农产品物流仍然是较为重要的物流资源。

② 美国制定《商品交易法案》，对商品流通的每一个环节进行规范。随着经济的发展，1974 年美国又对该法案进行了较大的修改，到 1992 年又进行了四次修订补充，其中把靠不公开情报进行内幕交易定为重罪。

③ 规定交通产业结构或交通科技进步的总目标是："建立安全、高效、充足和可靠的运输系统，其范围是国际性的，形式是综合性的，特点是智能性的，性质是环境友善的。"

安全管理方面，美国联邦政府相关部门及机构依法行使监督职能，各项职责非常明确，监督分工十分具体。如食品安全检验服务局，主要检验其生产的鱼类、谷类以及动植物类产品是否符合质量标准要求。环保署严格监督生产环节中是否对空气、水源、土壤等生态环境构成污染，对没有达到标准或违规的生产者进行严厉的处罚[200-205]；同时，在监督中强调科学性、公开性和透明度，建立有序的预防机制，从而构筑了较为完善的农产品质量安全管理体系，确保了美国农产品具有很高的质量安全水平和很好的公众信任度[206]。加拿大建立了职责划分清楚、目标明确、协同管理效果良好的农产品质量安全管理体制，重视农产品质量安全检测检验体系的建设，不断完善农产品品种、质量等级、化肥农药残留物、检验检疫、农业生产技术规程、农业投入品、农产品加工运输储存等物流环节的标准体系，强化对大宗谷物、农业投入品与农产品的质量安全监管。加拿大在加强农产品质量安全管理的同时，还非常注重对生产者、农产品经营者进行农产品标准化管理以及关键技术深入宣传、培训和教育，争取相关利益主体的参与和支持。加拿大企业在收购农产品时，往往与农场主签订合同，提出要求，如不得在农产品中掺杂任何化学物质、不得虐待牲畜等。例如，加拿大的 Wendy's International 公司（快餐连锁店）就向农场主提出要善待动物的特殊要求，并通过审计来检查是否满足了上述标准[207]。

（二）发达的农产品物流体系

1. 发达的农产品物流公共设施

美国政府在促进农产品物流发展过程中十分注重发挥公共基础设施服务农业的作用，并且不断优化基础设施网点布局和改造。美国拥有十分完备的公路、铁路以及水运交通运输设施，公路遍布城乡且呈现网状结构，能够便利地通往农村地区的每家每户；铁路运输十分方便，一些农产品收购站和仓库、加工厂建有专门的铁路线。美国的通信设施和网络发达，储运设备的机械化水平高，仅粮食的装卸设备就有螺旋式输送机、可移式胶带输送机及低运载量斗式提升机等。发达的物流基础设施和设备为美国农产品物流的有效组织提供了便利，为高效农产品物流提供了稳定的基础[208]。

2. 专业化的农产品物流主体

美国农产品物流主体主要是农场主与生产合作社，农产品物流主体的组织化、专业化、规模化程度较高，已经形成了一个完整的农场主合作社体系。全美约有150多万个农场主参加了美国农场主联盟和农业联合会，还有众多农户参加了不同类型的农业生产与销售合作社。根据美国1983年《农业统计》的资料，美国的农场主合作社分为供销合作社、服务性合作社和生产性合作社三类。其中每类都包括供销合作社、运销合作社、供给合作社若干种不同的合作社[209]。

3. 完善的农产品配送系统

美国有着发达的交通网、完善的服务体系和配送系统、先进的保鲜设备和快速的信息处理网络①，为农产品实现货畅其流创造了良好的条件[210]。通过使用条形码技术建立的追踪系统已广泛在农产品物流配送系统中使用，绝大部分包装食品和大宗物品（袋装橘子、苹果）使用条形码（bar code）帮助企业收集销售信息，这些条形码的设计让企业知道自己食品供应链的物流流出状况和模式，借此来对供应链上游物流的流入进行有效管理。除此之外，一些企业发展了基于质量安全的食品供应链的高新技术回溯（tracing）系统，比如农场主使用电子耳标识和相关数据收集卡来追踪食品或农产品的免疫记录、健康记录和饲养记录等[211]。这些基于食品供应链的信息能使食品或农产品在市场中得以实现其质量的价格。

4. 发达的农产品加工体系

美国把农产品的贮藏、保鲜、加工放在农业发展的首位，非常重视农产品加工及其深度利用技术，如美国的马铃薯和玉米深加工技术。20世纪70年代以来，美国的保鲜规模达70%[212]。冷链技术的发展使得发达国家的蔬菜、水果等生鲜农产品可以一直处于采摘后生理需要的低温状态，并形成特有的冷链物流，即农产品在田间采摘后按预冷—冷库—冷藏车运输—批发站冷库—超市冷柜—消费者冰箱的路径流动，因而，发达国家的蔬菜、水果等生鲜类农产品在物流环节的损耗率仅为1%—2%[213]。

（三）完善的物流金融市场环境

1. 农村合作金融体系

美国农村合作信贷体系成立于20世纪初叶。从19世纪来到20世纪30年代，特别是受20世纪30年代经济大危机的冲击，农产品过剩成为

---

① 在美国，农产品有78.5%是由产地通过配送中心直接到达零售店，农产品物流环节少、速度快、成本低、效率高。

美国农业发展的最大障碍，根据美国有关农业信贷的法律规定，支持和保护农业生产和农民利益的三家合作性质的政策性银行（联邦土地银行系统、联邦中期信贷银行系统、农村合作银行系统）相继在全美12个农业信贷区成立①。为了促进农村合作金融的发展，美国采取了不同于商业银行的管理模式，建立了由监管机制、行业自律协会、资金融通清算中心和互助保险集团构成的，目标一致、职能各异、相互独立、互为一体的农村合作金融管理体系。有力地支持了农产品物流，保证了农业生产资料供应、扩大了农产品销售、促进了农产品出口、开展了与农产品物流有关的业务活动的设备贷款、经营贷款、商品贷款。

2. 农村政策性金融体系

虽然，美国农村合作金融早期具有明显的政策性金融特征，但现代美国农村政策性金融主要是由20世纪30年代经济危机期间，为应付农业危机而形成的专门的农村政策性金融系统来实施，美国农村政策性金融机构主要包括农民家计局、商品信贷公司、农村电气化管理局与中小企业管理局以及农业政策性保险机构组成。由于美国农业保险具有其自身特殊性，本章将专门论述。这些农村政策性金融体系具有显著、强烈的政策性，缓和了农产品过剩危机，有力地支持了农产品物流。在提供贷款和支付补贴方面实行政府干预，对农场所有权贷款、经营支出贷款、为弥补自然灾害损失发放紧急贷款。此外，还对商业银行和其他金融机构向农民发放的贷款提供担保，并补贴由此而产生的利差。在农产品销售和生产方面实行政府调节，为小企业发展提供管理咨询和技术协助等服务，对促进包括小农场在内的小企业发展极为重要。

3. 农业保险体系

美国在农作物保险立法之前，曾进行了40多年的实践和研究，最终形成了一个在法律规范下，政府和民间相互协作，强制保险与自愿保险相结合，由政府政策支持，并给予经营管理费和保险费补贴，美国政府的联邦农作物保险公司（FCIC）和私营保险公司、农作物保险协会等共同参与开办、商业化运营的农业保险模式。

（1）美国农业保险组织体系

美国农业保险组织体系由政府、公司、行业协会组成，在功能上可以

① 由联邦政府的农业信贷管理局（Farm Credit Ad - ministration）领导、监督和管理，政策制定机构是联邦农业信贷委员会（Federal Farm Credit Board）。

划分为联邦农作物保险公司、有经营农作物保险资格的私营保险公司、农作物保险代理人和农险勘查核损人员三个层次及其支撑系统，是一个承担了从政策研究、立法论证、组织机构设置、产品设计开发，到保险品种销售、定损、统计、精算，以及相关宣传、推广和教育等职能的、分工明确、各司其职的完整系统。

（2）美国农业保险品种体系

美国农作物保险的主要险种有：多种风险农作物保险、团体风险保险、收入保险、冰雹险、其他险种。

（3）美国农业保险制度体系

美国农业保险制度包括法律和政策两部分。《联邦农作物保险法》《1994 年农作物保险改革法》等法律，为农作物保险的目的、性质、原则、开展办法和机构设置等提供了法律依据和保障。美国政府的农业保险政策，包括经济支持、再保险支持、补贴与免税等四个方面。

以上分析可以看出，在政府政策支持及完备的法律法规保护下，美国建立了发达的农产品物流体系、完善的物流金融市场环境，以农产品运销为主要内容，与美国农业发展相适应的农产品物流体系，构建了以政府可持续为主导，市场可持续为基础，政府、企业和民间相互配合，多种可持续手段综合运用，不同可持续主体分工明确，功能完善、行为规范的农产品物流可持续发展模式。美国农业高度发达，一些从事农产品生产、加工、销售一体化经营的大型国际化农业公司和农场，具备了接受经济性农产品物流服务的条件，不仅可以而且必须依靠经济性农产品物流机构提供的运输、存储、装卸搬运、包装、配送、流通加工、信息服务以及银行、保险、期货等现代农产品物流服务。但由于农业资金占用周期长、金额小、利率低、空间分散的特点，与经济性农产品物流机构的利润最大化目标不相吻合，加上经济性农产品物流在空间上远离农村，对农产品物流交易监督成本高，美国的经济性农产品物流同样难以满足整个农业发展的要求，尤其是农村广大中小型农业公司和农场的物流需求。为弥补经济农产品物流供给不足，美国政府依法发展了以农产品双向性和社会性物流为主体的农产品物流体系。农产品双向性物流是美国实施农业政策的重要物流渠道。农产品社会性物流按照政府的政策，提供诸如新创业农区、农产品销售、价格支持、农村社区发展等，其他经济物流机构不愿意或不能提供的长期资助物流。随着美国农产品物流制度不断完善，逐渐在北美农村经济发展中形成了以农产品双向物流为主体，以农产品社会物流为保障，以农产品经济物流为补充的“合同”一体化农产品物流模式。

二　北美发达国家农村经济发展中的“合同”一体化物流模式

以美国、加拿大为代表的北美模式是以“合同制”形式①将农产品的生产、供应、销售等环节有机地结合起来的农产品一体化物流模式[214]。

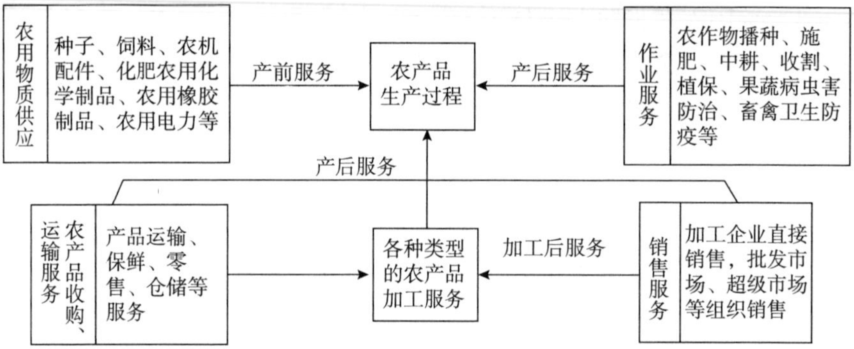

图4－1　以“合同制”为主体的产销一体化物流模式

资料来源：罗必良，《农产品流通体制改革：制度变迁与模式选择》，http：//xy. scau. edu. cn：8080/jingguan/zhidu/upload…179K，2006－9－13。

（一）横向一体化：“合同”联合体物流模式

“合同”联合体是“面对面”地签订合同，也被称为垂直的综合企业②，“合同”联合体物流采用期货交易模式[215]，其主要特点是：①农场主与私人工商企业均保持经济上、法律上的独立性，农场主与私人工商企业通

① 从1960年到1980年，这种一体化的农产品物流组织所创造的产值在美国农业总产值中的比重由25%上升到31%。1969年为美国农业提供服务的公司只有32565家，1975年增至4万家，1985年6.4万家，1987年达7.6万家。这种“合同制”的农产品物流模式中最为重要的是农业“合同”联合体物流模式、农场主合作社物流模式及农商联合体物流模式。

② “合同”联合体是北美国家农产品物流普遍采用的形式，实质上就是把农产品产供销的所有环节或其中的几个环节置于统一的领导之下，这也被称为垂直的综合企业。它一般是由一体化的产前和产后部门，尤其是食品加工部门构成的市场部门，通过与农场主签订协作合同，将产、销联合为一个有机的整体而形成的产供销一体化合同销售模式。一般来说，合同制农产品物流组织主要盛行于那些专业化、集约化程度较高，产品易腐又不易运输或产品用于大规模工业加工的农业部门。

过合同方式明确双方的权利和义务，构成合同制契约组织[216]。②农产品生产的合同销售从本质上讲属于期货交易，通常是农场主根据合同决定种植或养殖什么品种及其面积或数量[217]。③合同内容规范、标准。一般情况下，合同都会明确规定商品的品种、数量、种植或养殖的要求、价格、交货时间与地方、交易方式等等。农场主依合同生产出的农产品直接由签合同的加工企业或批发市场等收购。农场主通过合同方式明确与农业合作社之间、与私人公司之间、与各种行业管理委员会之间的权利和义务，以保证农产品的销路或收购。这在相当程度上避免了农场主生产的盲目性，增强了市场交易运行的有序性，能够有效地保证农产品供需平衡和价格稳定，从而减少农场主、农产品加工和销售者的市场风险，因而这种模式成为美国、加拿大农产品物流运行的有效模式之一[218-221]。

表 4-2　　美国“合同”联合体物流的区域分布情况①

主营物流类型	地理分布	典型特点
牧草乳酪物流区	东北部和滨湖各州	牛奶生产为中心，占全国 1/2
玉米物流州	北纬 40—45 度间	玉米占全国 3/4，养畜业占 2/3
小麦物流州	中部平原西部地区	春、冬小麦和牧草轮作
棉花物流州	美国东南部	棉花、水稻、甘蔗种植较多
山地放牧物流区	落基山高原山地区	粗放的专业化牧区
水果蔬菜物流区	太平洋沿岸南部	商品菜产量占全国 1/3

资料来源：赵勤，《中国现代农业物流问题研究》，东北林业大学博士论文，2006 年，第42～45 页。

（二）市场中介：农场主合作社物流模式

农场主合作社是“背对背”地由各种市场中介来联系。美国、加拿大是典型的人少地多、家庭农场占绝大多数的国家。1982 年，美国个人或家庭经营的农场占美国农场总数的 89%，如果把其他形式的家庭经营计算在内，以家庭为单位经营的农场占农场总数的 95%[222]。加拿大 2006 年农场总数约为 25.4 万个，其中 91.5% 是个人及家庭所有[223]。为了解

① 美国畜牧业合同化组织程度高于种植业，而在种植业中用于工业加工的易腐的又不便运输的蔬菜、水果、马铃薯、甜菜和甘蔗等经济作物生产的合同化组织程度又较谷物种植业为高。1980 年美国的合同销售占种植业销售额的 14%，牲畜产品的 38%，甜菜、加工蔬菜、柑橘分别达到 98%、85%、65%，鲜牛奶和肉鸡高达 89%。

决单个农场难以办到的问题，就需要各种非营利的合作社提供各种服务，有效沟通农户与政府之间、农户与市场之间的关系，通过批发市场、期货市场、集贸市场、超级市场等进行市场交换，以降低产品生产成本。这种合作社的经营目标不是获取合作组织的利润最大化，而是通过为其成员服务，使参加者从合作经营中获取最大收益。其典型特征如图4－2所示。

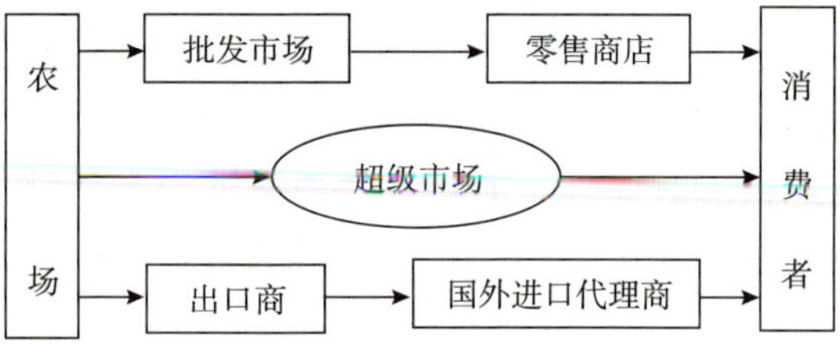

图4－2　美国农产品物流运行流程

1. 以销售和加工合作社为主

2001年，美国共有3229个农业合作社，其中约有2000个是农产品销售合作社[224]；加拿大2006年有农业销售合作社169个，萨斯客彻温省的小麦销售合作社就拥有6万名社员，其销售的小麦占全省小麦总产量的60%[225]。农产品合作社是农场主参与农产品物流、走向市场的重要依托①。

2. 以专业性与规模性强为基础

美国农田产业公司拥有遍及美国19个州、占全美农户总数1/5的成员，同时负责销售成员谷物达到25%—30%；美国中、西部150个粮食仓储中心出口量占美国粮食出口量的30%[226]；加拿大共有各类合作社7683个，合作社企业146785个，涉及农业、消费、金融、信用、保险、医疗和住宅等诸多领域。在加拿大2730万人的总人口中，有1530万人是合作社社员，合作社生产的牛奶占国内市场的66%，乳制品占20%，谷物和种子占51%，牲畜、家禽占48%，食品占51%[227]。

3. 以政府的政策支持为主导

为支持农产品合作社的发展，美国政府在法律、财税、金融及组织方

① 农产品销售合作社的主要功能是提供农产品加工和销售服务，同时为家庭农场主提供市场价格信息服务。它们在各个地区都拥有大量的谷物转运站（仓库），专门负责玉米、大豆、小麦等农产品的储存、加工和销售。同时，农产品合作社每天向各地的转运站发布现货基差和收购价格信息，而转运站则通过网络为每个家庭农场主提供现货和期货的价格信息服务。

面给予了各种优惠和扶持。建立了农业信贷合作体系，提供赋税的各种减免待遇等。在加拿大，联邦政府还设立了专门分管合作社事务的合作社秘书处，在投资、税收方面给予合作社优惠政策；设立投资局，对合作社投资项目提供需要的资金支持[228]。在政府政策支持下，美国、加拿大的农场主合作社发展迅猛。

（三）纵向一体化：农工商联合体物流模式

20 世纪 50 年代以后，随着农业生产专业化、社会化的发展形成了美国、加拿大农工商联合体物流模式[229,230]。通常是工商业企业直接介入农业，把农业生产资料的制造、供应和农业生产紧密结合起来，并通过农产品加工、储运及流通配送等环节的有机结合，进而形成纵向一体化的综合经营模式[231]。这种模式被称为综合农产品物流模式，也叫垂直一体化物流模式。其典型性特征是：单一经济实体能够提供集仓储、运输、包装、装卸、流通加工、配送和信息处理等多种功能服务，减少了中间环节，加快了农产品进入加工领域和投放市场的速度①。这类企业数量虽然不多，但拥有自己的庞大销售集团和网络系统，资本集中度相当高。美国通过立法限制农工商联合体企业从事农产品物流活动②，保护了家庭农场。

第二节 欧盟农产品物流可持续发展的典型——农产品物流可持续发展的欧盟模式

一 欧盟发达国家农产品物流可持续发展概况

与北美发达国家农产品物流发展的特点相比，欧盟的农业生产规模相对较小，以法国、德国、荷兰为代表的欧盟农产品物流可持续发展主要表

① 如美国的嘉吉公司，其经营范围涉及农用生产物资的供应，粮食的生产、加工、销售。嘉吉公司与大陆粮食公司、邦济公司、路易斯·德莱福斯公司、安德烈公司和加纳克粮食公司等五家大粮食私营贸易公司的粮油出口就占了全美的 60% 左右。

② 1974 年美国农业普查资料表明，当时农工商联合体企业仅占全美农场总数的 1.7%，但用地面积却占了 10.6%，农产品销售额占 18.2%。到了 1982 年，美国农业普查资料显示上述三个指标分别提高到 2.5%、16.3%、23.9%。

现在以下领域。

（一）政府政策支持及完备的法律法规

法国、德国、荷兰政府高度重视农业发展，农产品物流的快速发展来自于政府政策支持及完备的法律法规。荷兰对农产品物流配送中心的企业给予资金支持或贷款贴息，制定了标准的农产品生产链，建立了专业化程度很高的生产资料供应商、购销商与农户紧密连接的农产品购销体系。同时，法国、德国、荷兰高度重视农产品质量安全。德国农产品保鲜物流行业有关的规定和技术标准。

1. 食品卫生规定《EGNr. 852/2004》

这是一个将欧盟发布的食品安全指令转化为国家法律规定的文件，对食品的卫生标准做出了明确规定。为了保证食品安全，该文件对食品生产、加工和流通的每一个环节都有严格规定和具体要求。

2. 德国安全标准《GSl》

这是南欧洲贸易研究所和工商界一起制定的标准[①]，在物流程序中如何对保鲜产品进行交接也有详细说明。从农产品保鲜物流的专业来看，《GSl》是一部针对性很强的、颇具操作性的安全技术标准。

3. 德国工业标准《DIN》10508 和 8959

前者对食品的环境温度进行规范，对运输中的冷藏冷冻制定基础性标准；后者对使用的运输手段列有温控标准。荷兰具有完善的农产品安全管理体系，该体系由三部分共同构成：第一部分是农业、自然管理和渔业部；第二部分是健康、卫生、体育部；第三部分是一些专业协会[②]。各部

---

① 德国安全标准《GSl》主要罗列了易腐的肉类制品、鲜肉和香肠在运输中的法定冷藏标准和测试条件，对保鲜物流系统中的各阶段都提出具体的温控要求。对上述商品的各种运输工具也有专门的规定，包括容器和托盘等。

② 农业、自然管理和渔业部主要负责农产品生产过程中的安全标准政策制定、动植物和动植物产品生产和销售的检测和监测、农业生产和市场流通链的质量卫生控制，食品污染物、兽药、饲料添加剂、农药等的监测体系建设与发展，动物疾病控制以及农产品质量风险分析、风险管理等。健康、卫生、体育部下设了专门负责食品质量安全管理的总巡查员机构及若干地区分支机构，主要负责农产品质量安全法律建议、计算机信息处理、人力资源培训、食品检测、兽医指导、宣传、管理和质量控制、农产品质量安全终审投诉的处理和电话调查等工作。独立机构和专业协会包括农药授权委员会、荷兰奶制品委员会、荷兰肉类委员会和动物饲料生产委员会等，通过相关信息收集与统计、质量规则制定和市场规则执行，对农产品质量起到重要的管理监测作用。

分职责分工明确，相互协作，已建立起主要农产品质量控制体系，包括：GMP① 饲料的质量控制体系；IKB②、ISO、GMP 和 HACCP 猪肉的质量控制体系；GMP 和 KKM③ 奶制品的质量控制体系。

（二）发达的农产品物流体系

1. 发达的农产品物流公共设施及布局合理的物流网点

法国、德国、荷兰政府在促进农产品物流发展过程中都十分注重发挥公共基础设施服务农业的作用，并且不断优化基础设施网点布局和改造。荷兰的铁路、海运和公路运输发达便利，并且拥有非常合理的大规模农产品批发市场布局④。

2. 完善的农产品配送系统

法国、德国、荷兰农业的发展依靠高质量的农产品物流管理系统。德国有非常发达的农产品保鲜物流信息共享平台[232,233]。①德国冷库和冷藏物流企业协会网站。定期通报当前各会员在本国和欧洲的业务发展情况，及时提供在保鲜物流方面的统计数据和市场数据。②德国运输报。这是一份专业性很强的行业报纸，经常报道农产品保鲜物流方面的消息。③《保鲜物流》德文期刊。专业杂志，刊登专家文章，发表研究成果，常有行业问卷调查。④德国制冷和空调技术协会。⑤数个互为补充又都颇具规模的农业展览会⑤。农产品保鲜物流作为不可忽略和不可分割的一部分，在这些展会中占有一席之地。这些展会除展示企业产品外，还通过论坛、研讨会和时尚秀等各种形式构建国际性的专业物流信息交流平台。荷兰不仅具有非常先进的制冷和冷冻技术设备的冷冻行业，工作效率高日常

---

① GMP 是“Good Manufacturing Practices”的简称，GMP 合格证是建立在 ISO 9002 质量管理标准和 HACCP 技术标准的基础上的，荷兰的 GMP 体系于 2000 年 10 月 1 日生效。

② IKB 是荷兰语 Integrale Keten Beheersing 的简称，意思是“食物链整体控制”。

③ KKM 是荷兰语 Keten Kwaliteit Melk 的简称，意思是“奶业链条质量控制”，KKM 体系在 2000 年初建立，主要是为了保证牛奶产品质量指标的实现。

④ 荷兰有谢尔伯机场等六个航空港以及鹿特丹港，尤其是鹿特丹港，不仅周围分布着重要的蔬菜和水果种植区，港区四周高速公路纵横交错，水路运输网络也十分发达，且靠近欧盟国家水果进出口中心所在地巴伦德雷赫，可以迅速便捷地将荷兰 58% 以上的蔬菜与鲜花等鲜活植物运往巴黎、伦敦、东京和中国香港地区等世界各大城市。通过充分利用其交通设施便利的优势，荷兰的花卉产业目前已占领了全球 65% 的花卉市场。

⑤ 德国每年举办很多农业方面颇具规模和影响力的大型会展，如柏林绿色周、柏林国际果蔬展、科隆食品和饮料展、杜塞多尔夫国际冷冻食品及制冷技术展、法兰福肉类食品加工展等。

开支低，而且具有非常发达的航空货运业，据统计，全世界65%的花卉贸易就是通过荷兰进行的[234]。

3. 发达的农产品加工体系

20世纪70年代以来，法国、德国、荷兰的保鲜规模达60%[212]。根据德国各类农产品在保鲜物流总量中占有的比重和相关统计，2007年，德国农产品在保鲜物流总量中占的比重同比增加1.5%。其中水果（+1.5%）、冰淇淋（+1.7%）和猪肉（+1.1%）的物流量有少许增加，禽、野味、羔羊（-4.4%）有所减少。2006年，德国在册的冷藏和冷冻运货车有55521辆，2005年为55461辆，同比增加60辆。冷藏和冷冻拖挂车增加显著，2006年达到44915辆。同比增加3194辆。2006年冷藏和冷冻货车在吨位上第一次超过100万吨，同比增加7.4万吨[235]。据德国冷库和冷藏物流企业协会统计，德国保鲜物流企业目前约有890万立方米的冷藏仓库。加上不制冷的仓库，总容量可达1180万立方米230万个欧盟标准托盘位。荷兰拥有发达的农产品加工业，进入市场的农产品都经过不同程度加工，因而具备了较高的农产品深加工、精加工的水平和能力。

（三）完善的物流金融市场环境

1. 农村信贷模式

法国农村信贷体系是在政府支持下，在民间信用合作组织基础上，分三个层次构成的农业信贷互助银行体系，其在体制上实行半官半民、上官下民、官办为主，合作性和政策性相结合的典型模式，在管理上实行中央集权与地方分权相结合的模式。这是法国农村金融发展的最大特点。法国农业信贷互助银行系统，在核算上，实行两级核算，自负盈亏，总行为一级，省及其以下为一级，各层次的机构均为独立核算单位，相互关系以经济手段处理。在管理上，实行中央集权与地方分权相结合的管理模式，地方行和地区行都是群众性合作组织，其相互关系是互助合作性质。总行与地方行的连接点是官办与民办的结合部。农业信贷互助银行系统的资金主要依靠自有资金的来源以来，法国唯一享受政府贴息的银行是农业信贷互助银行体系。这种合作性和政策性相结合的典型模式，有力地支持了农产品物流，保证了农业生产资料供应、扩大了农产品销售、开展了与农产品物流有关的业务活动的领域发放短、中、长期的普通或优惠贷款。

2. 中小企业设备信贷银行和农业保险体系

中小企业设备信贷银行总部设在巴黎，并在全国各地设有分支机构，是给中小企业提供专项资金的政策性金融机构，在法国农业和农村企业发展中发挥了重要作用。其主要职能是为中小企业发展提供设备专项贷款、补贴性贷款、再投资贷款等政策性中长期优惠贷款；此外，还为政府合同提供预付款担保，并为中小企业发展提供信息和专家咨询等服务①。

以上分析可以看出，在政府政策支持及完备的法律法规保护下，法国建立了发达的农产品物流体系、完善的物流金融市场环境，由农产品社会性物流向整个农产品物流领域推行市场化，促进农产品物流机构开展更激烈的市场竞争以及经营业务的多样化，并逐渐在欧盟农村经济发展中建立了垂直合作一体化的市场运行体系。

二　欧盟发达国家农村经济发展中的典型农产品物流运行模式

以法国、荷兰为代表的欧盟模式，农场主倾向于市场化经营，建立了垂直合作一体化的市场运行体系，农产品物流的专业化程度越来越高，其中法国的农业公司化物流模式、荷兰以“拍卖市场”为中心的农产品物流运营模式在欧盟国家中极具代表性，在相当大程度上代表了欧盟农产品物流业发展的最高水平[236]。

（一）法国模式

法国是欧盟国家中农产品物流最发达的国家之一，也是当今世界的农产品出口大国。法国不仅已成功地实现了农业产业化经营，而且在农业科技、物流科技成果的利用与推广方面也积累了相当丰富的经验。法国农产品物流经营的模式较多，但最具代表性的是以下三种。

---

① 继 1960 年 7 月 10 日，法国以法律形式规定了农业保险后，1964 年建立了农业损害保证制度，拓宽了农业保险的范围，并由“国家农业灾害基金”负责补偿受灾农民的损失。该基金的 50% 来源于火灾险保费的 10%。其他财产险保费的 5%，另外 50% 由法国政府从财政拨付。20 世纪 80 年代的赔付率达 224%。1982 年法国又依法对自然灾害险实行强制保险，保险范围包括火灾、暴风雨、冰雹和雷灾造成的建筑物及其内部财产、牲畜损失以及冰雹造成的农作物损失。

1. 公司制一体化物流模式

公司制一体化物流模式是指法国的工业、商业、金融和农业企业，通过公司之间的参股控股将农产品生产与农产品加工、储运、销售及农业生产资料供应等环节有机结合在一起实行统一经营的农工商综合体，其目的在于获取最大的投资回报，这是法国农产品物流运行的最新形式之一。这种一体化物流运作主体由于资金实力雄厚，经营规模巨大，加上供、产、加、销各个环节的有机衔接，能够极大地提高农产品经营效率，同时降低农产品物流费用。因此，在法国农产品物流组织体系中占有日益重要的地位。据估计，1975 年法国公司制的农工商综合体拥有 500 万就业人口，占法国就业人口的 23%；农工商综合体的增加值约占国内生产总值的 15%；农产品食品出口额约占法国出口总额的 1/6[237]。

公司制的农工商联合体组织有的还是规模巨大的跨国公司，综合经济实力和市场竞争能力较强。如法国国有矿化公司所组织的联合体，就是由法国农业合作总联盟、法国国有矿化公司、银行集团和格尔底聂家族集团相互参股所组成的，联合体共有工矿企业、商业运输公司、技术服务公司等 50 多家及 400 多个农业合作社。经营范围从农产品生产、加工、采购、储运、出口，直到矿山、化肥农药、机器制造及科研服务等，目前它已发展成跨国集团，在美国、比利时、加拿大、刚果都有它的分公司。

2. 合同制一体化物流模式

合同制一体化物流模式主要是以一两个工商企业为核心（少数以合作社或大农场为核心），通过合同关系，把工业、商业、金融等与农业有关的部门组织起来，从而形成的一种综合体，这种综合体分为紧密型和松散型两种[238]。紧密型的一体化合同是指任何决策都由综合体的龙头企业集中作出；松散型的一体化合同一般是由食品加工厂或农产品销售商与农场主签订，对商品的价格、数量、质量和收购时间作出规定，决策集中程度是相对的而且有限。在法国，约有 1/4 的农户与私人公司、合作社或国家机构签订此类合同[238]。签约的农户必须按照合同要求进行专业化生产、经营，按时、按质、按量提供农产品；而工商业资本家则必须按合同向农户提供生产资料、技术、信贷服务等，从而把供、产、销各环节稳定地联系在一起，极大地提高了农产品物流效率。

3. 合作社一体化物流模式

在法国，农业合作社类型多种多样，如购销合作社、农产品加工合作社、服务合作社、制造生产资料合作社、农业生产合作社等。其中，流通领域的一体化合作社是法国农业合作社的主要形式。具体包括农业生产前阶段（如供应农用生产资料、种子、饲料、幼畜雏禽，以及人工配种、生产设计、农田建设等）和农业生产后阶段（如运输、加工、仓储、销售、烘干、冷冻、出口等）的合作社。这类合作社由所在地域范围内有关农业经营者构成，最少不能少于7家，它们均是独立经营的实体，加入合作社后仍是本企业的所有者。合作社成员通过与合作社签订合同的方式将自己的全部或部分产品交合作社经营。合作社则通过自己在技术、设备、消息、市场等方面的优势使会员获得最大经济效益。据法国农业部的资料，2001年法国有3700个工业和经济性的合作社，13300个服务合作社，13300个共同使用设备合作社，60个人工授精合作社。法国60万个各类农场中有90%与合作社有联盟关系。农产品加工占合作社营业额的40%，主要经营牲畜屠宰、奶制品、动物饲料、罐头食品、制糖业、葡萄酒、蒸馏烈性酒等。从某种意义上说，法国农民通过合作社控制了自己生产农产品的深加工的1/2[239]。

合作社一体化物流模式可以使社员农场保持独立生产的积极性和创造性，集中精力改善和发展生产，大量节省在供销和加工等方面的人力、财力消耗，减少中间流通环节，缩短流通过程，降低农产品物流成本，提高农业生产经营效益；社员农场能够通过合作社更好地获得市场信息反馈，以利于指导和改革生产。合作社把市场机制引进农场生产，并突破地区、国土界限，扩大农场同市场的联系，加强了市场对农场生产的刺激作用。合作社还能从市场销售角度，对农场改善管理、发展生产、改良品种、规格和质量，进行最好的技术援助。因此，以农业合作社作为组织载体的法国农产品物流一体化发展模式，是对农民、农业更有利、更有效的模式。

（二）荷兰模式

荷兰是“通往欧洲的门户”，不位于中心却具有为欧洲地区巨大的食品和农产品市场提供物流服务的优越地理位置和良好的物流基地设施。充分利用这一有利条件、积极发展农业物流的荷兰人，成功运营了极具荷兰特色的农产品“拍卖市场”物流模式[240]。

1. 以“拍卖市场”为中心的农产品物流运营模式

拍卖市场与农户的连接是荷兰农产品物流一体化经营最富特色的模

式，国际上享有盛名的拍卖市场在荷兰农业一体化的农产品物流发展中发挥着非常重要的作用，在国际上也享有盛名。荷兰的农产品拍卖历史久远，起源于19世纪，20世纪获得了长足发展，目前，荷兰80%的蔬菜、82%的水果和90%的鲜花都是通过拍卖市场销售[241]，马铃薯、水产品等也大都通过拍卖市场销售，且拍卖市场具有专业性，即一个拍卖市场只拍卖一类产品。“拍卖市场”的具体运作程序是：农户按照质量标准规定→进行农产品分类、加工、包装→检验合格后→送入拍卖大厅由拍卖市场进行竞价拍卖→拍卖成交后→市场内部系统会自动进行货款的结算和商品的配送。例如，荷兰的阿斯米尔拍卖行，就是由农民合作社组织控制的，这家拍卖行约有5000家经营花卉、盆栽植物的公司[242]。在阿斯米尔参与拍卖的花农，其生产的鲜花，必须全部通过拍卖市场拍卖。经销商要买最好的花，必须通过拍卖，并在公开的竞争下提出最好的价格。每一年所有荷兰花农和花卉大盘商，还会拨出营业额的1%作为全球花卉推销基金，由花卉协会专职负责运用基金，行销全球[243]。

2. 以“农业合作社”为主体的农产品物流运营模式

在荷兰，农业合作社遍及农产品生产经营、储藏运输、加工销售等各个领域，农民可以选择在某个环节或多个环节上加入各种类型的合作社，以提高他们农产品生产、经营的抗风险能力，实现增加收入的目的。荷兰的农业合作社大体上可分为[241]：①供应合作社。也称为采购供销合作社，主要从事农具、种子、肥料、饲料等生产资料的联合批量采购和统一供应，以降低农产品生产成本。②信用合作社。其主要功能是提供农民购买生产资料、发展生产所需的资金。如荷兰合作银行（Rabobank）就是在1973年由数家农村信用合作社合并，从而发展成为现在具有强大实力的荷兰合作银行集团的。目前，荷兰合作银行是全球第一大农民贷款公司，截至2005年12月末，荷兰合作银行集团总资产额达5062亿欧元，拥有荷兰最广泛的银行业务网及网上银行，参与了87%有关农业、食品业的金融交易；约有40%的中小型企业与荷兰合作银行建立有业务往来[244]。③农产品加工合作社。主要是负责农畜产品的加工、销售。④销售合作社。最典型的销售合作社是通过农民合作组建拍卖市场，由拍卖市场负责将新鲜农产品及时推向市场，并在最短的时间内完成交易。在荷兰，80%—90%的鲜花、水果、蔬菜等农产品是通过拍卖市场销售的。⑤服务合作社。农民合作组建的农业机械公司、农产品仓储基地、农业管理辅导站、救济服务中心等，都能够为农民提供各种各样的优质服务。

随着荷兰农业合作社规模的逐渐扩大，专业化、市场化水平的不断提高，自20世纪50年代以来，荷兰农业合作社的数量逐渐减少，但市场占有率却大幅度上升。如1949年荷兰有18个花卉拍卖市场合作社，到1997年却仅剩下7个，但其市场占有率却由60%增至96%[245]。荷兰农业合作社有很强的独立性和自主性，具备独立的法人地位，不受政府干预。一般情况下，农民以缴纳会费形式自愿入社，而且可以同时参加3—4个合作社。随着农产品需求量的不断增加、农产品出口市场的拓展，荷兰有相当一部分合作社通过合并与重组，组建大型合作社，并进行统一的农产品储存、加工以及新产品的开发，使农产品附加值大幅提高。

3. 集散中心运营模式

荷兰是世界上重要的农产品出口国，其生产的奶制品、鲜花、水果等享誉世界。为了保证农产品的合理配送、及时运输，荷兰在农产品市场附近建立了各种各样的农产品和食品集散中心。通常，农产品是先集中到各集散中心，通过分类、调制、分割、包装和储藏，并及时配送到各个客户。例如，经营鱼、肉、水果等货物运输的鹿特丹物流中心、专门从事进出口可可豆的阿姆斯特丹港、经营水果批发的弗拉辛港等，是专业化分工不同的物流中心[246]。

4. 虚拟农产品供应链运营模式

为了满足消费者对产品的新鲜方便、品种多样化的要求，荷兰人发展了新式的电子交换式信息和订货系统。比如荷兰的花卉和园艺中心就已建立了新式的电子交换式信息和订货系统，这种新型电子互联网系统首先瞄准国际市场上的公司对公司的电子商务模式，通过互联网将花卉、园艺等产品的供应商、生产商、种植主、批发商、零售商连接起来，在全球许多国家向广大客户和消费者提供服务[247]。在此基础上，荷兰人建立了电子虚拟的现代农产品物流供应链管理体系。这种虚拟农产品供应链的运营，可以使消费者、农产品供应链企业及相关职能部门通过信息共享平台及时了解整个供应链信息，农产品信息的准确度、透明度和及时性得到较大程度的提高，农产品供应链更为活跃，对物流企业而言，借助信息共享平台，也使得及时改进农产品物流计划、管理、调配等操作变得更加现实。

第三节　东亚农产品物流可持续发展的典型——农产品物流可持续发展的东亚模式

一　日本农产品物流可持续发展概况

日本是在资源严重缺乏，经济高度发达，农业以个体经济、农户小规模家庭经营为主的条件下，成功地发展现代农业的典型。尽管农业在日本国民经济中的比重逐渐下降，但日本政府丝毫没有放松对农业的支持，始终把农业发展和农村进步放在重要位置，使农业成为基础扎实、保障充分、安全稳定的产业部门。农产品物流可持续发展主要表现在以下领域。

（一）政府政策支持及完备的法律法规

日本最早的农产品合作销售组织出现于1878年，日本农协始建于二战后不久的1947年，大致经历了三个发展时期，第一时期：战前的合作销售活动[①]。第二时期：战时的合作销售活动[②]。第三时期：战后的合作销售活动。包括国家控制下的农产品销售活动（1946年—1953年）、农协主导的合作销售活动（1954年—1975年）[③]。农协合作销售活动的一些

① 战前的农产品合作销售活动，按照其组织形式和业务范围的不同，可分为两个不同的阶段；第一阶段是从1878年到1920年，也称之为“农民专收销售协会”的发展阶段；第二阶段是从1921年到1931年，通常称之为“全国行业合作协会”的发展阶段。

② 战时的合作销售活动时间是从1931年到1945年。为了确保战争物资的供给，由政府一手组建的“农业会”替代了各种专业性销售组织的活动，特别是在粮食、棉花等战略物资的流通方面，政府通过强制性的命令，规定农民必须将几乎是全部的农产品通过“农业会”卖给政府。

③ 国家控制下的农产品销售活动（1946年—1953年）。尽管在1947年成立了农协组织，但在农产品的销售和流通上仍沿袭着战时国家管制的做法。当时的农协不过是协助和代理政府筹集农产品的机构。到了1949年，蔬菜的流通管制开始解除，1950年对木炭、菜籽、大豆、杂谷类农产品的流通管理也相继解禁。但由于当时中间商人的势力仍十分强大，农协的合作销售活动的发展仍非常缓慢。农协主导的合作销售活动（1954年—1975年）。进入20世纪50年代中期进入了新的发展阶段。特别是20世纪60年代后期的高速经济成长所带来的整个农村生产结构的变化和这一时期的各种大规模农产品基地的建设，农产品批发市场的建立，以及综合农协体系的确立等，从多方面促进了农产品合作销售活动的发展。

重要原则、制度也正是在这一时期里逐步形成和完善起来的。日本颁布了《中央批发市场法》《批发市场法》《食品流通审议会令》等；同时，为了适应现代物流的发展需要，日本不断通过政府宏观政策的引导，确立以现代物流发展带动社会经济发展的战略目标[248]。1996 年日本通产省制定和颁发了《综合物流政策宏观大纲》①，日本通过政府制定相关政策、法律法规和制度规范促进农产品物流发展。

（二）发达的农产品物流体系

1. 发达的农产品物流公共设施

日本政府在促进农产品物流发展过程中都十分注重发挥公共基础设施服务农业的作用，并且不断优化基础设施网点布局和改造。日本政府通过财政拨款对农产品运输、储存、加工和销售的项目进行补贴，包括修建道路、码头、仓库（包括冷库）和市场等基础设施[217]。

2. 专业化的农产品物流主体

日本从事农产品物流的主体的组织化、专业化、规模化程度较高。日本农协是一个拥有强大经济力量的遍及全国的民办官助的农民群众经济团体，作为组织农产品进入流通的关键性组织，它把各个分散的农户组织起来，极大地增强了农民作为卖方的讨价还价能力，保护了农民的利益。在日本，约有 97% 的农户加入了“农协”，90% 的农产品由农协销售，80% 的农业生产资料由农协采购。日本农协不仅设有完善的组织系统，而且拥有农产品保鲜、加工、包装、运输、信息网络等现代化的优势[219]。

3. 完善的农产品配送系统

日本的农产品物流设施以及保鲜、冷藏、运输、仓储、加工等服务体系十分完备。在推进物流化的过程中，日本充分利用其批发市场信息中心的功能优势，通过互联网在全国乃至世界范围内大力发展多渠道、多层次、多形式、工商齐办的现代化物流系统网络，实现了批发市场与全国乃至世界主要农产品批发市场的联网。最为明显的是以大型量贩店为中心的

---

① 明确了日本物流产业发展目标，并从放松规划、完善基础设施、物流系统升级、建立政府部门协调促进机制、加大政府投资力度等方面制定了相应政策。1999 年，日本政府又将物流产业发展纳入了日本流通再生战略之中。

网上订、发货系统的应用十分活跃，不必进行现场看货、实物交易，而实行只看样品的信息交易，实物则由产地直接向超市筹配中心运送，做到商物分离[249]。

4. 发达的农产品加工体系

日本都把农产品的贮藏、保鲜、加工放在农业发展的首位，非常重视农产品加工及其深度利用技术，如日本的稻谷加工技术[250]。20 世纪 70 年代以来，日本的保鲜规模达 70%[251]。日本的农产品加工和包装技术非常先进，一般在港口码头附近就有加工厂，再从其他国家进口的农产品，比如从中国进口的蔬菜到达港口之后，马上运到加工厂去进行加工和包装，然后运送到超市或者直接运到居民家里，在这个过程中大大增加了农产品的附加值[252,253]。

（三）完善的物流金融市场环境

1. 农协金融系统

日本农协（农业协同组合）是日本最大的农业合作性经济组织，在日本农业发展中具有十分重要的地位。农协金融系统是依附于农协的一个具有独立融资功能的金融子系统，也是日本农协的重要组织部门，是日本农产品物流可持续发展的重要组织形式。日本农协金融系统由独立核算、自主经营，上下级不存在领导与被领导关系，但上级组织对下级组织提供金融服务的三个层次组成。各级农协金融组织有着非常密切的业务联系，农户和农业团体直接入股参加基层农协，基层农协入股参加“农信联”，“农信联”入股参加农林中央金库，形成完整的系统。基层农协信用部门是农协金融的最低层次，直接与农户发生信贷关系；“信用协同组合联合会”是农协金融的中间层次，服务对象是所属会员即基层农协、相关的农、林、渔业的企业和资金需求大、时间长、基层农协无法满足的农户，在农协系统金融中起承上启下的作用。“农林中央金库”是农协金融的最高层次，其资金主要满足农信联的需求和向农业机械、化肥、农药等大型农业联合企业发放贷款。农协系统金融的资金融通业务包括制度金融和普通金融两部分。前者要在政府的一定干预下开展，属政府规定专项贷款，利率较低甚至无息，但可从政府得到补贴和担保；而后者则不受这种政策限制，但也得不到政府的补贴和担保，它按市场原则进行。

2. 农业制度金融

农业制度金融即“农业政策金融”①，其功能是提供商业银行、合作金融机构（农协金融）不愿意或不能提供的农业和农村信贷支持，并成为农业金融的最后贷款人。包括农林渔业金融公库和中小企业金融公库[254]。（1）农林渔业金融公库。根据日本《农林渔业金融公库法》，日本农林渔业金融公库（简称 AFFFC）是日本唯一专门支持农林渔业发展的农业政策性金融机构。资金运用于农林渔业金融公库融资、农业现代化融资、农业改良资金融资。农林渔业金融公库融资是为农林渔业者提供其他金融机构不愿意或不能提供的信贷、即在农林渔业者向一般金融机构筹资发生困难时，该公库提供低利率、长期资本以提高其生产力。（2）中小企业金融公库。中小企业金融公库是1953 年依据《中小企业金融金公法》组建的，目的是为缺乏长期发展资本，难以从一般金融机构融资的中小企业提供金融支持。其服务对象包括农村中小企业性质的农业生产经营者。其资金运用主要是为中小企业提供生产经营设备贷款；长期周转资金；中小企业特别贷款；中小企业投资育成公司（中小企业孵化器）贷款；中小企业设备租赁公司。贷款方式包括直接贷款和委托其他机构贷款两种方式。

3. 农业保险体系

日本的农业保险体系是日本农村金融体系的重要组成部分。日本农业保险制度也经历了希望通过商业性保障来解决农业灾害补偿问题的过程，但由于农业自身的特点，日本农业保险最终还是形成了由日本民间非营利性团体经营，政府给予补贴和再保险扶持，实行“三级”村民共济制度，“三重”风险保障机制，采取强制保险与自愿保险相结合的日本农业保险模式。根据《农业灾害补偿法》，农业保险组织体系主要由三个层次组成：市、町、村农业共济组合；都、道、府、县农业共济组合联合会以及政府农业保险机构——全国农业保险协会。农业保险基金由农民投保保费和政府补贴各占50%组成，一旦受损，投保农户可获得全部损失的85%左右的赔偿。1952 年，日本还建立了以各府农业相互救济协会联合会成

① 所谓日本的农业制度金融，是指“基于法律、政令、规则以及条例等，为现实政策目的，由国家或地方公共团体通过融通财政资金或对民间金融机构的贷款予以利息补贴，而进行的一系列政策性融资活动”的总称。

员的“农业相互救济基金会”，以通过联合会筹集资金，保持各种农业保险业务收入和支出在一个较长时期内的平衡。农业保险由区域性农业共济组合经营，主要农产品的保险是强制的，其他作物和饲养动物实行自愿投保。政府通过提供部分经营费用和再保险，构筑全国农业保险体系，逐渐形成了别具一格的日本农业保险模式。

以上分析可以看出，在法律保护和政策引导下，实行农产品社会性物流，形成了以民间双向性质的“农协物流系统”为主体，以政府主导的“农业制度物流”为保障，以兼营农产品物流业务的经济性物流为补充，经济性物流业务和社会性物流相分离的农产品物流体系。日本农产品物流在推进农业持续发展、农业结构优化、农业现代化等方面发挥了极其重要的作用。

二　东亚发达国家（地区）农村经济发展中的典型农产品物流运行模式

（一）日本以“农协”为主导的批发市场模式

日本农产品物流是一种典型的以农协为主体、以批发市场为主渠道、以拍卖为手段的模式。这种模式有利于买卖双方扩大运销规模和交易空间、节省交易成本，是解决小规模农产品生产与大市场、大流通之间矛盾的有效运营模式（见图4－3）。

日本农协，全称为日本农业协同组合，是根据1974年国会通过的《农业协同组织法》，由农户自愿联合组织起来、拥有强大经济力量、遍及全国的半官半民的农民经济组织[255]。它是组织日本农民进入农产品物流领域的关键组织，在农产品物流的各环节，如组建批发市场和集配中心，组织物流、商流、信息流及组织结账等方面发挥了不可替代的作用。日本农协的组织体系分为三个部分：农协的全国性组织、农协的县级组织和基层农协。以农协为主体的农产品物流运行流程是：生产者→农协→批发市场→中间商（大宗交易者）→零售商→消费者（见图4－4）。它通常是以基层农协（基层农协分为以农户为服务对象的综合农协和以特定农业生产者为服务对象的专业农协）为单位，基层农协一般都建有农产品集贸所，负责把单个农户生产出来的农产品集中起来，然后经过统一的

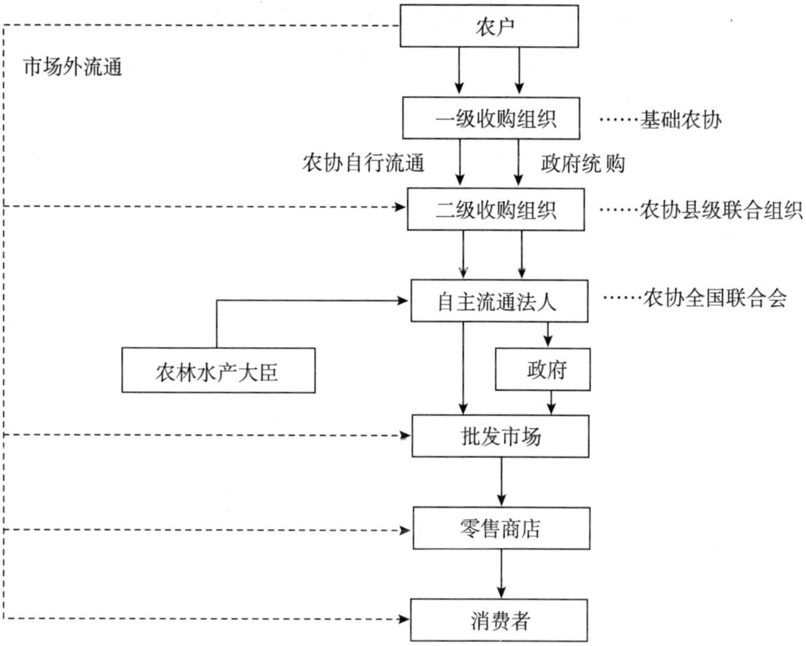

图4－3　日本以“农协”为主导的批发市场模式

品质检验和分类之后，再由农协统一组织上市。目前，日本农协系统共有集货所近3000个[256]。此外，农协系统还有全国运输联合会，下设众多运输组织，能够充分保证农产品以高保鲜度迅速运到批发市场。其具体运行模式主要有如下几种。

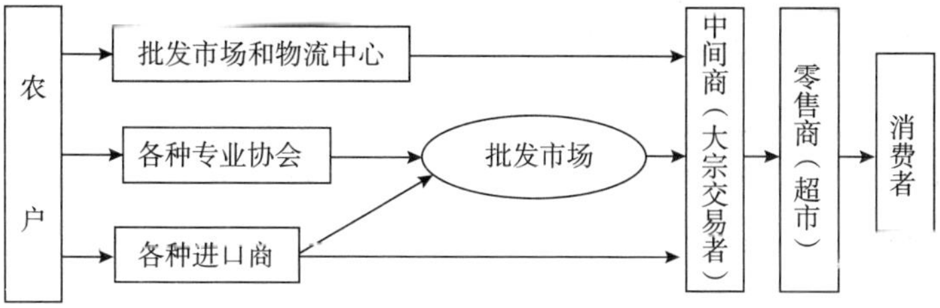

图4－4　日本农产品物流运行流程

1. 农协生鲜食品“集配中心”模式

20世纪60年代后期，日本农协为了进一步降低农产品物流成本，减少物流中间环节的耗费并提高所销售的农产品质量，开始采用农产品直销方式，并且在全国范围内布局设立生鲜食品“集配中心”。通常情况下，“集配中心”

采取预约定货、交易双方议价等方式，直接向超级市场、生活协同组合或者各种小规模生鲜食品零售店提供农产品。"集配中心"一般都设有低温仓库、常温仓库以及农产品包装加工设施等，货源全部来自农协系统。"集配中心"负责对农产品进行进一步的加工、小包装分解、分等分级及包装，同时开展农产品电子商务、配送、配套备货等业务。近年来，日本农协还进一步扩大了农产品物流配送范围，在全国范围内设立了更多、更为广泛的农产品物流集配中心，使得农产品配送更为合理。这样，大大削减了农产品的运送经费，进一步降低了农产品物流成本，形成农产品物流配送网络框架。

2. 生活协同组合模式

日本生活协同组合①的经营原则是三位一体，即会员们自己出资，自己利用，同时会员也参加经营，利益共享。至 2006 年，日本全国生协组织发展的地区生协、单位生协、大学生协、学校生协、医疗生协以及互助住宅生协组织有 526 家，参加会员人数达 2213 人，会员出资总额 5942 亿日元，总收入 32475 亿日元[257]。

3. 产地直销模式

日本除农产品批发市场以外的物流形式是产地直销物流，农产品直销形式很多，如早市、直销所、农户地头、合同、特约店、超市专柜销售等。按照农产品物流运营主体不同，早市和直销所物流可划分为几种类型：一是农协核心型，即农协承担了从组织运营到实际销售等全部物流作业；二是生产者核心型，即参加的农户承担了从组织运营到实际销售等全部物流作业；三是生产者与农协合作型，即价格决定和销售由参加的农户承担，组织运营由农协配合[258]。

4. 连锁超市模式

日本大型连锁超市的农产品采购灵活，可以大批量地直接从批发市场或市场外进货。批发市场外的采购渠道主要有农协配送中心、生产者、产

① 日本生活协同组合主要是城市消费者为维护自己利益、避免中间商盘剥而依法共同出资建立起来的消费合作社。一般情况下，生活协同组合组织主要有四种组织物流的方式：一是以"班"为单位的预约共同采购，这种形式通常是以近邻的三户以上人家组成班组进行采购，一个星期后以班组为单位送货，这种形式不需要店铺经营，而且能够直接送货上门，不仅成本低、方便会员，而且由于无库存，食品保鲜度好；二是直接利用生协开设商店销售农产品；三是以电子商务方式销售农产品；四是个人配送方式。生活协同组合组织作为消费者自己的组织，对农产品的安全性要求很高，通常设有农产品品质管理部负责对农产品的检查。

地集货组织、从事进口业务的商社等。大型连锁超市特点是规模大、资本厚、品种全、物流费用低、成本低、其商品售价比一般零售店低，而且由于超级市场品种齐全，便于挑选，深受家庭主妇的欢迎。

（二）中国台湾地区和韩国以“中介组织”为主体的农产品物流模式

以韩国、中国台湾地区为代表的新兴工业化国家和地区的农产品物流非常重视物流技术改进，批发市场在整个物流运行中起着重要的作用。韩国农产品是批发市场为核心的一体化供应链管理，可乐洞市场是目前世界上发展最成功的农产品批发市场①。我国台湾地区农产品运销的最主要的形式是中介组织（农会）②，“中介组织”农产品物流模式创造出了多成分、多渠道、分散生产和集中运销的农产品物流体系，为农户进入大市场创造了条件，有效地解决了小农户与大市场之间的矛盾[259]。

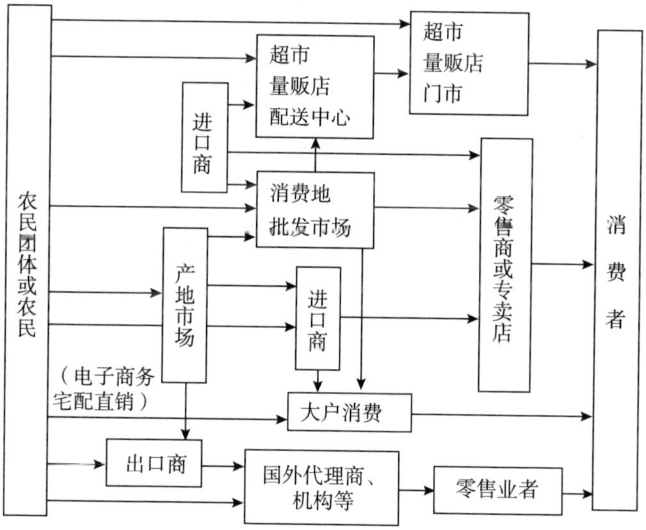

图4-5 中国台湾地区生鲜水果蔬菜物流运行流程

---

① 市场的开办主体是政府，其中中央政府占40%、地方政府占60%，这种政府主导型市场的优势在于，基础设施完善配套，管理先进，法制健全，为农产品物流的标准化和保障产品质量安全服务。目前政府加大对批发市场建设的投入力度，进一步改善市场的经营环境和状况。

② 乡镇以上的政府基本上都有农民自愿入会的农民组织——农会，在农产品流通方面，批发市场的建设和经营基本上是由农会参与主办的；同时农会还经营直销中心、配送中心、超市，办理共同运销。

1. 农产品一体化运销模式

从20世纪80年代初期至90年代中期，中国台湾地区农业生产从以家庭经营“小农经济”的生产模式转型为企业化运营。与此同时，消费市场需求多样化、优质化，农产品运营成本提高、农产品销售商品化和精致化的倾向逐渐明显。在农产品生产技术改进与营销推动下，出现了产地输出及终端消费一体化的农产品一体化运销模式[260]。

（1）直销模式。主要是农产品运销组织将产品包装或处理后，直接供应零售商，或由运销组织送货到家、机关团体，或社区居民主动集结共同购买。由于不需经过批发交易的阶段，减少了农产品运销层次，因而这种直销模式能够使生产者与消费者同享其利，销售比较稳定。至20世纪90年代后期，中国台湾地区已有100多家农产品直接供应中心，分布18个县市，大多是各级农会筹办[261]。

（2）共同运销模式。共同运销是指农户基于共同的利益，利用农民团体组织力量，自生产开始至销售之各阶段，集合成一个经济运销单位，将货品运销到消费地市场，以提高农民所得的一种一体化运作模式。从1973年开始，中国台湾地区农政部门就积极倡导农产品农民团体共同运销，根据台湾“农产品市场交易法”的规定，农民团体可以契约生产或契约供应的方式在农产品栽培较集中的产区办理共同运销，设置农产品分级包装集运中心，并由集运中心负责推广及运送至超市或专卖店等，也可直接供应消费者。共同运销的主要农产品有：果菜、渔产品、花卉、鸡蛋、羊只、毛猪、肉牛、肉用山羊、家禽等。1991年，台湾蔬菜的共同运销量为19.7万吨，其中农会运销量占50%，农业合作社（场）运销量占39.8%[261]。如“主妇联盟环保基金会”就是一个重要的农产品共同运销组织，其运行模式为：该联盟成员向农民采购后，将农产品配送到消费者小组的班长家中，再由小组成员自己到班长家中购买。

（3）计划运销模式。目前，中国台湾地区农产品计划运销主要以合同制为主，其目的在于促进生产专业化和运销秩序化，并保证供给稳定。合同制的实施步骤为：①决定核配原则和签订合同，遴选参加的农民团体、商定供应的品种、数量和期限等；②组织产销班和生产指导，实施共同运销；③调配集货和分级包装作业，与市场商定出货时间和数量等。

2. 农产品批发市场模式

批发市场是中国台湾地区农产品流通最主要的形式。根据“农产品市场交易法”的规定，批发市场是以服务为宗旨的非营利公共事业。因此，中国台湾地区农产品批发市场通常由政府出面征地，购置市场设备，然后委托农会、合作社或民营公司经营，具有明显的民间性和组织化特色。批发市场通常设在主要产区（产地批发市场）、主要居民地区（销地批发市场）和重要港口附近以及大城市，主要有以下功能：“迅速集货与分货功能；形成价格功能，使用电脑钟无线竞价拍卖，拍卖过程体现公平、公正、公开；清算货款功能，交易货款当日即以电汇方式汇往产地（供应人），市场内设有银行、合作金库、农会信用社等，无须现金往来；行情报道功能，每日交易的行情及时、准确报道，供供销双方参考。”[262] 市场上有固定的承销经纪人，为保证批发市场顺利运营，参与交易的供应人和承销人均需申请许可证，但不限制人数，并征收管理费和设备利用费。交易方式包括议价、拍卖、议价和拍卖结合的方式，视市场大小、发育程度不同而不同。同时，中国台湾地区建有完备的市场资讯报道系统，信息传递手段较为现代化，能够为生产者和消费者了解市场行情无偿提供信息服务。

第四节　发达国家（地区）农产品物流可持续发展的启示

一　发达国家（地区）农产品物流可持续发展的趋势

随着经济全球化步伐的加快，科学技术尤其是信息网络技术、通信技术的发展以及跨国公司的出现所导致的农产品本土化生产、全球化采购及全球化消费趋势的加强，农产品物流业已进入成熟阶段。在农产品物流内涵的拓展、过程延伸、覆盖面的扩大以及农产品物流管理的专业化、标准化和信息化都发生了极大的变化，出现了新的发展趋势。

1. 产销一体化趋势

随着农业生产经营竞争的加剧，产销一体化物流模式成为农产品流通态势发展的新类型，逐渐得到重视。产销一体化是指公司通过与农业生产者签订合同，通过合同把农业生产与“农业前部门”“农业后部门”连成一个综合体。产销一体化物流模式可以采取从最松散的纯粹市场交易到最紧密的一体化经营等一系列形式。目前，各国大多数产业依据各自的农产品特点，以不同紧密程度的合同形式进行一体化联合。这种一体化联合可以是农业资本（通常是农产品加工或者营销单位）通过契约合同与农户进行联合或者是投资建立农产品生产基地，也可以是农产品加工企业通过建立自己的物流运输渠道、营销渠道等或者与某些专门的营销公司进行联合以及农户组成合作社共同投资，参与农产品加工或销售，进入农产品的产后阶段的一体化联合方式。美国是产销一体化最早的国家，一些特定农产品（主要是蔬菜类）农产品合同生产或一体化经营的平均比例由 1960 年的 13% 提高到 1994 年的 18%[263]。

2. 物流运行虚拟化趋势

随着经济、信息网络技术应用的不断发展，虚拟经营势必会成为农产品物流运营的一种主要理念，有力地促进农产品物流业的进一步发展，提高农产品物流业的竞争能力和赢利能力。虚拟农产品物流模式是指具有不同资源与优势的农产品物流主体（包括第三方物流企业、中介组织、龙头企业、农村经合组织、产销大户、农户等），以网络为集散地，以计算机技术、现代信息技术为主要交流手段，以共同开拓市场为目标进行农产品物流运作与管理，实现企业间的物流资源共享和优化配置的农产品物流模式[264]。一般这种虚拟联合体由一个核心单位和几个成员单位组成，通过发展会员制，一端连接生产商会员实行集中采购，另一端连接批发商会员实行集中配送，并为它们提供资金、配送、市场信息、交易区等软硬件服务，提高了规模交易程度，减少了物流环节，降低了商品交易成本。同时，各物流主体在相互合作、组织协调的交易中，仍保持着各自的相对独立性，组织成员之间依然存在着竞争，主要是通过谈判形成比较密切的关系，而且，由于供求双方信息的透明、实时和高度的互动性，使得专门的技能和知识成为取得农产品物流控制权的重要影响因素，声誉和信用成为基本的组织要素，这有利于双方形成长期稳定的合作关系，有利于避免个别单位承担过高的组织管理费用，从而保持虚拟农产品物流各主体的内部活力，以适应市场变化，迅速获得成功。

3. 绿色物流发展趋势

绿色物流是可持续发展的需要，也是经济全球化的需要，与农产品质量安全相对应的绿色物流战略的事实，将极大地获得消费者的支持和青睐。绿色物流是指为了实现顾客满意，连接绿色需求主体和绿色供给主体，克服空间和时间限制的有效、快速的绿色商品和服务的绿色经济管理过程。它既包括对农产品物流系统污染进行控制，即在物流系统和物流活动的规划与决策中尽量采用对环境污染小的方案，如采用排污量小的货车车型、近距离配送、夜间运货（减小交通阻塞、节省燃料和减小排放）等，又包括建立农业和生活废料处理的物流系统。在发达国家，具备较强实力的农产品流通主体，正在朝此方向发展。

二　发达国家（地区）农产品物流可持续发展的特征

通过对美国、法国、荷兰、日本等发达国家农产品物流运营模式的比较分析，可以发现美、法、荷、日等国家在农产品物流发展方面各有特色，但从总体上看，这些国家农产品物流的发展又表现出一些共同特征。

（1）发达国家（地区）经济发展过程中都十分重视农产品物流的可持续发展，善于把握农产品物流与农村经济的关系。这些国家（地区）在农村经济与整个国民经济发展过程中，通过发展正规化的、经济性的农产品物流，或通过发展完全由政府包办的国有的、社会性的农产品物流来支持农村经济发展，充分认识到农产品物流与农村经济是互为条件的因果关系，彼此相互促进又相互制约，才能保持可持续发展。其认识形成于农村经济落后对国民经济发展的制约，完善于对农产品物流与农村经济关系的把握。已普遍形成了政府政策支持及完备的法律法规、发达的农产品物流公共设施及布局合理的物流网点、组织化与专业化以及规模化发展的农产品物流主体、完善的农产品配送系统、发达的农产品加工体系、高度重视农产品质量安全、完善的物流金融市场环境。

（2）发达国家（地区）都十分重视通过法律去规范农产品物流的可持续发展，可持续手段的选择经历了从单一的市场或政府协调到政府、市场等多种综合运用的过程。这些国家（地区）都非常重视通过法律手段保证农产品物流可持续发展，及时为农产品社会性物流的地位、功能与领域界定，为组织机构设置、运作和财政资金投入，以及促进农产品双向性物流在政府支持下，逐步发展为农产品物流主体提供了法律保障和规范。这一过程是政府基于对农产品物流和农村经济关系原理及其关系状态的正确认识和把握，不断地根据市场发育程度，及时、准确地界定政府与市场的边界，自觉地履行政府职能的过程。重要特点是以政府为主导，以市场为基础，以制度为前提，以双向性物流为主体，以社会性物流为保障，以经济性物流为补充，以政府机构、非政府组织、企业、准市场组织、社会关系网络等多种组织形式为载体，农户广泛参与，经济、法律和行政等多种手段配合运用，农产品物流的组织形式与结构、运作机制与管理模式、物流工具构成与创新等与农村经济规模、结构的发展相适应。

（3）发达国家（地区）都十分重视社会性物流和双向性物流在农产品物流可持续发展中的作用，并由狭义的运销支农逐步发展为以交易为特征的农产品物流与农村经济互惠发展。早期发达国家（地区）农产品物流发展无一例外地选择运销支农，并经历了因经济性运销支农失败，进而选择社会性运销支农，又因社会性运销支农不断增加政府财政负担，进一步转向通过制度诱导和保障民间双向性运销发展，逐步过渡到以社会运销为保障，双向运销为主体，经济运销为补充，注重农产品物流与农村经济互惠交易的可持续发展。在运销支农难以满足农村经济发展要求的背景下，一方面，将保险、期货等物流金融服务不断纳入农产品物流可持续发展的内容。在物流金融业务开展过程中，各参与者如资金出借方、资金需求企业、物流仓储企业注重的是如何采用先进的管理模式提高业务的执行效率，提升整体的效率，防范物流金融风险。物流金融服务提供商已经形成了一套科学有效的物流金融业务规范，在业务过程中采用了先进技术，建立了严格的规章制度和有效的业务流程。同时，具有发达资产评估、保险、资产处置、债权转让等市场，为物流金融的发展提供了有力支持，物流金融服务具有发达的市场环境。另一方面，则成立以农民为主体的农产品双向性经济组织或其他非政府组织，将农村基础设施建设、品种改良、新品种和新技术的推广与咨询、产品销售、扶贫开发、就业指导、教育培训等内容，与运销、保险、期货等物流服务有机结合，纳入可持续发展内容，并使双向性经济组织不断在政府的政策指导、资金支持和法律保障下，不断走上规范化道路。

（4）农产品物流可持续发展模式是可持续发展系统遵循可持续发展原理，在可持续发展主体推动下能动地适应其“生态环境”而不断演进的结果。不同国家以及同一国家在不同阶段，农产品物流可持续发展的模式及其特点并不相同，其差别主要取决于在特定经济发展目标下，农村经济发展水平、市场发育程度、资源禀赋状况以及社会文化背景。无论是美国模式、法国特点、还是日本和韩国的农协及其农协物流模式，无一不成长于特定的“生态环境”之中，无一不是以各国政府为核心的农产品物流与农村经济主体，为实现农村经济与国民经济可持续发展的目标，依靠制度创新，实现制度可持续，不断推动农产品物流可持续发展系统，能动地适应其“生态环境”的演进过程。虽然这些模式的表现形态因“生态环境”而各不相同，但其演进过程及其内部构造，完全符合总量可持续和结构可持续、宏观可持续和微观可持续、制度可持续和技术可持续、动态可持续和静态可持续相一致、制度可持续是关键的原则，其效果则取决于政府以及农产品物流与农村经济系统功能的发挥，而功能的发挥又取决于系统的内部构造、微观主体的治理结构和行为能力。

三　发达国家（地区）农产品物流可持续发展的启示

农产品物流可持续发展的国际经验，为西部地区农产品物流可持续发展提供如下启示性的结论。

（1）在经济发展过程中，必须始终正确认识农产品物流和农村经济的功能和地位，依靠有效的制度安排，始终确保农产品物流和农村经济与整个国民经济可持续发展。农产品物流的可持续发展需要市场和政府两种力量的推动。在对从农产品生产到最终消费者的物流链进行管理的过程中，政府的作用首先是为农产品物流的发展创造良好的外部环境；着力培养组织化、规模化发展的农产品物流主体；加快农产品批发市场的升级改造；加快区域农产品加工配送中心建设；大力支持现代农产品物流中心的建设；推进农产品交易方式变革；加强农产品质量安全管理；推动专业农产品物流金融服务发展方向。

（2）农产品物流可持续发展，必须始终坚持以可持续发展机理出发，通过制度可持续等多种可持续手段，使农产品物流优化资源配置，推进经济发展方式转变。一是调整物流需求结构。调整存量和做优增量，重在做大总量、提质升级；改造提升传统物流和培育发展现代物流，重在结构升级、增强持续发展能力；现实需求与潜在需求，重在技改调整、创造需求；实体经济与虚拟经济，重在强实扩虚、实虚结合。二是调整农产品产业结构。农产品现代加工产业坚持“龙头引领、配套协作”，实施“技术创新引领”战略；农产品加工业以“区域品牌 + 企业品牌”并举的思路，培育具有国际竞争优势的特色农副产品。三是变革农产品物流产业组织。加强农产品物流环节与农产品加工环节的产业组织体系建设。推动农产品现代化，通过大型农产品加工企业和农产品加工园区，实现农产品的深加工；设立专业农产品市场，推动各种农产品现货贸易公司和期货公司的发育，发展各种高效率的金融、中介企业，建设市场服务体系，促进农业生产与国际接轨，形成西部地区农产品国际竞争优势。

（3）农产品物流可持续发展，必须始终坚持以政府为主导，市场为基础，制度创新为前提，机制建设为重点，政府机构、非政府组织、企业、准市场组织、社会关系网络等多种组织形式为载体，农户广泛参与，多种可持续手段配合运用的原则。根据可持续发展的不同要求和外部环境，构造与之相适应的，社会性、双向性、经济性物流各尽其能，正规和非正规物流规范运行，农产品物流的组织形式与结构、运作机制与管理方式、物流创新与物流监管，与农村经济发展要求相适应的可持续发展模式。农产品物流可持续发展模式是一定环境条件下的产物，具有多样性、层次性、复合性和动态性特点。对于经济发达的工业化地区，可以通过培育农业产业化经营企业，培育农业经营公司、农产品加工企业、商贸型的龙头企业，以“公司 + 农户”“公司 + 中介组织 + 龙头企业”等模式，减少农户进入市场的交易成本，提高农民的收入。经济较为落后地区可以建立各种形式的专业合作经济组织和行业协会，让农民进入农产品物流供应链的各环节，从而引导农户和经营户走向规模化和企业化经营，通过规模经济获取农产品市场营销中的竞争优势。

（4）农产品物流可持续发展的关键在于以制度、组织和管理为内容的机制建设和模式选择，核心在于制度可持续，基础在于可持续发展主体的能力建设及其行为规范。一是借鉴发达国家（地区）制定和颁布有利于农产品物流运作的法律法规。二是借鉴发达国家（地区）农产品流通的主体形式，主要是企业化经营的农场、农产品批发与零售企业以及农户联合起来的协同组织，而非个人；同时，农工商一体化经营的程度较高。三是借鉴发达国家（地区）的批发市场运作模式，通过各种途径，切实加大对农产品批发市场的建设，把众多的农产品生产者、经营者联结起来，减少小农户的流通成本，提高农民的收入。四是借鉴发达国家（地区）的区域农产品加工配送中心的建设和运作，有效调控大宗农产品物流和各连锁超市生鲜区之间的物流联系，提高门店的农产品质量控制水平，加强采购谈判能力；并以生鲜加工配送中心为核心，重新整合生鲜产品供求双方的各种资源。五是借鉴发达国家（地区）综合型、专业型物流中心的建设经验，通过加快农产品中转站及综合型配送中心的建设，推动农产品物流中心的建立。六是借鉴发达国家（地区）的现代农产品交易方式，减少农产品现货交易中的暗箱操作，降低农产品交易费用，提高交易效率。七是借鉴发达国家（地区）对农产品质量安全管理的做法，以及像美国 UPS 那样的专业物流金融公司，这将是未来物流金融服务发展的方向。

第五章 中国农产品物流制度变迁的演化过程分析

"制度是重要的"，"发展"的过程本身就是制度变迁的过程。探求西部地区农产品物流可持续发展的机制与模式，必须对中国农产品物流制度变迁的演化过程进行深入考察。为此，本章将基于制度变迁与创新的理论和分析框架，考察我国农产品物流制度变迁的历程，探求其基本特征和影响因素，求解西部地区农产品物流与农村经济制度变迁的相互关系。

第一节 农产品物流制度变迁的初始条件

一 农产品物流制度变迁的历史背景

（一）近代中国农村经济发展的基本状况

中国古老的农村经济，自明清以后，逐渐转化为阻碍发展的沉重包袱。19 世纪后期的中国，人口压力激增、农业经济商品化加快，1905 年科举制度被废除，乡绅参与主流社会的路径发生变化。由此，几千年维系国家与农民关系的纽带开始断裂，中国传统小农经济难以自然延续，导致农村经济发展滞后[265]。这是中国农产品物流和农村经济制度变迁最为重要的初始条件。

1. 土地制度极不合理

地主土地所有制占主导的封建土地制度，是旧中国经济结构的基础，也是近代中国农村经济多重性障碍的根源。到 20 世纪 40 年代，其基本特征是占有高度集中，而经营却极端分散。占农村人口不到 10% 的地主、富农，占有50%以上的土地；而占农村人口90%以上的贫农、雇农、中农及其他农民，却总共只占有不到一半的土地[266]。占有土地者只凭借地权收取高额地租，而耕种者自身却不得温饱，农民的积极性受到严重挫伤，土地及其他生产条件严重恶化。同时，地主占有土地的全部和富农占有土地的一部分实行分割出租，分割出租的办法造成了极端分散的小农经营格局。小农经营格局为封建土地所有制的长期存在，提供了牢固的社会基础。

2. 小农生产方式极度落后

封建制度给中国农村经济带来的是土地占有结构和经营结构的双重障碍。在中国农村较长时期地保留着小农业与家庭手工业相结合的农户经营特色，这种经营结构具有相当强的稳固性，对自然经济的解体有着巨大的排斥力[267]。小农生产方式不仅为封建生产关系提供社会基础，而且也是中国农业生产力水平在特定阶段上的必然表现。在历史上它依附于封建生产关系而存在，一旦封建土地占有障碍消除之后，小农生产方式并不能迎刃而解，它的最终解决必须以一定的社会生产力水平为基础。

3. 农业生产力停滞衰落

在旧中国，农业几乎是农村经济的全部内容，全国90%以上人口在农村，90%的耕地种粮食[268]。生产工具自明清以来就没有重大改进，农业生产几乎陷入停滞状态。粮食严重短缺，农民所产的粮食即使全部自给性消费，也只能勉强维持农业生产和农村劳动力的简单再生产。经济作物的状况更糟，农业生产和农村经济衰落到了历史的最低点。经济发展的停滞和衰落总是同人口的严重超负荷联系在一起。落后的农村经济，不仅使其自身已经进入了难以为继的极端困境，而且成了一个人口大国谋求生存的焦点所在。

（二）近代中国农产品物流发展的基本情况

农产品物流发展与农村经济发展密切相关，自19世纪60年代晚清政府启动工业化以来，尤其是为了应付内祸外患和连连的战争赔偿，随着对乡村经济资源依赖和控制的加强，使得与传统中国小农经济的生产方式相适应的农产品物流，和传统中国的乡村经济一样遭到了政府权力的过度入侵，而不断失去原本具有的内生性[269]。几千年形成的国家农产品运销制度也和工业化中的农民、农村和农业一样，逐步衰败恶化，中国农产品物流和农村经济以及整个中国社会一样进入了空前的动荡之中[270]。新中国成立前期的中国农产品运销制度呈现出半殖民地半封建性质的总体特征，但不同的政权下又具有不同的特点。

1. 国民政府统治地区

抗日战争前（1927 年—1937 年），农产品运销经营主体的结构特征是官僚资本和买办资本逐步居于垄断地位，独占重要农产品的国内和进出口贸易；民族资本由主要地位而被排挤，最终破产或依附于买办资本；农民进入城镇集散中心出售农产品的数量增加，但被中间商控制。在农产品未统制以前，主要渠道是“中间商收购贩运批发—销地批发—零售”，对重要农产品统制以后，官僚买办资本成为商业主渠道，民族商业成为辅助渠道。1933 年以后，国民党政府对重要农产品陆续实施统制政策。1933 年实业部制定并公布了《实业四年计划》，将粮食、棉花、煤炭等产业物资统制起来；1934 年对棉花和蚕桑实行生产和销售统制；此外，还对烟叶、茶叶、糖料等商品实行统制。为了达到统制贸易和垄断出口的目的，政府对前述农产品采取了收购上的垄断低价和销售上的垄断高价。

抗日战争时期（1937 年—1945 年），垄断官僚买办资本成为农产品运销的绝对主体。为配合作战，农产品从生产到消费几乎全部纳入战时经济统制计划。1937 年国民政府公布《战时农矿工商管理条例》，1938 年经修改正式定为《非常时期农矿工商管理条例》，依此条例，棉、丝、麻、羊毛及其制品；食油、植物油、茶、糖等实行统制。1941 年国民政府公布《非常时期取缔日用重要物资囤积居奇办法》，禁止投机商人之投机活动。米、谷、麦、棉花、豆类、玉米等产品都在禁止之列。对麻、丝、茶、桐油、猪鬃等农产品实行统制的具体办法是由专设统制机构统制出口。对粮食运销的统制办法是在田赋之外实行粮食征购。国民政府的战时农产品运销制度使国民政府在抗日战争时期以低廉的代价获取了大量的粮食等农副产品，对统筹规划、统一调剂，以保证战时军粮的调拨、公教人员的粮食配给和民食的供应，起到了一定的作用。但另一方面掠夺性收购价格及办法又严重挫伤了农民的积极性，阻碍了农业生产力的发展，农业产量大大降低。

解放战争时期（1946 年—1949 年），官僚资本对国民经济的垄断控制和军事化统制大大加强。农产品运销制度具有掠夺性和强制性的特征。在农产品经营主体中，四大家族官僚资本占重要地位，地主、投机商人、高利贷资本也参与其中，美国垄断资本同四大家族官僚资本互相勾结，操纵中国农产品进出口。在国内农产品的流通上，国民党政府仍然实行抗日战争时期的限制物价和统制政策，而且管制的范围进一步扩大。1946 年 7 月 1 日，国民党政府恢复田赋征实、征借制度。1947 年 7 月，国民党政府命令对粮食等农产品实行征购征用，而且对其交易、价格、流通实行严格管制。这一时期，农产品的收购价、征购价、劝售价的制定全由政府和官僚资本集团所垄断[271]。

2. 革命根据地

抗日战争前（1927 年—1937 年），根据地农产品运销的特色就是：对内商业自由，对外贸易管制。根据地内的粮食买卖实行自由贸易政策，保护一般商人和合法经营买卖，私商、合作社均可经营。对于农产品的境外流通实行管制，在国民经济人民委员会下设立对外贸易局管理苏区对外贸易事宜。起初对于粮食等农产品的经营实行垄断，1933 年后也鼓励私人商业从事农产品的对外贸易，政府主要通过关税来调节农产品的私商活动。

抗日战争时期（1937 年—1945 年），根据地内仍采取“对内自由，对外管理”的政策。“对内自由”即取消日伪的农产品购销方面的统制，取消私商在贸易上的操纵垄断，在大力发展商业和征集补充商业参与管理农产品运销的同时，保护私营商业。“对外管理”即在农产品的对外贸易上实行管制，成立粮食委员会（1941 年山东省）统一筹粮，禁止粮棉出口。1938 年边区政府制定了《边区商业统制办法》《统制对外贸易执行》方案等法规，这些法规规定，从边区进口农产品尤其是粮食必须由边区贸易公司统一收购，然后转发给小商贩经营。1941 年边区制定了《关于粮食等八种物资运销紧急处置办法》《禁止粮食资敌规定六项紧急措施》以及《冀中区对外贸易暂行条例》等，规定粮食、榨油原料、棉花、皮毛等绝不许运销敌占区，违者治罪。对重要物资实行出口专卖制度，由解放区各县建立贸易局来管理，统制对外贸易，并实行许可证制度，对解放区之间实行贸易协调政策。在解放区里，公营商业、合作社商业所占的比重大大增加，地位也日益重要。到 1942 年晋察冀边区已发展公营商业店 46 个，附设分销所和生产单位 46 个。各个边区的合作商业有了广泛的发展。陕甘宁边区 1937 年有合作社 158 个，社员 57800 余人，到 1944 年发展到 690 个，社员 28 万人[272]。这些合作社配合公营商业，促进了解放区的物资交流，并减轻了社员的负担。根据地内允许私人经营粮食及规定以内的农产品，放开粮禁，使这一时期的私商也得到一定程度的发展。

解放战争时期（1946 年—1949 年），随着解放区的迅速扩大和大中城市的相继解放，根据地商业工作的重点从农村转向城市。1947 年 12 月，毛泽东在《目前形势和我们的任务》这一报告中，及时提出了新民主主义革命的三大经济纲领，指出："没收封建阶级的土地归农民所有，没收蒋介石、宋子文、孔祥熙、陈立夫为首的垄断资本归新民主主义国家所有，保护民族工商业。"按照这一纲领和"发展经济、保障供给，公私兼顾、劳资两利"的方针要求，这一时期公营商业的主要任务是：继续调动物资，筹集资金，支持解放战争；打击投机倒把，平抑物价，稳定新解放区市场；没收官僚垄断资本主义商业，壮大自己的力量。在完成上述任务的过程中，公营商业得到迅速发展，并联结成比较集中统一的系统，成为国内市场的主导力量。各新解放区军事管制委员会设立了贸易管理机构。公营商业的组织形式也做了较大的调整，除机关、部队办的商店并入政府的公营商业统一领导外，还将原来综合经营的公司改为专业公司。据不完全统计，1944 年，陕甘宁边区 80% 以上农民加入合作社。1945 年，山东根据地有合作社 4790 个，社员 100 万人。到 1949 年 10 月 1 日新中国成立前夕，全国公营商业共有机构 2000 多个，职工 8 万余人[272]。在购销政策方面，为了赢得解放战争的胜利，在军用粮食的采购上仍实行管制，由政府专营，其他农副产品实行自由贸易政策。在解放区，虽然也允许私人资本主义商业从事粮食等农产品的购销活动，但是，在活动范围、税收、市场价格、劳动条件等方面受到限制，使其只能获得一定的正当利润。粮食等主要农产品的对外贸易仍然采取统制政策。

3. 日本侵略区

1895 年中国台湾地区被日本强占，成为日本的殖民地。"九·一八"事变后东北进入了长达十多年的日本侵略时期。日本占领中国东北后，其势力逐渐向关内渗透，随着 1937 年"七·七"事变爆发，关内也有部分地区沦陷。沦陷区农产品运销制度是日本殖民统治的不可侵害的组成部分，其根本特征是殖民地经济。日本强占中国台湾后，对台湾经济采取了全面掠夺政策，制定了"工业日本，农业台湾"的总方针，妄图使台湾停留在农业社会，任其掠夺各种农副产品及原材料，在农副产品生产上实行作物种植计划，流通中实行专买专卖等统制制度。东北沦陷后，日本加紧在东北推行“日满经济一体化”的“国策”，置东北经济于日本经济的附庸地位来加以统制，东北一切经济活动均由日本根据自身经济利益的需要而加以控制和掌握。希望把东北变成日本的工业品和原材料产地，使东北经济完全殖民地化。在沦陷区，日本帝国主义提出“以战养战”“适地生产”的政策，大力发展军需作物。关内沦陷区的农业生产，必须服从于日本的军事经济需要，造成关内沦陷区农业生产的畸形化和殖民地化。

为把中国台湾变成其侵略东南亚的军事基地，日本侵略者对农产品从生产、流通到消费的专买专卖统制也大大加强。1939 年殖民当局推行“台湾重要作物增产 10 年计划”，限制台湾水稻种植面积、扩种棉花、甘蔗、黄麻、花生、番薯、香蕉、凤梨等作物，使台湾成为其侵华战争的军需地。日本殖民当局还颁布《暴利取缔令》《台湾物价委员会规则》《物价停止上涨令》等。

由于日本对江北贸易实行统制政策，并采取保护关税政策，抗日战争期间，东北进出口贸易很快成为日本独占市场的局面。例如 1938 年东北的输出贸易额中日本已占到78.5%[273]。1937 年日本侵略者公布《棉花统制法》，强迫农民把棉花卖给日本侵略者。1938 年公布《米谷管制法》，随之又公布了《满洲粮谷股份公司法》，对实行统制和对一切粮食均由满洲粮谷公司实行统一加工和购销。1939 年有《特产品专管法》，同时成立了“满洲特产专管公司”，对大豆、大麻子、苏子、小麻子、豆油、豆饼等实行“统一收购”。1939 年公布了《小麦及制粉业统制法》，对小麦和面粉实行统制。1940 年实行对农产品全面统制，1942 年进而公布《农产品强制出卖法》，以武力强迫“粮谷出荷”。所谓“出荷”，实际是对农民强掠粮食、油料等农产品。

日本对关内沦陷区的农产品运销亦严加统制。它采用各种手段，如军事政治勒索、低价收购等进行农产品的掠夺，限制农产品运销的自由，实行严格的贸易统制。例如在江南敌占区，无锡、常熟、芜湖等地，浙西、上海一带，粮食完全由三井、三菱及军部合作统制，日本除了在当地消费外，还大批地把粮食运走，粮食征收价格又极为低廉。据统计，平均征购价格要低于市价一半以上。再如蚕丝，中国蚕丝是日本蚕丝的劲敌，日本在占领江南蚕丝产区后，就设立了“慓中蚕丝”公司统制生丝的国内购销与国外输出。日本对其所需农产品，随时通过华北的“食粮公社”和华中华南的华商总会与各种贩卖组织，以极低价格搜刮棉花、小麦、稻谷、大豆、杂粮等。

二　农产品物流制度变迁的初始环境

中华人民共和国于 1949 年 10 月 1 日成立后，面对战后百废待兴的局面，中国共产党和中央人民政府选择了根据马克思主义和中国实践相结合，坚定不移地走社会主义道路。并根据当时的国际经济发展形势，以赶超为目标，极大地促进了生产力的发展，在政治上实行无产阶级领导下的人民民主制度。在经济上，实行社会主义计划经济体制；在产权上，实现社会主义公有制；在战略上，逐步实现工业化和现代化。这种选择是内外环境约束下的必然选择。首先，是对马克思主义经典理论和苏联计划经济模式取得成功的崇拜。其次，是应对国际政治、经济和军事竞争压力的需要。再次，对经济发展路径的选择和急于赶超世界发达国家的工业化目标。最后，是摆脱工业化面临市场需求约束的选择。优先发展重工业战略牺牲了农业、农村和农民的根本利益。农村经济制度反应是出现了人民公社制度、农产品统购统销制度和城乡分割的户籍管理制度[274]。农产品物流制度反应就是使农产品物流完全成为内生于经济发展战略的物流在农村的自然延伸，成为国家控制下向工业和城市输送农村经济资源与剩余的管道。

第二节　新中国成立以来的农产品物流制度变迁分析

一　农产品物流制度变迁的主要路径与基本内容

（一）新中国成立初期的农产品物流制度变迁（1949 年—1952 年）

1949 年至 1952 年新中国成立初期的农产品运销制度，形成自由购销时期是农产品物流起步阶段。在新中国成立初期，我国经济建设的方针和任务是使遭受战争破坏的国民经济恢复元气，同时改造半殖民地半封建的经济形态为新民主主义经济形态，并为由新民主主义经济形态向社会主义经济形态过渡奠定基础。与此相适应，农产品也由半殖民地半封建的运销制度改造为新民主主义的运销制度。

这一时期农产品流通体制和价格制度的总特征可概括为：农产品自由购销和市场调节价格为主的农产品流通体制和价格制度。从农产品购销政策上看，主要是以市场自由购销为主，购销经营活动主要是通过市场来完成的。从农产品购销经营主体结构上看，其性质是新民主主义性质的。国内市场上五种经济成分的商业并存，即社会主义国营商业、半社会主义性质的合作社商业、民族资本主义商业、个体商业、国家资本主义商业并存，其中，资本主义经济和个体经济占整个国民经济的90%。从流通渠道上看，通过私营商业购销是农产品流通的主渠道。从价格制度上看，则以市场价格为主，国营商业的价格只起引导和参考作用（只是挂牌价）。首先，对粮、棉、油等关系国计民生的重要农产品的购销政策是在坚持粮、棉、油商品自由购销的同时，积极通过国营商业和合作社商业在农村大力开展收购，以掌握足够的资源。为了多收购粮食，各级商业部门努力筹集资金，实现多收、多调。同时国家还通过农业税征收掌握大批粮食。统一粮食、棉花等重要物质的调度，把有限的资源用到最需要的地方。1950年国家颁布了《关于统一国家财政经济工作的决定》，实现了财政收支平衡，实施了物资、资金的统一调度和使用，从而更加有计划地统一组织粮食、棉花等重要物资的管理，实现了市场与物价的基本稳定。及时调整公私关系，保障私营粮棉商人的合法经营，促进粮、棉、油的顺利运销。其次，在重要农副产品方面，为加强对工业原料和出口物资的经营，1950年中央贸易部成立了土产公司和相应的外贸进出口公司，分管全国麻类、茶叶、蚕丝、猪鬃、畜产品等经营。通过这些公司来集中掌握大量的紧俏物资，加强国家对市场的调控能力。对其他重要农副产品和出口物资的采购，国家予以监督。根据《关于统一国家财政工作的决定》和《关于统一全国国营贸易实施办法的决定》规定，在采购上，有国营公司的，一般由国营公司收购，无国营公司的地方则委托供销社代购，国营公司和供销社的采购都采取自由采购的办法，但其调拨由中央贸易部统一指挥[275,276]。

新中国成立初期，国家除对粮、棉及若干种主要经济作物和出口物资的农产品的购销采取不同程度的管制外，对大量的一般农副土特产品采取自由购销办法，鼓励私营商业、合作社和农民去自由经营。值得注意的是，在1949年至1952年期间，虽然国营商业经营农产品的比重逐渐增加，左右市场的能力也越来越强，但该时期的国营商业主要是占领农产品批发环节，在零售环节，大部分农产品是通过城乡集市、庙会等渠道进行的[277]，因此从整体看仍然是市场调节在起作用，从而一定程度上保证了市场在刺激生产、搞活流通和保证农产品供应方面的重要功能。首先，从参与农产品流通经营的主体结构看，当时有五种经济成分的中间层组织者存在，包括国家所控制的社会主义国营商业、具有半社会主义性质的合作社商业、民族资本主义商业、个体商业和国家资本主义商业。各流通主体之间实行公平竞争，国家通过国营经济与其他主体公平、合法的竞争来逐步实现其在农产品市场上的主导地位和领导作用。其次，在农产品物流基础设施建设方面，在当时物流基础设施相当差、运输能力又十分有限的情况下，国家为了加快农产品的运输、降低农产品的损耗和运输费用，采用图上作业等物流技术，对铁路干线周围的农产品运输进行集体汇编，提高了农产品物流的运营效率。由此可见，新中国成立初期，政府推动的农产品物流制度的改变是保证城市居民生活和大力发展工业建设的基本制度要求。

（二）高度集中计划经济时期的农产品物流制度变迁（1953 年—1978 年）

1953 年至 1978 年高度集中的计划经济农产品运销制度，形成统购统销时期是政府完全控制物流活动阶段。1953 年起，为保证有计划经济建设的顺利进行，完成对私营工商业的社会主义改造，把分散的小农经济纳入到国家计划建设的轨道上来，实现由新民主主义商业到社会主义商业的转化，国家对农产品购销政策也做了相应的调整。对关系国计民生的粮食、油脂油料、棉花等重要农产品，国家先后实行统购统销政策。1953 年以后，国家为更多地掌握农副产品对茶叶、烤烟、大麻、苎麻等重要农产品及出口物资进行统一收购，规定只准国营专业公司或委托供销合作社收购。1955 年起对生猪实行派养派购政策。1956 年年初全行业公私合营后，因为农副产品几乎都由国营商业或供销合作社收购带来许多问题，因此 1956 年下半年国家又开放了农村自由市场，1956 年 10 月国务院颁布《关于放宽农村市场管理问题的指示》，1957 年 9 月国务院发布《关于由国家计划收购（统购）和统一收购的农副产品和其他物资不准进入自由市场的规定》，对进入自由市场的农产品作了具体规定。1958 年，商业上实行“大购大销”政策后，农副产品基本上都由国营商业独家收购。

1961 年 1 月中共中央发出《关于目前农产品收购工作中几个政策问题的规定》，明确提出把农副产品分为三类，实行不同的收购政策。第一类，粮食、棉花、食油，实行统购统销政策；第二类，其他重要农产品，实行合同派购政策；第三类，统购、派购以外的农副产品。文件还附了一个农产品收购分类表，表中共列出派购商品 24 个种类。1962 年 9 月，中共八届十中全会通过的《关于商业工作问题的决定》中指出："农副产品的收购，分别采取统购、派购和议购的办法。"国家实行统购的农产品，一直包括粮、棉、油 3 种。国家派购的农副产品品种，1962 年年底由国务院公布了一个目录，共列出 34 类，按细目算约 100 种左右，作为全国大体的统一规定，以后在较长一段时期内变化不大。其中，属于商业、粮食、供销、医药部门统一派购的农副产品一直在 80 种左右。1978 年，由商业部和供销合作总社管理的派购的农副产品（不包括地方增加的）共有 117 种。实行议购的农副产品品种，在 1961 年年初只是议购三类农副产品，且由国营商业负责，同年 3 月后主要由供销合作社负责，议购范围扩大到完成订购合同任务后的二类物资。1964 年，除粮食、食油为调剂品种和议价供应而继续保留了一些议购外，二类农副产品议购逐步停止，1967 年食油议购也被取消。1978 年，恢复食油议购，个别地区恢复了农村饮食业对猪、禽、蛋等商品的议购。国家在制定和执行农产品的统购，派购、议购的基本政策时，也实行了一些辅助政策如奖售、换购及加价收购政策。

与统购统销政策相适应，从 1953 年起主要农产品的价格也采取了计划价格形式。对统购统销的农产品，国家制定严格的统购牌价和统销牌价；对重要农副产品实行了国家统一收购牌价制度；而猪、牛、羊、蛋、菜、大宗水产和水果等主要副食品及燃料、蚕茧等工业原材料和中药材也执行国家规定的计划价格；与议购议销制度相适应的三类产品，采取议价的办法。国家对议价商品的管理在不同时期各有不同。如 1959 年国家对有的三类农产品规定了最高限价和最低限价；而在"文化大革命"期间，议价也基本上成了国家制定的价格，生产者和经营单位的定价权限很小。但总的趋势是由严到宽，由管到放，放中有管。

在 1953 年至 1978 年期间，我国农产品物流是国家计划主导为主，按行政区域进行资源分配和农产品供应，农产品流通几乎为国营商业公司和供销合作社完全垄断[278]，如图 5－1 所示。

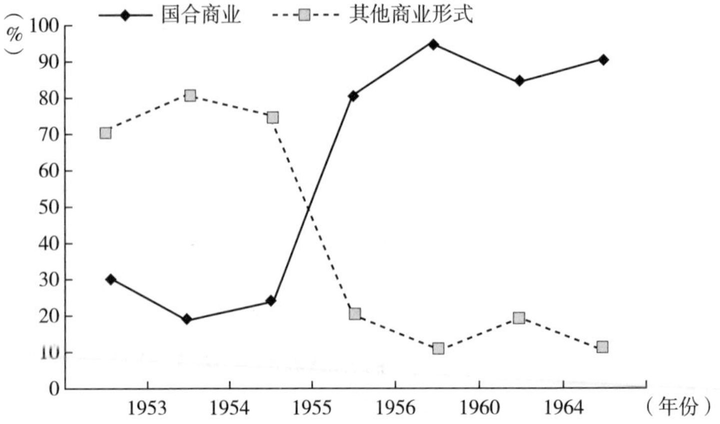

图 5－1 农产品购销主体份额比较

图 5－1 显示的是从 1953 年到 1964 年我国农产品购销主体份额的变化情况。从中可以看出，国营商业公司和供销合作社在 1956 年之后基本控制了鲜农产品的购销①。到 1958 年，国合商业已占农产品购销总额的 95%[279]。1963 年开始承担农产品物流活动（局限在储存和运输）主要是各级物资储运公司和商业储运公司②。由于物质储运公司、粮食企业、商业储运公司等物流主体间难以互通，农产品物流环节间割裂严重，系统性效率低[280]。与此同时，国家对物流基础设施建设投入了大量的资金③，铁路、公路、港口等取得了一定的发展，但也造成严重的重复建设[281]。这一时期物流的经济效益目标被放在了次要的位置。

---

① 在仓储设施方面，一些农资公司和国营商业流通部门建立了数量不多的运输车队，粮食收购部门建立了一些功能单一的粮库。此外，为了节省流通领域的费用，政府还根据农产品产销情况和交通条件，科学划分经济区域，在一部分农产品产销平衡的基础上，合理布局物资储运点，建立合理库存，编制并不断修改主要物资的合理流向图，提供利用各种运输方式及发展联运。从 1956 年 3 月开始，在全国主要交通干线试行 10 个品种的粮食分区产销平衡合理运输，由此规定农产品产销区及其流向和流动范围，并进一步限制和清除运输过远或者是运输对流和重复等不合理问题，以实现农产品物流最佳的经济效益和社会效益。

② 从 1963 年开始，国家提出“集中统一、全面管理、从生产出发、为生产服务”的方针，物资部门对中转供销仓库实行统一管理，主要农产品的物流活动基本上是由各级物资储运公司和商业储运公司承担。物资储运公司根据“以收抵支，收支平衡”的原则，按国家标准向用货单位收取一次性管理费用，而对物资系统的内部调拨物资一般不收取管理费用。

③ 到 1978 年年底，全国铁路运输线路长度 5.17 万公里，公路 89.02 万公里，内河 13.60 万公里，民航 14.89 万公里。

（三）改革开放以来农产品物流体制的演化（1979 年至今）

自 1979 年开始市场取向改革以来，为配合整个经济体制改革的推进和推动农村物流市场化的发展，与国家整个经济体制改革与转换的进展相适应，农产品正规物流体制也进行了一系列的改革，改革的总体方向是[282-285]：农产品统购统销的品种和范围不断减少和缩小，议购议销和自由购销的品种和范围不断增多和扩大，计划型物流模式向市场配置型物流模式转型，形成多样化农产品物流模式。其过程基本上经历了四个阶段。

1. 农产品物流体系的重构与调整（1979 年—1984 年）

1979 年—1984 年，在计划管理体制下逐步搞活流通，改革不合理的价格制度。1979 年开始的商品流通体制改革的方向，是针对计划经济体制的种种弊端，坚持以市场为取向，逐步扩大市场机制的调节作用。经过六年多的改革，突破了长达 30 年的高度集中的商品流通体制的限制，农产品物流模式开始从单一的国营模式向“三多一少”模式转型，农产品购销制度和市场交易制度的改革初步形成了农产品物流新格局[286]。

一是调整和改革农产品购销体制，减少统购派购的农产品品种。根据中共十一届三中全会的决定，从 1979 年起国务院及有关部门对农产品统购统销的范围和品种进行了重新规定。在统购范围上，1979 年国家规定，对于水稻地区口粮在 400 斤以下、杂粮地区口粮在 300 斤以下的，一律免除征购任务。1981 年国家首次对西藏地区取消了统购统销任务。1983 年国家又撤销了原来实行的关于粮食议购议销部分只由粮食部门统一经营，以及省级调剂议价粮需由省粮食厅（局）批准的各项规定。1984 年 7 月 19 日，国务院批准国家体改委、商业部、农牧渔业部《关于进一步做好农村商品流通工作的报告》，又将原商业部系统管理的一、二类农副产品由 21 种减为 12 种，即粮食、油脂油料、棉花生猪、黄红麻、苧麻、茶叶、牛皮、绵羊毛、毛竹、篙竹、蔬菜等。另外烟草、蚕茧的购销分别由烟草公司和丝绸公司实行统一经营，还有 24 种中药材也由国家指定的商业部门经营。1984 年 9 月，中共中央、国务院发布《关于尽快帮助贫困地区改变面貌的通知》，取消对贫困地区所有农副产品的统购和派购办法。这些改革措施的实施使统购统销的范围和品种明显缩小，在一定程度上冲击了原有的统购统销制度。1981 年 7 月，国家物价总局、商业部等 8 个单位联合颁发的《农副产品议购议销价格暂行管理办法》，共列出全国统一派购的二类商品 128 种，其中属于商业、粮食、供销、医药部门经营的共有 101 种，比 1978 年减少 16 种。为了进一步搞活流通，促进农业资源增殖和生产发展，1983 年 10 月 29 日，国务院批转商业部《关于调整农副产品购销政策，组织多渠道经营的报告》，将商业部主管的一、二类农副产品由 46 种减为 21 种，调下来的 25 种降为三类，实行市场调节，并将非主产区的杂粮、小油料由统购改为议购。到 1983 年连同其他部委管理的一、二类农副产品共剩 60 多种。

二是恢复、发展农村集贸市场、传统农副产品专业市场①，形成多种所有制相互竞争的物流渠道[287]。与缩小统购统销范围品种相对应的是开放集市贸易，允许部分产品实行议购议销和自由购销。1979 年 4 月后，国家放宽对集市贸易的限制，规定三类农副产品和除棉花外完成统购任务的一、二类农副产品，均可实行议购议销和上市自由购销。1983 年中共中央发出《关于当前农村经济政策的若干问题的通知》后，议购议销和自由购销的范围明显扩大，议购议销和有限度议购议销的农副产品均可到集市上自由购销。并且对农副产品开展了多渠道经营，从而打破了农副产品由主管部门及所属企业独家经营的格局。

总之，这一阶段农产品物流已注重农产品物流的系统运作，虽然零星放开了部分农副产品集市贸易，引入了市场调节的因素，但总体上仍未触动统购统销制度，真正意义上的现代农产品物流运作和现代农产品物流企业还没有出现。

2. *农产品物流“双轨制”运营的形成*（1985 年—1991 年）

1985 年后，取消统购派购制度，多种农产品开始自由流通体制。第一阶段的改革措施，并未彻底解决原有农副产品购销体制与农村商品经济的矛盾。1985 年 1 月 1 日，国务院颁布《关于进一步活跃农村经济的十项政策》，规定从 1985 年起，除个别品种外，国家不再向农民下达农产品

---

① 据统计，这一时期农村集贸市场数量由 1980 年的 37890 个迅速增加到 1984 年的 50356 个，成交金额增加了一倍，粮食成交量也由 1978 年的 25 亿公斤提高到 1983 年的 91.5 亿公斤。截至 1984 年，在农民出售的农副产品总额中，按国家计划牌价收购的比例由 84.7% 下降到 29.4%，而市场出售的比例则由 15.3% 上升为 60.6%。而且，集贸市场的发展、农产品上市流通量的迅速增大以及不同地区的农产品价格差异，又进一步诱发了农产品的贩运和流通，市场交易主体呈现出多元化发展态势，逐渐形成了国营、集体、个体等多种主体并存的结构，继而出现了多条通路运行的状态，改变了农产品物流的竞争环境。

统购派购任务，按照市场情况，分别实行合同定购和市场收购。另外，国家还对一些农副产品取消统购作了一些具体规定；如中药材中四个品种（甘草、厚仆、麝香、杜仲），只能由国家指定的商业公司收购。烟草仍实行由国家统一下达指令性的收购计划，并由烟草公司统一经营。棉花由供销合作社统一经营。定购部分的粮食由粮食部门统一经营，合同定购之外的自由经营，放管结合的政策正式形成。彻底改革农产品统派购制度，大大促进了农副业生产的发展、农村产业结构的调整以及商品经济的进一步发展。

1985 年到 1991 年，在家庭联产承包责任制与先行放开的农产品收购价格和集市贸易的相互配合下，我国农村经济获得了超常规发展，改变了农产品供应匮乏长期存在的状况，农产品产量大幅度提高，国家对重要农产品实行“双轨制”，促进了独立的农产品市场主体的形成、农产品市场体系的发育以及政府经济调控手段的变革。在集贸市场基础上建立农产品批发市场，形成了由批发商、农民经纪人、中介流通组织、农产品加工企业组成的市场流通大军。自由产销的新兴批发市场模式成为主要物流通道①，拉开了农产品物流市场化改革的序幕，也为农产品流通体制的市场化奠定了更进一步基础[288]。同时，《中国统计年鉴》中全国铁路、公路、内河、民航营业里程数据②，表明农产品物流基础设施建设有了很大的改善[289]。提高物流技术装备水平、建立粮食立体自动仓库，采用农产品多种运输方式实现了在市场取向的制度环境下农产品物流的基本价值，制度环境的改变是决定农产品物流制度变迁轨迹和边界的重要因素。

1991 年以前，放开的农产品由市场调节，未放开的部分农产品实行双轨制，在完成合同定购任务后允许议购议销，放开的农产品品种超过 90%，收购金额接近 60%。对计划管理的商品也进行了缩小指令性计划范围，完善指导性计划管理的改革。这里也应当指出，1985 年提出的彻

① 随着农产品生产量和品种的迅速增加、产销区域范围的扩大，国营和合作社经济逐渐退出了农产品流通领域，而小规模的集贸市场又无法组织和分销大规模农产品的异地交易。为了解决各类区域性、小规模集贸市场面临全国性农产品大流通的问题和困难，各地纷纷建立农产品批发市场，出现了中国农产品批发市场的大发展，全国农产品批发市场的数量由 1986 年的 892 个增加到 1991 年的 1509 个。

② 到 1991 年年底，全国铁路营业里程为 5.78 万公里，公路 104.11 万公里，内河 10.97 万公里，民航 55.91 万公里。

底改革农产品购销政策的目标并未完全实现，其主要原因是生产的不稳定而引发的市场的波动。这一时期农产品物流尚处于初步市场化的发展阶段，还没有完全消除计划型物流模式的痕迹①，处于计划型物流模式向市场型物流模式转型时期[290]。

3. 农产品社会性、经济性和双向性物流“三足鼎立”格局的形成（1992 年—1997 年）

从 1992 年开始，中国农村改革进入全面向市场经济转变阶段。1992 年以后，农产品购销政策进行了更加深入的改革，市场调节的农产品收购金额进一步扩大到 90% 以上。目前，只对 500 亿公斤国家定购粮食、棉花和烟叶保留着指令性流转计划，农产品购销政策进一步趋向自由购销[291]。从 1993 年起，粮食物流实现了双轨制向市场单轨制的转变。随着“菜篮子工程”建设的进展和流通条件的改善，1992 年，蔬果、食油、肉、蛋、菜、糖等农产品的价格在全国范围内放开[292]，开放市场，开放价格，鼓励竞争，实现了以上农产品由计划体制向自由市场流通体制的全面转换。尤其是随着我国农产品加工技术和农产品加工业的不断发展，形成了一批对农业产业链、农产品供应链有较强带动作用的龙头企业[293]。“农户 + 加工企业”“农户 + 运销企业”“公司 + 农户 + 保险”“公司 + 合作社”等契约型专业物流逐渐发展起来[294]。1992 年到 1997 年形成了农产品社会性、经济性和双向性物流“三足鼎立”的格局。此外，这一时期农产品物流基础设施建设速度不断加快。截止到 1997 年年底，全国铁路营业里程达到 6. 60 万公里，公路实现通车里程 122. 64 万公里，内河 10. 98 万公里，民航 142. 50 万公里[289]。

4. 新形势下农产品物流改革的深化与发展（1998 年至今）

1998 年，国家进行了“三项政策、一项改革”② 的粮食流通体制改革，但粮食类农产品放开相对较晚，直至 2004 年，国务院总理温家宝签

---

① 一是这一时期既存在着国家对农产品物流规模与流向的调控，同时，也存在以企业为主体的农产品物流运营，管理比较混乱，国家和企业对农产品物流的发展都存在着重新认识和探讨的过程；二是以企业为主体的第三方农产品物流已初步发展起来，但规模比较小，社会效益也不突出；三是政府重视农产品流通，粮食等重要农产品物流的计划定式被打破，新的物流模式又正在探索之中。

② “三项政策”是指粮食企业按保护价敞开收购余粮，粮食收储企业实行顺价销售，农业发展银行收购资金封闭运行；“一项改革”是指加快粮食收储企业自身改革。

署第407号国务院令，颁布《粮食流通管理条例》，全面放开粮食收购和销售市场，实行购销多渠道经营，清理和修改不利于粮食自由流通的政策法规，清理和剥离国有粮食企业财务挂账，推进国有粮食购销企业改革，使其真正成为市场主体[295-297]。这项改革意味着阻碍我国农产品流通体制改革的最后一个堡垒被攻克，我国多年探索的市场化流通体制真正形成。随着农产品流通全面进入市场化阶段，农产品流通体制改革进一步深化。国家实施了一系列加快农产品物流改革的措施：

一是加强农产品物流专业化、规模化发展方向。明确国家扶持的粮食品种按保护价收购，调整种植结构；加强对农产品加工增值、副产品综合利用以及新产品开发的研究，促使农产品资源得到充分、合理的利用；同时，这一时期还借鉴发达国家一些先进的农产品物流运营模式的做法，逐步向现代农产品物流转变，组建第三方物流企业使资源使用效率最大化[298]。截至2004年年底，通过调整布局和重组转制，全国国有粮食购销企业总数由1998年的30434个调整为2004年的20522个，国有粮食购销企业改制7027个，占全部购销企业总数的34%。其他多种所有制粮食经营企业达到10万个以上。广东、福建等一些开放比较早的省份，多种所有制市场主体所占比例达到甚至超过80%[299]。

二是加大基础设施的投资力度。增强全国冷藏仓储能力、农产品物流配套能力。1998年—2003年累计新建商业冷藏库2522万吨、粮食仓库1085万平方米，并配备了先进技术设备和管理手段[300]；国家投入巨额资金改善交通运输条件，到2005年年底，全国铁路营业里程为7.54万公里，公路193.05万公里，内河12.33万公里，民航199.85万公里[289]。实现了公铁、水铁运输方式一体化。此外，各级政府先后出台了大宗鲜活农产品运输的“绿色通道”办法，直接提高了农产品物流效率。

三是加大对农产品物流业的政策支持。2003年1月8日中央召开农村工作会议，专题讨论了加强农业流通体系的建设问题，《关于加快农产品流通设施建设的若干意见》为从根本上解决这一问题提供了政策导向。2004年—2007年，中央连续下发了4个“1号文件”。其中2004年2月中央1号文件《中共中央、国务院关于促进农民增加收入若干政策的意见》中又一次明确提出了要鼓励商贸企业、邮政系统和其他各类投资主体通过新建、兼并、联合、加盟等方式在农村发展现代流通业，要求供销合作社要创新服务方式，广泛开展联合、合作经营，加快现代经营网络建设，为农产品流通和农民生产生活资料供应提供服务，创造条件发展农产品物流。2004 年 9 月国家发展改革委、商务部、公安部、铁道部、交通部、海关总署、国家税务总局、中国民航总局、国家工商总局联合制定了《关于促进我国现代物流业发展的意见》；2005 年 1 月，交通部会同相关部门联合发布了《全国鲜活农产品流通“绿色通道”建设实施方案》；2005 年农业部印发了《关于加强农产品市场流通工作的意见》，对农产品市场流通基础设施建设的方向、内容、功能等提出了明确要求，为各地加强农产品市场建设提供了有力的指导。2005 年商务部等开展了“万村千乡”“双百市场”工程、农业部“百百万万”工程，质量检验检疫总局“5520”工程，商务部“信福工程”，全国供销合作总社的“新网工程”等，国家在文件中提出要加强物流发展。2005 年 8 月，农业部发布了《关于加快西部地区特色农业发展的意见》，发展西部特色农业七大举措。其中强调了通过发展特色农业，建设一批规模化的特色农产品生产基地，可以带动加工、储藏、运输等相关产业的发展，形成区域性的支柱产业，把独特的资源优势转化为经济优势，开辟新的就业渠道，增加就业机会，实现农民增收目标。要落实国家扶持重点龙头企业的各项政策，依托特色农产品标准化生产基地建设，培育一批从事特色农产品加工、销售等的农业产业化龙头企业。积极培育各类市场中介组织，发挥其在技术服务、产品销售方面的作用，推进农业产业化经营。2005 年 9 月国家计委、农业部等单位联合下发《关于加快农产品流通设施建设的若干意见》等相关文件。在 2009 年的 1 号文件中，也再次提出了要“加强农产品市场体系建设”，两会期间的十大产业调整振兴规划中，物流产业也列示其中，这是国家第一次全面提出关于物流业的建设规划，2009 年 3 月国务院印发《物流业调整和振兴规划》以来，物流业快速发展，产业发展水平不断提升。2010 年 4 月 7 日，国务院总理温家宝主持召开国务院常务会议，研究深入实施西部大开发战略的重点任务和政策措施，推进西部大开发战略。会议强调，今后十年是西部大开发承前启后的关键时期，必须以增强西部地区自我发展能力为主线，以保障和改善民生为核心，以科技进步和人才开发为支撑，进一步完善政策、加大投入、强化支持，坚定不移地深入实施西部大开发战略。国家发改委公布西部大开发七大任务，西部战略再次升级。国家将会从机械制造、物流经贸等多方面，推动西部地区经济社会跨越式发展。2011 年 6 月 8 日，国务院总理温家宝主持召开国务院常务会议，研究部署促进物流业健康发展工作。推出了推动物流业发展的八项配套措施，要切实减轻物流企业税收负担；要加大对物流业的土地政策支持力度；要促进物流车辆便利通行；要改进对物流企业的管理；要鼓励整合物流设施资源；要推进物流技术创新和应用；要加大对物流业的投入；要促进农产品物流业发展。这八项措施被业界称为物流业的“国八条”，是继2009年3月国务院颁布实施《物流业调整和振兴计划》之后的又一重大政策调整。会议要求各地区、各有关部门加强组织协调，细化政策措施，认真抓好落实。这一系列文件的出台和政策的调整，使我国各类农副产品商品化率大幅度提高，农产品物流环境进一步改善，为我国农产品物流产业的发展创造了良好的机会和条件。

由此可见，我国的农产品流通体制已经全面从计划经济模式向市场经济模式发展，并随着我国整体经济体制市场化改革的深入，市场化程度不断提高。在这个过程中，市场逐步发挥市场化价格调节机制对要素转移与重组的弹性作用，进行高效的资源配置，不断推动社会分工与协作的发展。农产品流通体制不仅决定着市场主体的行为，而且决定着农产品流通的速度、深度和广度以及农产品流通的方式和方法，因而直接或间接地影响着农产品市场的开放和我国农业的发展。

二　农产品物流制度变迁模式演进的动力机制

分析农产品物流制度变迁模式演进的动力机制是研究农产品物流制度变迁过程中的关系结构的前提。农产品物流产业的产生和发展演进，是基于竞争环境，在政府政策引导、市场需求拉动、物流基础设施建设和物流技术创新推动下发生的。

（一）制度变迁与农产品物流模式创新

农产品物流模式演进的诱因：外部利润的存在。“潜在利润”一般也称为“外部利润”，通常是由于现有制度安排难以将规模经济、交易费用、风险以及外部性等不确定性因素所带来的潜在收入内部化而产生的。因此，制度变迁也可以理解为一种效益更高的制度对效益较低的制度的替代过程。在我国农产品市场取向基调确立后，农产品物流制度的变迁可以说是对计划经济体制下统购包销不能实现的潜在利润追求的结果。在计划经济体制下，农产品生产价格和市场价格都是由政府主管部门控制，农产品产销的淡旺季、农产品品种及质量差价都不明显，依靠物流活动创造价值的努力根本无从谈起。因此外在于制度的潜在利润是巨大的，也是明显的。这些潜在利润主要体现在：农产品物流创造的时间价值、场所价值、功能价值[30,301-303]。在计划经济体制下，农产品物流功能更多的是体现在运输、装卸搬运方面，流通加工、物流信息等增值服务功能是不存在的。这除了受计划经济体制下统购包销流通体制的影响外，还与这一时期农产品流通系统之外的居民消费水平、农产品市场覆盖范围、物流技术支撑等社会、经济环境因素有关。

农产品产销关系主要有农产品生产者（主要是农户）和农产品纯消费者（主要是城市居民）两大比较特殊的利益主体，这两大利益主体覆盖范围之广以及主体内部利益实现机制之复杂，决定了我国的农产品物流制度变迁过程和变迁形式的复杂。物流活动作为农产品流通活动的重要组成部分，与之相关的制度结构也是农产品流通体制的重要内容。在1978年以前，我国农产品物流主体的性质和形式由于受到严格的强制性制度的限制，农产品物流主体、物流渠道是非常单调的，农产品物流功能的开发也缺乏激励，这就决定了计划经济时期我国农产品流通体制的一系列变迁主要是由政府提供的强制性制度变迁。1978年—1984年，我国制度环境发生了很大的变化，制度的松动引起了国营、个体等各类农产品物流主体的强烈反应，物流主体、物流渠道以及物流功能发生变化。在1985年初步市场化的农产品流通形成以后，农产品物流主体、渠道和功能更多地与实现农产品物流的时间价值、空间价值以及功能价值等潜在利润目标紧密相连，处于积极变动之中，农产品物流制度的变革回到了以利益为导向的轨道上来，进一步推动了我国农产品物流体系的演进[304]。

（二）城乡居民消费需求变动与农产品物流模式创新

1978年改革开放以来，随着城乡居民收入的增长，消费水平以及消费结构①不断提升导致了城乡居民消费需求的增长，由此带来的市场需求

① 消费结构是指人们在消费过程中所耗费的各种消费资料和劳务的构成或比例关系。消费结构及其变化是衡量居民生活消费质量变化状况以及内在构成合理化程度的重要标志，它反映了居民的消费特征及消费趋势，反映了居民生活水平的提高程度及社会经济发展的状况。

的扩大推动着农产品物流的发展。

1. 城乡居民收入的变化情况

改革开放以来，虽然城镇居民和农村居民收入还存在一定的差距，但与20世纪90年代相比我国城乡居民收入都有了显著的提高。从1979年起国家大幅调整了粮食、油脂油料、棉花、鲜蛋、生猪等18种农副产品的收购价格，1984年比1978年农产品收购价格提高了53.7%，1985年后，与购销政策变化相适应，国家逐步放开了农产品收购价格，这样就是为了确保农民收入[305-307]。随后国家又实行了敞开价收购粮食等政策。此外，退耕还林，粮食直补等政策都是确保农产品价格不会过低，农民收入达到一定水平。如图5-2所示：1978年中国农村居民人均纯收入为133.6元，2010年增加到5919元（可比价，以下同），比2009年增长14.9%，扣除价格因素实际增长10.9%。32年间增长了44.30倍；1978年中国城镇居民全年人均可支配收入为343.4元，2010年增加到19109元，比2009年增长11.3%，实际增长7.8%。32年间增长了55.6倍。这是1998年以来农村居民收入实际增速第一次超过城镇。城乡居民收入比从上年的3.33∶1缩小为3.23∶1。

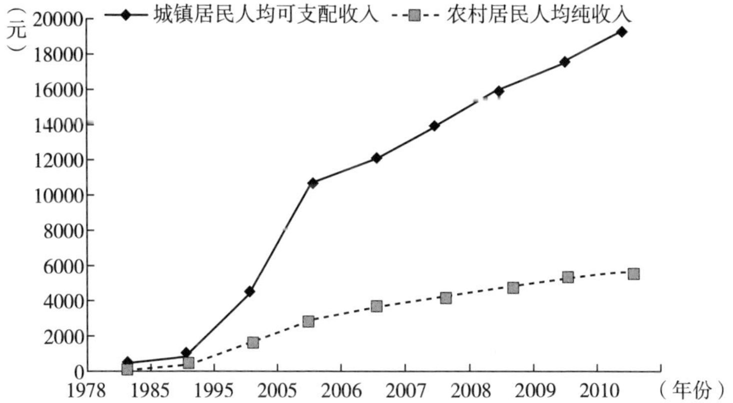

图5-2　中国城乡居民家庭人均收入变化

资料来源：根据1979年—2010年《中国统计年鉴》及2010年、2011年《国民经济和社会发展统计公报》相关资料整理。

2. 城镇居民农产品消费数量的变化情况

从表5-1可以发现，随着收入的增加，食物的消费数量也会发生变化[308]。当收入水平较低时，人们对初级农产品的需求较多，如粗粮、蔬菜等；随着收入水平的提高，人们对动物性、蛋白性农产品需求增加，如肉类、蛋类、家禽等。满足生存层次的消费需求是实现由贫困向温饱的过度，食物需求以粗粮、细粮及蔬菜为主，对肉、蛋等农产品需求较少。农村居民在生存层次的消费需求得到满足后，开始注重提高生活质量的消费，对肉类、蛋、家禽及水产品等需求增长较快。由此看出，我国农村居民食物消费由低层次向高层次逐渐演变的过程。这意味着现阶段乃至今后较长的一段时间内，生鲜农产品物流配送业将有很大的发展空间。

表 5－1　城镇居民家庭平均每人全年购买主要农产品数量　单位：千克

年份	粮食	鲜菜	猪肉	牛羊肉	家禽	鲜蛋	水产品	鲜奶	水果
1990	130.72	138.70	18.46	3.28	3.42	7.25	7.69	4.63	41.11
1995	97.00	116.47	17.24	2.44	3.97	9.74	9.20	4.62	44.90
1999	84.91	114.94	16.91	3.09	4.92	10.92	10.34	7.88	54.21
2000	82.31	114.74	16.73	3.33	5.44	11.21	11.74	9.94	57.48
2004	78.18	22.32	19.19	3.66	6.37	10.35	12.48	18.83	56.45
2005	76.98	118.58	20.15	3.71	8.97	10.40	12.55	17.92	56.69
2006	75.92	117.56	20.00	3.78	8.34	10.41	12.95	18.32	60.17
2007	77.60	117.80	18.21	3.93	9.66	10.33	14.20	17.75	59.54
2008	77.38	117.57	20.45	4.34	9.87	11.52	15.50	19.13	60.33
2009	76.16	115.54	19.36	4.43	8.83	10.22	14.32	18.58	59.20
2010	76.40	116.38	19.20	4.74	9.12	11.27	15.66	19.88	60.43

资料来源：《中国统计年鉴（2010）》，中国统计出版社，2010。

3. 城镇居民消费结构的变化情况

食物消费的最重要法则就是恩格尔法则（Engel's law），这个法则是由19世纪德国著名统计学家恩斯特·恩格尔提出来的[309]。这个法则指出，一个家庭收入越少，其总支出中用于购买食物的比重越大。随着家庭收入的增加，其总支出中用于购买食物的比重越小。也就是说，随着收入的增加，支出增加，食物支出也增加，但是食物支出的增加幅度，赶不上总支出的增加幅度，从而使食物支出在总支出中的比重下降，食物以外的其他支出，如娱乐、旅游等随意性支出比重将上升。图 5－3 说明了我国城乡居民的恩格尔系数都在下降，这个法则基于两点：一是人们对食物的需求是最基本的，食品消费所占比重将相对稳定。二是人们对食物的需求毕竟是有限的，当人们收入增加到一定程度时更加追求营养与健康，就必然会产生其他需求，而且随着收入的增加，其他需求会不断出现。消费结构是推动我国鲜活农产品物流快速发展的内部动力[310]。

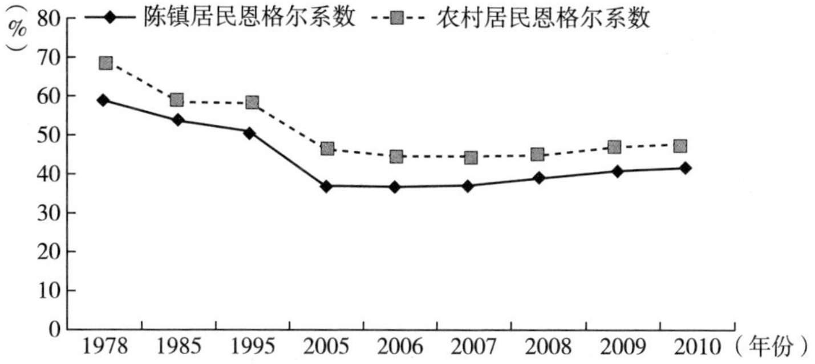

图 5-3　1979 年—2010 年中国城乡居民恩格尔系数

资料来源：根据 1979 年—2010 年《中国统计年鉴》及相关资料整理而得。

4. 城镇居民消费方式的变化

从表 5-2 可以发现，消费观念、消费方式、消费习惯变化，能够引起消费行为、消费需求的变化，这给农产品物流提供了市场基础与空间[311]。

表 5-2　　1997 年—2010 年我国社会消费品零售总额和餐饮业零售总额

单位：亿元、%

年份	社会消费品零售总额	餐饮业零售总额	餐饮业零售总额占社会消费品零售总额的比例
1997	31252.9	2488.2	7.96
1998	33378.1	2878.8	8.62
1999	35647.9	3270.3	9.17
2000	39105.7	3836.1	9.81
2001	43055.4	4465.2	10.37
2002	48135.9	5547.1	11.52
2003	52516.3	6191.4	11.79
2004	59501.0	7550.4	12.69
2005	67176.6	8886.8	13.23
2006	76410.0	10345.5	13.54
2007	89210.0	12352.0	13.85
2008	108488.0	15404.0	14.20
2009	107364.4	16244.2	15.13
2010	113785.2	17966.6	15.79

资料来源：据 1979 年—2010 年《中国统计年鉴》相关资料整理而得，2010 年数据来自 2011 年《国民经济和社会发展统计公报》。

5. 消费者对农产品质量安全认识的变化

表5－3表明，消费者对农产品质量的追求越来越多地表现在农产品的安全程度和新鲜程度上，尤其是在农产品质量安全上。随着社会进步和经济发展，不再为温饱发愁的消费者开始关注产品质量，多样性以及食品安全问题。合理的物流政策必须能保证尽可能少的制度漏洞，确保消费者食用到真正安全的食品。农产品物流政策改革，主要是进一步加强农产品质量标准建设，加强食品质量安全体系建设，现代农产品物流的相关研究会更加受到重视。

表5－3　　消费者对生鲜农产品不同特性的选择　　单位:%

重要程度	安全程度	新鲜程度	绿色环保产品	价格	品牌	方便程度	产地
第一	82.7	76.2	61.0	45.8	43.4	32.3	24.0
第二	4.0	10.7	16.0	16.7	21.4	24.5	15.2
第三	6.3	6.0	13.0	25.8	19.0	22.5	24.0
第四	5.0	3.7	4.7	6.4	7.1	9.7	11.1
第五	2.0	3.4	5.3	5.4	9.2	11.1	25.7
合计	100	100	100	100	100	100	100
平均值	4.6	4.5	4.2	3.9	3.8	3.5	3.3

资料来源：2002年5月“零售企业参与农业产业化和生鲜业务经营优化的发展战略研究课题组”所做的调查问卷。

（三）物流基础设施改善与农产品物流模式创新

随着我国改革开放以来商品经济的不断发展和农产品商品化率的不断提高，物流基础设施的作用不断凸显。换言之，农产品物流的发展对物流基础的依赖性越来越强[312－319]。新中国成立60年来，国家十分重视基础设施的更新改造。新中国成立初期，全国所有公路只有8万多公里。1952年全国县乡公路为4.7万公里，到1960年，全国县乡公路骤增20万公里，县乡公路里程达到26.8万公里，县乡公路网初步形成。到1978年年末，全国乡（镇）、行政村通公路的比例为91.5%和65.8%，县乡公路达到59.6万多公里，符合等级标准的公路约26万公里，全国公路总里程达到87万多公里。20世纪80年代以来，在以工代赈政策和交通扶贫资金的带动下，国家加大了基础设施建设力度。仅1995年到1997年的三年间，交通部共投资27.6亿元，地方配套46.3亿元，修建公路19228公里，桥梁206座、28282延米。到“九五”时期，国内年均新增公路4.2万公里，农村公路的技术等级和服务水平有了大幅度的提高。《2007年公路水路交通行业发展统计公报》数据显示，截至2007年年底，全国公路总里程达358.37万公里，比2006年年末增加（同口径比，下同）12.67万公里。其中，农村公路（含县道、乡道、村道）里程达到313.44万公里，路网结构进一步改善。特别是由于积极推进西部落后地区基础设施建设，物流基础设施已初具规模，成果显著。2001年开始实施的西部地区通县公路建设工程，涉及西部12个省区市及湖南、湖北、吉林的三个少数民族自治州和黑龙江大兴安岭地区共251个项目，建设总里程25766公里，总投资310亿元，这项工程已于2002年年底基本完成，大大改善了西部地区和少数民族地区的物流基础状况。在加速公路建设的同时，我国加快了高速公路的建设步伐。到2007年年底，我国已有高速公路5.39万公里[320]。长距离、远辐射和快捷、舒适、方便的交通环境为农产品在全国范围，甚至是全球范围内的自由流动、充分竞争提供了快车道，农村城镇化进程加快，农产品迅速增值，有力地推动了我国农产品物流产业的发展。

迄今为止，中国公路建设应该说成就斐然，而且许多农产品都是通过公路运输完成输送的。但在运输远程的、大量的、体积较大的和不易腐烂的农产品方面，铁路运输具有明显的比较优势。然而，铁路运输需求却往往难以得到满足。据铁道部运输局统计，至2008年3月，全国铁路日均装卸车已达15万车左右的较高水平，但全社会日均申请铁路货车车皮已达30万车左右，请车满足率近50%，与2004年请车满足率的35%相比有较大的提高。随着我国国民经济持续发展和工业化进程的加快，能源、原材料的需求将处于上升阶段，工业货运量的急剧升高必将拉动对货运车辆的需求。但由于总的运力有限，铁路运输仍然难以满足粮食和棉花等农产品的运输需求。

新中国成立初期，我国仅有港口泊位161个，到1978年年底，全国主要港口泊位数增加到735个，其中沿海港口深水泊位达到133个[321]。1979年以后我国港口建设进入快速发展阶段。《2007年公路水路交通行业发展统计公报》数据显示，至2007年年底，全国港口拥有生产用码头泊位35947个，其中万吨级及以上泊位1337个，沿海港口和内河港口分别为4701个和31246个，内河港口万吨级泊位分布在长江干流、珠江水系，分别为255个和4个。到目前为止，我国港口已初步形成码头种类齐、布局日趋合理的总体格局，而且我国部分海港的技术装备和管理水平总体上已接近世界先进水平，港口功能已由以装卸、集散货物为主的运输功能逐步扩展到仓储、加工和商贸等多个领域，为农产品物流产业的快速发展提供了良好的港口物流基础条件。

近几年我国信息业的发展速度也很快，网络建设取得了很大的成就，数据网、通信网、报纸、电视、广播等公共传媒得到了极大的发展。截至2007年年底，我国电话用户总数已经超过了9亿户，居世界第一位，其中固定电话达到了3.7亿户、移动电话达到了5.3亿户，移动电话超过了固定电话。农村的电“村村通”工程也取得了明显的成果，通话的行政村覆盖率已达到了99.2%，有25个省、自治区、直辖市实现了所有行政村通电话[322,323]。信息产业和通信业对农产品物流业的拉动作用非常明显，使得农产品物流信息、管理、控制的技术得以应用，在很大程度上提高了农产品物流效率，奠定了农产品现代物流发展的基础。我国交通运输、通信的快速发展，将有助于逐渐解决由于运力紧张、通信不畅而造成的农产品运输难度大、物流不畅等问题，运输、通信状况的改善将进一步推动我国农产品物流的发展，同时也会带动我国农业的整体全面发展。

（四）物流技术开发采用与农产品物流模式创新

在政府科学研究投入的推动下，我国农业科技投入强度（即农业科技投入占农业GDP的比例）近年增加较快。1985年—1997年全国农业科技投入强度从0.37%减至0.22%，年均减少0.01个百分点。1998年—2003年农业科技投入强度又以年均0.01个百分点的速度增长，2003年达到0.29%。2004年和2005年投入强度同比均有较大幅度提升，2005年达到0.49%[324]。随着农业生产和农业科技的发展，我国农业高新技术领域也取得了一定的成绩，科技进步对农业增长的贡献率分别是：“一五”时期19.9%，“二五”时期和三年恢复时期为负值（表明经济效益下降），“三五”时期为2.3%，“四五”时期为15.4%，“五五”时期为26.7%，“六五”时期为34.7%，“七五”时期为25.5%，“八五”时期为32.1%，“九五”时期为40.5%，“十五”时期为45.9%。“一五”时期到“十五”时期科技进步贡献率提高26个百分点（见图5-4）[325]。同时农业基础设施得到极大改善，农产品标准化进程加快，无公害、绿色食品生产规模不断扩大，农产品质量安全水平有了较为明显的提高[326,327]。

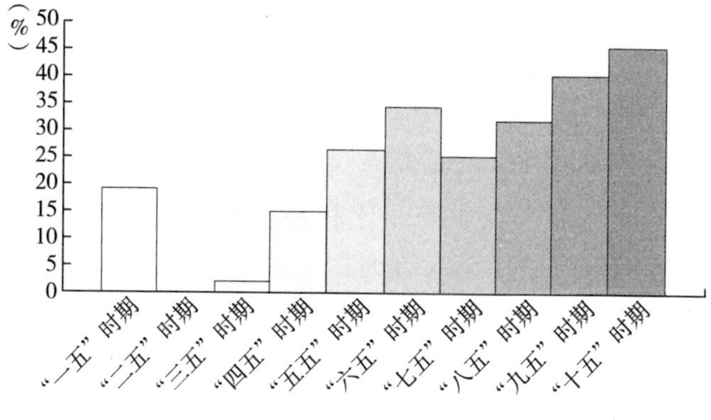

图 5-4　我国农业增长中的科技贡献率

资料来源：王启现、李志强、刘自杰，《我国农业科技进步与科研投资分析》，《科学管理研究》2007 年第 8 期，第 113~116 页。

物流科技开发与应用推动农产品物流模式创新可以归纳为两个维度：一是积累推动维度，二是创新推动维度，两个维度相互叠加，构成技术对农产品物流的推动。技术积累推动维度是在一定的技术和管理条件下，依靠农产品物流的再生产为物流经济提供积累性贡献，因而是对农产品物流实现量的推动；而创新推动维度是农产品物流技术和管理水平提升的一种推动方式，一旦物流技术或管理有质的进步或突破，将会促使积累推动维度在更高的水平上运转，也就是说将会使农产品物流发生跨越式的发展，实现农产品物流发展质的提升。创新维度相当于为农产品物流前进提供加速度，积累维度则能够保持农产品物流在一定时间内匀速前进，加速度会使农产品物流发展速度提升，这就是物流科技的开发与应用对农产品物流的推动原理。物流技术、信息技术及交通的变化对农产品物流的影响是潜移默化的。国际互联网的应用必然使农产品物流企业对信息的管理成本增加，这个成本包括硬件投资、维护成本和运行成本。而物流科技应用带来的收益主要是仓储成本的降低、指令的迅速传达和对市场的快速反应。这一领域的投资，总是有利可图的。因此在现代物流科技的支持下，企业总会选择最经济有效的物流模式，这就推动了农产品物流模式的演进。

（五）农产品物流组织与农产品物流模式创新

农产品物流组织是指介于农产品生产者与消费者之间，以农产品物流运作和管理为核心的实体性组织。农产品物流组织作为物流活动的组织者和协调者，是农产品物流活动有序、有效进行的基础和保障，也是农产品生产经营活动中最关键的微观主体之一[328-331]。

20世纪70年代末，尤其是农产品物流逐步市场化以来，农产品物流组织在我国广大农村得到了迅速发展，并在提高农民组织化程度、避免自然风险和市场风险、促进农业产业化和现代化方面发挥了无可替代的作用[332-336]。据中国农产品经纪人流通协会统计，截至2007年年末，我国农产品经纪人队伍已经发展到600万人，其中具有执业资格的40余万户，经纪执业人员逾100万人，全年经纪业务量超过2500亿元[337]。从目前看，这支经纪人队伍已成为我国农产品运销的重要力量。另据农业部统计，截至2006年年底，全国农民专业合作经济组织已超过15万个，农民专业合作组织成员数3878万户，占全国农户总数的15.6%，比2002年提高12.8个百分点。农民专业合作组织中，开展产加销综合服务的专业合作组织占总数的44.5%，以技术信息服务为主的占20.2%，以运销服务为主的占8.8%，以加工服务为主的占7.9%，以仓储服务为主的占2.1%，开展其他服务的占16.5%。2006年，农民专业合作组织统一组织销售粮食、蔬菜、瓜果、肉、蛋、奶、水产品等各类农产品1.7亿吨，开展各类技术培训3340万人次，经营服务盈余325亿元，其中22.5%的盈余73亿元返还给农民专业合作组织成员，23%的盈余75亿元用于股金分红，平均每个农民专业合作组织成员获得盈余返还和股金分红收入381元，农民成员收入普遍比非成员农户收入高出20%左右[338]。上述数据表明，农民专业合作经济组织在组织农民统一进入市场、增加农民收入、增强竞争力等方面发挥了重要作用，为我国建立适应各地农村经济发展特点、类型多元化、经营理念科学化、运行机制良好、具备国际竞争力的农产品流通组织提供了基础。

第三节　农产品物流制度变迁过程中的关系结构分析

本研究用“制度变迁模式”来概括农产品物流制度变迁过程中所表现出来的能代表其特征的运动方式，进而分析揭示农产品物流制度变迁过程中的关系。考察中国农产品物流制度变迁的主要路径与基本内容、农产品物流制度变迁模式演进的动力机制、农产品物流制度变迁的基本特征与影响因素，可以发现，农产品物流制度变迁过程中的关系结构主要表现在：农产品物流与农村经济制度变迁在模式上的不适应、结构上失衡和时间上的不一致。

一　农产品物流制度变迁的基本特征与影响因素

（一）农产品物流制度变迁的基本特征

农产品物流制度是农村经济制度的重要组成部分。依据制度变迁与创新理论，联系我国整体物流和农村经济制度变迁的实际，考察中国农产品物流制度变迁的主要路径和基本内容，可以发现，中国农产品物流制度变迁虽然也可以依据改革开放划分为两个阶段，但其变迁过程却具有与农村经济制度变迁不同的基本特征。

1. 农产品物流制度变迁在不同体制下总是表现为机构的不断反复调整

考察中国农产品物流制度历程可以直接发现一个基本事实，就是不论经济体制如何，农产品物流制度变迁表现为机构的不断反复调整。从新中国成立到现在，我国农产品流通在不同时期采取了不同的制度取向，这种制度取向和变迁基本反映了我国农产品流通的发展历程。本研究将我国农产品流通划分为6个主要阶段，这6个阶段在经历了一个计划与市场不断波动的漫长历程后，最终走向了市场化的发展道路。如图5－5所示。

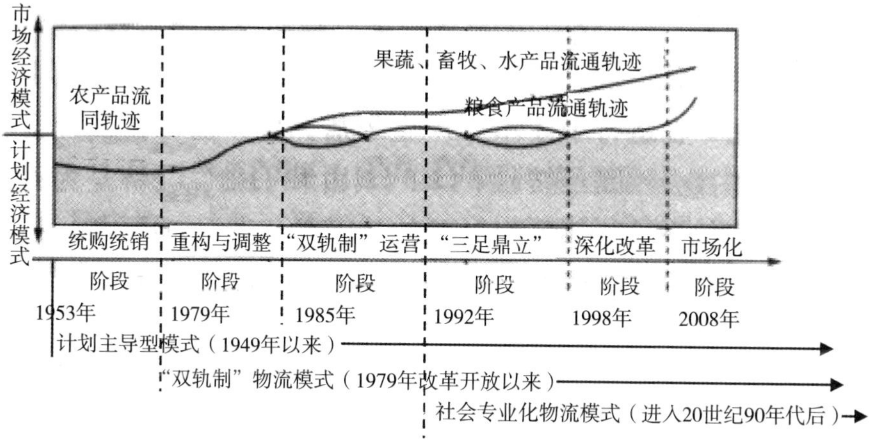

图5－5　农产品流通体制变动曲线

从农产品流通体制在计划与市场之间的变动曲线可以看出，我国农产品流通从计划经济模式向市场经济模式发展的过程中经过了一个相当艰难的历程。在农产品流通的市场化改革进程中，果蔬、畜牧、水产类是放开最早，推入市场最彻底的农产品。从 1985 年到现在，这 3 类农产品的生产一直保持着稳定的增长，流通顺畅，市场网络体系发展完善，社会化资源配置效率较高，证明了市场经济发展模式是经济发展的一种有效途径。

新中国成立以来，我国经济体制经历了从传统计划经济体制到双轨经济体制，再到市场经济体制三个阶段，这种制度取向和变迁不断推动社会分工与协作的发展，也引导着农产品物流机构的不断反复调整。如图 5－6 所示。本研究参考了彭芬[339]、陈丽芬[340]、王雷[341]等专家和学者的研究成果，将新中国成立 60 年来我国农产品物流组织的发展划分为四个阶段[342]。

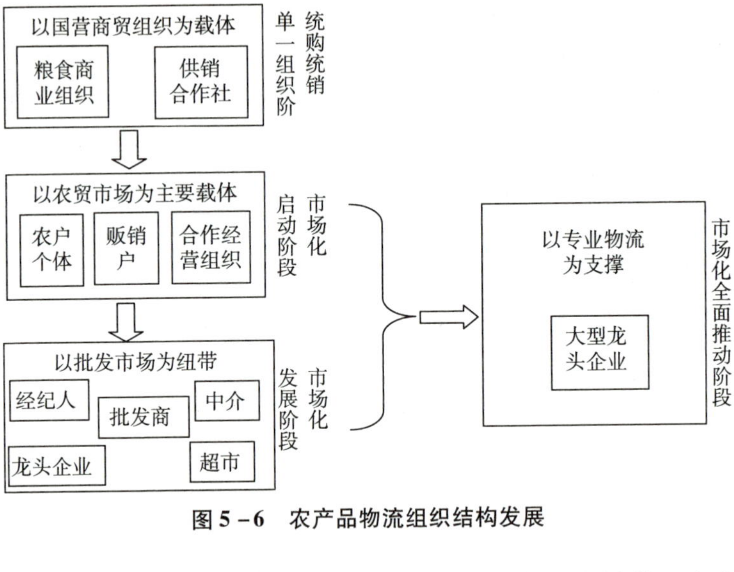

图 5－6　农产品物流组织结构发展

1949 年—1978 年以国营商贸组织为载体的计划购销单一组织阶段。农产品物流组织机构主要由粮食商业组织体系、供销合作社组织体系、其他相关国营商业和外贸组织构成，类型单一。

1979 年—1984 年以农贸市场为载体的市场化启动阶段。1978 年年底，提高农产品价格和恢复农村集市贸易。农产品实行自由流通、议购议销，形成“双轨制”雏形，农贸市场逐渐成为流通的主要载体。

1985年—1991年以批发市场为纽带的市场化发展阶段。国家对重要农产品实行“双轨制”，一些农产品批发市场便在集贸市场的基础上发展起来，以批发市场为载体的组织体系随之发展起来，形成了由批发商、农民经纪人、中介流通组织、农产品加工企业组成的市场流通大军。龙头企业、农业合作组织、农产品超市进入迅速发展阶段。该阶段的农产品物流组织结构呈现出多元化、体系化发展特点，形成了农产品生产—收购—批发—分销—零售的完整的农产品流通体系。

1992年至今以专业物流为支撑的市场化全面推动阶段。1992年到1998年粮食又在市场化和双轨制进行了反复。直至2004年颁布《粮食流通管理条例》，我国多年探索的市场化流通体制真正形成。农产品流通全面走向市场化，除了表现在价格体制的开放，还体现在零售业对外开放方面。1992年7月，国务院批准在北京、上海、天津、广州、大连、青岛6个城市和深圳、珠海、厦门、汕头、海南5个经济特区各试办1—2个中外合资或者合作经营的商业零售企业。1999年6月，零售业中外合资的试点范围扩大到所有省会城市。2004年12月11日，我国取消了投资零售领域的地域、数量和股权比例限制，外商企业进入速度加快。外商流通企业的进入，为农产品流通的市场体系构建起着巨大的推动作用。农产品流通体制变化促使流通模式逐渐由批发向现代物流转变。20世纪80年代中期以批发为核心的流通模式的主要功能是运输、存储，而包装、加工、保鲜等增值功能还没有完全开发出来，品牌产品比例较低，这导致了流通环节的利润主要来源于市场间的差价而不是加工增值。20世纪90年代后期，由于以物流配送为中心，以连锁超市为末端，以大量加工企业的快速发展为背景的新型现代农产品流通形式开始产生发展起来[342]。

2. 农产品物流制度变迁在三个不同层次上表现为二元结构系统的演进

从整体物流、农村经济和农产品物流三个不同层次上，考察中国农产品物流制度变迁的历程，可以发现，中国农产品物流制度变迁在三个不同层次的系统中，均表现出二元性特征。

首先，从整体物流系统来看，虽然在理论上农产品物流是中国整体物流系统中不可或缺的组成部分，但中国经济社会的“二元”结构特征，决定了中国农产品物流的“二元性”。表现出中国农产品物流制度变迁从属地位、时间、手段、内部结构与整体物流不对称。

其次，从农村经济系统来看，虽然在理论上农产品物流是中国农村经济系统中不可或缺的组成部分，但农产品物流系统的交叉性特征，中国政府对农产品物流以垂直治理为主、对农村经济以水平治理为主的特点，决定了中国农产品物流的“二元性”。表现出中国农产品物流制度变迁相对滞后于农村经济制度变迁。

再次，从农产品物流系统来看，中国农产品物流制度变迁存在外生（政府主导的依靠强制性制度变迁形成的农产品正规物流）与内生（民间自发的依靠诱致性制度变迁形成的农产品非正规物流）两种方式。两者具有互补性但始终存在冲突和对立，决定了中国农产品物流的“二元性”。中国农产品物流制度变迁就是这三个不同层次上具有二元性结构系统的演进过程[342]。

3. 农产品物流制度变迁以政府主导的自上而下的强制性制度变迁为主

考察中国农产品物流制度变迁历程可以发现，无论是计划经济时期的国营商业公司和供销合作社、其他相关国营商业和外贸组织“收了放，放了收、合了分，分了合”；再到国营物质储运公司、粮食企业、商业储运公司等基层机构；还是市场经济时期，政府实施的一系列农产品物流深化措施，诸如成立集贸市场及其商业化运营和经营、新建农产品批发市场及其业务调整等等，从单一的国营主导模式→农村集贸市场主导模式→批发市场主导模式的转型过程中，均采取了政府主导的、自上而下的、强制性变迁方式。这种制度安排在一定程度上稳定了农产品物流市场，但是未必能在较大程度上体现农民群众的意愿和农村经济发展的物流需求，原因在于政府（制度供给者）从实现自身目标的角度对农产品物流市场所做出的制度性安排，没有充分满足农产品物流需求者的物流需求，第一，农户资本积累能力较弱。第二，非专业化的流通形式不可避免地带来高的流通费用和流通的低效率。第三，个体经营组织市场行为的非规范造成物流无序及市场波动。表现出制度供给上的错位和不足，使得农产品物流服务的供给严重滞后于农产品物流需求[342]。

4. 农产品物流制度变迁是强制性制度变迁力量强于诱致性制度变迁的过程

从自由购销、统购包销、定购包销一直到市场化运作，从家庭分散经营、集体统一经营到农产品物流产业化发展，无法充分体现现代农产品物流专业化分工的基本特征，这些自发的、诱致性的农产品物流制度的变迁与创新转化为政府推动的强制性制度变迁，最终总是被政府强制性地升级。在农产品正规物流强制性制度变迁的压力下，从表层来看，由于缺少健全的市场和法律等普遍的信用要素，“农产品非正规物流”信用系统之间始终处于非正式、不规范的状态。从深层次来看，非政府力量建立起来的物流只能是非正规的，其结果是使农产品物流市场秩序处于更加混乱的现象。因此，在强制性物流制度变迁力量强于诱致性物流制度变迁的情况下，农产品正规物流与非正规物流的关系陷入了“恶性循环”。而第三方物流主导的多元化物流的出现正是一种诱致性制度变迁，可以有效增强小农生产与大市场的联合。第三方物流企业主导的多元化农产品物流模式创新，通过对农产品生产、运输、包装、储存、流通加工及销售等环节资源的优化整合，大大减少了农产品流通过程的中间环节和利益流失，相应的组织管理费用有所下降，交易效率大大提高，形成“良性循环”演进：诱致性变迁→强制性变迁→诱致性变迁→调动农民再创造的积极性→推进新农村经济的可持续发展。综上所述，以第三方物流企业为主导的多元化农产品物流模式创新，是适应我国农村经济改革、发展的一种组织制度创新，是社会主义市场经济条件下农户和企业的创造和选择，也是推进农产品现代物流发展的重要载体[342]。

（二）农产品物流制度变迁的影响因素

新中国成立迄今的农村经济制度的变迁，以 1978 年为分界线，可大致划分为改革开放前、后两个大的阶段。自新中国成立一直到 1978 年的计划经济时期，中国农村经济制度变迁和当时中国所有制度变迁一样，实际上是依靠国家权力而进行的一场强制性制度变迁，农村经济主体参与很少。1978 年至今，中国农村经济制度变迁的基本特征是诱致性变迁在前，强制性在后，两者反复交替，在摩擦和冲突中不断创新。这一制度创新不仅给中国农村经济的发展注入了新的活力，而且也显示出与改革开放以前截然不同的重要特征：一是农村经济制度变迁是农村经济主体基于利润动机的帕累托改进过程，二是农村经济制度变迁是诱致性变迁与强制性变迁的交互作用过程，三是农村经济制度变迁是一个不断由浅入深、由点到面的渐进式演进过程。任何制度变迁都不可能是孤立的，总是在一定初始条件和内外因素影响下的“路径依赖”过程。中国农产品物流制度的变迁同样如此。农产品物流系统作为物流与农村经济相交叉而形成的复合系统，中国农产品物流制度变迁的影响因素，除了具有和物流以及农村经济制度变迁相同的影响因素外，还具有以下特点：第一，在初始条件中，旧中国的农产品物流和解放区的物流制度安排构成了重要影响。第二，农产品物流制度变迁不仅和农村经济制度变迁一样，受发展战略和计划经济体制的影响，而且农产品物流制度还作为国家实施发展战略的手段和计划经济的工具，直接参与了对农村经济资源和剩余的吸取和控制。农产品物流制度变迁一直是在国家直接控制下强制性进行的。第三，在农产品物流制度变迁中，利益集团的影响主要发生在中央政府和地方政府、政府的农业部门和物流管理部门、农产品正规物流和农产品非正规物流，以及农产品正规内部经济性物流、社会性物流和双向性物流之间。

二　农产品物流制度变迁过程中的关系结构

（一）农产品物流与农村经济制度变迁模式互不适应

农产品物流制度变迁是与农村经济制度变迁不适应的强制性过程。自1979年以来，农村经济制度变迁以自下而上的诱致性变迁推动强制性制度变迁为特征。而与此形成了巨大反差的是，农产品物流制度变迁无论是在计划经济体制时期，还是在市场经济体制条件下，都是采用了强制性制度变迁压制和排斥强制性制度的方式，进而使制度变迁表现为自上而下的强制性变迁特征。农产品物流制度的变迁并没有给农产品物流带来大发展，也没有能有效地促进农村经济发展。在制度变迁的深度上，农产品物流制度的变迁则始终未能深入到产权关系这一制度变迁的内核[343]。

1. 制度变迁主体不同

虽然在计划经济体制时期，中国农产品物流和农村经济制度变迁主体都可分为政府和农村经济主体，但其主次和内部构成不同。在市场经济体制时期，农村经济制度变迁中，农村经济主体和地方政府已经不再是执行者，而且直接参与了自下而上诱导性制度变迁、推动了政府自上而下的强制性制度变迁。农村经济制度变迁主体出现多元化态势。而农产品物流制度变迁主体，虽然已出现地方政府的参与，但仍然是以中央政府为主，农产品正规物流主体依然只是制度执行者，农村经济主体推动的物流制度变迁还处于被打压状态。

2. 制度变迁过程不同

虽然在计划经济体制时期，中国农产品物流和农村经济制度变迁都是政府主导的自上而下的强制性变迁，但在农产品物流制度变迁的过程上农村经济主体自发的试图自下而上的诱致性制度变迁被压制状态表现得更加严重。在市场经济体制时期，农村经济制度变迁过程表现为农村经济主体自发的自下而上的诱致性制度变迁在先，在取得成功后很快被政府承认，并转化为政府推动的自上而下的强制性制度变迁，进而出现诱致性和强制性制度变迁互动进行的过程。而农产品物流制度变迁则仍然明显地表现出以政府主导的自上而下的强制性制度变迁为主，并不断压抑诱致性制度变迁的特征。

3. 制度变迁动因不同

虽然在计划经济体制时期，中国农产品物流与农村经济制度变迁都是政府为实现其发展战略而强制推动的结果，但在农村经济制度变迁的动因上地方政府更显重要。在市场经济体制条件下，由于农产品物流制度变迁主要是政府推动的强制性制度变迁，市场取向改革只是刚刚启动，其动因仍然是主要服从于政府的经济发展战略，所体现的主要是中央政府和地方政府、农产品正规物流和非正规物流，以及不同物流机构之间的利益关系，未能真正做到面向农村经济发展。而农村经济制度变迁所体现的主要是中央政府与地方政府、地方政府之间、农村与城市、农业产业与非农产业之间的利益关系，面向农村经济发展的趋势。

（二）农产品物流与农村经济制度变迁存在结构失衡

农产品物流制度变迁是从属于经济发展战略的强制性制度变迁过程。新中国成立后，物流成为计划经济体系的组成部分，从属于经济发展的计划物流十分自然地要强制性地延伸到农村，成为向工业和城市输送农村经济剩余的吸管。只有农村经济剩余难以支撑经济发展战略时，这种物流制度才能在中央政府的强制下朝有利于农村经济的方向变迁，一旦情形好转便又很快复原。改革开放以来，农产品物流制度变迁从属于经济发展战略的基本特征没有改变。只有农村经济问题开始影响国民经济发展和社会全体成员利益时，农产品物流制度变迁的方向才能在中央政府的强制下，做出暂时性的适当调整而非根本性的制度保障[344-346]。

1. 农产品物流与农村经济制度变迁的需求结构失衡

中国农产品物流制度变迁，一直是政府推动的强制性正规物流制度变迁压制农村经济主体自发的非正规物流制度变迁的过程。制度变迁的需求主要来自政府经济发展战略的需要，体现的是政府意志，近几年来的农产品物流改革则明显地表现出为农产品正规物流，特别是为国有物流自身“扶贫脱困”的特征。而农村经济制度变迁的需求，自改革开放以后，则主要来自农村经济主体对自身利益的追求，以及国家基于农业和农村经济与国民经济关系而对“三农”利益的保护和重视。

2. 农产品物流与农村经济制度变迁的供给结构失衡

农村经济制度变迁表现出不断增加农村经济微观主体生产经营自主权、不断维护其合法利益的制度供给特征，产权主体多元化、产权形式多样化的格局已经形成，从土地制度到农产品流通制度，从农产品价格形成制度到农村税费制度的改革，从农村产业结构调整到农业产业化发展，从乡镇企业到农村城镇化等等，无一不表现出这一特征。并且，农村经济主体和基层政府的诱致性制度供给比重不断增加。而农产品物流制度仍然停留在调整机构、规范管理等表层上，改革的措施主要是依靠政府的财政注入，产权改革还未真正启动，微观物流主体活力未能有效激发。

3. 农产品物流与农村经济制度变迁的区域结构失衡

不同地区农村经济发展水平是存在差异的，但由于中国农产品物流制度变迁是政府主导的自上而下的强制性制度变迁，各地农村经济发展的实际情况难以周全考虑，“一刀切”的现象依然十分明显。而在农村经济制度变迁中，由于诱致性制度变迁发挥了重要影响，在基本经济制度统一的前提下，农村经济主体和各级地方政府对农村经济制度变迁做了大量的实践，形成了多样化的制度变迁模式。总体而言，东部地区农村经济制度变迁时间早、程度深、速度快，而东部地区的农产品物流制度变迁尽管好于西部地区，但远不能适应农村经济发展的要求。而西部地区由于农村经济发展水平低，“一刀切”的农产品物流制度变迁也难以适应其农村经济实际。

上述农产品物流制度与农村经济制度变迁在模式上的不适应、结构上失衡，直接导致了农产品物流制度变迁在时间上滞后于农村经济制度变迁，使得农产品物流制约了农村经济制度变迁的进程。

第六章　转型时期西部地区农产品物流数量关系实证

依据新制度经济学的分析框架，农产品物流制度变迁及关系结构的不断积淀，必然表现为现实农产品物流与农村经济之间的数量关系。通过实证判断这种关系特征的状况，不仅是对中国农产品物流制度变迁及其数量关系绩效的检验，更是实现西部地区农产品物流可持续发展的重要依据。按本研究的定义，西部地区农产品物流可持续发展，必须与农村经济之间存在明确的关系：因果性→互动性→正向性→显著性。并且，这些不同层次的关系形态，都必须通过统计显著性检验。根据这些标准，本章将运用现代计量经济学方法和分析软件，对转型时期[①]西部地区农产品物流的数量关系状态进行实证分析和得出正确判断。

第一节　西部地区农产品物流数量关系的实证方法

一　西部地区农产品物流变量选择与数据来源

依据西部地区农村经济的现实[②]，结合国内相关研究的做法来计算农

① 本研究对“现实”的定义选择了“转型时期”，具体而言是指 1978 年以来的时期。其理由在第一章的“研究的背景”已有说明。由于判断西部地区农产品物流与农村经济关系的现实状况是本研究展开的重要依据，必须在研究之初进行，因此本研究的数据只能以 2008 年为限。根据资料的可得性，利用西部 12 个省级行政区（由于重庆只有 1997 年以来的数据，因此，将其数据加入到四川省进行分析）的人口数据和物流业产值数据，将时间跨度定为 1978 年至 2008 年，以求准确反映改革开放以来，在西部大开发过程中农产品物流演变轨迹。

② 本研究旨在反映西部地区农产品物流与农村经济的真实关系，相应地所涉及的变量也应当包含西部地区农产品物流与农村经济两个方面。对于西部地区农村经济发展水平的衡量，中国目前尚无官方统计指标与资料。

村增加值①（见表6－1）。在表6－1的基础上，图6－1显示了1978年—2008年西部地区第一产业增加值、乡镇企业增加值和农村增加值这三个变量的发展趋势。从中可以看出：1992年—2008年间西部地区农村经济发展水平的提高，更多地来自于乡镇企业发展的推动②。计量农村经济发展，农村投资与消费是必须关注的重要变量[347]。图6－2显示了1978年—2008年西部地区农村投资与消费的走势。从中可以发现，西部地区农村投资增长普遍低于农村消费增长，20世纪90年代中后期以后，西部地区农村投资增长与消费增长差距逐步扩大。

表6－1　1978年—2008年中国西部12省市区农村经济总量指标的时间序列③

类别 时间（年）	第一产业增加值（亿元）	乡镇企业增加值（亿元）	农村增加值（亿元）	农村投资（亿元）	农村消费（亿元）
1978	265.67	55.78	321.45	57.72	331.03
1979	398.51	66.09	464.60	62.68	381.73
1980	540.30	76.40	616.70	56.31	432.52
1981	594.30	102.48	696.78	32.46	494.18
1982	635.66	128.76	764.42	42.84	553.48
1983	675.80	154.88	830.68	54.00	625.27
1984	827.73	181.00	1008.73	71.93	722.94
1985	827.48	207.12	1034.6	88.00	885.30
1986	873.52	295.00	1168.52	106.51	972.73
1987	1109.63	383.28	1492.91	137.80	1100.03
1988	1401.91	471.28	1873.19	171.67	1355.52
1989	1567.96	559.25	2127.21	165.76	1490.85
1990	1283.77	672.30	1956.07	161.37	1554.27
1991	1393.86	797.91	2191.77	199.55	1709.03
1992	1514.31	1271.92	2786.23	259.79	1991.39
1993	1738.14	2270.30	4008.44	359.59	2384.00

① 如中国社会科学院农村发展研究所和国家统计局农村社会经济调查总队《中国农村经济形势分析与预测》（社会科学文献出版社，2003）等。国家统计局没有公布农村产值的数据，本研究用第一产业增加值和乡镇企业增加值之和估算农村经济总产出，即农村增加值。

② 1978年—2008年间西部地区无论是第一产业增加值和乡镇企业增加值，还是农村增加值都获得了长足的发展。尤其是1992年—1997年间，农村经济的发展保持了较高的水平。1997年以后，农业经济发展速度开始减缓。直到2000年实施西部大开发后，2002年—2008年间，农村经济的发展迅速提高。

③ 本表列出的西部地区12省市区，包括重庆、四川、贵州、云南、西藏、陕西、甘肃、宁夏、青海、新疆、广西、内蒙古。

续表 6－1

类别 时间（年）	第一产业增加值（亿元）	乡镇企业增加值（亿元）	农村增加值（亿元）	农村投资（亿元）	农村消费（亿元）
1994	2331.71	3098.91	5430.62	455.55	3123.73
1995	2798.05	3412.16	6210.21	568.25	3311.76
1996	3494.56	3753.38	7247.94	693.80	3416.25
1997	3696.93	3937.62	7634.55	746.33	3632.66
1998	3727.48	4335.65	8063.13	768.15	3680.66
1999	3652.40	4510.32	8162.72	795.15	3780.75
2000	3706.78	4756.85	8463.63	869.59	3999.35
2001	3833.07	4869.55	8702.62	936.66	4230.70
2002	4025.76	5054.48	9080.24	1040.40	4407.82
2003	4450.37	6193.72	10644.09	1266.93	4628.21
2004	5368.82	8051.83	13420.65	1486.92	4859.62
2005	5924.63	10628.42	16553.05	1737.34	5102.60
2006	6396.07	14029.52	20425.59	2159.71	5357.73
2007	7645.08	18518.96	26164.04	2579.25	6097.94
2008	9065.13	24074.65	33139.78	3158.34	7927.32

说明：农村增加值是相应各期《中国统计年鉴》《中国农村统计年鉴》《中国农业统计资料》的第一产业增加值、乡镇企业增加值，两者数值之和；农村投资是相应各期的《中国统计年鉴》按城乡分全社会固定资产投资中的西部地区 12 省的农村投资数值加总；农村消费是相应各期的《中国统计年鉴》各地区最终消费支出及构成中的西部地区 12 省的农村居民消费数值加总。

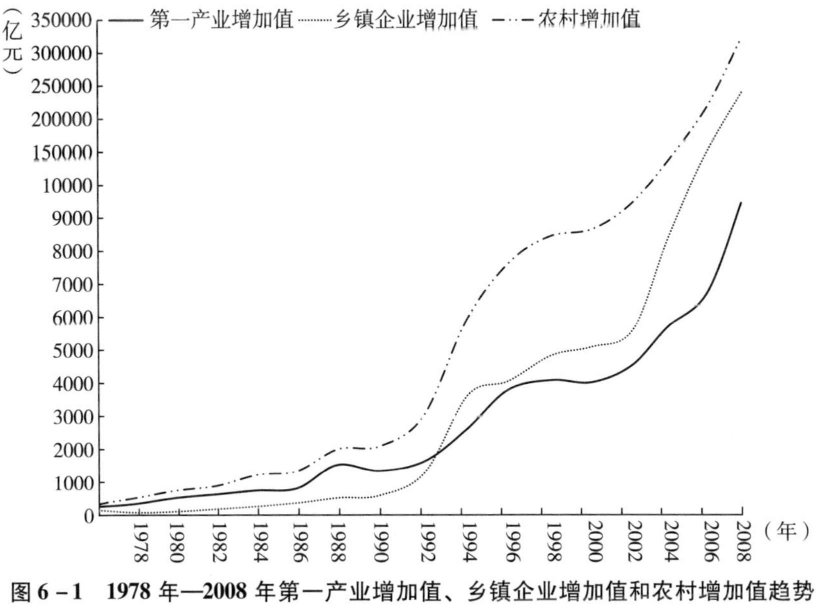

图 6－1　1978 年—2008 年第一产业增加值、乡镇企业增加值和农村增加值趋势

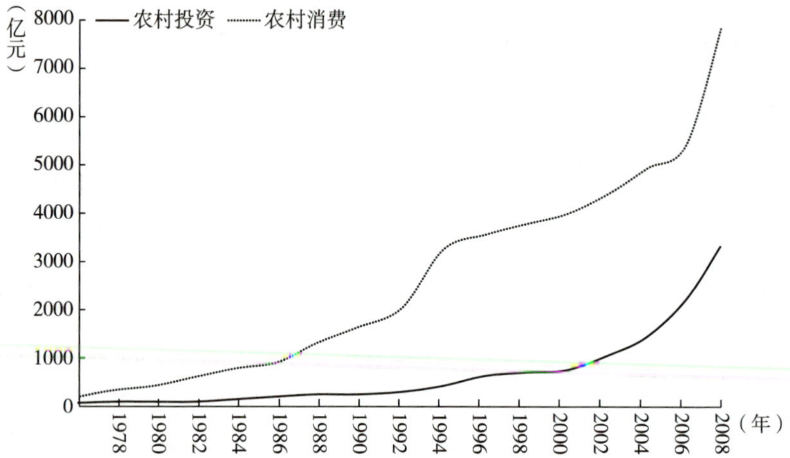

图 6－2　1978 年—2008 年农村投资与农村消费趋势

在上述总量指标的基础上，选择西部地区农村居民家庭人均纯收入予以反映西部地区经济发展水平（见表 6－2）。图 6－3 显示了 1978 年—2008 年西部地区农村人均 GDP、人均农业增加值和农民人均纯收入的变化趋势，从中可知，西部地区农村居民人均 GDP、人均农业增加值与农村居民人均纯收入的差距，从 20 世纪 90 年代开始逐渐拉大。图 6－4 显示了 1978 年—2008 年西部地区农村人均投资与人均消费的趋势图。与总量指标相吻合的是，20 世纪 90 年代中后期以后，西部地区农村人均投资与人均消费水平的绝对差距也扩大了。

表 6－2　1978 年—2008 年中国西部 12 省市区农村经济人均指标的时间序列

年份	农村年平均人口（万人）	农村人均增加值（元）	农村人均农业增加值（元）	农民人均纯收入（元）	农村人均投资（元）	农村人均消费（元）
1978	24581.0	130.77	108.07	126.90	23.48	134.66
1979	24697.0	188.12	161.35	152.57	25.38	154.56
1980	24783.0	248.83	218.01	182.19	22.72	174.52
1981	24916.5	279.64	238.51	212.76	13.03	198.33
1982	25011.5	305.62	254.14	208.13	17.13	221.29
1983	25141.5	330.40	268.79	238.30	21.48	248.70
1984	25167.5	400.80	328.88	273.30	28.58	287.25
1985	25171.0	411.02	328.74	305.85	34.96	351.71

续表 6－2

年份	农村年平均人口（万人）	农村人均增加值（元）	农村人均农业增加值（元）	农民人均纯收入（元）	农村人均投资（元）	农村人均消费（元）
1986	25296.5	461.92	345.31	326.00	42.10	384.53
1987	25432.0	587.02	436.31	352.42	54.18	432.53
1988	25623.5	731.04	547.11	415.32	67.00	529.01
1989	25863.5	822.47	606.24	458.46	64.09	576.43
1990	26141.5	748.26	491.08	523.09	61.73	594.56
1991	26472.0	827.95	526.54	539.83	75.38	645.59
1992	26574.5	1048.45	569.83	517.76	97.76	749.36
1993	26557.0	1509.37	654.49	608.72	135.40	897.69
1994	26674.0	2035.92	874.15	806.47	170.78	1171.07
1995	26796.0	2317.58	1044.20	1042.07	212.07	1235.91
1996	26935.0	2690.90	1297.40	1272.19	257.58	1268.33
1997	27043.0	2823.11	1367.05	1009.90	275.98	1343.29
1998	27110.0	2974.22	1374.94	1392.30	283.35	1357.67
1999	27169.5	3004.36	1344.30	1577.56	292.66	1391.54
2000	26211.5	3228.97	1414.18	1632.31	331.76	1525.79
2001	25047.0	3474.51	1530.35	1692.96	373.96	1689.10
2002	24656.5	3682.69	1632.73	1791.73	421.96	1787.69
2003	24016.0	4432.08	1853.08	1920.95	527.53	1927.13
2004	23658.0	5672.77	2269.34	2157.91	628.51	2054.11
2005	23295.0	7105.83	2543.30	2378.91	745.80	2190.42
2006	23044.0	8863.73	2775.59	2588.37	937.21	2325.00
2007	22883.0	11433.83	3340.94	3028.38	1127.15	2664.83
2008	22527.0	14711.13	6162.08	3517.75	1402.02	3519.03

说明：农村年平均人口是相应各期的《中国统计年鉴》各地区人口的城乡构成中的西部地区 12 省的乡村人口数加总，乡村年初人口数加总与年末人口数加总的平均值；农村人均“增加值、农业增加值、投资、消费”各值等于相应的总量值除以乡村年内平均人口；农民人均纯收入数据来源相应各期的《中国统计年鉴》各地区农村居民家庭人均纯收入中的西部地区 12 省的农村居民家庭人均纯收数加总。

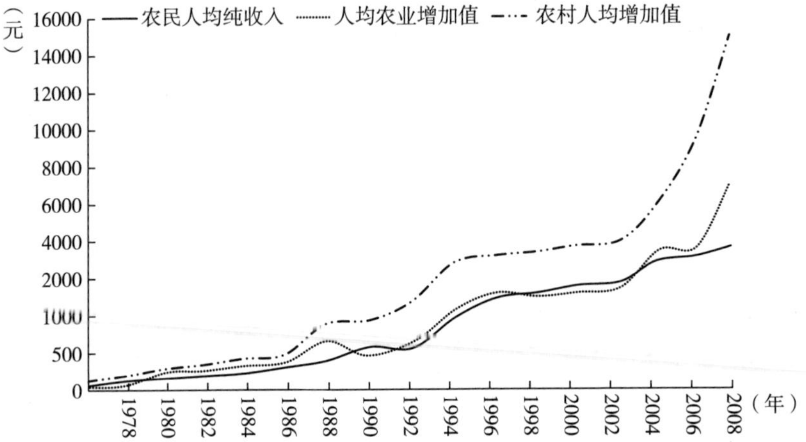

图 6－3　1978 年—2008 年农村人均增加值、人均农业增加值和农民人均纯收入趋势

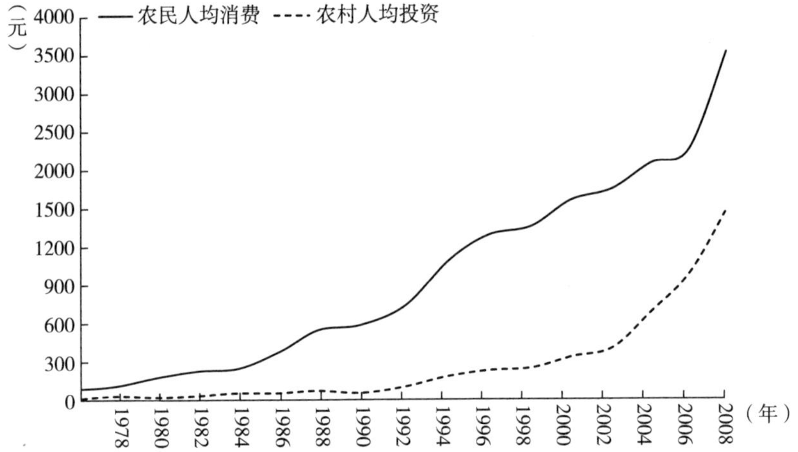

图 6－4　1978 年—2008 年农村人均投资与农村人均消费趋势

对于西部地区农产品物流发展的水平，主要衡量农产品正规和准正规物流机构的农产品运销，并从物流来源和物流运行两个角度加以分析[348]。从物流来源方面看，依据本研究的基本思路，可以选择物流供给指标①、物

① 物流服务的供给指标，物流的供给能力即“物流能力”，主要取决于物流的基础设施和经营服务能力指标（宗刚，2003）。物流供给指标包括该地区的物流基础设施状况、物流信息系统指标和物流企业服务能力指标等方面。

流需求指标[①]，本研究选取物流网络里程[②]、货物周转量[③]两个指标，图6－5显示的是1978年—2008年这两个指标的变动趋势。从物流运行方面看，应当选择物流成效这一指标[④]。然而，由于中国缺乏这一指标的官方统计数据，在实际分析中，本研究利用交通、仓储及通信业的总产值来构造物流产值指标的数据资料[⑤]，根据我国东中西三大地带的物流业产值比较来衡量西部地区物流发展的程度[⑥]。图6－6显示的是1978年—2008年我国东中西三大地带物流业产值指标的变动趋势。西部地区物流总量的所有相关数据参见表6－3。

表6－3　1978年—2008年中国西部12省市区物流总量指标的时间序列[⑦]

年份	物流网络里程（公里）	货运量（万吨）	货物周转量（亿吨公里）	物流产值指数	物流产值（亿元）
1978	17726.8（铁路）	26876.1	997.2	100.0	25.51
1979	18159.1（铁路）	28864.9	1155.1	108.3	27.63
1980	18360.5（铁路）	31000.9	1220.1	112.9	31.69

① 物流需求指标，主要反映社会经济产生物流需求状况及其对物流的发展推动力大小，物流的需求指标与经济增长速度密切相关（宗刚，2003）。物流需求是指社会经济活动在物流的各个环节（如运输、仓储、配送、流通加工等）所提出的有支付能力的需要，社会经济对物流的需求是通过各种物流需求量来反映的，但物流量并不完全代表经济社会活动对物流的需求。

② 考虑到数据的可得性和复杂性，仅选取物流网络里程这一指标来描述西部地区物流供给状况。物流网络里程是对物流网络的量化，指物质实体的通路，目前主要有铁路、公路、内河、航空和管道五种方式。从理论上讲，物流网络里程的度量应该是五种运输方式按实现的价值增加额的加权和，但限于数据的可得性和有效性，这里仅考虑物流网络里程中最主要的三种方式：公路里程、铁路营业里程和内河航道里程，并以其简单加总后的总和来度量物流网络发展状况。

③ 考虑到数据的可得性，可将货运量和货物周转量作为对物流需求的衡量指标，因货运量没有考虑到距离的因素，因此这里选取货物周转量作为反映物流需求的指标。

④ 物流发展成效的指标，主要是反映物流供给和需求共同作用所带来的物流实际发展情况（宗刚，2003）。物流成效指标包括很多方面，交通、仓储及通信业是物流业的主要部分，用于物流系统经济评价方法（魏国果等，2003）。

⑤ 考虑到价格因素对物流产值的影响，所以对于统计年鉴数据采用物流产值指数进行换算的方法，将其换算为1978年的不变价格。现代物流规模的增加主要体现在西部地区物流业的产值不断增加，交通运输、仓储和邮电通信业是物流业的支柱行业，所以可根据交通运输、仓储和邮电通信业的总产值的发展情况来看西部地区物流业的发展规模与发展速度。

⑥ 从时间角度看，东中西三大地带的物流业产值从1982年开始一直呈上升趋势，到1999年差距越来越大。东部地区物流产值增加尤为明显，中部地区增加也较快，都远远高于西部地区，西部地区物流产值增加缓慢，这与我国的经济发展政策有关，从1978年开始我国的经济开放政策一直倾向在东部地区，而西部地区的经济投资环境较差，经济发展优惠条件少，我国的经济发展政策为东部地区物流产业的快速发展注入了活力。

⑦ 数据来源于相应各期的《中国统计年鉴》《中国西部农村统计资料》。

续表 6-3

年份	物流网络里程（公里）	货运量（万吨）	货物周转量（亿吨公里）	物流产值指数	物流产值（亿元）
1981	18926.2（铁路）	33295.0	1231.9	115.0	33.27
1982	395032.0	35759.0	1357.1	128.1	38.40
1983	399393.3	40159.0	1515.1	140.2	45.32
1984	403268.7	39407.0	1726.8	161.1	89.30
1985	410836.3	39397.0	1929.5	183.3	111.84
1986	418030.2	39266.0	2043.2	208.8	128.90
1987	428725.0	40327.0	2239.3	228.9	185.81
1988	436640.6	40650.5	2345.9	257.5	188.15
1989	441912.2	107071.0	3272.0	268.3	224.22
1990	445816.3	191710.0	3243.3	290.7	252.71
1991	450334.7	189937.0	3325.7	321.4	194.45
1992	455001.0	196880.0	3541.1	353.7	371.64
1993	462592.0	241355.0	3869.2	398.1	351.51
1994	470183.0	253961.0	4197.3	432.0	425.39
1995	476741.0	276756.0	4386.0	479.4	536.03
1996	485352.0	286362.0	4543.4	532.4	664.93
1997	502383.0	290338.0	4706.4	581.3	443.82
1998	528662.0	293304.0	4706.5	642.9	547.94
1999	575918.0	294833.0	5183.6	721.2	682.50
2000	597859.0	306632.0	5423.2	783.0	756.71
2001	748329.0	313547.0	5862.5	852.0	863.28
2002	775968.0	330967.0	6385.9	912.7	970.96
2003	797197.3	348670.0	6939.1	968.6	1746.21
2004	815102.0	373744.0	7899.3	1108.9	2060.58
2005	838806.2	411824.0	8666.2	1233.7	2088.78
2006	1321014.0	453192.0	9580.9	1370.3	2424.76
2007	1399920.4	508874.0	10867.7	1547.8	2746.64
2008	1481710.8	627612.0	16403.0	1664.7	3159.39

说明：(1) 1978 年—1981 年物流网络里程是相应各期的《中国统计年鉴》“各地区运输线路长度”中的西部地区 12 省的铁路营业里程数值合计，加总。1982 年—2008 年物流网络里程是相应各期的《中国统计年鉴》“各地区运输线路长度”中的西部地区 12 省的公路里程、铁路营业里程和内河航道里程数值合计，加总。(2) 货运量是相应各期的《中国统计年鉴》“各地区货运量”中的西部地区 12 省的数值合计，加总。(3) 货物周转量是相应各期的《中国统计年鉴》“各地区货物周转量”中的西部地区 12 省的数值合计，加总。(4) 物流产值是相应各期的《中国统计年鉴》“按三次产业分地区生产总值”中的西部地区 12 省的交通运输、仓储和邮政业数值合计，加总。本表按不变价格计算。1978 年 = 100。交通、仓储及通信业产值已经剔除了价格因素，为可比价格。

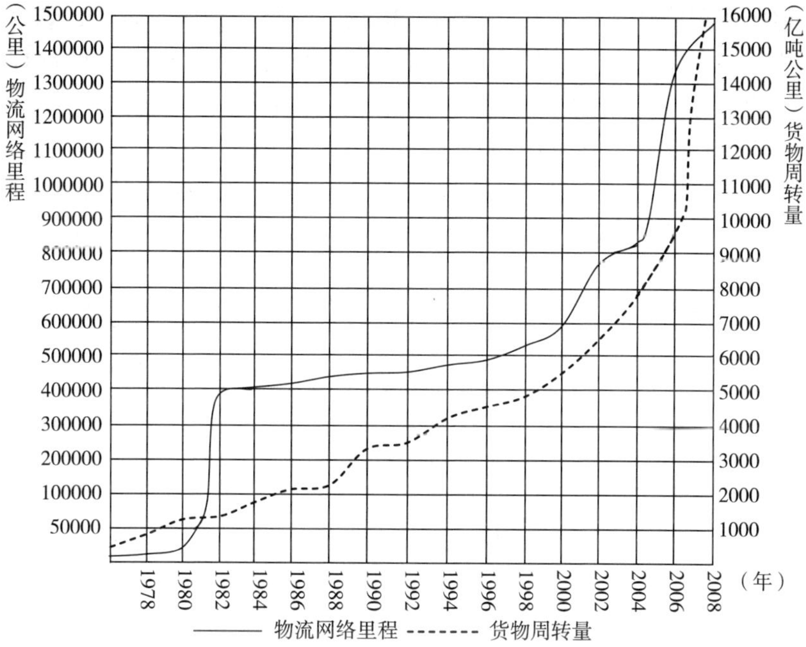

图 6－5　1978 年—2008 年西部地区物流网络里程、货物周转量趋势

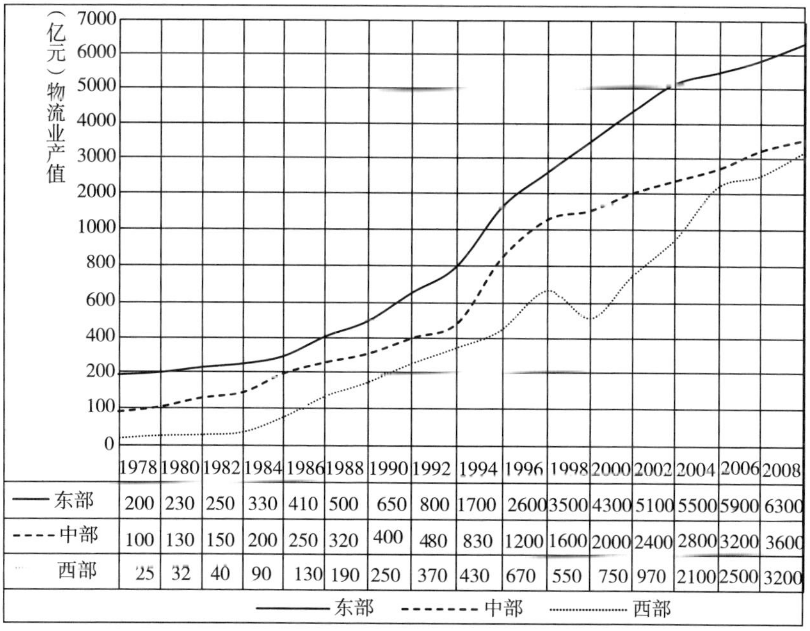

	1978	1980	1982	1984	1986	1988	1990	1992	1994	1996	1998	2000	2002	2004	2006	2008
—— 东部	200	230	250	330	410	500	650	800	1700	2600	3500	4300	5100	5500	5900	6300
- - - 中部	100	130	150	200	250	320	400	480	830	1200	1600	2000	2400	2800	3200	3600
西部	25	32	40	90	130	190	250	370	430	670	550	750	970	2100	2500	3200

——东部　- - - - - 中部　··········· 西部

图 6－6　1978 年—2008 年我国东中西三大地带物流业产值指标的变动趋势

西部地区主要农产品从粮食、油料、棉花、麻类、甘薯、甜菜、烟叶、蚕茧、茶叶、水果、肉类、奶类、禽蛋、水产类的产量增长看，西部地区已经成为全国最重要的糖料作物生产基地；西部地区是全国主要草原牧区①。与农村经济形势考察相适应，西部地区农产品物流发展水平的衡量，同样不能忽略人口因素。因此，还必须把前述指标转化为人均指标（见图6－7）。西部地区农产品物流的所有相关数据参见表6－4。

表6－4　1978年—2008年中国西部12省市区农产品物流人均指标的时间序列②

年份	农村年内平均人口（万人）	农村人均物流网络里程（公里）	农村人均货物周转量（吨公里）	农村人均物流产值（元）
1978	24581.0	0.72	405.6	10.37
1979	24697.0	0.73	467.7	11.18
1980	24783.0	0.74	492.3	12.78
1981	24916.5	0.75	494.4	13.35
1982	25011.5	15.79	542.5	15.35
1983	25141.5	15.88	602.6	18.02
1984	25167.5	16.02	686.1	35.48
1985	25171.0	16.32	766.5	44.43
1986	25296.5	16.52	807.7	50.95
1987	25432.0	16.85	880.5	73.06
1988	25623.5	17.04	915.5	73.42
1989	25863.5	17.08	1265.1	86.69
1990	26141.5	17.05	1240.6	96.67
1991	26472.0	17.01	1256.3	73.45
1992	26574.5	17.12	1332.5	139.84
1993	26557.0	17.41	1456.9	132.36
1994	26674.0	17.62	1573.5	159.47
1995	26796.0	17.79	1636.8	200.04
1996	26933.0	18.01	1686.8	246.86
1997	27043.0	18.57	1740.3	164.11
1998	27110.0	19.50	1736.0	202.11
1999	27169.5	21.19	1907.8	251.20
2000	26211.5	22.80	2069.0	288.69
2001	25047.0	29.87	2340.5	344.66

① 其他如新疆是我国最重要的长绒棉生产基地，四川、云南等地是全国重要的茶叶生产基地；内蒙古、青海、新疆等地是全国重要的奶制品生产基地；广西、云南、四川、陕西等是全国重要的水果生产基地；广西等是全国重要的水产品生产基地。

② 数据来源于相应各期《中国统计年鉴》《新中国五十年统计资料汇编》《中国农村统计年鉴》《中国物流年鉴》《中国物流行业年度报告》。

续表 6－4

年份	农村年内平均人口（万人）	农村人均物流网络里程（公里）	农村人均货物周转量（吨公里）	农村人均物流产值（元）
2002	24656.5	31.47	2589.9	393.79
2003	24016.0	33.19	2889.3	727.10
2004	23658.0	34.45	3338.9	870.98
2005	23295.0	36.00	3720.1	896.66
2006	23044.0	57.32	4157.6	1052.23
2007	22883.0	61.17	4749.2	1200.29
2008	22527.0	65.77	7281.4	1402.49

说明：（1）乡村年内平均人口是乡村年初人口与年末人口的平均值；（2）各人均指标由相应总量指标除以乡村年内平均人口求得。

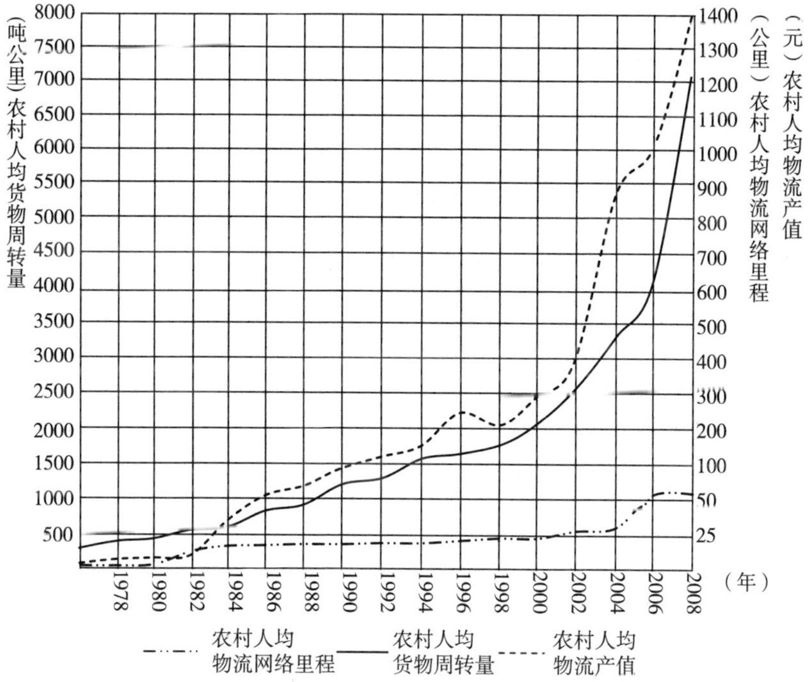

图 6－7　1978 年—2008 年西部农村人均物流网络里程、农村人均货物周转量、农村人均物流产值趋势

本研究还构造了西部地区农产品物流深化指标 WLSH（农产品物流产值/农村经济总产值），以此来反映农产品正规物流发展的程度；利用 Logistics efficiency 构造的物流相关效率 WLL 衡量整体物流发展水平；采用 GDP 及其增长率反映国民经济增长，对西部地区农产品物流与农村经济的发展效应进行实证。本研究的数据来源于《中国统计年鉴》（1981 年到2008年年历)、国家统计局农村社会经济调查司《中国农业统计资料汇编(1949—2004)》(中国统计出版社,2006)、国家统计局《历年中国国民经济和社会发展统计公报》(中国网,2007-2-28)、国家统计局国民经济综合统计司《新中国五十五年统计资料汇编》(中国统计出版社,2005)、《西部蓝皮书:中国西部经济发展报告》(社会科学文献出版社,2010)、《中国物流年鉴》(中国物资出版社,2005)、《2003年度中国行业发展报告:物流业》(中国经济出版社,2004)。

二 西部地区农产品物流数量关系的检验模型

(一)单位根检验①

本研究通过以下三个模型完成ADF检验[349-351]:

模型1: $$\Delta X_t = \delta X_{t-1} + \sum_{i=1}^{m} \beta_i \Delta_{t-i} + \varepsilon_t \tag{6-1}$$

模型2: $$\Delta X_t = \alpha + \delta X_{t-1} + \sum_{i=1}^{m} \beta_i \Delta_{t-i} + \varepsilon_t \tag{6-2}$$

模型3②: $$\Delta X_t = \alpha + \beta t + \delta X_{t-1} + \sum_{i=1}^{m} \beta_i \Delta_{t-i} + \varepsilon_t \tag{6-3}$$

(二)协整性检验③

$X_{1t}, X_{2t}, \cdots, X_{kt}$ 是 d 阶单整,存在 $\alpha = (\alpha_1, \alpha_2, \cdots, \alpha_k)$,使得 $Z_t = \alpha X_t' \sim$

① 为了避免模型出现“伪回归”,本研究首先采用迪凯和富乐(Dickey & Fuller,1981)提出的考虑残差项序列相关的ADF(Augment Dickey-Fuller)单位根检验法,检验变量的平稳性,对于非平稳性的变量进行处理,使之成为平稳时间序列。

② 模型3中的t是时间变量,代表了时间序列随时间变化的某种趋势。虚拟假设都是 H_0: $\delta=0$,即存在一单位根,模型1与另外两个模型的差别在于是否包含有常数项和趋势项。实际检验时从模型3开始,然后是模型2、模型1。何时检验拒绝零假设,即原序列不存在单位根,为平稳序列,则何时检验停止。否则,就要继续检验,直到检验完模型1为止。

③ 协整理论是分析非平稳时间序列的一个重要方法。恩格莱和格朗杰(R. F. Engle & C. W. J. Granger,1987)指出:如果两个或两个以上的非平稳时间序列(含有单位根的时间序列)的线性组合能构成平稳的时间序列,则称这些非平稳时间序列是协整的,称得到的平稳的线性组合为协整方程,可以认为协整方程的存在说明这些变量(即非平稳的时间序列)之间存在长期的均衡关系。如果变量是单整的,那么,本研究将对相关变量进行协整检验(Cointegration Test),以确定西部地区农产品物流发展与农村经济发展之间的长期关系。

$I(d-b)$ ，其中，$b>0$ ，$X_t=(X_{1t},X_{2t},\cdots,X_{kt})'$ ，则认为序列 $X_{1t},X_{2t},\cdots,X_{kt}$ 是 (d,b) 阶协整，记为 $X_t \sim CI(d,b)$ ，α 为协整向量[①]。

（三）因果关系检验[②]

1. 模型建立

$$\begin{cases} X_t = c_1 + \sum_{j=1}^{p} a_j X_{t-j} + \sum_{j=1}^{q} \beta_j Y_{t-j} + \mu_{1t} & (6\quad 4) \\ Y_t = c_2 + \sum_{j=1}^{p} \gamma_j Y_{t-j} + \sum_{j=1}^{q} \delta_j X_{t-j} + \mu_{1t} & (6-5) \end{cases}$$

（1）如果 $\beta_j=0$，$\delta_j=0(j=1,\ 2,\ \cdots,\ q)$，则 X_t、Y_t 互相独立；

（2）如果 $\beta_j=0$，$\delta_j\neq0(j=1,\ 2,\ \cdots,\ q)$，则 X_t 为 Y_t 的原因；

（3）如果 $\beta_j\neq0$，$\delta_j=0(j=1,\ 2,\ \cdots,\ q)$，则 X_t 为 Y_t 的原因；

（4）如果 $\beta_j\neq0$，$\delta_j\neq0(j=1,\ 2,\ \cdots,\ q)$，则 X_t、Y_t 互为因果。

2. F 检验

对于 $X_t = c_1 + \sum_{j=1}^{p} \alpha_j X_{t-j} + \sum_{j=1}^{q} \beta_j Y_{t-j} + \mu_{1t}$ 进行假设检验，设置：

$$H_0: \beta_j = 0$$

$$H_1: \beta_j \neq 0(j=1,2,\cdots,q)$$

首先对模型应用 OLS，记残差平方和为 $ESS(q,\ p)$，再对模型：

$$X_t = c_1 + \sum_{j=1}^{p} \alpha_j X_{t-j} + \varepsilon_t$$

应用 OLS ，记残差平方和为 $ESS(p)$。

构造统计量[③]：$F = \dfrac{[ESS(p) - ESS(q,p)]/p}{ESS(q,p)/(n-p-q-1)} \sim F(p,n-p-q-1)$ ；

① 本研究将采用约翰森（Johansen）提出的协整检验（JJ 检验）方法来检验变量之间的协整关系。从协整的定义可以看出，协整的经济意义在于：两个变量，虽然它们具有各自的长期波动规律，但是如果它们是协整的，则它们之间存在着一个长期稳定的比例关系。反过来，如果两个变量，具有各自的长期波动规律，但是它们不是协整的，则它们之间就不存在着一个长期稳定的比例关系。

② 格朗杰（Granger）因果检验是用于检验两个变量之间因果关系的一种常用方法。本研究将利用这一方法揭示西部地区农村经济与农产品物流两者之间是否存在因果关系。格朗杰因果检验的基本原理在于：给定一个信息集 A_t，它至少包含（X_t，Y_t），如果利用 X_t 的过去比不利用它时可以更好地预测 Y，称 X_t 为 Y_t 的格朗杰（Granger）原因。

③ 给定置信水平 α，查临界值 F_α，如 $F>F_\alpha$ 因果，拒绝 H_0，接受 H_1。实际应用时，需要对模型（6－4）、（6－5）同时检验，才能做出判断。在应用软件中给出了具体的存在因果关系的概率值。

3. 滞后期数的确定

本研究以 AIC 和 SC 确定最优滞后期数①。

第二节 西部地区农产品物流关系结构的数量特征

一 各时间序列的单位根检验

利用 Eviews 计量经济软件，对中国西部 12 省市区农产品的各物流指标和农村经济增长指标的进行单位检验，以确定各时间序列的平稳性[352]。各变量及其指标的相应对应关系如表 6-5。

表 6-5 各指标与变量间对应关系

指标	农村经济增加值	农民收入	农村投资	农村消费	物流网络里程	货物周转量	物流产值
变量	RGDP	FR	TZ	XF	WWL	HYZ	WLC

通过检验可以看出，时间序列的 FR 和 TZ 原序列的 ADF 统计量都大于该序列的检验值的临界值，说明 FR 和 TZ 时间序列都是平稳变量；而时间序列的 RGDP、XF、WWL、HYZ、WLC 原序列的 ADF 统计量都小于该序列的检验值的临界值，这说明 RGDP、XF、WWL、HYZ、WLC 时间序列均为非平稳变量。表 6-6 表明中国西部 12 省市区农产品的各物流指标和农村经济增长的时间序列为一阶非平稳序列②。

表 6-6 ADF 单位根检验结果③

变量	ADF 检验	检验类型（C，T）	滞后阶数（K）	显著水平	结论
RGDP	-2.3918	含时间趋势项和常数项	1	10%（-3.2602）	非平稳
△RGDP	-2.8057	含常数项	2	10%（-2.6417）	平稳

① 格朗杰因果检验中最重要的是滞后期确定，在实际分析中检验的功效取决于最优滞后期数的确定。如果滞后期数随机确定，会导致检验结果的错误。在该项研究中，最优滞后期数的确定是按阿凯克（Akaike）信息评价标准（AIC）和史瓦兹（Schwarz）评价标准（SC）确定的。

② 表示对非平稳变量采用差分算子进行检验，表中所有数据序列均为 10% 显著水平下的临界值都是平稳的。

③ 检验类型（C，T）分别表示单位根检验方程常数项，含时间趋势项；（K）表示单位根检验方程滞后阶数；△表示差分算子，△RGDP、△XF、△WWL、△HYZ 和△WLC 分别表示对相关变量取一阶差分值，△2XF 表示 XF 的二阶差分值。

续表 6－6

变量	ADF 检验	检验类型（C，T）	滞后阶数（K）	显著水平	结论
FR	－5.084	含时间趋势项和常数项	1	1%（－4.4691）	平稳
TZ	－5.1141	含时间趋势项和常数项	1	1%（－4.4167）	平稳
XF	－2.3334	含时间趋势项和常数项	2	10%（－3.2535）	非平稳
△XF	－2.6008	含常数项	1	10%（－2.6417）	平稳
△2XF	－402890	含常数项	3	1%（－3.78561）	平稳
WWL	－1.6586	含时间趋势项和常数项	2	10%（－3.6219）	非平稳
△WWL	－2.7734	不含时间趋势项和常数项	3	5%（－1.9566）	平稳
HYZ	－1.7289	含时间趋势项和常数项	1	10%（－3.6454）	非平稳
△HYZ	－2.0421	不含时间趋势项和常数项	1	5%（－2.6330）	平稳
WLC	－1.7146	含时间趋势项和常数项	3	10%（－3.6112）	非平稳
△WLC	－1.9608	不含时间趋势项和常数项	2	10%（－1.9574）	平稳

二　协整性检验

根据时间序列的单位根检验分析结果，可以看出农村经济增加指标（GDP）与物流供给能力指标（物流网络里程）和物流成效指标（物流产值）都是单整的，呈现出非平稳特征。本文选取常用的 Johansen 检验（JJ 检验）方法对这些变量之间是否存在长期稳定的关系进行检验①。表 6－7 协整性检验的结果表明存在协整关系②。

表 6－7　　中国西部 12 省市区农村经济总产值与物流网络里程和物流产值的协整检验结果

假设的协整方程数	最大特征值	似然比	临界值	
			5%显著水平	1%显著水平
None *	0.883335	49.00970	30.79	36.76
At most 1	0.578153	15.36407	16.52	21.15
At most 2	0.102555	1.05715	4.87	7.76

说明：* 表示在 1%显著水平拒绝零假设。

① Johansen 协整检验是一种基于向量自回归模型的检验方法，在检验之前，必须首先确定 VAR 模型的结构。根据 AIC 和 SC 准则可以确定 VAR 模型的最优滞后期数为 2。同时，利用 Q 统计量检验、怀特检验和 JB 检验进一步检验滞后期数为 2 的 VAR 模型，发现其拟合优度很好，残差序列具有平稳性，的确是最优模型。

② 这三个变量间存在着协整关系，即中国西部地区农村经济的发展与衡量农产品物流发展水平的物流网络里程和物流产值之间在 1978 年—2008 年间存在长期均衡关系。

表6－8确定的是西部12省市区农村经济总产值与物流网络里程和物流产值的均衡向量，得出 β＝(1.000000，2.443309，－2.720113)

表6－8　中国西部12省市区农村经济总产值与物流网络里程和物流产值的协整参数

Normalized cointegrating coefficients（std. err. in parentheses）		
RGDP	WWL	WLC
1.000000	2.443309	－2.720113
	(0.49081)	(0.36042)
Adjustment coefficients（std. err. in parentheses）		
	D（RGDP）	－0.003836
		(0.05166)
	D（WWL）	－0.325437
		(0.05725)
	D（WLC）	0.037932
		(0.05683)

则这三个变量之间的协整方程如下：

$$RGDP = -2.443309 * WWL + 2.720113 * WLC \quad (6-6)$$

(0.49081)(0.36042)

Log likelihood：159.4889

通过协整检验确定的上述三个变量之间的长期均衡关系[353]，可以发现1978年—2008年间，农村经济增加值GDP与物流网络里程之间存在着负相关关系，而农村经济增加值GDP与物流产值之间存在着正相关关系。这说明1978年—2008年间，从总体上来看，物流产值对农村经济之间是正向作用关系，物流产值的上升有利于农村经济的发展；而物流网络里程的增加，在转轨时期，对农村经济总产值的增加显然是一个不利因素，这与我国政府主导的农产品运销活动效率低下也是密切相关的。

根据时间序列的单位根检验分析结果，可以看出农村经济增加指标（GDP）与物流需求能力指标（货物周转量）和物流成效指标（物流产值）也都是单整的，呈现出非平稳特征。本文同样选取常用的Johansen检验（JJ检验）方法对这些变量之间是否存在长期稳定的关系进行检验。表6－9协整性检验的结果表明，这三个变量之间并不存在协整关系，农产品正规物流机构货物周转量水平和农村经济发展之间不存在长期均衡关系。

表 6－9　　中国西部 12 省市区农村经济总产值与物流网络里程和货物周转量的协整检验结果

假设的协整方程数	最大特征值	似然比	临界值	
			5%显著水平	1%显著水平
None *	0.737363	33.81887	43.55	49.56
At most 1	0.355423	10.489363	26.43	31.56
At most 2	0.211009	3.706090	13.36	17.37

说明：* 表示在 1% 显著水平拒绝零假设。

三　格朗杰因果检验

（一）西部地区农村经济总产值与农产品物流相关变量的格朗杰因果检验

表 6－10 表示西部地区农村经济总产值与农产品物流相关变量的格朗杰因果检验[①]。

表 6－10　西部地区农村经济总产值与农产品物流相关变量的 Granger 检验结果

变量	零假设	最优滞后期		自由度	F 统计量	P－值
		m	n			
△WLC	△WLC 不是△RGDP 的 Granger 原因	1	4	20	48.0015	7.00E－6
	△RGDP 不是△WLC 的 Granger 原因	1	3	21	0.5653	0.6457
△WWL	△WWL 不是△RGDP 的 Granger 原因	1	1	23	0.3629	0.5537
	△RGDP 不是△WWL 的 Granger 原因	1	1	23	0.6492	0.4299
△HYZ	△HYZ 不是△RGDP 的 Granger 原因	1	1	23	0.0322	0.8594
	△RGDP 不是△HYZ 的 Granger 原因	1	1	23	0.1605	0.6930

表 6－11 建立 VAR 模型，确定物流产值对农村经济总产值作用的符

① 在最优滞后期时，△WWL 和△HYZ 都不是△RGDP 的 Granger 原因，△RGDP 也不是△WWL 和△HYZ 的 Canger 原因。这说明在 1978 年—2008 年期间，物流网络里程和农产品正规物流机构货物周转量的增长与农村经济发展之间并不存在明显的因果关系。虽然，△RGDP 是△WLC 的 Granger 原因被拒绝，但是，在 1% 的显著水平下，可以发现△WLC 是△RGDP 的 Grange 原因，这说明在 1978 年—2008 年期间，物流产值的增长是农村经济发展的原因。检验结果说明：物流网络里程和农产品正规物流机构货物周转量的增长与农村经济发展之间并不存在明显的因果关系；物流产值的增长是农村经济发展的原因。

号关系[①]。该模型说明在 1978 年—2008 年期间，物流产值的增长是促进农村 GDP 增长的正向原因。

表 6－11　　西部地区农村经济总产值与物流产值的 VAR 分析结果

变量	系数	Std. Error	t－Statistic	Prob
△RGDP（－1）	1.563069	0.170480	8.671672	0.0000
△RGDP（－2）	－0.719335	0.169435	－3.7451672	0.0032
△WLC（－1）	0.222268	0.055554	2.405062	0.0304
C	0.664905	0.189754	2.655837	0.1234
R－squared	0.998931		因变量均值	7.199015
Adjusted R－aquared	0.998587		因变量标准差	1.254951
S.E. of regression	0.168369		赤池信息量准则	－2.829357
Sum squared resid	0.173642		贝叶斯信息准则	－2.631870
Log likelihood	34.15287		F－统计量	2788.440
Durbin－Watson stat	1.877120		PROB（F 统计量）	0.000000

（二）西部地区农民收入与农产品物流相关变量的格朗杰因果检验

表 6－12 表示西部地区农民收入与农产品物流相关变量的格朗杰因果检验[②]，检验结果说明：物流产值和农产品正规物流机构货物周转量的增长是农民收入变化的原因。

表 6－12　西部地区农民收入与农产品物流相关变量的 Granger 检验结果

变量	零假设	最优滞后期		自由度	F 统计量	P－值
		m	n			
△WLC	△WLC 不是△FR 的 Granger 原因	2	1	22	3.780	0.0424
	FR 不是△WLC 的 Granger 原因	3	3	21	2.4647	0.1052

① VAR 模型的拟合优度较好，也通过了各项检验。从模型中可以看出：与协整检验结果一致，物流产值的增长与农村经济总产值增长之间是正相关关系。

② 在最优滞后期时，△WLC 和△HYZ 都是 FR 的 Granger 原因；FR 是△WWL 和△HYZ 的 Granger 原因，则被拒绝。这说明在 1978 年—2008 年期间，物流产值和农产品正规物流机构货物周转量的增长是农民收入变化的原因；而△WWL 与 FR 之间存在双向的 Granger 因果关系，这说明在 1978 年—2008 年期间，物流网络里程的增长是农民收入变化的原因，而农民收入的变化也引起了物流网络里程的增长。

续表 6-12

变量	零假设	最优滞后期		自由度	F 统计量	P-值
		m	n			
△WWL	△WWL 不是 FR 的 Granger 原因	2	2	22	5.7288	0.0164
	FR 不是△WWL 的 Granger 原因	1	3	21	5.7127	0.0295
△HYZ	△HYZ 不是 FR 的 Granger 原因	1	3	21	6.0329	0.0259
	FR 不是△HYZ 的 Granger 原因	2	1	22	0.01426	0.9859

表 6-13 建立 VAR 模型，确定物流产值、物流网络里程的增长对农民收入作用的符号关系①。该模型说明在 1978 年—2008 年期间，物流网络里程的增加是农民收入增长的负向原因，而物流产值的增长是促进农民收入增长的正向原因。

表 6-13　西部地区农民收入与物流产值、物流网络里程的 VAR 分析结果

变量	系数	Std. Error	t-Statistic	Prob
FR（-1）	1.318098	0.153650	8.578595	0.0000
FR（-2）	-0.331316	0.141597	-2.339856	0.0310
△WLC（-1）	0.321653	0.078733	4.085363	0.0007
△WWL（-1）	-0.103788	0.040442	-2.566332	0.0194
C	0.032747	0.055866	0.586161	0.5650
R-squared	0.996081		因变量均值	2.590262
Adjusted R-aquared	0.997657		因变量标准差	0.164729
S.E. of regression	0.008931		赤池信息量准则	-6.456012
Sum squared resid	0.002173		贝叶斯信息准则	-6.127164
Log likelihood	78.19692		F-统计量	1687.898
Durbin-Watson stat	2.590176		PROB（F 统计量）	0.000000

表 6-14 建立 VAR 模型，确定农产品正规物流机构货物周转量增加对农民收入变化的作用关系②。该模型说明在 1978 年—2008 年期间，农产

---

① VAR 模型的拟合优度达到 0.997657，也通过了各项检验。从模型中可以看出：农民收入与物流网络里程的增长呈负相关关系，而与物流产值的增长呈正相关关系。

② VAR 模型的拟合优度较好，也通了各项检验。从模型中可以看出：农产品正规物流机构货物周转量增加农民收入之间呈正相关关系。

品正规物流机构货物周转量增加是促进农民收入增长的正向原因；而物流网络里程的增加与表6－13的模型一致，仍然是农民收入增长的负向原因。

表6－14 西部地区农民收入与货物周转量、物流网络里程的VAR分析结果

变量	系数	Std. Error	t－Statistic	Prob
FR（－1）	0.846284	0.040931	20.67612	0.0000
△HYZ（－1）	0.138331	0.032769	4.221361	0.0004
△WWL（－1）	－0.140556	0.040237	－3.493209	0.0023
C	0.909181	0.152790	5.950520	0.0000
R－squared	0.996743	因变量均值	6.026115	
Adjusted R－aquared	0.997816		因变量标准差	0.505366
S. E. of regression	0.032391		赤池信息量准则	－4.532904
Sum squared resid	0.021657		贝叶斯信息准则	－4.435263
Log likelihood	58.53911		F－统计量	2326.287
Durbin－Watson stat	2.322761		PROB（F统计量）	0.000000

表6－15建立VAR模型，确定农民收入变化对物流网络里程增长的作用关系①。该模型说明在1978年—2008年期间，农民收入的增加是物流网络里程增长的正向原因。

表6－15 西部地区物流网络里程与农民收入的VAR分析结果

变量	系数	Std. Error	t－Statistic	Prob
△WWL（－3）	0.601329	0.079753	7.539889	0.0000
FR（－1）	1.205548	0.311508	3.870041	0.0010
C	－3.698236	1.431872	－2.74565	0.0203
R－squared	0.988914		因变量均值	7.896212
Adjusted R－aquared	0.989573		因变量标准差	1.321335
S. E. of regression	0.143344		赤池信息量准则	－1.078125
Sum squared resid	0.2232265		贝叶斯信息准则	－0.855827
Log likelihood	14.89986		F－统计量	932.3746
Durbin－Watson stat	1.394640		PROB（F统计量）	0.000000

① VAR模型的拟合优度较好，通过了各项检验。从模型中可以看出：物流网络里程与农民收入之间呈正相关关系。

（三）西部地区农村投资与农产品物流相关变量的格朗杰因果检验

表6－16表示西部地区农村投资与农产品物流相关变量的格朗杰因果检验[①]，检验结果说明：物流产值的增长是农村投资变化的原因；农村投资变化是物流网络里程增长的原因；农产品正规物流机构货物周转量的增长与农村投资之间并不存在明显的因果关系。

表6－16　西部地区农村投资与农产品物流相关变量的Granger检验结果

变量	零假设	最优滞后期		自由度	F统计量	P－值
		m	n			
△WLC	△WLC不是TZ的Granger原因	3	1	21	5.9758	0.0051
	TZ不是△WLC的Granger原因	4	3	20	1.4910	0.2601
△WWL	△WWL不是TZ的Granger原因	4	2	20	0.6654	0.6264
	TZ不是△WWL的Granger原因	1	3	20	13.4906	0.0025
△HYZ	△HYZ不是TZ的Granger原因	4	3	20	0.9980	0.4410
	TZ不是△HYZ的Granger原因	1	1	23	0.2136	0.6489

表6－17建立VAR模型，确定物流产值增加对农村投资作用的符号关系[②]。该模型说明在1978年—2008年期间，物流产值增加对农村投资的增加是正向的促进作用。同样，由表6－16的结果表明：农村投资变化是物流网络里程增长的原因。但建立物流网络里程关于农村投资的VAR模型，确定两者之间的符号关系后，在实际分析中发现无法获得能够通过检验的模型（见表6－17）。图6－8是物流网络里程增长对农村投资相关冲击的动态反应[③]。从图中可以看出：给农村投资一个冲击后（图中虚线的变化），物流网络里程增长主要是下降趋势（图中实线的变化），农村投资对物流网络里程增长主要是负面影响，说明在1978年—2008年期

---

① 在最优滞后期时，△WLC是TZ的Granger原因；TZ是△WLC的Granger原因，则被拒绝。这说明在1978年—2008年期间，物流产值的增长是农村投资变化的原因；而△WWL是TZ的Granger原因，则被拒绝。相反，TZ是△WWL增长的Granger原因，说明在1978年—2008年期间，农村投资变化是物流网络里程增长的原因；在最优滞后期时△HYZ不是TZ的Granger原因，TZ也不是△WWL和△HYZ的Granger原因。这说明在1978年—2008年期间，农产品正规物流机构货物周转量的增长与农村投资之间并不存在明显的因果关系。

② VAR模型的拟合优度达到0.987898，通过了各项检验。从模型中可以看出：农村投资与物流产值的增长呈正相关关系。

③ 利用冲击—反应（impulse－response）分析探索两者之间的关系。

间，农村投资增加并没有促进物流网络里程的相应增长。

表 6－17　　　　西部地区农村投资与物流产值的 VAR 分析结果

变量	系数	Std. Error	t－Statistic	Prob
TZ（－1）	1.032926	0.081663	12.64857	0.0000
△WLC（－1）	1.003255	0.198244	5.060700	0.0001
C	－0.226699	0.070072	－1.695358	0.2216
R－squared	0.989834		因变量均值	2.051009
Adjusted R－aquared	0.986788		因变量标准差	0.251859
S. E. of regression	0.028477		赤池信息量准则	－4.128131
Sum squared resid	0.001245		贝叶斯信息准则	－3.824527
Log likelihood	49.31374		F－统计量	327.5270
Durbin－Watson stat	1.511126		PROB（F统计量）	0.000000

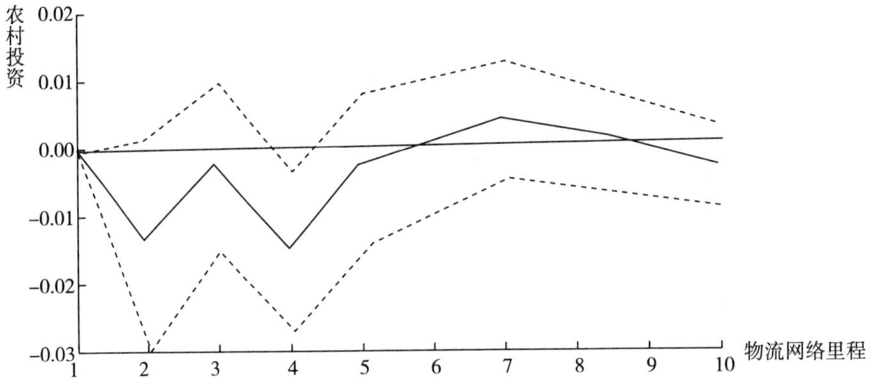

图 6－8　物流网络里程增长对农村投资相关冲击的动态反应

（四）西部地区农村消费与农产品物流相关变量的格朗杰因果检验

表 6－18 表示西部地区农村消费与农产品物流相关变量的格朗杰因果检验①，检验结果说明：农产品正规物流机构货物周转量的增长与农村消

① 在最优滞后期时，△WWL 和△HYZ 都不是△2XF 的 Granger 原因，△2XF 也不是△WWL 和△HYZ 的 Granger 原因，这说明在 1978 年—2008 年期间，农产品正规物流机构货物周转量的增长与农村消费增长量增加之间并不存在明显的因果关系；而△WLC 与△2XF 之间却存在双向的因果关系，这说明在 1978 年—2008 年期间，物流产值的增长是农村消费增长量增加的原因，农村消费增长量比上一期的增加同样也是物流产值增长的原因。

费增长量增加之间并不存在明显的因果关系；物流产值的增长是农村消费增长量增加的原因，农村消费增长量比上一期的增加同样也是物流产值增长的原因。

表 6－18　西部地区农村消费与农产品物流相关变量的 Granger 检验结果

变量	零假设	最优滞后期		自由度	F 统计量	P－值
		m	n			
△WLC	△WLC 不是Δ^2XF 的 Granger 原因	1	2	22	7.7253	0.01544
	Δ^2XF 不是△WLC 的 Granger 原因	3	3	21	3.2511	0.04567
△WWL	△WWL 不是Δ^2XF 的 Granger 原因	1	2	22	2.9041	0.1066
	Δ^2XF 不是△WWL 的 Granger 原因	1	1	23	1.4748	0.2395
△HYZ	△HYZ 不是Δ^2XF 的 Granger 原因	1	1	23	0.1658	0.6884
	Δ^2XF 不是△HYZ 的 Granger 原因	1	1	23	1.1825	0.2904

表 6－19 建立 VAR 模型，确定物流产值增加对农村消费作用的符号关系。该模型拟合效果并不是很理想，说明模型遗漏了其他重要相关变量。但是从模型中还是可以看出：两者之间的系数为正，说明在 1978 年—2008 年期间，物流产值的增长与农村消费增长量增加之间互为正向原因。

表 6－19　西部地区物流产值与农村消费的 VAR 分析结果

变量	系数	Std. Error	t－Statistic	Prob
△WLC（－1）	0.535230	0.306389	1.746896	0.0960
△XF（－2）	0.679948	0.132584	5.334552	0.0000
R－squared	0.329753		因变量均值	0.067304
Adjusted R－aquared	0.289396		因变量标准差	0.041325
S. E. of regression	0.044036		赤池信息量准则	3.896289
Sum squared resid	0.032833		贝叶斯信息准则	－3.789017
Log likelihood	44.78806		F－统计量	1.716345

第三节　西部地区农产品物流数量关系影响与评价

一　转型时期西部地区农产品物流数量关系的影响

表6-20反映的是转型时期西部地区农产品物流发展与农村经济发展的相互影响。采用WLSH（农产品物流产值/农村经济总产值）作为西部地区农产品物流深化指标，反映农产品正规物流发展的程度。由于WLSH包含了农村经济总产值这一变量，所以利用WLSH与农民收入（FR）之间的弹性分析来揭示西部地区农产品物流发展与农村经济发展的相互影响。从表6-20可以发现：WLSH对FR产生的是负面的影响，即农产品正规物流深化，反而抑制了农民收入增长。但FR的提高将对WLSH产生正面影响。

表6-20　　西部地区农产品物流发展与农村经济发展的相互影响

Vector Autoregression Estimates
Sample (adjusted): 1979　2008
Included observations: 30 after adjusting Endpoints
Standard errors & t-statistics in parentheses

	FR	WLSH
FR (-1)	1.007980	0.080677
	(0.01639)	(0.04205)
	(36.8602)	(1.71863)
WLSH (-1)	-0.292835	0.655299
	(0.05720)	(0.12142)
	(-4.26735)	(4.96029)
C	0.228117	0.034180
	(0.02035)	(0.05973)
	(7.34782)	(0.53482)
R-squared	0.997027	0.926523
Adj. R-squared	0.995534	0.919510
Sum sq. resids	0.003278	0.007159
S. E. equation	0.011298	0.018711

续表 6－20

	FR	WLSH
F－statistic	3395. 294	134. 2729
Log likelihood	77. 56355	61. 65537
Akaike AIC	－6. 214665	－4. 887783
Schwarz SC	－6. 066209	－4. 740526
Mean dependent	2. 611229	0. 763131
S. D. dependent	0. 174566	0. 069215
Determinant Residual Covariance		2. 63E－09
Log Likelihood		141. 2712
Akaike Information Criteria		－11. 26159
Schwarz Criteria		－10. 96798

表 6－21 反映的是转型时期西部地区农产品正规物流发展与国民经济发展的相互影响。从表 6－21 可以发现：GDP 与 WLSH 之间是正的弹性关系，即 WLSH 的提高将有助于 GDP 的增长。综合表 6－20、表 6－21 可以确定，转型时期西部地区正规农产品物流发展，一方面制约了农村经济的发展，另一方面却又促进了整个国民经济的发展。表 6－21 同时还显示：西部地区农产品物流虽然为国民经济发展做出了重要贡献，但是 GDP 增长对西部地区农产品物流发展的贡献却微乎其微。这说明西部地区正规农产品物流发展存在功能异化（非农化）问题，因此，不仅没有对西部地区农村经济发展给予有效支持，反而加剧了农村资金流失，成为向非农经济单向输出农产品物流资源的管道。

表 6－21　　西部地区农产品物流发展与国民经济发展的互相影响

Vector Autoregression Estimates
Sample（adjusted）：1979　2008
Included observations：30 after adjusting
Endpoints
Standard errors in（　）& t－statistics in［　］

	GDP	WLSH
GDP（－1）	0. 953911	0. 002947
	(0. 02985)	(0. 00386)
	[50. 1607]	[0. 19478]

续表 6－21

	GDP	WLSH
WLSH（－1）	0. 313958	0. 849462
	（0. 10892）	（0. 08233）
	[2. 61043]	[9. 11367]
C	0. 024672	0. 110067
	（0. 04515）	（0. 03271）
	[0. 44858]	[2. 51088]
R－squared	0. 990085	0. 916265
Adj. R－squared	0. 997016	0. 910592
Sum sq. resids	0. 014431	0. 008304
S. E. equation	0. 026096	0. 020041
F－statistic	3705. 199	116. 4365
Log likelihood	54. 07082	60. 08178
Akaike AIC	－4. 254739	－4. 756633
Schwarz SC	－4. 107482	－4. 609376
Mean dependent	4. 341083	0. 763154
S. D. dependent	0. 487559	0. 069215
Determinant Residual Covariance	3. 17E－08	
Log Likelihood（d. f. adjusted）	111. 3197	
Akaike Information Criteria	－8. 784566	
Schwarz Criteria	－8. 490051	

表 6－22 显示了西部地区农产品物流发展与整体物流发展的相互影响。从中可以发现：ZWL 与 WLSH 之间是负的弹性关系，即西部地区农产品正规物流发展与整体物流发展施加负面影响，这说明转型时期，中国整体物流发展以抑制西部地区农产品物流发展为代价。表 6－22 同时还显示出：整体物流发展对西部地区农产品物流发展的促进作用同样是微弱的，这说明转型时期，中国物流存在城乡分割和地位不平等的“二元物流结构”，西部地区农产品正规物流在整体物流中处于从属的地位和被隔离的状态。

表 6-22　　西部地区农产品物流发展与整体物流发展的相互影响

Vector Autoregression Estimates
Sample (adjusted): 1979 2008
Included observations: 30 after adjusting
Endpoints
Standard errors in ( ) & t-statistics in [ ]

	ZWL	WLSH
WLL (-1)	1.091101	0.002128
	(0.02415)	(0.00823)
	[31.0648]	[0.34160]
WLSH (-1)	-0.378116	0.841056
	(0.32606)	(0.07683)
	[-1.91452]	[9.60153]
C	0.230129	0.122354
	(0.19853)	(0.04363)
	[1.09310]	[2.25140]
R-squared	0.989491	0.916586
Adj. R-squared	0.988572	0.908745
Sum sq. resids	0.137989	0.008260
S. E. equation	0.081102	0.020022
F-statistic	1104.240	116.9339
Log likelihood	27.83942	60.12846
Akaike AIC	-2.069936	-4.760523
Schwarz SC	-1.921670	-4.613267
Mean dependent	1.964328	0.763119
S. D. dependent	0.797252	0.069215
Determinant Residual Covariance		2.12E-07
Log Likelihood		88.60255
Akaike Information Criteria		-6.884453
Schwarz Criteria		-6.588851

二　转型时期西部地区农产品物流数量关系的评价

（一）转型时期西部地区农产品正规物流未能促进农村经济发展

根据本章第一节分析思路，对于西部地区农产品物流发展的水平，主要衡量农产品正规和准正规物流机构的农产品运销，从物流来源和物流运行两个角度加以分析。从物流来源方面看，可以选择物流供给指标——物流网络里程、物流需求指标——货物周转量；从物流运行方面看，应当选择物流成效指标——物流产值。

（1）西部地区农产品物流来源未能促进农村经济发展。第一，物流网络里程对农村经济发展各项指标均有促进作用，农产品正规物流机构物流产值有利于农民收入增长。从表面上看，这一结果符合帕特里克经典的“供给领先”模式，似乎说明了转型时期西部地区农产品物流促进了农村经济发展。但依据本研究的实证结果，物流网络里程的增加并不必然代表农村经济发展。从西部地区农产品物流与农村经济制度变迁的角度看，在西部农村经济发展中农产品物流的有效产值来源仍然处于自我积累阶段；从西部地区农产品物流发展与整体物流和国民经济发展相互影响的角度看，西部地区农产品物流没有发挥促进农村经济发展的功能，而将农产品的物流产值输出到了非农经济部门[354]。第二，农产品货物周转量不仅没有促进农村经济的发展，反而阻碍了农民收入和农村经济总产值的增长。结合上述其他实证结果和西部地区农产品物流与国民经济发展和整体物流发展的相互影响，可以发现同时存在两种情况：农产品货物周转量仅在名义上存在，实际投向了非农化；或者由于西部地区农产品正规物流机构缺乏应有的物流能力，其结果是农产品货物周转量效率低下[355]。

（2）西部地区农产品物流运行未能促进农村经济发展。第一，农产品物流产值与农民收入以外的其他农村经济发展指标没有明显关系。说明农产品物流产值或是没有运用，或是非农化运用，或是没有被有效运用于农村经济发展。西部地区农产品物流发展与整体物流和国民经济发展的相互影响的实证显示：大量农产品物流产值被非农化运用。第二，农产品物流产值占农村经济总产值的比重（WLSH）提高，即农产品物流深化对农民收入（FR）增长产生的是负面的影响。直接说明了西部地区农产品物流发展不仅不能促进农村经济发展，反而抑制了农村经济发展。

（二）转型时期西部地区农村经济未能促进农产品正规物流发展

根据本章第一节分析思路，针对西部地区农村经济的现实，结合国内相关研究的做法来计算农村增加值，用第一产业增加值和乡镇企业增加值之和估算农村经济总产值。计量农村经济发展，农村投资与消费是必须关注的重要变量。

（1）西部地区农村经济发展未能直接促进农产品物流发展。第一，农村经济总产值与农民收入增长有利于提高农产品货物周转量水平。从表面上看，这一结果符合帕特里克经典的"需求追随"模式，似乎说明转型时期西部地区农村经济发展促进了农产品物流发展。但依据本研究的定义，从功能物流角度看，农产品货物周转量水平的提高并不必然代表农产品物流发展。不能转化为农村有效投资的农产品货物周转量增长，只能是功能异化的农产品物流发展，充其量只是农产品物流机构自身的发展，而非农村经济发展所需要的农产品物流发展，同时说明了农民收入增长源于农产品正规物流之外的因素[356]。第二，农村经济总产值增长不能促进农产品物流产值增长。一方面这一结果直接说明了转型时期西部地区农村经济发展，包括农业和乡镇企业发展，并没有对农产品正规物流发展起到需求诱导的作用。这和新古典经济学"需求创造供给"的论点是相悖的，依据新制度经济学的解释，说明转型时期西部地区农产品物流与农村经济关系存在制度障碍。另一方面，也说明了转型时期西部地区农村经济增长的动力只能从农产品物流以外的其他因素中寻找，这一结论再次表明了转型时期西部地区农产品物流未能促进农村经济发展。

（2）西部地区农村经济发展未能间接促进农产品物流发展。第一，农村消费与农产品货物周转量、农产品物流产值不存在重要联系。首先，与前述农村经济对农产品货物周转量的直接作用相同，说明农村消费并没有提高农产品货物周转量，未能真正促进农村经济发展。其次，与前述农村经济对农产品物流的直接作用一样，这一点同样说明：在转型时期，西部地区农村消费没有形成足以诱导农产品正规物流发展的有效需求，依据新制度经济学的解释，说明两者之间存在制度障碍。从另一方面也说明农村消费增长仍然处于自给自足阶段，农产品物流没能促进消费的增长和市场的扩大，进而拉动农村经济发展。第二，农村投资与物流网络里程、农产品物流产值不存在重要联系。首先，在前述物流网络里程对农村经济发展各项指标均有促进作用的基础上，可以发现，农村投资与物流网络里程不存在重要联系，关键是农村投资没能有效地促进农村经济增长，说明农村投资效率不高，这既可能与西部地区农产品物流引导投资的功能不足有关，也可能与财政的农村投资效率不高有关。其次，农村投资增长不利于农产品物流产值增长。农村投资源于财政、农村贷款、农村经济主体的自我积累，投资应该拉动农产品物流产值。这一结果说明由于农产品正规物流机构的物流能力不足，致使财政性投资和农村经济主体的自给性投资对物流性投资具有“挤出效应”。

（三）转型时期西部地区农产品物流与农村经济关系受外因制约

（1）综合西部地区农产品物流发展与农村经济发展、与国民经济发展、与整体物流发展的相互影响，分析表明：第一，西部地区农产品正规物流发展（WLSH 的提高）对农民收入（FR）增长产生的是负面的影响，但农民收入（FR）的提高对农产品正规物流的发展（WLSH 的提高）产生正面影响。第二，西部地区农产品正规物流的发展（WLSH 的提高）将有助于 GDP 的增长，但 GDP 增长对西部地区农产品正规物流发展（WLSH 的提高）的贡献却微乎其微。第三，西部地区农产品正规物流发展（WLSH 的提高）与整体物流发展（ZWL 的提高）施加负面影响，而整体物流发展（ZWL 的提高）对西部地区农产品正规物流发展（WLSH 的提高）的促进作用同样是微弱的。

（2）这些结果联系前述西部地区农产品物流与农村经济关系失调的分析，可以清楚地显示：第一，转型时期的西部地区农产品物流与农村经济关系受整体经济发展和整体物流发展的制约，西部地区农产品物流在整体物流中处于从属地位和被整体物流隔离的状态，“二元物流结构”制约了农产品正规物流向农村经济发展所需要的方向发展。第二，转型时期的西部地区农产品物流与农村经济关系失调，主要是由于国民经济发展通过“二元物流结构”中的农产品正规物流，实施了对农村经济的极化效应[357]。2011 年《中国物流配送研究报告》指出：我国城乡物流业发展极不平衡，落后的农业和农村经济与现代工业、发达的城市经济并存，以文盲、半文盲、文化水平低的群众为基础的落后科学与世界先进科学技术并存，广大的不发达地区、贫困地区和经济发达、比较发达地区并存，而且我国正处于实现工业化、现代化双重任务下，这种国情决定了城乡在经济、消费、观念等诸多方面存在着很大的差距。物流企业、物流设施、物流活动高度集中在交通极为发达的大城市中，形成辐射功能极强的物流中心城市，而在乡村地区物流业的发展比较缓慢，使城市物流与乡村物流在过程上相脱节，甚至少数乡村物流几乎为零，造成物流市场的地域化、畸形化。无论在我国的东部地区还是中西部地区都是在城市首先发展起物流业，然后沿着交通运输线例如铁路、河流、公路等为纽带形成物流节点，向周围地区主要包括乡村地区辐射。

总之，转型时期的西部地区农产品物流与农村经济关系不仅未能实现相互促进的可持续发展，反而陷入了相互制约的失调状态。因此，必须从西部地区农产品物流、农村经济系统及其外部制度环境角度入手，深入剖析导致西部地区农产品物流与农村经济关系失调的直接原因、深层原因和根本原因，进而依据可持续发展机理，构建实现可持续发展的机制与模式。

第七章　西部地区农产品物流关系结构失调原因分析

西部地区农产品物流可持续发展系统的复杂性，决定了其失调原因多样化、复杂化。根据西部地区农产品物流可持续发展的理论内涵与实现机理，以及前述基于制度和数量的实证分析，本研究认为：导致西部地区农产品物流关系结构失调的原因，不外乎政府职能不到位，导致可持续发展系统的制度缺乏弹性、结构不合理；西部地区农产品物流与农村经济之间系统的功能不足，导致技术进步与结构变迁不同步，资源配置不合理。据此，本章以政府、西部地区农产品物流主体、农村经济主体为对象，从宏观制度环境、农村经济发展和西部地区农产品物流发展三个方面，综合分析中国西部地区农产品物流关系结构失调的原因。

第一节　宏观制度环境约束是根本原因

一　初始条件不足和发展战略使然

（一）计划经济时期农产品物流

新中国成立后，在内外环境约束下实施计划经济体制的重工业和城市发展战略是巩固和发展新兴社会主义国家的“理性”和必然选择。实施计划经济体制下的重工业和城市发展战略的“计划”，只能计划“计划者”所拥有或控制的资源，计划经济的“计划者”是国家或代表国家的集体，因此，在产权上物流只能是以国家所有为特征的公有制物流。从这一意义上看，计划经济下的物流内生于经济体制和发展战略①。表7－1（a）、（b）显示了国民经济恢复阶段的农产品物流基本情况。

表7－1（a）　国民经济恢复阶段的农产品物流规模与分布情况

	市场主体：国营商业、国营粮食企业、供销合作社、国营外贸公司				
年份	全国性国营商业公司	国营商店	商店职工人数	达到全国商品批发总额	达到全国商品零售额
1949	15家	11094家	17万人	30%	11.5%
1952	28家	33282家	53万人	60%	34.4%
年份	全国基层供销合作社	社员	零售额	达到全国商品批发总额	达到全国商品零售额
1949	17351个	1.0亿人	10亿元	11.4%	6.7%
1952	35096个	1.5亿人	50亿元	33.5%	23.8%

表7－1（b）　国民经济恢复阶段的农产品物流基础设施的建设情况

单位：万公里

年份	铁路由铁道部实行统一管理	公路水运由交通部进行管理		航空由民用航空局管理
	全国铁路营业里程	公路里程	内河航道	民航航线
1949	2.18	8.07	7.36	—
1950	2.22	9.96	7.36	1.14
1951	2.23	11.44	7.36	1.05
1952	2.29	12.67	9.50	1.31

资料来源：国家统计局，《中国统计年鉴》（1983）、《新中国五十年统计资料汇编》（1999），中国统计出版社。

但是，中国在这一时期面临发展资本高度密集的重工业资本短缺的矛盾，这种内生于经济发展战略的财政性物流自然要延伸到农村，强制性地

① 这一时期农产品物流的主体、流向、规模及分布都发生了变化，国营农产品经营机构加入到物流主体的行列，并逐渐占据最重要的地位。城市新增人口以及工矿企业的农产品需求扩大是农产品物流变化压力的主要来源，顺应新中国成立初期保证城市居民生活和大力发展工业建设的基本制度要求，由政府推动的农产品物流制度的改变就成为理所当然。物流，在功能上实际成了政府财政的一部分，在产权上必然是以公有制的物流制度安排。

使农产品物流服从于计划经济体制和经济发展战略。从农村经济看，新中国农产品正规物流一开始就是外生的①。表 7－2（a）、（b）显示了计划经济时期的计划型农产品物流基本情况。计划经济体制时期，物资部门统一管理中转供销仓库就是其最好的说明。

表 7－2（a） 计划经济时期的计划型农产品物流规模与分布情况

年份	市场主体	统购统销	仓储设施
1953—1956	国营商业、国营粮食企业供销合作社，国营外贸公司	粮食、油料棉花、棉布、生猪、鲜蛋、烟叶及皮革、中药材等重要农产品	农资公司和国营商业流通部门建立运输车队 粮食收购部门建立了一些功能单一的粮库
1956—1978	国合商业	基本控制农产品的购销	规定农产品产销区及其流向和流动范围
1963—1978	物资部门	统一管理中转供销仓库	布局物资储运点、建立合理库存
	各级物资储运公司、商业储运公司	承担农产品的物流活动	编制物资流向图、提供各种运输工具及发展联运

表 7－2（b） 计划经济时期的计划型农产品物流基础设施的建设情况

单位：万公里

年份	全国铁路营业里程	公路里程	内河航道	民航航线
1953	2.38	13.71	9.50	1.40
1954	2.45	14.61	9.50	1.52
1955	2.56	16.73	9.99	1.55
1956	2.65	22.63	10.36	1.91
1957	2.67	25.46	14.41	2.64
1958	3.02	42.18	15.20	3.30
1959	3.23	50.79	16.30	3.72
1960	3.39	51.00	17.00	3.81
1961	3.45	47.70	17.20	3.91
1962	3.46	46.35	16.19	3.53

① 这一时期我国农产品物流基本上是由国家主导的，资源分配和组织供应是按行政区进行的，物流环节相互割裂，系统性差；物流活动仅限于对商品的储存和运输，其主要目标是保证国家指令性计划分配指标的落实，物流的经济效益目标被放在了次要的位置。

续表 7-2（b）

年份	全国铁路营业里程	公路里程	内河航道	民航航线
1963	3.50	47.51	15.72	3.57
1964	3.53	47.92	15.69	3.85
1965	3.64	51.45	15.77	3.94
1966	3.78	54.36	14.72	3.50
1967	3.86	55.75	14.78	3.51
1968	3.88	57.17	14.78	3.94
1969	3.93	60.06	14.81	3.93
1970	4.10	63.67	14.84	4.06
1971	4.28	67.54	14.16	4.21
1972	4.39	69.99	14.06	4.25
1973	4.43	71.56	13.88	4.54
1974	4.51	73.79	13.74	8.13
1975	4.60	78.36	13.56	8.42
1976	4.63	82.34	13.74	9.78
1977	4.74	85.56	13.74	13.21
1978	4.86	89.02	13.60	14.89

资料来源：国家统计局，《中国统计年鉴》（1983）、《新中国五十年统计资料汇编》（1999），中国统计出版社。

（二）转型经济时期农产品物流

基于计划经济体制下发展起来的物流体制和结构，虽然伴随着市场化进程而有所改善，开始出现计划型物流模式向市场配置型物流模式的转型。但考察改革开放以来中国物流与经济关系，可以发现，1978 年开始的中国农村改革最终并没有能诱导出农村经济的内生物流①。表 7-3（a）、（b）

① 这一时期我国农产品物流模式开始从单一的国营模式向“三多一少”模式转型，即“多种经济成分、多种流通渠道、多种经营方式、少环节”的农产品物流体制改革目标模式。据统计，从 1979 年到 1983 年，我国农贸市场成交金额增加了 1 倍，农产品上市流通量的迅速增加以及不同地区的农产品价格差异，诱发了农产品贩运和流通，形成了一批集贸市场，并随之出现数量有限的专业户，从而奠定了农产品物流的市场基础。但中国物流发展仍然没有沿着自身内在的逻辑展开和扩展，农村经济发展也自然没有成为农产品物流发展的重要目标。

显示了转型经济时期集贸市场主导型物流基本情况。在市场经济条件下集贸市场无法有效组织农产品的规模化交易，同样是有力的说明。

表7－3（a） 转型经济时期的集贸市场主导型物流规模与分布情况

	市场主体：国营、集体、个体			
年份	农村集贸市场数量	农贸市场粮食成交量	国家计划牌价收购的比例	市场出售的比例
1978	37890个	25亿公斤	84.7%	15.3%
1984	50356个	91.5亿公斤	29.4%	60.6%

表7－3（b） 转型经济时期的集贸市场主导型物流基础设施的建设情况

单位：万公里

年份	全国铁路营业里程	公路里程	内河航道	民航航线
1978	5.17	89.02	13.60	14.89
1979	—	—	—	—
1980	5.33	88.83	10.85	19.53
1981	5.39	89.75	10.87	21.83
1982	5.33	90.70	10.86	23.27
1983	5.46	91.51	10.89	22.91
1984	5.48	92.67	10.93	26.02

资料来源：国家统计局，《中国统计年鉴》（1983）、《新中国五十年统计资料汇编》（1999），中国统计出版社。

1985年国家进一步展开对农产品统购统销制度的改革。国有物流开始逐步退出农村和农业，农村领域的合作社业务非农化，导致了国家对农产品物流调控下的正规物流机构缺乏效率、以企业为主体的农产品物流规模较小缺乏社会效益、政府控制某些重要商品价格限制非正规物流发展①。表7－4（a）、（b）显示了转型经济时期批发市场主导型物流基本

① 这一时期对粮食、棉花、食油等由国家实行指令性计划管理，在形式上取消统购统销制，改为合同收购（后来又改为国家定购），其定购基数、价格由国家计划决定，以保证城市居民的需要；水果、蔬菜、畜产品、水产品等鲜活农产品逐步走向宏观调控下的自由流通和市场调节。自由产销的新兴批发市场逐渐取代了国营、合作社商业的传统封闭式批发网络而成为主要物流通道，并得到了社会的广泛认可，从而拉开了农产品物流市场化改革的序幕。

情况。这一时期的农产品物流多头无序，西部地区农产品物流自然难以可持续发展。

表7-4（a）　转型经济时期的批发市场主导型物流规模与分布情况

	市场主体：个体经营者、批发商、零售商、加工企业、中介组织	
年份	全国农产品批发市场的数量	市场出售的比例
1986	892个	65.3%
1991	1509个	86.3%

表7-4（b）　转型经济时期的批发市场主导型物流基础设施的建设情况

单位：万公里

年份	全国铁路营业里程	公路里程	内河航道	民航航线
1985	5.52	94.24	10.91	27.72
1986	5.58	96.28	10.94	32.43
1987	5.60	98.22	10.98	38.91
1988	5.62	99.96	10.94	37.38
1989	5.70	101.43	10.90	47.19
1990	5.79	102.83	10.92	50.68
1991	5.78	104.11	10.97	55.91

资料来源：国家统计局，《中国统计年鉴》（1983）、《新中国五十年统计资料汇编》（1999），中国统计出版社。

（三）市场经济时期农产品物流

1992年以后农村改革开始向市场经济全面转变。中共十四大确定了社会主义市场经济的改革目标，打破传统的粮食统销物流格局，"菜篮子工程"的实施加强了企业的市场主体地位，农产品物流得到快速发展。表7-5（a）、（b）显示了市场经济时期的契约型农产品物流基本情况。

表7-5（a）　市场经济时期的契约型农产品物流规模与分布情况

年份	市场主体	投资建设	物流模式
1992	加工企业	农产品生产基地	"加工型企业+农户"
1997	龙头企业	农产品生产基地	"运销型企业+农户""公司+合作社""农户+公司+保险"

表 7－5（b）　市场经济时期的契约型农产品物流基础设施的建设情况

单位：万公里

年份	全国铁路营业里程	公路里程	内河航道	民航航线
1992	5.81	105.67	10.97	83.66
1993	5.86	108.35	11.02	96.08
1994	5.90	111.78	11.02	104.56
1995	6.24	115.70	11.06	112.90
1996	6.49	118.58	11.08	116.65
1997	6.60	122.64	10.98	142.50

资料来源：国家统计局，《中国统计年鉴》（1983）、《新中国五十年统计资料汇编》（1999），中国统计出版社。

1998 年进一步推动农产品物流模式由计划型向市场型的转变。“三项政策、一项改革”为重点，粮食流通自由，粮价实现市场调控，标志着我国农产品全面的市场化流通体制的真正形成[①]。表 7－6（a）、（b）显示了市场经济时期的专业化农产品物流基本情况。

表 7－6（a）　市场经济时期的专业化农产品物流规模与分布情况

1998 年至今	市场主体	加工企业、连锁企业、中介组织、第三方物流企业
	物流模式	第三方农产品物流模式、农业联盟模式
1998—2003 年	投资建设	商业冷库 2522 万吨、粮仓 1085 万平方米、先进技术设备及管理手段
1998—2004 年	重组转制	国有粮食购销企业 20522 家，其中改制 7027 家 其他多种所有制粮食经营企业 10 万家以上

表 7－6（b）　市场经济时期的专业化农产品物流基础设施的建设情况

单位：万公里

年份	全国铁路营业里程	公路里程	内河航道	民航航线
1998	6.64	127.85	11.03	150.58
1999	6.74	135.17	11.65	152.22
2000	6.87	140.27	11.93	150.29

① 这一时期农产品物流体制改革的核心问题是加强农产品物流管理水平、信息化系统建设和数据共享建设，提升物流企业战略联盟及专业化服务水平。为了进一步减少费用、降低成本，国家采取一系列措施加快了农产品第三方物流模式改革的步伐。

续表 7-6（b）

年份	全国铁路营业里程	公路里程	内河航道	民航航线
2001	7.01	169.80	12.15	155.36
2002	7.19	176.52	12.16	163.77
2003	7.30	180.98	12.40	174.95
2004	7.44	187.07	12.33	204.94
2005	7.54	334.52	12.33	199.85
2006	7.71	345.70	12.34	211.35
2007	7.80	358.37	12.35	234.30
2008	7.97	373.02	12.28	246.18

资料来源：国家统计局，《中国统计年鉴》（2010），中国统计出版社。

虽然这一时期农产品物流得到较快发展，但从全国社会物流来看，农产品物流在社会物流总值中所占比重却很小。农业部农村经济研究中心（2006）的研究显示：2003 年我国农产品物流发展的差距悬殊，总值低于全国社会物流总值 27% 的增长幅度。本研究发现 2004 年以后这种差距进一步加大，2008 年农产品物流总值低于全国社会物流总值 48% 的增长幅度，农产品物流所占比例下降至 2.1%。表 7-7 显示了 1991 年—2008 年我国农产品物流的发展状况，农产品物流总值是反映农产品物流整体发展规模和水平的重要指标。1991 年—2008 年，农产品物流总额 175999 亿元；1991 年—2008 年，社会物流总额 4809410 亿元；1991 年—1999 年，农产品物流所占社会物流平均比为 7.9%；农产品物流同比平均增长率为 14.8%。2000 年—2008 年，农产品物流所占社会物流平均比仅为 3.5%；农产品物流同比平均增长率仅为 8.4%。分析看出，2000 年—2008 年与 1991 年—1999 年相比，农产品物流所占社会物流平均比不升反降，农产品物流同比平均增长率越来越低。结果表明 1991 年—2008 年间，中国农产品物流整体处于低水平运行，农产品物流总值占社会物流总值的比例不超过 4%，反映出农产品物流发展效率较低，不适应经济发展的要求。2000 年实施西部大开发战略，受农产品物流整体影响西部地区农产品物流无法发挥应有的市场功能，制约了西部地区农业产业化的发展。

表 7－7　　1991 年—2008 年中国农产品物流的发展状况

年份	农产品物流总额（亿元）	社会物流总额（亿元）	农产品物流所占比例（%）	农产品物流同比增长率（%）
1991	3252	30291	10.7	—
1992	3335	39188	8.5	2.6
1993	4281	54475	7.9	28.4
1994	6104	79237	7.7	42.6
1995	7951	102230	7.8	30.3
1996	8618	110614	7.8	8.4
1997	8996	124138	7.2	4.4
1998	9160	119388	7.1	1.8
1999	9138	139717	6.5	-0.2
2000	9634	171427	5.6	5.4
2001	10291	195442	5.3	6.8
2002	10986	233597	4.7	6.8
2003	11261	296595	3.8	2.5
2004	11970	383829	3.1	6.3
2005	12748	481983	2.6	6.5
2006	13546	595976	2.3	6.3
2007	15849	752283	2.1	17.0
2008	18879	899000	2.1	17.6

数据来源：中国物流与采购联合会，《中国物流年鉴（2008）》，中国物资出版社。

以上分析表明：我国过去的农业发展历程中，很长一段时期用农业的简单积累来哺育和扶持工业的发展，在重工业和城市发展战略之下，通过工农业产品“剪刀差”从农业和农村获取大量的农村经济剩余[358]，造成了工农差异、城乡差别，形成了重视城市轻视农村的格局，使“三农”问题逐步突出。农产品物流可持续发展自然处于国家发展总目标之外，西部地区农产品物流与农村经济关系失调是特定条件下的一种历史必然。

二　二元经济约束和分层治理冲突

（一）二元经济与二元物流结构约束

新中国成立后，面对落后的、以小农为主的经济基础，为应付外来竞争压力，以赶超为目标，必然使得经济系统呈现“二元结构①”，二元结构中内生于发展战略的中国农产品物流，也必然是一个二元结构系统。表7－8显示了1978年—2008年我国城乡居民家庭人均收入及恩格尔系数状况，城市居民家庭人均可支配收入和农村居民家庭人均纯收入是衡量城乡居民收入水平的重要指标。在表7－8的基础上，图7－1显示的是1978年—2008年中国城乡居民收入的比较情况，说明中国具有“二元结构”的典型特征，存在明显的城乡差别，在20世纪90年代中期以后城乡居民收入之间差距表现得更加突出。在表7－7的基础上，图7－2显示的是1991年—2008年中国农产品物流与全国社会物流发展水平比较。说明中国农产品物流总额与全国社会物流总额存在较大的差距，而与城乡经济发展差别相吻合，农产品物流与全国整体物流发展水平的差距在20世纪90年代以后也进一步拉大了[359]。在这种二元经济和二元物流结构的背景下，西部地区经济系统中的农产品物流也必然同样是一个二元结构系统，在西部地区农产品物流发展中同时存在物流扩张和物流抑制，而且一定表现为城市物流优先于农产品物流。因此，促进西部地区农村经济发展，必须改进现行中国及其西部地区物流的结构和功能，增强农产品物流在物流发展中的影响，强化农产品物流服务于农村经济的功能。

表7－8　1978年—2008年中国城乡居民家庭人均收入及恩格尔系数状况

年份	城镇居民家庭人均可支配收入		农村居民家庭人均纯收入		农村与城市人均收入的比例	城镇居民家庭恩格尔系数（%）	农村居民家庭恩格尔系数（%）
	绝对数（元）	指数（1978＝100）	绝对数（元）	指数（1978＝100）			
1978	343.4	100.0	133.6	100.0	38.92	57.5	67.7
1980	477.6	127.0	191.3	139.0	40.05	56.9	61.8
1985	739.1	160.4	397.6	268.9	53.80	53.3	57.8
1990	1510.2	198.1	686.3	311.2	45.44	54.2	58.8
1991	1700.6	212.4	708.6	317.4	41.67	53.8	57.6
1992	2026.6	232.9	784.0	336.2	38.69	53.0	57.6

① 刘易斯（W. Arthur Lewis）1954年在《劳动无限供给条件下的经济发展》一文中，将布克（J. H. Booke）于1933年提出的用于描述发展中国家社会经济现象的“二元结构”理论引入经济分析，从而开辟了经济分析的“结构主义”。

续表 7－8

年份	城镇居民家庭人均可支配收入		农村居民家庭人均纯收入		农村与城市人均收入的比例	城镇居民家庭恩格尔系数（%）	农村居民家庭恩格尔系数（%）
	绝对数（元）	指数（1978＝100）	绝对数（元）	指数（1978＝100）			
1993	2577.4	255.1	921.6	346.9	35.76	50.3	58.1
1994	3496.2	276.8	1221.0	364.3	34.92	50.0	58.9
1995	4283.0	290.3	1577.7	383.6	36.84	50.1	58.6
1996	4838.9	301.6	1926.1	418.1	39.80	48.8	56.3
1997	5160.3	311.9	2090.1	437.3	40.50	46.6	55.1
1998	5425.1	329.9	2162.0	456.1	39.85	44.7	53.4
1999	5854.0	360.6	2210.3	473.5	37.76	42.1	52.6
2000	6280.0	383.7	2253.4	483.4	35.88	39.4	49.1
2001	6859.6	416.3	2366.4	503.7	34.50	38.2	47.7
2002	7702.8	472.1	2475.6	527.9	32.14	37.7	46.2
2003	8472.2	514.6	2622.2	550.6	30.95	37.1	45.6
2004	9421.6	554.2	2936.4	588.0	31.17	37.7	47.2
2005	10493.0	607.4	3254.9	624.5	31.02	36.7	45.5
2006	11759.5	670.7	3587.0	670.7	30.50	35.8	43.0
2007	13785.8	752.5	4140.4	734.4	30.03	36.3	43.1
2008	15780.8	815.7	4760.6	793.2	30.17	37.9	43.7

资料来源：国家统计局，《中国统计年鉴》（2010），中国统计出版社。

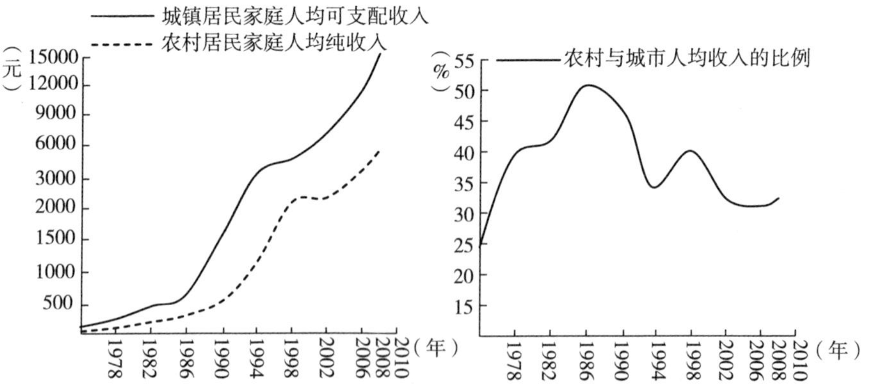

图 7－1　1978 年—2008 年中国城乡居民收入的比较

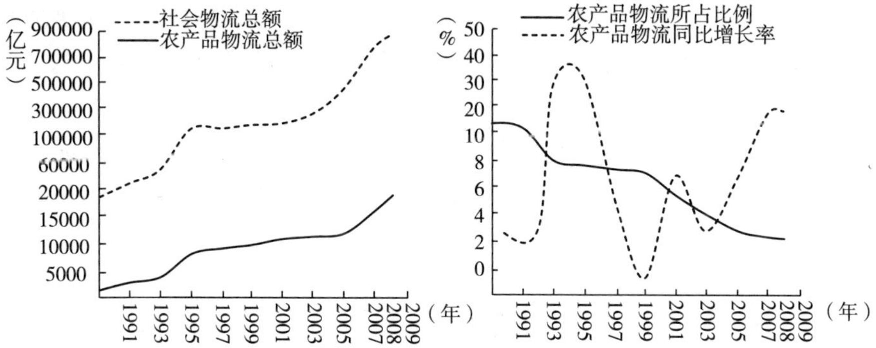

图 7－2　1991 年—2008 年中国农产品物流与全国社会物流发展水平比较

（二）分层治理中政府行为相互冲突

农产品物流可持续发展取决于农产品物流、农村经济两者的相互协调。从 1982 年—1986 年中央政府率先出台 5 个关于农村问题的“1 号文件”，2004 年—2007 年中央连续下发了 4 个“1 号文件”，到 2009 年出台的“1 号文件”再次提出“加强农产品市场体系建设”，最好地说明了中央政府协调两者关系采取的率先行动[360]。但中央决策层作为监督者并不能直接决定农产品物流可持续发展，决策层需要在分层治理系统中依靠委托—代理、命令—服从的方式落实，由于过长的信息链与过多的层级，加之中央决策层的监督不力，地方政府作为“经济人”具有短期行为与机会主义特征[361]，必然形成地方政府的行为顺序是“城市经济→农村非农业经济→农业经济”“农村大型非农企业→农业产业化组织→农村小型个体私营企业→以农业为主的农户经济”。因此，与中央政府相比，地方政府具有更强烈的工业化冲动。各级政府制定了物流发展规划，以及配套的扶持政策，形成重视城市物流、工业品物流发展而忽视了农产品领域的物流发展现象。由于我国物流是分部门管理，如铁路、民航、公路、水运都是分割的，现有的铁路网与公路网接点不同，各自规划，甚至完全分离，相互转换起来很困难，使得各物流主体很难根据市场需求对各种运输方式优化组合，在重重关卡下只能选择单一的运输方式。并且由于我国财政“分灶吃饭”，地方政府对本地农产品保护主义盛行，公开“设租”“寻租”，行政垄断在各地屡见不鲜，阻碍了农产品资源顺应经济规律的合理流通，忽视了农产品物流企业的发展，形成了西部地区物流产业组织结构存在的产业集中度低、规模效益低、产业进入壁垒低而导致的地区垄断与过度竞争并存，地方政府对区域内农产品物流组织缺乏足够的调控能力的情况[362]，直接影响到产业的核心竞争力。因此，进一步规范地方政府行为，切断竞争机制扭曲的体制根源，建立农产品行政物流（政府垂直治理）和农村经济（政府水平治理）管理部门之间的可持续发展机制意义十分重大。

三　思想认识不足和传统观念限制

（一）对农产品物流发展的内涵认识不清

农产品是人们生活所需的必需品，农产品物流是为满足人们对这种必需品的需求而提供的更优质的服务[363-365]。农产品物流一方面能更好地满足消费者的消费需求，另一方面它能促进生产者的商品转化，对农业生产具有积极的引导和促进作用。因此，农产品物流是一项既对生产者有利、又对消费者有益、同时还对政府有助的社会化事业，具有一定福利性的特点[366,367]。长期以来，对西部地区农产品物流的服务理解不仅停留在“运销”这一外在形式上，忽视了以利益、幸福为基础的福利性内核这一特征，而且对利益的理解也过于强调其道德含义。忽视了道德是交易中反复博弈的结果，信用关系是产权关系、社会福利关系的延伸；对物流的理解不仅停留在“资金流”这一表面层次上，忽视了以信任和安全感为基础的信用是物流的内核这一物流的制度属性，而且计划经济下的流通影响了农产品物流自身的可持续发展。因此，在市场经济条件下，对西部地区农产品物流的认识不具备“交易物流”“产业物流”和“功能物流”的概念内涵。

长期以来，无论是整体经济环境还是行业经济环境都是从“增长”角度看“经济发展”，对西部地区农产品物流发展也仅仅是片面地理解为“增长”意义上的“物流发展”，忽视了“转型时期”以产权为基础的制度结构在西部地区物流发展中的重要性，而且，对西部地区农产品物流制度和结构属性认识不全面。西部地区农产品物流制度仅被狭义地理解为宏观意义上的物流系统运行制度和微观意义上的物流机构管理制度，因此，对物流产权制度和以此为基础的物流治理结构的重要意义认识不足。片面地将物流安全和物流功能的发挥与国家对物流机构的所有权和控制权画上等号，忽视了合理的产权结构是物流有效治理结构的基础，有效的治理结构才是物流安全和物流功能发挥的保障。

（二）对农产品物流发展中的关系认识不足

从全国社会物流总值看，对经济发展中的工农关系认识不稳定，如表7－9所示。国家发展改革委、国家统计局、中国物流与采购联合会公布《2008年全国物流运行情况通报》显示：2008年，全国社会物流总额89.9万亿元，同比增长19.5%，仍然保持了较快增长态势，但增幅比2007年回落6.7个百分点。从社会物流总额的构成看，工业品物流总额79.86万亿元，同比增长20.8%，占社会物流总额的比重为88.8%，仍然是带动社会物流总额增长的主要因素。进口物流总额7.86万亿元，同比增长8.2%，占社会物流总额的比重为8.7%。再生资源物流总额和单位与居民物品物流总额分别增长3.8%和14%。农产品物流总额1.88万亿元，同比增长仅为17.6%，占社会物流总额的比重为2.1%，低于全国社会物流总额19.5%的增长幅度[368,369]。由此看出，近些年来，我国重视农业的发展，对农业的支持力度也在逐步加大，但目前工业品物流与农产品物流仍然存在明显差距。

表7－9　　2004年全国社会物流总值

项目	物流总值（亿元）	同比增长（%）	增幅（%）	物流总值比例（%）
全国社会物流总值	383000	29.9	2.9	—
工业品物流总值	325000	30.2	3.4	84.86
进口货物物流总值	46000	35.9	－4.1	12.01
农产品物流总值	12000	6.3	3.8	3.13
再生资源物流总值	325	16.8	－1.5	0.08
单位与居民物品物流总值	190	21.1	—	0.05

数据来源：中国物流与采购联合会，《中国物流年鉴（2005）》，中国物资出版社。

从相关行业发展环境看，一是交通运输业。社会分工使得农产品的商品化程度越来越高，区域化、专业化的优质高效生产也再度促进了农产品的商品化，但农产品的商品化离不开交通运输业对物流的支持[370]。西部大开发10年以来，交通运输的基础设施建设取得了很大的发展，交通运输条件也有了很大的改善，支持了农产品物流的发展，但西部地区交通运输在发展过程中也还存在一些政策上和体制上的问题，对农产品物流的发展形成了一定的制约。二是信息通信产业。伴随着知识经济的发展，物流产业也由科学化发展时期走向了现代化发展时期。信息流是商流和物流产生的前提和基础，所以信息产业的发展对农产品物流的现代发展有着极为重要的推动意义[371,372]。无论是电子信息产业还是通信业，在结构与规模、东部与西部、城市与农村之间都存在着不同程度的不协调问题，西部和农村的计算机、电话的普及率以及网络的覆盖率都还不高，需要加强信息和通信产业支持西部地区农产品物流发展的力度[373,374]。目前，在认识农产品物流与国民经济其他产业的关系上，忽视了在市场经济条件下这种关系应该是平等的交换关系，于是只要农产品产销有问题，出现“菜贱伤农”“卖难买贵”的事件，就指责农产品物流的运作，却很少关注农产品物流与相关行业关系是否健康、失调以及能否可持续发展[375]。因此，全面正确地认识两者关系对西部地区农产品物流可持续发展十分重要。

第二节　农村经济发展制约是深层原因

一　西部地区农村经济在波动中增长，但发展水平极不平衡

西部地区农村经济发展状态可以概括为表 7－10，以及据此形成的图 7－3 所示。1978 年我国 GDP 为 3645.2 亿元到 2008 年增长为 300670.0 亿元，1978 年西部地区农业生产总值为 265.67 亿元到 2008 年增长为 9065.13 亿元。1978 年—2008 年我国 GDP 平均值为 71386.2 亿元，而 1978 年—2008 年西部地区农业生产平均值为 2766.63 亿元。在 1978 年西部地区农业生产总值占全国 GDP 的比重为 7.23%，2008 年仅有 3.01%。其中，1991 年—1999 年，西部地区农业生产总值所占全国 GDP 平均比为 4.93%；2000 年—2008 年，西部地区农业生产总值所占全国 GDP 平均比为 3.00%。分析看出，2000 年—2008 年与 1991 年—1999 年相比，西部地区农业生产总值所占

全国 GDP 平均比有所降低。说明西部地区农业生产总值在波动中增长，相对于国民经济发展，西部农业经济发展总体水平偏低。

表 7－10　1978 年—2008 年中国 GDP 和西部地区农业生产总值及其发展速度

单位：亿元

时间（年）	GDP	西部地区农业生产总值	GDP 环比发展速度（%）	西部地区农业生产总值环比发展速度（%）	西部地区农业生产总值占全国比重（%）
1978	3645.2	265.67	118.36	126.03	7.23
1979	4062.6	398.51	111.45	150.00	9.81
1980	4545.6	540.30	111.89	135.58	11.89
1981	4891.6	594.30	107.61	109.99	12.15
1982	5323.4	635.66	108.83	106.96	11.94
1983	5962.7	675.80	112.01	106.31	11.33
1984	7208.1	827.73	120.89	122.48	11.48
1985	9016.0	827.48	125.08	99.97	9.18
1986	10275.2	873.52	113.97	105.56	8.50
1987	12058.6	1109.63	117.36	127.03	9.20
1988	15042.8	1401.91	124.75	126.34	9.32
1989	16992.3	1567.96	112.96	111.84	9.23
1990	18667.8	1283.77	109.86	81.88	6.88
1991	21781.5	1393.86	116.68	108.58	6.34
1992	26923.5	1514.31	123.61	108.64	5.62
1993	35333.9	1738.14	131.24	114.78	4.92
1994	48197.9	2331.71	136.41	134.15	4.84
1995	60793.7	2798.05	126.13	119.99	4.60
1996	71176.6	3494.56	117.08	124.89	4.90
1997	78973.0	3696.93	110.95	105.79	4.68
1998	84402.3	3727.48	106.87	100.82	4.42
1999	89677.1	3652.40	106.25	97.98	4.07
2000	99214.6	3706.78	110.64	101.49	3.74
2001	109655.2	3833.07	110.52	103.41	3.50
2002	120332.7	4025.76	109.74	105.03	0.85

续表 7－10

时间（年）	GDP	西部地区农业生产总值	GDP 环比发展速度（%）	西部地区农业生产总值环比发展速度（%）	西部地区农业生产总值占全国比重（%）
2003	135822.8	4450.37	112.87	110.55	3.28
2004	159878.3	5368.82	117.71	120.64	3.36
2005	183217.4	5924.63	114.60	110.35	3.23
2006	211923.5	6396.07	115.67	107.96	3.02
2007	257305.6	7645.08	121.41	119.53	2.97
2008	300670.0	9065.13	116.85	118.57	3.01

资料来源：1978 年—1998 年的数据来源于《新中国五十年统计资料汇编》，1999 年—2008 年的数据来自于 2000 年—2009 年各期《中国统计年鉴》。

说明：本表列出的西部地区农业生产总值为西部地区 12 省市区：重庆（只有 1997 年以来的数据）、四川、贵州、云南、西藏、陕西、甘肃、宁夏、青海、新疆、广西、内蒙古农业生产总值之和。环比发展速度以上年为 100。将时间跨度定为 1978 年至 2008 年，以求准确反映改革开放以来，尤其是西部大开发时期西部农村经济发展轨迹。

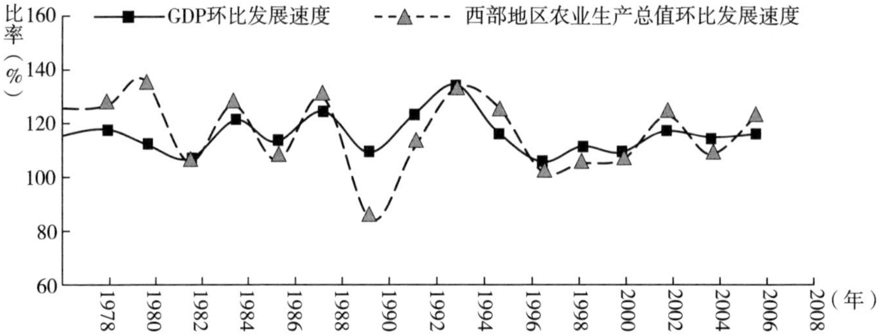

图 7－3　1978 年—2008 年西部农业经济与国民经济环比发展速度比较

此外，西部农村经济发展水平极不平衡。中国三大地区农村经济相比，西部地区农村经济发展水平低于中部、东部地区农村经济发展水平，形成了西部地区农村经济中较小的农产品流通量，西部地区农村经济对农产品物流的有效需求也就偏小，必然会制约西部地区农产品物流业务发展空间，导致农村经济与农产品物流呈现出低水平均衡状态[376]。图 7－4、图 7－5 反映了我国东部、中部、西部农村经济发展水平的不平衡导致了西部地区农产品物流发展差异[①]。图 7－4 显示的是 1978 年—2008 年中国三大地区物流发展差异比率，图 7－5 显示的是三大地区区际差异对总体差异的贡献比率的比较情况[②]。

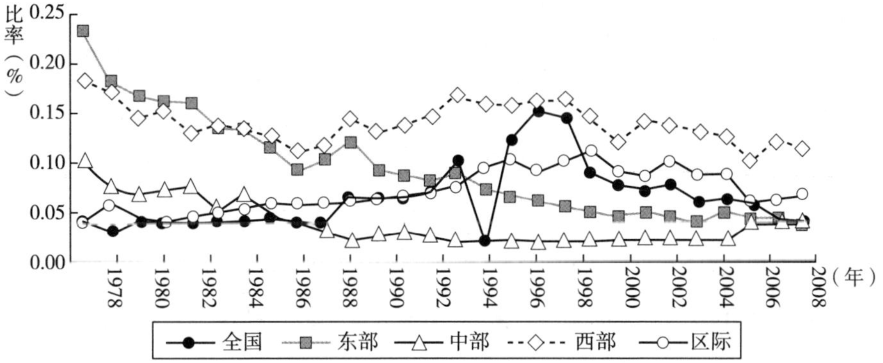

图 7－4　1978 年—2008 年三大区域间的区际差异的泰尔指数值的变动趋势

二　西部地区农民收入稳步增长，但城乡人均收入极不平衡

表 7－11 所示：1978 年，西部地区农村居民人均纯收入为 126.90 元，城市居民人均可支配收入为 326.1 元，农村居民人均收入只有城市居民人均可支配收入的 38.91%；在 1978 年—1993 年间，这项比例在 1982 年达

① 西部地区乡镇企业发展滞后，第一产业比重高，农村经济发展水平低。加之自给自足的小农经济在农业和农村经济发展中依然占有相当比例，因此农业经济和农村经济的物流程度也较低，于是决定了农业和农村经济中较小的农产品物流量。农产品物流业务空间就会受到制约，因而，农村经济与农产品物流就会陷入低水平均衡的陷阱。

② 本文采用泰尔指数（Theil），它是唯一满足可分解性的一类不平等测度指标。在三大地区中，西部地区变化幅度最大，波动也最为剧烈，从 1994 年开始，超过东部，在 1997 年达到最大值 0.1537 之后开始下降。西部地区泰尔指数起落的时间和全国泰尔指数变化的时间基本一致，但远远低于全国的差异。1999 年以后西部地区的泰尔指数逐渐下降，在 2007 年下降到较低的 0.0367，说明随着 1999 年西部大开发战略的实施，西部地区获得了更多的投资和政策优惠，基础设施建设空前发展，这使得对基础设施依赖度极高的物流业获得了快速发展，从而缩小了西部地区内部物流业发展的省际差异。我国区域物流发展的总体（省际）差异是不断缩小的，但这是由于三大地区内部差异的不断缩小所引起，而三大地区之间的差距则不断扩大，尤其是东部与中、西部之间的差距越来越大。

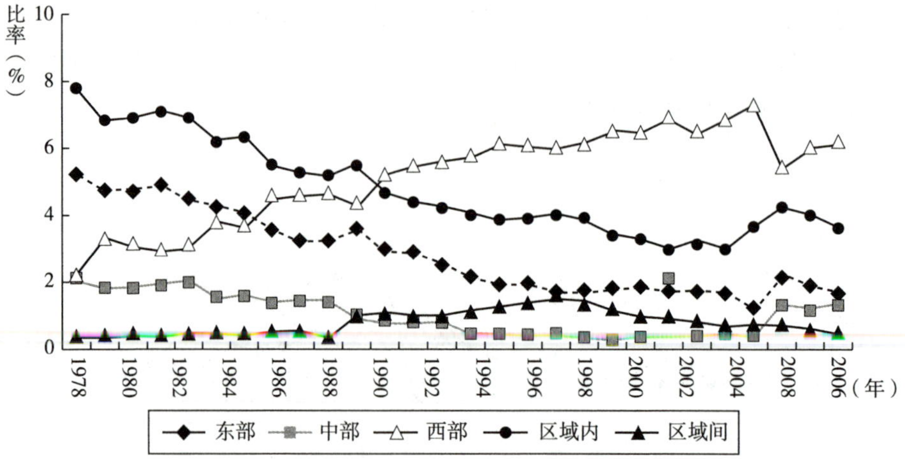

图 7－5　1978 年—2008 年三大地区区际差异对总体差异的贡献比率的比较

到最高，达到城市人均收入的 41. 41%；2003 年，农村居民人均纯收入为 1920. 95 元，而城市居民人均可支配收入为 7235. 39 元，农村居民人均收入只有城市居民人均可支配收入的 26. 55%，达到最低点。农村居民人均纯收入 2003 年是 1978 年 15. 14 倍，而城市居民人均可支配收入 2003 年是 1978 年 22. 19 倍。2003 年是农业恢复性增长较快的一年，但也只实际增长了 4. 3%，1997 年—2003 年的 7 年间年均增长仅为 3. 9%，仅为城镇居民收入增量的 16%，年均增长速度不到城镇居民的 50%，城乡居民收入差距绝对额，从 1978 年的 199. 23 元扩大到 2003 年的 5314. 44 元、到 2008 年的 9453. 43 元，其中 1978 年至 1985 年平均每年扩大量在 50—60 元之间；1985 年至 1992 年平均每年扩大量在 100—200 元之间；1992 年以后平均每年扩大量在 500—600 元之间；2004 年以后平均每年扩大量达到 1000 多元。2008 年城镇居民人均可支配收入 12971. 18 元，农村居民人均纯收入 3517. 75 元，农民收入水平比城镇落后了 8—10 年。1978 年地区农村居民家庭食品消费占生活消费支出的 70% 以上（恩格尔系数），2008 年恩格尔系数下降为 47. 7%。

以上分析可以看出，西部地区农民收入绝对水平低，必然导致西部地区农产品储运率低和资金短缺，西部地区农产品物流发展面临物流资源约束，难以满足农村经济发展的物流需求。西部地区农产品物流与农村经济处于低水平的均衡状态。西部地区农民收入相对水平低，必然导致城乡物

表 7－11　1978 年—2008 年西部地区农民收入和城镇居民收入及其发展速度

单位：元

年份	农村居民人均纯收入	城市居民人均可支配收入	农村与城市人均收入的比例	农村居民家庭恩格尔系数（%）	城市居民家庭恩格尔系数（%）
1978	126.90	326.13	38.91	71.7	61.5
1979	152.57	367.57	41.51	67.8	61.5
1980	182.19	457.48	39.82	65.5	61.3
1981	212.76	469.62	45.30	63.2	61.1
1982	208.13	502.65	41.41	65.8	60.9
1983	238.30	538.25	44.27	67.6	60.9
1984	273.30	621.68	43.96	67.2	61.0
1985	305.85	648.92	47.13	65.9	56.8
1986	326.00	789.84	41.27	64.3	57.1
1987	352.42	879.92	40.05	62.8	58.2
1988	415.32	1037.26	40.04	60.9	55.9
1989	458.46	1207.85	37.96	61.7	59.3
1990	523.09	1325.94	39.45	67.0	58.4
1991	539.83	1493.11	36.15	61.7	57.9
1992	517.76	1462.18	35.41	61.6	57.0
1993	608.72	1859.58	32.73	62.1	53.9
1994	806.47	2522.49	31.97	62.9	53.7
1995	1042.07	3090.16	33.72	62.7	54.2
1996	1272.19	3491.24	36.44	60.3	52.8
1997	1009.90	3765.06	26.82	59.1	50.4
1998	1392.30	4062.69	34.27	57.4	48.7
1999	1577.56	5341.51	29.53	56.6	46.1
2000	1632.31	5486.21	29.75	53.1	43.4
2001	1692.96	6017.49	28.13	51.7	42.2
2002	1791.73	6674.82	26.84	50.2	41.7
2003	1920.95	7235.39	26.55	49.9	40.5
2004	2157.91	7996.08	26.99	49.9	38.9

续表 7－11

年份	农村居民人均纯收入	城市居民人均可支配收入	农村与城市人均收入的比例	农村居民家庭恩格尔系数（%）	城市居民家庭恩格尔系数（%）
2005	2378.91	8783.17	27.08	49.8	38.1
2006	2588.37	9728.45	26.61	46.5	36.9
2007	3028.38	11309.45	26.78	46.6	38.9
2008	3517.75	12971.18	27.12	47.7	40.8

资料来源：1978 年—1998 年的数据来源于《新中国五十年统计资料汇编》，1999 年—2008 年的数据来自于 2000 年—2009 年各期《中国统计年鉴》。

说明：本表列出的西部地区农民收入和城镇居民收入为西部地区 12 省市区：重庆（只有 1997 年以来的数据）、四川、贵州、云南、西藏、陕西、甘肃、宁夏、青海、新疆、广西、内蒙古的农民收入总值之和与城镇居民收入总值之和。恩格尔系数是食品与生活消费总支出之比。将时间跨度定为 1978 年至 2008 年，以求准确反映改革开放以来，尤其是西部大开发时期西部农村经济发展轨迹。

流发展不协调，更加剧了西部地区农产品物流资源的短缺和外流，西部地区农产品物流和农村经济关系必然进入相互制约的恶性循环。

三　西部地区农村产业结构发生变化，但农村经济比较利益低下

西部地区农村典型现象是一多、一少、一集中，即多“农村人口”、少“农村耕地”①、集中“农村贫困人口”②。西部地区农村贫困人口占全国的比重还在增加，2005 年西部地区农村绝对贫困人口占全国农村绝对贫困人口的比重由 2004 年的 50% 上升到 50.8%，西部地区农村低收入人口占全国农村低收入人口的比重由 2004 年的 48.1% 上升到 52.1%。2005

① 中国西部地区土地面积 538 万平方公里，占全国国土面积的 56%，目前有人口约 2.87 亿人，占全国人口的 22.99%，1/3 的县人均耕地面积小于 0.8 亩，1/4 的县小于 0.5 亩，已经降至联合国所规定的耕地对人口的最低保障线。

② 据对全国 31 个省区市 6.8 万个农村住户的抽样调查，2005 年年末全国农村绝对贫困人口为 2365 万人，贫困发生率为 2.5%。在目前的农村绝对贫困人口中，东部地区为 324 万人，中部地区为 839 万人，西部地区为 1202 万人，各地区贫困发生率分别为 0.8%、2.5% 和 5.2%。2005 年初步解决温饱但还不稳定的农村低收入人口，全国为 4067 万人，占全国农村人口的比重为 4.3%，其中东部地区为 577 万人，中部地区为 1372 万人，西部地区为 2118 万人，占各地区农村人口的比重分别为 1.5%、4.2% 和 9.2%。因此，西部地区是目前我国最主要的农村贫困人口分布地区。

年 592 个国家扶贫重点县中，有 375 个在西部地区[377]。西部地区的农村贫困、城市化程度低，非农产业不发达，农村剩余劳力转移困难，过剩的农村人口被束缚在第一产业内，从而导致农业小规模、低效益经营。

西部地区农业资源短缺，与发达地区相比主要表现在农业生产率的差异。从农业资源的分布看，西部地区农业用地面积占全国的 67%，耕地占全国的 38.12%，牧草地占全国的 97.9%，林业用地占全国的 57.36%，乡村劳动力占全国的 32.07%，但农林牧渔总产值占全国的 24.3%，其中农业总产值占全国的 25.7%，林业总产值占全国的 27.7%，牧业总产值占全国的 27.1%，劳均产出西部地区是最低的，主要农产品产量占全国的比重也和其丰富的非农业资源不相称[377]。西部地区农业生产率低，当然和其农业资源的匹配有关系，如西北地区水资源短缺，严重制约了农业的发展，西南地区山高谷深，水土流失严重，农业基础设施薄弱，农业技术进步缓慢，也是影响西部地区农业生产率提高的重要因素。此外，农业生产周期长，自然风险和市场风险等多种风险并存，以及长期实施的向工业和城市倾斜战略致使西部地区农业生产手段落后，农村经济主体发育远不能适应市场要求。西部地区农业生产的基本单位主要是千家万户的小农经济[378]，分散的小农难以获得平等的贸易地位和收益，规模利益难以提升，导致西部地区农业生产比较利益低下。

四　西部地区农业生产条件进一步改善，但农村市场主体发育不良

农户的市场主体地位尚未完全形成。西部地区是全国主要的农产品生产基地，在西部 36729 万总人口中，农业人口占到 60% 以上。农户是西部地区农产品物流可持续发展的微观基础，其发育状况意义重大。在农民的组织化程度方面，由于历史和自然的原因，农产品物流的城乡“二元结构”相当严重，西部地区农户物流需求仍然是小农经济模式[379]，由于农村普遍缺乏具有独立产权的代表农民利益的经济组织，分散、细小的生产经营方式限制了农产品的交易，农民呈无组织分散状态进入市场，缺乏市场竞争力和自我保护能力。在农民文化素质方面，据 2004 年中国农业统计资料显示，在中国西部地区，大部分农村人口的受教育水平还处于初中、甚至小

学以下。人口平均受教育年限为7.4年，有近32%的人是小学以下文化程度[380]。由于西部地区农民的组织化程度、文化素质偏低，只能长期处于信息失灵的环境之中，市场主体意识难以形成，是典型的弱势群体。在农村经济、农村信用的共同约束下，西部地区农产品物流发展所面临的不仅是农户物流需求不足的限制，而且很容易造成农产品物流机构的不良风险[381]。

农村企业和农业组织产业化进程缓慢。农村企业规模较小，技术和管理水平不高，市场占有率低是西部地区普遍存在的现象。虽然，在农业产业化过程中，形成了一些具有一定规模的龙头企业，但其治理结构不合理，规模、质量和效益都不够高。原因在于市场开拓能力不强，企业与农户的利益联结机制不完善，龙头带基地带农户能力有限[382]。西部地区农业产业化龙头企业绝大多数为生产加工型企业，部分龙头企业兼营销售业务，而专门从事农用物资、农产品物流的龙头企业几乎为零，只是有为数不多的农产品流通企业。如陕西省79家省级以上农业产业化重点龙头企业中仅有6家大型农产品市场，其中果品批发市场只有2家，这与陕西省作为全国第一水果生产大省的地位极其不符，影响了陕西省农业产业化的深化。其直接原因是治理结构不合理、国家的税收优惠政策和农业产业化龙头融资的“软约束”和“道德风险”。而对于发展初期的龙头企业，由于缺乏健全的正规物流需求主体条件，资金短缺成为主要约束因素。

农村经济主体生产方式落后，政府投入不足。本研究在实地调查过程中发现：传统的生产要素和技术手段在西部地区农业生产中仍然占很高比重，尤其是在西部欠发达地区，农业生产的诸环节仍是以人畜力为主的传统技术工具。西部地区农业生产条件的差距大，科技进步在农业增长的贡献份额很低①。当前西部地区农业生产中，物质投入偏低，化肥、农机、农药等投入水平均低于发达国家。表7－12是中国西部地区与发达国家（地区）农业投资结构对比表[383]。农业投入不足直接导致农业基础设施条件差，流通效率低下。西部农村普遍存在“藏粮于民”的传统观念和习惯对发展农产品物流形成了一个很大的障碍。由于农户家庭储粮的设施

① 目前我国具有物流师资格的从业人员约1.7万人，而具有高级物流师职业资格仅292人。物流人才的短缺已成为制约我国农产品物流发展的瓶颈，特别是在教育水平相对落后的西部欠发达地区，人才欠缺的问题尤其严重，中、高级物流管理人才和工程技术人才极度缺乏。就国内范围比较，西部以身体素质为主的搬运和装卸工等从业人员的水平要明显低于东部具有专业知识技术的大专院校从业者。

简陋，损失严重。据调查结果显示，小麦储存3—5个月平均损失率为9%；玉米储存6—12个月，平均损失率为7%，再加鼠害、霉变等损失，平均每年储粮损失率为10%左右[384]。如果再将收获时的洒落，原粮作为饲料的隐性浪费包括在内，西部地区每年在农产品物流过程中造成的数量损失巨大。

表7-12 中国西部地区与发达国家（地区）农业投资结构对比

比较项目	发达国家（地区）	中国西部地区
果蔬产品损耗率	1%—2%	25%—30%
产中投资比例	30%	80%
产后投资比例	70%	20%
加工前后增值比	1∶3.8	1∶1.5

第三节 农产品物流功能不足是直接原因

一 西部地区农产品物流深化改革滞后

经过30年的改革，形成于计划经济体制下、重工业和城市倾斜战略的国有物流“大一统”格局已被打破，基本形成了多元化的物流机构构成的物流组织体系。虽然，在这一过程中，国家启动了农村流通市场化改革，初步确立了农产品物流主体行为的基本规范，逐步完善了农产品流通机制。但从整体上看，西部地区农产品物流发展存在多元化农产品物流结构不合理，农产品社会性物流发展不到位，农产品双向性物流发展难度大，农产品经济性物流发展不协调等问题。西部地区农产品物流深化改革滞后于整体物流、滞后于农村经济，西部地区农产品物流交易的市场机制还未形成。

（一）多元化农产品物流结构不合理

1. 农产品物流多重属性，不同主体同台竞争

从农产品经济属性影响的角度来看，农产品物流的经济属性是农产品

物流产生的根源和前进的动力。物流本身的价值创造活动是基于农产品的空间位移和时间价值所创造的，物流创造的价值最终赋予到农产品身上，这样经过多个物流、加工、销售等环节，价值不断被创造，农产品不断增值，并逐渐向消费者方向运动。消费者支付农产品的消费成本后，经济利益回流到价值创造的各组织中，使各组织进行下一生产或服务循环，也使各组织产生发展的动力，如图 7－6 所示。

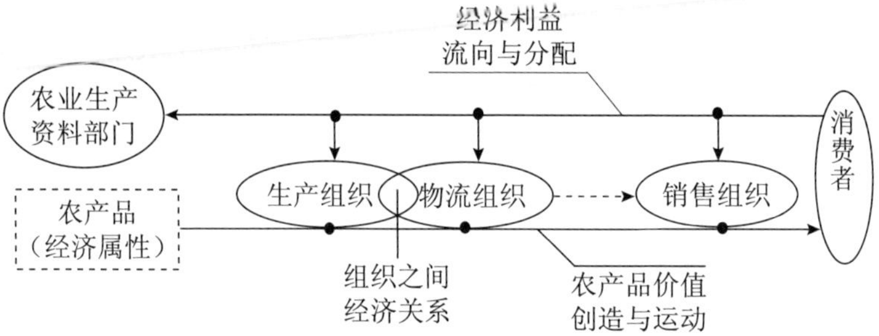

图 7－6　农产品经济属性是物流产生的根源

从农产品功能属性影响的角度来看，对农产品物流具有决定作用。农产品的功能属性主要有充饥、营养、健康、享受这四个大的方面，随着人们生活水平的提高，农产品消费逐渐从充饥（内核）向享受（外延）发展，因此也出现了农产品的优质生产和结构调整。消费影响的质量结构和种类结构的变化，促进了农产品区域化的优质高效生产，于是也促进了农产品区域间的互补，使原来低水准的“地产地销”主导模式发展到了全国大市场的“优势互补”主导模式，区域间物流的动因由“数量余缺调剂”逐步向“质量品种调剂”转化，区域间农产品出现了“双向性物流”。出现这种“双向性物流”的根本原因：一是区域功能双向性。如“南菜北运”的大物流现象，在市场经济条件下农产品会始终按着优势梯度进行流动，只要区域间存在优势互补，就应该存在这种“互补性物流”，物流的流向由“地产地销”的“支线环流”逐步向“优势互补”的“干线物流”方向发展，最终形成资源优势决定生产优势，生产优势决定产品优势，产品优势决定市场优势，资源与市场优势决定物流流向的“优势”决定论，如图 7－7 所示。二是主体功能双向性。如“供销合作社”的物流形态，它既代表国家利益又代表农民利益，是连接农业与工业、乡村与城镇、生产和消费的重要纽带。

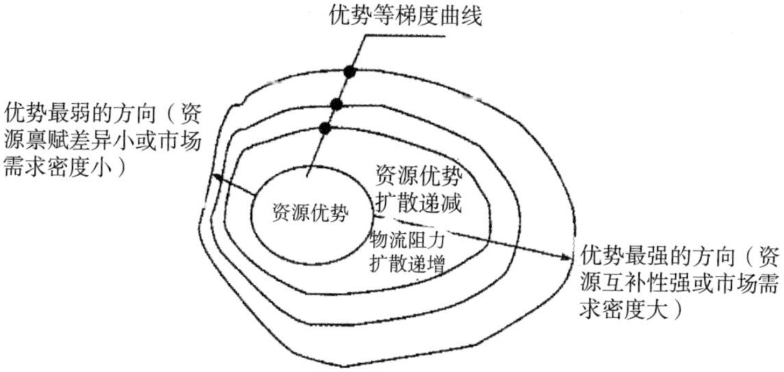

图 7－7　农产品物流流向优势决定模型

从农产品社会属性影响的角度来看，农产品的社会属性涉及了人们的基本生活保障和经济发展与社会稳定的前提问题，因而决定了农产品物流不单纯具有经济性，还应该具有社会性。农产品物流的社会性体现在农产品物流应具备战略物流、社会物流、福利物流、安全物流等特点，其重要意义远超过一般商品的物流。农产品物流既为生产者服务，也为消费者服务，其实质是为人们的生活保障服务，因为农产品不是社会某个群体的消费，而是普遍意义上的消费，具有社会福利最基本的基础性与广泛性，因而农产品物流具有较强的社会性和福利性，如图 7－8 所示。

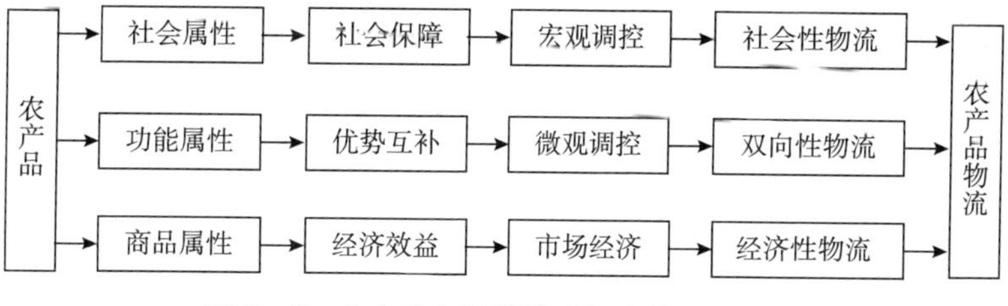

图 7－8　农产品多重属性对物流的综合影响

目前，西部地区农产品物流的社会属性、功能属性、经济属性之间联合性差、层次低，没有形成社会性物流、双向性物流、经济性物流有效运行的机制。在成熟的物流市场上，社会化、专业化的物流企业是构成物流市场的竞争主体。但是由于目前农产品物流企业还处于发展期，无法承担起全部的责任，于是以各种形式存在的物流服务提供者更多地充当了物流企业的角色。农产品物流市场鱼龙混杂，形成了多方物流与工商企业、个体物流同台竞争的多元化格局。①社会性物流，即政策性的非营利性物流。主要是指传统的国有流通企业，如国有粮食企业、国有商业公司。②双向性物流，即合作性的非营利性物流。主要是指以满足经济和社会需求为目的的自治组织，如农村供销合作社。③经济性物流，包括正规的营利性物流、非正规的营利性物流。前者主要是传统运输领域全国性的国有企业，如中外运、中国邮政、铁路系统、中远、中储等；后者包括如农户、加工型企业的自营物流、个体私营运输类或仓储运输公司、专业化的第三方物流公司、各种联合会、经纪人等民间物流活动。现有的农产品物流主体形态可以看出，一方面过低的进入障碍使得行业里存在着参差不齐的竞争者，随着新加入者的不断涌入，产业内的竞争日益升级。另一方面由于农产品生产具有周期性特点，相对于处于变化中的需求来说，有较高的资产专用性，存储、运输和加工等设备往往是针对一种农产品或农产品再次加工中的一个环节进行的，除此之外很难再有其他用途，退出障碍过高。处于这一尴尬状态的企业无疑会在过低进入障碍和过高退出障碍的双重作用下苦苦支撑，尽可能地延长这些资产的使用寿命，从而形成了农产品物流行业的“低收益和高风险”性。在这种多元化物流主体格局里，各物流主体之间分工不明确，导致主体间功能严重错位。

2. 产权结构、组织结构和服务功能单一

产权制度的建立就是通过权利的界定来明确当事人的预期收益，规范市场行为。产权结构是物流治理结构及其功能发挥的基础[385]。在产权结构上，中国农产品物流，无论是社会性的传统国有流通企业（国有粮食企业、国有商业公司等），还是双向性的农民合作经济组织（农村供销合作社），正规的经济性的传统运输领域全国性的国有企业（中外运、中国邮政、铁路系统、中远、中储等），都是国有或准国有物流机构，具有国有企业的典型特征和痼疾。就是近几年粮食流通体制改革和国有流通企业改革出现的国有粮食公司和供销社逐步演变成的物流企业，也基本是以国有或准国有为主体的产权结构。与农村经济主体产权多元化，农村私营、民营经济迅速发展相比，农产品物流产权结构单一，非正规的经济性的民营物流发展滞后（自营物流、中介组织、专业化的第三方物流公司等）。在组织和功能结构上，由于中国物流实行分业经营制度，功能结构只能通过组织结构体现，现行农产品物流主要由提供产品转移与储存服务的运输机构组成，农产品质量分级和标准化、市场信息、风险承担、融资等非运输业务发展严重不足。这种单一的组织结构导致西部地区农产品物流增值服务缺乏[386]。西部地区农产品物流就其功能而言就是西部地区农产品运输，服务功能不能满足实际需要。

第一，西部地区农产品的物流长期处于短缺经济，需要运用农产品质量分级和标准化来化解矛盾[387]。农产品受自身生物特性的影响，在消费者和生产者之间有关质量信息不对称的现象尤为突出[388]。很多产品的交易建立在双方对产品的实体查检之上，产品定价通常也是根据统货定价，不对产品进行分级，并不按照分级的基础定价，这在很大程度上降低了农产品的物流效率，使得优质农产品得不到优价，打击了农户的生产积极性[389]。当产品的价格和分级标准产生争议时，更缺少争议的仲裁机构。

第二，西部地区农产品物流系统决策效率和运营效率不高，需要完善市场信息系统。我国西部地区农产品信息的收集、处理和发布存在很多困难，缺乏准确、及时、全面的农产品物流市场信息。首先，农产品及其加工品品种繁多，信息繁杂并且市场信息变化快，这就造成信息的收集和沟通的困难。尤其是在我国西部地区，由于缺乏农产品质量标准，有关价格的信息几乎很难进行沟通。此外，信息的收集和提供成本高昂[390]。因此，对于农产品物流系统的任何参与者，尤其是单独的一个农户，独自收集所需要的、用以制订产品物流计划的全面和准确的信息是异常艰难的，或者说是几乎不可能的。

第三，西部地区农产品及其加工品面临较高的自然风险和市场风险，需要通过物流保险来分散风险，促进投资。由于各种类型的风险使经营决策变得非常困难，农户在决定生产决策时，面临自然灾害和价格波动等风险[391]。当农产品的交易行为发生时，伴随产品所有权的转移，风险也随之转移。农产品运销各环节的成员由于其性质不同，所承担的风险大小有着差异。对一些仅协助所有权的转移的经纪人、代理商而言，所承担的风险比较小。而农户、贸易商以及加工商、批发商、零售商等成员由于拥有产品的所有权，风险较大。农业保险或其他的险种的存在可以在一定程度上降低或转移农产品物流过程中的风险[392]。从国家统计局等三部门公布的地区耕地分布的情况看，西部地区受灾面积超过东部地区、中部地区和东北地区①。虽然中国人民保险公司1982年就开办农业保险业务，目前有20多个险种，但这种纯商业农业保险的运行很不成功[393]，制约了西部地区农产品物流保险发展，不能满足农村经济发展和农业结构调整的需要。

第四，西部地区农产品及其加工品的特性使得物流过程，需要大量的资金支持。作为农业生产经营的主体是分散的农户，无力承担大型农产品储藏、运输机械等生产要素的购置费用，急需农产品物流金融服务，然而西部地区目前农产品物流金融公司还未诞生[394-397]。

3. 区域结构失衡，农产品物流金融服务缺失

在区域上，笔者对东西部地区进行长时段追踪调查，东部地区选择河北、山东、浙江、广东、福建，西部地区选择重庆、四川、贵州、云南、广西、陕西、甘肃、青海、宁夏、西藏、新疆、内蒙古的调查显示：农产品物流发展具有与农村经济发展相一致的路径，但同时又受到过于单一的物流政策制约。东部经济发达地区，农产品业务性物流组织体系比较完善，具有一定的经营规模，业绩相对较好。在全国粮食流通体制改革和国有流通企业改革过程中，许多国有粮食公司和供销社向股份制、合作制物流企业演变较为顺利。形成农产品社会性、双向性和经济性物流相互配合的局面，在沿海经济发达地区出现了农产品物流园区的运营模式[398-402]。在中西部经济发展落后地区，以粮食生产为主的农业是农村经济的主体，而社会性物流发展不到位，经济性物流供给相对不足，物流服务比较单一。大多数农户和农村企业的物流需求只有通过农村供销合作社的垄断性供给和发展并不规范的自营物流来满足[403-405]。因此，农产品物流组织功能的区域失衡现象严重。

在西部地区农产品物流机构的规模上，受农产品物流金融服务缺失的制约。首先，西部地区农产品物流发展的资金供给存在制度缺口。农产品物流主体无论是贫瘠型→维持型→富足型的农户，还是小型→一定规模→龙头的企业，农产品物流主体从小到大发展过程中都需要农村金融提供传统的、新兴的、全面的金融服务[406]。农户与企业对农村金融层次性的需求特征如表7-13所示。从经济学的角度看，这种资金需求的多层次决定了一个功能

---

① 第二次全国农业普查主要数据第6号公报显示，截至2006年10月31日，全国耕地面积（未包括香港、澳门特别行政区和台湾省的数据）为12177.59万公顷。西部地区分布的耕地较多，占36.9%；东部地区、中部地区和东北地区分别占21.7%、23.8%和17.6%。2007年全国共有23个省（自治区、直辖市）发生了不同程度的洪涝灾害，全国农作物受灾面积364.2万公顷，成灾189.4万公顷。雪灾以及“5·12”四川地震已累计导致农作物受灾面积达1180万公顷左右。

健全的农村金融体系也应是多层次的，但西部地区农村金融供给政策的局限性导致了农村金融市场的卖方垄断。造成了市场分割背景下的卖方垄断格局，新生的“邮政储蓄银行”和“村镇银行”金融组织制度缺失①，专项的现代农产品物流金融产品“土地仓”尚未开发和运用②。其次，西部地区农产品物流发展的资金供需缺口严重。从资金供给状况看，信贷资金供给主体严重缺乏、信贷供给功能错位或弱化、资金供给总量不足、农村金融机构业务功能单一[407]。农村保险业停滞倒退以及农村金融产品欠开发和运用，

表 7－13　　农户及农产品供应链企业信贷需求特征与满足方式

农户	传统型	生活基本开支及小规模农产品生产贷款需求	民间小额贷款、商业性小额信贷、财政性扶贫资金
	兼业型	同上	上述之外还包括：自有资金、小额信用贷款
	市场型	规模化农产品、工商业贷款需求	自有资金、商业性信贷资金
生产、流通加工企业	小型生产企业、流通加工企业	启动市场资金需求与扩大规模资金需求	自有资金筹措、民间金融贷款、商业性信贷资金及政策性金融资金
	一定规模的生产企业、流通加工企业	生产贷款需求、规模扩张贷款需求、流动资金需求	自有资金筹措、商业性信贷资金、民间金融贷款、高利贷
	生产与流通加工龙头企业	规模化生产贷款需求、技改资金需求	商业性信贷资金
第三方物流企业	中小物流企业	规模化经营资金需求	商业性信贷资金、典当资金、担保融资及民间借贷资金
	大型第三方物流企业	规模化经营贷款需求	信用贷款、商业性信贷及资本市场运作

① 2007年以来，部分省市成立了“邮政储蓄银行”，但由于“邮政储蓄银行”自身组织制度的缺陷，还难以完全满足农产品供应链企业的金融需求。2006年以来，国家鼓励发展的村镇银行、贷款公司、小额贷款公司和资金互助社等四类新型农村金融机构，由于限定了民间资本和其他类型的国有资本参与提供农村金融供给的空间，加之缺乏规范的运作机制及较高的筹资和用资成本，同样难以担当满足现代农产品物流业发展的金融需求重任。

② “土地仓”制度是我国现代农产品物流金融发展的新范式。但由于缺少专业的担保基金或机构提供担保，加之农业保险萎缩，“土地仓”分散风险机制不健全，广大农户手中的土地经营权、林权等难以作为动产质押产品获得农村金融机构贷款。

不能满足西部地区现代农产品物流建设对金融的需要。从资金需求状况看，主要是农户资金需求、中小型农产品加工企业、运输仓储、流通配送企业及龙头企业的资金需求、农产品流通企业平稳扩张对资金的需求、物流基础设施建设对资金的需求。由于农产品产业链的延伸，越来越多的龙头企业和中介组织加入农产品物流供应链，使得固定资产、产品基地建设等方面的投入逐渐加大，项目的生产经营周期和回收期更长，从而导致中长期资金需求呈现增长趋势。此外，随着农产品国际贸易的日益频繁，汇兑、结算等金融需求也成为农产品物流企业的基本金融需求。而且，第三方农产品物流建设也迫切需要金融系统提供巨额资金支持和保障。

西部地区农产品物流金融困境根源在于：首先，城市倾斜和部门偏向政策妨碍农村金融市场的发展。主要受农村金融的二重制度结构、农村融资工具单一、农村金融机构布局不合理、农村正规金融组织的利率管制等影响。其次，资源配置准则与农产品物流业特征之间的矛盾[408]。农产品物流业自身的脆弱性和发展的滞后性，制约了农村金融对农产品物流业的资金支持，客观上造成农户和农产品供应链企业融资的困难。具体表现在：农产品物流业本身属于弱势产业，面临着自然和市场双重风险；金融机构从自身的赢利与资金安全考虑，不愿意向农产品物流产业提供贷款；金融服务分散化与金融的集约经营化矛盾的制约。再次，对农产品物流发展的支持性财政与税收政策不到位。资金的趋利性与农产品物流投入期限长、回报低的现实矛盾，决定了在缺乏政府扶持和优惠政策的前提下，商业银行的信贷资金是不会轻易投放到农产品物流业中的。从目前情况看，国家对农产品物流业发展的金融扶持政策也仅仅局限于农村信用社的“50%的贷款利率上浮权（改革试点地区可上浮70%）”和支农再贷款支持，对其他金融机构来说并没有太多的优惠政策。这就使得农村金融机构缺乏支持农产品物流业的积极性，加剧了农产品物流发展的资金供给抑制程度。最后，信息不对称与信用缺失。当前，我国农产品物流市场上社会信用严重缺失，这严重破坏了农产品物流业的社会信用基础；而且由于农产品供应链企业财务报表可信度低，银行无法依据其财务报表对客户资金和经营情况作出客观判断，加剧了银企之间的信息不对称矛盾，影响了农村金融机构发放贷款的积极性[409]。

（二）农产品社会性物流发展不到位

1. 农产品社会性物流的外延和功能界定过于狭窄

农产品社会性物流的功能，源于对社会性物流外延的确定。农产品社会性物流外延的确定，不仅决定了社会性物流机构业务范围的大小，进而决定其功能领域，而且还涉及其风险的缓解问题，在一定程度上还可以增加其盈利的可能性，进而影响到社会物流的功能发挥。在理论上，农产品社会物流的外延就是那些市场机制不能完成或完成成本较高的农产品物流领域。实践上，在市场经济条件下，农产品社会性物流的外延是由政府依据其对发展农村经济的职能认识，在权衡自身能力的基础上，通过对社会性物流机构的业务范围确定来决定的。但在现实中，“农产品社会性物流”等同于国家粮棉油购销，物流活动仅仅局限在对农产品的储存和运输，其主要目标是保证国家指令性计划分配指标的落实，经济效益目标不明确。致使农产品社会性物流不仅发展迟缓，而且这种狭隘的界定造成农村经济发展对社会性物流的需求无法得到充分满足。

国有粮食企业、国有商业公司成立之初的功能定位和中国社会性物流的外延是一致的，但从 1979 年起国务院及有关部门对农产品统购统销的范围和品种进行了重新规定，调整了国有商业公司的业务范围，将原商业部系统管理的一、二类农副产品由 21 种减为 12 种，即粮食、油脂油料、棉花生猪、黄红麻、苧麻、茶叶、牛皮、绵羊毛、毛竹、篙竹、蔬菜等。另外烟草、蚕茧的购销分别由烟草公司和丝绸公司实行统一经营，并且对农副产品开展了多渠道经营。因此，全国性国有商业公司、国有粮食企业的功能仅仅对粮棉等少数农副产品流通给予了支持，并没有充分发挥出支农的作用，即使在支持粮棉流通方面，由于购销市场化、主体的多元化，一方面以购销为主的全国性国有商业公司、国有粮食企业业务也出现规律性的明显下降；另一方面，随着粮棉流通体制改革的深化，对国有粮食企业、国有商业公司提出了从收购、加工到销售全方位物流服务的要求。此外，由于农产品及其加工品是一个充满自然风险的产业，农产品保险对农业、农村、农民发展尤为重要，发达国家普遍把农产品保险纳入社会性物流范围。而中国农产品社会性物流至今未包含农产品保险，致使农产品物流保险发育严重滞后。同时，制约了西部地区农产品物流保险发展，影响了西部地区农业投资的积极性，降低了西部地区农产品物流需求的规模。

2. 农产品社会性物流存在政策性和经营性的矛盾

国有粮食企业、国有商业公司的社会性是不言而喻的。社会性物流是政策性的非营利性物流，但社会性不代表亏损，社会性并不能抹杀公司的经营性。只要是公司，经营性就不能被忽略，经营性是物流机构的本质属性，也是一个公司成功运作的基础。但多年来，全国性国有商业公司、国有粮食企业实际上只是粮棉农副产品“法定的、唯一的”购销供应者，其功能停留在被动地执行政策上，经营自主权小，经营能力差，经营性没有得到体现。在资金运用方面，粮食企业根据“保护价敞开收购农副产品”的政策，一方面粮食企业从农业发展银行获得贷款后并没有还贷的激励和压力，2001年年底，粮食流通企业的不合理占用资金余额在4000亿元左右。另一方面与农民的交易谈判中国有粮食企业又掌握定价主动权，可以从两方面同时受益，并极易产生不良贷款，进而影响到农产品社会性物流资金链良性循环。虽然原有的商粮供应企业仍然是农产品物流（特别是大宗农产品）的核心力量，但随着粮食流通体制改革的深化，全国很多粮库被撤销或合并，由于国有流通企业模糊的产权制度，落后的管理体制，单一的物流功能在市场经济的大环境中越来越显现出不协调：主观上看，国有流通企业经营机制不合理，企业缺乏内在动力和压力，经营方式被动保守；客观上看，它作为企业却要承担政府该做的稳定市场的责任，它的税收、离退休职工负担等都高于其他经济成分的商业企业。经过这些年的发展，传统国有流通企业作为多元流通渠道中的一种保存了下来，但市场占有率已经显著下降，在大部分品种中已经不能称为主渠道。在全国粮食流通体制改革和国有流通企业改革过程中，西部地区一些国有粮食公司和供销社开始逐步向物流企业演变。

（三）农产品双向性物流发展难度大

1. 农产品双向性物流合作原则未能充分体现

供销合作社曾是我国农村市场商品流通的主渠道，供销合作社系统负责经营棉花、麻类、茶叶、蚕茧、土副产品等的购销业务，以及部分农业生产资料和农村生活资料的供应。它是连接农业与工业、乡村与城镇、生产和消费的重要纽带，一方面它代表国家利益，承担国家的购销任务，保证国家计划的执行，负责安排农村市场；另一方面又代表农民利益，为农民推销产品，供应生产资料和生活资料，提供各种服务，支持农民发展多种经营及农村工业[410]。但在重工业和城市倾斜战略下，国家自然要加强对农村流通体系的控制，合作由自愿变成了强制，合作物流事实上一直没有在农村供销合作社得到充分体现。在西部地区参与农村供销合作社的农民长期得不到运销优惠，不能实现农产品运销规模化、系列化、集约化，没有提高农民进入市场的组织化程度，没有提高农产品流通效率。这样一来，以农民为主体的权利得不到保护，合作物流的互助共济性和民主管理性自然就得不到体现。进一步还会导致农村供销合作社的资源配置能力就会被严重削弱或配置失当，广大农民的物流需求得不到正常满足，从而影响到农村经济的正常发展。

农村供销合作社“商业化”“非农化”倾向严重。合作组织是通过自愿联合起来的企业，以满足经济和社会需求为目的的自治组织。目前，世界上很多国家和地区都拥有强有力的农民合作组织，它们不但代表联合起来的农民集体采购农业生产资料，对农业生产进行技术指导，还在农产品加工和销售、产品品牌形成维护及促销等方面发挥重要作用。在各种合作组织中，农产品销售合作社是最重要的农业合作组织形式[411]。理论上农村供销合作社是不以盈利为目的的农民合作互助性物流组织，为“三农”服务是农村供销合作社的法定目标①。但由于农村供销合作社的合作原则未能有效体现，作为物流企业自然也具有追求利润的自利性动机。在农产品物流改革中，政府把服务“三农”的任务，一厢情愿地“赋予”了已经“商业化”的、在农产品物流中具有准垄断性地位的农村供销合作社[412]。近年来，农村供销合作社为了自己脱困，也开始了走规模经营、撤并集中之路，其决策权限也已经被上收。例如陕西省在2011年全省供销社系统有11个市（含杨凌区）级供销社，103个县级供销社，1220个基层供销社，900个独立核算企业。经营网点遍布城乡，总数超过2万个。全系统现有职工113414人，其中在岗48409人、下岗分流35186人、离退休29819人。省供销社直属企事业单位12个，其中直属公司9个，由省供销社控股或参股的有限责任公司22个；全日制中专和技工学校3所。省供销社及其企事业单位共有职工3516人，其中在岗1664人、下岗分流787人、离退休1065人。省供销社机关2002年定性为省政府直属事

① 由从事同类产品生产经营的农户自愿组织起来，在技术、资金、信息、购销、加工、储运等环节实行自我管理、自我服务、自我发展，以提高竞争能力、增加成员收入为目的。

业单位，人员编制65人，参照公务员管理，经费由财政全额拨付。虽然，目前陕西省农村供销合作社已超过2万家，但存在规模普遍较小、经营方式传统的问题，主要是因为理念、技术、资金的限制，因此“一体化经营”已名存实亡，形成巨大压力。

2. 农产品双向性物流功能难以发挥

中国区域发展的不平衡和农民对专业合作组织认识深度的不同，使得农产品双向性物流很多功能还没有完全发挥。为摸清西部地区农村合作经济组织运行状况，课题组对广西壮族自治区、甘肃省玉门市、陕西省关中大荔县和蒲城县荆姚镇以及陕南汉滨区进行了追踪调研。

调研案例7-1：广西壮族自治区农民专业合作经济组织发展情况

广西壮族自治区农民专业合作组织的发展开始于20世纪90年代末，到2000年年底，全区有农民专业合作组织100多个。根据区农业厅统计，截至2006年年底，全区农民专业合作经济组织发展到1678个，入会农户356776户，参与农民数140余万人，拥有各类固定资产7.91亿元。区域分布上，农民专业合作经济组织最多的5个市依次为桂林市501个、玉林市258个、南宁172个、柳州164个、钦州113个。行业分布上，种植业占65.2%；养殖业占22%；其他行业占12.8%。在经营服务类型上，“种养+销售”形式占74.5%，“收购+加工+销售”占10%，“种养+加工+销售”占9.4%，其他服务类型占6.1%。在组织领办主体上：农民经济能人牵头领办占49.7%，村委组织成立占34.1%，企业牵头领办占7.2%，由其他人员和服务部门牵头领办占9.1%。2006年全区农民专业合作组织实现会员收入51.8亿元，会员增收13.33亿元，会员户均增收3735.5元，人均增收952元；带动非会员农户132.8万户，增收29亿元，户均增收2188元。

广西壮族自治区农民专业合作经济组织发展存在的主要问题。从2007年统计数据上看，广西壮族自治区农民合作经济组织的入会农户仅为356776户，农户覆盖率比较低；74.5%的合作组织服务形式只是简单的组织生产和销售，经营服务形式比较单一，产业链比较短；65.2%的协会产生于种植业，行业分布不均匀；将近73%的组织拥有各类资产在10万元以下，将近15%的协会组织没有任何资产，大多数合作组织规模小、积累薄、带动弱；合作经济组织所得到的优惠政策很少，外部发展空间狭窄。具体而言，广西壮族自治区农民专业合作经济组织的发展还存在以下几大问题：①农民专业合作经济组织发展的外部环境存在缺陷。一是全区多数农民专业合作经济组织得不到财政、信贷、外贸等方面的扶持以及税收上的优惠，只能在“夹缝”中生存。二是少数领导干部对发展农民专业合作经济组织认识不足，不把其当成是农村经济体制的重大变革、解决农村“三农”问题、解决农村生产关系不适应生产力发展需要而组织起来的，因而对发展农民专业合作经济组织采取观望态度，不积极去引导扶持。三是《中华人民共和国农民专业合作社法》实施前，合作组织登记不规范导致农民专业合作组织的经济性质难以确定，影响了组织业务的开展。②农民专业合作经济组织内部运作机制不健全，不规范。一是章程不规范，许多流于形式，有的甚至没有。二是组织机构不健全，相当一部分组织的理事会、监理会等必要机构不健全。三是内部管理制度不够健全，民主意识淡薄，资金积累制度和风险保障制度缺乏。四是会员的利益关系不够紧密，突出表现在盈余分配比例小，有的甚至没有分配。五是股金层次低，市场竞争力不强，服务基本停留在信息、技术、咨询等层次上。③大多数专业合作经济组织较为松散，合作作用发挥不大。不论是领办人还是农民，由于缺乏创办合作组织的基本知识，没有掌握建立合作组织的基本原则，合作意识还比较淡薄，合作组织的作用没有发挥出来。如来宾市，2005年统计的时候登记在册的合作组织、协会有190家，但是到2007年7月统计时，有将近一半已经名存实亡。这些合作组织大多是由村委组织起来的专业协会，主要为了开展农业技术帮扶合作，由于没有收益、缺乏资金、组织不力等原因，很少开展服务，农民也逐渐失去参与的积极性，协会最终名存实亡。④组织规模小、自我发展能力不强。广西壮族自治区农民专业合作经济组织大部分是近年白手起家发展起来的，相当部分没有收入来源，积累甚少。目前，将近73%的组织拥有各类资产在10万元以下，将近15%的协会组织没有任何资产。合作组织发展生产、引进优良品种、推广先进技术、培训社员提高技术水平、注册商标打造品牌、农产品的加工、包装、销售等等，都需要资金投入。在政府财政扶持有限，合作组织自身积累又少的情况下，合作经济组织抵御市场风险能力弱，制约了其为会员服务的能力，也影响自身的发展。⑤对《农民专业合作社法》《农民专业合作社登记管理条例》的贯彻实施进展缓慢。《农民专业合作社法》已于2007年7月1日起正式实施，但是贯彻实施的进度比较缓慢。

调研案例7－2：甘肃省玉门市推动农民专业合作组织发展情况

目前，甘肃省玉门市共发展农民专业合作经济组织52家，拥有会（社）员9980人，带动农户14850户，拥有资产1710万元，会均32.88万元。在现有的农民专业经济组织中经工商局登记注册的农民专业合作社33家，注册资金2993万元，加入专业合作社的社员6130人，带动农户9830户，带动生产基地10万亩，2009年完成交易总额8200万元。33家合作社中获省级无公害蔬菜产地认证的合作社4家，省工商局注册商标的合作社3家。玉门市农民专业合作经济组织发展呈现出五个方面特点：一是组建类型呈现多样，服务区域不断扩大。随着市场的不断开拓，玉门市农民专业合作组织已开始跨区域开展合作，服务社员（会员）的范围已从本乡本村为主转向跨乡镇、跨县域、跨省拓展。二是合作层次不断提升。越来越多的农民专业合作组织从单一的生产资料购买、生产技术服务、农产品流通等合作向开展标准化生产、无公害产地认证、农产品质量安全保障及产品市场流通、整理加工、品牌包装等经营领域的合作拓展。三是组织运行逐步规范。目前，玉门市的农民专业合作组织形成了5种发展类型和模式，其中，龙头企业带动型8家，行业带动型8家，产业带动型16家，能人带动型的9家，乡村筹办型的11家。

甘肃省玉门市推动农民专业合作组织发展存在的困难和问题。①组织化程度不高，总体实力较弱。从当前玉门市农民专业合作组织发展的总体情况来看，多数农民专业合作社处于合作的初级阶段，规模小，组织化程度低，产销衔接不够紧密，重盈利轻服务，社员之间的合作关系有待进一步巩固和提高。②部分农民合作意识不够强，对发展合作的重要性缺乏足够的认识，缺乏联合创市场的意识，部分农民对合作带有很大的随意性，缺乏诚信意识，有利则合，无利则散，在一定程度上阻碍了合作组织的发展壮大。③农民专业合作组织经营资金普遍缺乏。由于农民专业合作组织多数原先是一些服务型的组织，自身没有资金积累，后期虽发展了一些经营性的农民专业合组织，但由于经营时间短，留作滚动发展的资金很少；另外没有抵押资产，不能满足金融部门贷款条件，因此资金不足是当前合作社普遍反映比较强烈的问题。④人才、技术、信息缺乏。大多合作社缺乏有实践经验、有合作理念、有市场知识的牵头人，也没有专门的技术人员为其服务。大部分发起人信息来源渠道比较窄，不能获得更多有用的市场信息。⑤推动农民专业合作组织发展合力不够强劲，部门协作联运机制需要进一步完善。

调研案例 7－3：陕西省关中和陕南农民专业合作组织发展调查走访

（1）大荔县下寨镇新堡村

在大荔县下寨镇新堡村，课题组看到一家农户的门口挂着渭南诚意麦业合作社的牌子。那么，他们究竟给社员提供了什么服务呢?

课题组：提供良种吗?

渭南诚意麦业合作社 任万福：原来提供，后来人都在村会计那儿办，和农资部门谈。

课题组：管销售吗?

渭南诚意麦业合作社 任万福：销售市场放开着呢，由别人收，村上三轮车收，不管销售。

成立合作社最重要的目的就是解决农副产品销售问题。而这家合作社却连最基本的服务都无法提供，村民们说，现在，他们基本都不信任他们的合作社。课题组了解到，在当地，像这样有名无实的合作社不在少数。这种现象还比较普遍，有的合作社仅仅就是挂了一块牌子，有的合作社成立之初的目的就是为了获得国家的资金支持，这样往往就会使农民失望或者误解。根据合作社法的规定，六人以上就可以在工商部门注册成立合作社。而大荔县 415 个行政村，就成立了 600 多家农民专业合作社。

大荔县农业局经管站副站长 杨红敏：我们县有一个乡有一个村同一个产业，就有三个的合作社。从发展一村一品来说都是不怎么好的。

因为没有什么门槛，有些合作社就只有几名社员，内部带动能力弱，市场营销推广也难有作为，而众多小合作社之间又加大了竞争，难免互相拆台。

大荔县荔农果蔬专业合作社理事长 汪战仓：大荔县有600多家农民专业合作社，光果蔬这一块就有200多家。

规模太小、服务又差的合作社自然无法获得村民的信任，而有些合作社由于管理不规范，离真正意义上的合作社相差甚远。

（2）汉滨区吉河镇

汉滨区吉河镇的吉缘养羊专业合作社成立两年多了，但是课题组发现合作社和社员之间连最基本的交易合同都没有。

课题组：你这个合作社和社员之间是一种什么样的关系，你们之间有没有签一个合同？

吉缘养羊专业合作社理事长 党小虎：基本上有协议。有养羊协议，只是一个养羊协议。

课题组：你们那个协议怎么规定？

吉缘养羊专业合作社理事长 党小虎：打个比方，我给你直接说确凿一点，他喂我的羊，我那是个公羊，他拉去做种羊，还有些多少是口说为凭。

合作社与社员之间没有按照法律规定建立规范的交易关系，相互的信任缺乏必要的约束。许多社员只记得利益共享，而忘了风险共担，安康、渭南很多合作社成立之初，都出现过社员违反合作社规定的事。

汉滨区务实蔬菜专业合作社理事长 潘应斌：农民看的事情比较短，当时菜价比较高，他（就把该卖给合作社的菜）偷偷卖一点。

柞水县石瓮镇东甘村生态合作社理事长 张庆平：有时农民把次品交到了合作社，他认为我是合作社成员，应该帮我把这个卖出去。

根据合作社法的要求，社员必须以现金或者能够处置的生产资料入股。所有收益严格按股份分红，盈余部分还要按比例返还给所有社员。但是，许多社员所以往往不愿意用现金出资。

柞水县豆制品加工农民专业合作社理事长 霍开智：他们觉得风险太大。

大荔县农业局经管站副站长 杨红敏：相对运作规范的也就100

多家，当然能达到示范社的也就是五六十家。

没有社员的支持，合作社的生存都成问题，就更谈不上扩大再生产了。由于诸多因素的影响，目前许多合作社的运营都不够好。所以，眼下获得社员的信任，成为合作社发展的当务之急。

(3) 蒲城县荆姚镇

在蒲城县荆姚镇许家庄村玉女土织布专业合作社调研时，合作社邀请的县工商局联络员正在对40多名新社员进行《农民专业合作社法》培训。

蒲城县工商局注册分局工作人员 党家顺：咱们通过培训，让合作社的成员对他们要承担的权利和义务更加了解。

蒲城县玉女土织布专业合作社理事长 张玉女：专业合作社不规范，就没人相信你。成立时候，我说今年如果赔了，算我一个人的，不叫大家负担。

果然，合作社的带头人张玉女就在承诺提供全面的原料和销售服务的同时，对大家的收益作了保证。玉女合作社不仅给社员们提供全面的服务，还常常邀请管理部门来讲政策，合作社也一天天赢得了社员的信任。

蒲城县玉女土织布专业合作社理事长 张玉女：今年分红的时候，我问下一年赔了咋办，大家都说，一起承担。

如今，玉女土织布专业合作社的社员从最初的6个人发展到200多人，从一个村辐射到了几个乡镇，合作社还注册了自己的商标，去年销售达到680万元，付给社员的加工费就达近200万元，合作社还被评为陕西省百强示范社。

蒲城县玉女土织布专业合作社理事长 张玉女：没有成立合作社时，农民单家独户创市场，就像渔民的小船，遇到风浪，就被打翻了。成立了合作社，就像咱造了个大船，抵御市场风险的能力就强了。

而大荔县的一些合作社，也正在谋划对全县的200多家果蔬合作社进行整合，增强实力。

大荔县荔农果蔬专业合作社理事长 汪战仓：通过几年的共同协商工作，未来可能会成为四五十家大的合作社，这样抗风险的能力就强了，一个拳头出击力量会更大一点。

渭南市工商局局长 张自录：农民专业合作社做大做强了，市场的竞争力就会更强，让农民增收的步子会更快一些，农民增收的效果就会更好。

实地考察发现，各地在推动农民专业合作组织发展中都存在组织化程度不高，总体实力较弱；农民专业合作组织经营资金普遍缺乏；人才、技术、信息缺乏；发展合力不够强劲，部门协作联运机制需要进一步完善的困难。典型的大荔县下寨镇新堡村渭南诚意麦业合作社有名无实、汉滨区吉河镇的吉缘养羊专业合作社与社员之间连最基本的交易合同都没有。事实上，在市场经济中，合作社往往能起到政府起不到的作用，目前西部地区很多地方农民组建合作社的热情很高，但真正运营好的并不多，合作社并不是一“合”就灵，其中的问题不容忽视，一些农民专业合作经济组织，并没有给加入的社员提供生产资料、技术信息、市场销售等服务，无法克服家庭经营规模小、与市场脱节等不足，缺少农业、工商等部门联合帮助他们规范运作、科学发展，还没有做到合作社真正发挥应有的功能作用，并没有意识到产前的生产资料选择和产中的技术规程操作以及产后的质检监测是农产品产业链的重要环节，也是农产品双向性物流服务的主要对象，无法让依托于合作社的成员真正受益。

（四）农产品经济性物流发展不协调

1. 正规的农产品经济性物流供给不足

正规的农产品经济性物流主要是传统运输领域全国性的国有企业，如中外运、中国邮政、铁路系统、中远、中储等，在各自的行业、领域处于垄断地位。由于其内生于经济体制和政府的发展战略，而始终外生于农村经济，加上长期的行政化运行和国有企业的痼疾所致，随着市场化改革进程的加快，尤其是中国加入 WTO 后，其自身的生存与发展遇到了挑战。为此，2004 年商务部等四部门提出要引导现有农产品物流企业改造升级，推动其向产业化、规模化方向发展。截至 2004 年年底，通过对过去的运输公司或者仓储公司的调整布局和重组转制，全国国有粮食购销企业总数由 1998 年的 30434 个调整为 2004 年的 20522 个，国有粮食购销企业改制 7027 个，占全部购销企业总数的 34%。其他多种所有制粮食经营企业达到 10 万个以上。需要强调的是，由于传统运输领域全国性的国有企业资金实力雄厚、物流设施齐全，提供全部的基本物流业务和部分的增值服务，但价格较商业储运公司稍高，因此并不适合农产品物流市场。近两年，虽然其中的一些国有企业已经开始改变经营模式，将业务延伸到农产品物流市场。例如以信函、包裹、报刊等投递为主的邮政业，将“邮政物流”介入农业高新技术产品的营销还处于试点阶段，从而使正规的农产品经济性物流供给不足，甚至在西部地区部分县和县以下的经济性物流服务出现了真空地带。原因在于，正规的农产品经济性物流运行机制落后。从外部因素看，由于前述思想认识和观念上的问题，农产品经济性物流仍然是国有物流占主体。农产品物流产权改革，不仅和农村经济产权主体多元化不相适应，而且也远远落后于国有企业的产权改革进程，造成当前农产品经济性物流运行的宏观机制仍然带有很强的行政化倾向。从内部因素看，农产品经济性物流具有传统国有企业的一般特征和痼疾。管理体制的僵化、经营方式的不灵活、漠视地方物流需求变化，致使农产品物流创新严重滞后，自身发展战略难以实施，服务于农村经济的物流功能难以发挥。

2. 非正规的农产品经济性物流发展不规范

首先，非正规的农产品经济性物流异常活跃。非正规的农产品经济性物流其内生于农村经济发展过程中，根据农村经济发展的实际需要而自发产生的农产品物流活动及其组织机构。如农户、加工型企业的自营物流、个体私营运输类或仓储运输公司、专业化的第三方物流公司、中介组织[413-418]、各种联合会、经纪人等民间物流活动[419,420]。

（1）个体私营运输类或仓储类企业正在成为农产品物流的重要力量，他们一般依托原来的仓储系统，并拥有简单的运输工具，形式灵活，价格低廉，大多在西部本地区提供基本物流服务，控制了大部分市场份额。

（2）专业化的第三方物流公司是物流产业发展的必然趋势，但是农产品市场的不成熟性，以及第三方物流公司过高的从业标准令很多物流服务提供者望而却步，真正的第三方物流公司在西部地区并不多见。

（3）行业协会在我国是贯彻政府物流政策的半行政组织，在农产品物流中发挥着不可替代的作用。据统计截至 2008 年 6 月，四川省已登记和备案的农村经济协会有 5396 个，注册资金和固定资产达 1.95 亿元，协会自身年收入 28.3 亿元，394 万入会农民家庭平均年收入增幅达到 30% 左右，成为农村区域经济发展的强大助推器。

（4）农村经纪人队伍是我国进入市场经济之后，市场机制仍不完善的特定历史时期所产生的一个特殊群体，以其形式灵活、服务价格低廉的特点赢得了分散的小规模农户的青睐，在农村市场异常活跃。截至2008年8月，重庆共有各类农村经纪组织10937户，执业人员总数达到15978人。其中公司经纪人391户，个体经纪人10000户，合伙经纪人73户，个人独资经纪人184户，其他组织经纪人289户。

其次，西部地区传统自营物流发展不规范。根据本研究的调查和上述制度分析结果发现，从绝对数量看非正规的农产品经济性物流主体虽然很大，但由于众多的参与个体从事小规模、原始、孤立的物流活动，层次低，离散性强，联合性差，对农产品的采购、运输、加工、仓储、包装、配送没有形成规范的系统管理与控制，难以实现农产品物流现代化。据调查，西部地区以传统自营物流为主，为农产品供需双方提供完整意义的第三方物流服务的企业屈指可数。虽然农产品自营物流在西部地区农村改革全面向市场经济转变阶段曾经发挥了重要的作用，但随着市场化进程的推进，农产品自营物流的各种弊端开始凸显：

（1）自营物流必须具备与生产能力相符的运输力量和仓储容量，这会给企业带来资金方面的负担，而且由于市场的不确定性还给企业带来一系列风险，尤其是在销售淡季，因为大量的运输和仓储设施闲置会造成极大浪费。

（2）由于企业内部物流部门与其他许多相关部门存在一定联系，而各部门之间又有着相互独立的利益，致使管理难度加大。

（3）物流的运作要求具备专业物流知识和实践能力，企业选择自营物流，往往会因为物流不是企业主营业务，不具备相应优势，而致使物流成本高、服务水平低。

（4）无法进行准确的效益评估。由于许多自营物流的企业采用内部各职能部门彼此独立的完成各自的物流，没有将物流分离出来进行独立核算，因此企业无法计算出准确的产品的物流成本，无法进行准确的效益评估。

目前，在西部地区农产品物流市场上，不论是农户，还是农产品生产企业，仍然热衷于自营物流，虽然也会向运输公司或运输个体户购买运输服务或向仓储企业购买储藏服务，但这些都只限于一次性、临时、分散的物流服务。物流企业缺乏足够的客户，无法实现规模效益，高成本已经成为制约西部地区农产品物流业进一步发展的“瓶颈”。尤其是缺乏专业化的第三方物流公司，物流的集约化程度和社会化程度很低。一方面，农产品物流活动的社会总需求大幅度增长；另一方面，却是小规模的零星运输大行其道。从宏观角度来看，这种物流方式造成了城市交通设施拥挤、农产品废弃物大量增长，污染了环境，加大了城市负担。从微观角度来看，大量存在的低效率往复迂回运输，增加了企业成本并降低了竞争力。农产品市场流通的不畅还大大增加了流通成本，降低了流通能力，许多农产品不能及时送到消费者手中，无法直接进入市场。农产品经销商队伍大都力量薄弱，经营规模小，抵御市场风险能力差，资金匮乏，无力组织好大宗农产品流通。因此，农产品物流业有必要改革自营物流占主导的局面，逐步引进农产品第三方物流。相对于自营物流而言，第三方农产品物流的具备了功能服务专业化、物流信息网络化、关系契约化、物流服务个性化、合作联盟化的基本优势[421]。随着我国物流业的调整振兴、农产品贸易量的不断扩大，农产品生产者和消费者对农产品物流服务的需求将会急剧增加，自营物流将越来越难以满足居民多样化、差异化的需要。而且，随着物流国际化的发展，国内物流业会面临越来越激烈的竞争，必将迫使国内传统物流企业向第三方物流快速转变。因此，在物流全球化和国际金融危机的背景下，西部地区应加快传统储运企业、粮食购销企业的改造，大力培育和支持第三方农产品物流企业的发展，以谋求我国第三方农产品物流业更大的发展空间。

二　西部地区农产品物流市场体系建设不完善

从交易视角看西部地区农产品物流功能不足，其实就是西部地区农产品物流交易条件不足。西部地区农产品物流交易最重要的条件就是西部地区农产品物流市场。国家为适应农村经济发展，对物流服务提出了全方位、多层面的要求，加快了西部地区农产品物流市场体系建设，并取得了一定的成效，但总体而言，目前西部地区农产品物流市场体系依然很不完善。

（一）西部地区农产品物流市场上物流交易规模小

农产品物流交易规模小，主要表现在农产品物流成本高，农产品物流信息体系不健全，农产品物流技术水平较低，农产品物流投资结构不尽合理，农产品物流交易方式不灵活[422]，在总量和结构上均无法满足农村各种经济主体多层次的物流需求。

1. 农产品物流成本高

当前，西部地区多数农户的生产经营是单户经营的形式，这种单户“物流”很难达到经济规模[423]。调查发现，西部地区物流成本一般占总成本的30%—40%，而鲜活产品则占60%左右，甚至更多；而世界发达国家物流成本一般控制在10%左右[424]。过高的物流成本迫使消费者要付出比农产品生产成本高得多的费用，大大削弱了西部地区农产品的国际竞争力，也影响到农民收入的提高。

2. 农产品物流信息体系不健全

西部地区农产品物流链众多环节之间信息共享度低，信息流通不畅，市场调节的盲目性大[425]。虽然县级以上政府的信息网络较健全，信息量也较大，但缺乏一个把政府、市场、客户和生产者有效连接起来的网络，市场供求信息不能快速传递，农民获取市场信息的成本较高；同时对农民的信息服务不到位，大多数农民因自身素质原因缺乏对信息的分析、选择能力，造成农产品供给、流向与流量常常带有盲目性，赶不上市场变化。信息不对称加大农民的弱势地位，农户家庭经济对市场信息难以做出准确的判断和预测，同时由于缺乏组织功能削弱了其价格形成能力，自身利益难以保护[426]。农产品物流渠道缺乏信息沟通引导，由于信息没有在生产者到消费者之间有效地流动，在批发市场中，中介组织、经纪人市场营销队伍人数庞杂，基本上是自发、松散、无序状态，经营手段落后，无法体现批发市场功能与规模效率优势。因此，从规模和市场竞争力上很难应对来自市场和大型现代物流企业的冲击，更难以与具有先进物流理念和现代管理模式的大型跨国物流公司竞争。

3. 农产品物流技术水平较低

首先，西部地区农产品流通以常温和自然物流形态为主，缺乏冷链物流设施和装备。在生鲜农产品的加工、储存等环节，冷藏、保温设施严重不足，且未形成链环系统[427]。据初步统计，生鲜农产品从田间采收到消费者餐桌需经过众多环节，其间损耗率高达25%—30%，而发达国家果蔬损耗率则控制在5%以内[428]。其次，西部地区适应现代物流运作要求的农产品仓储设施严重不足。许多20世纪五六十年代的老旧仓库仍在使用；仓储保管技术落后、机械化程度不高；农产品的包装、分拣、搬运等物流作业大都为手工操作，“四散”（即散装、散卸、散存、散运）现象大量存在，储备库布点不科学。通用仓库比较多，专用仓库不足，特种仓库，如低温库、冷藏库、立体仓库等严重短缺，导致简易仓库储藏和混藏、农民分散储藏，甚至露天堆放的问题相当突出[429]。最后，西部地区农产品综合运输网络不发达。农产品从生产地到消费地运输，从内陆运输到海上运输，从汽车运输到火车运输的多式联运交通网络尚未形成。此外，西部地区农产品物流规格化、标准化程度低。加入 WTO 西部地区农产品面临国际市场的冲击，农产品包装从材料到包装管理都没有统一标准，给农产品的储存、运输和加工造成一定困难。

4. *农产品物流投资结构不尽合理*

从产业结构与经济结构来看，西部地区农产品加工严重滞后。目前，西部地区农产品产中投资比例与全国 80% 相同，而发达国家只有 30%。西部地区农产品产后投资比例低于全国 20%—30%，较发达国家 70% 的比例有很大差距。发达国家养殖业产品产后投资比例 30%，西部地区不足 5%；西部地区农产品加工前后增值比为 1∶1.5，低于全国 1∶1.8 的水平，更低于发达国家 1∶3—1∶4 的水平。从农产品产业化整体来看，西部地区在农业生产上的投入较大，但保鲜技术和绿色物流等农产品后续处理加工方面却明显相对投入不足[430,431]。欧美、日本等地区和国家 90% 以上的蔬菜都经过了商品化加工处理后进入流通领域。在加工深度上，发达国家为 95%，发展中国家为 50%，西部地区低于全国 30%。农产品绝大多数在生产地以原始产品的形式销售，农产品物流过程增值能力非常弱。

5. *农产品物流交易方式不灵活*

当前，西部地区农产品交易基本上采用现货交易，还没有采用拍卖交易、仓单交易、远程合约交易、网络交易、期货交易等交易方式。现货交易方式往往存在着产品价格信息不公开、商流与物流不分离等缺陷，加大了农产品现货交易中的暗箱操作，增加了农产品交易费用，增加欺诈行为，无法形成对生产和消费具有重要指导意义的权威价格信息。目前，西部地区农产品仓单交易仅限于期货交易所，而大量以家庭为单位进行生产经营、流通销售的农产品仍然采用现货交易方式。这种交易方式由于在交易过程中农产品所有权经常发生转手，农产品实体在不同所有者之间多次流动，会大大地增加农产品的运输、装卸等交易费用，而且小农户只能被动接受收获季节的较低价格，独自承担价格下降的风险。由于农产品物流交易方式采用单一的现货交易，无法达到交易成本低、交易效率高、交易透明化，难以优化农产品管理与调配向消费者提供更为优质的服务。

（二）西部地区农产品物流市场体系发育不健全

1. 西部地区农产品物流市场处于抑制与分割状态

西部地区农产品物流市场存在物流抑制。物流服务产品价格政策严重滞后，导致农产品物流组织在执行的价格上出现恶性竞争和无序竞争。由于政府对货运依然实行较严格的管制，农产品物流供求的市场价格形成机制不健全，货运不能真实反映市场上物流的供求状况，货运弹性不足，面对信用和风险不同的交易主体，难以做到差别化定价，风险和收益处于不对称的状态，从而导致物流供给主体与需求主体的物流被抑制[432,433]。同时，西部地区农产品物流市场处于分割状态。农产品物流立法滞后，导致物流活动的规范化和法制化程度比较低。资源分配和农产品供应完全是按行政区域进行的，农产品物流环节相互之间割裂严重，系统性差。由于没有按经济区划设计，由此造成人为割裂物流，使流通和供应链渠道不畅。现有物流管理体制促使条块分割、地区分割、城乡分割、内外贸分割等现象严重，公平竞争的物流市场环境尚未形成。西部地区农产品物流市场上的物流供给主体均偏少，物流供给的垄断程度很高，没有形成有效的竞争机制，无法实现发展农村经济对农产品物流的层次性需求，缺乏系统化、综合化和一体化的运作体系，缺乏农产品市场与基地对接整合力度，制约农业生产集约化、农产品分销规模化、产加销一体化的发展，西部地区农产品物流创新被抑制[434]。从生产到销售物流粗放化，不合理的物流成本造成极大浪费，直接影响到农民的收益。

2. 西部地区农产品批发市场物流系统规划设计缺失

受城乡居民总体消费水平、消费观念和意识的制约，我国农产品集贸、批发市场在未来一段时间内仍将成为农产品物流主要经营业态，市场对于农产品的需求亦主要集中于此。农产品摆放在摊上，由业主和客户相互叫价降价进行对手交易。这样做不仅导致价格波动大，不利于农产品供需平衡；还使商流与物流混杂，物流成本与损耗很高。另外，由于农产品集贸、批发市场物流系统规划设计的缺失，限制了市场的升级与功能扩展。市场保鲜设施不足，使得交易双方只能采取即时现货交易模式；市场库存能力不足，迫使农产品必须在最短时间内全部售空，却难以避免物流环节的巨大消耗；缺乏一体化的现代农产品物流系统支持，使得农产品集贸、批发市场的物流活动粗放、分散、低效。农产品集贸、批发市场物流系统的缺陷，如电子商务、市场信息服务、拍卖交易、期货交易、绿色环保、质量卫生标准和检测体系等，直接影响到农产品物流的增值能力[435]。

3. 西部地区农产品加工配送中心运作效率差距大

西部地区农产品加工业仍处于起步阶段，存在的问题较多：农产品加工基本处于低级、粗放、零散的状态，运销保鲜技术、加工增值比重还比较低，农产品损耗和资源浪费严重。目前，西部地区农产品产加销联结机制不完善，订单农业履约率只有1/3左右，龙头企业带动农户只占农户总数的1/4，农民受益有限；农产品加工制品质量标准体系不健全，农药、兽药残留超标，ISO 9000、ISO 14000等质量标准体系的认证率较低。可以看出，西部地区农产品加工存在着很大的差距，无法有效调控大宗农产品物流和各连锁超市生鲜区之间的物流联系，降低了门店的农产品质量控制水平与采购谈判能力；无法以生鲜加工配送中心为核心向农副产品供应链的上游延伸，难以重新整合生鲜产品供求双方的各种资源。

4. 西部地区农产品物流园区布局存在明显地域差别

西部地区农产品物流的发展不仅受限于农产品生产的地域性与消费的普遍性、农产品生产的季节性与消费的全年性、农产品生产的局限性与消费的全球性等诸多因素的影响，而且由于西部地区农产品集散市场目前还处于初级阶段，拥有储藏、加工和信息开发利用能力的市场为数不多，因此农产品供给与消费之间的矛盾更为突出。根据西部地区实际情况，其比较优势在于发展劳动密集型产业。借鉴国内外经验，物流园区能够实现劳动密集型企业向产业化、集约化、规模化发展。农产品物流园区发展可充分发挥园区的整体优势和规模效益，既有效地解决了农村居民的就业问题，又增加了税收，最终极大地推动、促进农村经济发展。据中国物流与采购联合会和中国物流学会联合发布的第二次全国物流园区（基地）调查报告显示：至2008年上半年我国已拥有物流园区475个，已经运营的122个，占25.7%；在建的219个，占46.1%；规划中的134个，占28.2%。物流园区建设规模比较大，其中投资规模：1亿元—10亿元的占53.8%，10亿元—20亿元的占17.3%，20亿元—30亿元的占11.6%，

30 亿元以上的占 10.2%，1 亿元以下的占 7.1%；占地面积：0.1—1 平方公里的占 54.3%，1—2 平方公里的占 15%，5—10 平方公里的占 11.2%，2—3 平方公里的占 6.6%，3—5 平方公里的占 6.6%，10 平方公里以上的占 6.3%。从目前我国已建成或在建的物流园区规划功能看，已有一部分物流园区把发展农产品物流纳入规划。物流园区分布比较广，但地域差别明显。现有物流园区主要分布在：东部沿海经济区（20.4%）、南部沿海经济区（20.2%）、北部沿海经济区（14.1%）、西南经济区（11.8%）、东北经济区（10.1%）、黄河中游经济区（9.9%）、长江中游经济区（9.1%）和西北经济区（4.4%）（如图 7－9）。东部、南部以及北部三大沿海经济区的物流园区总量为 260 个，占全国总量的 54.7%。从上述分析可以看出，目前，西部地区的物流园区总量稀少，农村经济发展的比较优势不能充分发挥，无法推动农村经济发展、农民收入增加。

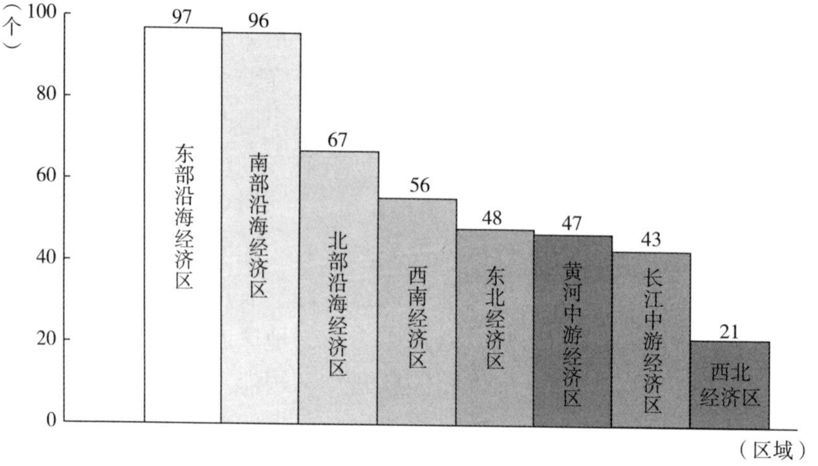

图 7－9　物流园区地理分布情况

数据来源：根据《第二次全国物流园区（基地）调查报告》相关数据整理。

三　西部地区农产品物流监管与调控体系功能不强

（一）西部地区农产品物流监管体系构造不完备

西部地区农产品物流监管体系，是指对西部地区农产品物流组织和西部地区农产品物流市场进行有效监督和管理的各种监督和管理机构、制度、运行机制等有机构成的动态统一体。西部地区农产品物流监管体系不完善，体现在西部地区农产品物流监管主体不明确、西部地区农产品物流监管体制僵化。

1. 西部地区农产品物流监管主体不明确

现代物流是一个新兴的复合型产业，涉及运输、仓储、货代、联运、制造、贸易、信息等行业，政策上关联许多部门。农产品物流涉及领域极为广泛，包括出入境检验检疫、税务、海事、国土规划、商贸、交管、港务、港口、机场和铁路等职能部门。目前，西部地区缺少发展现代物流业的综合组织协调机构，更缺少西部地区农产品物流监管主体，没有明确建立领导组织机构、监管部门、联席制度，没有理顺责权关系，无法以监管部门为主负责规划、统筹、协调农产品物流发展，从而对西部地区农产品物流监管的有效实施必然产生消极作用。

2. 西部地区农产品物流监管体制僵化

针对当前西部地区传统条块分割式的物流管理存在的弊端，现行政策法规相互之间有矛盾且难以统一的情况，说明不仅缺乏在实践中的经验积累，而且缺失有效的监督机制，反映出西部地区农产品物流监管体制还没有发挥其指挥、调度和监管的功能，无法改变当前物流资源分散、无序、低水平竞争的状况，无法促进西部地区农产品物流发展步入规模化、集约化的轨道；缺少制定地区统一的物流企业监管办法和认定标准，还没有建立一套反映西部地区农产品物流发展状况的统计指标体系，没有达到每年发布一次农产品物流产业组织发展状况的统计公报。可以说农产品物流政策体系远没有建立和完善，能否充分有效地发挥作用很大程度上取决于政策的具体实施效果。因此，强化监督、保证农产品物流政策的切实实施是促进农产品物流产业发展的一个关键问题。政府不仅需要尽快建立政策体系框架，保证地区物流市场有序、高效的发展，还要从全局出发，实施中心城市与周边区域的协调与合作，发挥自身优势，整合共同资源，形成共同开发、协作竞争、共同服务的区域农产品物流发展格局。

（二）西部地区农产品物流调控体系功能不强

西部地区农产品物流调控体系，是指为西部农村经济发展而实施的西部地区农产品物流政策及政策制定、传导机制等有机构成的动态综合体。西部地区农产品物流调控体系最大的不足就在于政策的制定与传导未能体现农村经济发展的特殊要求。西部地区不仅城乡经济呈现出典型的“二元结构”，就是在农村，由于地理条件、历史条件、资源禀赋等存在巨大的差异，经济发展的水平也呈现多层次性。东部地区与西部地区的农村状况不同，实施差别化的物流政策，基于物流与经济可持续发展的原理建立有区别的物流调控体系。

1. 需要建立西部地区农产品物流政策宏观调控的系统化

农产品物流的宏观调控是一项系统工程，调控过程中需要同财政、金融、生产、流通等部门进行密切配合，其中涉及不同的调控方式、调控手段，需要建立系统化的农产品物流政策体系。运用系统化的理论和方法对物流政策体系进行改造、加强同有关部门的配合是强化流通政策作用的必要手段。对于相关的农产品物流技术、质量安全、信息系统、技术标准、认证体系及市场准入和退出等都必须有明确的调控政策、调控责任者、调控承担者。目前，农产品质量安全管理及技术性贸易措施组织体系还是一个比较松散的、尚缺乏高度统一协调机制和有待进一步完善的体系，应加快农产品质量安全监管的法律法规立法步伐。只有加强农产品物流政策宏观调控的系统化与调控力度，才能提高物流政策体系的作用与效率。

2. 需要适合西部地区的农产品物流政策设计与论证程序

政策设计与论证的规范化是保证农产品物流政策体系延续与发展的必要条件。目前，西部地区物流政策设计与论证没有一个统一的、标准的程序，导致地方与国家的很多物流政策缺乏连贯性。因此，必须规范农产品物流政策的设计与论证，建立一个适合西部地区各区域统一的政策设计与论证程序，西部地区的物流政策制定都必须严格按照统一的程序进行。如实施差别化的物流政策，建立物流市场的监测与预警体系，将检测结果经统计分析后作为政策制定的重要依据。还可以建立政策论证的专家听证制度，并且把这种制度程序化、标准化及系统化，以此来保证政策的科学性、可行性。

第八章　西部地区农产品物流可持续发展的模式创建

实现西部地区农产品物流可持续发展，从根本讲是西部地区农产品物流可持续发展机理的生成和运行，达到农产品物流关系结果理想状态的过程。实现西部地区农产品物流可持续发展，必须根据可持续发展目标和要求，依据可持续发展的概念内涵和实现机理，针对西部地区农产品物流关系结构失调的原因，创新构建可持续发展的模式，并给出相应的运作手段和运行战略，进而针对实际中存在的问题，通过制度设计加以解决，使可持续发展机理得以发挥作用。为此，本章将基于“模式”的基本构成、“模式”的框架建立，创新构建西部地区农产品物流可持续发展模式。

第一节　西部地区农产品物流可持续发展模式的基本构成

一　西部地区农产品物流可持续发展模式内涵与构成

本研究依据克里斯托弗·亚历山大范式①，认为“模式”是揭示事物本质特征、更好地认识和改造客观事物的科学思维与操作方法[436]。“模式”

① 克里斯托弗·亚历山大（Christopher Alexander）认为，“模式”是在某种特定的场景下某个不断重复出现问题的解决方案，在研究一个多种因素交错的复杂现象时，一个良好的模式，能排除事物次要的非本质的部分，将其重要因素、关系、状态和过程突显出来，而对事物主要的、有特色的部分进行研究，有助于一个优良的设计方案的形成和理想目标的实现，运用模式的研究方法是现代科学研究的重要手段。

既可以从理论出发，通过假设、抽象、类比、演绎、分析等理论形成再现事物本质特征的理论模式，也可以从实践出发，通过对现实中的成功经验进行概括、归纳、综合而形成各种实践模式。理论模式经过实践检验便可指导实践，实践模式运行机理得到证实便可反过来指导实践。本研究认为：西部地区农产品物流可持续发展模式，是针对市场经济条件下，西部地区农产品物流可持续发展目标，借鉴已有的可持续发展经验，依据西部地区农产品物流可持续发展的概念内涵和实现机理，将西部地区农产品物流可持续发展的要素加以抽象、概括、类比、分析和逻辑演绎而构建的，以指导西部地区农产品物流可持续发展实践为目的的一种框架性的理论方案。

克里斯托弗·亚历山大认为“模式”有场景、动机、方案三个构成要素。因此，西部地区农产品物流可持续发展模式，应包括实现西部地区农产品物流可持续发展的背景、目标、可持续发展系统、可持续发展主体、可持续对象及其相互关系、作用方式与可持续手段等可持续机制实现形式的抽象表达。西部地区农产品物流可持续发展模式的创建，就是将理论分析和实践经验总结的内容具体化，但这种“具体化”与“实际操作”的要求相比，仍然是基于方法论层面，具有原则性和相对稳定性，理论模式的框架建立，可以提供政策思路的抽象性概括。而“实际操作”则是在此基础上，结合具体情况的实际安排，不仅更加具体，而且具有多样性、多变性和可操作性，既可以丰富理论模式，也可以指导新的实践模式的创建。因此，理论模式与实践模式都必须是理论和实践的统一。

二　西部地区农产品物流可持续发展模式构建的内容

（一）西部地区农产品物流可持续发展模式构建的目标

西部地区农产品物流可持续发展模式构建的目标，从根本上讲，就是西部地区农产品物流可持续发展的目标，即通过构建西部地区农产品物流可持续发展模式，实现农民、农业和农村经济与国民经济可持续发展，满足国民经济可持续发展对农村经济发展的要求[437,438]。这一目标的内容具体表现在以下四个方面：

（1）以实现农村经济总体发展战略为目标。一是农产品物流的发展要服从农村经济总体发展战略的要求。农业是农村经济与国民经济的基础产业，农产品在某种程度上是关系到国计民生的战略性物资，农业的基础地位和农产品的重要程度决定了发展农产品物流的重要意义，因此农产品物流发展战略要服从于农村经济总体发展战略的要求。二是农产品物流要在农业结构调整的基础上进行发展。为满足农产品消费需求的变化，农业生产结构调整要根据资源禀赋实现优质生产而进行。生产结构调整对农产品物流产生了重大影响，但农业生产结构调整是一种满足消费需求的必然性调整，因此农产品物流要在农业结构调整的基础上进行发展。

（2）以依托社会整体物流发展为基础。一是农产品物流要依托社会物流基础而发展。农产品物流不是一个封闭的体系，农产品物流产业链跨越了很多行业，这些行业奠定了物流发展的基础，农产品物流就是在这些行业的基础上通过资源整合走向专业化的发展道路，因此农产品物流要依托社会物流的基础来实现发展。二是农产品物流的发展要依靠现代物流管理、技术以及创新。物流是依靠现代科技与管理思想发展而来的，是无形价值链对实体价值链的创新推动产生了“第三利润”[439]。农产品流通向现代物流的方向发展，主要是通过现代物流的技术和管理思想来改善流通，创造新的价值。三是农产品物流要通过物流产业链协调、物流供应链优化、物流价值链提升来对农产品物流资源重组，流程改进，流向优化。农产品物流的发展要依靠“三链”的协调、优化与提升，这不仅是农产品物流可持续发展的思想，也是整个物流业可持续发展的基本思想。

（3）以完善农产品物流市场体系建设为重点。一是农产品物流的可持续发展要充分发挥自组织的内在推动作用与市场的外部有效调节作用。农产品物流的发展有内外两个大环境，内部系统环境主要靠自组织作用的积极发挥，外部市场环境应遵从市场经济规律，发挥市场的资源配置作用和市场的有效调节作用。二是农产品物流的可持续发展要从整合农产品物流资源出发。依靠现有资源的整合与重组、改革与提升，通过农产品市场与基地联盟整合，实现农业生产集约化发展、农产品分销规模化发展、产加销一体化发展。通过计算机、信息网络技术运用订单农业、契约合作、产业联盟，加大各流通主体间配合，加强各流通环节间整合，实现农产品物流链总体效果最大化、效率最优化。

（4）以加强农产品物流监管与调控体系功能为保证。一是完备农产品物流监管体系构造。要有利于不断降低农产品物流可持续发展成本，要有利于农产品物流可持续发展的制度弹性得到充分发挥，使制度弹性具有良好的可持续性。这就要求农产品物流可持续发展模式，在保持稳定性的基础上，必须具备良好的自我调节机制，能适应不同时间、空间和不同环境条件的要求。二是加强农产品物流调控体系功能。要适应不同区域条件下农村经济社会发展的要求。这就要求农产品物流可持续发展模式，在保持基本一致性的基础上，必须具有良好的区域适应性。实施差别化的物流政策，建立有区别的物流调控体系，农产品物流可持续发展应该采取逐步的、系统的、有梯度的渐进式发展方式。由于农业产业是个覆盖面广、牵涉行业较多、整体发展相对迟缓的一个相对特殊的领域，因此农产品物流很难在相当短的时间内取得全面性的、跨越式的发展，因而这种渐进式的发展方式主要通过重点突破、关键突破，以点促面地来推动系统的前进，不同区域的经济环境和发展环境不同，还可以因地制宜地采取不同的发展策略，通过发达地区带动落后地区，通过梯度发展来促动西部地区农产品物流的可持续发展。

在理论分析和实践经验总结的基础上，将以上这些内容具体化，基于方法论层面，这一目标的原则具体表现在，“目标”遵循总量可持续与结构可持续、宏观可持续和微观可持续、制度可持续和技术可持续、动态可持续和静态可持续相一致的原则；“思路”坚持整体性、综合性、主导性、结构性、动态性相统一的原则；“手段”坚持以市场为基础，以制度为保障，以政府为先导，以社会为补充，以市场主体的多种组织形式为载体，政府、市场、社会、企业、准市场组织、关系网络等各种组织形式和制度安排相配合的原则；“行为”坚持政府行为与市场主体行为相互可持续的原则。

（二）西部地区农产品物流可持续发展模式的运作手段

依据西部地区农产品物流可持续发展的概念内涵和实现机理，分析发现，西部地区农产品物流可持续发展模式的有效运行，必须采取相应的运作手段。西部地区农产品物流可持续手段可以概括为市场可持续、政府可持续、企业可持续、准市场组织可持续、关系网络可持续和社会可持续[440-442]。

（1）市场可持续具体形态有各种形式的垄断组织，合资、合作、合营，参股、入股，市场交换等，是众多的、分散的市场主体基于自身利益和各自占有的市场信息，在市场的供求机制、价格机制、竞争机制，以及信息揭示、披露和激励约束机制的作用下，进行分散决策后经过市场传递的结果[443]。市场可持续是“后期渐进式可持续”，在所有可持续手段中是最为基础的可持续手段。依据熊彼特的理论，市场可持续是通过市场机制对创新的刺激来实现的[52]。由于市场可持续是全部市场主体共同作用的结果，因此，其具有市场影响度高的特点。又由于市场可持续所依赖的是既有信息，其决策效果也需经过市场机制的不断传递才能形成最后的共同作用，因此，其可持续具有时间反应性低的特点。此外，市场可持续是通过市场剧烈的波动来实现的，很少是平静而稳定的，并不是在任何地方都是效率最高、成本最小的，并且市场可持续的唯一目的是作出立即的交易决定，而不关注长远战略问题，加上“市场失灵”的存在，使其可持续范围不能覆盖西部地区农产品物流与农村经济全部范围，需要市场制度约束市场主体行为，而市场制度又需要政府维护、建设，以及市场主体的共同遵守。因此，市场可持续不能是唯一的可持续形式，必须和政府可持续相配合。

（2）政府可持续具体形态有各种形式的出资、控股，产业政策，法律法规、物流政策，财政支持等，是政府依据预期目标和所占有的信息，支持与协助市场可持续，并在市场可持续失败或可持续成本过高的领域进行直接协调[444]。同时，政府可持续还为所有可持续手段提供最终强制，是整个可持续手段的最高权威者，承担可持续手段的实施提供规则并实施处罚的职能。政府可持续是“前期渐进式可持续”。因此，政府可持续具有市场影响度高和可持续时间反应性高的特点。但由于政府和市场一样，其本身也是一种制度安排，都因节约交易成本而产生，因此，政府可持续的核心问题不在于要不要政府可持续，而在于政府可持续能力如何的问题。政府的可持续能力就是执政能力，在本研究中就是驾驭市场经济条件下，西部地区农产品物流与农村经济关系的能力，其直接决定了可持续系统的运行成本和效率。可持续需要信息，获取信息需要成本，市场是提供和处理信息成本最低的制度安排，因此，政府可持续必须以市场可持续为基础，注意主动发挥各种可持续手段的比较优势，即厘定各自的边界。社会可持续作为基于信任、互惠、义务、责任以及道义、情感等因素的制度安排，受“非经济理性”支配[87]，不仅是市场可持续和政府可持续的有效补充，而且还为其有效运行提供了环境背景。

（3）企业可持续具体形态有各种形式的垂直型公司、控股公司、独资企业等，是通过科层制组织降低交易成本的反应，但随着企业对市场的替代，因企业规模而上升的企业组织管理成本，将阻止其可持续的继续进行[445]。企业可持续是政府和市场可持续的组织形式和微观基础。企业可持续作为微观的“前期渐进式可持续”，不难理解其具有市场影响度低、可持续时间反应性高的特点。企业作为一种可持续形式，需要以有效的企业治理结构为前提，而企业治理结构的有效性又与企业产权制度安排密切相关[446]。

（4）社会可持续是基于情感、责任、义务、道义和爱心等利他性因素，而非自身利益的横向可持续，由于缺少有效的约束，其效果取决于社会文明程度，一般其市场影响度和可持续时间反应性均不高。网络可持续也称关系可持续，具体形态有各种形式的战略伙伴，长期协作，业缘、地缘、血缘关系网等，是既相互依赖又相互平等的行为主体，基于自身利益或社会责任和义务，而结成的一种平等的、各自具有独立自主权的、无组织的、具有网状联系特征的可持续手段，是各类行为者，包括个人、企业、准市场组织、政府乃至国家或国家集团，在长期交易基础上形成的一种多边可持续，但其受到关系的广度和深度制约，通常不具稳定性[447]。准市场组织可持续具体形态有各种形式的寡头垄断组织；战略联盟、联合体、一体化经营、合作社、协会；业务代理、法人俱乐部、联席会议等，是介于网络可持续和企业可持续之间的可持续手段，同样是多边可持续，由于是建立在利益之上，因此，一旦目标实现，其可持续组织形式就随之解体，可持续功能消失。准市场组织可持续和网络可持续的市场影响度，在时间反应性上，介于政府与社会、市场与企业交叉线的中间[448]。

事实上，上述任何一种手段都无法实现西部地区农产品物流可持续发展，西部地区农产品物流可持续发展必须综合运用以上各种手段，按扬长避短、优势互补的原则，根据西部地区农产品物流关系结构状况，通过有效的制度安排和体制创新，综合发挥其功能，使农产品物流与农村经济主体相互合作并发展相互间联盟关系，实现西部地区农产品物流可持续发展。

（三）西部地区农产品物流可持续发展模式的运行战略

根据前述分析，建立西部地区农产品物流可持续发展模式的运行战略，如图 8－1 所示。可持续发展模式的运行战略体系中横向为农业战略体系，纵向为物流战略体系，中心圆为西部地区农产品物流活动的实施战略体系，左端为协调战略体系。农业战略体系主要从农业推动的角度做出的发展战略，其中包括基础推动战略→节点带动网络战略和梯度推进战略；物流战略体系主要从物流推动角度做出的发展战略，其中包括创新推动战略→区位化物流联盟战略、组织推动战略→供应链区域协控战略；协调战略体系是从社会环境出发作出的可持续发展战略。

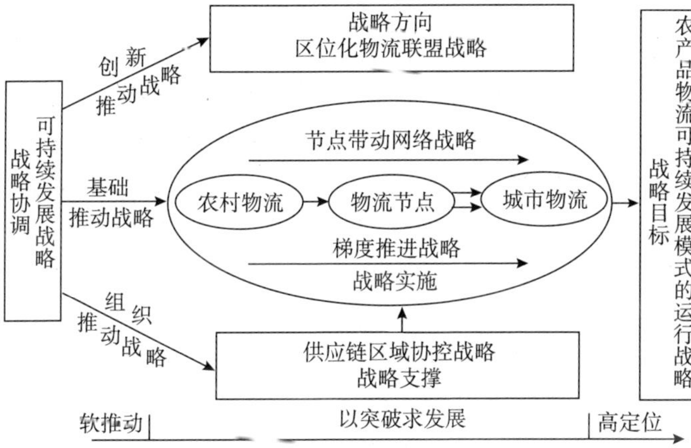

图 8－1　西部地区农产品物流可持续发展模式的运行战略

按照各种子战略的主要功能，又可分为方向性战略、支撑性战略、协调性战略、推动性战略和实施性战略。其中区位化物流联盟战略为方向性战略，代表西部地区农产品物流可持续发展模式运行的方向；供应链区域协控战略为支撑性战略，是西部地区农产品物流可持续发展模式运行的保障平台；可持续发展战略为协调性战略，为西部地区农产品物流可持续发展模式的运行提供良好的环境；基础推动战略、创新推动战略和组织推动战略为推动性战略，为西部地区农产品物流可持续发展模式的运行提供原动力和核心动力；节点带动网络战略和梯度推进战略为实施性战略，是西部地区农产品物流可持续发展模式运行的行动战略。这些功能战略按一定的结构构成了运行战略体系：以可持续发展为主线，以区位化物流联盟为发展方向，以基础推动、创新推动和组织推动为原动力，以供应链区域协控发展为支撑，以节点带动网络和梯度推进为手段，实现西部地区农产品物流可持续发展模式构建的目标。

第二节　西部地区农产品物流可持续发展模式的框架建立

一　西部地区农产品物流可持续发展模式的总体框架

依据西部地区农产品物流可持续发展的内涵与机理，本研究认为西部地区农产品物流可持续发展模式，是西部地区农产品物流可持续发展实现机理的外在表现，其形态取决于可持续发展的具体目标、可持续发展的外部环境约束、可持续发展手段的最优组合、可持续发展主体的自身能力等因素，应依据可持续发展的实现机理，在可持续发展模式总体框架下探索不同条件下的具体实现形态。基于此，构建西部地区农产品物流可持续发展模式的总体框架（见图 8 -2）。图 8 -2 是一个典型的前期—后期渐进式可持续系统，图中西部地区农产品物流可持续发展模式的背景是正处于“转型”和完善之中的社会主义市场经济体制；目标是满足经济可持续发展对农村经济发展的要求，即通过西部地区农产品物流与农村经济可持续发展，实现农业和农村经济与国民经济可持续发展；可持续发展系统由政府、西部地区农产品物流和农村实体经济（农村经济）构成，作为可持续发展基础的系统功能取决于微观经济主体能力和行为的规范性，能力取决于其拥有的人力资本，行为规范性则取决于系统内部的治理结构，或者说取决于制度约束的有效性；可持续主体是政府、西部地区农产品物流和农村经济主体。这里的主体首先是一个系统。作为可持续发展的政府是中央政府以及垂直分层治理的各级农产品行政物流部门和水平分层治理的各级政府农村经济管理部门构成的政府系统，其可持续发展功能是通过一定治理结构下政府组成人员的行为来实现的。西部地区农产品物流系统由农产品行政物流主体和农产品业务物流主体构成。农产品行政物流主体是政府在西部地区农产品物流系统中对农产品业务物流主体行为监督管理。农产品业务物流主体是指为农村经济提供物流服务功能的物流机构、组织或个人在西部地区农产品物流系统中具体从事业务活动的微观物流主体，其行为取决于一定制度约束下的自身所追求的目标。农村经济系统由政府的农村经济管理部门和农村经济活动主体构成。可持续发展方面主要是主体建设（主体构成、主体行为、治理结构）、交易方式、交易规模、产业结构、技术进步、区域分工、规模经济、外部经济、交易风险、成本收益等；西部地区农产品物流系统方面主要是主体构成、供给结构、供给价格、收益风险、经营能力等。在不同条件下，其可持续发展内容的侧重点不同，但概括起来不外乎制度、结构、规模和速度的可持续发展。

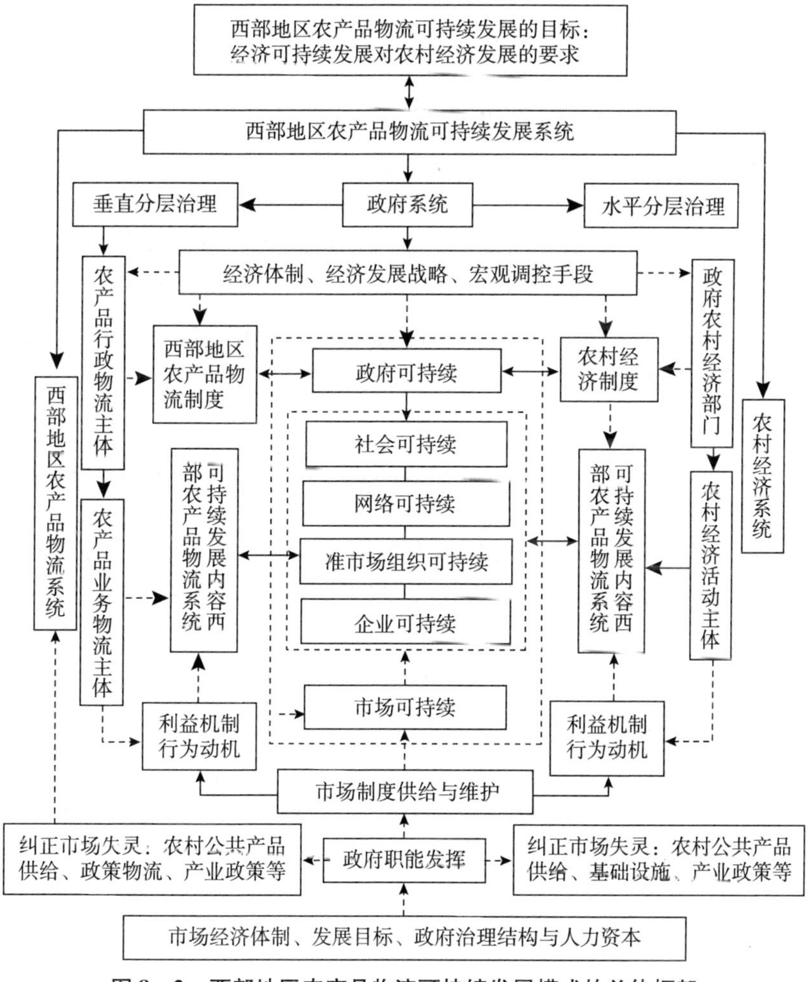

图8－2　西部地区农产品物流可持续发展模式的总体框架

说明：“实线”是指构成关系；“虚线”是表示作用方式或手段的相互机制；“箭头”是指作用或构成的方向；“矩形”是指模式的构成或影响要素。

在可持续发展过程中，一方面，政府系统在经济体制、经济发展战略和宏观调控手段基础上，依靠西部地区农产品物流制度与农村经济制度对西部地区农产品物流和农村经济主体的行为施加影响和控制，从而构成政府可持续；除此以外，政府可持续还包括垂直分层治理与水平分层治理结构之间的目标、行为和功能可持续。另一方面，政府系统又在经济体制、发展目标和政府治理结构以及政府人力资本的约束下，通过发挥政府的市场制度供给和维护，以及公共产品供给、基础设施建设和产业政策等纠正"市场失灵"的政府职能，促进西部地区农产品物流与农村经济主体依靠追求自身利益的行为动机，进行市场交易，从而构成市场可持续。政府在可持续主体中占有十分重要的地位。可持续手段除政府可持续和市场可持续之外，还存在介于两者之间的企业可持续、准市场组织可持续、网络可持续以及社会可持续及其实现手段，这些可持续手段和实现手段共同对西部地区农产品物流与农村经济系统的主体行为、总量、结构等参数施加影响和控制，进而实现可持续发展目标。因此，可持续发展的关键在于通过有效的制度安排，来调整各种可持续手段。所以，可持续手段归根到底是制度可持续，即通过制度安排实现可持续，这些制度也可称为可持续发展制度。

二 西部地区农产品物流可持续发展模式的基本类型

在西部地区农产品物流可持续发展模式的总体框架下，西部地区农产品物流可持续发展实践，因不同的环境条件将出现各种可持续发展的模式[449-453]。这些具体形态或表现为可持续发展中运行战略的侧重不同，或表现为可持续发展运作手段的配合使用方式不同，或表现为可持续发展目标的重点不同，如此等等。因此，在严格意义上说，并不存在一个统一的可持续发展模式，或者说上述总体框架只是一种理论抽象。据此，本研究依据可持续发展中运行战略的侧重不同，从农业推动的角度、物流推动的角度可以将可持续发展模式大致分为以下几种类型。

（一）基础推动战略的梯度推进与节点带动模式

依据可持续机理中政府和市场的配合方式，可以将西部地区农产品物流可持续发展模式大致分为以下三种类型：市场主导模式、政府主导模式、政府扶植模式。

1. 市场主导模式

这种模式特征是：农产品物流与经济主体行为主要受市场竞争的约束。其环境条件是农村经济、物流市场化程度和市场开放程度高，农村实体经济产业高度化、规模化，农业企业产业化程度高，农产品物流和农村经济主体市场意识强，信用程度高，农村经济组织化程度高，农村市场体系健全，农产品物流结构现代化、内生性程度高，物流创新能力强，市场监管有效，区域经济具有较强的辐射力，能通过外溢效应和示范效应向外扩散。可持续发展机制是：以市场可持续为主，政府的主要任务是市场监管和维持西部地区农产品物流安全、营造良好的市场环境、建立与经济结构相适应的物流结构。在西部地区，这种模式主要适用于国家已经确定的西部七大特色农业基地（七条农业产业带），以及西部开发区域规划中七条经济增长带：成渝经济区、关中—天水经济区、北部湾经济、呼包银经济区、兰西格经济区、新疆天山北坡经济区和陕甘宁经济区。

2. 政府主导模式

这种模式特征是：西部地区农产品物流与经济主体行为主要受政府行为的约束。其环境条件是农村市场开始形成，但发育不充分，开放程度一般，农村经济结构仍然以农业为主，但农业发展水平较高，西部地区农产品物流结构仍是传统形态，政府对微观经济、物流主体行为具有较高的约束力，能控制并对市场施加较大影响，农产品物流资金来源主要依靠政府动员机制。可持续发展机制是：以政府和市场结合为主，政府必须主导市场可持续，并不断培育西部地区农产品物流市场。在西部地区，这种模式一般主要适用于西部的比较发达地区。

3. 政府扶植模式

这种模式特征是：农村市场发育滞后，经济发展水平较低，农村市场主体未能真正形成，农产品物流需求层次低，交易规模小，农产品正规物流外生性强，农产品物流交易主要以社会性物流、自营物流为主，经济性物流发展比较困难。可持续发展机制是：以非市场化的政府和社会可持续为主，政府的主要任务是维持物流正常运转，加强农产品社会性物流和自营物流的有效性，注意培育农产品双向性物流。在西部地区，这种模式一般主要适用于西部欠发达地区和交通闭塞地区。

（二）创新推动战略与组织推动战略的综合模式

根据在农产品物流中的流程和物流中发挥核心作用的企业主体不同，可以将西部地区农产品物流可持续发展模式大致分为以下几种类型：以批发市场为中心的发展模式——批发市场主导模式；以加工企业（产销一体化组织）为中心的发展模式——供应链一体化模式；以物流园区为中心的发展模式——物流园区主导模式；以农业合作组织为中心的农产品物流发展模式——农业合作组织模式或中介组织主导模式。

1. 批发市场主导模式

批发市场主导模式减少了汇聚物流和产区市场交易这样一次转换，产品可以从生产领域直接通过主渠道物流进入销地市场，交易环节和物流转换的减少使得交易成本和物流成本都大大降低，物流效率也大大提高。这种物流模式称为“产—销”二段式物流模式，或“中心市场”模式[453]。优势体现在供应链间的组织地位均等，系统处在一个平衡发展状态，农业系统的整体社会效益和经济效益最优。

2. 农业合作组织模式

农业合作组织模式通过农业合作组织来整合分散的农业生产者，使其具备规模化组织的特点，从而具备实现“中心市场”二段式物流发展模式的条件。优势体现在提高农业生产的组织化程度，培育农民以更高的组织形式和主体进入市场，克服小生产与大市场、大物流之间的矛盾。

3. 中介组织主导模式

中介组织主导模式用中介组织来代替市场的中介功能，组织既可以进行交易，又可以组织物流的实施，而且还可以实现信息流、商流、物流的一体化。优势体现在把分散的生产集中起来进行产品加工，然后利用组织分销渠道直接将产品运送到终端市场进行销售，从中减少了很多物流的中间环节，实现了物流一体化，提高了农产品的物流效率，降低了物流成本。

4. 供应链一体化模式

农业合作组织模式和中介组织模式以及批发市场模式是对整个农产品物流的局部优化和提升，而从农产品物流供应链一体化发展的思想看，还应该进一步对“生产—流通—消费”进行一体化整合，这样就形成了供应链一体化模式和现代市场型物流模式，两种模式都是基于全局流程优化的发展模式。供应链一体化模式中的中介组织是一个广义的中介概念，包括批发商，也包括加工企业。现代市场型物流模式主要是指在传统批发市场功能的基础上，以信息化为手段的信息沟通与共享、现代交易方式（如拍卖、期货、电子商务等）的创新[450]。采用该模式的优点：一是能够提高生产环节的规模性与稳定性。二是突破组织边界，实现供应链整合，可以取得供应链上的整体竞争优势。三是供应链可以使经济组织之间形成明确稳定的契约关系，减少了各成员单位经营的不确定性。四是建设供应链信息平台，加强信息沟通，提高供应链的协调能力和反应速度，降低供应链成本。

5. 农产品物流园区主导模式

农产品物流园区发展模式是基于农产品物流活动集约化、一体化的思想而提出的。农产品物流园区是指由分布相对集中的多个农产品物流组织和物流设施，以及服务功能不同的专业化农产品物流及加工企业等构成的，能实现农产品物流规模化、功能化的农产品物流组织区域[451]。农产品物流园区是农产品供应链资源与物流活动的整合，是农产品物流系统的重要组成部分，也是农产品物流一体化的集中体现。通过发展农产品物流园区，将众多服务功能不同的物流企业集聚在一起，实现物流信息和物流基础设施的共享，形成企业间紧密的协作关系，可以解决我国农产品物流资源分散、单个农产品物流企业竞争力薄弱的问题。通过农产品物流园区，更好地发挥农产品专业化物流的作用，提供单独一家农产品物流企业所做不到的全方位的物流服务，实现农产品物流的集约化经营，可以提高农产品物流的规模效应，降低物流成本。农产品物流园区模式主要是对农产品物流供应链资源与物流活动进行部分整合优化，是对批发市场功能的拓展，但仍不是农产品物流供应链的整体优化[452]。

由于农产品种类繁多、属性各异，再加上地区性的环境差异（经济环境、地理环境等），所以短期内很难形成一种完全通用的西部地区农产品物流模式，因此西部地区农产品物流在相当长的时间内会有几种模式并存，这几种主要模式构成了西部地区农产品物流发展的综合模式。但随着社会进步，分散的农户会向农业合作组织方向发展，批发市场会向功能更强大的物流园区方向发展，农产品零售组织会向连锁的方向发展，本研究依据可持续发展中运行战略的侧重不同，从物流推动角度可以形成“创新推动战略的区位化物流联盟模式”和“组织推动战略的供应链区域协控模式”两种主流的物流发展模式，呈现出西部地区农产品物流可持续发展模式的综合形态及发展趋势，如图8－3。

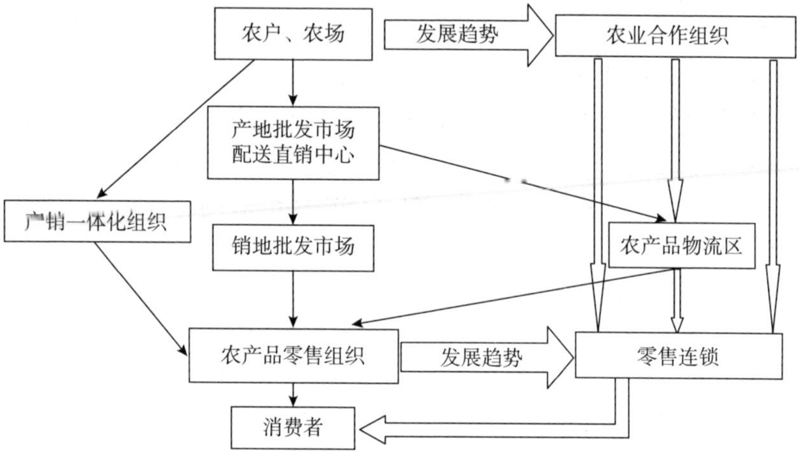

图8－3　西部地区农产品物流可持续发展模式的综合形态

事实上，以上划分在理论上完全可以根据前述可持续发展模式的运作手段分为市场可持续模式、政府可持续模式、企业可持续模式、准市场组织可持续模式、关系网络可持续模式、社会可持续模式，但由于这些模式在实际可持续发展过程中并不是孤立存在、单一运行的，而是相互配合进行的，因此，以上模式实质上是这些模式或手段的一种配合方式而已。除此以外，可持续发展模式还可以从目标上、时间上等不同角度划分。总之，西部地区农产品物流可持续发展模式具有内在机理一致性、外在形态多样性的特征，在现实中以上这些模式的划分往往相互交叉，并形成不同的中间形态。

第三节　西部地区农产品物流可持续发展模式的创新构建

西部地区农产品物流发展模式的多样化，并不代表西部地区农产品物流可持续发展模式没有规律可循，这种规律除表现在上述基本框架所反映的理论模式内在机理的一致性外，还表现在可持续发展实践模式构建或探索过程的一致性。依据本研究第三章所揭示的可持续发展的概念内涵和实现机理，围绕西部地区农产品物流可持续发展模式的基本构成与框架建立，发挥西部地区特殊优势，实现方法论意义上的可持续发展模式的提升策略与结构创新。

一　西部地区农产品物流可持续发展模式的提升策略

（一）完善西部地区农产品物流的交易方式

目前，西部地区农产品市场的交易方式基本上为面对面的议价交易，现货对手交易份额占据绝对市场份额，但这种交易方式交易效率低、交易成本高、物流成本也较高，因此在一定程度上限制了农产品物流的可持续发展。要适应农业的快速发展，提高西部地区农产品的国际竞争力，就必须针对不同农产品的特点，丰富和创新农产品交易方式，发挥各种交易方式的优势，形成良好的价格形成机制和交易机制，减少农业生产的盲目性，提高农产品价格的透明度，减少买难和卖难问题。通过交易方式的选择，实现商流、物流、货币流的分离，减少落地交易次数，缩短物流时间，提高流通效率，实现整个农产品物流系统的优化。国内外实践证明，期货交易适合粮食、棉花、油料等大宗耐储存农产品的交易，拍卖交易适合生鲜农产品的即期交易；同时随着技术的不断进步和供应链关系的逐步改善，远期交易、电子商务等新型交易方式对于农产品供需双方降低搜寻成本和规避市场风险都有着不可低估的作用。

（二）提高西部地区农产品物流信息化水平

运用现代信息技术可以提高信息的对称性、及时性，改变交易方式，改善物流流程，大大提高物流效率。因此，现代物流是一种现代经济活动的新模式，物流信息技术是物流业发展的基础和现代物流的重要标志。而农产品物流由于农产品的鲜活易腐性，以及下游企业、消费者对农产品物流整个过程透明性的要求，使得 GIS、GPS、RFID 等最新信息化技术在农产品物流领域具有广阔的应用空间。农产品物流信息化就是利用现代信息技术、信息平台、信息装备等，围绕农产品的生产、采购、运输、储存、保管、配送、服务等物流全过程进行信息的采集、交换、传输和处理，实现农产品的供应方、需求方、配送方、储存方等的有效协调和无缝连接，构造出高效率、高速度、低成本的农产品物流供应链，从而达到全面满足经济发展的目的。实现农产品物流信息化，必须建立起相适应的技术支撑体系，这一体系主要由信息化标准、基础信息技术及设施、事务处理系统、信息管理与决策系统、电子商务系统、资源计划系统等构成，为物流服务提供全方位的支持。

（三）提升西部地区农产品物流标准化程度

农产品标准化包括农产品质量分等分级和农产品质量安全两部分。农产品质量是指农产品的效用、意愿、价值等主观特性。一方面，由于农产品的生物特性，农产品质量千差万别，它们的味道、色泽、鲜嫩、大小、形状和湿度等性质构成了从高级到低级不同的农产品质量，称之为垂直质量差异。另一方面，在现实中质量又体现了消费者的主观偏好，比如，感官质量不同的产品，对不同的消费者同样具有吸引力，称之为水平产品差异。这种质量是由生产者：消费者偏好决定的。制定质量标准的目的是更好地满足消费者对不同质量产品的需要，而不是保证高质量产品的市场销售。农产品质量分级根据农产品的质量标准，将不同质量的农产品进行分级、归类。等级明确地反映了农产品功能用途及其相应的费用与价格，体现了消费者对农产品预期认可的不同质量要求。它的广泛应用能够降低市场的交易费用，促进市场竞争，更是农产品期货市场、批发拍卖市场运行的基础。农产品物流标准化包括农产品标准化、农产品物流技术标准化、农产品物流作业标准化、农产品物流信息标准化、农产品物流管理标准化和农产品物流服务标准化等。

二　西部地区农产品物流可持续发展模式的结构创新

（一）西部地区农产品物流区位化双层物流联盟的思想基础

“策略联盟”的核心思想是有效地结合各公司的强项及各自的特殊区域市场优势，着重降低成本、降低风险、减少流通环节，实现组织的联盟发展，快速获得规模效益。策略联盟已成为全球竞争策略的重要环节，其实起源于企业在面临国际竞争压力时，基于本身资源及能力的不足，期望透过合资，共同研发，交互授权，物流协议等方式，结合各自稀缺的有限资源，共同分担研发的成本及风险，掌握市场流通，制定产业标准。策略是从属于战略的，战略应该是方向性的把握，而策略则是具体的动作。“战略联盟”的概念最早由美国 DEC 公司总裁简·霍普兰德（J. Hopland）和管理学家罗杰·奈格尔（R. Nigel）提出，他们认为，战略联盟指的是由两个或两个以上有着共同战略利益和对等经营实力的企业，为达到共同拥有市场、共同使用资源等战略目标，通过各种协议、契约而结成的优势互补或优势相长、风险共担、生产要素水平式双向或多向流动的一种松散的合作模式。在技术产业中，由于竞争激烈，产品生命周期短，研发及销售开发不但投资额巨大，而且费时长久、风险大，并常涉及国际行销、国际专利权及其他法规等考验，因而策略联盟常成为一项快速有效的方式——它能够协助企业进入特定的市场、产品、科技领域或弥补本身在价值链中的短处。在当前经营环境瞬息万变的挑战下，策略联盟所具有的快速性、互补性、效果相乘等特质，已成为企业反应管理变化的一剂良方。以策略联盟构筑西部地区农产品物流区位化双层物流联盟是为了保证西部地区农产品物流顺畅，有效地结合物流各节点的强项，发挥特殊区域优势，降低物流总成本与风险而建立的相对稳定的合作伙伴体系，是多个具有资源互补的包括农产品生产、技术管理及从事物流和商流的成员企业。为了实现资源共享、风险共担、优势互补等特点的战略目标，可以在较短的时间内，通过外部资源的有效整合，实现对农产品市场机遇的快速响应，使参与区位化双层物流联盟的物流组织通过高效合作，顺利完成农产品物流任务而形成的贯穿整个物流的协调机制和优化规划的合作体系。

以策略联盟构筑西部地区农产品物流区位化双层物流联盟模式，其一是产业链层面的物流联盟，其二是绿色通道层面的物流联盟，使物流功能得到完善和充分发挥[375]，具有以下特点：组织的灵活性、行为的战略性、合作的平等性、范围的广泛性、管理的复杂性。区位化双层物流联盟治理结构是股权式联盟（合资、相互持股）、契约式联盟（生产，研发，销售等环节）；价值链的角度是横向（绿色通道层面的物流联盟）与纵向（产业链层面的物流联盟）的混合联盟；合作的正式程度是实体联盟、虚拟联盟，通过农产品物流企业间组建动态联盟进行合作。区位化双层物流联盟根据特定的市场环境，集成了各类伙伴企业（农产品运输、仓储、流通加工、包装、配送及物流信息等组织）以满足联盟体系所需的相关核心资源。连接不同区位、不同物流职能、运作模式的成员企业，借助于现代物流技术、网络资源、管理技术整合集成的共有信息平台和基础设施，通过共同参与物流经营活动，实现区位化的物流业务协作与合作。西部地区农产品物流区位化双层物流联盟，可以在较短的时间内，通过外部资源的有效整合，实现对农产品市场需求的快速响应，它是传统农产品物流组织及运作模式所无法达到的。通过区位化双层物流联盟模式建立各个物流节点的农产品物流企业稳定的合作关系，不仅扩大了各经营主体的经营范围，也在一定程度上克服了条块分割、地方保护和行业规制政策的制约。并且由于区位化双层物流联盟模式合作方式灵活，有较大的柔性，因此非常适合西部地区弱小农产品物流主体之间的联合，不仅可以规避风险，还可以借助联盟伙伴的力量来增强自身的优势。

（二）西部地区农产品物流区位化双层物流联盟的框架创新

由西部地区农产品物流可持续发展模式的综合形态及发展趋势可以看出，在当前农产品物流产业链由原来的生产推动升级为市场拉动的情况下，需要逐步形成满足农产品快速、高效需求的从市场到生产基地的流通模式，即需要实现基于策略联盟的西部地区农产品物流区位化双层物流的高效联盟[375]。要形成高效联盟，必须解决区位化双层物流联盟的模式、机制优化两个问题。

1. 选择合理集约化、绿色化的农产品联盟模式

第一层面：产业链层面的物流联盟。流通连接农产品产销链条，是产销联盟过程中重要环节。因此，应该基于当前农产品物流发展趋势，选择集约化、绿色化生产与消费的产业链层面的物流联盟模式①。产业链层面的物流联盟以市场化为指导，通过在联盟内部形成完善的实物流、信息流、资金流通路，确保农产品及其加工品运销网路的高效和有序畅通。西部地区农业合作组织运销联盟是建立区域内农产品高速高质流通机制的组织保障，也是西部地区农产品物流区位化双层物流联盟模式的运作基础。

---

① 产业链层面的物流联盟既包含横向的农业合作组织运销联盟，也包含这一横向联盟或者其局部与相关农业企业、贸易商和第三方物流企业达成的纵向物流联盟。

第二层面：绿色通道层面的物流联盟。随着农产品消费观念发生改变，消费结构向绿色、有机、天然及功能性和方便化发展。联盟模式的选择还应该结合西部地区农产品的特性，包括结合农产品绿色生产特性和绿色物流特性两个方面，针对性地选择绿色通道层面的物流联盟①。绿色通道层面的物流联盟是关系西部地区农产品运销时效的重要环节，能够提高优势农产品流通效率，扩大农产品出口，是改善农产品流通环境建设物流网络的重要方面。西部地区与周边十多个国家接壤，陆地边境线长达12747公里，聚居的少数民族比较集中。边境线长为西部地区发展农产品外向型物流合作提供了天然条件。西部地区可以发挥区域地理优势，建立西部地区便捷、高效的公路、铁路、航空等综合运输系统与立体交通运输网的现代物流网络体系。引进先进的农产品物流设施和保鲜冷冻链技术等具备国际先进水准的物流工艺、技术和设施，并整合已经形成的“米”字形高速公路网络与纵横交错的铁路运输网络。同时，充分发挥西部内陆港——西安国际港务区优势，进一步建立和疏通西部地区农产品绿色通道的物流联盟，降低农产品运销成本，建立统一有序的农产品流通大市场[454]。

2. 在选择合理联盟模式的基础上，需要对保障农产品高效流通的各种机制进行优化

“机制”现在已成为一个泛指的概念，其含义是“系统内部的有机制约关系及其运行机理”[440]。本研究探讨的西部地区农产品物流可持续发展模式的联盟机制是农产品从生产到消费的集约化物流组织之间，以提高农产品物流整体效率为目标，以信息化、资源共享、科技创新为手段，使农产品物流组织之间各相关联因素可持续运行的过程，本研究就是针对该过程的制约关系及运行机理的研究。如图8－4所示。

针对联盟机制各种要素在农产品联盟中发挥的不同作用，构建西部地区农产品物流区位化双层物流联盟机制研究的理论体系。联盟体系的研究最终目的是实现减少农产品流通环节的损耗、提高流通效率，满足西部地区农产品物流“大生产、大流通”的需求。

① 绿色通道层面的物流联盟是关系西部地区农产品运销时效的重要环节，它包含电子口岸对接、检验检疫和快速通关机制、农产品安全预警机制、专业化仓储设施和配送中心建设、设立农产品保税专区等。

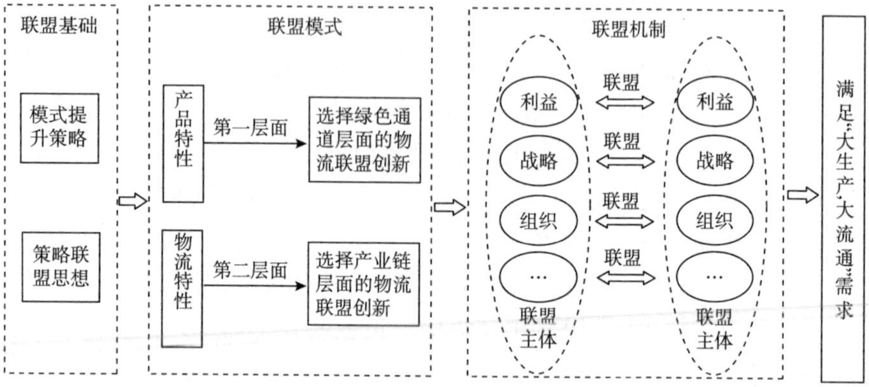

图8－4　西部地区农产品物流区位化双层物流联盟的框架创新

（三）西部地区农产品物流区位化双层物流联盟的模式优化

1. 西部地区农产品物流区位化双层物流联盟模式的层次优化

基于策略联盟思想，通过对西部地区农产品物流发展现状、存在问题以及发展趋势的分析可以看出，为了降低成本，提高物流效率，需要对传统农产品物流模式进行创新，实现从市场到生产的高效联盟。由于联盟各方活动性质不同，联盟方式形成纵向联盟与横向联盟[455,456]。而创新可以分为两个层次：一个是"点"的层次，即各个环节的创新；另一个是"线"的层次，即农产品物流供应链层次的创新[457,458]。西部地区农产品物流区位化双层物流联盟的层次创新主要体现在以下两个方面：

产业链层面的物流联盟创新。一是产地物流的规模集约化体现在集约生产、农业生产基地化发展的纵向联盟。通过合作组织、农业协会，将分散的农民组织起来，通过区域化种植形成生产的外部规模，提高生产效率。二是中转物流的规模集约化体现在纵向联盟和横向联盟一体化。三是销地物流的规模集约化体现在超市连锁化发展的纵向联盟。最终实现源头（生产基地）→核心（物流中心、龙头企业）→终端（零售连锁）产业链层面的物流联盟各环节与在整条链的创新[459]。

绿色通道层面的物流联盟创新。一是产地物流的绿色化体现在绿色生产、农业生产绿色化发展的纵向联盟。通过合作组织、农业协会，将分散的农民组织起来，通过区域化种植形成无公害农产品、绿色食品、有机农产品生产的外部规模，建立农产品安全预警体系，保障西部地区农产品绿色、有机农产品质量安全。二是中转物流的绿色化体现在纵向联盟和横向联盟一体化。通过设立农产品专用绿色通道、绿色化仓储设施和配送中心等，建立农产品检验检疫和快速通关体系，保障西部地区农产品运销时效。三是销地物流的绿色化体现在零售终端绿色化发展的纵向联盟。最终实现源头（产地物流）→核心（中转物流）→终端（销地物流）绿色通道层面的物流联盟各环节与整条链的创新[460]。

由此可见，物流联盟的各环节与整条链集约化、绿色化发展，缩短了从基地（即生产环节）到市场流通环节，实现西部地区农产品物流区位化双层物流联盟的高效联盟。生产基地、龙头企业、物流中心、零售连锁将逐渐发展成农产品流通的主体，在农产品流通中发挥越来越大的作用。同时，基于节点集约化、绿色化发展的集成上，形成西部地区农产品物流区位化双层物流联盟的模式优化[460]，如图 8－5 所示。

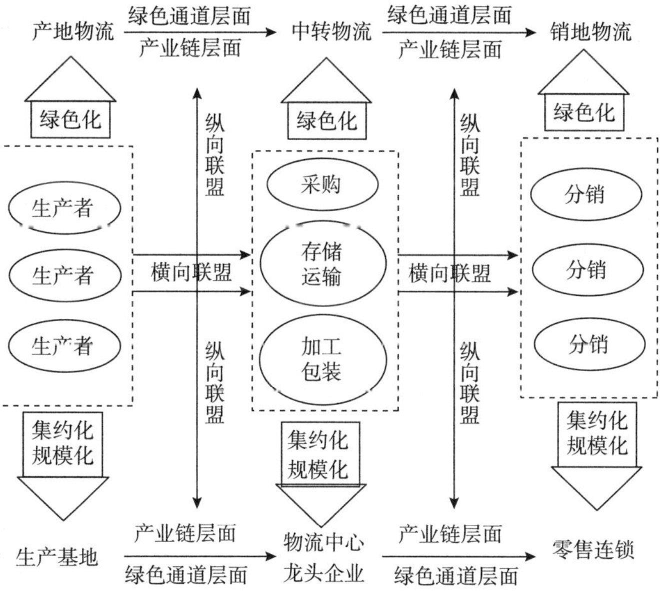

图 8－5　西部地区农产品物流区位化双层物流联盟的模式选择优化

2. 西部地区农产品物流区位化双层物流联盟模式的典型特征

上述分析可以看出，随着农业产业化、信息化提高，西部地区的农产品物流将由传统的批销模式走向现代的绿色化、集约化、规模化、一体化模式，将生产与消费通过两端的组织化、中间的电子商务化实现联盟。西部地区农产品物流区位化双层物流模式与相应的农产品特性、物流特点和主体的规模实力相关，适应于不同的情况，具有不同的特点：

（1）直接联盟模式。即“生产基地＋零售连锁”模式。生产与市场直接联盟，流通环节少。适用于不需要复杂加工的农产品，如生鲜果蔬、大批量粮食等，经过简单处理后直接运往零售连锁[461]。由于生产基地和零售连锁的加工、库存能力有限，一般流通范围不会很大。这种模式多以零售连锁为核心[462]。

（2）龙头企业模式。即“生产基地＋龙头企业＋（物流中心）＋零售连锁”模式。适用于需要专业加工的农产品，如肉制品、奶制品等。龙头企业一般以专业加工为主业[463]。流通范围根据龙头企业规模确定，可能局限于当地，也可能面向全国。这种模式多以龙头企业为核心[382]。

（3）物流中心模式。即“生产基地＋物流中心（配送中心）＋零售连锁”模式。物流中心型适用于流通体系生产、销售组织化相对较弱的情况，需要物流中心实现物流功能的集成，实现农产品的集散、批发、流通功能[464]。这种模式多以物流中心为核心。

（4）一体化模式。即大型连锁超市、龙头企业延伸产业链的模式。一体化企业通过长期契约、资本方法及向上或者向下的一体化方式，形成生产、加工、销售一体化[419]。一般企业选择需要高加工、高流通的农产品进行一体化，以获得高进入门槛，赢得更大的竞争优势。这种模式适用于具有较强加工、组织、资本实力的流通企业[433]。

西部地区农产品物流区位化双层物流联盟模式的构建，并不是摒弃现有物流资源，建立一个全新的系统，而是充分利用现有物流资源，通过对现有物流体系的不断整合、重组、补充、改造、提升，逐步发展成为适应西部地区经济发展和物流自身发展需要的新型的、先进的物流体系。由于西部地区市场发育程度不均衡，经济状况、自然条件也不尽相同，因此，西部地区农产品物流区位化双层物流联盟模式的构建，一方面应充分考虑现有物流资源的充分利用，结合不同区位的实际情况、不同农产品种类的具体需求；另一方面，通过构筑有利于农产品物流发展的基础设施、信息平台，以及各种机制的设计，作为整合现有物流资源的有效措施，推动高效区位化双层物流联盟体系的形成与发展。

（四）西部地区农产品物流区位化双层物流联盟的机制优化

西部地区农产品物流区位化双层物流联盟模式是在农产品现代物流“大生产，大流通”要求下，为适应目前消费结构和消费趋势的变化，农产品物流主体之间通过新型组织形式的深度联合，通过一定的措施、方法和机制解决联盟中各主体（不同的利益主体，相互独立的组织）之间的利益冲突，满足活动涉及的各个组织之间的相互利益需求或者达到设定的共同目标，使整个系统达到可持续的运作状态。因而运行机制的设计也将围绕联盟要素的联盟来构建。联盟要素包括，战略、利益、组织、流程、信息、标准、文化。

1. 西部地区农产品物流区位化双层物流联盟模式的战略联盟

战略联盟就是具有业务关联的企业在确定长期目标、发展方向和资源配置的战略管理过程中，从提高总体利益、企业彼此协同发展的目标出发，进行战略制定。通过企业的战略联盟，使企业之间在技术、资源等方面进行共享与协同，在提升总体利益的同时，获得各自企业整体业绩的提升，最终达到“1 + 1 > 2”的效果[465]。根据面对对象的不同，整个联盟体系的战略分为总战略、子战略和职能战略三个层次[466]，一是总战略：即西部地区农产品物流区位化双层物流整个联盟体系的竞争战略。该战略以整个链条体系满足顾客需求作为总体目标。二是子战略：即各个企业的战略，如生产基地、龙头企业、物流中心、零售组织各自的战略，主要是各自的竞争战略。三是职能战略：企业内部各个具体业务职能单元的战略，如生产战略、供应战略、市场战略、财务战略、人力资源战略、信息战略等。因此，战略联盟主要包括前两个层次[467]：其一是个体战略与总体战略的联盟，其二是子战略之间的联盟，战略联盟层次如图 8 – 6 所示。

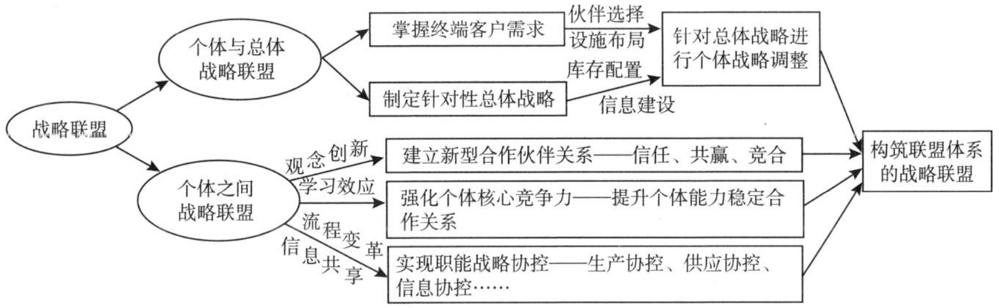

图 8 – 6　战略联盟层次

2. 西部地区农产品物流区位化双层物流联盟模式的利益联盟

作为农产品供应链中的利益相关群体，不论是生产者、加工运输、零售等中间环节还是消费者都有利益最大化的需求，存在各种利益冲突，需要建立农产品链间的共享利益、分担风险的机制。西部地区农产品物流区位化双层物流联盟模式的利益联盟体系如图 8－7 所示。

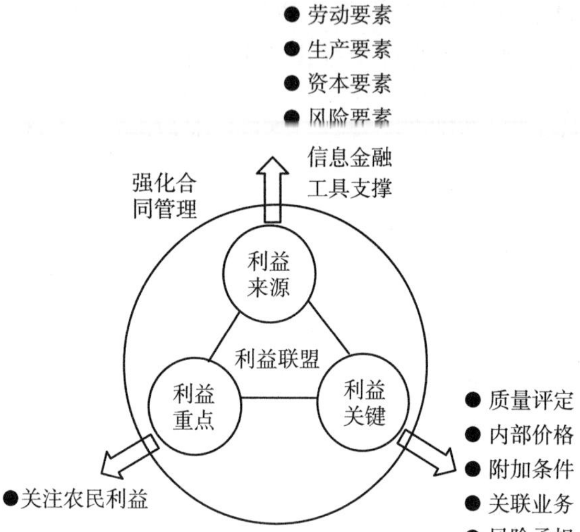

图 8－7　利益联盟体系

科学评价联盟体系中增值来源，着重关注生产基地相关环节的利益联盟。从生产到最后销售，农产品物流涉及生产、加工、运输、分销零售几个大的环节，各个环节之间都存在利益联盟问题。一般来说，从生产到零售端，是一个市场化水平逐步递进的过程，加工、运输及分销零售环节，其组织化程度、市场化程度相对较高，对市场信息掌握程度更广泛，因此具有更强的产品定价的话语权。而生产基地环节，虽然通过各种中介组织增加了其组织程度，但由于其具体的个体是农户，其市场意识、信息掌握有限，因而在利益分配中往往处于弱势地位，利益联盟的矛盾也多发生在这一环节。因此，应进行多种利益分配方法与机制的创新，保护农户利益。经过实践证明实行股份合作、实施保护价格、利润返还三种利益分配方式正逐渐被采用[468]。

3. 西部地区农产品物流区位化双层物流联盟模式的组织联盟

西部地区农产品物流区位化双层物流联盟体系中的每一个主体都是

一个独立的组织，不同的组织有不同的规模、结构、功能和管理体制等。当前，联盟体系各主体之间存在的诸多矛盾、低效，与组织联盟不顺畅有关。如组织化程度低造成整体效率低下、单调的科层结构使得组织效率低下等，为了建立快速反应、流通高效的联盟体系，应从组织方面实现高效联盟。所谓组织联盟就是在外部环境不断发展变化的情况下业务主体有效联盟，以提升企业竞争能力以及整个联盟体系的联盟效率。组织联盟主要包括规模、结构、功能、制度方面的联盟，如图8－8所示。

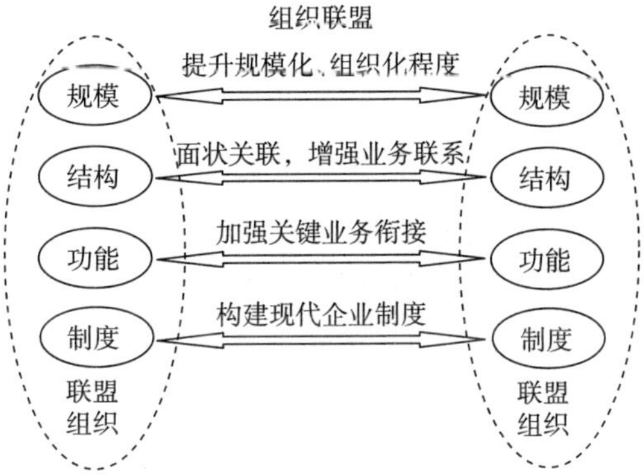

图8－8　组织联盟体系

（1）组织规模联盟。西部地区农产品物流区位化双层物流联盟模式构建的生产基地能够提高生产环节的组织程度。在我国东部一些地方，出现了“加盟连锁农场”模式，进一步加大了生产环节的组织化程度。除了生产环节这个组织程度最低的环节外，其余几个环节都应提高其主体的组织化程度，如加工企业、销售商，可以通过重组、联合、连锁经营等方式提升规模和竞争力。通过提高各环节主体的组织程度，才能提升组织效率，这是组织联盟的基础。

（2）组织结构联盟。组织结构联盟包括两个方面的工作：其一是组织内部，改善管理层次较多的传统科层结构；其二是组织之间，改善联盟形式，基于信息平台，增加联盟面。当前的农产品组织，由于产业化时间不长，组织化程度低，因此组织结构除了零售环节，其余环节大多以传统的科层结构为主。而西部地区农产品物流区位化双层物流联盟体系是一个强调快速响应、讲究时效的供应链，需要流程导向型的组织结构。联盟体系组织之间的伙伴关系，可以改善联盟方式，由蝴蝶型转化为钻石型，将组织之间的点状关联改善为面状关联，增加组织之间的业务往来，有利于促进组织联合，推动知识与技术创新。

（3）组织功能联盟。组织功能联盟即提高关联业务效率，包括双方的供货及接收方式、结算的时间及方式、双方生产系统及信息系统的联盟方式、新产品开发中的配合方式或者以合作进行科研创新来提高产品质量、降低成本的方式等。

（4）组织制度联盟。产权制度是西部地区农产品物流区位化双层物流组织制度联盟的核心问题，尤其要促进民营物流企业建立法人治理机制，渐进式自主制度创新与组织结构、组织规模、组织功能等联合，真正形成联动式组织联盟体系。

4. 西部地区农产品物流区位化双层物流联盟模式的流程联盟

随着企业运作和管理的日益规范，流程的概念也开始渗透到农产品物流企业管理的方方面面，如新的农产品的研发流程、生产流程、配送流程、客户服务流程、人力资源管理流程、财务管理流程等。由此可见，企业中所发生的任何一项活动都有其所对应的流程环节。流程的特点：第一，流程由若干环节所组成，而这些环节相互关联，共同为完成某一任务服务；第二，构成流程的环节是有限的，它有起点，也有终点；第三，在流程的起点处需要输入资源，终点处须输出成果。

（1）合理开放业务流程。流程开放建立在合理性、必要性基础上，通过高效的管理信息系统和技术支撑体系来准确、及时和快速地处理信息，使得联盟体系的合作伙伴及时了解有关流程处理的状态。

（2）确定核心业务流程。①客户服务：从联盟体系整体而言，下一个环节都是上一个环节的客户，都包括售前和售后的服务，产品的信息、产品到达时间以及客户意见等。但整个联盟体系面对的最终客户是消费者，这里的客户服务指的是针对消费者需求满意程度的服务。一般客户需求从与消费者直接接触的超市获得，包括对产品的意见、对产品的需求等。②订单管理：从联盟体系的最终端连锁超市那里得到具体产品的消耗和需求信息，自动触发订单管理系统，实现后续环节：加工企业加工备货、物流中心的仓储流程、生产基地的供货流程将根据订单情况进行相应的处理。③仓储管理：包括分拣和存货管理。当各部分接到上一环节的产品订单后，根据订单内容承担分拣、包装任务。存货管理包括存货及存货的补给工作，保证仓库合理的库存。④运输与交付：运输与交付流程一般对应相邻环节的订单管理和仓储管理，包括如何处理运输需求、涉及运输路线、运输的实施等，通过 Gis 软件和 Internet 对货物运输状态进行实时跟踪的服务。⑤退货管理：腐烂变质或没有达到质量需求的产品的退货处理，涉及对产品质量的检测和回收处理等。退货流程一般与上一环节的运输与仓储流程、客户服务流程联盟。目前必须通过属于不同主体的流程的联盟，使得整体联盟体系的运作更加优化。

5. 西部地区农产品物流区位化双层物流联盟模式的信息联盟

（1）物流信息是农产品联盟体系的核心因素之一。农产品信息联盟是农产品信息在西部地区农产品物流区位化双层物流联盟各主体内部和各主体之间的有效生成、流动、共享、利用，从而提高各主体及整个联盟体系的流通效率。信息联盟依赖信息技术与管理手段，涉及联盟体系的所有主体，主要体现在：信息化基础薄弱；缺乏信息生成、共享机制；信息技术落后，缺乏农产品信息追溯、安全监控手段；没有统一规划和标准；缺乏对信息的深层挖掘应用。因此实现信息的高效联盟，对于整个联盟体系的效率提高有着重要的意义。

（2）信息联盟体系构建。按照信息联盟体系从下到上，将信息联盟分成三个层面进行描述：第一个层面是基础层面：包括设备基础和标准基础；第二个层面是信息生成、共享、传递层面，即基于网络建立统 的数据平台以及各主体的应用系统；第三个层面是信息功能深层应用层面，即对应用系统产生的信息数据进行处理和深层挖掘。体系结构如图 8－9 所示。

第一个层面：基础建设层面。首先，政府主导进行网络设备、数据共享交换平台、信息安全服务等入网设备的网络基础建设的推进，尤其是农村地区的信息化发展和信息应用意识的提高。其次，是相关标准的制定。需要政府部门发挥主导作用，制定相应的信息化标准、信息安全标准、信息生成、使用、管理制度等。

第二个层面：信息平台层面。建立信息技术基础设施与统一的信息平台。考虑到具体实施的可行性和当前西部地区物流信息技术的发展现状，此处的用户不包含政府部门，只包括联盟体系中有业务关联的主体：生产基地组织、龙头企业、物流中心、零售连锁以及消费者。其应用系统也是针对以上用户的，主要通过以下应用系统，进行内部数据生成并共享。①农产品基础信息维护：该功能针对所有用户。从生产环节到最后销售环

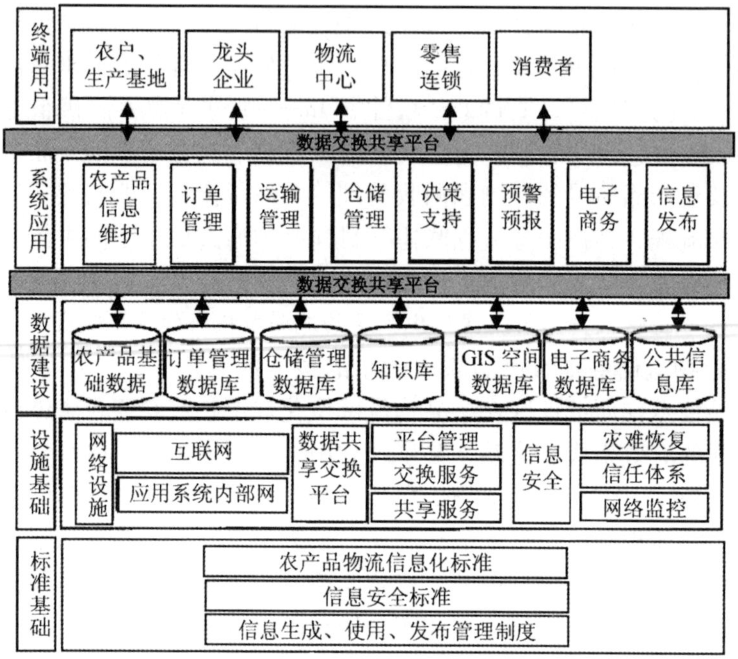

图8-9　信息联盟体系结构

节，对农产品的基本信息进行描述，如品牌、品质、数量情况等。②订单管理系统：对于长期合作的联盟主体，都需要进行订单管理，并可以共享有关信息。如生产加工企业可以根据超市提供的销售信息，分析农产品需求，向其上游的生产基地发布生产信息，并通过订单系统层层进行订单管理。③运输管理系统：运输管理，可以是物流中心等第三方物流企业，或者超市、加工企业内部的运输部门。④仓储管理系统：通过信息平台的搭建，能够完成农产品基础信息的建库和基础管理工作，为功能的深入开发奠定基础。

第三个层面：信息深层应用层面。除了以上对信息的基本应用，对于有条件的主体，还能对信息进行深层加工与应用，一般包括以下四个方面。①预警预报系统：可以通过历史销售数据预测未来销量，通过对市场需求进行有效的预测，控制农产品的有效库存。②决策支持系统：对农产品生产、流通、销售信息进行统计分析，为企业的管理决策提供支撑。③电子商务系统：通过信息平台实现网上拍卖等先进的交易方式，如果还连接海关和银行，可以实现网上支付等。④信息发布系统：面对公众建立相应的门户网站，使消费者能够对农产品基本信息进行查询。通过信息平台的应用，通过基于网络的信息平台，实现了农产品物流企业之间、企业与客户之间的农产品物流信息和农产品物流功能的共享。对于联盟主体而言能够解除产销困境，促进经济效益。

6. 西部地区农产品物流区位化双层物流联盟模式的标准联盟

先进经验、科研成果、新技术等只有通过简化、统一、协调、选优的原则，用标准的形式加以规定，才能促进其普及推广，提高劳动效率。保证从生产、管理到销售整个过程规范高效。农产品物流的标准包括很多内容，根据一些学者整理[469]，农产品物流标准有的应用于生产、流通、销售的某个物流环节中，如装备标准、作业标准，有的贯穿整个联盟体系的始末，如基础标准、信息标准、管理标准、服务标准等，用于传递信息、协调资源、促进主体之间的分工协作，需要多个联盟主体共同遵循。本研究讨论的标准联盟主要指后者，即指与所有联盟主体相关的、为了保证在西部地区农产品物流区位化双层物流联盟体系各主体的协调配合、准确的信息传递，各主体应遵守统一的流通标准，其重点在于如何实现各主体之间的无缝衔接。通过各主体间的标准联盟，能够实现农产品物流的全过程一体化、规范化，对于提高流通效率、降低流通损耗具有非常重要的作用。西部地区农产品物流区位化双层物流联盟体系围绕实物流和信息流进行，如图 8－10 所示。

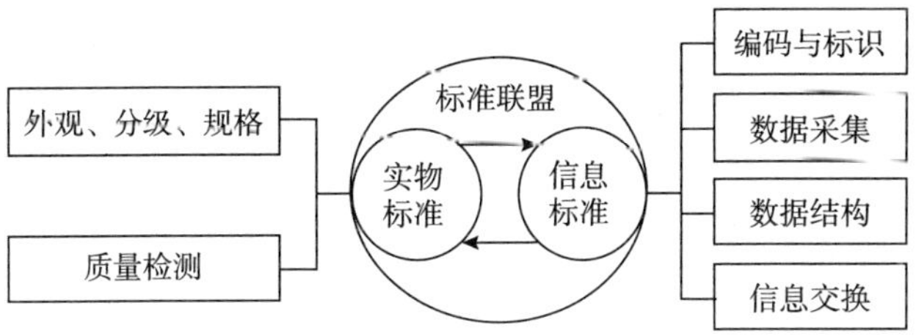

图 8－10　标准联盟体系结构

（1）实现物流的标准联盟。物流就是农产品的实物流动，在农产品生产和经营过程中，农产品标准化问题一直是困扰产销问题主要原因之一，其中在农产品出口和连锁超市生鲜区经营过程中，农产品标准化问题反映的尤为突出。①农产品外观标准，包括农产品的等级分类标准、规格标准。目前我国西部地区等级规格标准严重不全。既不便于储藏和搬运，而且由于外观质量差，也无法实现优质优价。因此，需要通过制定和推行农产品等级规格标准，引导、激励生产者和经营者按照标准生产和加工农产品，提升我国西部地区农产品档次和竞争力，扩大农产品出口。②农产品质量及质量检测标准。建立农产品质量及质量检测标准可有效防止突发性或群发性食品安全事故的发生[470]。

（2）实现信息流的标准联盟。物流信息标准联盟应该包括四方面内容的标准建设。①编码与标识标准。编码与标识即农产品代码编制所遵循的规则，编码与标识的标准化是实现物流信息追踪、信息自动采集和电子数据交换的前提，是物流信息标准化的第一步。从目前国内应用情况来看，代表农产品标识的条码标签的应用在农产品供应链各个环节存在严重脱节的现象。即从生产、仓储、运输、销售这一系列过程中，供应链各方参与者大部分都需要重新对货物进行分类、编码、标识、贴标签、信息录入等大量重复性作业，以致整个过程中的信息流通不顺畅、效率低下，没有发挥条码的最大功效。究其原因，主要有以下两种情况：一是农产品没有自带条码；二是条码标签类型不一致，以致无法扫描识别。因此，要从源头开始直至终端销售统一农产品的编码与标识标准，标准条码标签体系的应用，不仅有利于企业自身提高管理效率，也有利于供应链上下游企业之间的衔接配合。②数据采集标准。各环节进行信息化建设时，首先需要进行数据收集，需对采集内容、采集方式、传输渠道等进行一些约定，为进一步进行信息交互奠定基础。③物流数据与结构标准。创建数据库时也要遵循标准，譬如 E、R 实体关系及有多少属性表、字段、字段类型长度以及主外键关系、集联删除等，也是为了进一步实现数据交互与共享。④物流信息交换标准。不同主体的数据存在于不同的数据库中，大多为异构数据载体。数据交互标识就是多个异构数据载体之间进行数据交换时所遵循的标准，目前大部分采用规定好格式的 XML 文件进行数据交换。由于西部地区农产品物流区位化双层物流联盟之间大多数是多对多的网状结构，因此，在标准采纳时最好适应国际物流趋势，物流信息标准化更应该与国际接轨。可以将推广三大物流信息国际标准体系作为物流信息标准化工作的切入点。三大国际物流信息标准体系是指：一是实现标准化的物流编码与标识，包括国际物流单元编码标准 SSCC、国际物流位置编码标准 GLN、国际贸易货品分类编码标准 GTIN 等；二是实现标准化的物流智能识别，包括条码扫描 POS 标准、RFID 标准等；三是实现标准化的电子数据交换，包括 EDI 标准、EANCOM、XML 标准等。这三大国际物流信息标准体系的推广应用可以提高物流系统运作效率。西部地区农产品物流区位化双层物流联盟的建立，真正的农产品标准制定主体仍然是政府相关部门，政府必须给予足够的重视和经费的投入，并通过法律法规保障农产品各种标准的制定和实施。

7. 西部地区农产品物流区位化双层物流联盟模式的文化联盟

企业文化是现代企业品牌经营的重要内容之一，具有约束、导向、融合、凝聚和辐射等作用。与有形资源的整合相比，隐性的、根植于企业管理和员工脑海中的观念与文化的整合要困难得多。构成西部地区农产品物流区位化双层物流联盟体系的主体，由于其从事作业、组织方式、管理理念等存在诸多不同。因此，具有由不同形态的文化特质构成的企业，在合作中一定会产生一定的文化冲突。在联盟体系构建过程中，如果不重视文化冲突引发的问题，不仅达不到联盟体系总体战略所追求的共赢效果，而且还有可能因处理不当而影响到企业的正常运行。因此，在联盟体系运行中，要考虑文化联盟问题。

文化联盟就是联盟体系各主体在长期合作过程中，为了达到整体效率最高的目标，逐渐形成的共同信念，它包括价值观、经营哲学、道德准则、管理制度、员工心态，以及由此表现出来的企业共同的风范和精神。文化联盟是整个联盟体系顺畅运行的文化基础[471]。如果联盟体系没有一个共同的文化基础，各节点企业的文化便会互相抵触，从而影响供应链的管理。因此，必须实现各主体之间文化的联盟，增强其间的亲和度，以便有效地消除联盟体系中各种文化的摩擦以及由此造成的系统内耗。

通过对前面战略、利益、组织、流程、信息、标准、文化等要素联盟机制优化的分析，可以看出联盟体系中各要素的联盟并不是同步发展、一蹴而就的，而是一个循序渐进的过程，伴随着主体之间合作关系的深入，不断深化发展。可以将以上联盟要素分为不同的实施层次：第一层次：是实现战略与利益层次的联盟，这是联盟体系构建的基础，各主体通过战略联盟，能够使得各主体统一发展目标，实现资源配置合理化，资源运用最大化。同时按照公平合理的比例在各主体之间进行利益分配，这是合作的基础，是联盟体系建立初期首先要实现的。第二层次：是组织联盟和流程联盟，也可以理解成战术层面的联盟，随着联盟体系合作关系的深化，各主体能够进行更加深入的中观和微观层次的要素联盟。实现组织结构、组织功能、组织制度等方面的有效衔接，以及生产流程、配送流程、客户服务流程、库存管理流程等关键流程的联盟，有着积极的推动作用。第三层次：是信息及标准的联盟。因为只有在组织与流程联盟的基础上，才能进一步实现信息的联盟。而把标准联盟放在这个层次，也是由于标准的联盟需要建立在信息共享的基础上。第四层次：即最高层次是文化联盟。因为不同企业都有不同的文化，彼此的融合需要较长时间。只有通过长期合作后，才可能达到真正意义上的文化联盟。以上四个层次的联盟实现后，整个联盟体系发展到更高层次，则可能面临着战略、组织等的不断优化，进入更高的发展阶段。由此可见，整个联盟体系的联盟过程是一个不断发展、不断螺旋上升的过程。

第九章　西部地区农产品物流可持续发展的模式运行

西部地区农产品物流可持续发展的具体实现形态取决于模式创建要有基础运行平台作保证，应依据“模式”的提升策略与结构创新，设计西部地区农产品物流区位化双层物流联盟的运行平台——西部地区农产品供应链的区域协控中心。首先探索西部地区农产品物流可持续发展模式的运行设计（西部地区农产品供应链的区域协控中心的运行体系、形成机制、实现机制、约束机制）；在此基础上分析西部地区农产品物流可持续发展模式的运行管理（基于区域协控中心的区位化双层物流联盟的运作风险、空间优化）；最后进行西部地区农产品物流可持续发展模式的综合评价（西部地区农产品物流可持续发展评价指标体系的构建、综合评价方法）。为此，本章将基于“模式”的运行设计、运行管理、综合评价的分析，通过整合各成员的资源、技术与信息，科学设计西部地区农产品区域协控中心的运行平台，以保障西部地区农产品物流区位化双层物流联盟模式的优化实施，整个运行体系表现出集成化的运行管理和一体化的运行保障，实现西部地区农产品物流可持续发展。

第一节　西部地区农产品物流可持续发展模式的运行设计

一　西部地区农产品供应链的区域协控中心的运行体系

西部地区农产品物流可持续发展的模式运行，需要西部地区农产品物流区位化双层物流联盟的基础平台作保证，因此，当前应致力于推动西部地区农产品供应链的区域协控中心的保障运行。西部地区农产品供应链的区域协控中心是一个系统，系统整体功能发挥程度既受到系统结构的制约，也受到外部环境变化的制约。西部地区农产品供应链的区域协控中心的结构是系统功能的内在基础，功能是系统结构的外在表现。因此，要更好地发挥西部地区农产品供应链的区域协控中心的整体功能，需要研究其运行结构与运行系统。

（一）西部地区农产品供应链的区域协控中心的运行结构

1. 西部地区农产品供应链的区域协控中心的内涵

本研究通过农产品供应链与供应链协同的观点建立西部地区农产品供应链的区域协控中心的运行结构。农产品供应链是围绕核心企业，通过对信息流、物流和资金流的控制，把农产品从农资供应、农产品生产、采购、加工、运输，最后由销售网络把产品送到消费者手中，进而将生产者、核心企业、分销商直到消费者连成一个整体的功能性网链结构模式[375]。供应链协同（SCC）是指供应链中各节点企业为了提高供应链的整体竞争力而进行的彼此协调和相互努力。各节点企业通过公司协议或联合组织等方式结成一种网络式联合体，在这一协同网络中，供应商、制造商、分销商和客户可动态的共享信息，紧密协作，向着共同的目标发展[375]。

结合以上观点，西部地区农产品供应链的区域协控中心就是西部地区农产品供应链中各节点实体为了实现西部地区农产品物流可持续发展模式的共同目标，提高模式创新体系——“区位化双层物流联盟”的整体竞争力，通过基础保障平台——“区域协控中心”而进行彼此协调和互助努力。西部地区农产品供应链的区域协控中心的运行结构是各节点通过协议或联合组织等方式结成一种整体的协控网络式联合体。西部地区农产品供应链的区域协控中心、区位化双层物流联盟之间充分利用现代化技术，在基础保障平台→模式创新体系→共同目标的过程中，通过可动态地共享信息、相互合作、整体优化降低供应链的成本，提高供应链运行效率和经济收益的管理模式，向着共同的目标发展。这样，通过西部地区农产品供应链的区域协控中心对西部地区农产品物流区位化双层物流联盟的整合管理，物流活动的每一环节为了共同的目标保持协调一致，有效地提高了农产品物流的效率和服务水平；通过建立信息网络化的电子商务对接平台、契约网络化的产销标准与规范对接平台、实体物流网络化的电子口岸对接平台等服务平台，控制农产品源头的绿色安全，确保农产品安全质量体系的良好运行，实现西部地区农产品快速调配和优化，强化西部地区农产品生命周期管理和质量安全追溯体系；通过建立内部支撑体系、外部支撑体系，供应链每个节点之间依靠协控运作来降低西部地区农产品物流成本，提高竞争力，使供应链上的企业得到更大的收益。因此，西部地区农产品供应链的区域协控中心的运行结构强调战略合作伙伴关系，每个节点集中精力和各种资源从事比竞争对手更擅长的关键性业务，有效地提高了产业链层面物流联盟、绿色通道层面物流联盟的效率和服务水平，为提升西部地区农产品物流区位化双层物流联盟的整体绩效、实现西部地区农产品物流可持续发展奠定了保障基础[375]。如图 9－1 所示。

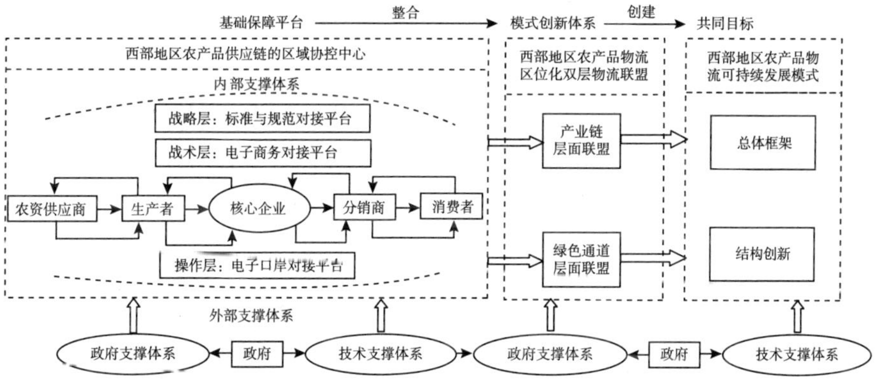

图 9－1　西部地区农产品供应链的区域协控中心的运行结构

2. 西部地区农产品供应链的区域协控中心的运作平台

（1）战略层：契约网络化的标准与规范对接平台。战略层负责统筹整个西部地区农产品供应链的区域协控中心的农产品物流活动，对整个农产品物流活动进行战略规划设计，负责制定统一的物流标准、操作规程和管理规范，提升农产品物流标准化程度。战略层对战术层、操作层起着协控性的作用，有效整合农产品产销过程。用契约来维护区域协控中心物流企业的顺利运行，规定成员的权利与义务，区域协控中心组织成员间契约的集合构成契约网络。区域协控中心的标准与规范对接平台包括农产品标准化、农产品物流技术标准化、农产品物流作业标准化、农产品物流信息标准化、农产品物流管理标准化和农产品物流服务标准化等的对接。西部地区与港澳台可以率先制定并推行共同的农产品市场准入机制；借助农业合作组织对接平台，制定共同的运输政策，达成农产品安全及互认机制；建立农产品加工原料协作把关机制和异地备案基地制度；并就西部地区与港澳台农产品生产、加工、运销过程的标准达成统一规范和实施制度。如互派专门机构接受业界委托设点，对西部地区与港澳台农产品进行检验检疫，或者通过西部地区与港澳台农产品检验检疫机构的有效衔接，就检验检疫结果互认的具体程序和范围等达成协议。再如台湾农委会已经着手建构台湾农产品生产履历咨询系统。消费者利用网际网路查询生产履历资料——消费者在市场上购得的具有农产品产销识别码的产品后，可利用电脑直接在网络上看到生产者的相片与联络方式、产销班资讯、生产地点以及完整的生产过程记录。优先鼓励“吉园圃”产销班与“有机”农场有意愿尝试记录生产履历的农民。西部地区可以透过农业产业化龙头企业和专业合作组织试点来尝试这个经验做法。总之，西部地区与港澳台农业合作组织在两地农产品认证、标准、包装规范、检验检疫等方面有所作为的同时，还要推动相关的制度性协调机制的形成，为今后供应链体系整合消除操作瓶颈[472]。

（2）战术层：信息网络化的电子商务对接平台。战术层是农产品加工企业、零售企业、第三方物流企业和信息服务公司、咨询公司等第三方企业在西部地区农产品供应链的区域协控中心建立的“农产品电子商务平台”上实现互动式交流，提高农产品物流信息化水平。现代网络技术的迅速发展和广泛应用，极大地加速了区域协控中心伙伴间的信息交换，充分利用信息网络能使区域协控中心将处在不同地理位置上的伙伴连接起来，以较低的成本，快速地实现组织成员的合作与协调整个西部地区农产品物流区位化双层物流联盟。区域协控中心的电子商务对接平台是实现企业和物资需求者的供需关系，其核心是产销信息系统和安全资信系统。包括建立西部地区农产品检验检疫电子平台、及时的供求信息交换平台、制定西部地区农企和品牌农产品资信等级评价体系平台、对信用好的农产品实行快速通关办法等[473]。西部地区在建设农业合作组织网络平台的实践中，可以借助卫星宽频主干网，实现多媒体实时视频传播，而且由于这项技术通讯费用低，适合西部地区丘陵多山的县域推广应用，并能确保与西部与港澳台卫星体系的贸易实体平台对接后的信息畅通。

（3）操作层：实体物流网络化的电子口岸对接平台。操作层是西部地区农产品供应链的区域协控中心根据消费者的需求，把农产品物流的采购、储运、加工等功能安排给“农产品电子口岸平台”相应成员来实施，各成员企业以集成化农产品供应链的区域协控中心为主导，维护整个农产品物流运作流程，完善农产品物流的交易方式。实体物流网络化的电子口岸对接平台是在信息网络化的电子商务对接平台和契约网络化的产销标准与规范对接平台的支撑下，西部地区农产品物流网络运作的实体。区域协控中心的电子口岸对接平台是提高农产品物流时效，保障西部地区绿色通道层面的物流联盟顺利进行的基础平台。区域协控中心可以在新疆边境口岸与中南亚（哈萨克斯坦、吉尔吉斯斯坦、塔吉克斯坦、巴基斯坦、蒙古、印度、阿富汗）及俄罗斯共建农业物种风险评估制度，并制定共同的有害生物的风险管理方案的基础上，通过动植物检验检疫机构的电子化对接，统一农产品检验检疫的标准化机制和便捷通关机制。还可以把西部内陆港——西安国际港务区鲜活农产品直接贸易试点机制作为突破口，试行电子口岸对接的相关事宜，共同探讨建立包括供应港澳台地区鲜活农产品的生产基地管理、运销路经、通关、检验检疫、税费收取等方面的电子资讯系统。可以进一步探讨国际标准化组织提出的“一个标准、一次检验、全球通行”的农产品快速流通理念的制度建设和具体实施路径，逐步实现西部地区农产品的快速通关和双向保税功能，从而不断完善西部地区边境口岸、内陆港的电子化监督与服务体系[454]。

以上分析可以看出，西部地区农产品供应链的区域协控中心的运行结构是综合性、专业化、集成化、一体化的物流服务，需要强大的支撑体系来保障整个系统顺畅、高效地运行。首先是内部支撑体系。作为主导节点的区域协控中心一定要综合考虑各个成员间的利益分配问题，建立配套的农产品供应链内部支撑体系，主要对供应链中的其他节点从市场、服务、技术、渠道等各方面进行全方位的系统支持，来保证农产品供应链体系的稳定性[474,475]。其次是外部支撑体系。一方面，需要强大的技术体系支持，包括信息技术、物流技术、管理技术等，政府对农产品基础设施平台和信息平台的建设负有责任；另一方面，需要一定的政策体系予以支撑，政府通过法律、法规和财政政策、税收政策、货币政策和利率政策推动西部地区农产品供应链的区域协控中心对各协控企业的集成运作，真正做到协作、调控供应链间的成员运行方式[476]，更好地将集成化的西部地区农产品供应链的区域协控中心各节点“无缝”连接，实现对西部地区农产品物流区位化双层物流联盟的整合管理。

（二）西部地区农产品供应链的区域协控中心的运行系统

从西部地区农产品供应链的区域协控中心的运行结构可以看出，农产品供应链中节点企业较多，但是各节点在产业环境、组织文化、技术能力、信息传递、物流系统等诸多层面所涉及的标准、格式、规则、原则和态势上存在着广泛的不一致性，为了实现西部地区农产品供应链的区域协控中心的整体功能和效用，各节点必须相互协作、控制。另一方面，根据系统原理，西部地区农产品供应链的区域协控中心也是一个经济系统，是一个由相互作用、相互依赖的若干组成部分结合而成的具有特定功能的有机整体，具有整体性、层次性和协控性，具有智能化的自组织性[477]，对这个复杂系统进行管理的实质是协控与共赢。因此，建立西部地区农产品供应链的区域协控中心，对农产品供应链的区域协控机制进行研究具有十分重要的意义。

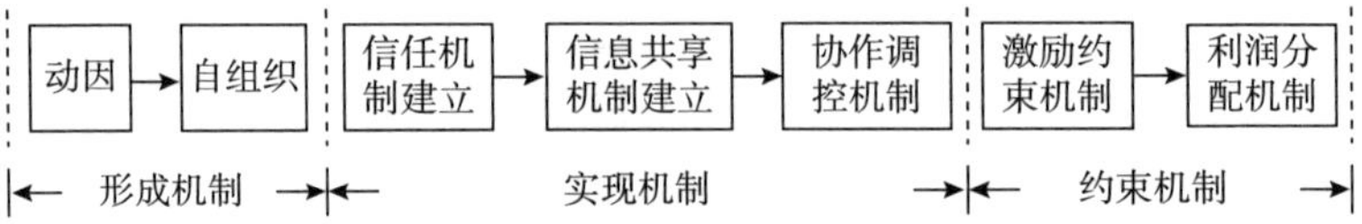

图 9－2　西部地区农产品供应链的区域协控中心的运行系统

西部地区农产品供应链的区域协控中心的运行系统如图 9－2 所示，主要包括三类机制：第一类西部地区农产品供应链的区域协控中心形成机制。是分散的实体形成供应链的区域协控中心动因以及通过自组织形成农产品供应链的区域协控中心机理[478]。第二类西部地区农产品供应链的区域协控中心实现机制。包括供应链中信任机制的建立、信息共享机制的形成、各节点间的协作调控机制。第三类西部地区农产品供应链的区域协控中心约束机制。是如何通过激励机制保证整条供应链的正常运转、农产品供应链的利益应如何在各节点之间进行分配[479]。

二　西部地区农产品供应链的区域协控中心的形成机制

（一）西部地区农产品供应链的区域协控中心的动因

1. 降低西部地区农产品物流区位化双层物流联盟的运行费用

西部地区农产品供应链的区域协控中心形成的根本原因和目标是降低

交易费用。从农产品物流交易主体的行为来看，农民没有能力收集物流提供商的信息，与物流商的交易活动往往不够理性，加之物流商彼此之间存在信息不对称而产生欺诈行为。从物流交易过程来看，农产品物流各方具有一定的依赖性，一方违约将给另一方造成巨大的损失，主要是场地、设施设备、人力等资源已经投入而交易却终止，所投入的资金将无法挽回。而且，由于市场环境的变化，交易双方信息的不对称，将导致交易的不确定性。农民作为个体，其农产品物流因无法产生规模经济效益，且物流商之间频繁的讨价还价，其签约将导致较高的交易费用。而西部地区农产品供应链的区域协控中心作为代表着农民利益的市场主体之一，与农产品供应链各节点结成战略伙伴关系，这种关系能大大降低搜寻交易对象信息的费用；区域协控中心伙伴间的经常沟通与协商有助于减少合作伙伴的冲突，降低机会主义行为发生的概率，有效地避免用于解决纠纷而产生的费用，可以形成区域协控中心信息传递迅速的经济性；区域协控中心伙伴间长期的合作能够建立长久的契约关系，减少因谈判、制定协议等产生的费用，并为合作伙伴之间带来稳定的业务来源，同时还有助于西部地区个性化物流的建立，物流活动在区域协控中心内进行，可以使交易费用内部化，将大大降低农产品物流的费用、提高物流质量，这是保证西部地区农产品物流区位化双层物流联盟能够生存的必要的前提条件[473]，如图9－3所示。

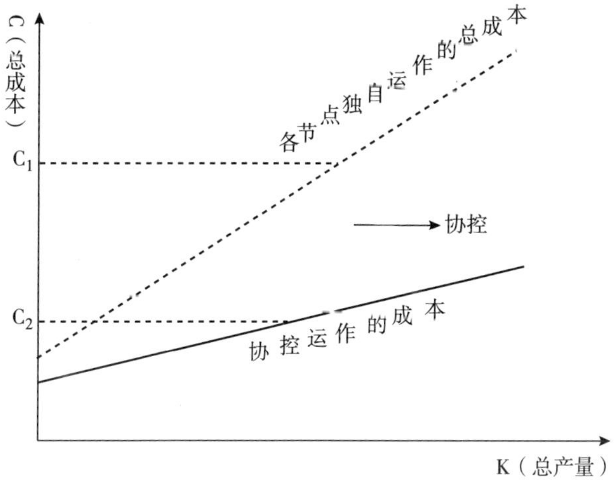

图9－3　西部地区农产品供应链的区域协控中心成本效应

2. 确保西部地区农产品物流区位化双层物流联盟的稳定

西部地区农产品供应链的区域协控中心形成的主要原因是有助于筛选物流商，消除“逆向选择”，确保区位化双层物流联盟的稳定，形成规模效应。农产品物流是一个连续的过程，其间任意一个物流环节的运行出问题或参与的物流提供商能力偏低，将有可能导致整个物流链条的断裂给组织带来巨大的损失，同时若个别物流商采取“搭便车”的策略将使整个物流运作增加不必要的负担[480]。因此，必须认真选择物流商，建立西部地区农产品供应链的区域协控中心。然而我国农产品生产者的基本单位是农户，规模较小。由于小农户的生产经营与大市场的矛盾，在选择物流商时易产生“逆向选择问题”，稳定性差、效率较低。区域协控中心在选择物流伙伴时，对物流商进行客观的评估，可从其财务状况、技术创新能力、物流水平及其在行业内的口碑等进行综合的考察，例如，一些有关潜在物流企业的变量可以充当质量水平的强信号：①质量承诺，是指潜在合作伙伴以今后将承担维修费用或赔偿费用为代价，传递产品与服务的高质量特性。②企业声誉，有助于鉴别潜在合作伙伴的质量水平。企业声誉的机会成本包括沉淀成本和未来成本。沉淀成本是指企业为建立自己良好的声誉所花费的成本，未来成本是指一旦被发现所传递的信息与事实不符而将蒙受的损失。③第三方认可，政府相关部门、各种市场中介等组织的认可或被优秀供应链接纳则可以较为有效地传达代理人的质量信息。进一步建立相应的评价指标体系，根据科学的决策方法选择区域协控中心物流伙伴，从而确保西部地区农产品物流区位化双层物流联盟的稳定[481]。

3. 保障西部地区农产品物流区位化双层物流联盟的利益

西部地区农产品供应链的区域协控中心形成的关键原因是风险共担、利益均沾。西部地区农产品物流区位化双层物流联盟的每一个层次都试图使自身的利益最大化，但这是以损害其他层次为代价的，这并不能给区位化双层物流联盟带来利益最大化。西部地区农产品供应链的区域协控中心合作双方会制定一个长期的合约，且一般会设置一个参考的约定价格，这个价格是不变的，确定这个价格，物流企业组织会考虑到其效率变化和能获得的效益。物流行业的效率是不断变动的，也就是未来市场上的物流服务价格会是个变数[482]。假设目前的市场平均波动$\triangle X$，约定的价格为X。当价格上升时，以区域协控中心的两个实体农协、第三方物流公司为例，农协具有选择权，为维系合同的稳定关系，第三方物流公司应该给予农协

一定的补偿，其补偿额应为 min（C_1，$|\triangle X|$）；当价格下降时，第三方物流公司具有选择权，为维系合同的稳定关系，农协应给予第三方物流公司一定的补偿，其补偿额应为 min（C_2，$|\triangle X|$）。C_1是农协购买看涨权（买权）应付出的代价，由合作的第三方物流公司所获得；C_2是农民合作组织购买看跌权（卖权）应付出的价格，由农协所获得。C_1，C_2根据布莱克·舒尔斯模型对期权定价的公式来确定[483]。以上分析可以看出，只有当供应链的区域协控中心制定合理的利益分享计划时，供应链的节点企业之间才能获得更高的利润，才能保障西部地区农产品物流区位化双层物流联盟的利益。

（二）西部地区农产品供应链的区域协控中心的自组织

西部地区农产品供应链的区域协控中心的共同利益，驱使着潜在的合作者在“没有人为干预”的情况下自发地向供应链的区域协控中心聚集，成为现实供应链的区域协控中心合作者，这个过程是一个自发聚集的过程，是一个从无序到有序的过程。若把西部地区农产品供应链的区域协控中心看成一个系统，可称其为自组织。当有序的西部地区农产品供应链的区域协控中心结构体形成后，合作者共同制定并遵循共同的“游戏规则”协控运作。

在西部地区农产品供应链的区域协控中心形成时，可能是下面的状况：各节点要素自发结成“虚拟企业”，因为加入西部地区农产品供应链的区域协控中心所获得的效益要远大于单个组织单独经营所获得的效益。由于农产品供应链的区域协控中心各节点要素的控制者是具有思考能力的人（具有智能），人们由于识别了这种效益，从而自发地加入西部地区农产品供应链的区域协控中心系统。

我们可以从数理的角度来分析西部地区农产品供应链的区域协控中心的自组织过程，建立供应链的区域协控中心系统的自组织模型。假定西部地区农产品供应链的区域协控中心只有两个实体：农协与物流提供商，没有政府的存在，且两者都是理性的。农协与物流提供商建立长期的战略联盟关系，以联盟的利益最大化为目标使双方获得利益大于以各自利益最大化为目标的获得利益。可以建立一个完美信息动态博弈模型[484-486]。

第三方物流（3PL）提供商先确定单位农产品物流价格，农协再决定农产品物流量。设第三方物流商的利润为 $\pi_1(p,q)=qr(p)$，p 表示单位农产品物流价格，q 表示物流量，$r(p)$ 表示单位农产品物流第三方物流商的收益，显然 $\pi_{1p} > 0, \pi_{1q} > 0$ ，物流商的目标是最大化 π_1 ；农协的利润函数是 $\pi_2 = R(q) - pq$ ，假定 $R(q)$ 是严格的凹函数，即 $R' > 0, R'' < 0$ ，农协的目标是最大化 π_2 。这是一个完美信息动态博弈。

农协视 p 既定，要实现最大利润，决策变量 q 必须满足一阶条件 $\frac{\partial \pi_2}{\partial q} = R'(q) - p = 0$ ，即 $R'(q) = p$ ，设此时 $q = q*(p)$ 。边际收益等于边际成本。因为边际收益是递减的，上述一阶条件表明农协的物流需求随物流价格递减。

物流商预期农协将会根据上述一阶条件选择 $q = q*(p)$ ，物流商的最优化一阶条件是：$\pi_{1p} + \pi_{1q}q_p^* = 0$ ，即 $-\frac{\pi_{1p}}{\pi_{1q}} = q_p^*$ 。此一阶条件表示物流商将选择物流单价 $p*$ ，使 $p*$ 点自己的等利润曲线与农协的物流需求曲线相切，子博弈精炼纳什均衡的结果是 $(p*, q*(p*))$ ，如图 9－4 所示。

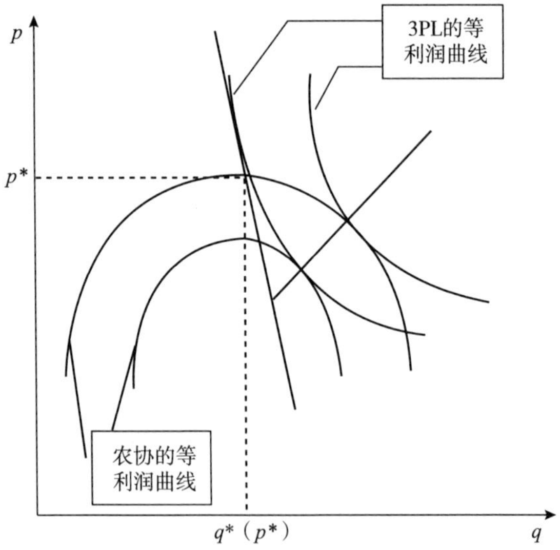

图 9－4　信息动态博弈曲线

从图 9－4 可以看出它并不是帕雷托最优点。如果 $p*$ 和 $q*$ 在图中所示阴影部分，农协和物流商的利润均会增加。一个帕雷托最优，一定满足农协的等利润曲线的斜率与物流商等利润曲线的斜率相等。即 $-\frac{\pi_{2p}}{\pi_{2q}}=\frac{R'(q)-p}{q}=-\frac{\pi_{1p}}{\pi_{1q}}$。

假定农协与物流商追求协控的利益最大化，对物流单价、物流量同时进行磋商，并最终达成协议。那么 $\max\pi_1\pi_2$ 的最优化一阶条件是：

$$\pi_{1p}(R(q)-pq)-\pi_1 q=0,\pi_{1q}(R(q)-pq)+\pi_1(R'-p)=0$$

整理得：$-\frac{\pi_{2p}}{\pi_{2q}}=\frac{R'(q)-p}{q}=-\frac{\pi_{1p}}{\pi_{1q}}$，显然得到了一个帕雷托最优解。博弈双方得到的利益大于不合作得到的利益，即建立西部地区农产品供应链的区域协控中心实现双方利益最大化。

上述模型简单描述了西部地区农产品供应链的区域协控中心实体间的自组织过程，在自组织的过程中，各实体一方面会自觉地调整个体结构和行为，使其向着适应供应链整体目标的方向发展，这是一种自组织和智能理性的自适应性。另一方面，由于个体经济利益的驱动，各实体的行为可能发生与供应链整体利益的悖逆，这是一种“非理性”或者“有限理性”的行为，需要采用“被组织”的方式进行调控[487]。

三　西部地区农产品供应链的区域协控中心的实现机制

（一）西部地区农产品供应链的区域协控中心的信任机制建立

在西部地区农产品供应链中，节点和节点之间的信任机制没有建立。例如，核心企业与农民一直是一种松散的关系，核心企业选择生产基地一般是委托乡镇农技站与农民签订单，农技站对种子、技术把关，企业按实收的农产品给农技站服务费。这样的运作过程无疑拉大了核心企业与农户之间的距离，信任机制难以建立。而信任是西部地区农产品供应链的区域协控中心对各节点协控运作的前提，是供应链的区域协控中心正常运转的支柱。农产品供应链由于其复杂性、不确定性、脆弱性，使得节点之间的信任机制进一步成为保障西部地区农产品供应链的区域协控中心内部协控运作的根基[488]。

（二）西部地区农产品供应链的区域协控中心的信息共享机制

在我国西部地区，农产品的生产大多分散在千家万户，这导致供给方面的信息常常很零散和不准确，与此同时，来自零售终端的需求信息也很难直接到达分散的生产者。在农产品供应链中，“牛鞭效应”和“信息滞后”最终造成的后果往往是市场需求旺盛的产品供应不上，而大量上市的产品又堆积如山无人问津，这势必会严重挫伤生产者的积极性[489]。农产品链的信息包括与农产品生产、经营、销售有关的一切消息、情报、数据、资料等的总称，是农情和商情的综合反映。它具有信息的一般特点，如客观性、有价性、时效性、共享性、传播性和可加工性等，还具有季节性、区域性、渗透性和分散性等独有特征。在西部地区农产品供应链中，可通过区域协控中心来实现信息共享，进一步形成区域协控中心的电子商务供应链网络的结构，实现中心内部的协控运作[490]。

农产品物流信息平台系统能够使农户、经销商和加工企业等参与主体之间进行有效的信息协调与控制，促进供应链节点的相互信任，提高快速反应能力，降低牛鞭效应。为了使信息在农产品供应链上顺畅流通，减少供应链信息传递的不确定性，需要建立我国西部地区农产品供应链的区域协控中心的电子商务供应链网络结构，实现合作“双赢”。所谓双赢源于“win - win”，这主要是针对单纯的输赢关系（lose - win）而言的[491]。单纯的输赢关系认为市场中企业的竞争只出现一种结果，即一方损失而另一方收益。在这种观念下的供应链必然存在局部优化，而未达到整体最优的问题。合作的双赢策略是供应链各个成员的首选策略。结成战略合作伙伴关系很关键的一点就是供应链各方的信任。通过分析市场竞争环境、确立合作伙伴选择目标、制定合作伙伴评价标准、成立评价小组、合作伙伴参与、评价合作伙伴、实施供应链合作关系的战略合作伙伴的综合评价、选择步骤，建立大范围的网络组织，信息网络自然成为支撑和维持这个组织网络的重要基础。

电子商务供应链（virtual supply chain，VSC）旨在开发一个电子信息系统，以使最后消费者能够直接从农产品企业组成的供应链虚拟联盟中订货。它被看作是：合作伙伴基于专门的信息服务中心提供的技术支持和服务而组建的动态供应链[492]。根据系统原理，西部地区农产品供应链的区域协控中心的电子商务供应链网络也是一个经济系统，是一个由相互作用、相互依赖的若干组成部分结合而成的具有特定功能的有机整体，具有整体性、层次性和协控性。农产品电子商务供应链网络系统的模式可以分为七个步骤：市场信息收集；电子商务供应链发起与组织；合同投标与获取；农产品生产与配送；售后服务与产品回收；利益分配；电子商务供应链的解散[493]。农产品电子商务供应链一般是一种网状结构，它可以通过VSC信息服务中心（包括VSC服务系统），分别支持目标、任务、信息和技术等方面来完成。如图9－5所示。

网状结构中心点O——VSC信息服务中心（包括VSC服务系统：VSC服务器、VSC数据库）：供应商、生产商、承运商、分销商、零售商、消费者、其他伙伴；

网状结构扩散点A——任务：市场信息获取、电子商务供应链组织、农产品生产与配送、售后服务与产品回收、利益分配、电子商务供应链的解散；

网状结构扩散点B——信息：消费者与市场信息、供应商、生产商信息、承运商、分销商、零售商信息、其他伙伴信息；

网状结构扩散点C——目标：全面满足消费者需要、降低供应链成本、提高影响速度和效率、提高产品和服务质量、降低资源消耗与环境影响、实现合作伙伴“双赢”；

网状结构扩散点D——技术：Internet技术、数据库技术、合作伙伴选择技术、供应链优化、运作和管理技术。

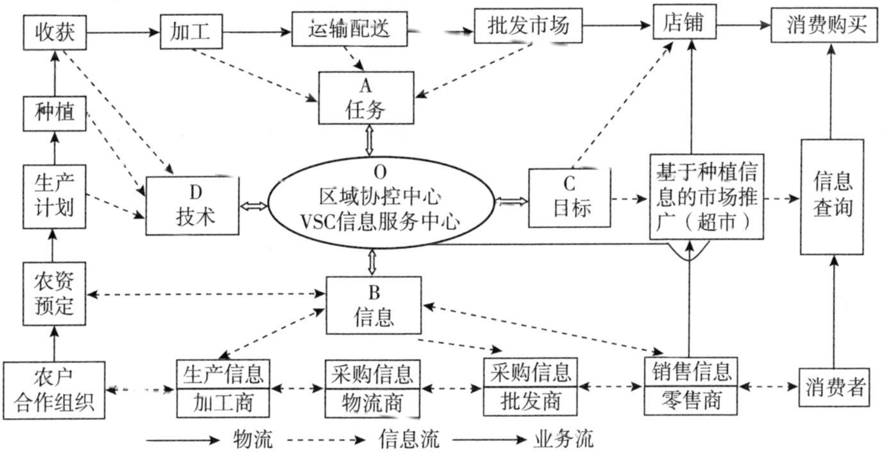

图9－5　西部地区农产品供应链的区域协控中心信息共享综合模式

西部地区农产品供应链的区域协控中心的信息共享模式能够降低西部地区农产品物流成本，防范农产品价格巨幅波动，尤其是建立农户合作组织能更好实现西部地区农产品快速调配和优化，提高整体竞争力。首先，农户合

作社的集体信誉代替了农户个体信誉。避免了分散的农户个体与上下游企业进行信息交换时所产生的“道德风险”和“逆向选择”行为，提高了信息的准确性，保护了农户和其他节点的利益。农户合作社作为一个主体，由于契约和制度的作用，要向整个供应链提供准确的信息，对于其他节点，由于农户合作社可实施集体惩罚，也要向农户组织提供准确的信息。其次，作为农户合作组织，可以统一对当地农户的生产信息进行发布，对农户的需求信息进行设计，并通过各种方式获得外部信息并及时反馈给农户。再次，农户合作组织在信息设备的投资上具有优势，还可以聘请专业人士对信息设备进行管理，也可以聘请专人负责农产品信息的获取和发布工作，及时获得和传递准确信息，提高农户信息共享的速度和准确度[494]。

（三）西部地区农产品供应链的区域协控中心的协作调控机制

西部地区农产品供应链的区域协控中心委员会建立目标制、准时制等供应链管理方法的协作调控机制。西部地区农产品供应链的区域协控中心对目标进行分解，建立一套完整的目标体系。将目标分解和任务界定后，区域协控中心的协作调控工作就变成了为满足目标任务的实现而采取的伙伴物流组织间的管理措施，即实现目标管理。目标管理是一种参与式管理，要求所有的核心能力伙伴和部分外围伙伴物流组织参与整体目标的建立及其分解工作，同时要求合作伙伴的物流组织，在各自的职能发挥中实行自我调控，并努力完成工作目标。区域协控中心任务或目标在执行过程中，同样受到其他多方面条件的限制和约束，如区域协控中心的业务发生过程中，要求物流组织的合作伙伴之间能够默契配合，实现由采购、运输、仓储到配送等一系列上下游业务过程的适时、顺利的衔接。同时，在采用准时制与供应链管理方法，不仅是业务过程的需要，同时也可以规范伙伴物流组织的业务行为，减少伙伴物流组织间因业务问题而产生的矛盾，以保证西部地区农产品供应链的区域协控中心运转的协调控制机制的建立。

四　西部地区农产品供应链的区域协控中心的约束机制

（一）西部地区农产品供应链的区域协控中心的激励约束机制

农产品供应链是围绕核心企业构建的功能网链结构，其中，核心企业作为供应链的发起者充当委托人的角色，其他节点充当代理人的角色。由于供应链各节点是独立的个体，拥有自身的核心利益，而这种利益可能和供应链的整体利益是不一致的，因此它们可能会向供应链中的合作者隐瞒部分信息，所以在农产品供应链中信息是不对称的。要充分发挥农产品供应链的整体功能，第一条途径是建立可靠的信息共享渠道，消除信息不对称。第二条途径是建立一种激励约束机制，在不改变信息结构的情况下，通过委托方对代理方实施利益协调和让渡，消除代理方进行机会主义行为的利益动机[494]。

1. 西部地区农产品供应链的区域协控中心激励约束机制的建立

从微观经济学和博弈论的角度来看，激励机制实际上是一种对供应链成员企业适用的契约或合同，是用来规范成员企业行动的约束或制度。激励约束机制应是核心企业（委托方）按照如下程序建立的：第一，委托方要分析并建立自己的收益与代理方的行为（道德风险）之间的关系。第二，委托方应考虑提升代理方行为的积极性（与整条供应链和委托方的绩效为负相关），或者阻止其相关行为（与整条供应链和委托方的绩效为负相关）。首先，委托方的收益必须分析监督并分析监督成本，因为代理方的行为总是期望减少代理方支付共享信息的成本。其次，代理方的行为（道德风险）影响委托方的希望行为（道德风险）的效用。最后，委托方与代理方实现双赢要求委托方必须对代理方提供大于代理人不接受合同时能够获得的最大收益的激励。

2. 西部地区农产品供应链的区域协控中心的激励方式

西部地区农产品供应链的区域协控中心激励机制的目标是建立链间的战略合作伙伴关系，相互信任、信息共享，每个成员都充分发挥自己的核心竞争力，以实现资源的整合优势，增加供应链的总效益。西部地区农产品供应链的区域协控中心可利用的激励方式有：

（1）合同激励。西部地区农产品供应链的区域协控中心合同的签署是具有法律效力的，它是供应链契约的一种具体形式。能促进成员企业按照合同行事，促进农产品供应链节点之间的协控运作。

（2）信任激励。西部地区农产品供应链的区域协控中心节点间的相互信任可达成战略层协控、战术层协控和操作层协控。通过合理的利益分配机制，使这种相互信任的合作伙伴关系得以稳定。同时又进一步增强互信，从而使各成员在长期合作关系中获得最大利益。

（3）信息激励。在西部地区农产品供应链的区域协控中心，如果一节点企业能够准确、快捷地获得合作企业的需求信息，并主动采取措施提供优质服务，会使合作方的满意度大大提高。供应链成员在信息不断产生的条件下，始终保持对信息的渴望，也更加关注合作方的运行状况，不断寻求解决新问题的方法。

（4）价格激励。西部地区农产品供应链的区域协控中心的上游企业和下游企业，应根据供应链不同节点的具体情况和特征，分别采用不同的价格激励方式。例如，西部地区农产品供应链的区域协控中心的加工企业为了保障农产品原料供应的稳定性和农户的生产积极性，可设定最低收购价来保护和激励农户进行农产品的种植和生产。

（5）信誉激励。无论对农户（农户合作组织）、加工企业还是零售企业来说，信誉都极其重要。从委托代理角度来看，代理人的业务量取决于其过去的代理质量与合作水平，因此，代理人要积极地提高产品质量和运作水平，从而来提高自己的信誉。

（6）淘汰激励。为了不被供应链所淘汰，西部地区农产品供应链的区域协控中心节点成员就必须承担一定的责任和义务，对自己承担的供货任务负有全方位的责任。

（二）西部地区农产品供应链的区域协控中心的利益分配机制

西部地区农产品供应链的区域协控中心各节点利益分配不合理的表现主要是各成员之间的相互利益冲突。造成利益分配不合理的原因很复杂，但总体而言主要是没有建立有效的薪酬决定制度，或制度虽有，但执行不力。从广义上说，西部地区农产品供应链的区域协控中心是由农户、龙头企业、加工商、物流企业、批发商、经销商、零售商等利益相关者共同建立维系的。区域协控中心的发展需兼顾各方利益，处于强势的主体（如龙头企业、加工商、物流企业）不应剥夺弱势主体（农户）的正当利益。强势群体之间也应着眼于长远发展。缓解强弱主体之间的利益冲突主要对策是对强势的主体进行制衡，防止其滥用控制权。对弱势主体的利益加强保护，让弱势的主体也能分享西部地区农产品供应链的区域协控中心发展的利益。

西部地区农产品供应链的区域协控中心在建立合理利益分配和监督机制要做到以下两个方面：第一，建立“以人为本”的理念，重人轻利；

第二，重视制度建设，建立起区域协控中心的利益相关者如何参与利益分配的机制，并重视制度落实。如果没有合理的利益分配机制和监督机制，西部地区农产品供应链的区域协控中心将失去相关主体的支持，区域协控中心发展不可持续。因此，建立西部地区农产品供应链的区域协控中心的合理的利益分配机制和监督机制是农产品物流正常运行的前提，是西部地区农产品物流可持续发展的保障。

第二节　西部地区农产品物流可持续发展模式的运行管理

从西部地区农产品物流可持续发展的模式运行设计可以看出，西部地区农产品供应链的区域协控中心是一个基于资源整合、降低成本、提高整体效率为目的的系统工程。这一系统功能的顺利实现，需要有效的管理来确保农产品物流可持续发展模式的运行安全。构建区域协控中心作为一种现代物流管理模式，在其酝酿、组建、运行及解体等不同阶段都存在一定的风险，尤其是在市场、法律环境尚未完善的条件下，基于区域协控中心的区位化双层物流联盟成员间容易出现互不信任和不规范的行为，从而导致区域协控中心管理模式的中途失败，给农产品物流活动带来不必要的损失。因此，在提出西部地区农产品物流可持续发展模式的运行设计的基础上，需要对其实践中消除基于区域协控中心的区位化双层物流联盟运作风险和不断优化其空间结构进行必要的探索。

一　基于区域协控中心的区位化双层物流联盟的运作风险

（一）风险类型

基于区域协控中心的区位化双层物流联盟风险是指面对西部地区农产品物流复杂的内外部环境，在西部地区农产品供应链的区域协控中心运作过程中，由西部地区农产品物流区位化双层物流联盟成员不顾联盟利益和外部环境的不确定因素，导致区位化双层物流联盟偏离预定目标或利益损失。风险可以分为基于区域协控中心的区位化双层物流联盟内部环境引致的风险和农产品物流本身的外部环境所产生的风险两类。

1. 外部风险

（1）政策风险。一方面，政府由于宏观调控或体制改革而引起的政策方向、法律法规的调整可能会带来风险，比如，国家取消现有对农业财税、金融、土地使用等扶持政策，农产品进口国对农产品进口标准的提高等；另一方面，地方政府还可能出于其他原因直接干预物流市场，影响基于区域协控中心的区位化双层物流联盟企业实现既定目标。

（2）市场风险。需求变动：由于不可控因素可能导致某种农产品产量过大，价格下降，物流需求过低，减少基于区域协控中心的区位化双层物流联盟组织的规模收益。同时，市场油价升高，会增加农产品物流成本。

（3）金融风险。利率的变动：可能会影响农户贷款成本的增加，物流企业、农产品销售企业融资成本的增加；汇率的变动：直接影响农产品的出口收益；全球或地区性的金融危机：可能导致农户、农产品物流企业、农产品销售企业筹资困难，并直接导致农产品价格和销量的下降。

（4）自然风险。由于未知的自然灾害导致农产品的物流时间被延长，导致农产品在运输过程中变质，同时也会增加物流成本。

（5）技术风险。第三方物流企业在包装、加工或运输上技术水平有缺陷，或者办事人员的疏忽，会导致农产品的损耗，影响基于区域协控中心的区位化双层物流联盟企业的经营成果。

2. 内部风险

（1）沟通风险。由于联络渠道的阻塞或相互沟通的积极性不足，导致时间进程安排上的脱节，甚至可能出现联盟伙伴错误的理解指令，导致基于区域协控中心的区位化双层物流联盟组织在时间上和资源上的浪费。

（2）组织管理风险。由于各个成员有各自不同的企业文化和管理模式，因而在相互协作中可能会出现一些在管理和组织方面的冲突，这些冲突如果解决不好，有可能使得组织协调失衡、管理失控，最终导致基于区域协控中心的区位化双层物流联盟组织解体、失败。

（3）道德风险。基于区域协控中心的区位化双层物流联盟的成员之间主要以契约的形式联系起来，同时也是建立在伙伴间相互信任的基础上。由于存在信息不对称性，不排除个别伙伴出现单方面违约，弄虚作假、欺骗伙伴，或泄露合同机密的可能性。另外，农产品供应链下游企业在明知农产品在物流过程中已经变质的情况下，为了自身利益帮助上游隐瞒，最终将威胁民众的生命安全。

（4）流动性风险。包括联盟伙伴的退出以及成员中技术人员的流失和管理人员的变动。核心成员的中途退出会导致项目延误，甚至联盟组织瓦解；一些核心技术人员的流失，将直接导致成员核心能力的削弱，进而影响基于区域协控中心的区位化双层物流联盟的进程；成员企业管理人员发生变动，由于管理者个人偏好的不同，这将影响其参与区域协控中心的区位化双层物流联盟的积极性。

（5）激励风险。基于区域协控中心的区位化双层物流联盟的一个好处是其“双赢”性或“多赢”性，这也是不同主体能够相互结盟的物质前提，但如果在伙伴间不能公平公正地进行利益分配，会导致伙伴参与的积极性降低，甚至出现相互掣肘的局面。

（6）战略柔性丧失风险。由于区域协控中心的区位化双层物流联盟中的伙伴总是拿出自己的核心能力参与协作，往往其自身也比较看重自己的核心能力在目前联盟企业中的地位和重要性，而对自身的非核心能力的重视程度降低，战略管理趋于“刚性化”。当区域协控中心的区位化双层物流联盟企业解体或外部环境发生变化时，则由于缺乏灵活性，无法克服来自联盟企业内部环境的惯性力，出现企业经营“柔性”丧失、在市场上生存能力被削弱的危机。

（二）风险预警

预警是指根据系统外部环境及内部条件的变化，对系统未来的不利事件或风险进行预测和报警。为了有效地防止上述各种物流作业风险，必须建立一个风险预警系统，主要包括基于区域协控中心的区位化双层物流联盟风险的预警指标体系和风险评估方法。

1. 风险指标体系

根据前述的风险类型，可以得到风险预警指标，如图9-6所示。

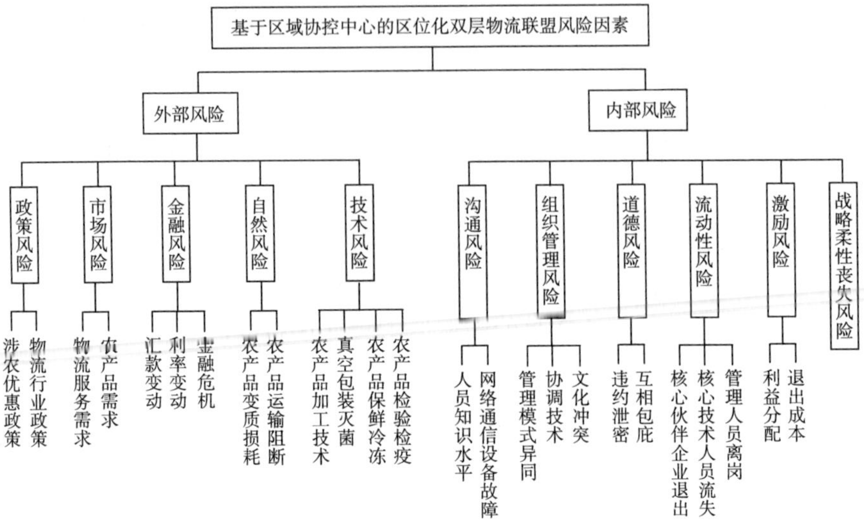

图 9－6　基于区域协控中心的区位化双层物流联盟风险预警指标

2. 风险评估方法

基于案例的推理方法（Case－based Reasoning，CBR），由美国耶鲁大学的教授 Roger Schank 于 1982 年首次提出，是人工智能领域一项重要的推理方法。它是利用过去的案例和经验来解决新问题的一种方法，该技术的最大特点是充分利用已有的案例经验来分析和解决问题，并通过吸收新的案例来增加知识，具有自学习功能，使系统尽量减少人为因素的干扰，CBR 处理流程如图 9－7 所示[495]。

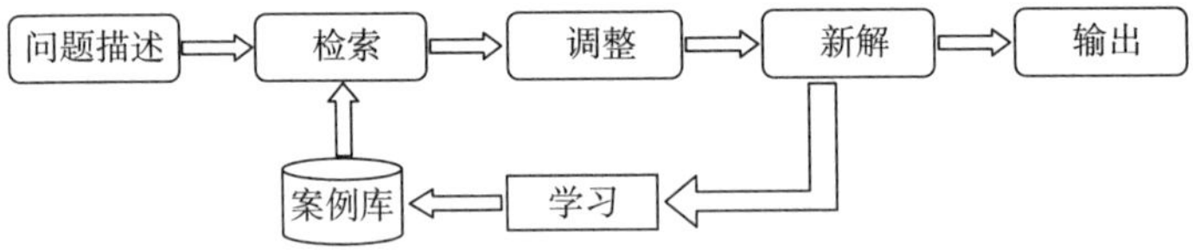

图 9－7　CBR 流程

（三）风险防范

除了建立风险预警机制，有针对性地进行风险控制，更重要的是在日常工作中做好风险防范，采取科学的策略，减少基于区域协控中心的区位化双层物流联盟的不和谐因素。

1. 采用期权理论减少农协与核心物流伙伴的风险

选择第四方物流运作方式可以帮助农协与核心战略合作伙伴，减少农民以及农协和区域协控中心的区位化双层物流联盟之间的合作风险。具体运作形式：建立以第四方物流集成化供应链组织、第三方物流执行组织、农协及农产品生产者在内的利益协作共同体。第四方物流对基于区域协控中心的区位化双层物流联盟运作中技术、信息及相关资源的全面整合，并设计出高效率、高效益的物流执行方案；第三方物流是农产品物流的具体执行载体，承担区域协控中心的区位化双层物流联盟的运输、仓储、装卸搬运、流通加工、包装、配送及相关信息实施者；而农协及农产品生产者是上述运作方式的起点和物流活动发生的源泉。因此，只有建立以第四方物流为核心区域协控中心的区位化双层物流联盟，实现利益均沾、风险共担，信息、技术等资源的共享，才能最大限度地降低合作风险。

2. 促进伙伴企业员工交流，创建“共赢”的文化氛围

建立合作伙伴诚信合作关系，加强契约规定等规范建设，通过建立培训体制、网络论坛创造核心伙伴交流的机会，减少沟通障碍、文化摩擦，培养核心伙伴之间互相信任、互相尊重的环境，树立“共赢”的组织文化。制订对基于区域协控中心的区位化双层物流联盟整体贡献的成员企业间共赢的分配方案，也可在各成员合作所得的基础上设计转移支付机制，将部分收益在成员之间重新分配，从而达到多赢的效果，加快区域协控中心的区位化双层物流联盟对市场需求的响应，维护其稳定和协调发展。同时，建立可靠的信息共享渠道，及时进行信息披露，建立有效的“信誉”机制。宣传农产品物流安全的重要性，建立奖惩机制，宣扬诚信，增加长远利益在伙伴心中的比重。

3. 建立风险管理组织，科学选择供应链合作伙伴

为有效地规避和应对基于区域协控中心的区位化双层物流联盟风险，农户组织、批发商企业和零售商企业都可以建立风险管理组织。风险管理组织可以采取矩阵结构形式，企业各个部门的人员共同参与风险管理，共同承担风险管理的责任。在此之上建立对风险管理负有全部责任的风险管理委员会，管理协调各部门的工作。基于区域协控中心的区位化双层物流联盟的节点企业在选择合作伙伴时，应建立全面的评价指标体系并采用科学的方法对合作伙伴进行选择，设计柔性的多头供应链，使得产生“有害选择”的概率大大降低。

二 基于区域协控中心的区位化双层物流联盟的空间优化

（一）空间的区位分类

基于区域协控中心的区位化双层物流联盟空间是大量在地理位置上集中且与农产品的生产、加工、交易、出口相互关联的产业、企业、中介组织、农产品贸易组织及综合服务机构等，在一定的地域上形成以农户或产地为发端，以西部地区一级、二级物流中心为连接点，以区域协控中心为供应链的核心，以国内外物流中心为依托点，形成的网链式物流框架体系，提供农产品区位化双层物流联盟一体化系列服务的产业群体广域性空间组合的经济现象。西部地区农产品物流区位类型如表 9－1 所示。

表 9－1　西部地区农产品物流区位类型

区位类型	主要功能	布局特点	优势和劣势
区域协控中心物流产业集聚区	整箱、整件集聚、流通加工、短期仓储、包装、运输等	与一级农产品物流中心具有铁路、公路快速通达的干线或支线，分布于沿区域协控中心城区	农产品外贸物流枢纽和外贸规模的优势；对一级、二级物流中心要求较高
一级物流中心或集聚区	集散、整理、配货、流通加工、包装、冷冻冷藏、信息服务等职能	与二级农产品物流中心有快速通道，汇集区域性农产品向区域协控中心集结，分布于省市中心	借助其将所辐射的服务半径形成规模优势；但受所在区域专业化种植规模的限制
二级物流中心或集聚区	邻近农产品产区，集中专业化种植区农产品，简单的拣选、整理及粗加工	连接产地零星的单一物流职能组织（私营物流企业和个人），分布于乡镇一级区域内	临近产区，即可直通区域协控中心，又可集聚于一级中心；易受产区规模和自身组织化程度制约
龙头企业农产品纵向一体化物流组织	集产、供、销、物流一体化，并形成自己的农产品交易与物流体系	绿色化、集约化、规模化种植区域，产业化、组织化程度高，单一品种生产规模大	易发挥产、供、销、贸一体化的优势；产业链过长，外部协作化水平低，影响成本降低
第三方农产品物流组织	具有区域性物流公司的性质，市场自发型衍生的农产品专业物流中心	分布于农产品流通中心和交易中心附近地区，兼有农产品内外贸一体化性质	专业化、一体化物流水平较高；但分布多集中在城市一级的地区，局限性大
农业集团或公司与农户的农产品物流组织	产与销联盟的农产品物流系统，采取一条龙的运作模式	分布于产业化比较高的专业化种植区域以公司带动区域化的种植基地形式存在	直接面对农户，可发挥连接市场与指导农户的作用；但受专业化物流条件约束，成本较高

西部地区农产品物流空间可以分为四种类型：①腹地型：位于农业生产作业区附近的二级物流中心空间；②边缘型：位于市级城市周边的一级物流中心空间；③临近型：位于临近区域协控中心周边的物流空间；④内部型：位于区域协控中心作业区内部的物流空间。

（二）空间结构的优化

作为农产品生产的现代农业示范基地、高科农业园区、产业化“龙头”企业、农产品出口基地和特色农产品基地及农户，从产前至产后，涉及相对广泛而复杂的物流业务，并纳入农业生产的综合服务体系之中，而基于区域协控中心的西部地区农产品物流则涵盖了包括区域协控中心、物流中心或集聚区以及其他物流组织复合型物流集成的经济活动，且在地域上构成了以区位化双层物流联盟为主轴的相互关联性产业集群。结合西部七大特色农业基地已形成七条产业带的状况，以及西部后续开发期间依托重点支持的大型农业产业化500家“龙头”企业的要求，根据产业区域空间布局状况，显现出优势产业带在农业资源结构和空间结构所呈现的区域特点，具体如表9－2所示。

表9－2　西部七大特色产业带物流的不同区域组合特征

区域	农业资源结构	农业产业结构	产业空间结构
新疆优质棉花生产基地	以对象型资源为主，交通的进步使资源在区域空间内重新配置，区域的协作化水平凸显，技术资源的作用日益重要	协作互动型产业结构调整思路，关键把农业产业化经营和县域经济发展与加强农业综合生产能力建设等结合起来，用产业化的办法提升农业，实现工农业互动	空间结构程凝聚状态，随纺织工业的集中，形成了少数大型节点。部分地区得到极化，社会经济发展水平呈现出依资源的不同而形成地域上的分异现象，空间差异缩小
云南、内蒙古和新疆糖料生产基地	以产业整合和建立增值链，形成较大规模的农业产业集群，培育农产品加工技术组合能力，在整体上增强区域技术创新能力	结构导向型的产业结构是通过调整区域产业结构，建立起以主导产业为核心，农业资源的综合开发和加工制造协调发展的产业结构，带动区域经济的全面发展	空间扩散成为主流，区域内小型节点快速成长，大中型节点的通道建设加快，生产力流量扩大，跨区域节点间由通道连接的水平网络形成，区域内由不同等级通道连接的多级垂直网络形成，等级体系较完整

续表 9-2

区域	农业资源结构	农业产业结构	产业空间结构
新疆瓜果、云南元谋、甘肃河西走廊和青海蔬菜生产基地	以推动产业转移找准自己在地区产业链中的定位。依靠科学技术充分利用两个市场资源，推动区域资源整合技术	技术导向型产业结构是使区域产业结构向高度技术、高附加值方向转变，大力增强特色产业在整个产业结构中的比重，直到成为主导产业	空间结构在扩散力和积聚力的双重引导下迅速重组。一方面出现大型特色产业聚集区等高级节点；另一方面城乡一体化和城乡融合过程迅速推进，有形通道内价值流比重迅速增加
云南、内蒙古和新疆花卉生产基地	以资源的深度开发利用为重点，实现经济增长由资源—产品—产业链的多向性过渡，朝着产业的纵向一体化的渐进式循环过程转变	内生型产业结构为调整方向，增强产业自我发展和自我提升的内在动力；大培育产业链和产业簇群，通过“龙头”产业带动，形成具有技术优势和市场竞争力的产业或产业集群	以价值链空间布局区域产业集群，形成层次不同的外向空间、承接空间、腹地空间三种形态，构建一个按照“进口（创新）—生产—出口”的产业空间结构，并以全方位、多层次、梯度性展开，产业的纵向延伸在空间结构呈财富创造的“经济马赛克”现象——产业集群化
宁夏、甘肃、新疆、青海中药材生产基地	以技术资源优势为可持续发展的动力，建立山岭、邱地等资源的协控开发机制，注重纵向一体化的产业联动效应	互动型产业结构调整思路，关键是采用现代农业种植技术，加强农业综合生产能力建设的结合，加大了产业的技术、信息等含量的推广力度	由地缘空间链接的经济合作区域，不仅有区位条件、更具有跨地缘联系的市场兼容。靠市场推动，包括通过“梯度转移”“自由化贸易”“经济区位空间结构整合”等作用推动
云南烟叶生产基地	以区位条件为发展根基，禀赋地区技术资源，促进产业的多元化发展，通过机制创新实现产业的梯度转移	联动型产业结构为发展方向，强化产业之间的波及和联动效应，培育综合产业服务体系，通过农业企业集团以带动农户和基地的方式，实现产业结构的纵深化	空间结构以区域内部空间结构的有序化以及与地区主流空间的紧密连接，为社会、经济实现可持续发展的目标，产业之间的关联性促使地区产业空间的布局呈一体化发展倾向
西南地区热带水果基地	以热带经济为立足点，建立多元化交叉型经济发展模式，通过技术改造实现标准化，实施热带经济作物立体化联合开发体系	引导型产业结构为调整方向，将技术、资金投入作为产业可持续发展的动力，注重于产业链条的培育和衔接，并将热带资源作为农业产业结构优化调整的手段	空间结构以热带经济资源为依托，产业“区域空间结构优化”波及至技术的创新成为市场扩散的主要手段，形成具有鲜明特色的优势产业带，逐步适应国际化合作与竞争的农业产业空间体系

续表 9－2

区域	农业资源结构	农业产业结构	产业空间结构
西北地区优质水果生产基地	以传统优势产业资源为重点并向多极化综合产业体系的转变，依靠科学、网络信息手段完成产业一体化的飞跃和升级	资源导向型的产业结构朝高加工度方向发展，资金和技术含量迅速增加，农业的集约化程度提高，农村服务业中生产性服务迅速发展	产业空间以优势农产品为基点，衍生出地域广阔分布的产品加工制造产业集群，且与知识、技术、信息等产业组织节点的耦合性增强，空间分布增长极大，产业体系趋于完备和国际化

随着全球经济一体化时代的到来，中国农业产业化发展的外向型经济发展战略必然要求西部地区农业产业融入全球经济的主流空间。西部地区农产品物流空间结构依托区域协控中心资源具有强烈的辐射效应，加速农产品物流效率，适时优化区位化双层物流联盟空间结构，使西部地区农产品内外贸物流空间达到最佳状态，实现西部地区农业资源配置、获取最大的空间联盟效应和提高总要素生产力。如图 9－8 所示，西部地区农产品物流网络流程的上游为“节点”代表农户；中游为一级、二级物流中心（批发市场或加工组织）、区域协控中心；下游目的地为国内的农产品商贸企业（贸易代理组织或批发）的物流中心及消费终端、国外的农产品进口商贸企业（贸易代理组织或批发）的物流中心及消费终端。连接上、中、下游直至零售终端的公路、铁路、水路及航空等运输方式，构成农产品物流网络的“路线”。

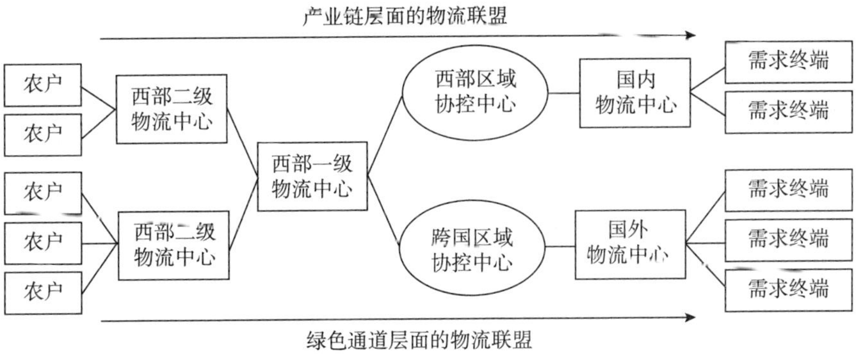

图 9－8　基于区域协控中心的区位化双层物流联盟空间结构的优化

（三）空间结构的层次优化

以区域协控中心为核心的西部地区农产品物流区位化双层物流联盟空间结构的层次包括区域空间体系、区域协控中心—腹地物流协作的空间体系及国际物流空间体系三个层面结构优化与创新。

第一层面：区域体系的空间优化。各级物流中心彼此之间的分工与协作体系的进一步优化，整体上要形成布局合理、层次清晰、功能明确的物流网络体系的布局。扩大区域性农产品物流中心的多向辐射，并形成向区域协控中心结集的运作格局，统筹铁路、公路、航空等运输资源，明确分工，错位经营，扬长避短，体现各自的功能特色。将区域协控中心的综合功能开发与农业产业集群的物流紧密结合起来，完成“纵横相交”的“米”形区位化双层物流联盟空间主干框架网络体系（“一纵”是指产业链层面联盟。“一横”是指绿色通道层面联盟。“相交”是指链间点与线对接，即节点带动网络、干线带动支线），实现农产品物流可持续发展规划相衔接和统一。

第二层面：区域协控中心—腹地空间体系的优化。加快区域协控中心—腹地物流一体化进程，发挥腹地农产品物流中心的集散功能和辐射作用，进一步发挥区域协控中心在区域经济社会以及国民经济发展的影响力。以区域协控中心为核心是推动西部地区农产品物流区位化双层物流联盟集约化、网络化的重要内容和途径，但还要正视西部地区农产品供应链的区域协控中心发展过程中来自外部的一系列挑战，特别是在资源整合、管理体制、服务功能、部门条块分割、设施建设、运行效率、竞争秩序等方面还存在较多的问题。一方面要加快区域协控中心与腹地的物流网络统一规划，具体是区域协控中心服务职能的延伸、物流资源结构调整、物流区位优化、技术和制度创新；另一方面是区域协控中心—腹地的公共服务设施与基础设施建设的同步发展，实现区域协控中心—腹地区域、区域协控中心—城市区域物流组织的区位化双层物流联盟，最终实现区域协控中心—腹地的内外贸物流一体化目标。

第三层面：农产品国际物流空间体系的优化。以订单农业为基点，借助西部地区农产品供应链的区域协控中心整合产区、农业产业集群、城乡第三方物流、国内外物流中心等物流资源，通过协同经济的增量效益从而实现创新的集群经济共同发展的道路。明晰西部地区农产品供应链的区域协控中心中物流产业组织的分工，实现上游与下游组织之间的互动发展，建立农产品物流需求链，延伸扩大区域协控中心—腹地范围。采取柔性化的产业聚集，形成具有适应市场变化而快速反应能力的跨国物流虚拟组织的区域协控中心。一是区域协控中心物流组织内部农产品生产加工作业与管理方式的柔性化。具有能适应国外不同客户与不同规模物流定制要求的高灵活性。二是与国外物流中心及终端客户的衔接。在空间上形成跨国界的物流组织间协作与合作分工体系，实现彼此间业务关系的柔性化。以区域协控中心整合实现价值增值的西部地区农产品物流区位化双层物流联盟，使物流链上中下游的组织之间形成一个互动的利益共同体。通过实现供应链环节中各企业的信息沟通、数据互换和协同作业，改造和优化外贸物流的业务流程，通过缩短交货周期、降低周转库存，降低产业集群的运行成本，实现区域规模经济和范围经济效益，提高西部地区农产品的国际竞争力。

第三节　西部地区农产品物流可持续发展模式的综合评价

西部地区农产品物流可持续发展完成模式的创建和运行后，应该进行西部地区农产品物流可持续模式的综合评价，通过评价能够对体系的运转效率、发展前景、存在问题进行评估，成为西部地区农产品物流可持续战略体系机制调整、不断优化的基础。

一　西部地区农产品物流可持续发展评价指标体系的构建

（一）体系构建原则

为了能科学、客观地反映评价对象，应该建立与农产品物流产业运行机制相配套的实效性强、覆盖面广、结构合理的指标体系，在设立指标的过程中，既要立足于我国的国情，又要与现阶段的西部地区发展水平相适应，并符合国家政府的发展方针，还要逐步与国际农产品物流相接轨。因此，应发挥西部特殊优势以及区域协控中心与区位化双层物流联盟的特点，本研究认为建立有效的西部地区农产品物流可持续发展评价指标体系应遵循以下原则：

1. 科学性原则

评价指标体系是理论和实际结合的产物，它必须是对客观实际的抽象描述。农产品物流可持续发展涉及的因素很多，如何对其进行高度的抽象、概括，如何在抽象、概括中抓住最重要、最有代表性的东西，是设计指标体系的关键和难点。

2. 系统性原则

对农产品物流可持续发展的评价是一个涵盖多因素、多目标的复杂系统，评价指标体系应力求全面反映农产品物流的综合情况，既能反映系统的内部结构与功能，又能正确评估系统与外部环境的关联，组成一个相互联系、相互对应的有机整体。

3. 客观性原则

要求指标能客观地反映农产品物流可持续发展的内涵，各子系统和指标之间应该相互联系，并能较好地量化农产品物流可持续发展目标的实现程度。评价的目的是为了决策，因此评价的质量影响着决策的正确性，所以必须弄清评价资料是否全面、正确、可靠。

4. 可比性原则

我国到目前为止没有进行专门的西部地区农产品物流统计指标，仍然处于摸索阶段，因此设计指标的内涵、外延、设计口径、计量标准，既要保持相对的独立，又要与国际标准保持一致，这样才可以与国外的资料进行对比分析。

5. 针对性原则

西部地区农产品物流可持续发展指标体系的建立应与西部地区农产品物流发展特征和行业发展状态相适应，能够满足西部地区现实需求。评价指标应尽量包括评价对象的各个方面，同时要结合区域协控中心、区位化双层物流联盟、可持续发展能力的特点和评价重点进行，对关键的统计指标进行重点分析。

(二) 评价指标体系

西部地区农产品物流可持续发展评价指标体系的分析框架，根据西部地区物流业发展现状及现阶段关注的重点，指标体系包括区域协控中心、区位化双层物流联盟、可持续发展能力共3个一级指标、7个二级指标、45个三级指标[496-499]，如表9-3所示。

表9-3　西部地区农产品物流可持续发展评价指标体系

一级指标	二级指标	三级指标
区域协控中心 A_1——内部运行	B_1——标准与规范对接平台	C_1——农产品深加工技术水平
		C_2——冷藏与保鲜技术水平
		C_3——包装与检测技术水平
		C_4——协控技术的综合化水平
		C_5——协控中心网络组织合同生效比例
		C_6——组织主体间协议的信任与公平度
		C_7——组织成员间权利与义务维护度
	B_2——电子商务对接平台	C_8——农产品信息动态共享率
		C_9——农产品信息集中协控率
		C_{10}——农产品信息传递有效率
		C_{11}——农产品信息利用价值率
		C_{12}——网上订单信息实现率
	B_3——电子口岸对接平台	C_{13}——风险评估与风险管理方案
		C_{14}——快速通关和双向保税功能
		C_{15}——电子化监督与服务体系
		C_{16}——新型交易方式采用灵活度
区位化双层物流联盟 A_2——外部运行	B_4——产业链层面与绿色通道层面	C_{17}——战略层的战略联盟
		C_{18}——战略层的利益联盟
		C_{19}——运作层的组织联盟
		C_{20}——运作层的流程联盟
		C_{21}——运作层的信息联盟
		C_{22}——运作层的标准联盟
		C_{23}——文化层的文化联盟

续表 9－3

一级指标	二级指标	三级指标
可持续发展能力 A_3——综合运行	B_5——农产品物流目标维度	C_{24}——制度可持续
		C_{25}——结构可持续
		C_{26}——规模可持续
		C_{27}——速度可持续
	B_6——农产品物流价值维度	C_{28}——商品完好率
		C_{29}——交货合格率
		C_{30}——订单满足率
		C_{31}——采购计划完成率
		C_{32}——供货计划完成率
		C_{33}——交货产品新鲜度
		C_{34}——客户投诉率
		C_{35}——产品满意程度
	B_7——农产品物流发展维度	C_{36}——农产品跨地区销售受限程度
		C_{37}——农产品市场交易规范化程度
		C_{38}——经营环境竞争的公平性
		C_{39}——法律制度的完善性
		C_{40}——政府服务的高效性
		C_{41}——物流各方遵守交易契约的信用度
		C_{42}——农产品物流综合服务组织的协作性
		C_{43}——员工专业技术培训比例
		C_{44}——高级专业技术人才比例
		C_{45}——流程、技术、管理创新

二　西部地区农产品物流可持续发展模式的综合评价方法

对农产品物流的综合评价可以采取两大类评价方法：一类是以特尔菲法专家评价为代表的主观赋权综合评价方法；另一类是以因子分析为代表的客观赋权的综合评价方法[500,501]。本研究采用因子分析方法。

基于西部地区农产品物流可持续发展评价指标体系，具有多层次、多因素的特点，且不确定因素较多。因子分析以最少的信息丢失把众多的原始变量浓缩成少数的几个因子变量，用它们来概括和解释具有错综复杂关系的大量的观测事实，从而建立起最简洁、最基本的概念系统，揭示出事物之间最本质的联系。因子分析法对于指标体系中存在较多无法准确量化的指标比较适用。因此，本研究将选用因子分析综合评价方法进行西部地区农产品物流可持续发展模式的评价。在进行指标权重计算中，决定采用三角模糊数法进行权重计算。

（一）因子分析的综合评价方法

设有 N 个样本，P 个指标变量，存在 m 个潜在的公共因子，原公共因子变量为 B_1，B_2，…，B_m。经标准化后的公共因子变量记为 $F=$（F_1，F_2，…，F_m）T，变换后的新变量均用 C 表示，$C=$（C_1，C_2，…，C_p）T，则模型为：

$$\begin{cases} C_1 = \alpha_{11}F_1 + \alpha_{12}F_2 + \cdots + \alpha_{1m}F_m + \varepsilon_1 \\ C_2 = \alpha_{21}F_1 + \alpha_{22}F_2 + \cdots + \alpha_{2m}F_m + \varepsilon_2 \\ \cdots \\ C_p = \alpha_{p1}F_1 + \alpha_{p2}F_2 + \cdots + \alpha_{pm}F_m + \varepsilon_p \end{cases}$$

矩阵形式为：

$$C = RF + \varepsilon, 其中\ R = \begin{bmatrix} r_{11} & r_{12} & \cdots & r_{1m} \\ r_{21} & r_{22} & \cdots & r_{2m} \\ \cdots & \cdots & \cdots & \cdots \\ r_{p1} & r_{p2} & \cdots & r_{pm} \end{bmatrix}$$

其中，C_1，C_2，…，C_p表示 p 个均值为 0、标准差为 1 的原有变量；F_1，F_2，…，F_m表示 m 个因子变量；矩阵 $R=$（r_{ij}）称为因子载荷阵。找出公因子就是采用某种方法找出因子载荷阵 R。r_{ij}为指标变量 x_i（$i=1$，2，…，p）在公共因子 F_j（$j=1$，2，…，m）上的载荷，为特殊因子。数学上可以证明，因子载荷 α_{ij} 就是第 i 变量与第 j 因子的相关系数，反映了第 i 变量在第 j 因子上的重要性。ε_1、ε_2、…、ε_p 为特殊因子，特殊因子起着残差的作用，但被定义为彼此不相关而且和公共因子也不相关。对所得到的各因子，先观察它们在哪些变量上的载荷较大或较小，再根据载荷大的变量本身的内容来说明因子额含义。然后将每个公因子表示为变量的线性组合，并用变量的观测值来估计各个因子的得分。

（二）三角模糊数法的评价步骤

为了使各指标具有可比性，并有利于综合因子的解释，本研究采用三角模糊数方法。三角模糊数法在综合决策中①，指标因素的权重处于非常重要的地位，它反映了各个指标因素在综合决策过程中所起的作用，直接影响到综合决策的结果[502,503]。下面介绍用三角模糊数确定 AHP 指标权数的主要步骤[504,505]。

（1）根据问题的总目标，建立分层指标体系。

（2）专家对评价指标进行两两比较，即针对第 k 层全部指标与 $k-1$ 层某一指标进行两两比较，用三角模糊数构造模糊判断矩阵。设判断矩阵评分邀请 T 位专家，第 t 位专家给出的第 k 层判断矩阵为 $A^{(t)}=(a_{ij}^{(t)})_{n\times m}$，其中 $a_{ij}^{(t)}=(l_{ij}^{(t)},m_{ij}^{(t)},u_{ij}^{(t)})$。根据公式

$$a_{ij}=\frac{1}{T}\otimes(a_{ij}^{(1)}\oplus a_{ij}^{(2)}\oplus\cdots\oplus a_{ij}^{(t)})=\left[\frac{\sum_{t=1}^{T}l_{ij}^{(t)}}{T},\frac{\sum_{t=1}^{T}m_{ij}^{(t)}}{T},\frac{\sum_{t=1}^{T}m_{ij}^{(t)}}{T}\right] \tag{9-1}$$

（3）对于各模糊判断矩阵，计算各个元素的综合重要程度 S_j。可以计算出第 k 层全体元素针对第 $k-1$ 层中第 h 个元素的综合模糊判断矩阵。再根据公式：$S_i^k=\sum_{j=1}^{n_k}a_{ij}\otimes\left(\sum_{i=1}^{n_k}\sum_{j=1}^{n_k}a_{ij}\right)-1$，计算出第 k 层第 i 个元素针对第 $k-1$ 层中第 h 个元素，相对于其他元素的综合重要程度值。

（4）层次单排序。根据三角模糊数基本计算法则，

当 $m_1<m_2$ 时，

$$V(M_1\geq M_2)=\begin{cases}\dfrac{l_2-u_2}{(m_1-u_1)-(m_2-l_2)},(l_2<u_1)\\0,(\text{其他})\end{cases} \tag{9-2}$$

① 荷兰学者 Van Laarhoven 于 1983 年提出了用三角模糊数表示模糊比较判断的方法，把 AHP 拓展为能够在模糊环境下适用的 FAHP。通过把模糊数学的方法引入到 AHP 判断矩阵构造中，可以在充分考虑个人判断的模糊性的基础上使判断矩阵构造更加合理，同时避免了一致性检验这一步骤，这种模糊 AHP 的方法被称为三角模糊数层次分析法。

当 $m_1 > m_2$ 时，$V(M_1 \geq M_2) = 1$

$$d'(C_i) = V(M_i \geq M_1, M_2, \cdots, M_{i-1}, M_{i+1}, \cdots, M_n) = \min V(S_i \geq S_k), \\ k = 1, 2, \cdots, i-1, i+1, \cdots, n \tag{9-3}$$

对各模糊判断矩阵，计算第 i 个元素 A_i 要重要于其他原则的可能程度。由此得到所有准则的权重向量为

$$w' = (d'(C_1), d'(C_2), \cdots, d'(C_n))^T$$

经过归一化处理，可以得出每个准则的归一化权重值

$$w = (d(C_1), d(C_2), \cdots, d(C_n))^T$$

（5）层次总排序。总排序向量是将评价对象相对于评价指标的权重矩阵与评价指标相对于总目标的权重向量相乘的结果。这样计算的结果，能消除众多信息的重复信息，避免了主观确定权数的随意性，从信息量和系统效应角度来确定权重，比较客观、实际。

综合上述，使用因子分析进行综合评价可以发现各个变量的相关关系，可以找出影响农产品物流效果的主要因素和制约环节。因此，本文构建的农产品物流可持续发展模式运作的综合评价体系，为现阶段西部地区农产品物流产业政策规划的制定、政策实施效果的监测提供具有一定操作性的参考建议。当然，这套综合评价体系须得到国家有关部门的认可，并组织相关力量收集有关数据，再按因子分析的原则和步骤进行分析，一定能得出切合实际的结论。这对西部地区农产品物流运行水平和质量提高，加快农产品物流的可持续发展必定有所裨益。

第十章　西部地区农产品物流可持续发展的机制建设

实现西部地区农产品物流可持续发展，重要的是，在构建可持续发展模式的基础上，建设科学合理的可持续发展机制。西部地区农产品物流可持续机制由政府、农产品物流、农村经济系统的功能与相互关系构成，其核心是制度，关键是政府。因此，可持续发展机制建设，在本质上，就是通过制度设计，使三大系统的功能和相互关系达到理想状态的过程。为此，本章将针对西部地区农产品物流关系结构失调的原因，在确立西部地区农产品物流可持续发展机制建设的基本思路上，坚持以观念创新和政府职能转变为前提，制定和实施可持续发展战略。目标是实现可持续发展，中心是制度可持续，重点是政府行为，手段是制度设计，从宏观制度环境、农村经济和农产品物流这三个方面，展开本研究形成的以营造宏观制度环境为保证，建立综合决策机制加快体制创新；以化解西部地区农村经济约束为基础，建立立体保障机制改善发展质态；以强化西部地区农产品物流功能为突破，建立整体运行机制实现管理创新的可持续发展机制的建设路径。

第一节　西部地区农产品物流可持续发展机制建设的基本思路

西部地区是全国主要的农产品生产基地，在西部 36729 万总人口中，农业人口占到 60% 以上。西部大开发战略实施 10 年来，西部特色农业得到快速发展，国家确定了重点发展西部七大特色农业基地，形成优势产业布局，农产品生产能力显著提高。农产品不仅在国内市场而且在国际市场上都有一定的竞争力。西部地区的区位优势使其区域地位将会更加突出。此外，农产品生产的集中性、地域性与农产品消费的分散性、全球性特点，使得农产品的跨地域流通成为必然。因此，在西部地区农产品物流可持续发展思路上，以观念创新和政府职能转变为前提，制定和实施可持续发展战略。必须以“三个转变”为抓手，走适度开发、高效种养、精深加工、标准化、规范化、生态化、产业化的农产品物流发展道路，逐步把传统的农产品物流，改变为以提高资源配置效率及其再生产能力的现代的农产品物流。

一　由“效率优先、兼顾公平”向“公平高效、规范透明”转变

西部地区农产品物流可持续发展是经济社会可持续发展的内在要求和重要内容。应在“公平”基础上，构建高效率、规范透明的市场经济体制。就西部地区农产品物流可持续发展而言，西部地区农产品物流关系结构失调的原因，在本质上，是西部地区农产品物流与农村经济主体长期受到约束。实现可持续发展，就是赋予西部地区农产品物流与农村经济主体公正平等、规范透明的选择自由和发展机会。一是切实赋予并保护好西部地区农民公正平等、规范透明的市场主体地位。将宪法赋予的公民权真正地落实到实处，并给予制度保护。切实赋予并维护好农民自由选择、自愿交换、自愿合作的市场交易权利。积极稳妥地将农民依法组织起来，实现农民利益代言人制度化和利益集团相互制衡。二是切实赋予并保护好西部地区农产品物流与农村经济公正平等、规范透明的产业地位。市场经济条件下产业具有平等地位和追求效益的权利，认可西部地区农业和农村经济及其农产品物流与其他产业相同。合理区别财政支农、农产品社会性物流和农产品经济性物流之间的关系，加强财政和物流支农的协调配合与可持续，发挥其诱导性机制，保证西部地区农产品物流监管与农村经济发展对西部地区农产品物流创新要求的可持续。三是切实赋予并保护好西部地区不同产权主体公正平等、规范透明的市场地位。西部地区农产品物流关系结构失调的一个重要原因，不仅在于西部地区农产品物流主体与农村经济

主体的产权结构不对称，而且也在于不同产权主体市场地位的不平等。实现西部地区农产品物流可持续发展，不仅要加快西部地区农产品物流产权改革，构建多元化的西部地区农产品物流产权主体，使其产权结构与农村经济发展要求相适应，而且要依法赋予不同产权主体以平等的市场地位。

二　由“城乡分割、相对独立”向“城乡统筹、空间集聚”转变

新中国成立以来，由于初始条件、外部环境和思想认识的限制，尤其是对经济发展中的工农关系认识不牢固，具有强烈的工业和城市倾向，过度获取农村经济资源和剩余，这是导致中国经济、物流二元结构的根源，也是导致西部地区农产品物流关系结构失调最为重要的根本原因。因此，实现西部地区农产品物流可持续发展，必须建立基于交易视角和功能范式的农产品物流发展观。西部地区农产品物流可持续发展既符合可持续发展的一般原理，又具有自身的独特性。必须从西部地区经济发展的全局着眼，通盘考虑，统一决策，彻底改革现行的“城乡分割、相对独立”局面，从根本上解决“三农”问题。一是以可持续发展为原则制定和实施经济发展战略。必须树立科学发展观，从可持续发展角度，正确认识和把握西部地区经济发展中的工农关系、城乡关系，注意维护占人口绝大多数、但仍属于弱势群体的农民权益。在充分发挥地方政府间的经济竞争对中国经济发展重要作用的基础上，以可持续发展为标准，以市场机制的建立和完善为重点，建立有效的政府业绩考核办法和干部任用机制，防止行政区域间过度的经济竞争和地方政府官员片面的政绩观，导致对经济增长的片面追求和短期行为。二是以城乡统筹为手段化解农产品物流二元结构。对西部地区农产品物流可持续发展而言，要充分认识经济系统中工农、城乡必须保持一致可持续发展；要充分认识西部地区农产品物流关系结构失调是受二元性制度压制结果的必然反映；要充分认识城乡统筹发展的重要性，切实实行工业反哺农业、城市支持农村和“多予少取放活”的方针，改善农村基础设施和生态环境条件、落实科技进村入户。三是以空间集聚为方法实现农产品物流关联效益。要走出“以农业论农业”的狭窄圈子，由过去相对独立、二元化的传统农产品物流向空间集聚、一体

化发展的现代农产品物流转变。过去农业的产业化问题，是在二、三产业中将农民排斥出去，现在要打破一、二、三产业的界限，形成一个多元化、多功能的产业体系；要明确把发展“特色农业”“绿色农业”“观光农业”“立体农业”“订单农业”“四季农业”作为富裕西部百姓、加快城乡一体化进程的重要举措之一。以农民增收为目标，重点建设现代特色农业示范基地，全面带动整个西部地区的农业发展现代化水平，建成全国知名的西部地区农产品物流基地；要在全力促进农业循环发展，实现经济效益、生态效益、社会效益最大化的基础上，以现代农业科技示范园为中心，发展种植、畜牧、养殖、粮食、蔬菜加工等产业，不断延长产业链条，建立“种、养、加、销”一体化的现代农产品物流发展模式，使种植业、养殖业、加工业联合成一个整体，实现西部地区农产品物流整体效益，形成以农养畜、以畜带工，以工保经，以经促农的良性循环。

三　由“粗放型、不协调发展”向“集约型、可持续发展”转变

经济转型过程中，西部地区农产品物流关系结构失调的原因复杂多样。实现西部地区农产品物流可持续发展关键在于机制与模式构建。可持续发展的基础是市场经济条件下，政府、西部地区农产品物流主体和农村经济主体功能的发挥，核心在于制度可持续，重点是政府行为与市场行为的可持续。发挥政府职能，实现“集约型”“差别物流”是走出“失调陷阱”、走向“可持续发展”的切入点。但治本在于现代市场制度在西部农村的确立和完善，以及“二元”经济、物流结构的“一元化”。当前应立足西部地区农产品物流的现实情况，走具有西部特色的农产品物流现代化道路。一是建立西部地区农产品物流区位化双层物流联盟的组织模式。打造产业链层面的物流联盟、绿色通道层面的物流联盟，标准化生产型、科技展示型、产业加工型、休闲观光型等，综合体现着生产、加工、冷链物流、农业休闲等多种层级功能，使物流功能得到完善和充分发挥。二是建立西部地区农产品供应链的区域协控中心的运行平台。用现代工业理念做大农业，用现代流通理念做活农业，用现代金融理念做强农业，用现代生态理念做好农业。西部地区独特资源优势，积蓄现代农产品物流未来的

"核心竞争力"。西部地区除了独一无二的环境品牌，生物多样性的资源，也决定了一种多元化的农产品物流开发格局，例如，杨凌代表着干旱、半干旱地区示范辐射的核心地位，汉中是中国南北分界线上最独特的农业品种区。把多样性的资源优势，与多元化的市场需求全面对接，将特色农产品供应链的区域协控中心在西部地区错位布局，着力提高资源产出率、农产品商品率，降低物流成本提高竞争力、实现农产品快速调配和优化、强调农产品生命周期管理和质量安全追溯体系。三是建立健全以生态评价为中心的矛盾梳理体系。找准市场定位，关注生态资源价值，立足全产业链支撑，聚拢核心科技行业地标，最优组合各种生产要素，增强现代农产品物流园区集群力量、扩大辐射半径，以园区为极核丰富多种功能，让区域特色产业有序衔接、循环发展，以实现市场开放共赢，最终实现农民收入的稳步提高，收获经济效益、生态效益和社会的全盘效益。生态评价化解"生态文明"与"经济增长"的矛盾，以控重于治的策略，能够使农产品物流可持续发展过程从"自发"到"自觉"，从"异化"到"本真"，从"失调"到"协调"，有利于整个社会的和谐发展实现。

第二节　以营造宏观制度环境为保证，建立综合决策机制加快体制创新

一　以"制度建设"为核心，构建和完善可持续发展体制

良好的制度环境才能实现西部地区农产品物流可持续发展。就当前而言，就是必须建立和完善社会主义市场经济体制。西部地区农产品物流的健康发展要依赖于良好的外部环境。这主要包括：稳定的政治环境；高效的市场经济环境；健全的制度环境。西部地区农产品物流的健康运营要依赖于良好的制度基础，包括物流制度、信用制度、法律制度、内控制度等。农产品物流产业组织体系必须加快自身的内控制度建设，按行业组织经营范围与特点建立起适应风险防范与发展要求的内控制度，促进农产品

物流产业内各农产品物流企业能协调健康发展。

（一）平衡“生态文明”与“经济增长”的价值取向

西部地区农产品物流可持续发展的价值目标是农产品物流部门在促进农村经济和整个经济可持续发展的前提下，形成的农产品物流与农村实体经济系统，在各自内部组成要素持续协调，以及两者在总量和结构上分别相互持续协调的基础上，实现农产品物流利益的最大化与整体经济、物流系统演进保持可持续的系统演进过程，最终实现经济和社会的和谐发展。经济发展中农产品物流可持续发展模式的表现形态因“生态环境”而各不相同，具有多样性，但成长路径具有一致性。其中最重要的是经由社会制度的作用而实现生态文明。马克思主义生态价值观认为，在人与自然的关系中，不仅人是主体，在某种意义上自然也是主体；不仅人依靠自然，所有生命也都依靠自然。因而人类要尊重生命和自然界。为了缓解不断增加的生态问题与环境危害，应建立可持续发展法规，致力于对供应链与生态链关系的把握；并由狭义的产品生产、加工、贮运、消费逐步发展为以产品生态安全、资源安全、提高制造业综合效益为特征的制造商的供应链与生态链互惠发展。

加快体制创新步伐，建立资源、环境与发展相协调的综合决策机制。在制定规划、调整产业布局时，要综合考虑社会效益、经济效益、生态效益，进行充分论证，避免决策失误，从源头上控制对资源、环境的破坏。一是完善西部地区农产品物流工程可行性论证和西部地区农产品物流环境评估制度；二是建立西部地区农产品物流区位化双层物流联盟（产业链层面、绿色通道层面）的污染总量控制和达标排放“双控”制度；三是建立起与西部地区农村资源总量相适应的农产品供应链区域协控中心的强度控制制度；四是进一步建立、健全法律法规体系，完善监察制度。例如成立西部地区农产品物流综合管理机构，综合协调西部地区12省市区，包括重庆、四川、贵州、云南、西藏、陕西、甘肃、宁夏、青海、新疆、广西、内蒙古农村资源的开发利用和保护，负责西部地区农产品物流总体规划的制定，草拟农产品物流管理的地方性法规及组织重大农产品物流科技攻关，维持农村开发和生产的秩序，监督和保护农村环境与资源，协调处理农产品物流运营中的矛盾，为科学、合理地开发西部地区资源提供保障。

（二）构建“市场为基础”与“政府为主导”的实现平台

发挥市场在可持续发展中的基础性作用。建立规范的西部地区农产品物流市场体系，第一，培育农产品物流市场主体。农产品物流市场参与主体最重要的是农产品物流机构、企业和农民。第二，大力培育农产品物流市场体系。积极为企业可持续、准市场组织可持续、关系网络可持续和社会可持续等可持续形式的发展创造条件。完善农产品物流市场体系是一项长期而复杂的系统工程，既要从硬件着手，又要从软件进行。第三，严格规范农产品物流市场。第四，逐步开放西部地区农产品物流市场。

发挥政府在可持续发展中的主导性作用。以促进农业和农村经济与国民经济可持续发展，以维护社会、农村经济和市场的公平与稳定为目标，提高西部地区农产品物流政策之间的协调性。农产品物流政策按职能不同，可以划分为农产品的物流产业组织政策、物流技术与现代化政策、物流财政金融政策、物流信息政策、物流基础设施设备政策、物流调节与储备政策、物流项目与网点规划政策，等等。这些不同的物流政策之间必须很好地相互配合、相互协调。应力求在西部地区乃至全国范围内保持政策的一致性与协调性，对于一些相互矛盾的政策应尽快加以修改。提高西部地区农产品物流可持续发展的制度创新，以及驾驭市场经济条件下西部地区农产品物流与农村经济关系的宏观调控能力，主动实现政府行为与市场行为的协调，填补市场空缺，弥补市场不足。

二　以“能力建设”为重点，强化政府的可持续发展职能

在市场经济条件下，西部地区农产品物流可持续发展，固然必须要发挥市场的基础性作用，并要充分调动企业、准市场组织、社会和关系网络等各方面力量，但政府是关键。因此，西部地区农产品物流可持续发展重点是通过“能力建设”对政府的可持续发展职能进行强化。

（一）科学界定可持续发展中的政府职能

政府在西部地区农产品物流可持续发展中的职能主要体现在，一是营造好西部地区农产品物流可持续发展的宏观制度环境，为市场机制的有效运行

提供制度框架。当前重点是构建公平高效的社会主义市场经济体制，制定和实施经济社会可持续发展战略。二是通过经济的、行政的和法律的手段，及时纠正“市场失灵”[506]。当前重要的是统筹城乡社会经济发展，就西部地区农产品物流可持续发展而言，必须把西部地区农产品物流可持续发展纳入经济发展的战略规划；必须颁布西部地区农产品物流可持续发展的法律法规；必须把西部地区农产品物流可持续发展列入政府的考核目标。

（二）优化可持续发展中的政府治理结构

对西部地区农产品物流可持续发展而言，当前重要的工作是加强分层治理结构的政府可持续。首先，要通过改进对各级政府和政府官员的考核和任用办法，防止其行为短期化、政绩片面化、竞争过度化，减少利益集团对政府决策的影响。其次，要加强垂直的西部地区农产品物流系统和水平的农村经济系统可持续的制度化。为此，必须构建西部地区农产品物流可持续发展的组织制度。一要在西部地区各级政府成立物流可持续发展委员会，推进西部地区农产品物流可持续发展的领导和宏观决策机构的形成与运行。二要在继续坚持和完善物流垂直治理的基础上，一方面，要以联席会议、信息互通、重大决策共议，以及必要的沟通、会商形式，加强中央与各级地方政府的协调与监管[507]。另一方面，积极鼓励各级地方政府和物流部门，尤其是农产品社会性物流、经济性物流、双向性物流相互配合，利用各种财政配套支持的方法，达成物流交易满足农村经济发展的需要，实现地方政府促进农村经济发展的目标。三要加强西部地区农产品物流可持续发展的理论和政策研究，形成可持续发展的决策智囊。建立政府的西部地区农产品物流可持续发展预警监控体系和应急救援机制。

第三节　以化解西部地区农村经济约束为基础，建立立体保障机制改善发展质态

一　建立西部地区农村经济发展的基础，加大西部地区农村资金筹集和管理

中国西部地区农业和农民不具有获取竞争性资源的优势，农村资金的

供给，主要是通过农民自愿或非自愿地自筹资金来实现的。农村资金供给不足，导致农村经济发展基础不牢，进而使西部地区农产品物流交易条件不足、交易风险过高。要解除西部地区农产品物流可持续发展的农村经济约束，必须在营造宏观制度环境的基础上，按城乡统筹的要求，从农村资金的特性、政府责任和农村经济发展的需要出发，建立与之相适应的供给机制，奠定西部地区农村经济发展的基础。

（一）改变农村资金投入方式，建立“土地银行”

要按照城乡统筹的发展要求，重点调整财政资金支出结构和使用方向，向“三农”倾斜，逐年加大财政支农资金、农业基本建设投资、扶贫开发资金的投入力度。健全财政转移支付制度，加大向农村转移支付力度。在保持农村基本经营制度不变的前提下，通过成立“土地银行”的方式，逐步推行“合并调整、反租倒包、企业租赁、自愿互换、入股合作”等五种土地流转模式。通过“土地银行”对土地进行流转以及财务管理，在运作过程中，接受政府、农户的监督，流转过程公开透明，实现规范运营。通过推行适合西部地区的农村土地流转模式，使得粗放耕作的土地、闲置或半闲置的土地向专业大户集中，先进农业生产技术也得到进一步推广和应用。这不仅能够调整和优化原有土地的功用，吸引更多资本投入到农村地区和现代农业领域，提升土地的利用价值，实现土地规模化经营，还能够催生出一批掌握先进的耕作和管理技术，拥有较强的市场经营能力，善于学习，更能适应和推动现代农业产业化发展的“职业农民”。西部地区要通过培育和发展“土地银行”，按照“政府主导监管、企业化运营、农户自愿参与”体制创新农村土地流转模式，在确保农用地合法使用和充分保障农民权益的基础上，可使自身土地“流出”的农户既获得固定的租金收入，也可通过外出务工或从事其他行业来获取收入，还可到土地“流入”大户或企业中就业来增加收入。近年来，杨凌园区共吸引32个涉农企业的项目投资，合同引资超过12亿元，其中投资过亿元项目4个[508]，为杨凌更好地发挥国家级农业高新技术产业示范区的“引领示范”作用提供了土地资源支撑。

（二）广拓农村资金筹集渠道，建立“专项基金”

西部地区农村资金需求，单靠政府供给无法满足，应积极利用市场、社会、农村社区和非政府组织力量。要按照“谁引进、谁收费，谁投资、谁收益，谁受益、谁补偿，谁破坏、谁修复”的原则，加大改革创新力度，建立专项基金：加大政府投入——设立政府专项基金；广开资金渠道——设立农村开发基金；降低研发风险——设立农村科技风险基金；加大污染治理——设立农村综合治理基金。通过制度安排来激活民间资本，培育和壮大其他社会供给主体。合理调整投入结构，要按照WTO的要求，加快清理现有的财政支农政策和法规，建立政府对农业的支持保护体系[509]。对投入的要素进行优化组合，确立新的集经济效益、生态效益、社会效益于一体的综合性的评价标准，并通过制定相应的法规和实施必要的政策措施，使农村基础设施、农村教育、人才、科研和技术推广、农产品质量建设、动植物防疫检疫等投入有必要的保证。

二　改善西部地区农村经济发展的质态，加速西部地区农村生产要素流动

生产要素的优化配置以其流动性为前提，流动性取决于交易成本。由于产权界定不清、保护不力，以及利益集团施压等制度原因，西部地区农村生产要素流动，尤其是农村劳动力转移、农村土地承包经营权流转的交易成本过高，流动不畅，致使西部地区农村经济发展质态不佳，进而制约了西部地区农产品物流发展。

（一）引导农村剩余劳动力转移，促进农民就业

大力发展劳动密集型产业。必须充分认识到农村剩余劳动力转移是西部地区经济发展过程中一项不可回避的长期而艰巨的任务，劳动力资源丰富是西部地区的比较优势。在经济结构调整中，必须正确处理好发展高新技术产业与劳动密集型产业的关系，既要抓住新型工业化的机遇，有选择地发展高新技术产业，又要充分发挥西部地区劳动力资源优势，鼓励发展城乡劳动密集型和技术密集型结合的方向发展，包括发展劳动和技术密集型农业，尤其是西部地区农产品物流建设，为农村剩余劳动力转移提供广阔的就业空间，同时也提供了西部地区“回乡创业”新的平台。以陕西勉县为例，近3年农民工回乡创业人数达1853人，提供就业岗位12741个，

共计2.9亿元的回流资金更丰富了农产品物流多元化的社会投资体系[510]。

积极鼓励中小企业的发展。目前，我国全民所有制大型、中型、小型企业的资金有机构成之比为1.83∶1.23∶1，资金就业率之比为0.8∶0.66∶1，可见，小企业的创立和管理成本低，且小企业中单位资金所安排的劳动力人数远远多于大企业[511]。对于资金相对缺乏而劳动力成本低的西部地区，中小企业的发展对于增加地方财政收入，提高自我积累和自我发展能力具有重要的促进作用，特别是在解决就业及推进城镇化方面具有大企业不可替代的作用。一是农业发展中的技术进步将会产生大量的剩余劳动力，而中小企业的发展将起到吸收随生产率提高而出现的剩余劳动的任务。二是与大企业建立紧密的协作配套及专业化分工联系的中小企业若能得到较好的发展，将有利于大企业进行合理的产业、产品结构调整，改变“大而全”的生产结构，帮助这些大企业走出困境。

加强农村劳动力就业培训。建立政策引导、财政扶持、民间兴办、社会参与的农村劳动力就业培训机制。要在帮助农民转变思想观念，树立市场经济意识，提高维护自身权利能力的基础上，根据劳动力市场需求，一是有针对性地开展农村劳动力转移前的“订单式”就业技能培训，将就业培训和就业指导、引导相结合。二是要在办好普通高等教育分流农村劳动力的同时，发展农村职业技术教育，尤其是积极引进民间资本，发展校企合作型、订单式的职业技术教育，实现农村就业与创业机会。

（二）立足农业和农村全产业链，提升比较优势

农业是西部大开发的基础和重要组成部分，发展特色农业是实施西部大开发战略的重点任务。特色农业首先是要求具有明显的区域比较优势，即该地区生产的某种农产品，无论是在产量还是品质上都具有其他地区所无法比拟的优势。西部地区地域辽阔，光、热、水、土资源丰富，物种资源多样，尤其是水能蕴藏总量占全国的82.5%，已开发水能资源占全国的77%，有着发展农业生产必不可少的自然优势，其独特的区位优势构成了发展特色农业的基础。据相关资料统计，我国西南地区和西北地区的自然资源丰裕度分别名列第一名和第二名，但分布不均匀。西部各省区市可以利用其丰富的农业资源，依托其独特的气候条件和地理环境，因地制宜，大力发展特色农产品和产业，培育具有西部特色的农业产业带和产业群，通过农业产业化经营带动当地经济的全面发展[129]。

西北地区生态环境脆弱，应把农业发展与环境保护结合起来。西北地区的许多地方能够因地制宜，大力发展以耐旱节水农业、多样化农业为重点的生态农业。例如，内蒙古凉城县大量种植以耐旱、抗寒的豆、粟、小米为主要特色的杂粮作物，全县现已有 9 个品种的 30 多万亩（2 万多公顷）农产品被认证为无公害生产基地；新疆地区依托其特色优势资源，着力于发展“红色产业”，现已建成了工业番茄、啤酒花、红花、枸杞等区域性特色农产品生产、加工和出口基地。目前，新疆特色农产品发展方兴未艾，已发展成为全国最大的啤酒花和番茄酱生产基地，其番茄酱出口量占国际贸易量的 1/4，啤酒花产量已占到全国总产量的 70%，枸杞占 50% 以上；另外，新疆、甘肃还利用其绿洲边缘地带较好的光热、温差条件，种植一些宜于沙地栽培的瓜类、蔬菜，如新疆的“哈密瓜”，甘肃民勤县的沙地“甜瓜”和景泰县的旱沙地马铃薯等；陕西渭北高原光照充足，昼夜温差大，其独有的气候资源特征和土壤条件，使得这里生产的苹果无论是品质还是外观都在国内居于前列，现已成为国内有名的苹果生产优势区，苹果产业带的集中度更以每年 5 个百分点的速度递增。目前全国共有浓缩苹果汁生产及贸易企业约 70 家，我国浓缩苹果汁总产量 105 万吨。其中，陕西和山东是国内最主要的两个产区，陕西地区产量约占总产量的 60%[130]。

西南地区由于受太平洋和印度洋的暖湿气流的影响，水资源相对丰富，在农业产业化的过程中，许多地方已经注重发展具有特色的立体农业、观光农业、珍稀农业和生态农业。以广西为例，松香、玉桂和八角是其最具特色和优势的经济农林产品，其种植面积、产品产量、产品质量、产品的内外贸易在全国都处于优势地位，是广西传统的出口拳头产业。近年来广西特色农产品价格普遍提升较快，对促进从业农民的收入增长起到了积极作用。

云贵地区的地貌、气候类型多样，是适宜粮食生产的地区，在稳定粮食生产的同时，一些地方发挥当地独特的自然风景资源优势和奇特的少数民族风情，加快发展观光旅游业并重点发展质优量少、高价热销的精品农产品和高档鲜花、优质烟叶、绿色水果等特色产品，为旅游提供优质农产品，变资源优势为经济优势。以云南省为例，全省已初步形成了以滇中、滇东北为主的烟草、畜牧、花卉、中药材、马铃薯产业区；以滇南、滇西南为主的优质稻米、甘蔗、茶叶、橡胶和咖啡产业区；以滇南、滇东南为主的热果、药材产业区。烟草、甘蔗、茶叶和橡胶已经形成了区域化布局与专业化生产。

总之，西部地区农产品在贸易中已经占据重要地位，但尚需进一步通过农业产业化经营，提升农产品比较优势。当前解除西部地区农产品物流发展的农村经济约束，要求做到下列几点。一要立足全产业链支撑体系的思路，不断优化农业产业结构。在 WTO 框架下，将各种要素集合，农民经济合作组织、配套设施、龙头企业、金融服务等，资源集约利用、要素高度集聚、产业有机融合，以实现更大空间的要素富集，提升优势产业集聚效应。在确保食品安全基础上，以扩大优质农产品的规模为重点，调整优化种植业结构；以扩大养殖业规模为重点，调整农业内部结构，发展粮、经、饲三元结构，发展好果蔬生产，加快发展优质、专用、无公害农产品、绿包食品和特色产品。二要综合西部地区自然资源、区位特点、经济社会条件等方面优势，提高农村核心竞争力。推进农村土地规模化经营，实现规模经济，开展综合经营，形成西部地区区域特色，大力发展西部地区农村经济的特色产业带，形成区域规模，拉长产业链，形成产业集群，不断提高农产品竞争力，把潜在的优势转化为现实的竞争优势。三要大力发展农村经济结构调整的支撑体系。当前重点是推广农业标准化生产，积极鼓励有条件的农民自主创业，发展农村民营经济。健全农村流通组织，支持农民合作社承担涉农项目、兴办农产品加工企业或参股龙头企业，探索跨产业、跨地域、跨行业的合作社联合模式，特别是外销网络。培育农民经纪人队伍，通过组织创新，构建适应市场竞争的新型主体，建立农村市场体系，以产销订货、“订单农业”等形式促进西部地区农产品物流。

（三）聚拢农业和农村核心科技，打造行业地标

2012 年中央“1 号文件”锁定农业科技，把推进农业科技创新，作为农产品生产保供和现代农业发展的支撑，强调逐步提高农业研发投入占农业增加值的比重，建立投入稳定增长的长效机制。目前，改变西部地区农业结构趋同化状况，不能只着眼高精尖科技，一整套农业科技体系的完善才是基石。应积极配合国家治理西部生态环境的各项重大举措，改变自清代中叶以来形成的在旱地陡坡上广种薄收的方式，积极发展林业、畜牧业，适当降低粮食生产在农业经济中所占的比重，使农、林、畜牧业协调

发展。应加强农业基础设施建设，改善农业生产条件，注重发展“低投入、低污染、高产出、高质量、高效益、节水源、节土地”的可持续发展的现代化农业，加强农产品、畜产品、林产品、土特产品及其他副产品的深度技术开发和系列技术开发。如通过陕西杨凌农业示范区的建立和发展，充分发挥其农业科技优势的带动和示范作用，提高农业生产的综合能力，大力发展出口创汇农业，真正把农产品及至整个农业生产带入市场，实现多层次增值的目标，增加农村经济收入，为农业发展积累资金，推动农业向商品化、专业化、现代化发展。

专利技术奠定行业地位，地标性的大企业对全产业链具有辐射带动能力。要打造西部地区行业地标的位子，就必须促进农业和农村科技进步，为此必须做到如下几点。一要建立整套的农业和农村科技体系，全面提高农业和农村核心科技覆盖率。完成基层农技推广服务体系改革，建成农技推广、畜牧兽医、农业机械、农产品质量安全检测中心、特色产业技术推广机构，推进农业和农村核心科技进村入社、到企驻园。二要促进西部地区农业和农村经济增长方式，由“资源依存型”向“科技依赖型”的转变。开展重大技术攻关和集成创新，重点培养一批中青年农业科研人才队伍，加强农业科研创新团队建设。成为农业和农村科技创新、技术示范和成果转化的综合样板，聚拢西部地区农业和农村核心科技未来“核心竞争力”[512]。三要建立稳定的农业和农村科技投入资金的力度与来源，完善农业和农村科技成果转化机制。对使用西部地区农业和农村核心科技资金必须依法加强监管，提高投入效率。加快农村科技成果交易市场体系建设，鼓励科技人员下乡，积极实施“科技入户工程”，建立与农村产业结构调整、规模经营相配套的农村科技成果推广和转化模式。

三　激发西部地区农村经济发展的活力，壮大西部地区农村市场经济主体

创新是经济发展的动力，以农村市场经济主体持续不断的创新能力为条件，而这种持续不断的创新能力则取决于农村市场经济主体成长和发育程度。因此，无论从理论上，还是从现实的角度讲，西部地区农业和农村经济可持续发展的约束化解，都必须壮大西部地区农村市场经济主体。

（一）增加农村经济主体的人力资本，强化市场能力

发展经济学认为：人力资本是经济发展的重要因素，壮大农村市场经济主体，必须增加其人力资本。因此，树立人力资本观念是关键。在技术飞速发展和知识经济兴起的今天，土地、能源、矿产等自然资源对经济增长的作用相对下降，从世界范围看，资源开发导向型国家的经济增长比较缓慢，而知识开发导向型国家的经济增长要快得多，像日本、新加坡及西欧一些国家，它们的自然资源极其匮乏，但人力资本却非常丰富，经济发展就较快。由于资源性产品需求弹性低，且易受外部市场需求变化的影响，造成经济增长的不稳定性。而知识开发则有较强的灵活性和适应性，随着知识经济的兴起，这一趋势越来越明显。我国西部地区与东部发达地区在发展上的差距，实质上主要是知识、教育、技术、观念上的差距。据第五次人口普查资料统计，西部不识字或识字很少的人口数占在业人口数比重为 39.5%，高出全国平均水平 8 个百分点，高出东部地区 11 个百分点。西部 90 年代在业人口受教育年限仅相当于东部 80 年代的水平。教育水平相对落后和由此带来的价值观念、劳动者素质不高等问题，已成为影响西部经济发展的主要制约因素。面对以知识经济为主导的世界经济发展大趋势，实施西部大开发战略，必须把着眼点从以往只重视“物的开发”，转到重视知识、信息、教育、技术等“人的开发”上来。开发西部最根本的是人才，靠发展教育加快培养人才，靠环境和政策留住、吸引人才。因此，增加农村经济主体的人力资本，首先要建立选拔、竞争和学习机制。其次要增加农村经济主体从事市场交易的人力资本投入，以提高其获得市场信息、提高政策信息的能力[513]。它包括有关市场经济的法律知识、经营管理知识教育和能力培养，尤其是针对农民教育和培训，以及对农村中小企业经营者提高经营管理水平的教育和培训。这些教育和培训，不仅开展学校式的传统教育，更重要的是要通过典型示范发挥“干中学”的效应。

（二）优化农村经济组织的运行模式，增进市场运作

农村经济组织的发展有助于缓解农户小规模经营与农业现代化的矛盾，改变农业小生产者在现代大市场的弱势地位，并带动农业产业化水平的提升。西部地区要解决“三农”问题，扩大农业经营规模，提高农业

劳动生产率和农业的比较优势，改善农村落后的社会经济面貌，就必须加快农村合作经济组织发展，并以此来推进农民组织化程度的提高和农村产业化规模的创新。一是需要政府推动，建立农村经济主体的市场意识，按照在农村合作经济组织组建和运作过程中起主导作用的主体以及组织类型，归纳划分农村合作经济组织模式。合作组织帮助农民集中生产和销售农产品，提高经营能力，加强农产品增值性经营活动。如甘肃农村合作经济组织建立了四种运行模式：政府主导型协会、能人主导型协会、公司主导型协会、专业合作社[514]。二是完善农村经济组织在内部组织机构、决策程序、分配制度等方面政策，按照《农民专业合作社法》的实施进行规范。三是把合作社发展成为一体化农业产业化龙头企业。农村经济组织主要以提供产前、产中、产后服务为主，在有盈余的合作组织中，其盈余主要来源于初级产品销售，而来源于真正能延长农业产业链的农产品储运、加工等方面的组织极少。四是通过合作社创办加工型经济实体，以“合作社＋公司”模式延长农业产业链条。合作社的壮大、合作社实力的增强以及把其他一些不规范的合作组织或可能改造的利益联结体，改造为能够承担起农业产业化龙头角色的合作组织，既依赖于经济发展水平的不断提升，也依赖于政府鼓励和扶持政策的不断完善[515]。

第四节　以强化西部地区农产品物流功能为突破，建立整体运行机制实现管理创新

一　形成现代物流观念，把握西部地区农产品物流改革意义

西部地区农产品物流功能不足的根源，一方面有其极为深刻和复杂的历史与现实原因，另一方面主要是西部地区农产品物流改革不到位。正如前述第七章的“原因分析”中指出，西部地区农产品物流改革滞后于农村经济和整体物流。在此，依据本研究对功能范式框架下西部地区农产品物流的分析，应从建立制度物流、功能物流和产业物流等现代物流观念方

面加以分析。

（一）建立制度物流观念，按物流发展规律推进西部地区农产品物流改革

西部地区农产品物流改革长期以农产品公有物流机构为主，以计划管理和行政干预的治理结构为基础，导致了西部地区农产品非公有物流发展缓慢，压制了农产品非正规物流发展。西部地区农产品物流不仅存在“市场风险”和“信用风险”，而且还存在“垄断”“委托—代理”带来的“道德风险”“逆向选择”等“制度风险”，严重制约其功能发挥。因此，强化西部地区农产品物流功能必须把握西部地区农产品物流发展的制度内涵，遵循物流发展的内在规律，促进西部地区农产品物流改革。西部地区农产品物流改革重在制度建设，关键在信息、信任、信用和信誉机制的建立，构建西部地区农产品物流制度的产权基础是核心，完善西部地区农产品物流发展的法治体系是保证[381]。

（二）建立功能物流观念，按农村经济需求推进西部地区农产品物流改革

西部地区农产品物流改革被误解为“西部地区农产品物流就是西部地区农业物流或农村物流，西部地区农产品物流发展就是西部地区农产品物流机构增加”，导致了西部地区农产品物流改革内容单调而且没有引起足够的重视，西部地区农产品物流供给主体界定不清，西部地区农产品物流政策传导机制失灵，西部地区农产品物流功能难以正常发挥作用。为此，必须依据“斯密定理”[516]，清楚地认识到只有创造西部地区农产品物流交易条件才是解决西部地区农产品物流功能不足问题的重点。这就要求基于交易视角，构建西部地区农产品物流改革的功能范式，即遵循西部地区农产品物流的交易属性和农村经济系统的环境与目标→农村经济发展对西部地区农产品物流的功能需求；遵循西部地区农产品物流系统的环境和目标→西部地区农产品物流实现其功能和目标的具体形态及其结构优化途径。基于此，从农村经济发展角度理解西部地区农产品物流，拓展西部地区农产品物流改革的政策范围，既要区别于整体物流，还要区别于内部物流。因此，西部地区农产品物流供给政策应在实行差别化的基础上结合西部地区农村经济现实来制定。

（三）建立产业物流观念，按产业发展规律促进西部地区农产品物流改革

西部地区农产品物流改革受计划经济物流观的影响，尚不具备“产业物流”内涵，致使西部地区农产品物流不具备服务农村经济的功能。为此，首先，必须充分认识到市场经济中物流运行具有独立规律；其次，必须充分认识到将西部地区农产品物流作为一个独立的产业而发展壮大；最后，必须充分认识到核心竞争力所具有的价值性、独特性、难以模仿性和不可替代性，西部地区农产品物流发展过程需要打造核心竞争力①。因此，必须尊重西部地区农产品物流追求自身利益的权利，注重提高西部地区农产品物流产业的规模效应。

1. 建立农产品综合生产防范体系，推进西部地区农产品产销链的产前变革

农产品产销困境问题主要是解决农产品从生产到销售的整体物流链条问题，要从产前防范开始运作，这样才能真正解决产销大环境下物流的根本问题。农产品综合生产防范体系是在消费结构和消费趋势变化下，预防农产品供需缺乏弹性，忽视消费特点；预防农产品自然风险和市场风险，避免盲目投入；预防对农业范畴内的农产品属性与影响关系认识的局限；预防农村普遍存在“藏粮于民”的传统观念和习惯对发展农产品物流形成的障碍。因此，建立防范体系一是必须在产前加强对农产品供给与需求的调查研究，提高农产品综合生产的风险防范能力，打造综合型的农产品“五制”生产体系，即产前预测制—产前认证制—产前评估制—产前培训制—产前保险制，培育产销平衡的优质农产品。充分认识到农产品供给缺乏弹性，但延展性消费仍富有弹性；农产品数量需求缺乏弹性，但结构性消费仍富有弹性。此外，我国各地的民风习俗存在着很大的差异：南甜北咸、西辣东酸，这对农产品物流也是有一定影响的，而且在一定程度上决定了农产品物流的流向。农产品及其加工品面临较高的自然风险和市场风险，通过物流保险来分散风险，促进投资，加强农业生产中化肥、农机、农药等物质投入。二是必须在产前加快推进农业科技进步和创新，提高农

---

① 西部地区农产品物流产业核心竞争力是指西部地区农产品物流不仅包括企业核心竞争力，而且还包括培育和整合企业竞争力的制度竞争力和政策竞争力。前者是指西部地区农产品物流发展制度环境的优势，后者是指西部地区农产品物流产业政策的有效性。

产品综合生产能力，打造综合型的农产品“三基”生产体系，即原料基地—加工基地—研发基地，培养特色精品农产品。建立西部地区农产品基地、农业园区、农产品企业技术开发创新体系，制定动力机制、激励约束机制、利润分配机制等，通过产学研相结合提高新型名牌农产品产品综合开发能力。三是必须在产前高度重视农产品源头的质量安全检验检测体系建设，大力发展西部地区无公害农产品、绿色食品、有机农产品，保障绿色、有机农产品质量安全。[375]

2. 建立农产品物流运行虚拟化治理模式，推进西部地区农产品产销链的产后变革

随着经济、信息网络技术应用的不断发展，虚拟经营势必会成为农产品物流运营的一种主要理念，有力地促进农产品物流业的进一步发展，提高农产品物流业的竞争能力和赢利能力。虚拟农产品物流治理模式是一个全产业链的解决方案，可以为龙头企业等各类产业化组织提供信息发布、宣传展示、在线交易、即时配送、物流金融、追踪溯源等服务。由信息网、联盟网、商城网、追溯网共同组成。农业产业化信息网为信息发布平台，主要收集发布产业化扶持政策、工作动态、行业发展等方面的信息，同时收集发布各类产业化组织产品、资源、供求、招商等信息。农产品产销联盟网为渠道整合平台，可以对企业发布的原料、产品、供求、招商等信息进行自动筛选、配对，实现营销渠道的纵向优化；可以利用企业发布的销售网络信息，进行销售网络的横向整合。农产品商城网为产品交易平台，龙头企业可以进行在线开店、在线交易、在线支付、在线结算，通过交易、配送实现信息流、商流、物流、资金流的四流合一。农产品质量追溯网为质量追溯平台，可以整合各类质量管理资源，将龙头企业的内部管理外化于形，实现龙头企业与消费者的互动。四大网站通过服务不同的对象，将农业产业链条中的各个环节、各类主体有机地结合起来，形成农产品产销联盟，对整体宣传企业，展示农产品，打造农产品品牌，提高农产品竞争力，扩大农产品市场份额具有举足轻重的作用。[375]

这种虚拟联合体由一个核心单位（龙头企业）和几个成员单位（第三方物流企业、中介组织、农村经合组织、农户等）组成，成员主要是通过谈判形成比较密切的关系，声誉和信用成为基本的组织要素，这有利于双方形成长期稳定的合作关系，有利于避免个别单位承担过高的组织管

理费用，从而保持虚拟农产品物流各主体的内部活力，以适应市场变化，扩大交易规模，降低交易成本。从欧美发达国家的农产品物流产业发展情况来看，农产品供应链物流运行虚拟化已经成为主流趋势，它通过对信息流、物流、资金流的控制，从采购原料到生产农产品，最后由销售网络把农产品送到消费者手中，其涵盖的范畴远超过传统农产品物流，是更为高级的物流发展阶段[493]。传统农产品物流因其准入门槛较低而竞争激烈，而农产品供应链管理各方面要求相对更高，因而避免了过多的新进入者，也保证了利润率。借鉴发达国家的经验，农产品供应链物流运行虚拟化是西部地区农产品物流产业目前发展的必然趋势。

3. 农产品物流体系重构，产销一体化破解“菜贱农伤”之困

随着农业生产经营竞争的加剧，产销一体化物流模式成为农产品流通态势发展的新类型，逐渐得到重视。产销一体化是指公司通过与农业生产者签订合同，通过合同把农业生产与“农业前部门”“农业后部门”连成一个综合体。产销一体化物流模式可以采取从最松散的纯粹市场交易到最紧密的一体化经营等一系列形式。目前，各国大多数产业依据各自的农产品特点，以不同紧密程度的合同形式进行一体化联合。这种一体化联合可以是农业资本（通常是农产品加工或者营销单位）通过契约合同与农户进行联合或者是投资建立农产品生产基地，也可以是农产品加工企业通过建立自己的物流运输渠道、营销渠道等或者与某些专门的营销公司进行联合以及农户组成合作社共同投资，参与农产品加工或销售，进入农产品的产后阶段的一体化联合方式。美国是产销一体化最早的国家，一些特定农产品（主要是农产品类）农产品合同生产或一体化经营的平均比例由1960 年的 13% 提高到 1994 年的 18%。[375]

借鉴发达国家的经验，目前应着力推动以下几个方面：第一，发挥农产品物流微观主体作用，重点培养组织化、规模化发展的西部地区农产品物流主体。首先是农产品物流微观主体的组织形式、层次、市场分工及其物流工具、物流服务和运作方式等经营形式具有多元化、动态性特征，能动态地适应农村经济发展的要求。其次是在对农产品物流市场进行细分的基础上，农产品物流主体间市场分工明确，相互间协作、配合默契。在此基础上，整合农资生产企业、农家店等资源，形成“从田头到餐桌”的完整产业链，由市场有效需求带动农业产业化，提高农业生产区域化、专业化、规模化水平。第二，西部地区农产品物流发展以“普遍主义信用”

为主体，充分发挥“特殊主义信用”[123]，着重建立信誉和诚信机制。以多元化、多层次的农产品物流组织形式，多样化、低成本的农产品物流工具和物流服务，以及分布广泛、服务及时的农产品物流服务网络为手段，形成适应于农村经济发展要求的物流资源动员、组织与运用能力。第三，发挥经济区域特殊优势，以策略联盟构筑其西部地区区位化双层物流联盟的组织模式。第一层是产业链层面的物流联盟，第二层是绿色通道层面的物流联盟，使农产品物流功能得到完善和充分发挥，实现农产品市场与基地的高效对接。产业链层面的物流联盟首先是产地物流的规模集约化体现在集约生产、农业生产基地化。通过合作组织、农业协会，将分散的农民组织起来，通过区域化种植形成生产的外部规模，提高生产效率。其次是中转物流的规模集约化体现在纵向联盟和横向联盟一体化。销地物流的规模集约化体现在超市连锁化发展。绿色通道层面的物流联盟是关系区域农产品运销时效的重要保证，它包含检验检疫和快速通关机制、农产品安全预警机制、专业化仓储设施和配送中心建设、农产品保税专区建设等。西部地区区位化双层物流联盟体系最终目的是实现减少农产品流通环节的损耗、提高流通效率，解决农业产业化经营统一市场开拓能力不足、营销渠道整合能力不够、农产品产销缺乏竞争力等问题，促进产地与销地、生产与加工、加工与流通的有机结合，满足农产品物流“大生产、大流通”的需求。

4. 建立西部地区农产品物流突发事件应急机制，消除产销失控现象

建立西部地区农产品物流突发事件应急机制，及时应对市场变化。西部地区农产品物流在应急环节上具有滞后性，应尽快实现物流企业流通过程的产业化、集约化，增强抵御市场风险的能力。建立西部地区农产品物流协控中心的应急机制，加强对仓储中心、运输与配送、检验与检疫、支撑性服务的协调控制。基于整个供应链间信息共享，科学设计区域协控中心的运行平台，实行统一、协调、控制的物流运作，强调农产品生命周期管理和质量安全追溯体系，推动农产品电子商务平台、运销标准与规范平台对接。西部地区农产品物流突发事件应急机制在市场波动时是政府控制和平抑农产品价格的有效应急手段，同时也可以作为供需双方重要的应急缓冲。能有效地控制在途物流与质量，也可以通过增加批量和减少空返来降低物流成本提高竞争力，实现区域农产品快速调配和优化，彻底消除产销失控现象。[454]

二　优化西部地区农产品物流结构，重构西部地区农产品物流组织体系

西部地区农产品物流功能不足，从表现形式上看，是西部地区农产品物流系统的有效供给不足；从交易视角看，其实就是西部地区农产品物流交易不足。强化西部地区农产品物流功能，重要的是在功能范式框架下，优化西部地区农产品物流结构，重构西部地区农产品物流组织体系。西部地区农产品物流结构具有多维性，可以从不同角度分析，依据本研究对西部地区农产品物流关系结构失调原因的分析，应从产权结构、业务结构和产业结构方面加以分析。

（一）建立西部地区农产品物流组织体系的制度基础，优化农产品物流产权结构

1. 确立西部地区农产品物流发展的制度基础

首先，建立西部地区农产品物流的发展法规、暂行条例及管理办法等政策体系。具有前瞻性和系统化的政策法规是规范和推动农产品物流发展至关重要的制度保证。一是政府积极研究制定西部地区扶持农产品物流产业发展和物流基地发展建设的政策意见，包括法规、暂行条例及管理办法，在市场准入、企业用电、投资、融资、配送车辆管理、人才流动、行业标准、技术标准等方面给予有力的政策支持。二是建立和完善农产品物流技术标准体系，加快制定和推进物流基础设施、技术装备、管理流程、信息网络的技术标准。建立农产品质量安全标准、运输标准质量认证、仓储标准质量认证、流通加工及包装认证等体系；广泛采用标准化、系列化、规范化的运输、仓储、装卸、包装机具设施和条形码、信息交换等技术；规范物流企业分类标准，设立工商登记代码；尽快建立西部地区社会物流统计与核算体系。三是加快制定物流产业政策，从产业发展的角度来统筹规划、整合资源，实现农产品物流的整体推进。物流发展的产业政策包括产业促进、产业组织、企业布局规划、相关行业协调政策，以及相配套的市场准入和金融政策等。产业政策的主要作用在于弥补市场的缺陷；实现产业的超常规发展，缩短赶超时间；促进产业结构合理化与高度化，实现产业资源的优化配置；增强产业的国际竞争力。其次，建立西部地区农产品物流政策体系的执行保障系统[517]。一是完善财政税收政策：统一农产品物

流企业的营业税税率、降低农产品物流企业的所得税负担、对农产品物流企业开具专用运输发票、避免向部分农产品物流企业重复征税、减免农产品物流企业进口必需的设备关税、建立规范的财税管理机制。二是建立融资政策：政府直接投资、政府与民间资本共同投资、政府管制下的私人投资。三是建立健全土地征用政策、开发区物流行业的扶持政策、农产品物流园区规划与建设的相关配套扶持政策、第三方物流大型企业集团的重点扶持政策、技术创新政策、物流专业人才培养和储备政策、物流设施改造政策、物流信息网络化政策、交通管理政策、项目审批政策。再次，建立西部地区农产品物流市场综合治理的配套政策[518]。一是建立健全信用体系，营造促进现代物流业发展的良好环境。进一步扩大开放，加快与国际物流市场接轨，鼓励外商以各种方式投资建设、经营物流设施项目。建立信用机制，加强现代物流业诚信建设。二是建设诚信市场，营造物流市场发展的良好环境。开展企业诚信评选，引导行业诚信经营，为诚信经营的企业创造良好的条件。弘扬诚实守信的价值观念，强化诚信的激励机制和约束机制，打破地区分割和垄断，统一执法力度，促进统一货运市场的形成。三是建立城乡物流市场的准入制度，避免低水平的恶性竞争。四是发挥场站点的综合功能，场站建设规划和改造要纳入西部地区物流的整体规划当中。五是成立农产品物流行业协会，充分发挥中介组织的特殊作用。最后，从政府开始实施物流法治化，即不仅要建立政府“以法”的法治，而且要建立政府“依法”的法治。为确保西部地区市场体系拥有一个良好的法律环境，要确立以市场主体、市场行为、市场秩序、市场监测调控与管理及信用管理法律制度为主要内容的流通法律体系建设目标[519]。

2. 优化西部地区农产品物流发展的产权结构

首先，培育多元化西部地区农产品物流产权主体。一是要逐步放宽西部地区农产品物流市场的准入限制，尤其是要放开对西部地区农产品民间物流的限制，打破所有制和行业界限，积极将民间资本、产业资本、海外资本等引入西部地区农产品物流市场。二是要鼓励农户间成立互助物流机构，引导非正规物流正规化。三是积极引导非国有产权主体，构建多元化西部地区农产品物流主体平等竞争的西部地区农产品物流市场格局。其次，深化西部地区农产品公有制物流产权改革。一是要积极推进国有商业物流股份化改造，建立现代企业制度，赋予国有经济性物流拥有选择逐步退出农产品竞争性物流市场的权利，同时积极通过社会性物流参与西部地区农产品物流交易。二是政府要积极履行农产品社会性物流直接支农的功能。同时对国有经济性物流机构从事西部地区农产品物流业务，给予政策倾斜发挥其支农的功能。三是要继续深化农村供销合作社改革，使农村供销合作社等农村合作组织成为专门化的农产品营利性物流机构[520]。在此基础上，按西部地区农村经济发展的不同要求，探索农村供销合作社改革的不同模式。在西部地区经济较发达地区，重点是将农村供销合作社发展为股份制、合作制的农产品商业物流；在西部地区经济落后地区，重点是发挥好其双向性的特点，注重开展综合经营。

（二）扩展西部地区农产品物流组织体系的服务范围，优化农产品物流业务结构

1. 扩展西部地区农产品物流服务的业务领域

首先，完善现有西部地区农产品运销业务，将农产品物流发展从农产品扩展到整个农村经济。不仅包括农产品运销需求，还包括农产品保险、农产品质量分级和标准化、市场信息、风险承担、融资等物流需求。当前重点是要将农产品物流技术开发、农产品企业加工和物流基础建设，尤其是农产品保险纳入西部地区农产品社会性物流的范围，加快发展西部地区农村保险。建立农村供销合作社改革的思维框架，全方位推进西部地区农产品物流改革，构造完整的西部地区农产品物流供给体系，使得西部地区农村经济发展的物流需求得到满足。其次，西部地区农产品物流改革不仅要区别于整体物流，而且西部地区农产品物流内部也同样应实行差别化。重点是在产业上，要区分农业物流与农村非农物流及其内部构成；在功能上，要区分农产品行政物流与业务物流；在业务物流上，要区分社会性（非营利性）物流和营利性物流，并界定各自的功能，给予相应的政策设计。

2. 拓宽西部地区农产品物流机构的经营与业务范围

首先，拓宽西部地区农产品营利性物流机构的经营范围。通过建立战略联盟、业务代理等方式，逐步探索专门化的地方性农产品营利性物流机构，提高西部地区农产品物流机构的范围经济和规模经济。其次，拓宽西部地区农产品社会性（非营利性）物流机构的业务范围。一是要将西部地区农产品社会性物流的外延确定为市场机制不能完成或完成成本较高的西部地区农产品物流领域，并由政府依据其对发展农村经济的职能认识，在权衡自身能力的基础上，通过有关法律程序使之制度化。二是要认识到

西部地区农产品社会性物流具有公共产品性质的西部地区农产品物流需求，应通过直接支持方式予以满足，准公共产品性质则通过诱导性机制，诱导经济性物流机构提供物流供给。

3. 成立西部地区慈善性质的农产品物流机构形成特色的可持续扶贫的道路

农产品物流不单纯具有经济性，还应该具有社会性。农产品物流的社会性体现在农产品物流应具备战略性、福利性、安全性等特点，其重要意义远超过一般商品的物流。农产品物流既为生产者服务，也为消费者服务，其实质是为人们的生活保障服务，因为农产品不是社会某个群体的消费，而是普遍意义上的消费，具有社会福利最基本的基础性与广泛性，因而农产品物流具有较强的社会性和福利性。目前，立足可持续发展战略，依托华夏文明发展区域经济，在西部地区形成农产品慈善性物流基地，为企业实现经济效益和社会效益双赢搭建一个平台，将扶贫与可持续发展结合起来，走一条有中国农产品物流特色的可持续扶贫的道路。要积极引进民间资本，按国际成功经验，成立西部地区慈善性质的农产品物流机构，推进其可持续发展。一是法治的逐步完善。慈善性质的农产品物流是扶贫的有效方式，同时也是物流的特殊形式。通过完善法治促进慈善性质的农产品物流事业快速健康发展。二是平台的合理搭建。建设“西部地区农产品慈善性物流基地”的基础，设立“西部地区农产品慈善性物流基金”，将西部地区农产品慈善性物流的善款全部返回西部地区农产品专门化营利性物流机构的资金来源，积极鼓励西部地区农产品慈善性物流在农村贫困地区开展业务。开展政府扶贫、慈善性质的农产品物流分工与合作。三是产业的广泛联动。根据西部地区农村经济发展水平，对西部地区各类农产品慈善性物流机构的管理方法进行适时调整，不断提高西部地区农产品慈善性物流机构的经营水平，以创业就业促进产业发展，实现经济增长。[375]

（三）提高西部地区农产品物流组织体系的核心能力，优化农产品物流产业结构

1. 提高西部地区农产品物流制度核心竞争力

一是要在完善西部地区农产品物流产权制度和相关法律法规的基础上，针对中国西部地区农产品物流需求多样化、多层次的特点，培育各种规模的西部地区农产品物流机构，发展以民营为主的西部地区农产品物流机构，

引导农产品非正规物流规范化发展，建立综合性的西部地区农产品物流市场体系。二是要构建西部地区农产品物流机构之间以及物流机构和实体经济之间的关系网络，促进西部地区农产品物流交易方式的发展，不断改善农村信用关系，加强西部地区农产品物流的各种可持续形式的配合，创新西部地区农产品物流可持续发展模式。三是要优化西部地区农产品物流区域结构，实施差别化的西部地区农产品物流区域发展战略。以基础推动战略的梯度推进与节点带动模式是根据政府与市场的关系可以分为“市场主导模式”“政府主导模式”“政府扶植模式”。以创新推动战略与组织推动战略的综合模式是根据在农产品物流中的流程和物流中发挥核心作用的企业主体不同可以分为“批发市场主导模式”“农业合作组织模式”“中介组织主导模式”“供应链一体化模式”“农产品物流园区主导模式”。实现以策略联盟构筑区位化双层物流联盟的组织模式创新及其区域协控中心的运行体系优化，使西部地区农产品物流功能得到完善和充分发挥。[375]

2. 提高西部地区农产品物流企业的核心竞争力

一是要推行西部地区农产品物流机构按业绩分配制度，加快企业化进程。西部地区农产品物流企业结构与其承担的功能相吻合，注意物流的特殊性决定了物流政策应维持物流市场的适度竞争，要规避无序或恶性竞争。二是要积极促进产业资本和物流资本融合，提升西部地区农产品物流机构的资金实力。对国有商业物流进行股份制改造，鼓励国有经济性物流机构在社会性物流引导下开展西部地区农产品物流业务，并按西部地区农产品物流业务对农产品国有物流机构进行整合与重组。三是要强化以人为本的管理理念，实施西部地区农产品物流发展的企业形象战略。提升西部地区农产品物流企业经营理念，注重团队精神、培养企业文化，激发员工潜能，重视诚信文化、社会责任的个性化理念，并注重运用理念的表达、传播与规范行为功能[521]。加强企业的成本和质量管理，要重视基于企业形象和流程再造的西部地区农产品物流机构经营创新。

三　改进西部地区农产品物流监管，提高西部地区农产品物流运行效率

中国西部地区农产品物流功能不足的另一个重要原因是西部地区农产

品物流监管失范。由于计划经济物流观和计划经济物流监管体制仍然深刻地影响着西部地区农产品物流监管，与市场经济条件下现代物流意识相适应的西部地区农产品物流监管理念还未能完全确立，监管组织还不健全，监管制度还不完善。因此，强化西部地区农产品物流功能，需要对西部地区农产品物流监管进行改进。

（一）建立西部地区农产品物流监管方式：刚性管理与柔性管理

西部地区农产品物流监管体系是一个以“有效监管”和“高效运作”为目标导向、事关物流全面建设和全面发展的系统工程。西部地区农产品物流监管体系是一种广泛的监督和管理系统，既包括宏观监督和管理，也包括物流微观主体的自我监督和管理，以及物流行业自律式的监督和管理。总体框架既包括横向业务职能的重组和纵向三级事权的科学划分，也包括业务流程再造和业务改革整合[522]，是现行西部地区农产品物流改革整合的继续。探索构建西部地区农产品物流监管体系，存在多种视角和切入点，重点要增强西部地区农产品物流工作整体性和协调性，侧重解决西部地区农产品物流监管链条缺失、横向协同不力的问题。在市场经济条件下，实施西部地区农产品物流的有效监管，必须创新监管方式。对西部地区农产品物流的刚性管理，表现的是政府通过运用强制性的手段来维护和实现所需要的物流市场秩序。强制性在政府建构和情势危机时可以发挥重要的作用，但并不能成为一种常态性的工具。因此，政府对西部地区农产品物流的刚性管理只能是一种应急的管理方式。所以，当前西部地区农产品物流的监管方式创新，绝不是简单要求政府在西部地区农产品物流监管方式上增添“刚性”的因素，而其核心是要求政府通过进一步地诉求合法性，加强与物流组织之间的对话、沟通与协商，做到由被动式监管向互动式监管转变、由处罚性监管向引导性监管转变、由两端式监管向全程式监管转变。实施风险管理，以企业为监管单元，根据现代物流的特点，在特定的时间内对企业物流、资金流、信息流、经营状况、纳税记录等运用现代信息技术进行分析和开展稽查，对企业实行全过程的监督，改变以往物流监管只注重前期审核和后期核销的状况，转变为整体的、动态的过程管理，在对风险信息分析运用的基础上，进行有重点的监控，尽可能保证物流畅通，真正实现“一线放开，二线管住”的监管理念，使西部地区农产品物流监管更具“柔性”。本研究认为当前西部地区农产品物流的监管方式创新的基本方向，就是要在新的历史时期建构出一种政府主导的、规范有序的自上向下、自下向上的平行轨道的“双轨”格局。

（二）优化西部地区农产品物流监管模式：大通道管控与双窗口开放

大通道是指联结中国东部与西部、联结亚欧大陆的通道，它东起我国连云港，经陇海线、兰新线横穿亚欧大陆腹地，直达大西洋东岸的荷兰鹿特丹港。双窗口是指联合中国东部、西部两个窗口，开放式走西口。联合要做到：部地区各个省区联合，而且要东、西两地区的全国性联合，实行“东西合作”“西西合作”，把西北作为我国向西开发的前沿。走西口要做到：一是向西开放，主要是指原苏联的哈萨克、乌兹别克、吉尔吉斯、土库曼、塔吉克五个共和国，乃至西亚、中东、东欧和整个欧洲的贸易。目前中亚五国的总体产业结构的特点是重视工业，轻视农业；重视重工业，轻视轻工业，基本上属于重工业型，轻工业与农产品加工能力明显不足。农牧业产品特别是面粉、肉类长期以来不能自给，食品自给率普遍不到70%，有“东部粮仓”之称的哈萨克每年也要从外地调进大量食品。中亚五国的农产品不仅在总量上全面短缺，而且品种单一，加工落后，不能满足多样化的市场需求[523]。我国西部地区农产品资源丰富，其中部分产品居世界领先地位，可提供充足的出口资源。并且西部地区光能资源丰富，光合产物积累多，黑夜低温，呼吸消耗少，而且棉花绒长质地好，果实着色浓，瓜、果、甜菜糖分含量高，具有发展经济作物和园艺作物生产优势。如南疆的长绒棉、北疆的甜菜、吐鲁番的葡萄、哈密的瓜，陕西的苹果、酥梨，四川的柑橘和云贵的烤烟等，均驰名于世。这些工业原料作物及瓜果等园艺作物以及牧业生产等均有较大潜力，有能力向中亚五国出口服装、食品等产品，且质优价廉，适合中亚五国的消费层次和结构[524]。二是走西口并不放弃东口，应实行两个窗口双向开放，由东口引进必要的粮食和先进的农业技术和装备，由东、西两个窗口出口适应于东、西两个市场不同需求的农产品及其加工产品，这样才能促进西部农业振兴。

创新西部地区农产品物流监管模式，提高监管效能。

（1）以信息化建设为基础。一是完善西部地区农产品物流信息监控系统。开发和建设西部地区农产品物流信息监控系统，实现监管区域、场所的物流企业和加工贸易企业与海关联网，及时了解西部地区农产品进、出、转、存等物流信息，对西部地区农产品物流进行全过程、动态的监管。二是建设封闭式的物流监管运行模式[525]。按照统一、规范的原则建设和完善卡口的集装箱号识别系统、车牌识别系统、电子地磅系统、U卡识别系统等通道式智能系统，实现自动信息数据采集、传输、运行、管理。建设和配套闭路电视监控系统和GPS监控系统，对监管区域、场所实施24小时监控，并对运输海关监管货物的车辆实施GPS全过程监控。促进农产品在不同监管区域、场所间有序地流动。三是深化陆路口岸通关作业改革。推行EDI无纸报关、多点报关、集中报关等通关运行机制，满足企业不同的通关需求，提高通关效率。推进西部地区与周边国家通关便利化合作，促进口岸及配套设施上水平，加快电子口岸建设，实现信息共享。积极配合国家与周边国家在检验检疫标准、海关制度、国际运输法律等方面形成一系列制度性安排。建设大通道管控与双窗口开放联合走西口的“9+1”监管框架（9项监管重点和1个中心建设），即运输工具监管、运单管理、进口农产品账册管理、出口农产品跟踪监管、转关运输农产品监管、拼箱农产品管理、空箱监管、转运过境通运农产品监管、运输工具自用物料和运输人员自用物品监管以及农产品物流监控指挥中心建设。监控指挥中心汇总整合西部地区农产品物流监管信息，对物流监控和突发事件进行协调指挥、统一处置。

（2）建立区域间联动机制。推进区域一体化建设在确保有效监管的前提下，整合作业流程，简化手续，疏通西部地区农产品物流在监管区域、场所间的合理流转渠道，构建西部地区农产品物流全方位、多层次的立体监管体系及通关一体化机制，实现监管区域、场所间的整体联动，通过优势互补，提高区域竞争力[526]。西部地区农产品物流要依托大通道与双窗口优势，大力发展窗口经济、通道经济，形成一个由极点增长模式和带状发展模式结合的“双窗口—大通道—区域间联动—沿腹地轴线纵深型”的西部地区农产品物流开放带。促进区域间的协调发展，更好地适应西部地区农产品物流的可持续发展。

（三）完善西部地区农产品物流监管机制：提升人力资本与强化行为规范

提升西部地区农产品物流监管主体的人力资本。一是全面导入现代人力资源管理。按照现代人力资源管理的理念、方法和技术对物流监管主体进行开发和管理，政府应该构建一个科学的西部地区农产品物流监管主体培训体系，合理地进行人力资本投资。树立明确的人力资本投资目标，创新培训途径和方式，丰富完善培训内容，建立培训激励机制，健全培训制度和法制。二是推行专业监管人员专业化。在各级专门的监管机构中必须配备真正懂物流的骨干来负责组织和领导监管工作，理论和政策研究部门应成为相关监管决策机构的智囊。三是疏通专业监管人员流动渠道。除人力资源配置的内部化方式外，政府部门还应充分利用各级人力资源市场进行外部化配置，降低专业监管人员的人身关系依附性，进一步健全完善选拔录用制度。不同监管机构之间可以在一定范围内开展业务骨干交流挂职，以更好地交流信息，熟悉业务规程，提高合作效率。四是发挥舆论和社会监督作用。利用各种传播媒介和采取多种形式，加强对西部地区农产品物流监管知识的宣传、普及和相关农产品物流监管状况的报道，有利于调动群众积极性、有利于问题解决、有利于和谐稳定。

强化西部地区农产品物流监管机构的行为规范。首先，加强西部地区农产品物流不同监管机构的分工合作。一是要理顺垂直监管机构基于不同目标的纵向关系，要明确水平监管机构基于不同分工的横向关系，重点是明确各自的职责和行为边界，关键是政府监管系统要履行好监管职责和发挥最终的强制力。二是要形成监管合力，建立起统一高效、多层次监管体系，防止监管真空地带的出现。本研究建议，在西部地区成立的“物流与经济可持续委员会或领导小组”，应是其日常综合办事机构，地方政府的物流与经济可持续组织应主要对地方性农产品物流进行监管，并与政府垂直监管系统相配合一致[527]。其次，依靠制度建设规范西部地区农产品物流监管行为。西部地区农产品物流监管从根本上讲应通过规范地遵守法规制度，而不是靠行政命令来进行。虽然中国已经形成了系列物流法规，如《中华人民共和国合同法》《中华人民共和国公路法》《汽车货物运输规则》《中华人民共和国铁路法》《铁路货物运输管理规则》等，但仍缺少系统化与全面化，而且对西部地区农产品物流监管的针对性不强，导致了西部地区农产品物流实际监管中运用法规进行监管难度大。因此，需要参阅国标监管标准，制定西部地区农产品物流监管制度和政策；建立农产品物流合作、激励、风险预警、防范、处理与补救机制。必须在完善相关法律体系，尽快制定有关西部地区农产品物流监管实施细则的基础上，加强执法力度。建立西部地区农产品物流监管与西部地区农产品物流市场的可持续发展，是目前西部后续开发背景下实现西部地区农产品物流可持续发展的有效途径。

第十一章　研究结论与政策运用

本项目是关于西部地区农产品物流可持续发展政策的研究。本研究从理论和方法层面，确立了西部地区农产品物流研究的逻辑起点；针对既有分析范式的缺陷，从交易视角和功能范式上，界定了“西部地区农产品物流”，并深化了对“西部地区农产品物流发展”的理解；同时界定了研究的基本范畴和分析基点，进而通过理论和实证分析得出了研究结论和政策建议。

第一节　研究结论

一　西部地区农产品物流可持续发展的内涵与机理：是西部地区农产品物流理想状态的实现过程，受产业环境、信用关系和微观基础的约束

1. *交易视角的西部地区农产品物流内涵*

“西部地区农产品物流”是在信息约束、信任约束、信誉约束和制度约束的共同作用下形成“规模经济”的信用交易，包括这些活动在制度安排下所形成的经济系统（与其他经济系统具有平等交换关系的系统）、运动形式（农产品、资金、信息的流出方和流入方，连接两者的农产品物流中介机构和农产品物流市场，形成产品流、资金流、信息流、信用流，提高生产效率、满足客户需求的形式）总称。西部地区农产品物流实质是信用关系制度化的产物。功能意义上的西部地区农产品

物流，一是具有促进西部农村经济发展功能的物流。二是西部农村经济与整体物流的交叉系统。三是内部功能结构复杂多样的系统。针对农产品物流的交易特点创造交易条件，才是解决农产品物流供给不足问题的根本所在。

2. 西部地区农产品物流发展的制度内涵

从西部地区农产品物流发展过程可以看出，西部地区农产品物流发展是信用的发展，实质就是农产品物流制度的完善过程：（前提）实体经济存在规模经济 + 经济主体追求规模收益 + （根本）信息→信任→信用→信誉 + （保证）减少交易不确定性 + 降低交易风险 + 降低交易成本 = （完善）农产品物流制度。功能意义上的西部地区农产品物流发展，一是促进结构调整推动整个农业系统均衡协调发展的重要基础。二是提高居民生活质量、增加农民收入的重要内容。三是已成为开发利用西部地区内陆港（无水港）、解决农村资源短缺的重要途径。四是农业实现区域化、专业化生产和产业化发展，提高农产品的市场竞争能力的重要保证。五是农村剩余劳动力转移的战略重点。

3. 西部地区农产品物流可持续发展的概念内涵

从“概念界定”看，西部地区农产品物流可持续发展是保持西部农村经济发展，适应西部经济发展要求的西部地区农产品物流与农村实体经济关系理想状态及其实现过程。农产品物流与农村实体经济之间的相互关系是相互依存、相互制约、平等互利的产业经济关系。西部地区农产品物流可持续发展的内涵是在不损害后代利益的前提下，利用市场机制适度地开发利用农产品物流资源，保证当代人对物流产品及服务的需求，实现农产品物流资源供需平衡和良性循环。其本质是农村资源在农产品物流与农村实体经济部门的可持续性优化配置。从“基本特征”看，西部地区农产品物流可持续发展，是西部地区农产品物流与农村经济可持续发展主体，在制度可持续框架下，综合运用各种可能的可持续发展手段，使西部地区农产品物流与农村经济关系达成理想状态，具有在开放系统中制度、技术作用下西部地区农产品物流通畅，其总量、结构和速度配合适当构成良性循环的理想状态特征。其实现过程是一个不断受西部经济发展的要求和外部干扰因素影响、不断进行关系状况判断，具有内部结构复杂、多层次相交叉、在变革—创新中不断循环往复的“前期—后期渐进式”系统运动过程。

4. 西部地区农产品物流可持续发展的实现机理

从“均衡过程”看，是宏观制度环境下西部地区农产品物流与农村经济相互促进达成的最优供求均衡。西部地区农产品物流与农村经济的相互作用机理是在宏观经济、物流环境和相应的制度安排下，西部地区农产品物流和农村经济的交易主体，在一定交易环境中进行相应交易活动的结果。宏观制度通过改变交易环境影响西部地区农产品物流发展与农村经济发展的关系，并不是西部地区农产品物流与农村经济的所有均衡关系都是可持续发展，只有在西部地区农村经济发展和西部地区经济社会发展相适应条件下的均衡才是可持续发展，而且这种均衡不仅表现在总量上，还要表现在结构上，并且是具有高度稳定性的长期均衡，即西部地区农产品物流供给的主体结构与农村经济的物流需求结构的相互适应。可持续发展的均衡机理是一种理想状态的抽象，因此，实现西部地区农产品物流可持续发展的关键在于制度可持续。实现可持续发展必须通过制度创新，创造西部地区农产品物流可持续发展系统运行的理想条件。从“内在规律”看，西部地区农产品物流可持续发展，必须以良好的产业环境、信用关系和微观基础为条件。产业环境：农村经济主体参与西部地区农产品物流“交易”的最高价格承受水平，由其生产经营活动的收益分布状态和机会成本决定。信用关系：存在信用风险的条件下，西部地区农产品物流需求主体更多地选择参加西部地区农产品物流交易，而西部地区农产品物流供给主体参与交易的约束更加苛刻，将更多地选择退出交易。微观基础：第一，在西部地区农产品物流可持续发展中，市场发育、非农产业发展、农户思想观念的转变直接决定了农户的经济行为，农村企业和产业化组织的治理结构直接决定其物流行为。第二，在西部地区农产品物流可持续发展中，农产品正规营利性物流不可能完全满足西部地区农产品物流需求，而且其难以适应农村人际信任环境。农产品正规非营利性物流主体中，农产品社会物流主体所承担的功能可以通过市场机制来解决；农产品双向性物流必须采取符合合作制原则的组织形式，形成有效的双向物流制度。农产品非正规物流存在的种种局限，在经济发展中应加以引导和予以规范。第三，在西部地区农产品物流可持续发展中，适时地判断市场经济的发育程度，界定政府行为在西部地区农产品物流与农村经济中的作用领域、方式和程度，包括政府退出的领域、方式和程度。加强人力资本投入，形成学习机制，真正行使政府职能对西部地区农产品物流可持续发展同样重要。

二　农产品物流可持续发展的国际经验借鉴与启示：经济发展中农产品物流可持续发展模式具有多样性，但成长路径具有一致性

1. 发达国家（地区）农产品物流可持续发展的趋势

随着经济全球化步伐的加快，科学技术尤其是信息网络技术、通信技术的发展以及跨国公司的出现所导致的农产品本土化生产、全球化采购及全球化消费趋势的加强，农产品物流业已进入成熟阶段。在农产品物流内涵的拓展、过程延伸、覆盖面的扩大以及农产品物流管理的专业化、标准化和信息化都发生了极大的变化，出现了新的发展趋势。一是产销一体化趋势。随着农业生产经营竞争的加剧，产销一体化物流模式成为农产品流通态势发展的新类型，逐渐得到重视。二是物流运行虚拟化趋势。随着经济、信息网络技术应用的不断发展，虚拟经营势必会成为农产品物流运营的一种主要理念，有力地促进农产品物流业的进一步发展，提高农产品物流业的竞争能力和赢利能力。三是绿色物流发展趋势。绿色物流是可持续发展的需要，也是经济全球化的需要，与农产品质量安全相对应的绿色物流战略的事实，将极大地获得消费者的支持和青睐。

2. 发达国家（地区）农产品物流可持续发展的特征

通过对美国、法国、荷兰、日本等发达国家农产品物流运营模式的比较分析，可以发现美、法、荷、日等国家在农产品物流发展方面各有特色，但从总体上看，这些国家农产品物流的发展又表现出一些共同特征。第一，发达国家（地区）经济发展过程中都十分重视农产品物流的可持续发展，善于把握农产品物流与农村经济的关系。第二，发达国家（地区）都十分重视通过法律去规范农产品物流的可持续发展，可持续手段的选择经历了从单一的市场或政府协调到政府、市场等多种综合运用的过程。第三，发达国家（地区）都十分重视社会性物流和双向性物流在农产品物流可持续发展中的作用，并由狭义的运销支农逐步发展为以交易为特征的农产品物流与农村经济互惠发展。第四，农产品物流可持续发展模式是可持续发展系统遵循可持续发展原理，在可持续发展主体推动下能动地适应其“生态环境”而不断演进的结果。

3. 发达国家（地区）农产品物流可持续发展的启示

农产品物流可持续发展的国际经验，为西部地区农产品物流可持续

发展提供如下启示性的结论。第一，在经济发展过程中，必须始终正确认识农产品物流和农村经济的功能和地位，依靠有效的制度安排，始终确保农产品物流和农村经济与整个国民经济可持续发展。第二，农产品物流可持续发展，必须始终坚持以可持续发展机理出发，通过制度可持续等多种可持续手段，使农产品物流优化资源配置，推进经济发展方式转变。第三，农产品物流可持续发展，必须始终坚持以政府为主导，市场为基础，制度创新为前提，机制建设为重点，政府机构、非政府组织、企业、准市场组织、社会关系网络等多种组织形式为载体，农户广泛参与，多种可持续手段配合运用的原则。农产品物流可持续发展模式是一定环境条件下的产物，具有多样性、层次性、复合性和动态性特点。第四，农产品物流可持续发展的关键在于以制度、组织和管理为内容的机制建设和模式选择，核心在于制度可持续，基础在于可持续发展主体的能力建设及其行为规范。

三　中国农产品物流制度变迁的演化过程分析：中国农产品物流与农村经济制度变迁模式不同，在时间、结构及其相互影响上失调

1. 中国农产品物流制度变迁的主要路径与基本内容

一是新中国成立初期的农产品物流制度变迁（1949 年—1952 年），新中国成立初期，政府推动的农产品物流制度的改变是保证城市居民生活和大力发展工业建设的基本制度要求。二是高度集中计划经济时期的农产品物流制度变迁（1953 年—1978 年），这一时期物流的经济效益目标被放在了次要的位置。三是改革开放以来农产品物流体制的演化（1979 年至今），其过程基本上经历了四个阶段：农产品物流体系的重构与调整，农产品物流“双轨制”运营的形成，农产品社会性、经济性和双向性物流“三足鼎立”格局的形成，新形势下农产品物流改革的深化与发展。我国的农产品流通体制已经全面从计划经济模式向市场经济模式发展，并随着我国整体经济体制市场化改革的深入，市场化程度不断提高。

2. 中国农产品物流制度变迁模式演进的动力机制

分析农产品物流制度变迁模式演进的动力机制是研究农产品物流制度

变迁过程中的关系结构的前提。农产品物流产业的产生和发展演进，是基于竞争环境，在政府政策引导、市场需求拉动、物流基础设施建设和物流技术创新推动下发生的。主要表现在，一是制度变迁与农产品物流模式创新。二是城乡居民消费需求变动与农产品物流模式创新。三是物流基础设施改善与农产品物流模式创新。四是物流技术开发采用与农产品物流模式创新。五是农产品物流组织与农产品物流模式创新。

3. 中国农产品物流制度变迁的基本特征与影响因素

农产品物流制度变迁的基本特征：一是农产品物流制度变迁在不同体制下总是表现为机构的不断反复调整。二是农产品物流制度变迁在三个不同层次上表现为二元结构系统的演进。三是农产品物流制度变迁以政府主导的自上而下的强制性制度变迁为主。四是农产品物流制度变迁是强制性制度变迁力量强于诱致性制度变迁的过程。农产品物流制度变迁的影响因素：第一，在初始条件中，旧中国的农产品物流和解放区的物流制度安排构成了重要影响。第二，农产品物流制度变迁不仅和农村经济制度变迁一样，受发展战略和计划经济体制的影响，而且农产品物流制度还作为国家实施发展战略的手段和计划经济的工具，直接参与了对农村经济资源和剩余的吸取和控制。农产品物流制度变迁一直是在国家直接控制下强制性进行的。第三，在农产品物流制度变迁中，利益集团的影响主要发生在中央政府和地方政府、政府的农业部门和物流管理部门、农产品正规物流和农产品非正规物流，以及农产品正规内部经济性物流、社会性物流和双向性物流之间。

4. 中国农产品物流制度变迁过程中的关系结构

一是农产品物流与农村经济制度变迁模式互不适应。农产品物流制度变迁是与农村经济制度变迁不适应的强制性过程。表现在农产品物流与农村经济制度变迁的主体、过程、动因不同。二是农产品物流与农村经济制度变迁存在结构失衡。农产品物流制度变迁是从属于经济发展战略的强制性制度变迁过程。表现在农产品物流与农村经济制度变迁的需求结构、供给结构、区域结构失衡。因此，农产品物流制度与农村经济制度变迁在模式上的不适应、结构上失衡，直接导致了农产品物流制度变迁在时间上滞后于农村经济制度变迁，使得农产品物流制约了农村经济制度变迁的进程。

四　转型时期西部地区农产品物流数量关系实证：转型时期西部地区农产品正规物流受内外因素影响，未能与农村经济相互促进可持续发展

1. 转型时期，西部地区农产品物流数量关系从西部地区农产品正规物流来看，未能促进农村经济发展

首先，西部地区农产品物流来源未能促进农村经济发展。一是物流网络里程的增加并不必然代表农村经济发展。在西部农村经济发展中农产品物流的有效资金来源仍然处于自我积累阶段，西部地区农产品物流没有发挥促进农村经济发展的功能，而将农产品的物流资金输出到了非农经济部门。二是农产品货物周转量不仅没有促进农村经济的发展，反而阻碍了农民收入和农村经济总产值的增长。说明农产品货物周转量仅在名义上存在，实际投向了非农化；或者由于西部地区农产品正规物流机构缺乏应有的物流能力，其结果是农产品货物周转量效率低下。其次，西部地区农产品物流运行未能促进农村经济发展。一是农产品物流产值与农民收入以外的其他农村经济发展指标没有明显关系。说明农产品物流产值或是没有运用，或是非农化运用，或是没有被有效运用于农村经济发展。二是农产品物流产值占农村经济总产值的比重提高，即农产品物流深化对农民收入增长产生的是负面的影响。直接说明了西部地区农产品物流发展不仅不能促进农村经济发展，反而抑制了农村经济发展。

2. 转型时期，西部地区农产品物流数量关系从西部地区农村经济来看，未能促进农产品正规物流发展

首先，西部地区农村经济发展未能直接促进农产品物流发展。一是农产品货物周转量水平的提高并不必然代表农产品物流发展。不能转化为农村有效投资的农产品货物周转量增长，只能是功能异化的农产品物流发展，充其量只是农产品物流机构自身的发展，而非农村经济发展所需要的农产品物流发展，同时说明了农民收入增长源于农产品正规物流之外的因素。二是农村经济总产值增长不能促进农产品物流产值增长。说明转型时期西部地区农产品物流与农村经济关系存在制度障碍，也说明了转型时期西部地区农村经济增长的动力只能从农产品物流以外的其

他因素中寻找。其次，西部地区农村经济发展未能间接促进农产品物流发展。一是农村消费与农产品货物周转量、农产品物流产值不存在重要联系。说明农村消费并没有提高农产品货物周转量，未能真正促进农村经济发展。同时说明农村消费增长仍然处于自给自足阶段，农产品物流没有能促进消费的增长和市场的扩大，进而拉动农村经济发展。二是农村投资与物流网络里程、农产品物流产值不存在重要联系。说明农村投资效率不高，这既可能与西部地区农产品物流引导投资的功能不足有关，也可能与财政的农村投资效率不高有关。同时说明由于农产品正规物流机构的物流能力不足，致使财政性投资和农村经济主体的自给性投资对物流性投资具有“挤出效应”。

3. 转型时期，西部地区农产品物流与农村经济关系，受外因制约

首先，综合西部地区农产品物流发展与农村经济发展、与国民经济发展、与整体物流发展的相互影响，分析表明：一是西部地区农产品正规物流发展对农民收入增长产生的是负面的影响，但农民收入的提高对农产品正规物流的发展产生正面影响。二是西部地区农产品正规物流的发展将有助于 GDP 的增长，但 GDP 增长对西部地区农产品正规物流发展的贡献却微乎其微。三是西部地区农产品正规物流发展与整体物流发展施加负面影响，而整体物流发展对西部地区农产品正规物流发展的促进作用同样是微弱的。其次，这些结果联系前述西部地区农产品物流与农村经济关系失调的分析，可以清楚地显示：一是转型时期的西部地区农产品物流与农村经济关系受整体经济发展和整体物流发展的制约，西部地区农产品物流在整体物流中处于从属地位和被整体物流隔离的状态，“二元物流结构”制约了农产品正规物流向农村经济发展所需要的方向发展。二是转型时期的西部地区农产品物流与农村经济关系失调，主要是由于国民经济发展通过“二元物流结构”中的农产品正规物流，实施了对农村经济的极化效应。总之，转型时期的西部地区农产品物流与农村经济关系不仅未能实现相互促进的可持续发展，反而陷入了相互制约的失调状态。因此，必须从西部地区农产品物流、农村经济系统及其外部制度环境角度，深入剖析导致西部地区农产品物流与农村经济关系失调的直接原因、深层原因和根本原因，进而依据可持续发展机理，构建实现可持续发展的机制与模式。

五　西部地区农产品物流关系结构失调原因分析：西部地区农产品物流关系结构失调源于制度环境、农村经济和农产品物流的共同约束

1. *宏观制度环境约束是西部地区农产品物流关系结构失调的根本原因*

一是初始条件不足和发展战略使然。我国过去的农业发展历程中，很长一段时期用农业的简单积累来哺育和扶持工业的发展，在重工业和城市发展战略之下，通过工农业产品“剪刀差”从农业和农村获取大量的农村经济剩余，造成了工农差异、城乡差别，形成了重视城市轻视农村的格局，使“三农”问题逐步突出。农产品物流可持续发展自然处于国家发展总目标之外，西部地区农产品物流与农村经济关系失调是特定条件下的一种历史必然。二是二元经济约束和分层治理冲突。首先，二元经济和二元物流结构约束。西部地区经济系统中的农产品物流也必然同样是一个二元结构系统，在西部地区农产品物流发展中同时存在物流扩张和物流抑制，并且一定表现为城市物流优先于农产品物流。而且在西部地区农产品物流内部也存在正规物流和非正规物流、国有物流和非国有物流的“二元结构”。其次，分层治理中政府行为相互冲突。中央决策层作为监督者并不能直接决定农产品物流可持续发展，决策层需要在分层治理系统中依靠委托—代理、命令—服从的方式落实，由于过长的信息链与过多的层级，加之中央决策层的监督不力，地方政府作为“经济人”具有短期行为与机会主义特征，必然形成地方政府的行为顺序是“城市经济→农村非农业经济→农业经济”；“农村大型非农企业→农业产业化组织→农村小型个体私营企业→以农业为主的农户经济”。因此，与中央政府相比，地方政府具有更强烈的工业化冲动。各级政府制定了物流发展规划，以及配套的扶持政策，形成重视城市物流、工业品物流发展而忽视了农产品领域的物流发展现象。由于我国物流是分部门管理，使得各物流主体很难根据市场需求对各种运输方式优化组合，在重重关卡下只能选择单一的运输方式。并且由于我国财政“分灶吃饭”，地方政府对本地农产品保护主义盛行，公开“设租”“寻租”，行政垄断在各地屡见不鲜，阻碍了农产品资源顺应经济规律的合理流通，忽视了农产品物流企业的发展，形成了西部地区物流产业组织结构存在的产业集中度低、规模效益低、产业进入壁

垒低而导致的地区垄断与过度竞争并存，地方政府对区域内农产品物流组织缺乏足够的调控能力，直接影响到产业的核心竞争力。导致垂直治理结构系统和水平治理结构系统产生冲突，最终背离可持续发展目标。三是思想认识不足和传统观念限制。首先，对农产品物流发展的内涵认识不清。具体表现为对农产品物流的内涵认识不清、对农产品物流发展的内涵认识不清。其次，对农产品物流发展中的关系认识不足。从全国社会物流总值看，对经济发展中的工农关系认识不稳定，目前工业品物流与农产品物流仍然存在明显差距。从相关行业发展环境看，在认识农产品物流与国民经济其他产业的关系上，忽视了在市场经济条件下这种关系应该是平等的交换关系。

2. *农村经济发展制约是西部地区农产品物流关系结构失调的深层原因*

一是西部地区农村经济在波动中增长，但发展水平极不平衡。西部地区农业生产总值在波动中增长，相对于国民经济发展，西部农业经济发展总体水平偏低。西部农村经济发展水平极不平衡，导致农村经济与农产品物流呈现出低水平均衡状态。二是西部地区农民收入稳步增长，但城乡人均收入极不平衡。首先，西部地区农民收入绝对水平低，必然导致西部地区农产品储运率低和资金短缺，西部地区农产品物流发展面临物流资源约束，难以满足农村经济发展的物流需求。西部地区农产品物流与农村经济处于低水平的均衡状态。其次，西部地区农民收入相对水平低，必然导致城乡物流发展不协调，更加剧了西部地区农产品物流资源的短缺和外流，西部地区农产品物流和农村经济关系必然进入相互制约的恶性循环。三是西部地区农村产业结构发生变化，但农村经济比较利益低下。首先，过剩的西部地区农村人口被束缚在第一产业内，从而导致农业小规模、低效益经营。其次，西部地区农业资源短缺，与发达地区相比主要表现在农业生产率的差异，西部地区农村经济结构调整困难。再次，分散的小农难以获得平等的贸易地位和收益，规模利益难以提升，导致西部地区农业生产比较利益低。四是西部地区农业生产条件进一步改善，但农村市场主体发育不良。农户的市场主体地位尚未完全形成；农村企业和农业组织产业化进程缓慢；农村经济主体生产方式落后，政府投入不足。

3. *农产品物流功能不足是西部地区农产品物流关系结构失调的直接原因*

一是西部地区农产品物流深化改革滞后。首先，多元化农产品物流结构不合理。农产品物流多重属性，不同主体同台竞争；产权结构、组织结构和服务功能单一；区域结构失衡，农产品物流金融服务缺失。其次，农产品社会性物流发展不到位。农产品社会性物流的外延和功能界定过于狭窄；农产品社会性物流存在政策性和经营性的矛盾。再次，农产品双向性物流发展难度大。农产品双向性物流合作原则未能充分体现；农产品双向性物流功能难以发挥。最后，农产品经济性物流发展不协调。正规的农产品经济性物流供给不足；非正规的农产品经济性物流发展不规范。二是西部地区农产品物流市场体系建设不完善。首先，西部地区农产品物流市场上物流交易规模小。农产品物流成本高；农产品物流信息体系不健全；农产品物流技术水平较低；农产品物流投资结构不尽合理；农产品物流交易方式不灵活。其次，西部地区农产品物流市场体系发育不健全。西部地区农产品物流市场处于抑制与分割状态；西部地区农产品批发市场物流系统规划设计缺失；西部地区农产品加工配送中心运作效率差距大；西部地区农产品物流园区布局存在明显地域差别。三是西部地区农产品物流监管与调控体系功能不强。首先，西部地区农产品物流监管体系构造不完备。西部地区农产品物流监管主体不明确；西部地区农产品物流监管体制僵化。其次，西部地区农产品物流调控体系功能不强。需要建立西部地区农产品物流政策宏观调控的系统化；需要适合西部地区的农产品物流政策设计与论证程序。

六　西部地区农产品物流可持续发展的模式创建：西部地区农产品物流可持续发展模式，特征表现为一致性的实现机理和多样性的实现形态

1. 西部地区农产品物流可持续发展模式的基本构成

一是西部地区农产品物流可持续发展模式内涵与构成。西部地区农产品物流可持续发展模式的含义，是针对市场经济条件下，西部地区农产品物流可持续发展目标，借鉴已有的可持续发展经验，依据西部地区农产品物流可持续发展的概念内涵和实现机理，将西部地区农产品物流可持续发展的要素加以抽象、概括、类比、分析和逻辑演绎而构建的，以指导西部地区农产品物流可持续发展实践为目的的一种框架性的理论

方案。西部地区农产品物流可持续发展模式的构成，包括实现西部地区农产品物流可持续发展的背景、目标、可持续发展系统、可持续发展主体、可持续对象及其相互关系、作用方式与可持续手段等可持续机制实现形式的抽象表达。二是西部地区农产品物流可持续发展模式构建的内容，包括确立西部地区农产品物流可持续发展模式构建的目标、运作手段和运行战略。

2. 西部地区农产品物流可持续发展模式的框架建立

一是西部地区农产品物流可持续发展模式的总体框架。西部地区农产品物流可持续发展模式，是西部地区农产品物流可持续发展实现机理的外在表现，其形态取决于可持续发展的具体目标、可持续发展的外部环境约束、可持续发展手段的最优组合、可持续发展主体的自身能力等因素，应依据可持续发展的实现机理，在可持续发展模式总体框架下探索不同条件下的具体实现形态。总体框架是一个典型的前期—后期渐进式可持续系统，目标是通过西部地区农产品物流对农村经济可持续发展，实现农业和农村经济与国民经济可持续发展。二是西部地区农产品物流可持续发展模式的基本类型。在这一总体框架下，西部地区农产品物流可持续发展实践，因不同的环境条件将出现各种可持续发展的模式。依据可持续发展中运行战略的侧重不同，从农业推动的角度、物流推动的角度可以将可持续发展模式大致分为：第一种类型是基础推动战略的梯度推进与节点带动模式，进一步根据政府与市场的关系可以分为“市场主导模式”“政府主导模式”“政府扶植模式”。第二种类型是创新推动战略与组织推动战略的综合模式，进一步根据在农产品物流中的流程和物流中发挥核心作用的企业主体不同可以分为“批发市场主导模式”“农业合作组织模式”“中介组织主导模式”“供应链一体化模式”“农产品物流园区主导模式”。

3. 西部地区农产品物流可持续发展模式的创新构建

一是西部地区农产品物流可持续发展模式的提升策略。完善西部地区农产品物流的交易方式、提高西部地区农产品物流信息化水平、提升西部地区农产品物流标准化程度。二是西部地区农产品物流可持续发展模式的结构创新。首先建立西部地区农产品物流区位化双层物流联盟的思想基础。其次是西部地区农产品物流区位化双层物流联盟的框架创新。选择合理集约化、绿色化的农产品联盟模式；在选择合理联盟模式的基础上，需要对保障农产品高效流通的各种机制进行优化。三是西部地区农产品物流区位化双层物流联盟的模式优化。西部地区农产品物流区位化双层物流联盟模式的层次优化，形成西部地区农产品物流区位化双层物流联盟模式的典型特征。四是西部地区农产品物流区位化双层物流联盟的机制优化。包括战略联盟、利益联盟、组织联盟、流程联盟、信息联盟、标准联盟、文化联盟。西部地区农产品物流区位化双层物流整个联盟体系的联盟过程是一个不断发展，不断螺旋上升的过程。西部地区农产品物流可持续发展的构建或探索过程具有一致性，有规律可循。

七　西部地区农产品物流可持续发展的模式运行：西部地区农产品物流可持续发展的模式运行体系，特征表现为集成化的运行管理和一体化的运行保障

1. 西部地区农产品物流可持续发展模式的运行设计

一是西部地区农产品供应链的区域协控中心的运行体系。首先建立西部地区农产品供应链的区域协控中心的运行结构。运行结构是各节点通过协议或联合组织等方式结成一种整体的协控网络式联合体。运作平台分为战略层→契约网络化的标准与规范对接平台、战术层→信息网络化的电子商务对接平台、操作层→实体物流网络化的电子口岸对接平台。其次提出西部地区农产品供应链的区域协控中心的运行系统。对区域协控机制进行研究具有十分重要的意义，运行系统主要包括三类机制：形成机制、实现机制、约束机制。二是西部地区农产品供应链的区域协控中心的形成机制。包括西部地区农产品供应链的区域协控中心的动因、自组织。三是西部地区农产品供应链的区域协控中心的实现机制。包括西部地区农产品供应链的区域协控中心的信任机制建立、信息共享机制、协作调控机制。四是西部地区农产品供应链的区域协控中心的约束机制。包括西部地区农产品供应链的区域协控中心的激励约束机制、利益分配机制。

2. 西部地区农产品物流可持续发展模式的运行管理

一是基于区域协控中心的区位化双层物流联盟的运作风险。首先是风险类型。风险可以分为基于区域协控中心的区位化双层物流联盟内部

环境引致的风险和农产品物流本身的外部环境所产生的风险两类。其次是风险预警。主要包括基于区域协控中心的区位化双层物流联盟风险的预警指标体系和风险评估方法。最后是风险防范。采用期权理论减少农协与核心物流伙伴的风险；促进伙伴企业员工交流，创建“共赢”的文化氛围；建立风险管理组织，科学选择供应链合作伙伴。二是基于区域协控中心的区位化双层物流联盟的空间优化。首先是空间的区位分类。可以分为四种类型，腹地型：位于农业生产作业区附近的二级物流中心空间；边缘型：位于市级城市周边的一级物流中心空间；临近型：位于临近区域协控中心周边的物流空间；内部型：位于区域协控中心作业区内部的物流空间。其次是空间结构的优化。结合西部七大特色农业基地已形成七条产业带的状况，以及西部后续开发期间依托重点支持的大型农业产业化500家“龙头”企业的要求，根据产业区域空间布局状况，显现出优势产业带在农业资源结构和空间结构所呈现的区域特点。最后是空间结构的层次优化。第一层面：区域体系的空间优化。第二层面：区域协控中心—腹地空间体系的优化。第三层面：农产品国际物流空间体系的优化。

3. 西部地区农产品物流可持续发展模式的综合评价

一是西部地区农产品物流可持续发展评价指标体系的构建。包括体系构建原则、评价指标体系。二是西部地区农产品物流可持续发展模式的综合评价方法。包括因子分析的综合评价方法、三角模糊数法的评价步骤。综合评价体系为现阶段西部地区农产品物流产业政策规划的制定、政策实施效果的监测提供具有一定操作性的参考建议。当然，这套综合评价体系须得到国家有关部门的认可，并组织相关力量收集有关数据，再按因子分析的原则和步骤进行分析，一定能得出切合实际的结论。这对西部地区农产品物流运行水平和质量提高，加快农产品物流的可持续发展必定有所裨益。

基于“模式”的运行设计、运行管理、综合评价的分析，通过整合各成员的资源、技术与信息，科学设计西部地区农产品区域协控中心的运行平台，以保障西部地区农产品物流区位化双层物流联盟模式的优化实施，整个运行体系表现出集成化的运行管理和一体化的运行保障，实现西部地区农产品物流可持续发展。

第二节 政策运用

一 西部地区农产品物流可持续发展机制建设的基本思路

1. 由“效率优先、兼顾公平”向“公平高效、规范透明”转变

西部地区农产品物流可持续发展是经济社会可持续发展的内在要求和重要内容。应在“公平”基础上，构建高效率、规范透明的市场经济体制。就西部地区农产品物流可持续发展而言，西部地区农产品物流关系结构失调的原因，在本质上，是西部地区农产品物流与农村经济主体长期受到约束。实现可持续发展，就是赋予西部地区农产品物流与农村经济主体公正平等、规范透明的选择自由和发展机会。一是切实赋予并保护好西部地区农民公正平等、规范透明的市场主体地位。二是切实赋予并保护好西部地区农产品物流与农村经济公正平等、规范透明的产业地位。三是切实赋予并保护好西部地区不同产权主体公正平等、规范透明的市场地位。

2. 由“城乡分割、相对独立”向“城乡统筹、空间集聚”转变

新中国成立以来，由于初始条件、外部环境和思想认识的限制，尤其是对经济发展中的工农关系认识不牢固，具有强烈的工业和城市倾向，过度获取农村经济资源和剩余，这是导致中国经济、物流二元结构的根源，也是导致西部地区农产品物流关系结构失调最为重要的根本原因。因此，实现西部地区农产品物流可持续发展，必须建立基于交易视角和功能范式的农产品物流发展观。西部地区农产品物流可持续发展既符合可持续发展的一般原理，又具有自身的独特性。必须从西部地区经济发展的全局着眼，通盘考虑，统一决策，彻底改革现行的“城乡分割、相对独立”局面，从根本上解决“三农”问题。一是以可持续发展为原则制定和实施经济发展战略。二是以城乡统筹为手段化解农产品物流二元结构。三是以空间集聚为方法实现农产品物流关联效益。

3. 由“粗放型、不协调发展”向“集约型、可持续发展”转变

经济转型过程中，西部地区农产品物流关系结构失调的原因复杂多样。实现西部地区农产品物流可持续发展关键在于机制与模式构建。可持

续发展的基础是市场经济条件下，政府、西部地区农产品物流主体和农村经济主体功能的发挥，核心在于制度可持续，重点是政府行为与市场行为的可持续。发挥政府职能，实现“集约型”“差别物流”是走出“失调陷阱”、走向“可持续发展”的切入点。但治本在于现代市场制度在西部农村的确立和完善，以及二元经济、物流结构的“一元化”。当前应立足西部地区农产品物流的现实情况，走具有西部特色的农产品物流现代化道路。一是建立西部地区农产品物流区位化双层物流联盟的组织模式。二是建立西部地区农产品供应链的区域协控中心的运行平台。三是建立健全以生态评价为中心的矛盾梳理体系。

二　以营造宏观制度环境为保证，建立综合决策机制，加快体制创新

1. 以“制度建设”为核心，构建和完善可持续发展体制

良好的制度环境才能实现西部地区农产品物流可持续发展。就当前而言，就是必须建立和完善社会主义市场经济体制。西部地区农产品物流的健康发展要依赖于良好的外部环境。这主要包括：稳定的政治环境；高效的市场经济环境；健全的制度环境。西部地区农产品物流的健康运营要依赖于良好的制度基础，包括物流制度、信用制度、法律制度、内控制度等。农产品物流产业组织体系必须加快自身的内控制度建设，按行业组织经营范围与特点建立起适应风险防范与发展要求的内控制度，促进农产品物流产业内各农产品物流企业能协调健康发展。一是平衡“生态文明”与“经济增长”的价值取向。二是构建“市场为基础”与“政府为主导”的实现平台。

2. 以“能力建设”为重点，强化政府的可持续发展职能

在市场经济条件下，西部地区农产品物流可持续发展，固然必须要发挥市场的基础性作用，并要充分调动企业、准市场组织、社会和关系网络等各方面力量，但政府是关键。因此，西部地区农产品物流可持续发展重点是通过“能力建设”对政府的可持续发展职能进行强化。一是科学界定可持续发展中的政府职能。二是优化可持续发展中的政府治理结构。

三　以化解西部地区农村经济约束为基础，建立立体保障机制改善发展质态

1. 建立西部地区农村经济发展的基础，加大西部地区农村资金筹集和管理

要解除西部地区农产品物流可持续发展的农村经济约束，必须在营造宏观制度环境的基础上，按城乡统筹的要求，从农村资金的特性、政府责任和农村经济发展的需要出发，建立与之相适应的供给机制，奠定西部地区农村经济发展的基础。一是改变农村资金投入方式，建立“土地银行”。二是广拓农村资金筹集渠道，建立“专项基金”。

2. 改善西部地区农村经济发展的质态，加速西部地区农村生产要素流动

生产要素的优化配置以其流动性为前提，流动性取决于交易成本。由于产权界定不清、保护不力，以及利益集团施压等制度原因，西部地区农村生产要素流动，尤其是农村劳动力转移、农村土地承包经营权流转的交易成本过高，流动不畅，致使西部地区农村经济发展质态不佳，进而制约了西部地区农产品物流发展。一是引导农村剩余劳动力转移，促进农民就业。二是立足农业和农村全产业链，提升比较优势。三是聚拢农业和农村核心科技，打造行业地标。

3. 激发西部地区农村经济发展的活力，壮大西部地区农村市场经济主体

创新是经济发展的动力，以农村市场经济主体持续不断的创新能力为条件，而这种持续不断的创新能力则取决于农村市场经济主体成长和发育程度。因此，无论从理论上，还是从现实的角度讲，西部地区农业和农村经济可持续发展的约束化解，都必须壮大西部地区农村市场经济主体。一是增加农村经济主体的人力资本，强化市场能力。二是优化农村经济组织的运行模式，增进市场运作。

四　以强化西部地区农产品物流功能为突破，建立整体运行机制实现管理创新

1. 形成现代物流观念，把握西部地区农产品物流改革意义

西部地区农产品物流功能不足的根源，一方面有其极为深刻和复杂的历史与现实原因，另一方面主要是西部地区农产品物流改革不到位。西部

地区农产品物流改革滞后于农村经济和整体物流，依据本研究对功能范式框架下西部地区农产品物流的分析，应从建立制度物流、功能物流和产业物流等现代物流观念方面加以分析。一是按物流发展规律改革西部地区农产品物流建立制度物流观念。二是按农村经济需求改革西部地区农产品物流建立功能物流观念。三是按产业发展规律改革西部地区农产品物流建立产业物流观念。主要包括：建立农产品综合生产防范体系，推进西部地区农产品产销链的产前变革；建立农产品物流运行虚拟化治理模式，推进西部地区农产品产销链的产后变革；农产品物流体系重构，产销一体化破解“菜贱农伤”之困；建立西部地区农产品物流突发事件应急机制，消除产销失控现象。

2. 优化西部地区农产品物流结构，重构西部地区农产品物流组织体系

西部地区农产品物流功能不足，从表现形式上看，是西部地区农产品物流系统的有效供给不足；从交易视角看，其实就是西部地区农产品物流交易不足。强化西部地区农产品物流功能，重要的是在功能范式框架下，优化西部地区农产品物流结构，重构西部地区农产品物流组织体系。西部地区农产品物流结构具有多维性，可以从不同角度分析，依据本研究对西部地区农产品物流关系结构失调原因的分析，应从产权结构、业务结构和产业结构方面加以分析。一是建立西部地区农产品物流组织体系的制度基础必须优化西部地区农产品物流产权结构。包括：确立西部地区农产品物流发展的制度基础；优化西部地区农产品物流发展的产权结构。二是扩展西部地区农产品物流组织体系的服务范围必须优化西部地区农产品物流业务结构。包括：扩展西部地区农产品物流服务的业务领域；拓宽西部地区农产品物流机构的经营与业务范围；成立西部地区慈善性质的农产品物流机构形成特色的可持续扶贫的道路。三是提高西部地区农产品物流组织体系的核心能力必须优化西部地区农产品物流产业结构。包括：提高西部地区农产品物流制度核心竞争力；提高西部地区农产品物流企业的核心竞争力。

3. 改进西部地区农产品物流监管，提高西部地区农产品物流运行效率

中国西部地区农产品物流功能不足的另一个重要原因是西部地区农产品物流监管失范。由于计划经济物流观和计划经济物流监管体制仍然深刻地影响着西部地区农产品物流监管，与市场经济条件下现代物流意识相适应的西部地区农产品物流监管理念还未能完全确立，监管组织还不健全，

监管制度还不完善。因此，强化西部地区农产品物流功能，需要对西部地区农产品物流监管进行改进。一是建立西部地区农产品物流监管方式：刚性管理与柔性管理。当前西部地区农产品物流的监管方式创新的基本方向，就是要在新的历史时期建构出一种政府主导的、规范有序的自上向下、自下向上的平行轨道的“双轨”格局。二是优化西部地区农产品物流监管模式：大通道管控与双窗口开放。大通道是指联结中国东部与西部、联结亚欧大陆的通道，双窗口是指联合中国东部、西部两个窗口，开放式走西口。西部地区农产品物流要依托大通道与双窗口优势，大力发展窗口经济、通道经济，形成一个由极点增长模式和带状发展模式结合的“双窗口—大通道—区域间联动—沿腹地轴线纵深型”的西部地区农产品物流开放带。促进区域间的协调发展，更好地适应西部地区农产品物流的可持续发展。三是完善西部地区农产品物流监管机制：提升人力资本与强化行为规范。提升西部地区农产品物流监管主体的人力资本，强化西部地区农产品物流监管机构的行为规范。建立西部地区农产品物流监管与西部地区农产品物流市场的可持续发展，是目前西部后续开发背景下实现西部地区农产品物流可持续发展的有效途径。

第十二章　附　录

附录一　西部地区农产品现代物流发展模式相关案例

一　案例1：宁夏四季鲜农产品综合批发市场模式

批发市场主要解决交易规模小、组织化程度低、信息不对称、品种结构单一等问题，因此对于小商品和农产品比较适合采用批发市场模式。而对于我国西部地区农业生产组织规模较小的情况，如果没有相当规模的合作组织或中介组织，则更适于采用批发市场模式。我国西部地区的农产品批发市场中产地批发市场明显多于销地批发市场就说明了这个问题。

以批发市场为中心的垂直一体化农产品物流系统通过“企业办市场，市场企业化”，实现了农产品物流系统创新。其系统模式如图12－1所示。

以西部地区较有代表性的蔬菜产地批发市场——宁夏四季鲜农产品综合批发市场为例来说明批发市场模式这种农产品物流模式。

2011年12月25日，辐射全区、连接区外的综合性批发市场——宁夏四季鲜农产品综合批发市场正式营业投入使用，它是由宁夏回族自治区供销社牵头组建、西北地区最大的宁夏四季鲜农产品综合批发市场。宁夏四季鲜农产品综合批发市场位于永宁县望远工业园，处于银川市场物流带。项目由宁夏回族自治区供销社牵头组建的宁夏四季鲜农产品公司实施，总建筑面积47.9万平方米，总投资9.4亿元，于2010年4月开工，是一个集农产品批发、加工包装、冷链储运、物流配送、商铺租赁、信息采发、检验检测、农技服务等为一体的综合性批发市场，建成后可提供5000多

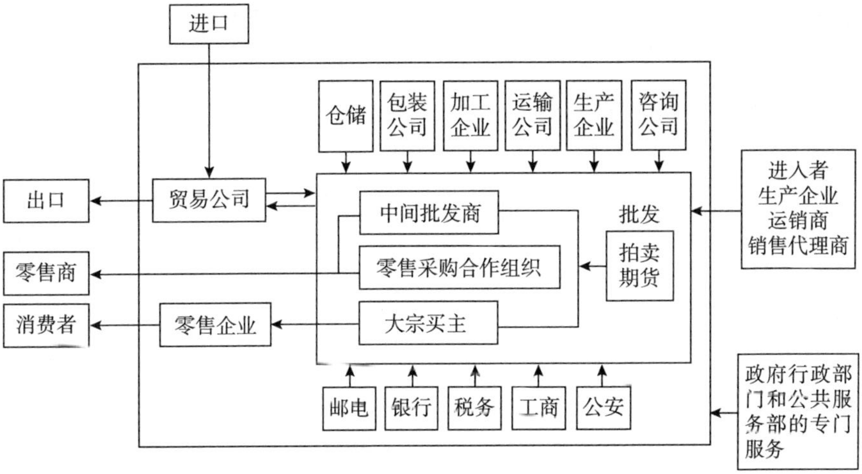

图 12－1　以批发市场为中心的发展模式

个就业创业岗位。

市场基本涵盖了现代物流企业的全部要素，市场分 11 个功能区，包括水果交易区、蔬菜交易区、地产菜交易区、干果炒货交易区、商务服务区、农产品展示区等。主要建设内容有大型封闭式交易大厅、拍卖大厅、电子结算中心、质量及农残检测系统。特别是运用市场先进的信息采集系统及全国农产品批发市场信息发布系统，为社会提供及时的农产品信息，引导农业生产结构调整、增加农业收入。而且，市场吸引了区内外一批农产品经营商户、企业入驻，截至 2013 年，来市场经商和入驻意向的区内外商户超过 600 户。

该市场是目前西北地区规模最大、功能最全、设施最优、信息化程度最高的全国一流区域性综合物流市场。这个市场投入营运后，预计每年的农产品吞吐量将达到 1 亿吨，年交易额 30 亿元左右，完全可以满足银川及周边地区农产品的集散，对丰富银川的“菜篮子”“果盘子”将起到保障作用。同时，市场还可以解决 4000 名至 6000 名失地农民和其他人员就业。市场对所有新进入市场的商贩给予免场地费、摊位费和最高补助 1 万元等优惠政策，并开展了为期一个月的新年购物节。2013 年，已有宁夏、内蒙古、甘肃、陕西等地的 600 多家商户进驻这个市场。

市场年上市品种有 300 多个，覆盖了宁夏 80 万亩（5. 33 万公顷）的蔬菜种植面积，带动了冬暖式大棚 30 万个，形成了万亩辣椒、万亩西红柿、万亩香瓜、万亩韭菜和3000多亩（200多公顷）无土栽培蔬菜等十几个成方连片的蔬菜基地。产地批发市场不但具有典型的集散功能，对区域化优质专业生产也有明显的带动作用。市场拉动激活各种生产要素，集聚了各类资本，促进了种养加、贸工农以及科研开发为一体的集约经营。市场的物流配套设施十分完善，有近10万平方米的交易服务大厅和大棚，有冷冻、冷储冷链系统，有完善的电子信息系统和电子商务平台，有完备的市场管理和完善的中介服务。市场的交易手段也比较领先，交易流程实行“一卡通”结算，蔬菜交易实现了全程电子化。市场还建有国内蔬菜电子拍卖市场，实现了以消费者参与的竞价机制进行交易。同时，市场有大型的农副产品质检中心，每周定期对上市蔬菜进行抽检，保证了农产品的质量，以包装规格化、重量标准化、质量等级化、客户会员化、交易电子化的“五化”模式促进了农产品现代物流的发展。

从宁夏四季鲜农产品综合批发市场的发展模式我们可以看出，农产品物流的批发市场模式是一个有效的、成熟的农产品物流模式，但批发市场的功能还需要不断地创新、不断地延展，以适应现代农业、现代物流和农产品消费的发展和变化。

（1）农产品流通体制改革必须坚持市场化的改革取向，并建立以批发市场为中心的市场体系。使市场和企业成为调控的直接手段，让农产品批发市场成为一个龙头，既服务于农业，又带动起一系列的服务业发展。

（2）重视中介组织的培育，并为之提供良好的制度环境。建立连接农民与市场的中介组织，实质上是农产品流通组织的创新，而这又是一个农产品物流和商流的规模结构不断扩大、优化的过程。必须依据农产品流通组织结构演变的内在要求来进行，不能用行政的方法按照某种固定的模式去硬性地塑造或堆砌。

（3）农产品流通体制的改革与建设应充分发挥多方面的主观能动性，打破单纯由国家或地方政府投资农产品市场建设的局面，建立起多元化投资主体的投资建设机制，并以股份制的现代企业制度明确各投资主体的权利和责任。

（4）打破单纯由政府职能部门管理市场的体制，由企业管理市场更有利于市场的长期发展，更有利于良好流通秩序的建立和市场交易水平的不断提高，由企业管理市场是市场管理体制的创新，这种创新带来的绩效是明显的。

（5）建立起多种经营主体并存的格局。一个市场的活力很大程度上取决于其竞争是否充分，而充分的竞争则需要充足的交易主体和交易量，因此，多种交易主体并存是市场充满活力的前提，对农产品批发市场尤其如此。

（6）健全的农产品流通法规是农产品有序流通、农产品大市场建立与运行的保障。农产品流通必须有相关的法律法规，这既是市场有序运行的保证，也是农产品市场规范化的依据。然而，我国至今仍没有一部专门的有关农产品批发市场的法律，批发市场的规范也只是借鉴国外农产品批发市场的经验来进行。对于单个的某一农产品市场来说，规模有限，企业化运行是高效的，但对于全国性的大市场来说，企业化运行将会大大增加其组织成本，因而它需要更高层次、更具权威性的制度即法律来维系。

（7）制度安排与环境的相容，是任何制度创新并有效运行的前提。任何制度都有其产生的特殊背景和运行的适宜外部环境，当这一制度与其所处的外部环境相容时，它能从与外部环境的物质、能量交流中获取更有利于自身发展的各种资源，通过自身对环境做出的贡献被环境所认可，在运行中减少由与环境摩擦引起的运行成本，从而有着较高的运行效率。相反，当某一制度与环境不相容时，在现实中必然是低效的。

二　案例 2：蒙牛乳业中介组织发展模式

蒙牛乳业是一个以奶业加工为主的企业，其后向收购物流与前向分销物流都在企业的组织模式下进行，在农产品物流中替代了批发市场的功能，充当了中介组织的角色。蒙牛乳业的“分散饲养、定点收购、集中加工、统一分销”模式对乳业生产的集约化、分销渠道的网络化和物流的一体化发展起到了重要的推动作用，属于较为典型的中介组织物流模式。

蒙牛乳业成立于 1999 年，集团总部设在呼和浩特市和林格尔盛乐经济园区，拥有总资产近 40 亿元，员工万余人。至 2008 年年底，主营业务收入实现 239 亿元，年均递增 104%，是全国首家收入超过 200 亿元的乳品企业。主要产品的市场占有率超过 35%；UHT 牛奶销量全球第一，液体奶、冰淇淋和酸奶销量居全国第一，乳制品出口量、出口的国家和地区居全国第一。

蒙牛乳业后向实行“公司 + 基地 + 农户”的发展模式，扩大了辐射范围，带动了乳业产业的集约化发展。蒙牛乳业成立以来，作为农业产业化国家重点龙头企业，蒙牛乳业集团已在全国各生产基地的周边地区建立奶站共计 3000 多个，联系奶农达百万户，累计收购鲜奶超过 1500 万吨，累计为农牧民发放奶款超过 400 亿元，累计创造产值超过 1000 亿元，累计缴纳税款超过 40 亿元，累计创造就业机会超过 30 万个。

蒙牛乳业生产基地在内蒙古区域内以呼和浩特为轴心，向西延伸至包头、巴盟等地区；向东延伸至兴安盟、通辽等地区；向外省延伸，进入北京、天津、山西、山东、湖北、河南、安徽、兰州、新疆、浙江、黑龙江等地区。

吉林省洮南市那金镇是洮南市乃至吉林省最为贫困落后的乡镇之一，素有“穷甲吉林”之称。那金镇资源贫乏、自然条件恶劣、生产力水平低下，农业生产“靠天吃饭”，广大农民生活极为贫困，年收入仅为数百元的贫困户占全镇农户的 2/3 以上，90% 以上的农户勉强维持温饱。2002 年年初，蒙牛集团在乌兰浩特市建立了乳品加工基地，那金镇距乌兰浩特市仅 40 多公里，且两地间有柏油公路相连，比邻的地理优势和“背靠蒙牛养奶牛”的市场机遇使那金镇成为蒙牛公司的“后院生产车间”，带动了那金镇的经济发展。4 年后，全镇奶牛养殖村已发展到 12 个，养奶牛农户达到 1014 个，建奶站 11 个，养殖奶牛 2570 头，日产鲜奶 16 吨。那金镇奶牛业总收入达到 2050 万元，占全镇当年农业总收入的 70%，养奶牛户人均收入 4000 元，全镇农民人均收入的 41% 来自奶牛业。奶牛养殖业已经成为这个镇农业经济的主要支柱和最大增收来源。

蒙牛乳业前向实行企业化组织的分销模式，通过建立直销、专业代理网络，借商业批发、连锁、零售等形式，使其产品走人了千家万户。

蒙牛乳业从原料生产开始，从收购、流通到分销的整个物流过程基本都是在企业的组织下进行的，整个产业链的协调、供应链的管理也是在企业的组织下完成的，从生产到消费的中间物流过程完全体现了组织中介的作用，是农产品物流组织中介发展模式的成功案例。

附录二 西部地区农产品市场与基地联盟相关案例

一 案例1：生产基地与物美超市连锁直接联盟

随着农业产业化的发展，优质农产品需要寻求更广阔的市场。传统的农产品销售方式难以在消费者心中建立起安全信誉，也难以确保生态农业基地生产的优质农产品的价值，从而把很多特色农产品局限在产地，无法进入大市场、大流通，致使生产与销售脱节。与此同时，城镇超市快速发展，商家需要优质农副产品进入超市，以吸引更多的消费者。消费者则希望在超市能够便捷地采购到优质安全的食品。以往，超市蔬菜、瓜果完全依靠中介公司或大型批发市场提供，那些菜一般要在运输、储藏过程中花上一两天时间，甚至更久，中间环节多，不仅难以保证农产品的质量，也提高了流通成本。

在这种情况下，越来越多的超市改变传统的采购渠道，通过多种方式与农产品供应基地建立合作关系，直接把自己的采购系统延伸到田头，直接向生产者采购产品，形成了“基地 + 超市”这种流通模式。物美集团经过两年多的调研和准备，于2009年5月初正式启动“新鲜蔬果直通车”专项工程，实现与西部地区部分蔬菜生产基地的“基地 + 超市”联盟。

物美集团是国内最早以连锁方式经营超市的专业集团公司之一，率先在北京创办大型综合超市，也是较早在零售业使用POS系统以及在北方地区店铺超百家的连锁企业，具有较强的实力。为丰富农产品品种，向消费者提供质量更优、价格更实惠的农产品，提升超市的核心竞争力，物美积极开发了对农产品生产基地进行直接采购农产品的模式，促进农产品市场的进一步发育与发展。

西部地区自然条件优越、农业门类齐全、产品种类丰富、产量规模很大、产品品质优良，西部地区七大名优特农产品生产基地是中国最大的农产品生产基地和出口基地。例如：新疆优质棉花生产基地；云南、内蒙古和新疆糖料生产基地；西南地区热带水果、西北地区优质水果生产基地；新疆瓜果、云南元谋、甘肃河西走廊和青海蔬菜生产基地；云南、内蒙古和新疆花卉生产基地；宁夏、甘肃、新疆、青海中药材生产基地；云南烟叶生产基地。

“基地+超市”联盟的本质是将现代流通方式引向广阔农村，将农产品生产规模化并与千变万化的大市场联盟起来，构建市场经济条件下的产销一体化链条，实现商家、农民、消费者共赢，带来了广泛而深刻的经济社会影响。

（一）联盟运行机制

1. 战略联盟

首先是需要在超市和基地之间建立长期合作意识。从超市角度看，可以对直供农产品建立追溯制度，实现农产品质量从农田到餐桌的全过程控制，提高农产品质量安全水平，从而提升超市的核心竞争力；从农民的角度看，由于有了超市的指导，农民生产技术和管理水平得到提高，有助于供货数量保证和质量提高，解决了销售难题，更能保证自身利益；从消费者角度看，消费者需要的是价格适中的新鲜蔬菜。因此，农产品进超市是我国经济发展的必然趋势，长期合作对于各方的发展都是有利的。目前，物美已经与部分生产基地初步建立了长期战略合作伙伴关系，针对满足消费者需求的共同目标，物美加大对生产基地的农产品采购力度，并在采购价格、结算方式以及技术支持等方面，提供优惠的条件和便利，并在产品规划、人才培养、技术创新等方面结合各自的发展规划共同进行。

2. 利益联盟

在传统的供应链采购模式下，介于农民和超市之间的中间环节分配了产品30%—40%的利润，而农民和超市只有10%—15%的利润。“基地+超市”联盟省掉中间环节后，农户、超市和消费者均可以获得一定程度的成本下降。在这种情况下，物美及生产基地对增值部分的来源进行详细评估，把劳动、生产要素、资本、经营风险等全部综合到利益分配的方案中去，在保证新鲜果蔬从田间地头直通到柜台不超过24小时的同时，将大部分增加的利益分给了农户和消费者，农户获得了比直接给返销户更多的利润，消费者在物美购买生鲜蔬菜的价格比农贸市场便宜20%—40%，很好地实现了利益在农超之间的“基地+超市”联盟。

3. 信息联盟

包括产品信息联盟和市场信息联盟。物美对直供的农产品在生产阶段就进行产品信息跟踪，了解产品的种植情况、农药播撒情况、产品质量安全信息等，实现农产品基本信息的联盟。同时超市也可根据市场行情，对生产领域进行适当干预、调整，避免盲目生产，减少不必要的浪费，充分发挥市场调节作用，将最有效的消费信息传递给生产者，指导生产。

4. 组织联盟

为了实现组织规模联盟，西部地区各省各级供销社将越来越多的农户组织成有一定生产规模的生产基地。为了保证直采产品质量，物美专门成立了从事农技指导、咨询和培训的团队，与当地供销社合作，共同为基地农民提供服务。也增加了农产品质量控制、现场直采的部门，拓宽与基地的合作层面，更好地与基地端进行合作。

5. 标准联盟

目前发展初期的标准联盟，主要体现在管理水平更高的超市将标准向生产端输出。物美依据超市对农产品的分类标准、规格标准以及质量检测标准等向生产基地提出要求，让生产基地提供满足超市要求的农产品。

6. 文化联盟

首先在超市和基地这个联盟体系内，产生一个共赢文化，让成员形成这样的共识：通过直接联盟的合作，对于超市、生产基地、消费者，是共赢的。事实也证明，各方都得到了价值实现。其次，形成顾客至上文化，联盟体系只有一个目标——提供满意的产品与服务给消费者，这就要求从生产开始，直至最终服务，所有成员都要关注产品质量。超市与生产基地通过以上文化的构建，营造友好协商的合作氛围，彼此信任，逐步形成农产品联盟体系的良好品牌和社会形象。

（二）支撑及发展机制

1. 政策支持

正是意识到“基地+超市”联盟是减少流通环节、降低农产品流通成本的有效手段，是解决鲜活农产品难卖的根本途径，2008 年 12 月，商务部、农业部联合下发了《关于开展农超对接试点工作的通知》，国务院办公厅发布了《关于搞活流通扩大消费的意见》，都明确指出要支持大型连锁超市、农产品流通企业与农产品专业合作社建立农产品直接采购基地，培育自有品牌，促进产销衔接。在相关政策的支撑下，财政、国土、税务、金融等有关部门的配套措施将进一步出台，都将为“基地+超市”

联盟的发展创造良好的宏观环境。

2. 技术支持

先进的信息化技术一直是物美集团的核心竞争力之一。从 1994 年开始使用 POS 机，到 2002 年的信息系统，再到 2006 年与 SAP 携手正式启动的 WINBOX 项目，物美一直都走在信息化的前列，并被国家信息化测评中心评为“重大企业信息化建设成就奖”，信息系统已经覆盖了采购、销售、物流、财务、人力资源和营销等各项业务，为“基地 + 超市”联盟的顺畅运行提供了技术支撑。通过信息技术的应用，配送中心实施给店铺多次供货，使配送中心对店铺订单的满足率得到提升，缩短了“基地—配送中心—店铺”之间供应链的空间和时间，有效控制了库存周转天数。同时能够清理并整合系统内的供应商信息，检查供应商的交易记录，将系统中庞大的供应商数据进行逐条梳理，使供应商管理更加规范化、精细化。

3. 资本支持

为了推动“基地 + 超市”联盟的运转，物美筹集资金进行相关建设。2010 年 9 月 18 日，物美集团在银川设立的首个大卖场占地近 2 万平方米，涵盖 6 万多种商品，拥有 3000 个停车位。物美将在未来 3 年时间，累计投资 45 亿元，在银川打造西北第一大商贸集团，做西北的超市引领者，建立西北最大的现代化物流体系，成为西北类型最全、规模最大的百货公司和行业领头羊。物美集团将在银川建设两大新地标，并自主经营两家高端、新型百货商店，一家标准大卖场样板店和一家现代量贩广场，还有一个西北最大的超市物流基地，在银川周边 500 公里范围内 7 个重点市、区开设 2 家百货公司、10 家大卖场、50 家生活超市和若干家购物中心，以及 3 个分销配送中心和恒温室，这是专门为“基地 + 超市”联盟方便储藏新鲜农产品而建的。在发展过程中，物美集团将在全区新增就业岗位近 4 万个。此外，物美集团还将借用自己的物流体系和销售终端，把宁夏的特色工业品、农产品推入北京、天津、杭州乃至其旗下全国各超市。

4. 人才培养

根据物美集团的规划，下一步将增加人才培养，尤其是采购端的质量检测、采购人员。同时和多家名优特农产品基地合作，进一步扩大蔬菜品种的引入，逐步推广到所有物美连锁门店。

当前，“基地 + 超市”联盟模式尚处于快速发展阶段，随着对直接联盟模式的深入探索，将会在组织、管理等方面不断创新，推动直接联盟模式的可持续发展。

二 案例2：四川聚和生态农业龙头企业型联盟

四川聚和生态农业发展有限公司是一家民营独资企业，注册资本6200万元，由三名自然人股东共同出资设立。公司位于四川省成都市龙泉驿区国家级经济技术开发区。主营市场开发、农副产品批发与零售、物流配送、水果蔬菜冷藏、分选加工、冷藏货运、进出口贸易等。聚和公司经过不懈的追求和努力，先后被评为了“农业产业化国家重点龙头企业”“省农业产业化先进营销组织”“农业部定点农产品批发市场”“国家发改委信息化系统定点建设市场”“管理创新十佳市场”“全国蔬菜批发十强市场”、商务部“双百市场”和“绿色市场”等荣誉称号。

四川聚和生态农业的销售终端包括零售连锁、商场超市、餐饮、批发和特供等，其中零售连锁是非常重要的渠道，尤其在大城市，是销售的主要渠道。四川聚和生态农业发展有限公司与多家超市连锁达成合作伙伴协议，直接向零售连锁供货，使得“生产基地—加工企业—零售超市”成为主要流通模式之一。

（一）联盟运行机制

1. 战略发展及利益联盟

四川聚和生态农业发展有限公司自成立以来，一直以农业产业化经营和带动农民增收为己任，秉承“让果蔬动起来，让农民富起来”的企业宗旨和“建市场带产业，活经济富百姓”的奋斗目标，于2003年在成都市龙泉驿区投资兴建了西部最大、功能最齐全、现代化水平最高的“成都龙泉聚和（国际）果蔬交易中心”。

聚和（国际）农产品物流中心以农产品流通为纽带，连接生产与消费，打造基地建设、农产品批发、气调保鲜、物流配送、分选加工、精品展示、电子商务、检验检疫、粮油批发、进出口贸易等为一体的产业链条，促进了农村市场繁荣，增加了农民收入，推动了农业经济的快速发展。聚和（国际）农产品物流中心一期占地325亩（21.67公顷），建筑面积16万平方米，已投资3亿元人民币建成了7.8万平方米蔬菜交易区，

2.3 万平方米水果交易区，1.1 万平方米特色精品展示交易厅，0.8 万平方米商务中心，1.5 万平方米综合楼，10000 吨德国、荷兰先进技术设备的气调保鲜冷藏库，8 吨/小时光电加工分选线以及电子结算中心、信息管理中心、检验检疫中心和安全监控中心，集农产品展示交易、电子拍卖、气调保鲜、贮藏加工、分选包装、物流配送、电子商务、无公害检验检测、进出口贸易等多功能配套服务为一体的大型农产品交易中心。

2. 组织联盟

为了提高与生产基地、零售连锁的关联，不仅要求供应销售部门与合作单位保持密切的联系，质管、检验部门也应保持紧密联系。四川聚和生态农业发展有限公司在组织上，改组成事业部制和对各销售公司实行专营制，加强各主要产品系列的直线管理和渠道管理的扁平化，缩减渠道的中间环节。并根据零售终端的经营规模、销量、服务与管理等不同特色，划分不同部门，进一步加强销售体系与各销售终端的联盟。

3. 质量、标准联盟

聚和（国际）农产品物流中心凭借完善的功能配套设施，运用先进的“功能齐全、经营安全、信息快捷”的物流理念以及场地设施租赁、交易管理、信息服务、气调保鲜、光电分选和第三方物流为主要经营模式。物流中心现日均吞吐量达 8500 吨，日车流量达 1700 辆次，日人流量 16000 人次，日交易额达 1900 万元，销售品种达 100 余种。2009 年实现交易量 320 万吨，交易额达 70 亿元，所销售农产品辐射全国甘肃、陕西、新疆、内蒙古、黑龙江、江苏、云南、贵州、青海等 20 余个省市，吸纳农民工就业 2000 余人，带动了人均年增收 2000 元，极大地丰富了成都乃至西南地区广大人民的“菜篮子”。项目全部投运后，预计年物流量达到 600 万吨，物流价值 100 亿元，极大地推动西部农产品的快速流通，提升了农产品从生产、储藏、运输到销售环节的附加值，改变了传统农业向现代农业的发展观念，带动了西部地区农产品种植业朝集约化、规模化、标准化的方向发展。此外，公司还充分利用种植基地、检测中心、气调保鲜库、分选加工车间等优势资源，发展农产品配送业务，为政府、学校、超市、“便民菜店”等团体配送安全、新鲜、价优的农产品。

公司以“市场＋合作社＋农户”的农业产业化合作模式，在四川省内组建了 10 余个标准化种植基地，覆盖面积 6000 多亩（400 多公顷），种植农户 3000 多户，还通过了四川省出入境检验检疫局注册建设了 1000

余亩（66.67 公顷）出口创汇基地。通过长期努力，聚和公司建立的部分基地已通过四川省商检局出口备案登记，并通过国家认监委认可的 GAP（良好农业规范认证）。公司对基地的土壤、种植、用药、采收等一系列环节进行全程监控，实行“统一农资供应、统一技术培训、统一生产管理、统一抽样检测、统一品牌包装”，使优质果率从 50% 提高达 80%，社员每亩农资投入降低 10% 以上，亩成本减少 300 元—500 元的生产投入，社员平均每斤水果销售价格提高 0.5 元左右，每亩果树收入增加约 1000 元左右，促进农业增产，农民增收。公司从事进出口贸易以来，与新加坡、泰国、印尼、马来西亚、澳大利亚、加拿大等诸多国家建立了长期的合作关系。去年又成功出口和通过香港转口柑橘类、枇杷、水蜜桃、猕猴桃、草莓、李类、梨、菌类等农产品 200 多吨水果到相关国家，实现销售收入 40 多万美元。

交易中心按照国家标准建设了检验检测中心，可在半小时内对 88 个蔬菜或水果的药物残留、有机磷、氨基甲酸酯等项目进行抽样检测。市场与区质监局、农发局、工商局建立了联合监测机制，制定了市场准入制度、农产品抽检制度、经销商管理制度、产品信息公示制度、商品清退制度和质检员管理制度等质量安全体系，明确规定了对检测不合格的产品进行退市处理，经过权威部门和认证机构认证的“无公害农产品”“绿色食品”“有机食品”可凭相关证书或检测报告直接进入市场销售；对实施购销挂钩的经营户建立购销挂钩关系，已明确供货主体和产品质量责任的可进入市场销售，有效遏制了不合格农产品进入批发市场交易，保障了农产品的质量安全，切实保护消费者的身体健康。

4. 文化联盟

自创立以来，四川聚和生态农业发展有限公司一直坚定地实施企业文化战略，充分发挥企业文化的导向、凝聚、激励、规范等功能，比较有代表性的有：“勤奋、务实、高效、创新”的企业精神；“让绩效优秀者名利双收，让滥竽充数者难以自容”的激励理念；“质量就是生命，责任重于泰山”的质量观。企业文化强有力地促进了公司事业的快速、健康发展。同时，四川聚和生态农业发展有限公司将之用于合作伙伴的选择，将绩效文化、共赢文化带人到整个联盟体系中，实现文化联盟。

聚和（国际）果蔬交易中心为给社会承担一份责任，为人民贡献一份力量，在 2008 年的雪灾和地震中，努力开展各项救灾活动。一是组织公司员工、商户捐款16.5万元，捐赠蔬菜500多吨，为灾区人民积极献爱心；二是承担了灾区蔬菜的调入和调出任务，到全国各地每天调入2000多吨蔬菜到市场供应，同时利用气调保鲜库进行储备蔬菜周转，确保市场和灾区的蔬菜需求，平抑了物价；三是在市场内设立了“灾区农产品直销点”，对进入市场的灾区蔬菜免收交易管理费，在雪灾和地震期间共免收交易费1000多万元；四是承担了灾区救灾物资在成都中转的光荣任务，安排布置了40000平方米的仓库作为救灾物资转运中心，周转品种上千种，周转量达到35000吨，保证了震灾物资第一时间送到灾区；五是公司调动冷藏保鲜车辆，深入到彭州、汶川、理县、茂县等灾区，以保护价收购各种蔬菜和甜樱桃5000多吨，帮助灾区人民的生产自救，降低灾区人民的损失。在抗震救灾工作中，聚和公司做了大量的工作，增强了灾区人民抗灾自救的能力，实现了农产品市场与受灾地区的有效联盟，在保障市场供给、稳定市场秩序、平抑农产品价格、恢复灾区生产、促进灾区农产品流通、保障农产品食品安全等方面都发挥了重要作用。

聚和公司自成立以来，严格遵守国家相关的法律法规，依法经营、诚信经商，认真履行企业义务，按时、照章纳税，不存在偷漏拖欠税的问题，每年向税务部门缴纳的税收200多万元。公司认真遵守国家颁布的劳动法规及相关规定，努力保障职工权益，每月按时足额地为员工缴纳社保基金，切实解决员工的后顾之忧。公司按时归还银行的贷款和利息，在融资信用方面信誉良好，各项指标体系较好，目前银行信用等级为AA级。公司积极参加社会公益事业，不定期为当地农民捐书捐物，提高农民的知识；同时为公司员工、社会人士、伤残人士捐助救治基金，努力现身于光彩事业，勇于承担多项社会责任。

（二）支撑与发展机制

1. 政策支撑

聚和公司被列为“农业产业化全国重点龙头企业”，在国家支持农业产业化发展的宏观环境下，使得聚和公司能够在财政资金、国债项目、减免税费、金融信贷、上市融资、立项审批等多方面得到国家的直接支持。各种政策支持，为聚和公司进行基地建设、技术引进创造了良好的外部环境。

2. 资本支撑

聚和公司发展过程、基地建设过程离不开资本支撑。根据农产品物流中心发展的需要，聚和将通过政府引导，市场化运作机制，大力整合西部地区资源，科学规划产业布局，高标准、高水平地构建中国一流的“成都市农产品交易中心”。该项目将主要以冷链生鲜物流中心、东盟农产品中西部集散中心、成都市净菜加工中心、有机农产品交易中心、电子商务交易及农产品价格指数发布信息中心、农产品拍卖中心等功能。项目建成投入使用后，预计可促进就业5000人，带动当地人均年增收2000元，预计年交易额达到200亿元人民币，将形成全国综合性的农产品物流大市场，成为“买全国、卖全国”交易平台，打造成为国际现代综合农产品物流中心。

3. 人力支撑

聚和公司汇聚了全国各地、世界各地的人才，建立了一支一流的人才队伍，先后聘用国外专家300多人次，累计投放几亿元资金。为了提高员工整体素质，聚和公司常年开设各种类型培训班，确保员工每年都要受到两次以上的培训。还与北京师范大学等大学联系，把大学办到了企业里。公司先后拿出上千万元将数百名干部、技术人员、优秀员工送到国外考察、学习，培养才干。多类型的人才为聚和公司的发展奠定了基础。

4. 技术创新

聚和公司产品的质量离不开先进的技术，聚和公司全套引进了世界先进生产线及其配套技术，同时组织专家实行技术攻关，消化、吸收、创新了国外技术。

5. 文化创新

聚和公司的文化创新就是在企业构建一种创新文化，就是让创新意识无所不在，只有创新的思想，才有创新的行为，进而推动制度创新、组织创新、管理创新和技术创新。正是基于这种创新意识，聚和公司不断进行经营模式创新、品牌创新以及技术创新等，都体现出创新已经成为推动企业发展的最重要的动力，并通过合作把这种文化向生产、零售端输出，使得“不断创新”成为一种习惯、一种规范，对农产品市场与基地联盟体系的后续发展，提供巨大的动力。

聚和公司在经营农业产业化事业过程中，极大地促进了农产品的“大进大出”，大大增强了农产品的物流功能，对增加农民自主谋业机会，实现以产业化为依托，保障农民收入持续增长，以市场化带动农业的产业化和现代化发展，推进城乡一体化和社会主义新农村建设等都起到了十分重要的推动作用。

三　案例3：陕西红果贸易有限公司一体化型联盟

陕西红果贸易有限公司（原名扶风县红果贸易有限公司），是2000年由扶风县果品销售公司联合扶风地区果品经销企业组建的集团公司，2001年实现股份制改造注册登记为有限责任公司。公司现拥有资产总额2415万元，其中固定资产1530万元。注册资金1000万元。该公司先后荣获“陕西省农业产业化重点龙头企业”“中华全国供销合作总社参与农业产业化重点龙头企业”“扶风县信用联社优秀信用企业”称号。

公司所在地扶风县是全国55个优质苹果生产基地县之一，位于北纬34°12′—34°37′、东经107°45′—108°0′，海拔850—1579米，平均气温12.4℃，年日照2136.5小时，积温4053.7℃，降雨量591.8毫米。土壤肥沃，昼夜温差大，为苹果生长提供了理想的环境，所产苹果，果型端正，含糖量高，色泽艳丽，香甜爽口，风味醇厚，而且硬度大，无污染，耐贮运，是名副其实的绿色苹果。

近年来，按照“公司+基地+农户”的产业化模式，不断健全生产，销售服务体系，注册了“法门寺”商标，申请了进出口自营资格，带动全县和周边地区果业的发展。2003年，公司被认定为陕西省农业产业化重点龙头企业和中华全国供销总社参与农业产业化重点龙头企业。并被扶风县信用联社评定为优秀信用企业。

陕西红果贸易有限公司地处国家AAAA级旅游景区法门寺，是从事苹果、梨、葡萄、猕猴桃、杂果、辣椒等农副产品购销、冷藏业务的果品流通企业。占地面积33000平方米，拥有冷库7座，冷藏能力1.2万吨。该公司年经销果品3万吨。在全国20多个大中城市有自己的销售窗口，并建立了160多家长期业务关系。组织200多人的果品经纪人队伍，产品远销广东、广西、福建、云南、湖北、湖南、四川、重庆及东南亚和俄罗斯等市场。由本公司牵头与扶风、岐山、凤翔、千阳、陇县等五县果业管理部门建设的九万亩绿色苹果基地，2003年产品检测全部合格，通过了中国绿色发展中心认证，以“法门寺”为品牌的红富士、秦冠、嘎拉、粉红女士苹果，获得绿色标志使用权。在凤翔、扶风建立优质精品苹果基地2000亩（133.33公顷），实行订单农业。通过科技承包，统防统治，套袋管理，使精品苹果全部进入高端市场。

红果贸易有限公司以农产品标准化、信息化为前提，从产前、产中绿色生产资料供应和产后绿色农产品营销工程两端入手，初步形成了“生产—加工—物流中心—销售”一体化的产业格局。目前，布局全国的各级物流中心的建设还在规划当中，通过红果贸易有限公司的探索，未来将建立以绿色食品为切入点的展示交易、加工保鲜、仓储配送、科研开发、信息处理、金融服务等内容为一体的现代农产品物流体系，并随着遍及全国的五级现代物流体系的建成，摸索出一体化的现代农产品物流模式。

链接资料：

2012年01月02日《陕西日报》“陕西成为水果生产第一大省 增加值突破200亿”

2011年12月28日，记者从省果业局获悉，2011年我省果业增加值预计将突破200亿元。在全省30个苹果基地县，果农人均苹果纯收入将达到6000元，而11个猕猴桃重点县的果农人均猕猴桃纯收入将高达7000元。

据省果业局调查统计，截至2011年底，全省水果总面积1714万亩，挂果面积1114万亩，产量1420万吨，成为全国水果生产第一大省。其中苹果面积959万亩，产量960万吨，面积、产量均居全国第一；猕猴桃面积90.9万亩，产量70万吨，成为全球最大的猕猴桃生产基地。全省果业发展呈现面积稳中有增、总产不断提高、农民收入持续增加的良好态势。

在果园面积和产量稳步提高的同时，我省果树品种结构趋于合理。目前，全省已建成渭北黄土高原苹果产业带、秦岭北麓猕猴桃产业带、秦岭南坡浅山柑橘产业带、黄河沿岸红枣产业带、大中城市近郊时令水果产业带，区域特色和优势不断凸现。

果园管理水平大幅提升。四项关键技术由最初的“行政推动”已基本转为果农的“自觉行动”。财政支持果业发展项目的积极实施和国家标准果园的创建，果园枝条粉碎发酵还田和“灯、板、带”防治技术的推广应用，有力推动了果业技术创新和标准化生产。全省标准果园、生态果园中80%以上悬挂配置“杀虫灯、黏虫板、诱虫带”等设施，果园病虫无害化防治水平进一步提高。全省经欧盟和国内认证认可的有机苹果20

万亩，通过认证的出口基地86万亩。

果农收入持续增加。据统计，延安市人均果业收入过万元的村有389个，涉及果农17万人；人均收入过万元的户有52047户，占全市果农户的23%。周至县种植猕猴桃的果农人均纯收入已达到8600元，楼观镇周一村90%以上的农户亩均收入过万元。一些种植优良品种、作务技术较高的农户，每亩收入甚至超过两万元。在果业提质增效工程带动下，2011年城固柑橘品质提升，每公斤收购价2.2元以上，高出往年20%，成为县域经济的支柱。

附录三　西部地区农业产业化龙头企业

一　第五批西部地区农业产业化国家重点龙头企业

表12－1　第五批西部地区农业产业化国家重点龙头企业名单

内蒙古通辽余粮畜业开发有限公司	内蒙古蒙都羊业食品有限公司
东乌珠穆沁旗草原东方肉业有限责任公司	鄂尔多斯市四季青农业开发有限公司
扎兰屯市蒙东牲畜交易市场有限责任公司	内蒙古民丰薯业有限公司
乌兰浩特市金谷粮油米业加工有限公司	内蒙古富川饲料科技股份有限公司
内蒙古通辽岳泰股份有限公司	广西巨东种养集团有限公司
横县桂华茧丝绸有限责任公司	广西来宾东糖集团有限公司
广西壮族自治区国有高峰林场	广西五丰粮食集团有限公司
广西金穗农业投资有限责任公司	广西梧州制药（集团）股份有限公司
广西金源生物化工实业有限公司	贺州嘉宝食品有限公司
广西凌云浪伏茶业有限公司	成都佳享食品有限公司
四川省丹丹调味品有限公司	四川徽记食品产业有限公司
四川逢春制药有限公司	四川国豪种业股份有限公司
四川回春堂药业连锁有限公司	四川省福元肉类食品有限公司
四川省犍为凤生纸业有限责任公司	峨眉山仙芝竹尖茶业有限责任公司
四川巴山雀舌名茶实业有限公司	四川江口醇酒业（集团）有限公司
四川仁寿玉泉食品有限公司	四川省五友农牧有限公司

续表 12－1

四川特驱投资有限公司	四川省味聚特食品有限公司
四川省畜科饲料有限公司	四川省花秋茶业有限公司
广元市申达实业有限公司	中食成都食品有限公司
四川永鑫农牧股份有限公司	四川省天兆畜牧科技有限公司
重庆市涪陵辣妹子集团有限公司	重庆周君记火锅食品有限公司
重庆市铜龙食品有限责任公司	重庆小天鹅百福食品有限公司
重庆五斗米饮食文化有限公司	重庆恒都农业开发有限公司
重庆南方金山谷农牧有限公司	重庆红蜻蜓油脂有限责任公司
内蒙古通辽余粮畜业开发有限公司	内蒙古蒙都羊业食品有限公司
贵州百灵企业集团制药股份有限公司	贵州省湄潭县栗香茶业有限公司
贵州湄潭盛兴茶业有限公司	贵州经典云雾茶业有限责任公司
贵州东太农业股份有限公司	遵义陆圣康源科技开发有限责任公司
云南宏斌绿色食品有限公司	云南惠嘉集团有限公司
云南锦苑花卉产业股份有限公司	云南爱俍农牧（集团）有限公司
云南龙润茶业集团有限公司	昆明华曦牧业集团有限公司
勐海茶业有限责任公司	西藏特色产业股份有限公司
陕西陕富面业有限责任公司	陕西欣绿实业股份有限公司
陕西福锦米业有限公司	陕西春光油脂有限公司
陕西苍山茶业有限责任公司	宝鸡祥和面粉有限责任公司
清涧县巨鹰枣业有限责任公司	陕西大匠农科产业（集团）有限公司
富县宏佳果贸有限责任公司	陕西大地种业有限公司
商洛市朝阳工贸有限责任公司	咸阳新阳光农副产品有限公司
甘肃达利食品有限公司	甘肃宏良皮业股份有限公司
甘肃陇原中天生物工程股份有限公司	甘肃三洋啤酒原料股份有限公司
静宁常津果品有限责任公司	甘肃康美现代农牧产业集团有限公司
天水众兴菌业有限责任公司	宁夏泰瑞制药股份有限公司
宁夏中杞枸杞贸易有限公司	宁夏厚生记食品有限公司
宁夏天瑞产业集团现代农业有限公司	银川市金河乳业有限公司
御马国际葡萄酒业（宁夏）有限公司	青海可可西里实业开发集团有限公司
柴达木羊绒有限公司	青海康普生物科技股份有限公司
青海清华博众生物技术有限公司	青海绿草源食品有限公司

续表 12－1

湟中弘大农副产品购销有限公司	新疆鸿锦枸杞实业有限公司
新疆恩利德生物科技有限公司	阿图什富江果业有限公司
新疆恒丰糖业有限公司	吐鲁番市宋峰物流有限公司
伊犁天药生物科技有限公司	昌吉回族自治州粮油购销（集团）有限责任公司
新疆瑞源乳业有限公司	新疆庄子实业有限公司
库尔勒利华棉业有限公司	新疆天海绿洲农业科技股份有限公司
新疆西部牧业股份有限公司	新疆银隆国际贸易股份有限公司
和田昆仑山枣业有限责任公司	奇台县春蕾麦芽制造有限公司

资料来源：中国农产品专家网。

二　西部地区农垦农业产业化国家重点龙头企业

表 12－2　　西部地区农垦农业产业化国家重点龙头企业名单

包头懋菲蒙奶业股份有限公司	广西明阳生化科技股份有限公司
广西农垦糖业集团有限公司	重庆市天友乳业有限公司
重庆市大正畜牧科技有限公司	贵阳三联乳业有限公司
云南天然橡胶产业股份有限公司	昆明雪兰牛奶有限责任公司
甘肃莫高实业发展股份有限公司	甘肃亚盛实业（集团）股份有限公司
兰州好为尔生物科技股份有限公司	宁夏回族自治区西夏王葡萄酒业（集团）公司
宁夏农垦贺兰山清真肉羊产业（集团）有限公司	新天国际葡萄酒业有限公司
新疆赛里木现代农业股份有限公司	新疆冠农果茸股份有限公司
新疆塔里木农业综合开发股份有限公司	新疆塔里木河种业股份有限公司
新疆伊力特集团有限公司	新疆天康畜牧生物技术股份有限公司
新疆中基实业股份有限公司	新疆石河子银河纺织有限责任公司
新疆康地农业科技发展有限责任公司	中国彩棉（集团）股份有限公司

资料来源：农业部信息中心 。

附录四　西部地区农业产业化示范单位

一　西部地区第一批国家农业产业化示范基地

表 12－3　　西部地区第一批国家农业产业化示范基地名单

呼伦贝尔岭东农牧业产业化示范园区	通辽市科尔沁农牧业产业化示范园区
赤峰市元宝山区平庄农产品加工园区	来宾市兴宾甘蔗园区
玉林市健康产业园区	重庆市长寿现代农业园区
成都市郫县中国川菜产业化功能区	眉山市东坡区泡菜产业示范基地
四川省南充市嘉陵区大风垭现代农业示范园区	宜宾市高县庆符—文江农产品加工园区
贵州省遵义市湄潭县绿色食品工业园区	云南昆明石林台湾农民创业园
云南（曲靖）国际农业食品科技园区	杨凌现代农业示范园
白水县苹果科技产业园	甘肃酒泉省级农业产业化示范基地
武威黄羊省级农业产业化示范基地	宁夏利通金银滩奶牛核心园区
西宁（国家级）经济技术开发区南川工业园区城	南绒毛工业园
昌吉农业科技园区	库尔勒经济技术开发区农副产品加工工业园

资料来源：农业部信息中心。

二　西部地区第十五批农业部定点市场

表 12－4　　西部地区第十五批农业部定点市场名单

乌兰察布市集宁区丰泰长信果品蔬菜批发市场	扎赉特旗石头城子农畜产品批发市场
成都濛阳（四川国际）农产品交易中心	自贡川南农副产品批市场
成都市金林湾花木交易市场	三联家禽有限责任公司
祥和九龙坡蔬菜批发市场	（荣昌）畜牧产品交易市场
毕节市洪南农产品专业批发市场	明骏骐干菜副食粮油批发市场
明金马正昌第二果品市场	定西市临洮县崖湾蔬菜批发市场

续表 12－4

凉市东郊蔬菜瓜果批发市场	都县东升果蔬产品交易市场
宁国际枸杞交易中心	吉将台马铃薯批发市场
吉市中亚农副农资批发市场有限责任公司	犁农副产品中心批发市场
羌县楼兰特色果蔬综合市场有限责任公司	团农十四师皮墨农产品批发交易市场
团农十三师红星一场农产品批发交易市场	团农四师六十一团阿力玛里农产品综合批发交易市场

资料来源：农业部信息中心。

参考文献

[1] 丁俊发."三农"问题与现代物流［J］. 经济，2004（4）：31～34

[2] 中国物流与采购联合会. 中国物流年鉴［S］. 北京：中国物资出版社，2008：273～274

[3] Franz Wiedmann. Georg Wilhelm Friedrich Hegel，Hamburg：Rowohlt Taschenbuch Verlag GmbH，1965：226

[4] 马克思. 资本论（第1卷）［M］. 北京：人民出版社，1975：362～376

[5] 马克思. 资本论（第1卷）［M］. 北京：人民出版社，1975：362

[6] 马克思. 资本论（第1卷）［M］. 北京：人民出版社，1975：393～395

[7] 谢富胜. 分工、技术与生产组织变迁［M］. 北京：经济科学出版社，2005：84～85

[8] 马克思. 资本论（第3卷）［M］. 北京：人民出版社，1975：671

[9] 马克思. 资本论（第3卷）［M］. 北京：人民出版社，1975：450

[10] 邹薇，庄子银. 分工、交易与经济增长［J］. 中国社会科学，1996（3）：4～13

[11] 李碧珍. 农产品物流模式创新研究［M］. 北京：社会科学文献出版社，2010：34～35

[12] 马克思恩格斯全集. 中文1版（第12卷）［M］. 北京：人民出版社，1962：749

[13] 马克思. 资本论（第1卷）［M］. 北京：人民出版社，1975：131

[14] 马克思. 资本论（第1卷）［M］. 北京：人民出版社，1975：106

[15] 马克思恩格斯全集. 中文1版（第46卷. 上）［M］. 北京：人民出版社，1979：210

[16] 马克思恩格斯全集. 中文1版（第46卷. 上）［M］. 北京：人民出版社，1979：437

[17] 马克思. 资本论（第2卷）［M］. 北京：人民出版社，1975：116

[18] 马克思. 资本论（第2卷）[M]. 北京：人民出版社，1975：127
[19] 马克思恩格斯全集. 中文1版（第49卷. 上）[M]. 北京：人民出版社，1979：297
[20] 马克思. 资本论（第1卷）[M]. 北京：人民出版社，1975：188
[21] 马克思. 资本论（第1卷）[M]. 北京：人民出版社，1975：130
[22] 马克思. 资本论（第1卷）[M]. 北京：人民出版社，1975：182
[23] 马克思. 资本论（第1卷）[M]. 北京：人民出版社，1975：995
[24] 中国大百科全书·经济学（Ⅱ）[M]. 北京：中国大百科全书出版社，1988：779
[25] 中国大百科全书·经济学（Ⅱ）[M]. 北京：中国大百科全书出版社，1988：786
[26] 马克思. 资本论（第2卷）[M]. 北京：人民出版社，1975：339
[27] 马克思恩格斯全集. 中文1版（第45卷）[M]. 北京：人民出版社，2001：40
[28] 朱占峰. 论马克思主义流通观视阈下的新流通模式的构建 [J]. 商丘师范学院学报，2007（11）：101～104
[29] 崔向阳. 对马克思流通理论的新认识 [J]. 商业研究，2005（15）：12～15
[30] 李碧珍. 马克思物流思想及其现实意义 [J]. 福建师范大学学报（哲社版），2006（6）：26～31
[31] 晏维龙. 马克思主义流通理论当代视界与发展 [M]. 北京：中国人民大学出版社，2009：36
[32] 李君如. 当代中国的马克思主义：邓小平理论 [M]. 河南：河南人民出版社，1994：39
[33] 黄爱民. 毛泽东商品经济思想与邓小平市场经济理论 [J]. 毛泽东思想论坛，1994（1）：21～23
[34] 毛泽东. 毛泽东文集（第7卷）[M]. 北京：人民出版社，1999：440；439
[35] 中共中央文献编辑委员会. 毛泽东著作选读（下册）[M]. 北京：人民出版社，1986：42～45
[36] 李碧珍. 农产品物流模式创新研究 [M]. 北京：社会科学文献出版社，2010：373
[37] 徐虎. 论邓小平流通经济思想的现实意义 [J]. 中国流通经济，2008

(11)：14～16
[38] 邓小平. 邓小平文选（第3卷）[M]. 北京：人民出版社，1995：103～110
[39] 邓小平. 邓小平文选（第3卷）[M]. 北京：人民出版社，1995：218～227
[40] 邓小平. 邓小平文选（第3卷）[M]. 北京：人民出版社，1995：367
[41] 邓小平. 邓小平文选（第3卷）[M]. 北京：人民出版社，1995：373
[42] 曹佩文. 国际物流会议与物流理论的发展 [J]. 铁道物资科学管理，1997（6）：48～49
[43]（美）斯蒂格利茨. 经济学（下）[M]. 北京：中国人民大学出版社，1997：253
[44]（英）W. 阿瑟·刘易斯. 经济增长理论 [M]. 上海：上海三联书店，1994：38～41
[45] 汪斌，董赞. 从古典到新兴古典经济学的专业化分工理论与当代产业集群的演进 [J]. 学术月刊，2005（2）：31～38；54
[46] 习李克. 关于分工、专业化和产权制度的一般均衡分析 [J]. 经济社会体制比较，2002（3）：37～44
[47] A. Young. Increasing Returns and Economic Progress. Economic. Journal, 1928（38）：527～532
[48]（英）亚当·斯密. 国富论 [M]. 谢祖钧等译，湖南：中南大学出版社，2003：13～24
[49] 杨小凯，黄有光. 专业化与经济组织 [M]. 北京：经济科学出版社，1999：74～93
[50] 杨小凯，张永生. 新兴古典经济学与超边际分析 [M]. 北京：社会科学文献出版社，2003：28
[51]（美）道格拉斯·C. 诺斯. 经济史中的结构与变迁 [M]. 陈郁，罗华平等译，上海：上海三联书店；上海人民出版社，1991：212
[52]（美）熊彼特. 经济发展理论 [M]. 北京：商务印书馆，1990：76
[53]（美）德尔伯格，赫里克. 经济发展 [M]. 上海：上海译文出版社，1986：215
[54]（印）布拉塔·贾塔克. 发展经济学 [M]. 北京：商务印书馆，1989：42～45
[55]（美）杰拉尔德·M. 迈耶. 发展经济学的先驱 [M]. 北京：经济科

学出版社，1988：313～315

[56]（美）唐·埃思里奇．应用经济学研究方法论［M］．北京：经济科学出版社，1998：64～68

[57]（美）唐纳德·J．鲍尔索克斯，戴维·J．克劳斯．物流管理——供应链过程的一体化［M］．林国龙，宋柏，沙梅译，北京：机械工业出版社，1999：247～251

[58]（美）戴维·J．布隆伯格，斯蒂芬·勒梅，乔·B．汉纳．综合物流管理入门［M］．雷震甲，杨纳让译，北京：机械工业出版社，2003：111～115

[59]（美）威廉姆森．资本主义经济制度［M］．北京：商务印书馆，2002：83

[60]（日）丸川知雄．关于企业集团中间性组织产生的理论依据［J］．中国工业经济研究，1992（9）：15～18

[61] 王询．论企业与市场间的不同形态［J］．经济研究，1998（7）：34～40

[62] 黄祖辉，刘东英．我国农产品物流体系建设与制度分析［J］．农业经济问题，2005（4）：2

[63] 马士华，林勇，陈志祥．供应链管理［M］．北京：机械工业出版社，2000：15～38

[64] Robert B. Handfield. Sourcing and Supply Chain Management［M］. United States：Prentice－Hall Inc，1999：81～93

[65] Robert B. Handfield，Ernest L. Jr. Nichols. Introduction to Supply Chain Management［M］. Upper Saddle RiverN. J：Prentice Hall，1998：311～320

[66]（英）马丁·克里斯托弗．物流竞争——后勤与供应链管理［M］．马越等译，北京：北京出版社，2001：515～520

[67]（美）菲利普·科特勒．营销管理：分析、计划、执行和控制［M］．梅汝和等译，上海：上海人民出版社和西蒙与舒斯特国司，1997：976～983

[68] 方福前．当代西方经济学主要流派［M］．北京：中国人民大学出版社，2004：15

[69]（英）安德鲁·坎贝尔，凯瑟琳·萨姆斯·卢克斯．战略协同［M］．任通海，龙大伟译，北京：机械工业出版社，2000：20

[70]（英）安德鲁·坎贝尔，凯瑟琳·萨姆斯·卢克斯. 战略协同［M］. 任通海，龙大伟译，北京：机械工业出版社，2000：67～68

[71]（英）安德鲁·坎贝尔，凯瑟琳·萨姆斯·卢克斯. 战略协同［M］. 任通海，龙大伟译，北京：机械工业出版社，2000：85～86

[72] 胡汉辉，邢华. 产业融合理论以及对我国发展信息产业的启示［J］. 中国工业经济，2003（2）：23～29

[73] 植草益. 信息通讯业的产业融合［J］. 中国工业经济，2001（2）：24～27

[74] 马健. 产业融合理论研究评述［J］. 经济学动态，2002（5）：78～81

[75] 吴万青. 现代物流的经济分析［J］. 科技情报开发与经济，2004（5）：89～91

[76] 王健伟. 传统物流与现代物流的经济比较分析［J］. 交通运输工程学报，2002（2，3）：114～117

[77] 洪银兴. 可持续发展经济学［M］. 北京：商务印书馆，2000：154

[78]（英）伊恩·莫法特. 可持续发展——原则、分析和政策［M］. 北京：经济出版社，2001：164～168

[79] 张坤民. 可持续发展论［M］. 北京：中国环境科学出版社，1997：325

[80] 余逊达. 邓小平与中国经济制度创新［N］. 人民日报，1995－03－30

[81] 林毅夫，蔡昉，李周. 中国的奇迹：发展战略与经济改革［M］. 上海：上海人民出版社，1994：158

[82] 胡钧，刘凤义. 马克思经济学与新制度经济学的比较［J］. 经济学动态，2001（6）：24～27

[83]（美）道格拉斯·C. 诺斯. 制度、制度变迁与经济绩效［M］. 上海：上海三联书店，1994：114

[84]（英）布赖恩·斯诺登. 现代宏观经济学发展的反思［M］. 北京：商务印书馆，2000：306

[85] 伍装. 西方经济学中制度变迁理论的演变［J］. 经济学动态，1999（8）：98～102

[86]（美）戴维·菲尼. 制度安排的需求与供给［M］. 北京：商务印书馆，1992：217

[87]（美）奥斯特罗姆，皮希特. 制度分析与发展的反思［M］. 北京：商务印书馆，1992：138

[88] (美) L. E. 戴维斯，道格拉斯·C. 诺斯. 财产权与制度变迁 [M]. 上海：上海三联书店；上海人民出版社，1994：174
[89] 拉坦，速水. 论诱致性制度创新理论 [J]. 发展研究，1984 (7)：77～80
[90] 汪丁丁. 经济发展与制度创新 [M]. 上海：上海人民出版社，1995：233
[91] (美) 道格拉斯·C. 诺斯. 经济史中的结构与变迁 [M]. 上海：上海三联书店；上海人民出版社，1994：563
[92] 马广奇. 制度变迁理论：评述与启示 [J]. 生产力研究，2005 (7)：25～30
[93] 林毅夫. 关于制度变迁的经济学理论：诱致性变迁与强制性变迁 [A]. R. 科斯，A. 阿尔钦，D. 诺斯等. 财产权利与制度变迁——产权学派与新制度学派译文集 [C]. 上海：上海三联书店；上海人民出版社，1994：385～387
[94] 周小亮. 论外在制度创新的差异性与多样性 [J]. 经济评论，2002 (3)：126～129
[95] (美) L. E. 戴维斯，道格拉斯·C. 诺斯. 制度创新的理论描述、类推与说明 [M]. 上海：上海三联书店，1991：421～425
[96] 李玉虹，马勇. 技术创新与制度创新互动关系的理论渊源 [J]. 经济科学，2001 (1)：104～107
[97] (奥) 哈耶克. 自由秩序原理 [M]. 上海：上海三联书店，1997：378
[98] 樊纲. 公共选择与改革过程 [A]. 盛洪. 中国的过渡经济学 [C]. 上海：上海三联书店，1994：333～338
[99] (美) 丹尼斯·缪勒. 公共选择 [M]. 上海：上海三联书店，1993：517
[100] (美) 道格拉斯·C. 诺斯. 论制度 [J]. 经济社会体制比较，1991 (6)：15～18
[101] (日) 青木昌彦. 什么是制度？我们如何理解制度 [J]. 经济社会体制比较，2000 (6)：76～80
[102] 刘元春. 交易费用分析框架的政治经济学批判 [M]. 北京：经济科学出版社，2001：213～217
[103] 秦代红，刘学. 加快发展农产品物流业提高农业竞争力——以四川省成都市为例 [J]. 农村经济，2002 (12)：63～65

[104] 梁琳娜. 西部农产品物流问题分析与对策研究 [J]. 甘肃农业，2006 (11)：42 ~45
[105] 李虹. 西部地区农产品物流发展现状及对策 [J]. 消费导刊，2008 (1)：96 ~99
[106] 张春颖，王秀云，李娜. 我国西部欠发达地区农产品物流发展及物流中心的现状与对策分析 [J]. 物流科技，2010 (8)：36 ~39
[107] 张春颖，王秀云，李娜. 我国西部特色农产品冷链物流的发展现状与策略研究 [J]. 物流科技，2010 (10)：50 ~54
[108] 戴伟娟. 农产品物流发展的内在动因与机制探析—以国际经验为例 [J]. 上海经济研究，2006 (5)：143 ~146
[109] 刘东英. 农产品现代物流研究框架的试构建 [J]. 中国农村经济，2005 (7)：88 ~92
[110] 王欣兰. 现代物流管理概论 [M]. 北京：清华大学出版社，2007：355 ~358
[111] 刘晓红. 陕西农业产业化中物流问题调研分析 [J]. 企业经济，2005 (3)：113 ~115
[112] 纪良纲，刘东英. 我国农产品流通中介组织发展的目标模式 [J]. 河北经贸大学学报，1999 (2)：57 ~64
[113] 叶兴庆. 社会主义市场经济中的农村经济体制 [M]. 青岛：青岛出版社，1996：53
[114] 祖田修. 农学原论 [M]. 北京：中国人民大学出版社，2003：76
[115] (法) 比尔基埃 (A. Burguiere). 家庭史 [M]. 北京：生活、读书、新知三联书店，1998：448
[116] (匈) 马扎亚尔. 中国农村经济研究 [M]. 上海：上海神州国光出版社，1932：117 ~119
[117] (美) R. 科斯，A. 阿尔钦，道格拉斯·C. 诺斯等著. 财产权利与制度变迁 [M]. 上海：上海人民出版社，1994：214
[118] 李碧珍. 农产品物流模式创新研究 [M]. 北京：社会科学文献出版社，2010：201
[119] 李建平，石淑华. 试析"诚信"与"信用"的联系与区别—再论信用本质上是一个经济问题 [J]. 东南学术，2004 (1)：84 ~90
[120] (美) 奥利弗·E. 威廉姆森. 资本主义的经济制度 [M]. 北京：商务印书馆，2002：332

[121] 李学工. 农产品物流框架体系构建 [M]. 北京：中国物资出版社，2009：62
[122] 姜子叶，杨瑞洁. 民间信用的效应分析 [J]. 财贸经济，2002 (11)：89 ~ 92
[123] 吴汉洪，徐国兴：信用本质的经济学分析 [J]. 中国人民大学学报，2004 (4)：53 ~ 56
[124] 夏君. 国土资源规划要先行 [N]. 人民日报，2000 - 04 - 03 (11)
[125] 苏楠，曹晅. 我国中、西部地区对外贸易与城乡居民收入差距的关系研究——基于省际面板数据的实证分析 [J]. 学习与实践，2010 (11)：75 ~ 79
[126] 杜林青. 中国农业和农村经济经济结构的战略性调整 [M]. 北京：中国农业出版社，2004：426
[127] 郑风田，姜克芬. 农村经济与管理 [M]. 北京：中央广播电视大学出版社，1998：255 ~ 258
[128] 安希伋. 我国农产品价格、生产成本与农民收入 [J]. 美国农业经济学会，1989：136 ~ 140
[129] 王静. 西部民族地区农产品品牌战略及其出口竞争力研究 [J]. 现代管理科学，2011 (9)：101 ~ 103
[130] 王静. 西部内陆港农产品外贸物流结构的优化与创新——以西安国际港务区为例 [J]. 宁夏社会科学，2011 (4)：54 ~ 57
[131] 夏英. 中国农业产业化问题研究 [M]. 北京：中国农业出版社，2002：213 ~ 217
[132] (英) W. 阿瑟·刘易斯. 劳动力无限供给条件下的经济发展 [M]. 北京：北京经济学院出版社，1989：45 ~ 47
[133] (美) 舒尔茨. 改造传统农业 [M]. 北京：商务印书馆，1987：553 ~ 557
[134] 雷海章. 现代农业经济学 [M]. 北京：中国农业出版社，2003：253 ~ 257
[135] 刘伟，杨云龙. 资源配置与经济体制改革 [M]. 北京：中央财政经济出版社，1989：412
[136] 熊德平. 农业产业机构调整的内涵、关键、问题与对策 [J]. 农业经济问题，2002 (6)：164 ~ 168
[137] 曾珍香. 可持续发展的协调性分析 [J]. 系统工程理论与实践，2001

(3)：24～27
[138] Saint - Paul, Gilles. Technological Choice, Financial Marketsand Economic Development. European Economic Review, 1992：36
[139] E. R. Weintraub. Microfoundations：the Compatibility of Microeconomics and Macroeconomics, Cambridge：Cambrige University Press, 1979：237
[140] C. Closs. Logistics strategy：does exist. Journal of Logistics, 1997 (1)：18
[141] J. Bryant. A simple rational expectation keynes - type model Quarterly Journal of Economics, 1983 (97)：525～529
[142] G. L. Cramer, Jensen C W, Southgate D D. Agricultural Economics and Agri - business. N. Y.：JohnWiley, 2001
[143] Creyer, H. Elizabeth, T. William, et al. Tradeoffs between price and quality：how a value index afects preforonce formation. Journal of Consumer Affairs (Winter), 1997：280～302
[144] F. R. David. Concepts of Strategy Management (6th. ed). Prentice Hall Inc, 1997
[145] A. Fiegenbaum, H. Thomas. Strategic groups as reference groups：theory, modeling and empirical examination of industry and competitive strategy. Strategic Management Journal, 1995：461～476
[146] D. C. North. Institutions, Institutional Change and Economic performance. Cambridge：Cambridge University Press. 1990
[147] Morash. Strategic logistics capabilities for competitive advantage and firm success. Journal of Business Logistics, 1996 (1)：17
[148] M. F. Neves. A Model for the distribution channels planning process. Journal of Business & Industrial Marketing , 2001 (16, 7)：518～539
[149] (加) 唐纳德·沃特斯. 物流管理概论 [M]. 刘秉镰，韩勇等译，北京：电子工业出版社，2004：97～103
[150] 王槐林，刘明菲. 物流管理学 [M]. 武汉：武汉大学出版社，2002：219～221
[151] 王之泰. 现代物流学 [M]. 北京：中国物资出版社，1995：411～414
[152] 武拉平. 中国农产品市场行为研究 [M]. 北京：中国农业出版社，2002：54～57

[153] 徐寿波. 商品物流新理论 [J]. 新华文摘, 2009 (19): 72 ~ 75
[154] (美) 杰拉尔德 · M. 梅尔, 詹姆斯 · E. 劳赫. 经济发展前沿问题 (第 7 版) [M]. 黄仁伟, 吴雪明等译, 上海: 上海人民出版社, 2004: 110 ~ 115
[155] 盛洪. 现代制度经济学 [M]. 北京: 北京大学出版社, 2004: 222
[156] 樊纲. 两种改革成本与两种改革方式 [J]. 经济研究, 1993 (1): 23 ~ 27
[157] 樊纲. 公共选择与改革过程 [J]. 经济社会体制比较, 1993 (1): 112 ~ 116
[158] 夏振坤. 发展经济学新探 [M]. 武汉: 武汉出版社, 19974: 302
[159] 徐寿波. 商品物流理论研究 [J]. 管理世界, 2009 (7): 1 ~ 9
[160] 张绪昌, 丁俊发. 流通经济学 [M]. 北京: 人民出版社, 1995: 98 ~ 102
[161] 傅殷才. 制度经济学 [M]. 武汉: 武汉出版社, 1996: 513 ~ 516
[162] 郝渊晓. 现代物流管理学 [M]. 广州: 中山大学出版社, 2001: 163 ~ 167
[163] 徐绪松. 复杂科学资本市场项目评价 [M]. 北京: 科学出版社, 2003: 342 ~ 346
[164] 李京文, 徐寿波, 王之泰等. 物流学及其应用 [M]. 北京: 经济科学出版社, 1987: 409 ~ 413
[165] 徐寿波. 关于物流的科学分类问题 [J]. 北京交通大学学报 (社会科学版), 2005 (4, 4): 11 ~ 15
[166] (日) 花房陵. 物流构造 [M]. 聂永有译, 北京: 文汇出版社, 2002: 253 ~ 257
[167] 傅家骥. 技术创新学 [M]. 北京: 清华大学出版社, 1998: 551
[168] 贾裕泉. 进化经济理论评述 [J]. 经济学动态, 2000 (6): 54 ~ 57
[169] 张昱. 农产品市场竞争力 [M]. 广州: 中山大学出版社, 2004: 87 ~ 91
[170] 赵黎明. 我国区域现代农业物流体系发展探要 [J]. 中国农业大学学报, 2003 (3): 137 ~ 140
[171] 赵敏. 农产品物流 [M]. 北京: 中国物资出版社, 2007: 238 ~ 242
[172] 陈宗胜. 中国经济体制市场化进程研究 [M]. 上海: 上海人民出版社, 1999: 753

[173] 林毅夫. 发展战略与经济改革 [M]. 北京：北京大学出版社，2004：154～157
[174] 谢家智. 区域资金配置研究 [M]. 北京：中国物价出版社，2004：203～205
[175] 温铁军. 农村基本经营制度研究 [M]. 北京：中国经济出版社，2001：113～115
[176] 罗必良. 经济组织的制度逻辑 [M]. 太原：山西经济出版社，2000：227
[177] 李军杰，钟君. 中国地方政府经济行为分析 [J]. 中国工业经济，2004 (4)：104～107
[178] (美) 施蒂格勒. 产业组织与政府管制 [M]. 上海：上海三联书店，1989：663～665
[179] 袁恩祯，张道根. 交易活动与经济关系演进 [M]. 上海：上海社会科学院出版社，2002：414～418
[180] J. Stiglitz, A. Weiss. Credit Rationing in Markets with Imperfect Information, American Economic Review, 1981 (71)：393～406
[181] (美) 冯皮斯克·J. D. 等. 发展中经济的农村金融 [M]. 汤世生，许均华，钱绪红等译，中国金融出版社，1990：612～613
[182] 江春. 我国民间信用中的产权问题 [J]. 经济科学，1998 (1)：47～51
[183] 侯建新. 农民、市场与社会变迁 [M]. 北京：社会科学文献出版社，2002：477～479
[184] 安希伋. 转型经济与农民 [M]. 北京：中国农业出版社，2004：317～323
[185] 侯石安. 国家与农民"取"与"予"的关系研究 [J]. 农业经济问题，2000 (6)：19～23
[186] 国务院关于支持农业产业化龙头企业发展的意见 [N]. 中国食品报，2012-03-29
[187] (美) 丹尼尔·F. 斯普尔伯. 市场的微观结构——中间层组织与厂商理论 [M]. 北京：中国人民大学出版社，2002：312～315
[188] 罗必良，李孔岳，王京安等. 农业产业组织：演进、比较与创新——基于分工维度的制度经济学研究 [M]. 北京：中国经济出版社，2002：511～514

[189] 罗必良，王玉蓉．农业经济组织的制度结构与经济绩效——一个理论框架及其应用分析［J］．农业经济问题，1999（6）：78～82
[190] 张建华．产业组织理论研究的新进展［J］．经济学动态，1996（5）：83～87
[191] 李长江，徐静，苏繁．供应链节点企业间的信任及实现机制［J］．工业工程与管理，2005（2）：89～96
[192] 黄继忠．省级财政支出制度：委托代理关系下的分析［J］．经济社会体制比较，2003（6）：52～55
[193] 马克思恩格斯选集（第1卷）［M］．北京：人民出版社，2001：253
[194] 列宁全集（第4卷）［M］．北京：人民出版社，1990：45～47
[195] 詹森，麦克林．企业理论：管理行为、代理成本和所有制结构［J］．金融经济学杂志，1976（3）：132～135
[196] 熊德平．农村金融与农村经济协调发展研究［M］．北京：社会科学出版社，2009：185
[197] 叶兴庆．社会主义市场经济中的农村经济体制［M］．青岛：青岛出版社，1996：147
[198] 查杏云，王春法等．西方国家农业现代化透视［M］．上海：上海远东出版社，1998：365
[199] 王新利．中国农村物流模式及体系发展研究［D］．西北农林科技大学博士论文，2003：76
[200] E. Avila. Intellectual property in agricultural biotechnology and agribusiness strategy：the problem of investment in R&D（Mexico）. Ph. D. The Ohio State University. 2002 Dissertation Abstracts International，Volume：63，Section：A，298
[201] C. R. Bertsch. Panama retail food sector. A Foreign Agricultural Service Global Agricultural Information Network Report，PNOO11，USDA. 2000
[202] Chang，Tung－Zong，R. W. Albert. Price，product information，and purchase intention：an empirical study. Journal of the Academy of Marketing Science，1994（22）：16～27
[203] G. Ghezan，M. Meteos，L. Viteri. Impact of supermarkets and fast－food chains on horticulture supply chains in Argentina. Development Policy Review，2002（20，4）：389～396
[204] F. A. Ghisi，A. L. Da Silva. The information technology on food supply

chain management. Management of Engineering and Technology. Portland International Conference，2001：169
[205] K. S. Huang. An inverse demand system for US composite foods. American Journal of Agricultural，1988（70）：902～909
[206] 王敏. 美国农产品质量安全管理的考察与启示［J］. 农业质量标准，2006（1）：40～43
[207] 李阳，李玉成，余捷. 加拿大农业与农产品质量安全考察报告［R］. 农场经济管理，2007（1）：19～21
[208] 范秀荣，李晓锦. 日、美、荷农产品物流组织的经验与启示［J］. 中外物流，2007（4）：94～96
[209] 何云峰. 美国物流组织模式的发展与变迁［J］. 物流技术，2003（4）：44～45
[210] 俞菊生，王勇等. 世界级城市的农产品市场体系建设模式［J］. 上海农业学报，2004（2）：1～5
[211] M. Cocucci，E. Ferrari，S. Martello. Milk traceability from farm to distribution. Italian Food and Beverage Technology. Pinerolo：Chiriotti Editrice，2002：15～20
[212] 陈淑祥. 西方国家农产品流通比较［J］. 重庆工商大学学报，2006（8）：19～23
[213] 王中军. 国外农产品物流的经验简述［J］. 世界农业，2007（4）：8～9
[214] 罗必良. 美国的农业服务组织及其效率特征［J］. 南方农村，1997（3）：40～44
[215] R. C. Blshop. Endangered Species and Uricertainty：the Economics of a Safe Minium Standard，American Journal Agricultarl Economics，1978（60）：10～18
[216] 张德化，汪上. 发达国家农产品流通组织的比较与启示［J］. 北方经贸，2005（4）：123～125
[217] 黄勇，易法海，杨平. 国外农产品物流模式及其经验借鉴［J］. 社会主义研究，2007（3）：133～135
[218] 黄祖辉，吴克象，金少胜. 发达国家现代农产品流通体系变化及启示［J］. 福建论坛，2003（4）：12～14
[219] 周发明. 中外农产品流通渠道的比较研究［J］. 经济社会体制比较，

2006（5）：116～120
[220] 孙剑．李崇光．美国和日本主要农产品营销渠道的比较［J］．世界农业，2003（3）：46～50
[221] 贺峰．世界农产品物流的比较分析［J］．世界农业，2006（5）：21～24
[222] 郭灿章．发达国家农业经营组织发展的形式及特征［J］．世界农业，2006（3）：7～9
[223] 张进．加拿大保护性耕作农业［J］．当代农机，2008（2）：26～28
[224] 郭红东．美国农业合作社发展面临的问题与启示［J］．世界农业，2004（7）：29～31
[225] 杨玲玲，辛小丽．加拿大合作社运动的起源、发展现状及未来趋势［J］．科学社会主义，2006（4）：121～124
[226] 侯立军等．中国粮食物流科学化研究［M］．北京：中国农业出版社，2002：265
[227] 加拿大的新型农业合作社和合作社改革［EB/OL］．http：//www.jncw.net.cn/html/196/78.html
[228] 中华全国供销合作总社赴加拿大、挪威考察团．加拿大、挪威合作社考察报告［R］．中国合作经济，2005（1）：15～17
[229] M. Boehjie, L. F. Schrader. The industrialization of Agriculture：Question of Coordination. Great Britain：The Ipswich Book Company，1988
[230] L. D. H. Weld. The Marketing of Farm Products READ BOOKS，2009
[231] C. J. Vaughn. The Price－Quality Relationship. Journal of Food Products Marketine，2000（6，1）：137
[232] 路建忠，武敏，马福婷．国外超市生鲜水果蔬菜经营发展趋势［J］．河北北方学院学报，2006（2）：45～48
[233] 吴勇民，杜文龙，樊雪梅．国内外鲜活农产品物流系统比较及启示［J］．商业经济，2008（2）：11～13
[234] 唐步龙．荷兰农产品物流的发展对中国的启示［J］．商场现代化，2008（1）：97～98
[235] 孔凡真．国外食品保鲜新技术［J］．粮油加工，2000（1）：51～54
[236] 孙烨．欧盟农产品流通体制的特征及启示［J］．调研世界，2003（2）：131～132
[237] 复旦大学世界经济研究所法国经济研究室．法国经济［M］．北京：

人民出版社，1985：59
［238］王引．欧盟农业产业化的背景、形式和绩效［J］．江西农业大学学报（社会科学版），2005（2）：18～21
［239］林涛．法国的农业合作机制［J］．全球科技经济瞭望，2002（2）：26～27
［240］厉为民．荷兰的农业奇迹［M］．北京：中国农业科学技术出版社，2003：116～118
［241］赵勤．中国现代农业物流问题研究［D］．东北林业大学博士论文，2006：47～50
［242］浙江大学中国农村发展研究院．荷兰农业发展及其对浙江的启示［DB/OL］．http：//www.card.org.cn/upfile/file_1155109118.doc
［243］丽华．法国、荷兰农业合作社发展简介［J］．中国花卉园艺，2005（23）：22
［244］荷兰合作银行［DB/OL］．http：//www.e－nw.shac.gov.cn
［245］罗鸣．荷兰农业合作社和农民合作组织［J］．世界农业，1999（4）：46～48
［246］周庆．中外物流园建设的比较分析［J］．商业时代，2005（17）：71～74
［247］谢如鹤，唐秋生．国外食品冷藏供应链发展概况［J］．物流技术，2002（6）：166～169
［248］俞菊生．日本的农产品物流和批发市场［J］．上海农村经济，2003（4）：43～44
［249］孟枫平．日本农业信息化进程的主要特点［J］．世界农业，2003（4）：113～115
［250］世经．日本的农业标准化［J］．中国质量技术监督，2004（2）：48～49
［251］M. McDonald. Food Firms and food flows in Japan 1945～1998. World Development，2000（28，3）：487～502
［252］甲裴渝，王志刚．关于中日蔬菜贸易摩擦和日本紧急进口限制的经济分析［J］．农村经济问题，2002（10）：87～89
［253］肖映林等．日本蔬菜产销状况［J］．中国果菜，2000（2）：51～54
［254］（日）家之光协会．日本农业年鉴［S］．日本农业年鉴刊行会编，1995：357

[255] 刘云，李时敏．日本农协在农产品流通中的作用与启示［J］．国外农业，2002（12）：108～109
[256] 潘立亚，贺盛瑜．日本农产品批发市场的发展对我国的借鉴［J］．农村经济，2006（8）：127～129
[257] 何平．日本生活协同组合会给我省直销社的启示［EB/OL］．http：//mt．rednet．cn
[258] D. Martin，C. Howard，P. Herbig．The Japanese distribution system．European Business Review，1998（2）：442～445
[259] 宏平．港台批发市场模式［J］．中国市场，2004（4）：36
[260] 方志权，顾海英．海峡两岸鲜活农产品流通体制若干问题比较研究［J］．上海农村经济，2003（1）：40～43
[261] 邱章泉．台湾农产品运销的形式及启示［J］．台湾农业探索，1999（2）：1～6
[262] 肖映林等．台湾蔬菜流通与制度建设［J］．绵阳高等经济技术专科学校学报，1999（6）：91～93
[263] 范秀荣，李晓锦．发达国家农产品物流组织的经验与启示［J］．中国流通经济，2007（1）：14～16
[264] Y. Wang，Y. Gerchak．Supply chain coordination when demand is shelf spaced ependent．Manufacturing & Service Management，2001（3，1）：82～87
[265] 陈道江，黄峰．制度变迁的演进论述评［J］．社会科学家，2003（9）：121～124
[266] 陈启峰．论中国农业的改革与发展［J］．福建农业大学学报（社科版），2001（4）：13～15
[267] 池泽新等．制度经济学的逻辑与中国农业经济组织形式的选择［J］．中国农村经济，2003（11）：36～40
[268] 陈百明等．中国农业资源综合生产能力与人口承载能力［M］．北京：气象出版社，2001：435～437
[269]（美）奥尔森．国家兴衰探源——经济增长、滞胀与社会僵化［M］．北京：商务印书馆，1993：105～107
[270] 徐彬．中国农业发展中的失范现象及其纠正［J］．调研世界，2003（9）：29～31
[271] 姚今观，纪良纲等．中国农产品流通体制与价格制度［M］．北京：

中国价格出版社，1995：78
[272] 农业部软科学委员会. 中国农业和农村经济规律性问题研究 [M]. 北京：中国农业出版社，1998：211～213
[273] 黄荣风. 农产品流通中存在的问题及对策初探 [J]. 农村发展论丛，1997（5）：11～15
[274] 林毅夫. 再论制度、技术与中国农业发展 [M]. 北京：北京大学出版社，2000：302～305
[275] 中华人民共和国农业部. 中国农业发展报告（2002）[R]. 北京：中国农业出版社，2002：155～158
[276] 国家统计局国民经济综合统计司. 新中国五十五年统计资料汇编 [S]. 北京：中国统计出版社，2005：755～758
[277] 国家统计局农村社会经济调查司. 中国农业统计资料汇编 1949～2004 [S]. 北京：中国统计出版社，2006：534～536
[278] 姚今观，纪良纲. 中国农产品流通体制与价格制度 [M]. 北京：中国物价出版社，1995：156～158
[279] 邓涛. 生鲜农产品业态变革研究 [D]. 华中农业大学硕士论文，2006：24
[280] 商业贸易·物资 [DB/OL]. http：//www.cyszw.com/cyzs/DATA/13－04－04.html
[281] 中国统计年鉴（2000）[S]. 北京：中国统计出版社，2000：435
[282] 潘耀国. 中国农业产业化的进展与组织创新 [J]. 经济研究参考，2003（1328）：35
[283] 刘成玉. 理顺农产品流通促进农业产业化 [J]. 中国流通经济，1997（3）：111～114
[284] 中共中央十五届三中全会. 关于农业和农村工作若干重大问题的决定 [M]. 北京：人民出版社，2000：112
[285] 宋洪远等. 改革以来中国农业和农村经济政策的演变 [M]. 北京：中国经济出版社，2000：252～255
[286] 樊纲，王晓鲁，张立文等. 中国各地区市场化相对进程报告 [R]. 经济研究，2003（3）：82～87
[287] 姚今观，纪良纲. 中国农产品流通体制与价格制度 [M]. 北京：中国物价出版社，1995：11
[288] 李泽华. 我国农产品批发市场的现状与发展趋势 [J]. 中国农村经

济，2002（6）：36～42
［289］中国统计年鉴（2007）［S］．北京：中国统计出版社，2007：626
［290］赵勤．中国现代农业物流问题研究［D］．东北林业大学博士论文，2006：4～5
［291］丁声俊．深化农产品流通体制改革的目标与思路［J］．农业经济问题，1997（7）：12～14
［292］崔传义，程言清，黄祖辉．农产品流通现状、问题及发展趋势［J］．价格理论与实践，2002（10）：59～72
［293］张厚义等．中国私营企业发展报告（2002）［R］．北京：社会科学文献出版社，2003：552～557
［294］李玉忠．农业产业化中“公司＋中介组织＋农户”经营模式探析［J］．北京农业，2006（12）：1～2
［295］丁振京．中国粮食流通制度变迁及创新决策［J］．农业经济导刊，2003（10）：41～45
［296］洪涛．中国粮食市场化大趋势［M］．北京：经济管理出版社，2003：115～157
［297］侯立军等．中国粮食物流科学化研究［M］．北京：中国农业出版社，2002：345～348
［298］陈善晓，王卫华．基于第三方物流的农产品流通模式研究［J］．浙江理工大学学报，2005（3）：85～89
［299］崔宁波，陈诗波，矫健．我国农产品物流主体的发展沿革及培育对策［J］．东北农业大学学报（社会科学版），2008（4）：28～31
［300］国家粮食局课题组．中国粮食批发市场发展研究报告［R］．北京：经济管理出版社，2003：352～357
［301］（德）汉斯，克里斯蒂安·波弗尔．物流前沿——实践创新前景［M］．张计划，李轶情，陈晖译．北京：机械工业出版社，2004：344～351
［302］艾伦·哈里森，瑞莫克·万·胡可．物流管理与战略［M］．方梅萍，魏清江等译．北京：电子工业出版社，2003：323
［303］阿齐·萧．市场流通中的若干问题［M］．哈佛大学出版社，1915：235
［304］付跃东，王继权．农产品流通制度变迁及其趋势分析［J］．新疆农垦经济，2002（2）：67～70

[305] 卢现祥. 西方新制度经济学 [M]. 北京：中国发展出版社，1996：113

[306] 刘东英. 我国生鲜蔬菜物流体系研究—制度、组织与交易效率 [D]. 浙江大学博士论文，2005：160～165

[307] 靳共元. 居民收入差距问题研究的新进展 [J]. 经济学动态，1996（8）：52～56

[308] 黄季琨. 社会发展、城市化和食物消费 [J]. 中国社会科学，1999（4）：13～17

[309] 欧阳文和，李元森. 恩格尔系数及其在中国适用问题的再思考 [J]. 湖南商学院学报，2005（2）：9～11

[310] 蒋和平，王克军. 21 世纪初中国主要农产品需求和生产的预测 [J]. 农业经济与科技发展研究，2002（6）：47～50

[311] 丁俊发. 发展农产品物流任重道远 [J]. 中国合作经济，2004（1）：47

[312] 许宝健. 从传统农业到现代农业 [N]. 中国县域经济报，2007－01－08

[313] 刘广登. 农民负担问题的若干思考 [J]. 学海，1996（1）：22～25

[314] 袁永康. 中国农产品流通体制改革前沿报告 [R]. 北京：中国农业出版社，2003：675～777

[315] 于洪祥. 对农产品流通问题的思考 [J]. 山东经济战略研究，1997（4）：209～211

[316] 赵艳丽，嵇国平. 我国农产品流通体系建设的现状、问题和新思路 [J]. 物流科技，2004（9）：83～85

[317] 秦代红，刘学. 加快发展农产品物流业提高农业竞争力 [J]. 农村经济，2002（12）：113～116

[318] 赵英霞. 中国农产品物流发展的问题及对策研究 [C]. 第五次中国物流学术年会论文集，2007：682～687

[319] 刘志雄. 中国农产品市场发育研究 [D]. 中国农业大学博士论文，2006：94

[320] 刘铮，周英峰. 改革开放以来我国基础产业和基础设施建设成绩斐然 [DB/OL]. http：// news.163.com

[321] 张浩. 我国港口业发展回顾与“十一五”期间发展展望 [DB/OL]. http://www.lyg.gov.cn

[322] 2007 中国通信产业 TOP 10 系列 [DB/OL]. http://www.c114.net
[323] 互联网发展现状与特点 [DB/OL]. http://www.e-gov.org.cn
[324] 王启，李志强，刘自杰. 我国农业科技进步与科研投资分析 [J]. 科学管理研究，2007 (8)：113~116
[325] 黄季坤等. 中国农业科技投资经济 [M]. 北京：中国农业出版社，2000：506
[326] 蒋和平，黄仁. 中国农业科技园区发展的现状及政策建议 [J]. 农业技术经济，1998 (6)：75~77
[327] 任坤秀. 采用标准化与促进农产品流通 [J]. 上海管理科学，2003 (4)：57~59
[328] 杜红梅. 我国农产品流通组织体制的理论和实证分析 [J]. 求索，2004 (7)：51~53
[329] 何坪华，杨名远. 农村市场中介组织的经济评价 [J]. 新疆农垦经济，2000 (3)：14~16
[330] 池泽新. 农村市场中介组织基础理论问题研究综述 [J]. 江西农业大学学报（自然科学版），2002 (10)：104~107
[331] 武云亮. 农产品物流组织形式及其发展趋势 [J]. 资源开发与市场，2007 (1)：68~70
[332] 张雪宁，刘莉. 物流发展与组织模式的演进及其规律 [J]. 深圳大学学报（人文社会科学版），2004 (21，4)：77~80
[333] 袁华. 构建以合作组织为纽带的农产品流通渠道 [J]. 科技情报开发与经济，2005 (5)：157~179
[334] 池泽新. 中介组织主导型市场农业体制探索 [M]. 北京：中国农业出版社，2004：367~367
[335] 赵荣，钟永玲. 农产品流通体制改革三十年回顾与展望 [J]. 农业展望，2008 (12) 25~29
[336] 张钢，孙明波. 关于组织创新研究的观点综述 [J]. 科研管理，1997 (4)：12~16
[337] 廉维亮. 农产品经纪人"破茧成蝶" [N]. 人民政协报，2008-01-18
[338] 王成慧. 我国农村流通——30 年发展之成就 [DB/OL]. http://news.qq.com
[339] 彭芬，张明玉，曹卫兵. 我国农产品物流组织历史演进研究 [J]. 物

流科技，2008（11）：5～7

［340］陈丽芬. 我国农村流通体制改革30年回顾与展望［J］. 市场营销导刊，2008（5）：11～15

［341］王雷. 回顾与展望——农村流通改革三十年［J］. 中国市场，2008（21）：22～23

［342］王静. 新中国成立以来农产品物流制度的变迁及其启示［J］. 陕西师范大学学报（哲学社会科学版），2012（1）：169～176

［343］罗必良. 中国农产品流通体制改革的目标模式［J］. 经济理论与经济管理，2003（4）：82～86

［344］罗小峰，朱信凯，雷海章. 农产品现代流通体制研究综述［J］. "三农"问题研究，2003（4）：134～137

［345］孟凡胜，金明华. 我国农产品物流落后原因初探［J］. 物流科技，2005（2）：148～152

［346］孟祥林，张悦想，申淑芳. 中国农业经济增长中的制度分析［J］. 江西农业大学学报（社会科学版），2003（12）：98～95

［347］柴军. 农业产业化状况的量化研究［J］. 农业技术经济，1997（3）：118～122

［348］贾卫丽，王成艳，赵瑞莹. 关于农产品物流的供求状况分析及对策［J］. 安徽农业大学学报（社会科学版），2004（5）：153～155

［349］杨伦标，高英仪. 模糊数学原理及其应用［M］. 广州：华南理工大学出版社，1995：574～578

［350］曹炳元. 应用模糊数学与系统［M］. 北京：科学出版社，2005：44～47

［351］胡宝清. 模糊理论基础［M］. 武汉：武汉大学出版社，2004：83～85

［352］何明珂. 物流系统论［M］. 北京：中国审计出版社，2001：205～208

［353］陈章武. 管理经济学［M］. 北京：清华大学出版社，1996：114～117

［354］张金隆. 农业物流的发展研究［J］. 科技进步与对策，2004（9）：32～35

［355］杨孚平. 农产品流通与国民经济成长［J］. 中国社会科学院研究生院学报，1990（3）：60～64

［356］杨瑞珍. 农民收入升降与国民经济可持续发展的正负效应［J］. 中国软科学，1997（5）：87～91

[357] 孙冶方．社会主义经济的若干理论问题［M］．北京：人民出版社，1984：225
[358] 冯海发，李激．我国农业为工业化提供资金积累的数量研究［J］．经济研究，1993（9）：122～124
[359] 李大胜，罗必良．关于农产品流通的若干问题［J］．南方农村，2002（1）：82～83
[360] 叶兴庆．社会主义市场经济中的农村经济体制［M］．青岛：青岛出版社，1996：215～218
[361]（美）奥尔森．集体行动的逻辑［M］．上海：上海三联书店，1994：456～459
[362]（美）乔治·J. 施蒂格勒．产业组织和政府管制［M］．上海：上海三联书店，1989：337
[363] 方天堃．畜牧业经济管理［M］．北京：中国农业大学出版社，2003：327～329
[364] 樊纲，王晓鲁．中国各省市场化程度的最新报告［R］．经济科学出版社，2004：412～425
[365] 侯彩云．试论农产品加工与食品加工［J］．农业工程学报，2002（3）：191～193
[366] 厉以宁．大力发展农产品物流产业［DB/OL］．中国农村研究网，http：//www. ccrs. org. cn
[367] 丁俊发．大力发展适应现代农业要求的物流产业［J］．经济界，2007（3）：9～13
[368] 郭华平，陈曦．论中国农产品加工面对经济全球化的发展［J］．农业经济，2002（11）：55～57
[369] 吴昊．交通运输对农业交易效率的影响［D］．北京交通大学博士学位论文，2004：331
[370] 郝玉强．WTO 框架下的我国农产品储运企业的出路——如何向农产品物流中心转变［J］．商品储运与养护，2005（1）：33～37
[371] 陈建国，陈琳．农业信息化的发展方向与途径［J］．农业图书情报学刊，2005（2）：11～13
[372] 蒋向东．我国农业信息化发展战略的分析［J］．农机化研究，2005（5）：123～125
[373] 胥爱贵．加快农产品信息化的建议［J］．农业经济问题，2002（4）：

170～174
［374］周剑云．建立健全我国农业信息化战略服务体系初探［J］．农业图书情报学，2005（2）：165～168
［375］王静．我国农产品产销困境下建立物流链支撑体系对策研究［J］．思想战线，2012（1）：53～57
［376］崔和瑞，赵黎明．区域农业可持续发展的系统分析及实现模式［J］．河北农业大学学报，2003（5）：43～47
［377］西部蓝皮书：中国西部经济发展报告［R］．社会科学文献出版社，2010：714～719
［378］易炼红．健全市场经济条件下的农业保护体系［M］．长沙：湖南人民出版社，1998：360
［379］Long，M. F.．Credit for Small Farmers：Indonesia，Malaysia and Thailand，US AID，Spring Review of Small Farmers Credit XV，Feb，1973
［380］国家统计局农村社会经济调查司．中国农业统计资料汇编 1949～2004［S］．北京：中国统计出版社，2006：339
［381］王静．新农村建设中农产品供应链信用风险特征及其防范［J］．经济问题，2011（2）：86～90
［382］姜昭，王凯．我国农户与龙头企业主要利益连接机制的优缺点分析［J］．现代经济探讨，2006（1）：71～75
［383］吴希宁．关于山区农产品流通问题的思考［J］．湖北经济，2002（10）：116～119
［384］李志萌．现代农产品流通体系的构建与完善［J］．江西农业大学学报（社会科学版），2005（3）：93～95
［385］（美）亚瑟·A．汤姆森，斯迪克兰迪 A.J．战略管理［M］．段盛华，王智慧主译，北京：北京大学出版社，2002：121～125
［386］孙剑，李崇光．运用农产品营销深化农业结构调整［J］．商业研究，2003（3）：143～148
［387］向清敏．农产品流通向标准化迈进［J］．农产品市场周刊，2006（18）：10～11
［388］王照明，刘静．不对称信息市场理论是现代信息经济学的核心［J］．数量经济技术经济研究，2002（7）：153～158
［389］于冷，顾海英．农业标准化监测管理体系设计［J］．农业现代化研

究，2002（3）：101～105
［390］胡希宁，步艳红．“信息不对称”与经济学的理论创新：2001 年度诺贝尔经济学奖理论评述［N］．光明日报，2001－11－02
［391］刘冀生．企业经营战略［M］．北京：清华大学出版社，1995：343～348
［392］寇平君，卢风君，沈泽江．构建我国农产品市场流通模式的战略性思考［J］．农业经济问题，2002（8）：13～17
［393］张杰，张红宇．关于金融支农问题的调研报告［R］．2004：11～15
［394］林汉川等．中小企业发展中所面临的问题［J］．中国社会科学，2003（2）：114～117
［395］（美）尼尔·格雷戈里，斯托伊安·塔涅夫．中国民营企业的融资问题［J］．赵红军，黄烨青译，经济社会体制比较，2001（6）：88～92
［396］李敏．我国农产品交易市场发展对策研究［J］．统计研究，2003（1）：73～75
［397］王凯等．中国农业产业链管理的理论与实践研究［M］．北京：中国农业出版社，2004：157～160
［398］焦必方，方志权．中日鲜活农产品流通体制比较研究［M］．上海：上海财经大学出版社，2002：504～508
［399］李良宏．农产品流通体系发展的金融对策研究［J］．经济师，2007（4）：252
［400］张文松．企业战略能力研究［M］．北京：科学出版社，2005：456～459
［401］刘联辉，文珊．我国农产品物流系统模式革新趋势及其构筑策略［J］．农村经济，2006（5）：111～113
［402］王凯．加强我国农业产业链管理的战略思考［J］．科技与经济，2004（1）：45～46
［403］黎元生．农产品流通组织创新研究［M］．北京：中国农业出版社，2003：8～11
［404］武云亮．我国农产品物流组织创新研究［J］．商品储运与养护，2006（6）：19～22
［405］徐国虎，许芳．合作博弈下的供应链供需经济批量模型［J］．中国储运，2004（5）：32～34
［406］胡愈，许红莲，岳意定．基于我国现代农村物流建设的金融供求研究

[J]. 湖南大学学报（社科版），2007（3）：67~70
[407] 熊军. 论农村经济发展的金融支持［J］. 商场现代化，2006（4）：169~171
[408] 陈彩凤. 论我国农村金融市场的构建［D］. 广西大学硕士论文，2006：14~15
[409] 刘彤. 中小企业融资中的信用缺失问题及解决［J］. 西南民族学院学报（哲学社会科学版），2003（4）：106~111
[410] 白红玲. 浅谈我国农产品流通中的中介组织［J］. 甘肃农业，2003（3）：51~54
[411] 杜吟棠. 合作社：农业中的现代企业制度［M］. 江西：江西人民出版社，2000：558~560
[412] 牛霞，安玉发. 农产品流通中介组织的职能、作用及制度基础［J］. 中国农业大学学报（社科版），2003（1）：40~44
[413] 牛若峰. 当代农业产业一体化经营［M］. 南昌：江西人民出版社，2002：271~272
[414] S. D. Ellinger. Marketing logistics integration and firm performance. International Hournal of Logistics Management，1999（1）：10
[415] M. S. Togar，S. Ramaswami. An integrative framework for supply chain collaboration The International Journal of Logistics Management，2005（2）：257~265
[416] 牛若峰. 农业产业一体化经营的理论框架［J］. 中国农村经济，1997（5）：51~54
[417] 孙剑，李艳军. 基于一体化战略的农产品物流系统模式［J］. 商业时代，2003（17）：117~119
[418] 姚今观等. 贸工农一体化经营——理论与实务［M］. 北京：中国物价出版社，1998：318~320
[419] 贺卫，段万春，王浣尘. 企业联盟：21世纪我国小企业的发展之道［J］. 经济问题探索，2000（5）：86~87
[420] 刘志英，王超. 核心竞争力基础上的物流联盟的建立［J］. 科技和产业，2004（8）：186~188
[421] 杜小芳，张金隆. 农产品的第三方物流管理模式［J］. 中国合作经济，2004（1）：48~49
[422] Sink，Langley. A managerial framework for the acquisition of Third -

Party logistics services. Journal of Business Logistics, 1997 (2): 18
[423] 舒辉. 集成化物流：理论与方法 [M]. 北京：经济管理出版社，2005：35～38
[424] 齐永智，漆雁斌. 农产品超市：未来农产品销售的主渠道 [J]. 经济论坛，2004 (21)：119～120
[425] 王宁，黄立平. 基于信息网络的农产品物流供应链管理模式 [J]. 农业现代化研究，2005 (2)：126～129
[426] 王静. 西部绿色农产品物联网结构模式与系统优化——以典型山区农业市商洛为例 [J]. 社会科学家，2011 (4)：59～63
[427] 吴远开，朱俊，朱道立. 全球物流环境下的冷藏链发展研究 [J]. 实用物流技术，2003 (2)：145～148
[428] 易学超. 食品保鲜技术的发展探讨 [J]. 制冷与空调，2001 (10)：91～94
[429] 谢如鹤. 保鲜链——食品物流的后起之秀 [J]. 中国物流与采购，2004 (5)：167～169
[430] 梁燕君. 辐照食品保鲜技术的现状及前景 [J]. 研究与探讨，1997 (4)：102～105
[431] 刘国信. 食品保鲜新技术 [N]. 中国食品质量报，2004-06-23
[432] 李连阁，朱道华. 农村工业化分散化空间结果的成因与聚集的条件 [J]. 中国农村经济，2000 (6)：33～35
[433] 奥斯特罗姆，皮希特. 制度分析与发展的反思 [M]. 北京：商务印书馆，1992：76～78
[434] 江若尘. 企业竞争的新模式——企业协调竞争：企业集群 [J]. 财贸研究，2000 (3)：63～67
[435] 夏文汇. 电子商务平台下农产品物流运作模式研究 [J]. 农村经济，2003 (7)：5～6
[436] 徐文静. 物流战略规划与模式 [M]. 北京：机械工业出版社，2002：398～403
[437] 邬文兵. 企业跨越式发展战略——理论、模式与实践 [M]. 北京：科学出版社，2005：183～186
[438] 王伯鲁. 产业技术跨越模式分析 [J]. 世界科技研究与发展，2000 (3)：98～103
[439] 包建民. 物流现代化 [M]. 上海：上海交通大学出版社，1997：

277 ~ 281
[440] （加）亨利·明茨伯格，布鲁斯·阿尔斯特兰德，约瑟夫·兰佩尔. 战略历程——纵览战略管理学派［M］. 刘瑞红，徐佳宾，郭武文译，北京：机械工业出版社，2002：78 ~ 80
[441] 李少军. 论战略观念的起源［J］. 世界经济与政治，2002（3）：132 ~ 136
[442] 姚小诗. 战略管理理论研究的发展历程与展望［J］. 预测，2003（6）：28 ~ 31
[443] 袁伯乔. 基于委托代理的供应链激励机制研究［J］. 重庆教育学院学报，2008（7）：34 ~ 36
[444] 钱刚毅，张子刚，陈金菊. 中间层组织的互补性博弈及其协调机制［J］. 科技进步与对策，2006（11）：167 ~ 169
[445] D. Gifford，L. Hall，W. Ryan. Chains of success：case studies on International and Australian food businesses cooperationing to compete in the global market. Canberra：Common wealth of Australia，1998
[446] D. C. Castel，H. L. Lee. Probability based supply chain model simulates business enterprise system from supplier through final distribution. Proceeding of the Industrial Engineering Research Conference，Publish by IIE，Norcross GA，USA，1993：762 ~ 766
[447] L. Norina，W. C. Bailey. Value analysis in the supply chain：case study of grain supply. Dynamics in Chains and Networks，2004：379 ~ 389
[448] A. Pyka，P. Windrum. The self – organisation of Innovation networks：an economist's view. The SEIN Project Papers，1999 – 10 – 06
[449] 谭涛，朱毅华，农产品供应链组织模式研究［J］. 现代经济探讨，2004（5）：127 ~ 128
[450] 佟姗姗. 果蔬农产品物流模式探析［J］. 全国商情：经济理论研究，2009（4）：44 ~ 45
[451] 耿松涛. 中国连锁超市物流的现状及其模式分析［J］. 物流技术，2004（5）：113 ~ 115
[452] 吴聪. 我国连锁零售企业物流运作模式选择决策研究［J］. 物流技术，2005（4）：93 ~ 96
[453] 杨顺江，彭鹰. 中国蔬菜流通模式构建：一个比较分析的启示［J］. 中国农村经济，2004（4）：146 ~ 149

[454] 王静. 西部地区农产品对外贸易的制约因素与可持续发展策略 [J]. 国际贸易探索，2011 (8)：25 ~ 32
[455] 李新春. 企业联盟与网络 [M]. 广州：广东人民出版社，2000：453 ~ 455
[456] 郭晓林，贺盛瑜. 囚徒困境情形下物流联盟的稳定性分析 [J]. 软科学，2005 (1)：100 ~ 104
[457] 郭日跻. 企业创新能力开发 [M]. 沈阳：东北大学出版社，2000：145
[458] 张耀辉. 产业创新的理论探索 [M]. 北京：中国计划出版社，2002：199 ~ 203
[459] 朱毅华. 农产品供应链物流整合实证研究 [M]. 南京：南京农业大学，2004：45 ~ 46
[460] 王静. 低碳经济的绿色物流模式下西部农产品发展措施 [J]. 甘肃社会科学，2011 (3)：233 ~ 236
[461] 刘勤生. 我国蔬菜加工与流通的现状及发展趋势 [J]. 粮油加工与食品机械，2000 (5)：17 ~ 21
[462] 宣亚男等. 我国生鲜农产品零售方式变化趋势、影响因素与对策初探 [J]. 农村经济，2003 (11)：178 ~ 181
[463] 陈超，罗英姿. 创建中国肉类加工食品供应链模型的构想 [J]. 南京农业大学学报，2003 (26)：192 ~ 193
[464] 包先建. 农副产品批发市场布局规律与现实问题的探讨 [J]. 安徽商贸职业技术学院学报，2003 (2)：83 ~ 85
[465] (英) 安德鲁·坎贝尔，凯瑟琳·萨姆斯·卢克斯. 战略协同 [M]. 任通海，龙大伟译，北京：机械工业出版社，2000：76
[466] 李勇，杨秀苔，张异等. 论供应链管理中的战略协同 [J]. 经济与管理研究，2004 (4)：57 ~ 60
[467] 项保华，李庆华. 波特模型及其改进 [J]. 中国工业经济，1999 (11)：96 ~ 99
[468] 公彦德，李帮义，李为相. 三级供应链协调和利润分配机制研究 [J]. 统计与决策，2008 (1)：185 ~ 186
[469] 韩松. 从基准理论出发构建我国农产品物流标准体系 [J]. 全国商情：经济理论研究，2008 (5)：23 ~ 25
[470] 王静. 关中—天水城市圈农产品物流产业集群建设布局研究 [J]. 城

市问题，2010（7）：68～72
[471] 杨俊生，张春玲．谈物流企业文化构建［J］．物流管理，2007（10）：20～21
[472] 杜赵伟，刘顺．农产品供应链的协调问题分析及对策研究［J］．现代商业，2007（6）：48～49
[473] 王静．供应链零库存方式下企业内在信用评级研究［J］．学术论坛，2011（2）：128～133
[474] 甘卫华．论农副产品供应链的构建组织［J］．物流技术，2004（4）：28～31
[475] 陈兵兵．SCM供应链管理——策略、技术与实务［M］．北京：电子工业出版社，2004：44～46
[476] 张敏．基于核心企业的农产品供应链分析［J］．物流技术，2004（5）：121～122
[477] 张彦等．系统自组织概论［M］．南京：南京大学出版社，1990：644～645
[478] 吴彤．耗散结构理论的自组织方法论研究［J］．科学、技术与辩证法，1998（6）：17～21
[479] 曹艳媚，王咏红，高瑛．农产品供应链绩效评价研究［J］．安徽农业科学（社科版），2008（36，8）：340～342.
[480] 慕继丰，陈方丽，冯宗宪．企业网络结构的效率［J］．科研管理，2002（5）：76～80
[481] 李纬澍．关于供应链经济系统性质的研究［J］．物流技术，2004（6）：52～54
[482] 蒋鹏飞，王震．三级供应链合作博弈分析［J］．山东大学学报（理学版），2008（1）：103～106
[483] 刘欠宁，刘亚相，单青松．一类三级供应链模型的研究［J］．西北农林科技大学学报（自然科学版），2006（11）：102～105
[484] J. S. Keebler，D. M. Ledyard，K. B. Manrodt. Keeping score：measruin the business value of logistics in the supply chain. Oak Brook：Council of Logistics Management，1999
[485] P. P. MichaeI，P. Ribbers，A. Tsalgatidou. Integrated value chains and their implications from a business and technology standpoint. Decision Support Systems，2000（29）：323～337

[486] Shuxiang Wang, Weiliang Zeng. Intangible value chain and its investment & management Proceedings of 2004 International Conference on Management Science&Engineering, 2004
[487] 严广全，吴清烈，何勇. 非对称信息条件下供应链协同的重复博弈分析 [J]. 工业技术经济，2008 (2)：33～37
[488] 王静. 基于 SWOT 的中小型农产品物流企业战略选择与发展对策 [J]. 经济问题，2012 (1)：78～82
[489] 程国平，汪波. 供应链中信息协同评价初探 [J]. 中国机械工程，2003 (3)：95～97
[490] 史丽萍，蔡歆. 电子商务环境下供应链整体绩效评价 [J]. 物流科技，2003 (26, 3)：14～16
[491] 蒋鹏飞，沙亚军，胡发胜. 二级供应链不同博弈研究 [J]. 山东大学学报，2007 (42, 2)：1～5
[492] K. Mertins, M. Rabe, F. W. Jakel. Distributed modelling and simulation of supply chains. International Journal of Computer Integrated Manufacturing, 2005 (18, 5)：342～349
[493] 王静. 中国农产品物流可持续发展模式的区位化创新战略 [J]. 河北学刊，2012 (4)：142～145
[494] 王静. 我国农产品物流电子商务供应链网络结构与运行机制 [J]. 学术论坛，2012 (2)：132～136
[495] M. Epsrein, P. Wisner. Using a balanced scorecard to implement stainability. Environmental Quality Management, 2002 (11, 2)：14～24
[496] 中国企业供应链管理绩效水平评价参考模型 (SCPRI. 0) [DB]. 电子供应链管理委员会，2003－10－17
[497] 徐贤浩，马士华，陈荣秋. 供应链关键绩效评价指标及优化 [J]. 华中理工大学学报，2000 (28, 3)：30～32
[498] 冷志杰，唐焕文. 大宗农产品供应链四维网络模型及应用 [J]. 系统工程理论与实践，2005 (3)：113～115
[499] 赵英霞. 中国农产品物流评价指标体系的构建 [J]. 商业研究，2007 (1)：211～213
[500] 龚迪. 生鲜物资物流配送绩效的模糊综合评价 [J]. 中国储运，2007 (5)：104～106
[501] 杜栋，庞庆华. 现代综合评价方法与案例精选 [M]. 北京：清华大

学出版社，2004：417～418

[502] Shuxiang Wang，Mingyu Zhang. Study on China agriculture development by system analying method. China－USA Business Riview，2003（10）：119～124

[503] Saty. The Analytic Hierarchy Process，New York：McGraw－Hill，1980

[504] 诸克军，张新兰. FuzzyAHP方法及应用［J］. 系统工程理论与实践，1997（17，12）：64～69

[505] 赵庆祯，王文宾，赵培忻. 农产品物流绩效评价的ANP方法［J］. 农产品系统科学和综合研究，2005（8）：237～240

[506] 成耀荣，胡小文. 物流政策的制定及其评估方法研究［J］. 综合运输，2004（2）：12～15

[507] 夏春玉. 中国物流政策体系：缺失与构建［J］. 财贸经济，2004（8）：94～98

[508] 耿苏强. 杨凌示范区辉煌十五年，现代农业看杨凌［N］. 农业科技报，2012－03－11

[509] 丁学东. 世界贸易组织与农业政策［M］. 北京：中国财政经济出版社，2001：235～240

[510] 魏建科，刘芝仙. 扶风县农产品生产现状与发展对策［J］. 陕西农业科技，2002（1）：114～116

[511] 黄祖辉，将文华. 农业与农村发展的制度透视［M］. 北京：中国农业出版社，2002：63～72

[512] 魏后凯. 市场竞争，经济绩效与产业集中［M］. 北京：经济管理出版社，2003：87～95

[513] 李艳，张敏. 物流系统的人力资本分析［J］. 物流技术，2005（2）：33～34

[514] 张学鹏. 甘肃省农村合作经济组织发展现状［J］. 甘肃农业，2004（10）：82～85

[515] 王凯. 中国农业产业链管理的理论与实践研究［M］. 北京：中国农业出版社，2004：41～45

[516]（美）迈克尔·迪屈奇. 交易成本经济学——关于公司的新的经济意义［M］. 北京：经济科学出版社，1999：473～476

[517] 海峰，张丽立，孙淑生. 我国现代物流产业政策体系研究［J］. 武汉大学学报，哲学社会科学版，2005（9）：158～161

[518] 赵娴. 我国物流业现行政策的分析与评价 [J]. 综合运输, 2004 (2): 18 ~ 22
[519] 陈代芬. 我国物流法规建设中的问题及建议 [J]. 中国物流与采购, 2002 (12): 41 ~ 43
[520] 温思美, 杨顺江. 论农业产业化进程中的农产品流通体制改革 [J]. 农业经济问题, 2000 (10): 77 ~ 81
[521] 傅晓. 论虚拟物流企业的企业文化建设 [J]. 物流科技, 2005 (4): 20 ~ 23
[522] (美) 亚瑟·A. 汤姆森, A. J. 斯迪克兰迪. 战略管理 [M]. 段盛华, 王智慧主译, 北京: 北京大学出版社, 2002: 306 ~ 309
[523] 陈芬森. 国际农产品贸易自由化与中国农业市场竞争策略 [M]. 北京: 中国海关出版社, 2004: 311 ~ 316
[524] 伊志宏. 消费经济学 [M]. 北京: 中国人民大学出版社, 2004: 154 ~ 158
[525] 李旭宏, 胡文友, 毛海军. 区域物流中心规划方法 [J]. 交通运输工程学报, 2002 (1): 77 ~ 81
[526] 肖三亮, 杨家齐. 论区域物流平台的构建 [J]. 武汉理工大学学报, 社会科学版, 2001 (6): 55 ~ 59
[527] 郑弼洙. 赵镇行, 朴勇安. 综合化物流管理体制和我国应对方案 [J]. 海运产业研究院, 1993

索　引

G

J

K

M

N

Q

后　记

《西部地区农产品物流可持续发展政策研究》是2010年经我向全国哲学社会科学规划办公室提出项目申请、获准立项，并于2012年年底主持完成的国家社会科学基金项目（10BJY075）“西部地区农产品物流可持续发展政策研究”的最终成果。2010年7月5日—6日，中共中央、国务院召开西部大开发工作会议，进一步深入推进西部大开发。以全面协调可持续发展的科学发展观为内核，围绕“深入推进、加快发展”这一主线，全面深入推进西部大开发战略，推动西部大开发迈出更大的步伐，取得更大的成就，使西部地区的发展再上一个新的台阶和水平，在缩小地区差距上取得实质性突破，实现全面建设小康社会的目标。新的发展阶段、新的战略思路，不仅为研究提供了思想和理论指导，而且进一步验证了选择和研究该课题方向上的正确性、时间上的及时性和价值上的重要性。研究工作自2010年7月正式启动，及时、认真地抓住这一机遇，认真贯彻落实，从而使资料准备、数据处理和理论研究得到了进一步深化。2011年上半年进行研究最关键的实际调研阶段。2012年上半年，研究初步成果形成，但并没有急于“完成任务”，而是进一步带着研究得出的初步结论和政策建议，再次深入到重庆、四川、贵州、云南、陕西、甘肃、宁夏、广西等实际调研地，征求实际工作部门的意见和建议，整理分析后进一步修改完善。2012年10月研究结论正式确立，在此后的定稿过程中，也没有满足于一般的文字工作，而是继续跟踪最新进展，进行充实和完善，最后形成本研究成果。

本课题的提出、研究计划的制订和研究工作的组织实施，以及本成果撰写修订由王静执笔完成。在研究过程中，得到了有关专家和单位的帮助支持，长安大学马天山教授、陕西师范大学马启明教授、上海交通大学赵旭教授、中国建筑第八工程局马荣全教授等都十分关心课题进展，并为研究提出宝贵建议。西北政法大学科研处、经济学院以及商学院；长安大学经济管理学院；陕西师范大学政治经济学院、陕西师范大学马克思主义博士后科研流动站；上海交通大学安泰经济与管理学院、上海交通大学管理科学与工程博士后科研流动站；中国建筑第八工程局博士后科研工作站等单位和领导对研究提供了支持。成果在全国哲学社会科学规划办公室组织的验收鉴定和这次成果文库出版申请中，得到了评审专家的一致好评。本成果是集体智慧的结晶。在此，表示衷心感谢。

王 静
2015 年 7 月 15 日
于西北政法大学雁塔校区